Beginning XML

Kurt Cagle
Dave Gibbons
David Hunter
Nikola Ozu
Jon Pinnock
Paul Spencer

Wrox Press Ltd.

Beginning XML

wrox

Published by Wrox Press Ltd, Arden House, 1102 Warwick Road, Acocks Green,
Birmingham, B27 6BH, UK
Printed in the United States
ISBN 1-861003-4-12

Trademark Acknowledgements

Wrox has endeavored to provide trademark information about all the companies and products mentioned in this book by the appropriate use of capitals. However, Wrox cannot guarantee the accuracy of this information.

Credits

Authors
Kurt Cagle
Dave Gibbons
David Hunter
Nikola Ozu
Jon Pinnock
Paul Spencer

Additional Material
Jerry Ablan
Chris Ullman

Technical Reviewers
Rich Anderson
Mark Birbeck
Barclay Blair
Michael Corning
Steve Danielson
Gerry Fillery
Steven Livingstone
Brian Loesgen
Michael Mason
Stephen Mohr
Simon North
Bruce Peat
Simon Perrott
Jon Pinnock
Paul Spencer
Andrew Watt

Technical Editors
Dianne Parker
Lisa Stephenson

Managing Editors
Joanna Mason
Dominic Lowe

Development Editor
Sarah Bowers

Project Manager
Jake Manning

Production Project Coordinator
Tom Bartlett

Additional Layout
Mark Burdett
Jonathan Jones
Laurent Lafon

Figures
William Fallon

Cover
Shelley Frasier

Index
Alessandro Ansa

About the Authors

Kurt Cagle

Kurt Cagle is a writer and developer specializing in XML and Internet related issues. He has written eight books and more than one hundred articles on topics ranging from Visual Basic programming to the impact of the Internet on society, and has consulted for such companies as Microsoft, Nordstrom, AT&T and others. He also helped launch Fawcette's XML Magazine and has been the DevX DHTML and XML Pro for nearly two years. In his free time he writes novels, draws comic books and tries to keep his two daughters out of mischief without much success. Kurt lives in Olympia, Washington, and can be reached via his shared website at http://www.vbxml.com, a web resource for Microsoft XML developers.

Dave Gibbons

Dave Gibbons is President of Cardboard String Media and creator of XMLephant.com. He has written over 20 books on technology. Dave lives in Hillsboro, Oregon, U.S., with his wife Tammy.

David Hunter

As a consultant and software architect for MobileQ.com, David Hunter has had extensive experience building scalable n-tier applications, using Internet technologies. David is never more at home than when playing with technologies nobody yet uses, and his peers have only just heard of.

David also provides training on XML, and software development best practices. Although currently enthralled with XML, he can't wait until it's commonplace, so that he can be enthralled with something else nobody's heard of.

First of all, I would like to thank God for the opportunity he has given me to write this book. I pray that the glory will go to him. I would also like to thank Wrox' editors; if this book is helpful, easy to read, and easy to understand, it's because the editors made it that way. Furthermore, I'd like to thank Lalit Canaran, and MobileQ.com, for the incredible support I was given.

And finally, I'd like to thank the person who never read a single word of this book, but was always willing – at a moment's notice – to make fun of my cover photo: my best friend Andrea. You helped me more than you'll ever know.

Nikola Ozu

Nikola Ozu is an independent systems architect who lives in Wyoming. Recent work has included an XML vocabulary for architects, and the design of a production and full-text indexing system for a publisher of medical reference books and databases. This system was also based upon XML, with a nod to content that was still in SGML and various proprietary markup languages. In the early 90s, Nik designed and developed the *Health Reference Center* and *InfoTrac* CD-ROM products. Previous work has ranged from library systems on mainframes to embedded microsystems (telecom equipment, robotics, toys, arcade games, and videogame cartridges).

When not surfing the 'net, he surfs the Tetons and the Pacific and climbs wherever there is rock and/or mountains – often accompanied by his 13-year-old son, a budding composer and rock guitarist, football goalkeeper, and all-around great guy.

To Noah: May we always think of the next (2^3-1) generations, instead of just our own 2^0.

I must give thanks to my editors at Wrox, the reference and IS staff at the Teton County Library, plus my friends Christopher Hoagland and Deanna Ingram. My work on this book would not have been possible without their kind and gracious assistance.

Jon Pinnock

Jonathan Pinnock started programming in Pal III assembler on his school's PDP 8/e, with a massive 4K of memory, back in the days before Moore's Law reached the statute books. After turning his back on computers for three years in order to study Mathematics at Cambridge University, he was forced back into programming in order to make a living, something that he still does from time to time. These days, he works as an independent developer and consultant, mainly in the City of London. He is the author of *"Professional DCOM Application Development"* and co-author of *"Professional XML"* and *"Professional Linux Deployment"*, but hopes that this will not be held against him.

Jonathan lives in Hertfordshire, England, with his wife, two children and a 1961 Ami Continental jukebox. His moderately interesting web site is located at **www.jpassoc.co.uk**.

Paul Spencer

When not sailing, Paul Spencer is senior partner and managing consultant at Boynings Consulting, which specializes in advising companies on the business and technical implications of XML. He has carried out work and provided XML training for several of the largest UK companies and is an XML advisor to the UK government. Paul has spoken at XML conferences organised by the GCA, Wrox, and Microsoft and is the author of the Wrox book *"XML Design and Implementation"*.

Paul has an MA from Cambridge University and gained an MBA with distinction from Lancaster University.

Table of Contents

Introduction   1

Who is this Book For?   1

What's Covered in this Book?   2

What You Need to Use this Book   4

Conventions   4
Downloading the Source Code   6

Tell Us What You Think   6

Errata & Updates   6

Chapter 1: What is XML?   9

Of Data, FIles, and Text   9
Binary Files   10
Text Files   11
A Brief History of Markup   12

So What *is* XML?   13
What Does XML Buy Us?   15
How Else Would We Describe Our Data?   15
XML Parsers   16
Why "Extensible"?   17
HTML and XML: Apples and Red Delicious Apples   18
Hierarchies of Information   18
Hierarchies in HTML   19
Hierarchies in XML   19
What's a Document Type?   21
No, Really – What's a Document Type?   21

Who is the World Wide Web Consortium?   22

What are the Pieces that Make Up XML?   23
Where is XML Used, and Where Can It be Used?   23
Reducing Server Load   24
Web Site Content   24
Remote Procedure Calls   24
E-Commerce   24

Summary   25

Chapter 2: Well-Formed XML   27

Tags & Text & Elements, Oh My!   28
Rules for Elements   31
     Element Names   33
     Case Sensitivity   34
     White Space in PCDATA   35

Attributes   38
Why Use Attributes?   41

Comments   42

Empty Elements   46

XML Declaration   47
Encoding   47
     Unicode   48
     Specifying Character Encoding for XML   48
Standalone   49

Processing Instructions   51
Is the XML Declaration a Processing Instruction?   51

Illegal PCDATA Characters   53
Escaping Characters   53
CDATA Sections   54

Parsing XML   57
     Microsoft Internet Explorer Parser   57
     James Clark's Expat   57
     Vivid Creations ActiveDOM   57
     DataChannel XJ Parser   57
     IBM xml4j   58
     Apache Xerces   58
Errors in XML   58

Summary   59

Chapter 3: XML in the Browser: Cascading Style Sheets   61

Why Do We Need Style Sheets?   62
The History of Styling HTML   63
     The Origins of Markup   63

Style Sheets and HTML — 65

Creating Styles in HTML — 66
The style Attribute — 67
The <STYLE> Element — 67
Cascading Styles — 68
Overriding Styles with Style Elements — 70
Comments in Style Sheets — 71
A Class Act in HTML — 71
Cascading Class Selectors — 75
Pseudo-Classes — 78
External Styles in HTML — 81
<LINK> — 81
The @import Directive — 82

Cascading Style Sheets and XML — 83

External Style Sheets in XML — 83
More on External Style Sheets — 85
Internal XML Cascading Style Sheets — 87
The Medium is the Message — 87
The @media Directive — 88
Media Groups — 89
The Box Model — 90
The display Property — 91
Other display Values — 91
The Difference Between display and visibility — 92
Setting Colors — 94
Hex Color Codes — 95
Building Borders — 96
Background Images — 99
Limitations When Working with Images — 100
Positioning and Repeating Background Images — 101
Specifying Multiple Background Properties — 102
Creating Backgrounds — 102
Understanding Positioning Schemes — 104
Static Position — 104
Relative Position — 104
Absolute Position — 104
Fixed Position — 105
Inherited Position — 105
Setting Positions and Units — 105
Width and Height — 107
Overflow — 108

Clipping 108
Floats 109
Lists and Tables 111
Working with Lists in XML 113
Supporting Tables in CSS 114
Text and Font Manipulation 116
font-size 116
font-style and font-weight 117
font-family and @font-face 117
font-variant, text-decoration, text-transform 119
Indentation, Padding and Margins 119
text-indent 119
Margins and Padding 120
Kerning and Spacing 121
letter-spacing 121
line-height 121
Alignment 122
text-align 122
vertical-align 122
Ruby Characters 122
Printing 122
Units – Pixels versus Points 123
The @page Directive 124
Page Breaks 124
Printing Using Scripting 125

Aural Style Sheets **125**

Summary **128**

Chapter 4: XSLT and XPath **131**

Running the Examples **132**
XT 132
MSXML 132

What is XSL? **133**
So How Do XSLT Style Sheets Work? 133
Associating Style Sheets Using Processing Instructions 134
Why is XSLT So Important for E-Commerce? 134

Imperative versus Declarative Programming — **137**

Imperative Programming — 137
Declarative Programming — 138
XSLT Has No Side Effects — 140

XPath — **141**

order.xml — 141
Node? What's a Node? — 142
Location Paths — 142
   Building Location Paths — 143
   But Why Doesn't XPath Use XML Syntax? — 144
   More Specific Location Paths — 144
XPath Functions — 146
   Node Functions — 146
   Positional Functions — 148
   Numeric Functions — 149
   Boolean Functions — 150
   String Functions — 152
Axis Names — 156

Summary — **161**

Chapter 5: XSLT – The Gory Details — **163**

Templates — **163**

XSLT's Order of Operations — 164
   Default Templates — 165
How Do Templates Affect the Context Node? — 165

XSLT Elements and their Use — **166**

<xsl:stylesheet> — 166
<xsl:template> — 167
   Template Priority — 167
<xsl:apply-templates> — 168
<xsl:value-of> — 171
<xsl:output> — 173
<xsl:element> — 175
<xsl:attribute> and <xsl:attribute-set> — 178
   Related Groups of Attributes — 179
<xsl:text> — 181
Conditional Processing with <xsl:if> and <xsl:choose> — 182
<xsl:for-each> — 187

<xsl:copy-of>	190
<xsl:copy>	192
<xsl:sort>	195
Modes	197
Variables, Constants, and Named Templates	201
<xsl:variable>	202
Named Templates	204
Parameters	205

Using XSLT with CSS — **208**
| CSS and XSL-Formatting Objects | 213 |

XSLT in the Real World — **213**

Summary — **214**

Chapter 6: The Document Object Model (DOM) — **217**

What is the DOM? — **218**
XML as an Object Model	218
The XML DOM	219
DOMString	219

DOM Interfaces — **220**
So What are Interfaces?	221
Implementing Interfaces	221
DOM Implementations	223
The DOM Core	224
Extending Interfaces	225

The DOM Core in Detail — **226**
Exceptions	226
DOMException	227
Node	227
Getting Node Information	227
Traversing the Tree	230
Adding and Removing Nodes	232
Document	235
DOMImplementation	238
DocumentFragment	239
NodeList	240
Element	242
NamedNodeMap	245

Attr 247
CharacterData and Text 249
    Handling Complete Strings 249
    Handling Sub-Strings 250
    Modifying Strings 250
    Splitting Text 251
Comment and CDATASection 254
ProcessingInstruction 256

Summary **259**

Chapter 7: The Simple API for XML (SAX)   261

What is SAX, and Why Was it Invented?   261
The Fabulous Lost Treasure of the Xenics 262
So What Does that Have to Do with SAX? 262
Where to Get SAX 263
Who is this Megginson Guy Anyway? 264

Using the SAX Interfaces   264
Preparing the Ground 264
How to Receive SAX Events 268
Extracting Character Data 273
Extracting Attributes 276
Error Handling 281
    More About Errors – Using the Locator Object 284
    Even More About Errors – Catching Parsing Errors 286
Other Methods in DocumentHandler 288
    ignorableWhitespace 288
    processingInstruction 289

Good SAX and Bad SAX   290

SAX 2.0   291

Summary   291

Chapter 8: Namespaces   293

Why Do We Need Namespaces?   293
Using Prefixes 294
So Why Doesn't XML Just Use These Prefixes? 296

How XML Namespaces Work — 297

Default Namespaces — 300
Namespaces of Descendents — 301
Canceling Default Namespaces — 303
Do Different Notations Make Any Difference? — 303
Namespaces and Attributes — 305

XSLT from a Namespace Point of View — 308

What Exactly are URIs? — 312

URLs — 312
URNs — 313
Why Use URLs for Namespaces, Not URNs? — 314
What Do Namespace URIs Really Mean? — 315

When Should I Use Namespaces? — 316

Summary — 317

Chapter 9: Basic Valid XML: DTDs — 319

Why Do We Need DTDs? — 320

XML Application Requirements — 320
Document Type Definitions — 321
Valid XML — 321
Validating Parsers — 322
Sharing DTDs — 324
A Simple Example — 324
Why Use XML to Do This? — 324
The Basic BookCatalog Data Model — 325

DTDs — 329

Internal versus External DTDs — 330
When to Use Internal and External Subsets — 330
Associating a DTD with an XML Document — 331
The XML Declaration (A Refresher) — 331
The Document Type (DOCTYPE) Declaration — 332

Basic DTD Markup — 337

Element Type (ELEMENT) Declarations — 338
Element Content Categories — 338
Content Models — 340

Attribute (ATTLIST) Declarations   349
   Attribute Types   351
   Attribute Defaults   356
   Extending the BookCatalog Data Model   358
Limitations of DTDs   373

Summary   **376**

Chapter 10: Valid XML: Schemas   379

Schemas versus DTDs   **380**
Syntax   381
Content Models   381
Data Typing   382
Extensibility   382
Dynamic Schemas   383

Basic Schema Principles   **383**
XML Parsers with Schema Support   384
Structures and Datatypes, or Chickens and Eggs   385

Datatypes   **385**
Primitive Datatypes   386
   Primitive Types for XML Schema   386
Dcrived Datatypes   387
   Built-in Derived Types for XML Schema   387
Atomic and List Datatypes   388
   Atomic Datatypes   388
   List Datatypes   388
Aspects of Datatypes   389
   Value Spaces   390
   Lexical Spaces   390
   Facets   390
   Fundamental Facets   390
   Constraining Facets   392

Associating Schemas with XML Documents   **395**
XML Schema Preamble – The <schema> Element   395
   Specifying the Namespaces   396
   Specifying the Version   396
XDR Preamble – The <Schema> Element   396

Structures   397

Datatype Definitions   397
     Simple Type Definitions   398
     Complex Type Definitions   400

Content Models   406
     Element Content Categories   407
     Cardinality – minOccurs and maxOccurs   407
     Choice and Sequence Groups – <choice> and <sequence>   408
     Mixed Content (Unsequenced Group) – <all>   409
     Content From Another Schema – <any>   410
     Model Groups – <group>   411

Element Declarations   411
     Element Constraints – <element>   412

Attribute Declarations   414
     Attribute Constraints – <attribute>   414
     Attribute Groups – <attributeGroup>   416

Annotations   418

Summary   419

Chapter 11: Advanced Valid XML   421

Entities   422

Entity References   423
     Character References   424

General Entities   424
     Parsed Entities   425
     Unparsed Entities   429

Parameter Entities   430
ISO and Other Standard Entity Sets   432

Non-XML Data (Notations)   434

     The <!NOTATION> Declaration   435
     The NOTATION Attribute Type   435
     The ENTITY and ENTITIES Attribute Types   435

Internal versus External DTD Subsets   438

     The standalone Attribute   439

Conditional Sections   439

Nesting Conditional Sections   443

Summary   443

Chapter 12: Linking XML   445

HTML Linking   446

XML Linking   447

XLink   448
XLink Attributes   449
  The type Attribute   450
  The href Attribute   451
  Semantic Attributes (role and title)   451
  Behavior Attributes (actuate and show)   452
  The from and to Attributes   453
Link Types   454
  Simple Links   454
  Extended Links   457
  Locator-type Elements   458
  Arcs   459
  Resource-type Elements   461
  Title-type Elements   463
Defaulting XLink Attributes   463

Pointing to Document Fragments with XPointer   464
Appending XPointer Expressions to URIs   465
  Using Multiple XPointer Expressions   465
XPointer Schemes   467
XPointer Shorthand Syntaxes   468
  Full Syntax   468
  Bare Names Syntax   469
  Child Sequence Syntax   469
Locations, Points and Ranges   470
  Points   470
  Ranges   471
  How Do We Select Ranges?   472
XPointer Function Extensions to XPath   474

Querying   475

Summary   475

Chapter 13: XML and Databases — 477

Databases, Yesterday and Today — 478
SQL — 479
Retrieving Data from Multiple Tables — 480
Normalization — 481

Making Use of What You've Got — 482
N-Tier Architecture — 482
Using XML in an N-tier Application — 484
Returning XML from a Data Object — 486

Integrating XML into the Database Itself — 487
Storing XML in a Database — 487
Using the Database — 488
An Even Simpler Data Object — 489

Database Vendors and XML — 490
Microsoft's XML Technologies — 490
MSXML — 490
Visual Basic Code Generator — 491
SQL Server — 491
Putting SQL Server to Work — 492
Oracle's XML Technologies — 494
XML Parsers — 494
Code Generators — 494
XML SQL Utility for Java — 494
XSQL Servlet — 495
Putting Oracle to Work — 496

Who Needs a Database Anyway? — 496

Summary — 498

Chapter 14: Other Uses for XML — 501

Serializing Object Models — 502
Suggestions for a Good Object Model — 508
Include Pretty-Printing Characters — 508
Allow Each Object to Serialize Itself — 510
Commit/Rollback Functionality — 517
Don't Return Anything from an Empty Object — 517
Keep Track of Historical Information, Including Errors — 518

XML-RPC   **519**
SOAP   521
The Poor Man's RPC   521

Stateless Objects   **526**

Resource Description Framework (RDF)   **528**
How Does It Work?   529

Schematron   **530**

Summary   **534**

Case Study 1: Lydia's Lugnuts Web Store   **537**

Complexity   538
Maintenance   540

Creating Order from Chaos   **540**
Designing the XML Structure   540
Creating XML Files   542
Grouping Products Together   544

Transforming and Displaying XML with XSL   **545**
The Existing Web Page   547
The XSLT Style Sheet   549

Incorporating Content from Multiple Sources   **557**
Product Listings   558
Nuts. Nuts? Nuts! Templates   561
The Nut Haus Templates   562
The New HTML Web Pages   563

The Future of Lydia's Lugnuts   **565**

Case Study 2: Discussion Group System   **567**

Designing the Architecture   **567**
An XHTML Framework System   568
A Note About the XMLPipes Framework   569
What Does the XHTML Framework Do?   570
Defining the Server   572

Defining Membership Directories   **573**

Designing the Message Boards — 576

Retrieving the Message Child Tree — 580
Retrieving the Message Ancestor Tree — 580
Retrieving the Message Sibling Tree – Next — 581
Retrieving the Message Sibling Tree – Previous — 582

Creating Messages — 583

Using Namespaces — 583

Editing and Deleting Messages — 590

Deleting a Message — 592

Viewing Lists of Messages — 593

A Few Thoughts on Online Editors — 599

Editing and Viewing Individual Messages — 600

Summary — 608

Case Study 3: XML for a Business-to-Business Application — 611

An E-Commerce Problem and Our Solution — 612

E-Commerce Requirements — 613
Why Doesn't EDI Achieve This? — 614
The eBIS-XML Concept — 615
So What (exactly) is eBIS-XML? — 617
An Existing eBIS-XML Application — 618
Decisions, Decisions — 619
DTD versus Schema — 620
Style Sheets and XSL — 620
Tools for Developing Schemas — 621

eBIS-XML Schemas — 624

Developing the v2.4 eBIS-XML Schemas — 624
Moving On Up – Version 3 — 627
The Final Schema — 632
Summary of Schema Development Tips — 635
A Reprise on the Tools Used — 635

eBIS-XML Style Sheets — 639

A Simple Invoice — 639
Push and Pull Models — 643
More About the Invoice Style Sheet — 644
Doing it the Easy Way? — 654
Summary of the Style Sheet — 655

Have We Met Arthur's Requirements?   **655**

Next Steps   **657**

Simple Routing   657

    The BizTalk Header   658

Choreography   659

More Futures   660

And If We Were to Start Now?   **660**

Summary   **661**

Appendix A: The XML Document Object Model   **663**

Fundamental Interfaces   **663**

DOMException   663

Node   664

Document   666

DOMImplementation   668

DocumentFragment   668

NodeList   668

Element   669

NamedNodeMap   670

Attr   671

CharacterData   671

Text   672

Comment   672

Extended Interfaces   **672**

CDATASection   672

ProcessingInstruction   673

DocumentType   673

Notation   673

Entity   674

EntityReference   674

Appendix B: SAX 1.0: The Simple API for XML   **677**

Class Hierarchy   **678**

Interface org.xml.sax.AttributeList   678

Interface org.xml.sax.DocumentHandler   681

Interface org.xml.sax.DTDHandler   685

Interface org.xml.sax.EntityResolver   687
Interface org.xml.sax.ErrorHandler   689
Class org.xml.sax.HandlerBase   691
Class org.xml.sax.InputSource   694
Interface org.xml.sax.Locator   698
Interface org.xml.sax.Parser   699
Class org.xml.sax.SAXException   702
Class org.xml.sax.SAXParseException   703

Appendix C: ASP Quick Start Tutorial   707

The Anatomy of the HTTP Protocol   708
Overview   708
The HTTP Server   708
Protocol Basics   709
   The Connection   709
   The Request   709
   The Response   712
   Disconnecting   712

Introducing Active Server Pages   713
How the Server Recognizes ASPs   713
ASP Basics   713
   The Tags of ASP   714
   <SCRIPT> Blocks   714
   The Default Scripting Language   714
   Mixing HTML and ASP   715
   Commenting Your ASP Code   716

The Active Server Pages Object Model   717
Collections   717
   Iterating the Contents Collection   718
   Removing an Item from the Contents Collection   719
The Request Object   719
   The Request Object's Collections   720
   Request Object Property and Method   724
The Response Object   724
   The Response Object's Collection   724
   The Response Object's Methods   725
   The Response Object's Properties   727

The Application and Session Objects 728
  Scope Springs Eternal 728
  The global.asa File 729
  The Application Object 729
  The Session Object 730
The Server Object 732
  Properties 732
  Methods 732
The ObjectContext Object 733
  SetAbort 734
  SetComplete 734

Using Active Server Pages Effectively **734**
Designing the Site 734
Creating the global.asa File 735
Creating our Main Page 735
The ASP/VBScript Section 736
The HTML Section 738

Summary **740**

Appendix D: JavaScript Quick Start Tutorial **743**

JavaScript and HTML **744**

JavaScript and Java **744**

Running the Examples in this Appendix **745**

Statements **746**
Comments 747
  Single Line Comments 747
  Multi-line Comments 747

Variables **748**
Data Types 749
Variable Names 750

Operators **751**
Mathematical 751
Assignment 752
Logical (Boolean) 752
Precedence of Operators 753

Functions — 754

Creating Functions — 754
Returning Information from a Function — 754
Passing Information to a Function — 755
Built-in Functions — 755

Program Flow — 756

Conditional Code — 756
  The if Statement — 756
  The switch Statement — 758
Loops — 759
  The for Loop — 760
  while and do ... while Loops — 760
  The break and continue Statements — 761

Objects — 762

String — 763
  The toLowerCase and toUpperCase Methods — 763
  Methods to Return Strings and Characters — 763
  Methods to Search Strings — 764
  Joining Strings — 764
Number — 764
Math — 765
Date — 766

Arrays — 766

Summary — 767

Appendix E: Support, Errata, and P2P.Wrox.Com — 769

The Online Forums at P2P.Wrox.Com — 769

How to Enroll for Online Support — 770
Why this System Offers the Best Support — 771

Support and Errata — 771

Wrox Developer's Membership — 771
Finding an Erratum on the Web Site — 772
Add an Erratum: E-mail Support — 773
  Customer Support — 774
  Editorial — 774
  The Authors — 774
What We Can't Answer — 774
How to Tell Us Exactly What You Think — 774

Appendix F: Useful Web Resources   **777**

Appendix G: XML Schema Datatypes   **783**

Primitive Types   **783**
string   784
boolean   784
decimal   784
float   785
double   785
timeDuration   785
recurringDuration   787
binary   787
uriReference   788
ID   788
IDREF   788
ENTITY   788
NOTATION   789
QName   789
Constraining Facets for Primitive Types   789

Built-in Derived Types   **790**
language   791
name, NCName   792
integer, negativeInteger, positiveInteger, nonNegativeInteger, nonPositiveInteger   792
byte, short, int, long   792
unsignedByte, unsignedShort, unsignedInt, unsignedLong   792
century, year, month, date   792
recurringDate, recurringDay   793
time, timeInstant, timePeriod   793
Constraining Facets for Derived Types   794

index   **797**

Introduction

Welcome to Beginning XML, the book I wish I'd had when I was first learning the language!

XML is a relatively new programming language, but one which is becoming more and more widely used in a vast range of applications. XML is a markup language, used to describe the structure of data, so anywhere that data is input/output, stored, or transmitted from one place to another, is a potential fit for XML's capabilities. Perhaps the most well known applications are web related (especially with the latest developments in handheld web access – for which the technology is XML-based). But there are many other non-web based applications where XML is useful – for example as a replacement for (or to complement) traditional databases or for the transfer of financial information between businesses.

This book aims to teach you all you need to know about XML – what it is, how it works, what technologies surround it, and how it can best be used in a variety of situations, from simple data transfer to using XML in your web pages. It will answer the fundamental questions:

❑ What is XML?

❑ How do I use XML?

❑ How does it work?

❑ What can I use it *for*, anyway?

Who is this Book For?

Since XML had a predecessor, SGML, many XML books have been written with the intention of helping SGML developers get used to the leaner syntax of XML, or were written by people who have moved from SGML to XML. I, on the other hand, started out fresh with XML, and am assuming that most of the readers of this book have not been introduced to SGML either. For that reason, I set out to write the book that I would have wanted when I was first learning XML. I have tried to structure the book in a way that will make sense to the beginner, and yet still quickly bring you to XML expert-status.

This book is for people who know that it would be a pretty good idea to learn the language, but aren't 100% sure why. You've heard the hype, but haven't seen enough substance to figure out what XML is, and what it can do. You may already be somehow involved in web development, and probably even know the basics of HTML, although neither of these qualifications are absolutely necessary for this book.

The word "Beginning" in the title refers to the style of the book, rather than the reader's experience level: there are two types of beginner for whom this book will be ideal:

❏ Programmers who are already familiar with some web programming or data exchange techniques. You will already be used to some of the concepts discussed here, but will learn how you can incorporate XML technologies to enhance those solutions you currently develop.

❏ Those working in a programming environment but with no substantial knowledge or experience of web development or data exchange applications. As well as learning how XML technologies can be applied to such applications, you will be introduced to some new concepts to help you understand how such systems work.

What's Covered in this Book?

I've tried to arrange the subjects covered in this book to take you from no knowledge to expert, in as logical a manner as I could. We'll be using the following format:

❏ First, we'll be looking at what exactly XML is, and why the industry felt that a language like this was needed.

❏ Once we've covered the *why*, the next logical step is the *how*, so we'll be seeing how to create well-formed XML.

❏ Because there are a number of related technologies surrounding XML, we'll next cover a few of the more common, and more powerful, technologies that you can make use of.

❏ Once you're comfortable with XML, and have seen it in action with these surrounding technologies, we'll go on to some more advanced things you can do when creating your XML documents, to make them not only well-formed, but valid. (And we'll talk about what "valid" really means.)

❏ We'll then move on to some of the surrounding technologies that don't actually exist yet, but are on the way.

❏ And finally, we'll finish off with some case studies, which should help to give you ideas on how XML can be used in real life situation, and which could be used in your own applications.

The chapters are broken down as follows:

Chapter 1: What is XML?

Here we'll cover some basic concepts, introducing the fact that XML is a markup language (a bit like HTML) where you can define your own elements, tags and attributes (known as a vocabulary). We'll see that tags have no presentation meaning – they're just a way of describing the structure of data.

Chapter 2: Well-Formed XML

As well as explaining what well-formed XML is, we'll take a look at the rules which exist (the XML 1.0 Specification) for naming and structuring elements – you need to comply with these rules if your XML is to be well-formed.

Chapter 3: XML in the Browser: Cascading Style Sheets

In this chapter we'll see that we can add styles to elements for presentation purposes using cascading style sheets (CSS).

Chapter 4: XSLT and XPath

XML can be transformed into other XML, HTML, and other formats using XSLT style sheets, which are introduced here. (A series of XSLT templates are applied to matching sections and these templates can extract/add/replace content.) The XPath language, used to locate sections in the XML document, is also covered in detail.

Chapter 5: XSLT – The Gory Details

Having seen what XSLT is, this chapter looks at the details of the XSLT elements, used to create the XSLT style sheets.

Chapter 6: The Document Object Model (DOM)

Programmers can use script to manipulate XML, using the Document Object Model's objects, interfaces, methods, and properties, which are described here.

Chapter 7: The Simple API for XML (SAX)

An alternative to the DOM is to use SAX as an interface. This chapter shows how to use SAX.

Chapter 8: Namespaces

Because tags can be made up, we need to avoid name conflicts when sharing documents. Namespaces provide a way to uniquely identify a group of tags, using a URL. This chapter explains how to use namespaces.

Chapter 9: Basic Valid XML: DTDs

We can specify how an XML document should be structured, and even give default values, using Document Type Definitions (DTDs). If XML conforms to the associated DTD it is known as valid XML. This chapter covers the basics of using DTDs.

Chapter 10: Valid XML: Schemas

An alternative to DTDs are XML Schemas, which are explained here.

Chapter 11: Advanced Valid XML

Some more advanced concepts of using DTDs are covered in this chapter.

Chapter 12: Linking XML

We can locate specific parts of the XML document using XPath and XPointer. When the technology becomes implemented, we will be able to link sections of documents and other resources using XLink. Both XPointer and XLink are described in this chapter.

Chapter 13: XML and Databases

XML is perfect for structuring data, and some traditional databases are beginning to offer support for XML. These are discussed, as well as a more general overview of how XML can be used in an n-tier architecture.

Chapter 14: Other Uses for XML

A catch-all chapter which covers some potential future developments, such as standard ways of describing the content of documents (Resource Description Framework) and using XML-RPC to transmit data across a network. We also take a look at an alternative method of validation, called Schematron.

Case Studies 1 to 3

Throughout the book you'll gain an understanding of how XML is/will be used in web, business to business (B2B), data storage, and many other applications. These case studies cover three example applications and show how the theory can be put into practice in real life situations.

Appendices

These provide reference material which you may find useful as you begin to apply the knowledge gained throughout the book in your own applications. JavaScript and ASP quick start tutorials are also included for readers who are not familiar with these subjects.

What You Need to Use this Book

Because XML is a text-based technology, all you really need to create XML documents is Notepad, or your equivalent text editor. However, to really see some of these samples in action, you might want to have Internet Explorer 5 or later, since this browser can natively read XML documents, and even provide error messages if something is wrong. For readers without IE5, there will be some screenshots throughout the book, so that you can see what things would look like.

If you do have IE5, you also have an implementation of the DOM, which you may find useful in the chapters on that subject.

If you want to try out the examples of using XML with web pages, you will need access to a web server, such as Microsoft's IIS (or PWS).

Throughout the book, other (freely available) XML tools will be used, and we'll give instructions for obtaining these.

Conventions

To help you understand what's going on, and in order to maintain consistency, we've used a number of conventions throughout the book:

When we introduce new terms, we **highlight** them.

These boxes hold important information.

Advice, hints and background information comes in an indented, italicized font like this.

Try It Out

After learning something new, we'll have a Try It Out section, which will demonstrate the concepts learned, and get you working with the technology.

How It Works

After a Try It Out section, there will sometimes be a further explanation, to help you relate what you've done to what you've just learned.

Words that appear on the screen in menus like the File or Window menu are in a similar font to what you see on screen. URLs are also displayed in this font.

On the occasions when we'll be running a command from the DOS command line, it will be shown as:

```
C:\>xt blah.xml blah.xsl
<root>
  <results/>
</root>
```

Keys that you press on the keyboard, like *Ctrl* and *Enter*, are in italics.

We use two font styles for code. If it's a word that we're talking about in the text, for example, when discussing functionNames(), <Elements>, and Attributes it will be in a fixed pitch font. If it's a block of code that you can type in and run, or part of such a block, then it's also in a gray box:

```
<html>
  <head>
    <title>Simple Example</title>
  </head>
  <body>
    <p>Very simple HTML.</p>
  </body>
</html>
```

Sometimes you'll see code in a mixture of styles, like this:

```
<html>
  <head>
    <title>Simple Example</title>
  </head>
  <body>
    <p>Very simple HTML.</p>
  </body>
</html>
```

In this case, we want you to consider the code with the gray background, for example to modify it. The code with a white background is code we've already looked at, and that we don't wish to examine further.

Downloading the Source Code

As we move through the chapters, there will be copious amounts of code available for you, so that you can see exactly how it works. We'll also be stopping frequently and trying it out, so that you can not only see how things work, but make them work yourself.

The source code for all of the examples is available for download from http://www.wrox.com – more on that in a while. You might decide that you prefer to type all the code in by hand. Many readers prefer this because it's a good way to get familiar with the coding techniques that are being used.

Whether you want to type the code in or not, we have made all the source code for this book available at our web site, at the following address:

http://www.wrox.com

If you're one of those readers who likes to type in the code, you can use our files to check the results you should be getting – they should be your first stop if you think you might have typed in an error. If you're one of those readers who doesn't like typing, then downloading the source code from our web site is a must!

Either way, it'll help you with updates and debugging.

Tell Us What You Think

We've worked hard to make this book as relevant and useful as possible, so we'd like to get a feel for what it is you want and need to know, and what you think about how we've presented things.

If you have anything to say, let us know at:

feedback@wrox.com

or:

http://www.wrox.com

Errata & Updates

We've made every effort to make sure there are no errors in the text or the code. However, to err is human, and as such we recognize the need to keep you informed of any mistakes as they're spotted and amended.

More details on obtaining support, finding out about errata, and providing us with feedback, can be found in Appendix E.

What is XML?

Extensible Markup Language (**XML**) is the latest buzzword on the Internet, but it's also a rapidly maturing technology with powerful real-world applications, particularly for the management, display and organization of data. Together with its display language (XSL) and the standardized Document Object Model (DOM), it is an essential technology for anyone using markup languages on the web or internally. This chapter will introduce you to some of the basics of XML, and begin to show you why it is so important to learn about it.

We will cover:

- ❑ The two major categories of computer file types – **binary files** and **text files** – and the advantages and disadvantages of each

- ❑ The history behind XML, including other markup languages – **SGML** and **HTML**

- ❑ How XML documents are structured as **hierarchies** of information

- ❑ A brief introduction to some of the other technologies surrounding XML, which you will be working with throughout the book

- ❑ A quick look at some areas where XML is proving to be useful

While there are some short examples of XML in this chapter, you aren't expected to understand what's going on just yet. The idea is simply to introduce the important concepts behind the language, so that throughout the book you can see not only how to use XML, but also why it works the way that it does.

Of Data, Files, and Text

XML is a technology concerned with the description and structuring of *data*, so before we can really delve into the concepts behind XML, we need to understand how data is stored and accessed by computers. For our purposes, there are two kinds of data files that are understood by computers: **text files** and **binary files**.

Binary Files

A **binary file**, at its simplest, is just a stream of **bits** (1's and 0's). It's up to the application which created a binary file to understand what all of the bits mean. That's why binary files can only be read and produced by certain computer programs, which have been specifically written to understand them.

For example, when a document is created with a word processor, the program creates a binary file in its own proprietary format. The programmers who wrote the word processor decided to insert certain binary codes into the document to denote bold text, other codes to denote page breaks, and many other codes for all of the information that needs to go into these documents. When you open a document in the word processor it interprets those codes, and displays the properly formatted text on the screen, or prints it to the printer.

The codes inserted into the document can be considered **metadata**, or *information about information.* (That is, "this word should be in bold", "that sentence should be centered", etc.) This metadata is really what differentiates one file type from another; the different types of files use different kinds of metadata.

For example, a word processing document will have different metadata from a spreadsheet document, since they are describing different things. But word processing documents from different word processing applications will also have different metadata, because the applications were written differently:

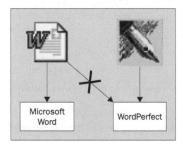

As the above diagram shows, a document created with one word processor cannot be assumed to be readable in or used by another, because the companies who write word processors all have their own proprietary formats for their data files. So Word documents open in Microsoft Word, and WordPerfect documents open in WordPerfect.

Luckily for us most word processors come with translators, which can translate documents from other word processors into formats that can be understood natively. Of course, many of us have seen the garbage that sometimes occurs as a result of this translation; sometimes applications are not as good as we'd like them to be at converting the information.

The advantage of binary file formats is that it is easy for computers to understand these binary codes, meaning that they can be processed much faster, and they are very efficient for storing this metadata. And, as we've seen, the disadvantage is that binary files are "proprietary". You might not be able to open binary files created by one application in another application, or even in the same application running on another platform.

Text Files

Like binary files, **text files** are also streams of bits. However, in a text file these bits are grouped together in standardized ways, so that they always form numbers. These numbers are then further mapped to characters. For example, a text file might contain the bits:

```
1100001
```

This group of bits would be translated as the number "97", which would then be further translated into the letter "a".

> *This example makes a number of assumptions. A better description of how numbers are represented in text files is given in the section on "Encodings" in Chapter 2.*

Because of these standards, text files can be read by many, many applications, and can even be read by humans, using a simple text editor. If I create a text document, anyone in the world can read it (as long as they understand English, of course), in any text editor they wish. This makes it much easier to share information with others.

The following diagram shows just some of the applications on my machine that are capable of opening text files. Some of these programs will just allow me to *view* the text, while others will let me *edit* it as well.

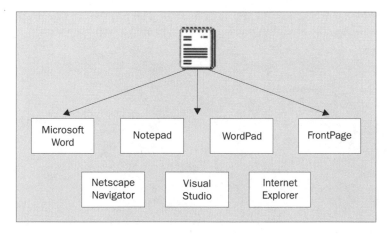

In its beginning, the Internet was almost completely text-based, which allowed people to communicate with relative ease. This contributed to the explosive rate at which the Internet was adopted, and to the ubiquity of applications like e-mail, the World Wide Web, newsgroups, etc.

The disadvantage of text files is that it's more difficult and bulky to add other information – our metadata in other words. For example, most word processors allow you to save documents in text form, but if you do then you can't mark a section of text as bold, or insert a binary picture file. You will simply get the words, with none of the formatting.

A Brief History of Markup

We can see that there are advantages to binary file formats (easy to understand by a computer, compact), as well as advantages to text files (universally interchangeable). Wouldn't it be ideal if there were a format that combined the universality of text files with the efficiency and rich information storage capabilities of binary files?

This idea of a universal data format is not new. In fact, for as long as computers have been around, programmers have been trying to find ways to exchange information between different computer programs. An early attempt to combine a universally interchangeable data format with rich information storage capabilities was **SGML** (**Standard Generalized Markup Language**). This is a text-based language that can be used to **mark up** data – that is, add metadata – in a way which is **self describing**. (We'll see in a moment what self describing means.)

SGML was designed to be a standard way of marking up data for any purpose, and took off mostly in large document management systems. It turns out that when it comes to huge amounts of complex data there are a lot of considerations to take into account and, as a result, SGML is a very complicated language. But with that complexity comes power.

The best known application of SGML is **HyperText Markup Language**, or **HTML**. Because the rules for creating SGML documents are so well laid out, and because SGML has been used so extensively in document management systems, it was a good fit to produce a specific vocabulary – HTML – to be a universal markup language for the display of information, and the linking of different pieces of information. The idea was that any HTML document (or **web page**) would be presentable in any application that was capable of understanding HTML (termed a **web browser**).

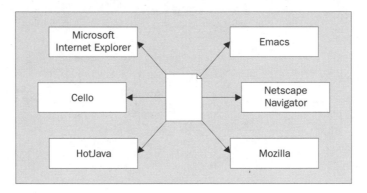

Not only would that browser be able to display the document, but if the page contained **hyperlinks** to other documents, the browser would be able to seamlessly retrieve them as well. A hyperlink is simply a pointer to another document somewhere on the web. Normally, when you click on a hyperlink in a web page the result is that the page pointed to replaces the current page in the browser window. This is what makes the World Wide Web a "web" – any HTML document can potentially link to any other HTML document. So if I were to create a web site on guitars, I could create a link to the web sites of my favorite guitar manufacturers, or my favorite guitar players, even though those sites are produced by other people I have no contact with.

Furthermore, because HTML is text-based, anyone can create an HTML page using a simple text editor, or any number of web page editors.

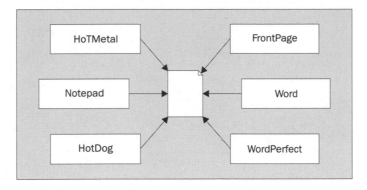

Even many word processors, such as WordPerfect and Word, allow you to save documents as HTML. Think about the ramifications of these two diagrams: any HTML editor, including a simple text editor, can create an HTML file, and that HTML file can then be viewed in any web browser on the Internet!

So What *is* XML?

Unfortunately, SGML is such a complicated language that it's not well suited for data interchange over the web. And, although HTML has been incredibly successful, it's also limited in its scope: it is only intended for displaying documents in a browser. This means that I could create an HTML document which displays information about a person, but that's about all I could do with the document. I couldn't figure out from that document which piece of information relates to the person's first name, for example, because HTML doesn't have any facilities to describe this kind of specialized information.

Extensible Markup Language (XML) was created for this reason.

Note that it's spelled "Extensible", not "eXtensible". This is a common mistake made by those new to XML.

XML is a **subset** of SGML, with the same goals (markup of any type of data), but with as much of the complexity eliminated as possible. XML was designed to be fully compatible with SGML, which means that any document which follows XML's syntax rules is by definition also following SGML's syntax rules, and can therefore be read by existing SGML tools. It doesn't go both ways though, so an SGML document is not necessarily an XML document.

It is important to realize, however, that XML is not really a "language" at all, but a standard for creating languages which meet the XML criteria. In other words, XML describes a syntax which you use to create your own languages. For example, suppose I have data about a name, and I want to be able to share that information with others. But I also want to be able to use that information in a computer program. Instead of just creating a text file like this:

```
John Doe
```

or an HTML file like this:

```
<HTML>
<HEAD><TITLE>Name</TITLE></HEAD>
<BODY>
<P>John Doe</P>
</BODY>
</HTML>
```

I might create an XML file like this:

```
<name>
  <first>John</first>
  <last>Doe</last>
</name>
```

Even from this simple example you can see why markup languages like SGML and XML are called self describing. Looking at the data, you can easily tell that this is information about a <name>; and you can see that there is data called <first> and more data called <last>. (I could have given the data any names I liked. However, if you're going to use XML, you might as well use it right, and give things *meaningful* names.)

You can also see that the XML version of this information is much bigger than the plain-text version. Using XML to mark up data will add to its size, sometimes enormously, but small file sizes aren't one of the primary goals of XML; it's only about making it easier to write software that accesses the information, by giving structure to data. However, this larger file size should not deter you from using XML. The advantages of easier-to-write code far outweigh the disadvantages of larger bandwidth issues. And, if bandwidth is a critical issue for your applications, you can always compress your XML documents before sending them across the network – compressing text files yields very good results.

Try It Out – Opening an XML File in Internet Explorer

If you're running IE5 or later, our XML from above can be viewed in your browser.

1. Open up Notepad and type in the following XML:

```
<name>
  <first>John</first>
  <last>Doe</last>
</name>
```

2. Save the document to your hard drive as name.xml.

3. You can then open it up in IE5 (for example by double-clicking on the file in Windows Explorer), where it will look something like this:

How It Works

Although our XML file has no information concerning display, IE5 formats it nicely for us, with our information in bold, and our markup displayed in different colors. Also, `<name>` is collapsible, like your file folders in Windows Explorer. For large XML documents, where you only need to concentrate on a smaller subset of the data, this can be quite handy.

This is one reason why IE5 can be so helpful when authoring XML: it has a default **style sheet** built in, which applies this default formatting to any XML document.

> *Style sheets are used to describe the display of certain types of documents. There are a variety of languages which can be used to create style sheets. In Chapter 3 we'll be looking at a style sheet language called Cascading Style Sheets (CSS), and in Chapters 4 and 5 we'll learn about a transformation style sheet language called Extensible Style sheet Language – Transformations (XSLT).*

As we'll see in later chapters, you can also create your own style sheets for displaying XML documents. This way, the same data that your applications use can also be viewed in a browser. In effect, by combining XML data with style sheets you can separate your data from your presentation. That makes it easier to use the data for multiple purposes (as opposed to HTML, which doesn't provide any separation of data from presentation – in HTML, *everything* is presentation).

What Does XML Buy Us?

But why would we go to all of the bother of creating an XML document? Wouldn't it be easier to just make up some rules for a file about names, such as "The first name starts at the beginning of the file, and the last name comes after the first space"? That way, our application could still read the data, but the file size would be much smaller.

How Else Would We Describe Our Data?

As a partial answer, let's suppose that we want to add a middle name to our example:

```
John Fitzgerald Doe
```

Okay, no problem. We'll just modify our rules to say that everything after the first space and up to the second space is the middle name, and the rest after the second space is the last name. Oh, unless there is no second space, in which case we'll have to assume that there is no middle name, and the first rule still applies. So we're still fine. Unless a person happens to have a name like:

```
John Fitzgerald Johansen Doe
```

Whoops. There are two middle names in there. The rules get more complex. While a human might be able to tell immediately that the two middle words compose the middle name, it is more difficult to program this logic into a computer program. (We won't even discuss "John Fitzgerald Johansen Doe the 3rd"!)

Unfortunately, when it comes to problems like this many software developers just throw in the towel and define more restrictive rules, instead of dealing with the complexities of the data. In this example, the software developers might decide that a person can only have *one* middle name, and that the application won't accept anything more than that.

This is pretty realistic, I might add. My full name is David John Bartlett Hunter, but because of the way many computer systems are set up, a lot of the bills I receive are simply addressed to David John Hunter, or David J. Hunter. Maybe I can find some legal ground to stop paying my bills, but in the meantime my vanity takes a blow every time I open my mail.

This example is probably not all that hard to solve, but it points out one of the major focuses behind XML. Programmers have been structuring their data in an infinite variety of ways, and with every new way of structuring data comes a new methodology for pulling out the information we need. With those new methodologies comes much experimentation and testing to get it just right. If the data changes, the methodologies also have to change, and the testing and tweaking has to begin again. But with XML there is a standardized way to get the information we need, no matter how we structure it.

In addition, remember how trivial this example is. The more complex the data you have to work with, the more complex the logic you'll need to do that work. It is in these larger applications where you'll appreciate XML the most.

XML Parsers

If we just follow the rules specified by XML, we can be sure that it will be easy to get at our information. This is because there are programs written, called **parsers**, which are able to read XML syntax and get the information out for us. We can use these parsers within our own programs, meaning our applications never have to even look at the XML directly; a large part of the workload has been done for us.

There are also parsers available for parsing SGML documents, but they are much more complex than XML parsers. Since XML is a subset of SGML, it's much easier to write an XML parser than an SGML parser.

In the past, before these parsers were around, a lot of work would have gone into the many rules we were looking at (like the rule that the middle name starts after the first space, etc.). But with our data in XML format, we can just give an XML parser a file like this:

```
<name>
  <first>John</first>
  <middle>Fitzgerald Johansen</middle>
  <last>Doe</last>
</name>
```

and it can tell us that there is a piece of data called <middle>, and that the information stored there is Fitzgerald Johansen. The parser writer didn't have to know any rules about where the first name ends and where the middle name begins. It didn't have to know anything about my application or <name>s at all. The same parser could be used in my application, or in a completely different application. The language my XML is written in doesn't even matter to the parser; XML written in English, Chinese, Hebrew, or any other language could all be read by the same parser, even if the person who wrote it didn't understand any of these languages.

But there's also another added benefit here: if I had previously written a program to deal with the first XML format, which had only a first and last name, that application could also accept the new XML format, without me having to change the code. So, because the parser takes care of the work of getting data out of the document for us, we can add to our XML format without breaking existing code, and new applications can take advantage of the new information if they wish. (Note that if we subtracted elements from our <name> example, or changed the names of elements, we would still have to modify our applications to deal with the changes.)

On the other hand, if we were just using our previous text-only format, any time we changed the data at all, every application using that data would have to be modified, retested, and redeployed.

Because it's so flexible, XML is targeted to be the basis for defining data exchange languages, especially for communication over the Internet. The language makes it very easy to work with data within applications, such as one that needs to access the <name> information above, but it also makes it easy to share information with others; we can pass our <name> information around the net, and even without our particular program they can read the data. They can even pull the file up in a regular text editor and look at the raw XML, if they like, or open it in a viewer such as IE5.

Why "Extensible"?

Since we have full control over the creation of our XML document, we can shape the data in any way we wish, so that it makes sense to our particular application. If we don't need the flexibility of our <name> example, and decide to describe a name in XML like this:

```
<designation>John Fitzgerald Johansen Doe</designation>
```

we are free to do so. If we want to create data in a way that only one particular computer program will ever use, we can do so. And if we feel that we want to share our data with other programs, or even other companies across the Internet, XML gives us the flexibility to do that as well. We are free to structure the same data in different ways that suit the requirements of an application or category of applications.

> This is where the *extensible* in Extensible Markup Language comes from: anyone is free to mark up data in any way using the language, even if others are doing it in completely different ways.

Of course, the benefits of XML become even more apparent when people use the same format to do common things, because this allows us to interchange information much more easily. There have already been numerous projects to produce industry-standard **vocabularies** to describe various types of data. For example, **Scalable Vector Graphics** (**SVG**) is an XML vocabulary for describing two-dimensional graphics; **MathML** is an XML vocabulary for describing mathematics as a basis for machine to machine communication; **Chemical Markup Language** (**CML**) is an XML vocabulary for the management of chemical information. The list goes on and on. Of course, you could write your own XML vocabularies to describe this type of information if you so wished, but if you use other, more common, formats, there is a better chance that you will be able to produce software which is compatible with other software.

HTML and XML: Apples and Red Delicious Apples

What HTML does for display, XML is designed to do for data exchange. Sometimes XML won't be up to a certain task, just like HTML is sometimes not up to the task of displaying certain information. (How many of us have Adobe Acrobat readers installed on our machines, for those documents on the web that HTML just can't do properly?) But when it comes to display, HTML does a good job most of the time, and those who work with XML believe that, most of the time, XML will do a good job to communicate information. Just like HTML authors sometimes give up precise layout and presentation for the sake of making their information accessible to all web browsers, XML developers will give up the small file sizes of proprietary formats for the flexibility of universal data access.

There is, of course, a fundamental difference between HTML and XML:

❑   HTML is designed for a *specific* application; to convey information to humans (usually visually, through a web browser)

❑   XML has no specific application; it is designed for whatever use you need it for

This is an important concept. Because HTML has its specific application, it also has a finite set of specific markup constructs (`<P>`, `<UL>`, `<H2>` etc.), which are used to create a correct HTML document. In theory, we can be confident that any web browser will understand an HTML document because all they have to do is understand this finite set of tags. (In practice, of course, I'm sure you've come across web pages which displayed properly in one web browser, but not another.)

On the other hand, if we create an XML document, we can be sure that any XML parser will be able to retrieve information from that document, but we can't guarantee that any application will be able to understand *what that information means*. That is, just because a parser can tell us that there is a piece of data called `<middle>`, and that the information contained therein is "Fitzgerald Johansen", it doesn't mean that there is any software in the world that knows what a `<middle>` is, or what it is used for, or what it means.

So we can create XML documents to describe any information we want, but before that XML can be considered useful, there must be applications written which understand it. Furthermore, in addition to the capabilities provided by the base XML specification, there are a number of related technologies, some of which we'll be covering in later chapters. These technologies provide more capabilities for us, making XML even more powerful than we've seen so far. Unfortunately, some of these technologies exist only in draft form, meaning that exactly how powerful these tools will be, or in what ways they'll be powerful, is yet to be seen.

Hierarchies of Information

We'll discuss the syntactical constructs that make up XML in later chapters, but before we continue, it might be useful to examine how data is structured in an XML document.

When it comes to large, or even moderate, amounts of information, it's usually better to group it into related sub-topics, rather than to have all of the information presented in one large blob. For example, this chapter is broken down into sub-topics, and further broken down into paragraphs; a tax form is broken down into sub-sections, across multiple pages. This makes the information easier to comprehend, as well as making it more accessible.

Software developers have been using this paradigm for years, using a structure called an **object model**. In an object model, all of the information that's being modeled is broken up into various objects, and the objects themselves are then grouped into a **hierarchy**. We'll be looking in more detail at object models in later chapters.

Hierarchies in HTML

For example, when working with **Dynamic HTML** (**DHTML**) there is an object model available for working with HTML documents, called the **Document Object Model** or **DOM**. This allows us to write code in an HTML document, like the following JavaScript:

```
alert(document.title);
```

Here we are using the `alert()` function to pop up a message box telling us the number of HTML elements in the document. That's done by accessing an object called `document`, which contains all of the information needed about the HTML document. The `document` object includes a property called `title`, which returns the title of the current HTML document.

> *The information that the object provides comes to us in the form of **properties**, and the functionality available comes to us in the form of **methods**. Again, this is a subject we'll come back to later on.*

Hierarchies in XML

XML also groups information in hierarchies. The items in our documents relate to each other in **parent/child** and **sibling/sibling** relationships.

> **These "items" are called** elements. **We'll see a more precise definition of what exactly an element is in Chapter 2. For now just think of them as the individual pieces of information in the data.**

Consider our <name> example, shown hierarchically:

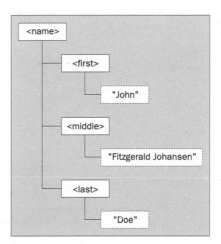

<name> is a parent of <first>, which is a child of <name>. <first>, <middle>, and <last> are all siblings to each other (they are all children of <name>). Note also that the text is a child of the element. For example "John" is a child of <first>.

This structure is also called a **tree**; any parts of the tree that contain children are called **branches**, while parts that have no children are called **leaves**.

Because the <name> element has only other elements for children, and not text, it is said to have **element content**. Conversely, since <first>, <middle>, and <last> have only text as children, they are said to have **simple content**.

Elements can contain both text and other elements. They are then said to have **mixed content**. For example:

```
<doc>
   <parent>this is some <em>text</em> in my element</parent>
</doc>
```

Here, <parent> has three children:

❑   A text child containing the text "this is some"

❑   An <em> child

❑   Another text child containing the text " in my element"

It is structured like this:

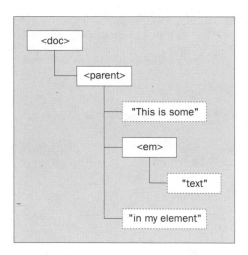

Relationships can also be defined by making the family tree analogy work a little bit harder: <doc> is an **ancestor** of <em>; <em> is a **descendant** of <doc>.

Once you understand the hierarchical relationships between your items (and the text they contain), you'll have a better understanding of the nature of XML. You'll also be better prepared to work with some of the other technologies surrounding XML, which make extensive use of this paradigm.

What's a Document Type?

XML's beauty comes from its ability to create a document to describe any information we want. It's completely flexible as to how we structure our data. But eventually, we're going to want to settle on a particular design for our information, and say "to adhere to our XML format, structure the data like this".

For example, when we created our <name> XML above, we created some **structured data**. We not only included all of the information about a name, but our hierarchy also contains implicit information about how some pieces of data relate to other pieces (our <name> contains a <first>, for example).

But it's more than that; we also created a specific set of elements, which is called a **vocabulary**. That is, we defined a number of XML elements which all work together to form a name: <name>, <first>, <middle>, and <last>.

But, it's even more than that! The most important thing we created was a **document type**. We created a specific type of document, which must be structured in a specific way, to describe a specific type of information. Although we haven't explicitly defined them, there are certain rules that the elements in our vocabulary must adhere to, in order for our <name> document to conform to our document type. For example:

- ❑ The top-most element must be the <name> element
- ❑ The <first>, <middle>, and <last> elements must be children of that element
- ❑ The <first>, <middle>, and <last> elements must be in that order
- ❑ There must be information in the <first> element and in the <last> element, but there doesn't have to be any information in the <middle> element

And so on.

In later chapters, you'll see that there are different syntaxes we can use to formally define an XML document type. Some XML parsers know how to read these syntaxes, and can use them to determine if your XML document really adheres to the rules in the document type or not.

However, all of the syntaxes used to define document types so far are lacking; they can provide some type checking, but not enough for many applications. Furthermore, they can't express the human meaning of terms in a vocabulary. For this reason, when creating XML document types, human-readable documentation should also be provided. For our <name> example, if we want others to be able to use the same format to describe names in their XML, we should provide them with documentation to describe how it works.

In real life, this human-readable documentation is often used in conjunction with one or more of the syntaxes available.

No, Really – What's a Document Type?

Well, okay, maybe I was a little bit hasty when labeling our <name> example a document type. The truth is that others who work with XML may call it something different.

One of the problems people encounter when they communicate is that they sometimes use different terms to describe the same thing. (Or, even worse, use the same term to describe different things!) For example, I might call the thing that I drive a car, whereas someone else might call it an auto, and someone else again may call it a G-Class Vehicle. Furthermore, when I say car I *usually* mean a vehicle that has four wheels, is made for transporting passengers, and is smaller than a truck. (Notice how fuzzy this definition is, and that it depends further on what the definition of a truck is.) When someone else uses the word car, or if I use the word car in certain circumstances, it may instead just mean a land-based motorized vehicle, as opposed to a boat or a plane.

The same thing happens in XML. It turns out that when you're using XML to create document types, you don't really have to think (or care) about the fact that you're creating document types; you just design your XML in a way that makes sense for your application, and then use it. If you ever did think about exactly what you were creating, you might have called it something other than a document type.

> The terms document type and vocabulary are ones we picked for this book because they do a good job of describing what we need to describe, but they are not universal terms used throughout the XML community. Regardless of the terms you use, the concepts are very important.

Who is the World Wide Web Consortium?

One of the reasons that HTML and XML are such great ideas is that they're **standards**. That means that anyone can follow these standards, and the solutions they develop will be able to interoperate. So who creates these standards?

The **World Wide Web Consortium** (**W3C**) was started in 1994, according to their web site (http://www.w3.org), "to lead the World Wide Web to its full potential by developing common protocols that promote its evolution and ensure its interoperability". Recognizing this need for standards, the W3C produces **recommendations** which describe the basic building blocks of the web. They call them recommendations, instead of standards, because it is up to others to follow the recommendations to provide the interoperability.

Their most famous contribution to the web is, of course, the HTML recommendation; when a web browser claims that it follows version 3.2 or 4.0 of the HTML recommendation, they're talking about the recommendation developed under the authority of the W3C.

The reason specifications from the W3C are so widely implemented is that the creation of these standards is a somewhat open process: any company or individual can join the W3C's membership, and membership allows these companies or individuals to take part in the standards process. This means that web browsers like Netscape Navigator and Microsoft Internet Explorer are more likely to implement the same version of the HTML standard, because both Microsoft and Netscape were involved in the evolution of that standard.

Because of the interoperability goals of XML, the W3C is a good place to develop standards around the technology. All of the technologies covered in this book are based on standards from the W3C, from the XML 1.0 Specification, to the XSLT Specification, to the XPath Specification, etc.

What are the Pieces that Make Up XML?

"Communicating information" is a pretty broad topic, and as such it would be futile to try and define a specification to cover it fully. For this reason there are a number of inter-related specifications (some of which are still in the early stages of development) that all work together to form the XML family of technologies, with each specification covering different aspects of communicating information. Here are some of the more important ones:

❑ **XML 1.0** is the base specification upon which the XML family is built. It describes the syntax that XML documents have to follow, the rules that XML parsers have to follow, and anything else you need to know to read or write an XML document. (It also defines DTDs, although they sometimes get treated as a separate technology. See the next bullet.)

❑ Because we can make up our own structures and element names for our documents, **DTDs** and **Schemas** provide ways to create templates for our document types. We can check to make sure other documents adhere to these templates, and other developers can produce compatible documents. DTDs and Schemas are discussed in Chapters 9, 10 and 11.

❑ **Namespaces** provide a means to distinguish one XML vocabulary from another, which allows us to create richer documents by combining multiple vocabularies into one document type. We'll look at namespaces in detail in Chapter 8.

❑ **XPath** describes a querying language for addressing parts of an XML document. This allows applications to ask for a specific piece of an XML document, instead of having to always deal with one large "chunk" of information. For example, XPath could be used to get "all the last names" from a document. We'll discuss XPath in Chapter 4.

❑ As we discussed earlier, in some cases we may want to display our XML documents. For simpler cases, we can use **Cascading Style Sheets** (**CSS**) to define the presentation of our documents. And, for more complex cases, we can use **Extensible Style sheet Language** (**XSL**), that consists of **XSLT**, which can transform our documents from one type to another, and **Formatting Objects**, which deal with display. These technologies are covered in Chapters 3, 4 and 5.

❑ **XLink** and **XPointer** are languages which are used to link XML documents to each other, in a similar manner to HTML hyperlinks. They are described in Chapter 12.

❑ To provide a means for more traditional applications to interface with XML documents, there is a document object model – the **DOM**, which we'll discuss in Chapter 6. An alternative way for programmers to interface with XML documents from their code is to use the Simple API for XML (**SAX**) which is the subject of Chapter 7.

Where is XML Used, and Where Can It be Used?

Well, that's quite a question. XML is platform and language independent, which means it doesn't matter that one computer may be using, for example, Visual Basic on a Microsoft operating system, and the other is a Unix machine with Java code. Really, any time one computer program needs to communicate with another program, XML is a potential fit for the exchange format. The following are just a few examples, and we'll be discussing such applications in more detail throughout the book.

Reducing Server Load

Web-based applications can use XML to reduce the load on the web servers. This can be done by keeping all information on the client for as long as possible, and then sending the information to those servers in one big XML document.

Web Site Content

The W3C uses XML to write their specifications. These XML documents can then be transformed to HTML for display (by XSLT), or transformed to a number of other presentation formats.

Some web sites also use XML entirely for their content, where traditionally HTML would have been used. This XML can then be transformed to HTML via XSLT, or displayed directly in browsers via CSS. In fact, the web servers can even determine dynamically what kind of browser is retrieving the information, and then decide what to do. (For example, transform the XML to HTML for older browsers, and just send the XML straight to the client for newer browsers, reducing the load on the server.)

Remote Procedure Calls

XML is also used as a protocol for **Remote Procedure Calls** (**RPC**). RPC is a protocol which allows objects on one computer to call objects on another computer to do work, allowing distributed computing. As we'll see in Chapter 14, using XML and HTTP for these RPC calls allows this to occur even through a firewall, which would normally block such calls, providing greater opportunities for distributed computing.

E-Commerce

E-Commerce is one of those buzzwords that you hear all over the place. Companies are discovering that by communicating via the Internet, instead of by more traditional methods (such as faxing, human-to-human communication, etc.), they can streamline their processes, decreasing costs and increasing response times. Whenever one company needs to send data to another, XML is the perfect fit for the exchange format.

When the companies involved have some kind of on-going relationship this is known as business to business (**B2B**) e-commerce. There are also business to consumer (B2C) transactions – you may even have used this to buy this book if you bought it on the Internet. Both types have their potential uses for XML.

And there are many, many other applications where XML makes a good fit. Hopefully, after you've finished this book, you'll be able to intelligently decide when XML works, and when it doesn't.

Summary

In this chapter, we've had an overview of what XML is and why it's so useful. We've seen the advantages of text and binary files, and the way that XML combines the advantages of both while eliminating most of the disadvantages. We have also seen the flexibility we have in creating data in any format we wish.

Because XML is a subset of a proven technology, SGML, there are many years of experience behind the standard. And because there are other technologies built around XML, we can create applications that are as complex or simple as our situation warrants.

Much of the power that we get from XML comes from the rigid way in which documents must be written. In the next chapter, we'll take a closer look at the rules for creating well-formed XML.

Well-Formed XML

We've discussed some of the reasons why XML makes sense for communicating data, so now let's get our hands dirty and learn how to create our own XML documents. This chapter will cover all you need to know to create "well-formed" XML.

> **Well-formed XML is XML that meets certain grammatical rules outlined in the XML 1.0 specification.**

You will learn:

- ❑ How to create XML **elements** using **start-** and **end-tags**
- ❑ How to further describe elements with **attributes**
- ❑ How to declare your document as being XML
- ❑ How to send instructions to applications that are processing the XML document
- ❑ Which characters aren't allowed in XML, and how to put them in anyway

Because XML and HTML appear so similar, and because you're probably already familiar with HTML, we'll be making comparisons between the two languages in this chapter. However, if you don't have any knowledge of HTML, you shouldn't find it too hard to follow along.

If you have Internet Explorer 5, you may find it useful to save some of the examples in this chapter on your hard drive, and view the results in the browser. If you don't have IE5, some of the examples will have screenshots to show what the end results look like.

Tags and Text and Elements, Oh My!

It's time to stop calling things just "items" and "text"; we need some names for the pieces that make up an XML document. To get cracking, let's break down the simple `<name>` document we created in Chapter 1:

```
<name>
  <first>John</first>
  <middle>Fitzgerald Johansen</middle>
  <last>Doe</last>
</name>
```

The words between the < and > characters are XML **tags**. The information in our document (our data) is contained within the various tags that constitute the markup of the document. This makes it easy to distinguish the *information* in the document from the *markup*.

As you can see, the tags are paired together, so that any opening tag also has a closing tag. In XML parlance, these are called **start-tags** and **end-tags**. The end-tags are the same as the start-tags, except that they have a "/" right after the opening < character.

In this regard, XML tags work the same as start-tags and end-tags do in HTML. For example, you would create an HTML paragraph like this:

```
<P>This is a paragraph.</P>
```

As you can see, there is a `<P>` start-tag, and a `</P>` end-tag, just like we use for XML.

All of the information from the start of a start-tag to the end of an end-tag, and including everything in between, is called an **element**. So:

- ❏ `<first>` is a start-tag
- ❏ `</first>` is an end-tag
- ❏ `<first>John</first>` is an element

The text between the start-tag and end-tag of an element is called the **element content**. The content between our tags will often just be data (as opposed to other elements). In this case, the element content is referred to as **Parsed Character DATA**, which is almost always referred to using its acronym, **PCDATA**.

> *Whenever you come across a strange-looking term like PCDATA, it's usually a good bet the term is inherited from SGML. Because XML is a subset of SGML, there are a lot of these inherited terms.*

The whole document, starting at `<name>` and ending at `</name>`, is also an element, which happens to include other elements. (And, in this case, the element is called the **root element**, which we'll be talking about later.)

To put this new-found knowledge into action, let's create an example that contains more information than just a name.

We're going to build an XML document to describe one of the greatest CDs ever produced, *Dare to be Stupid*, by Weird Al Yankovic. But before we break out Notepad and start typing, we need to know what information we're capturing.

In Chapter 1, we learned that XML is hierarchical in nature; information is structured like a tree, with parent/child relationships. This means that we'll have to arrange our CD information in a tree structure as well.

1. Since this is a CD, we'll need to capture information like the artist, title, and date released, as well as the genre of music. We'll also need information about each song on the CD, such as the title and length. And, since Weird Al is famous for his parodies, we'll include information about what song (if any) this one is a parody of.

Here's the hierarchy we'll be creating:

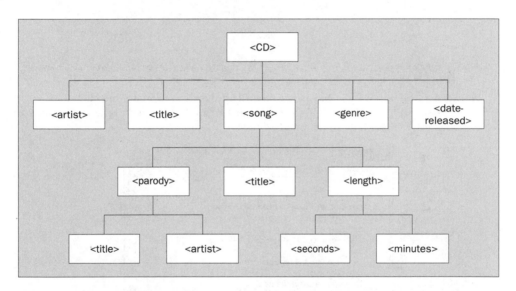

Some of these elements, like <artist>, will appear only once; others, like <song>, will appear multiple times in the document. Also, some will have PCDATA only, while some will include their information as child elements instead. For example, the <artist> element will contain PCDATA for the title, whereas the <song> element won't contain any PCDATA of its own, but will contain child elements that further break down the information.

2. With this in mind, we're now ready to start entering XML. If you have Internet Explorer 5 installed on your machine, type the following into Notepad, and save it to your hard drive as cd.xml:

```
<CD>
   <artist>"Weird Al" Yankovic</artist>
   <title>Dare to be Stupid</title>
   <genre>parody</genre>
```

```
<date-released>1990</date-released>
<song>
  <title>Like A Surgeon</title>
  <length>
    <minutes>3</minutes>
    <seconds>33</seconds>
  </length>
  <parody>
    <title>Like A Virgin</title>
    <artist>Madonna</artist>
  </parody>
</song>
<song>
  <title>Dare to be Stupid</title>
  <length>
    <minutes>3</minutes>
    <seconds>25</seconds>
  </length>
  <parody></parody>
</song>
</CD>
```

For the sake of brevity, we'll only enter two of the songs on the CD, but the idea is there nonetheless.

3. Now, open the file in IE5. (Navigate to the file in Explorer and double click on it, or open up the browser and type the path in the URL bar.) If you have typed in the tags exactly as shown, the cd.xml file will look something like this:

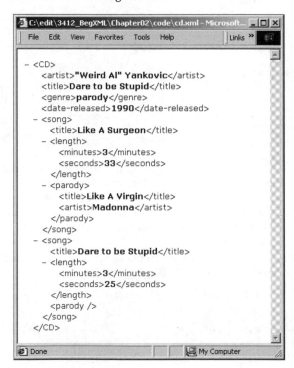

How It Works

Here we've created a hierarchy of information about a CD, so we've named the root element accordingly.

The `<CD>` element has children for the artist, title, genre, and date, as well as one child for each song on the disc. The `<song>` element has children for the title, length, and, since this is Weird Al we're talking about, what song (if any) this is a parody of. Again, for the sake of this example, the `<length>` element was broken down still further, to have children for minutes and seconds, and the `<parody>` element broken down to have the title and artist of the parodied song.

You may have noticed that the IE5 browser changed `<parody></parody>` into `<parody/>`. We'll talk about this shorthand syntax a little bit later, but don't worry: it's perfectly legal.

If we were to write a CD Player application, we could make use of this information to create a play-list for our CD. It could read the information under our `<song>` element to get the name and length of each song to display to the user, display the genre of the CD in the title bar, etc. Basically, it could make use of any information contained in our XML document.

Rules for Elements

Obviously, if we could just create elements in any old way we wanted, we wouldn't be any further along than our text file examples from the previous chapter. There must be some rules for elements, which are fundamental to the understanding of XML.

> **XML documents must adhere to these rules to be well-formed.**

We'll list them, briefly, before getting down to details:

- ❏   Every start-tag must have a matching end-tag
- ❏   Tags can't overlap
- ❏   XML documents can have only one root element
- ❏   Element names must obey XML naming conventions
- ❏   XML is case-sensitive
- ❏   XML will keep white space in your text

Every Start-tag Must Have an End-tag

One of the problems with parsing SGML documents is that not every element requires a start-tag and an end-tag. Take the following HTML for example:

```
<HTML>
<BODY>
<P>Here is some text in an HTML paragraph.
<BR>
Here is some more text in the same paragraph.
<P>And here is some text in another HTML paragraph.</p>
</BODY>
</HTML>
```

Notice that the first `<P>` tag has no closing `</P>` tag. This is allowed – and sometimes even encouraged – in HTML, because most web browsers can detect automatically where the end of the paragraph should be. In this case, when the browser comes across the second `<P>` tag, it knows to end the first paragraph. Then there's the `<BR>` tag (line break), which by definition has no closing tag.

Also, notice that the second `<P>` start-tag is matched by a `</p>` end-tag, in lower case. HTML browsers have to be smart enough to realize that both of these tags delimit the same element, but as we'll see soon, this would cause a problem for an XML parser.

The problem is that this makes HTML parsers much harder to write. Code has to be included to take into account all of these factors, which often makes the parsers much larger, and much harder to debug. What's more, the way that files are parsed is not standardized – different browsers do it differently, leading to incompatibilities.

For now, just remember that in XML the end-tag is required, and has to exactly match the start-tag.

Tags Can Not Overlap

Because XML is strictly hierarchical, you have to be careful to close your child elements before you close your parents. (This is called **properly nesting** your tags.) Let's look at another HTML example to demonstrate this:

```
<P>Some <STRONG>formatted <EM>text</STRONG>, but</EM> no grammar no good!</P>
```

This would produce the following output on a web browser:

Some **formatted *text*, *but*** no grammar no good!

As you can see, the `<STRONG>` tags cover the text `formatted text`, while the `<EM>` tags cover the text `text, but`.

But is `<EM>` a child of `<STRONG>`, or is `<STRONG>` a child of `<EM>`? Or are they both siblings, and children of `<P>`? According to our stricter XML rules, the answer is none of the above. The HTML code, as written, can't be arranged as a proper hierarchy, and could therefore not be well-formed XML.

If ever you're in doubt as to whether your XML tags are overlapping, try to rearrange them visually to be hierarchical. If the tree makes sense, then you're okay. Otherwise, you'll have to rework your markup.

For example, we could get the same effect as above by doing the following:

```
<P>Some <STRONG>formatted <EM>text</EM></STRONG><EM>, but</EM> no grammar no
good!</P>
```

Which can be properly formatted in a tree, like this:

```
<P>
  Some
  <STRONG>
    formatted
    <EM>
```

```
        text
      </EM>
    </STRONG>
    <EM>
      , but
    </EM>
    no grammar no good!
  </P>
```

An XML Document Can Have Only One Root Element

In our `<name>` document, the `<name>` element is called the **root element**. This is the top-level element in the document, and all the other elements are its children or descendents. An XML document must have one and only one root element: in fact, it must have a root element even if it has no content.

For example, the following XML is not well-formed, because it has a number of root elements:

```
<name>John</name>
<name>Jane</name>
```

To make this well-formed, we'd need to add a top-level element, like this:

```
<names>
    <name>John</name>
    <name>Jane</name>
</names>
```

So while it may seem a bit of an inconvenience, it turns out that it's incredibly easy to follow this rule. If you have a document structure with multiple root-like elements, simply create a higher-level element to contain them.

Element Names

If we're going to be creating elements we're going to have to give them names, and XML is very generous in the names we're allowed to use. For example, there aren't any reserved words to avoid in XML, as there are in most programming languages, so we have a lot flexibility in this regard.

However, there are some rules that we must follow:

- ❑ Names can start with letters (including non-Latin characters) or the "_" character, but not numbers or other punctuation characters.

- ❑ After the first character, numbers are allowed, as are the characters "-" and ".".

- ❑ Names can't contain spaces.

- ❑ Names can't contain the ":" character. Strictly speaking, this character is allowed, but the XML specification says that it's "reserved". You should avoid using it in your documents, unless you are working with namespaces (which are covered in Chapter 8).

- ❑ Names can't start with the letters "xml", in uppercase, lowercase, or mixed – you can't start a name with "xml", "XML", "XmL", or any other combination.

- ❑ There can't be a space after the opening "<" character; the name of the element must come immediately after it. However, there can be space before the closing ">"character, if desired.

Here are some examples of valid names:

```
<first.name>
<résumé>
```

And here are some examples of invalid names:

```
<xml-tag>
```

which starts with xml,

```
<123>
```

which starts with a number,

```
<fun=xml>
```

because the "=" sign is illegal, and:

```
<my tag>
```

which contains a space.

> **Remember these rules for element names – they also apply to naming other things in XML.**

Case-Sensitivity

Another important point to keep in mind is that the tags in XML are **case-sensitive**. (This is a big difference from HTML, which is case-insensitive.) This means that `<first>` is different from `<FIRST>`, which is different from `<First>`.

This sometimes seems odd to English-speaking users of XML, since English words can easily be converted to upper- or lower-case with no loss of meaning. But in almost every other language in the world, the concept of case is either not applicable (in other words, what's the uppercase of   ? Or the lowercase, for that matter?), or not extremely important (what's the uppercase of é? The answer may be different, depending on the context). To put intelligent rules into the XML specification for case-folding would probably have doubled or trebled its size, and still only benefited the English-speaking section of the population. Luckily, it doesn't take long to get used to having case-sensitive names.

This is the reason that our previous `<P></p>` HTML example would not work in XML; since the tags are case-sensitive, an XML parser would not be able to match the `</p>` end-tag with any start-tags, and neither would it be able to match the `<P>` start-tag with any end-tags.

> **Warning!** Because XML is case-sensitive, you could legally create an XML document which has both `<first>` and `<First>` elements, which have different meanings. This is a bad idea, and will cause nothing but confusion! You should always try to give your elements distinct names, for your sanity, and for the sanity of those to come after you.

To help combat these kinds of problems, it's a good idea to pick a naming style and stick to it. Some examples of common styles are:

❑   `<first_name>`

❑   `<firstName>`

❑   `<first-name>` (some people don't like this convention, because the "`-`" character is used for subtraction in so many programming languages, but it is legal)

❑   `<FirstName>`

Which style you choose isn't important; what is important is that you stick to it. A naming convention only helps when it's used consistently. For this book, I'll usually use the `<FirstName>` convention, because that's what I've grown used to.

White Space in PCDATA

There is a special category of characters, called **white space**. This includes things like the space character, new lines (what you get when you hit the *Enter* key), and tabs. White space is used to separate words, as well as to make text more readable.

Those familiar with HTML are probably quite aware of the practice of white space stripping. In HTML, any white space considered insignificant is stripped out of the document when it is processed. For example, take the following HTML:

```
<P>This is a paragraph.        It has a whole bunch
   of space.</P>
```

As far as HTML is concerned, anything more than a single space between the words in a `<P>` is insignificant. So all of the spaces between the first period and the word `It` would be stripped, except for one. Also, the line feed after the word `bunch` and the spaces before `of` would be stripped down to one space. As a result, the previous HTML would be rendered in a browser as:

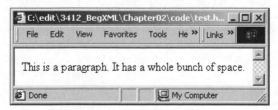

In order to get the results as they appear in the HTML above, we'd have to add special HTML markup to the source, like the following:

```
<P>This is a paragraph.       It has a whole
bunch<BR>
  of space.</P>
```

  specifies that we should insert a space (nbsp stands for **Non-Breaking SPace**), and the <BR> tag specifies that there should be a line feed. This would format the output as:

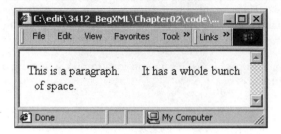

Alternatively, if we wanted to have the text displayed exactly as it is in the source file, we could use the <PRE> tag. This specifically tells the HTML parser not to strip the white space, so we could write the following and also get the desired results:

```
<PRE>This is a paragraph.        It has a whole bunch
   of space.</PRE>
```

However, in most web browsers, the <PRE> tag also has the added effect that the text is rendered in a fixed-width font, like the courier font we use for code in this book.

White space stripping is very advantageous for a language like HTML, which has become primarily a means for displaying information. It allows the source for an HTML document to be formatted in a readable way for the person writing the HTML, while displaying it formatted in a readable, and possibly quite different, way for the user.

In XML, however, no white space stripping takes place for PCDATA. This means that for the following XML tag:

```
<tag>This is a paragraph.        It has a whole bunch
   of space.</tag>
```

the PCDATA is:

This is a paragraph.   It has a whole bunch
   of space.

Just like our second HTML example, none of the white space has been stripped out. As far as white space stripping goes, all XML elements are treated just as the HTML <PRE> tag. This makes the rules much easier to understand for XML than they are for HTML:

> **In XML, the white space stays.**

Unfortunately, if you view the above XML in IE5 the white space will be stripped out – or will seem to be. This is because IE5 is not actually showing you the XML directly; it uses a technology called XSL to transform the XML to HTML, and it displays the HTML. Then, because IE5 is an HTML browser, it strips out the white space.

End-of-Line White Space

However, there is one form of white space stripping that XML performs on PCDATA, which is the handling of **new line** characters. The problem is that there are two characters that are used for new lines – the **line feed** character and the **carriage return** – and computers running Windows, computers running Unix, and Macintosh computers all use these characters differently.

For example, to get a new line in Windows, an application would use both the line feed and the carriage return character together, whereas on Unix only the line feed would be used. This could prove to be very troublesome when creating XML documents, because Unix machines would treat the new lines in a document differently than the Windows boxes, which would treat them differently than the Macintosh boxes, and our XML interoperability would be lost.

For this reason, it was decided that XML parsers would change all new lines to a single line feed character before processing. This means that any XML application will know, no matter which operating system it's running under, that a new line will be represented by a single line feed character. This makes data exchange between multiple computers running different operating systems that much easier, since programmers don't have to deal with the (sometimes annoying) end-of-line logic.

White Space in Markup

As well as the white space in our data, there could also be white space in an XML document that's not actually part of the document. For example:

```
<tag>
  <another-tag>This is some XML</another-tag>
</tag>
```

While any white space contained within <another-tag>'s PCDATA is part of the data, there is also a new line after <tag>, and some spaces before <another-tag>. These spaces could be there just to make the document easier to read, while not actually being part of its data. This "readability" white space is called **extraneous white space**.

While an XML parser must pass all white space through to the application, it can also inform the application which white space is not actually part of an element's PCDATA, but is just extraneous white space.

So how does the parser decide whether this is extraneous white space or not? That depends on what kind of data we specify <tag> should contain. If <tag> can only contain other elements (and no PCDATA) then the white space will be considered extraneous. However, if <tag> is allowed to contain PCDATA, then the white space will be considered part of that PCDATA, so it will be retained.

Unfortunately, from this document alone an XML parser would have no way to tell whether <tag> is supposed to contain PCDATA or not, which means that it has to assume none of the white space is extraneous. We'll see how we can get the parser to recognize this as extraneous white space in Chapter 9 when we discuss content models.

Attributes

In addition to tags and elements, XML documents can also include **attributes**.

> **Attributes are simple name/value pairs associated with an element.**

They are attached to the start-tag, as shown below, but not to the end-tag:

```
<name nickname='Shiny John'>
  <first>John</first>
  <middle>Fitzgerald Johansen</middle>
  <last>Doe</last>
</name>
```

Attributes must have values – even if that value is just an empty string (like " ") – and those values must be in quotes. So the following, which is part of a common HTML tag, is not legal in XML:

```
<INPUT checked>
```

and neither is this:

```
<INPUT checked=true>
```

Either single quotes or double quotes are fine, but they have to match. For example, to make this well-formed XML, you can use one of these:

```
<INPUT checked='true'>
<INPUT checked="true">
```

but you can't use:

```
<INPUT checked="true'>
```

> *Because either single or double quotes are allowed, it's easy to include quote characters in your attribute values, like* `"John's nickname"` *or* `'I said "hi" to him'`. *You just have to be careful not to accidentally close your attribute, like* `'John's nickname'`; *if an XML parser sees an attribute value like this, it will think you're closing the value at the second single quote, and will raise an error when it sees the* `"s"` *which comes right after it.*

The same rules apply to naming attributes as apply to naming elements: names are case sensitive, can't start with "xml", and so on. Also, you can't have more than one attribute with the same name on an element. So if we create an XML document like this:

```
<bad att="1" att="2"></bad>
```

we will get the following error in IE5:

Try It Out – Adding Attributes to Al's CD

With all of the information we recorded about our CD in our earlier Try It Out, we forgot to include the CD's serial number, or the length of the disc. Let's add some attributes, so that our hypothetical CD Player application can easily find this information out.

1. Open your `cd.xml` file created earlier, and resave it to your hard drive as `cd2.xml`.

2. With our new-found attributes knowledge, add two attributes to the `<CD>` element, like this:

```
<CD serial=B6B41B
    disc-length='36:55'>
  <artist>"Weird Al" Yankovic</artist>
  <title>Dare to be Stupid</title>
  <genre>parody</genre>
  <date-released>1990</date-released>
  <song>
    <title>Like A Surgeon</title>
    <length>
      <minutes>3</minutes>
      <seconds>33</seconds>
    </length>
    <parody>
      <title>Like A Virgin</title>
      <artist>Madonna</artist>
    </parody>
  </song>
  <song>
    <title>Dare to be Stupid</title>
    <length>
      <minutes>3</minutes>
      <seconds>25</seconds>
    </length>
    <parody></parody>
  </song>
</CD>
```

3. If you typed in exactly what's written above, when you display it in IE5 it should look something like this:

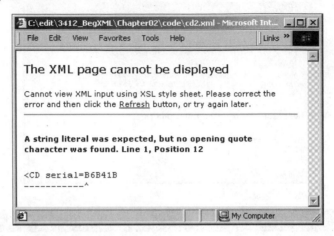

4. Now edit the first attribute, like this:

```
<CD serial='B6B41B'
    disc-length='36:55'>
```

5. Re-save the file, and view it in IE5. It will look something like this:

How It Works

Using attributes, we added some information about the CD's serial number and length to our document:

```
<CD serial=B6B41B
    disc-length='36:55'>
```

When the XML parser got to the "=" character after the `serial` attribute, it expected an opening quotation mark, but instead it found a B. This is an error, and it caused the parser to stop and raise the error to the user.

So we changed our `serial` attribute declaration:

```
<CD serial='B6B41B'
```

and this time the browser displayed our XML correctly.

The information we added might be useful, for example, in the CD Player application we considered earlier. We could write our CD Player to use the serial number of a CD to load any previous settings the user may have previously saved (such as a custom play list).

Why Use Attributes?

There have been many debates in the XML community about whether attributes are really necessary, and if so, where they should be used. Here are some of the main points in that debate:

Attributes Can Provide Metadata that May Not be Relevant to Most Applications Dealing with Our XML

For example, if we know that some applications may care about a CD's serial number, but most won't, it may make sense to make it an attribute. This logically separates the data most applications will need from the data that most applications won't need.

In reality, there is no such thing as "pure metadata" – all information is "data" to *some* application. Think about HTML; you could break the information in HTML into two types of data: the data to be shown to a human, and the data to be used by the web browser to format the human-readable data. From one standpoint, the data used to format the data would be metadata, but to the browser or the person writing the HTML, the metadata *is* the data. Therefore, attributes can make sense when we're separating one type of information from another.

What Do Attributes Buy Me that Elements Don't?

Can't elements do anything attributes can do?

In other words, on the face of it there's really no difference between:

```
<name nickname='Shiny John'></name>
```

and:

```
<name>
  <nickname>Shiny John</nickname>
</name>
```

So why bother to pollute the language with two ways of doing the same thing?

The main reason that XML was invented was that SGML could do some great things, but it was too massively difficult to use without a fully-fledged SGML expert on hand. So one concept behind XML is a simpler, kinder, gentler SGML. For this reason, many people don't like attributes, because they add a complexity to the language that they feel isn't needed.

On the other hand, some people find attributes easier to use – for example, they don't require nesting and you don't have to worry about crossed tags.

Why Use Elements, if Attributes Take Up So Much Less Space?

Wouldn't it save bandwidth to use attributes instead?

For example, if we were to rewrite our `<name>` document to use only attributes, it might look like this:

```
<name nickname='Shiny John' first='John' middle='Fitzgerald Johansen'
last='Doe'></name>
```

Which takes up much less space than our earlier code using elements.

However, in systems where size is really an issue, it turns out that simple compression techniques would work much better than trying to optimize the XML. And because of the way compression works, you end up with almost the same file sizes regardless of whether attributes or elements are used.

Besides, when you try to optimize XML this way, you lose many of the benefits XML offers, such as readability and descriptive tag names. And there are cases where using elements allows more flexibility and scope for extension. For example, if we decided that `first` needed additional metadata in the future, it would be much simpler to modify our code if we'd used elements rather than attributes.

Why Use Attributes when Elements Look So Much Better? I Mean, Why Use Elements when Attributes Look So Much Better?

Many people have different opinions as to whether attributes or child elements "look better". In this case, it comes down to a matter of personal preference and style.

In fact, *much* of the attributes versus elements debate comes from personal preference. Many, but not all, of the arguments boil down to "I like the one better than the other". But since XML has both elements and attributes, and neither one is going to go away, you're free to use both. Choose whichever works best for your application, whichever looks better to you, or whichever you're most comfortable with.

Comments

Comments provide a way to insert into an XML document text that isn't really part of the document, but rather is intended for people who are reading the XML source itself.

Anyone who has used a programming language will be familiar with the idea of comments: you want to be able to annotate your code (or your XML), so that those coming after you will be able to figure out what you were doing. (And remember: the one who comes after you may be you! Code you wrote six months ago might be as foreign to you as code someone else wrote.)

Of course, comments may not be as relevant to XML as they are to programming languages; after all, this is just data, and it's self-describing to boot. But you never know when they're going to come in handy, and there are cases where comments can be very useful, even in data.

Comments start with the string `<!--` and end with the string `-->`, as shown here:

```
<name nickname='Shiny John'>
  <first>John</first>
  <!--John lost his middle name in a fire-->
  <middle></middle>
  <last>Doe</last>
</name>
```

There are a couple of points that we need to note about comments. First, you can't have a comment inside a tag, so the following is illegal:

```
<middle></middle <!--John lost his middle name in a fire--> >
```

Second, you can't use the string `--` inside a comment, so the following is also illegal:

```
<!-- John lost his middle name -- in a fire-->
```

The XML specification states that an XML parser doesn't need to pass these comments on to the application, meaning that you should never count on being able to use the information inside a comment from your application.

> **HTML programmers have often used the trick of inserting scripting code in comments, to protect users with older browsers that didn't support the `<SCRIPT>` tag. That kind of trick can't be done in XML, since comments won't necessarily be available to the application. Therefore, if you have text that you need to get at later,** *put it in an element or an attribute*!

Try It Out – Some Comments On Al's CD

Since we've only included a couple of the songs from this fine album in our document, perhaps we should inform others that this is the case. That way some kind soul may finish the job for us!

1. Open up your `cd2.xml` file, make the following changes, and save the modified XML file as `cd3.xml`:

```
<CD serial='B6B41B'
    disc-length='36:55'>
  <artist>"Weird Al" Yankovic</artist>
  <title>Dare to be Stupid</title>
  <genre>parody</genre>
  <date-released>1990</date-released>
  <!--date-released is the date released to CD, not to record-->
  <song>
```

```
        <title>Like A Surgeon</title>
        <length>
          <minutes>3</minutes>
          <seconds>33</seconds>
        </length>
        <parody>
          <title>Like A Virgin</title>
          <artist>Madonna</artist>
        </parody>
      </song>
      <song>
        <title>Dare to be Stupid</title>
        <length>
          <minutes>3</minutes>
          <seconds>25</seconds>
        </length>
        <parody></parody>
      </song>
    <!--there are more songs on this CD, but I didn't have time to include
        them-->
  </CD>
```

2. View this in IE5:

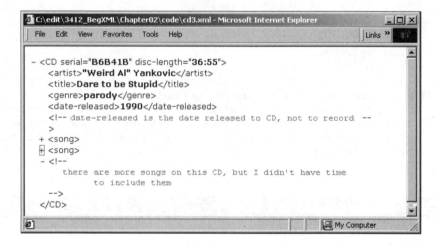

How It Works

With the new comments, anyone who reads the source for our XML document will be able to see that there are actually more than two songs on "Dare To Be Stupid". Furthermore, they can see some information regarding the <date-released> element, which may help them in writing applications that work with this information.

In this example, the XML parser included with IE5 *does* pass comments up to the application, so IE5 has displayed our comments. But remember that a lot of the time, for all intents and purposes this information is only available to people reading the source file. The information in comments *may or may not* be passed up to our application, depending on which parser we're using. We can't count on it, unless we specifically choose a parser that does pass them through. This means that the application has no way to know whether or not the list of songs included here is comprehensive.

Try It Out – Making Sure Comments Get Seen

If we really need this information, we should add in some real markup to indicate it.

1. Modify cd3.xml like this, and save it as cd4.xml:

```
<CD><!--our attributes used to be here-->
  <songs>11</songs>
  <!--the rest of our XML...-->
  <artist>"Weird Al" Yankovic</artist>
  <title>Dare to be Stupid</title>
  <genre>parody</genre>
  <date-released>1990</date-released>
  <song>
    <title>Like A Surgeon</title>
    <length>
      <minutes>3</minutes>
      <seconds>33</seconds>
    </length>
    <parody>
      <title>Like A Virgin</title>
      <artist>Madonna</artist>
    </parody>
  </song>
  <song>
    <title>Dare to be Stupid</title>
    <length>
      <minutes>3</minutes>
      <seconds>25</seconds>
    </length>
    <parody></parody>
  </song>
</CD>
```

2. This XML is formatted like this in IE5:

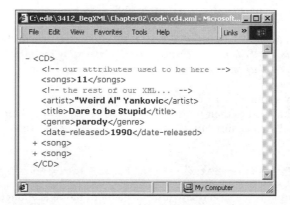

This way, the application could be coded such that if it only finds two <song> elements, but it finds a <songs> element which contains the text "11", it can deduce that there are 9 songs missing.

Empty Elements

Sometimes an element has no data. Recall our earlier example, where the `middle` element contained no name:

```
<name nickname='Shiny John'>
  <first>John</first>
  <!--John lost his middle name in a fire-->
  <middle></middle>
  <last>Doe</last>
</name>
```

In this case, you also have the option of writing this element using the special **empty element** syntax:

```
<middle/>
```

This is the one case where a start-tag doesn't need a separate end-tag, because they are both combined together into this one tag. In all other cases, they do.

Recall from our discussion of element names that the only place we can have a space within the tag is before the closing ">". This rule is slightly different when it comes to empty elements. The "/" and ">" characters always have to be together, so you can create an empty element like this:

```
<middle />
```

but not like these:

```
<middle/ >
<middle / >
```

Empty elements really don't buy you anything – except that they take less typing – so you can use them, or not, at your discretion. Keep in mind, however, that as far as XML is concerned `<middle></middle>` is *exactly* the same as `<middle/>`; for this reason, XML parsers will sometimes change your XML from one form to the other. You should never count on your empty elements being in one form or the other, but since they're syntactically exactly the same, it doesn't matter. (This is the reason that IE5 felt free to change our earlier `<parody></parody>` syntax to just `<parody/>`.

> *Interestingly, nobody in the XML community seems to mind the empty element syntax, even though it doesn't add anything to the language. This is especially interesting considering the passionate debates that have taken place on whether attributes are really necessary.*

One place where empty elements are very often used is for elements that have no (or optional) PCDATA, but instead have all of their information stored in attributes. So if we rewrote our `<name>` example without child elements, instead of a start-tag and end-tag we would probably use an empty element, like this:

```
<name first="John" middle="Fitzgerald Johansen" last="Doe"/>
```

Another common example is the case where just the element name is enough; for example, the HTML `<BR>` tag might be converted to an XML empty element, such as the XHTML `<br/>` tag. (XHTML is the latest "XML-compliant" version of HTML.)

XML Declaration

It is often very handy to be able to identify a document as being a certain type. XML provides the **XML declaration** for us to label documents as being XML, along with giving the parsers a few other pieces of information. You don't need to have an XML declaration, but you should include it anyway.

A typical XML declaration looks like this:

```
<?xml version='1.0' encoding='UTF-16' standalone='yes'?>
<name nickname='Shiny John'>
  <first>John</first>
  <!--John lost his middle name in a fire-->
  <middle/>
  <last>Doe</last>
</name>
```

Some things to note about the XML declaration:

❑   The XML declaration starts with the characters <?xml, and ends with the characters ?>.

❑   If you include it, you must include the version, but the encoding and standalone attributes are optional.

❑   The version, encoding, and standalone attributes must be in that order.

❑   Currently, the version should be 1.0. If you use a number other than 1.0, XML parsers that were written for the version 1.0 specification should reject the document. (As of yet, there have been no plans announced for any other version of the XML specification. If there ever is one, the version number in the XML declaration will be used to signal which version of the specification your document claims to support.)

❑   The XML declaration must be right at the beginning of the file. That is, the first character in the file should be that <; no line breaks or spaces. Some parsers are more forgiving about this than others.

So an XML declaration can be as full as the one above, or as simple as:

```
<?xml version='1.0'?>
```

The next two sections will describe more fully the encoding and standalone attributes of the XML declaration.

Encoding

It should come as no surprise to us that text is stored in computers using numbers, since numbers are all that computers really understand.

> A character code **is a one-to-one mapping between a set of characters and the corresponding numbers to represent those characters. A** character encoding **is the method used to represent the numbers in a character code digitally, (in other words how many bytes should be used for each number, etc.)**

One character code/encoding that you might have come across is the **American Standard Code for Information Interchange** (**ASCII**). For example, in ASCII the character "a" is represented by the number 97, and the character "A" is represented by the number 65.

There are seven-bit and eight-bit ASCII encoding schemes. 8-bit ASCII uses one byte (8 bits) for each character, which can only store 256 different values, so that limits ASCII to 256 characters. That's enough to easily handle all of the characters needed for English, which is why ASCII was the predominant character encoding used on personal computers in the English-speaking world for many years. But there are way more than 256 characters in all of the world's languages, so obviously ASCII can only handle a small subset of these. This is reason that **Unicode** was invented.

Unicode

Unicode is a character code designed from the ground up with internationalization in mind, aiming to have enough possible characters to cover all of the characters in any human language. There are two major character encodings for Unicode: **UTF-16** and **UTF-8**. UTF-16 takes the easy way, and simply uses two bytes for every character (two bytes = 16 bits = 65,356 possible values).

UTF-8 is more clever: it uses one byte for the characters covered by 7-bit ASCII, and then uses some tricks so that any other characters may be represented by two or more bytes. This means that ASCII text can actually be considered a subset of UTF-8, and processed as such. For text written in English, where most of the characters would fit into the ASCII character encoding, UTF-8 can result in smaller file sizes, but for text in other languages, UTF-16 should usually be smaller.

Because of the work done with Unicode to make it international, the XML specification states that all XML processors must use Unicode internally. Unfortunately, very few of the documents in the world are encoded in Unicode. Most are encoded in **ISO-8859-1**, or **windows-1252**, or **EBCDIC**, or one of a large number of other character encodings. (Many of these encodings, such as ISO-8859-1 and windows-1252, are actually variants of ASCII. They are not, however, subsets of UTF-8 in the same way that "pure" ASCII is.)

Specifying Character Encoding for XML

This is where the `encoding` attribute in our XML declaration comes in. It allows us to specify, to the XML parser, what character encoding our text is in. The XML parser can then read the document in the proper encoding, and translate it into Unicode internally. If no encoding is specified, UTF-8 or UTF-16 is assumed (parsers must support at least UTF-8 and UTF-16). If no encoding is specified, and the document is not UTF-8 or UTF-16, it results in an error.

Sometimes an XML processor is allowed to ignore the encoding specified in the XML declaration. If the document is being sent via a network protocol such as HTTP, there may be protocol-specific headers which specify a different encoding than the one specified in the document. In such a case, the HTTP header would take precedence over the encoding specified in the XML declaration. However, if there are no external sources for the encoding, and the encoding specified is different from the actual encoding of the document, it results in an error.

If you're creating XML documents in Notepad on a machine running a Microsoft Windows operating system, the character encoding you are using by default is windows-1252. So the XML declarations in your documents should look like this:

```
<?xml version="1.0" encoding="windows-1252"?>
```

However, not all XML parsers understand the windows-1252 character set. If that's the case, try substituting ISO-8859-1, which happens to be very similar. Or, if your document doesn't contain any special characters (like accented characters, for example), you could use ASCII instead, or leave the encoding attribute out, and let the XML parser treat the document as UTF-8.

If you're running Windows NT or Windows 2000, Notepad also gives you the option of saving your text files in Unicode, in which case you can leave out the encoding attribute in your XML declarations.

Standalone

If the standalone attribute is included in the XML declaration, it must be either yes or no.

❑ yes specifies that this document exists entirely on its own, without depending on any other files

❑ no indicates that the document may depend on other files

This little attribute actually has its own name: the **Standalone Document Declaration**, or **SDD**. The XML specification doesn't actually require a parser to do anything with the SDD. It is considered more of a hint to the parser than anything else.

This is only a partial description of the SDD. If it has whetted your appetite for more, you'll have to be patient until Chapter 11, when all will be made clear.

It's time to take a look at how the XML declaration works in practice.

Try It Out – Declaring Al's CD to the World

Let's declare our XML document, so that any parsers will be able to tell right away what it is. And, while we're at it, let's take care of that second `<parody>` element, which doesn't have any content.

1. Open up the file cd3.xml, and make the following changes:

```
<?xml version='1.0' encoding='windows-1252' standalone='yes'?>
<CD serial='B6B41B'
    disc-length='36:55'>
  <artist>"Weird Al" Yankovic</artist>
  <title>Dare to be Stupid</title>
  <genre>parody</genre>
  <date-released>1990</date-released>
  <!--date-released is the date released to CD, not to record-->
  <song>
    <title>Like A Surgeon</title>
    <length>
      <minutes>3</minutes>
      <seconds>33</seconds>
    </length>
    <parody>
      <title>Like A Virgin</title>
      <artist>Madonna</artist>
    </parody>
```

```
    </song>
    <song>
      <title>Dare to be Stupid</title>
      <length>
        <minutes>3</minutes>
        <seconds>25</seconds>
      </length>
      <parody/>
    </song>
    <!--There are more songs on this CD, but I didn't have time
        to include them!-->
  </CD>
```

2. Save the file as cd5.xml, and view it in IE5:

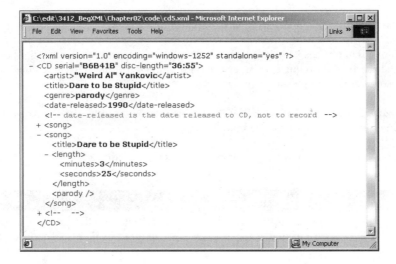

How It Works

With our new XML declaration, any XML parser can tell right away that it is indeed dealing with an XML document, and that document is claiming to conform to version 1.0 of the XML specification.

Furthermore, the document indicates that it is encoded using the windows-1252 character encoding. Again many XML parsers don't understand windows-1252, so you may have to play around with the encoding. Luckily, the parser used by Internet Explorer 5 does understand windows-1252, so if you're viewing the examples in IE5 you can leave the XML declaration as it is here.

In addition, because the Standalone Document Declaration declares that this is a standalone document, the parser knows that this one file is all that it needs to fully process the information.

And finally, because "Dare to be Stupid" is not a parody of any particular song, the <parody> element has been changed to an empty element. That way we can visually emphasize the fact that there is no information there. Remember, though, that to the parser <parody/> is exactly the same as <parody></parody>, which is why this part of our document looks the same as it did in our earlier screenshots.

Processing Instructions

Although it isn't all that common, sometimes you need to embed application-specific instructions into your information, to affect how it will be processed. XML provides a mechanism to allow this, called **processing instructions** or, more commonly, **PIs**. These allow you to enter instructions into your XML which are not part of the actual document, but which are passed up to the application.

```
<?xml version='1.0' encoding='UTF-16' standalone='yes'?>
<name nickname='Shiny John'>
  <first>John</first>
  <!--John lost his middle name in a fire-->
  <middle/>
  <?nameprocessor SELECT * FROM blah?>
  <last>Doe</last>
</name>
```

There aren't really a lot of rules on PIs. They're basically just a "<?", the name of the application that is supposed to receive the PI (the **PITarget**), and the rest up until the ending "?>" is whatever you want the instruction to be. The PITarget is bound by the same naming rules as elements and attributes. So, in this example, the PITarget is nameprocessor, and the actual text of the PI is SELECT * FROM blah.

PIs are pretty rare, and are often frowned upon in the XML community, especially when used frivolously. But if you have a valid reason to use them, go for it. For example, PIs can be an excellent place for putting the kind of information (such as scripting code) that gets put in comments in HTML. While you can't assume that comments will be passed on to the application, PIs always are.

Is the XML Declaration a Processing Instruction?

At first glance, you might think that the XML declaration is a PI that starts with xml. It uses the same "<? ?>" notation, and provides instructions to the parser (but not the application). So is it a PI?

Actually, no: the XML declaration isn't a PI. But in most cases it really doesn't make any difference whether it is or not, so feel free to look at it as one if you wish. The only places where you'll get into trouble are the following:

❑ Trying to get the text of the XML declaration from an XML parser. Some parsers erroneously treat the XML declaration as a PI, and will pass it on as if it were, but many will not. The truth is, in most cases your application will never need the information in the XML declaration; that information is only for the parser. One notable exception might be an application that wants to display an XML document to a user, in the way that we're using IE5 to display the documents in this book.

❑ Including an XML declaration somewhere other than at the beginning of an XML document. Although you can put a PI anywhere you want, an XML declaration must come at the beginning of a file.

Try It Out – Dare to be Processed

Just to see what it looks like, let's add a processing instruction to our Weird Al XML:

1. Make the following changes to cd5.xml and save the file as cd6.xml:

```
<?xml version='1.0' encoding='windows-1252' standalone='yes'?>
<CD serial='B6B41B'
    disc-length='36:55'>
  <artist>"Weird Al" Yankovic</artist>
  <title>Dare to be Stupid</title>
  <genre>parody</genre>
  <date-released>1990</date-released>
  <!--date-released is the date released to CD, not to record-->
  <song>
    <title>Like A Surgeon</title>
    <length>
      <minutes>3</minutes>
      <seconds>33</seconds>
    </length>
    <parody>
      <title>Like A Virgin</title>
      <artist>Madonna</artist>
    </parody>
  </song>
  <song>
    <title>Dare to be Stupid</title>
    <length>
      <minutes>3</minutes>
      <seconds>25</seconds>
    </length>
    <parody/>
  </song>
  <?CDParser MessageBox("There are songs missing!")?>
</CD>
```

2. In IE5, it looks like this:

```
<?xml version="1.0" encoding="windows-1252" standalone="yes" ?>
- <CD serial="B6B41B" disc-length="36:55">
    <artist>"Weird Al" Yankovic</artist>
    <title>Dare to be Stupid</title>
    <genre>parody</genre>
    <date-released>1990</date-released>
    <!-- date-released is the date released to CD, not to record -->
  + <song>
  + <song>
    <?CDParser MessageBox("There are songs missing!")?>
  </CD>
```

How It Works

For our example, we are targeting a *fictional* application called `CDParser`, and giving it the instruction `MessageBox("There are songs missing!")`. The instruction we gave it has no meaning in the context of XML itself, but only to our `CDParser` application, so it's up to `CDParser` to do something meaningful with it.

Illegal PCDATA Characters

There are some reserved characters that you can't include in your PCDATA because they are used in XML syntax.

For example, the "<" and "&" characters:

```
<!--This is not well-formed XML!-->
<comparison>6 is < 7 & 7 > 6</comparison>
```

Viewing the above XML in IE5 would give the following error:

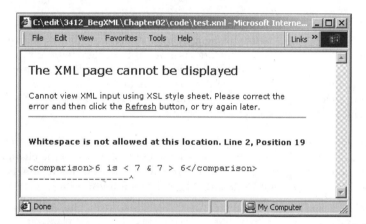

This means that the XML parser comes across the "<" character, and expects a tag name, instead of a space. (Even if it had got past this, the same error would have occurred at the "&" character.)

There are two ways you can get around this: **escaping characters**, or enclosing text in a **CDATA section**.

Escaping Characters

To escape these two characters, you simply replace any "<" characters with < and any "&" characters with &. The above XML could be made well-formed by doing the following:

```
<comparison>6 is &lt; 7 &amp; 7 > 6</comparison>
```

Which displays properly in the browser:

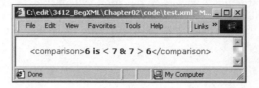

Notice that IE5 automatically un-escapes the characters for you when it displays the document, in other words it replaces the < and & strings with < and & characters.

< and & are known as **entity references**. The following entities are defined in XML:

❑   & – the & character

❑   < – the < character

❑   > – the > character

❑   ' – the ' character

❑   " – the " character

Other characters can also be escaped by using **character references**. These are strings such as &#*nnn*;, where "*nnn*" would be replaced by the Unicode number of the character you want to insert. (Or &#x*nnn*; with an "x" preceding the number, where "*nnn*" is a hexadecimal representation of the Unicode character you want to insert. All of the characters in the Unicode specification are specified using hexadecimal, so allowing the hexadecimal numbers in XML means that XML authors don't have to convert back and forth between hexadecimal and decimal.)

Escaping characters in this way can be quite handy if you are authoring documents in XML that use characters your XML editor doesn't understand, or can't output, because the characters escaped are *always* Unicode characters, regardless of the encoding being used for the document. As an example, you could include the copyright symbol ( ) in an XML document by inserting © or ©.

CDATA Sections

If you have a lot of "<" and "&" characters that need escaping, you may find that your document quickly becomes very ugly and unreadable. Luckily, there are also **CDATA sections.**

> **CDATA is another inherited term from SGML. It stands for** Character DATA.

Using CDATA sections, we can tell the XML parser not to parse the text, but to let it all go by until it gets to the end of the section. CDATA sections look like this:

```
<comparison><![CDATA[6 is < 7 & 7 > 6]]></comparison>
```

Everything starting after the `<![CDATA[` and ending at the `]]>` is ignored by the parser, and passed through to the application as is. In this trivial case, CDATA sections may look more confusing than the escaping did, but in other cases it can turn out to be more readable. For example, consider the following example, which uses a CDATA section to keep an XML parser from parsing a section of JavaScript:

```
<script language='JavaScript'><![CDATA[
function myFunc()
{
    if(0 < 1 && 1 < 2)
        alert("Hello");
}
]]></script>
```

If you aren't familiar with JavaScript and want to know what the above script does, take a look at the tutorial in Appendix D.

This displays in the IE5 browser as:

Notice the vertical line at the left hand side of the CDATA section. This is indicating that although the CDATA section is indented for readability, the actual data itself starts at that vertical line. This is so we can visually see what white space is included in the CDATA section.

If you're familiar with JavaScript, you'll probably find the `if` statement much easier to read than:

```
if(0 &lt; 1 &amp;&amp; 1 &lt; 2)
```

Try It Out – Talking about HTML in XML

Suppose that we want to create XML documentation, to describe some of the various HTML tags in existence.

1. We might develop a simple document type such as the following:

```
<HTML-Doc>
  <tag>
    <tag-name></tag-name>
    <description></description>
    <example></example>
  </tag>
</HTML-Doc>
```

In this case, we know for sure that our <example> element is going to need to include HTML syntax, meaning that there are going to be a lot of "<" characters included. This makes <example> the perfect place to use a CDATA section, meaning that we don't have to search through all of our HTML code looking for illegal characters. To demonstrate, lets document a couple of HTML tags.

2. Create a new file and type this code:

```
<HTML-Doc>
  <tag>
    <tag-name>P</tag-name>
    <description>Paragraph</description>
    <example><![CDATA[
<P>Paragraphs can contain <EM>other</EM> tags.</P>
]]></example>
  </tag>
  <tag>
    <tag-name>HTML</tag-name>
    <description>HTML root element</description>
    <example><![CDATA[
<HTML>
<HEAD><TITLE>Sample HTML</TITLE></HEAD>
<BODY>
<P>Stuff goes here</P
</BODY>/HTML>
]]></example>
  </tag>
  <!--more tags to follow...-->
</HTML-Doc>
```

3. Save this document as `html-doc.xml` and view it in IE5:

```
C:\edit\3412_BegXML\Chapter02\code\html-doc.xml - Microsoft Internet Explorer
File   Edit   View   Favorites   Tools   Help                    Links »

 - <HTML-Doc>
   - <tag>
       <tag-name>P</tag-name>
       <description>Paragraph</description>
     - <example>
         <![CDATA[ <P>Paragraphs can contain <EM>other</EM> tags.</P>
           ]]>
       </example>
     </tag>
   - <tag>
       <tag-name>HTML</tag-name>
       <description>HTML root element</description>
     - <example>
       - <![CDATA[
           <HTML>
           <HEAD><TITLE>Sample HTML</TITLE></HEAD>
           <BODY>
           <P>Stuff goes here</P
           </BODY>/HTML>
           ]]>
       </example>
     </tag>
     <!-- more tags to follow... -->
   </HTML-Doc>

Done                                              My Computer
```

How It Works

Because of our CDATA sections, we can put whatever we want into the `<example>` elements, and don't have to worry about the text being mixed up with the actual XML markup of the document. This means that even though there is a typo in the second `<example>` element (the `</P` is missing the `>`), our XML is not affected.

Parsing XML

The main reason for creating all of these rules about writing well-formed XML documents is so that we can create a computer program to read in the data, and easily tell markup from information.

> *According to the XML specification (http://www.w3.org/TR/1998/REC-xml-19980210#sec-intro): "A software module called an **XML processor** is used to read XML documents and provide access to their content and structure. It is assumed that an XML processor is doing its work on behalf of another module, called the **application**."*

An XML processor is more commonly called a **parser**, since it simply parses XML and provides the application with any information it needs. There are quite a number of XML parsers available, many of which are free. Some of the better known ones are listed below.

Microsoft Internet Explorer Parser

Microsoft's first XML parser shipped with Internet Explorer 4 and implemented an early draft of the XML specification. With the release of IE5, the XML implementation was upgraded to reflect the XML version 1 specification. The latest version of the parser (March 2000 Technology Preview Release) is available for download from http://msdn.microsoft.com/downloads/webtechnology/xml/msxml.asp. In this book we'll be mainly using the IE5 version.

James Clark's Expat

Expat is an XML 1.0 parser toolkit written in C. More information can be found at http://www.jclark.com/xml/expat.html and Expat can be downloaded from ftp://ftp.jclark.com/pub/xml/expat.zip. It is free for both private and commercial use.

Vivid Creations ActiveDOM

Vivid Creations (http://www.vivid-creations.com) offers several XML tools, including ActiveDOM. ActiveDOM contains a parser similar to the Microsoft parser and, although it is a commercial product, a demonstration version may be downloaded from the Vivid Creations web site.

DataChannel XJ Parser

DataChannel, a business solutions software company, worked with Microsoft to produce an early XML parser written in Java. Their website (http://xdev.datachannel.com/directory/xml_parser.html) provides a link to get their most recent version. However, they are no longer doing parser development. They have opted instead to use the xml4j parser from IBM.

IBM xml4j

IBM's AlphaWorks site (http://www.alphaworks.ibm.com) offers a number of XML tools and applications, including the xml4j parser. This is another parser written in Java, available for free, though there are some licensing restrictions regarding its use.

Apache Xerces

The Apache Software Foundation's Xerces sub-project of the Apache XML Project (http://xml.apache.org/) has resulted in XML parsers in Java and C++, plus a Perl wrapper for the C++ parser. These tools are in beta, they are free, and the distribution of the code is controlled by the GNU Public License.

Errors in XML

As well as specifying how a parser should get the information out of an XML document, it is also specified how a parser should deal with errors in XML. There are two types of errors in the XML specification: **errors** and **fatal errors**.

- ❑ An error is simply a violation of the rules in the specification, where the results are undefined; the XML processor is allowed to recover from the error and continue processing.

- ❑ Fatal errors are more serious: according to the specification a parser is *not allowed to continue as normal* when it encounters a fatal error. (It may, however, keep processing the XML document to search for further errors.) Any error which causes an XML document to cease being well-formed is a fatal error.

The reason for this drastic handling of non-well-formed XML is simple: it would be extremely hard for parser writers to try and handle "well-formedness" errors, and it is extremely simple to make XML well-formed. (HTML does not force documents to be as strict as XML does, but this is one of the reasons why web browsers are so incompatible; they must deal with *all* of the errors they may encounter, and try to figure out what the person who wrote the document was really trying to code.)

But draconian error handling doesn't just benefit the parser writers; it also benefits us when we're creating XML documents. If I write an XML document that doesn't properly follow XML's syntax, I can find out right away and fix my mistake. On the other hand, if the XML parser tried to recover from these errors, it may misinterpret what I was trying to do, but I wouldn't know about it because no error would be raised. In this case, bugs in my software would be much harder to track down, instead of being caught right at the beginning when I was creating my data.

Summary

This chapter has provided you with the basic syntax for writing well-formed XML documents.

We've seen:

- ❑ Elements and empty elements
- ❑ How to deal with white space in XML
- ❑ Attributes
- ❑ How to include comments
- ❑ XML declarations and encodings
- ❑ Processing instructions
- ❑ Entity references, character references and CDATA sections

We've also learned why the strict rules of XML grammar actually benefit us, in the long run, and how some of the rules for authoring HTML are different from the rules for authoring well-formed XML.

Unfortunately – or perhaps fortunately – you probably won't spend much of your time just authoring XML documents. But once you have the data in XML form, you still have to be able to use that data. In the chapters that follow we'll learn some of the other technologies surrounding XML, which will help you to make use of your data, starting with one of the most common: display.

XML in the Browser: Cascading Style Sheets

So far we've seen what XML is and hinted at where it can be used, and we know the basics of how we can create well-formed XML documents. Unfortunately, on its own the usefulness of this knowledge is fairly limited. As we've seen, XML is concerned with the *structure* of data and not its *presentation*, but it's the visual presentation of data that drives much of the software that exists today. XML, whether in either data or document format, still often needs some mechanism to display the tags in a representation that communicates the intentions of the tags more effectively to your readers..

Style sheets in general serve that purpose of improving the expression of XML data, and **cascading style sheets** (**CSS**) in particular can be used to set most media characteristics, for example font-size and family, the way a document flows, the aural qualities of spoken text, to name but a few.

In this chapter we'll introduce cascading style sheets by first studying how they are used with HTML. This is obviously an XML book, not an HTML book, but CSS is a language that can be readily used by both markup languages. Because in some cases it's easier to understand the impact of CSS in HTML than it is in XML, this chapter begins with the HTML application of cascading style sheets – we'll then see how the same properties can be applied to the XML world. This will include looking at:

- ❑ How to create style sheets for XML documents
- ❑ How to use CSS with XML
- ❑ Where some of the limitations are
- ❑ How you can use CSS to provide very sophisticated effects in your documents for web pages, printed pages, speech engines, and other media

> **Most of the screenshots in the chapter were generated using the IE5 parser, but unfortunately IE5 doesn't support a completely accurate version of CSS. Ideally we'd recommend you use the Netscape Navigator 6.0 Beta, the Opera 4.0 Beta, or the W3C Amaya browsers to run the examples, all three of which have close to perfect support for the W3C spec.**

Why Do We Need Style Sheets?

One of the most common questions that many people new to XML ask when they encounter XML is this: if I create an arbitrary tag in XML, then how does the browser know what that tag looks like on the screen. In other words, how does it know what to display? The answer is perhaps not terribly comforting – it doesn't!

Imagine if I create a nested XML structure that looks like this, for display on the web:

```
<document>
    <head>
        <title> Cascading Style Sheets</title>
        <author>Kurt Cagle</author>
        <date>15 March 2000</date>
    </head>
    <body>
        <para>One of the most common questions that many people new to
        XML ask when they encounter XML is this: <quotation>If I create
        an arbitrary tag in XML, then how does the browser know what
        that tag looks like on the screen - in other words, how does it
        know what to display?</quotation>. The answer is perhaps not
        terribly comforting - it doesn't!</para>
        <para>Imagine if I create a nested XML structure that looks
        like this:</para>
        <!-- and so forth -->
</document>
```

There's nothing within the browser that would intrinsically recognize such tags as <author> or <date>, although many browsers would probably pick up on tags that had names similar to their HTML counterparts, such as <title> or <body> and interpret them wrongly. (Perhaps I want the title to appear in large letters at the start of the document, rather than appearing in the window title bar as it would in Navigator or Internet Explorer.)

In fact, this is one of the central behaviors that differentiates XML and HTML. The HTML tags have very definite meanings, and an HTML browser will usually have an implicitly defined style sheet for the HTML tags – the specific format may change, but there will be some kind of associated style.

> *Typically, by default, the <H1> or Heading 1 style displays text in a 24 pt Times Roman font, although there is no requirement that it uses that specification – the header simply implies that it's the most prominent header in the document, and so should be drawn in such a way as to always appear as the most prominent element on the page. Similarly, other tags have implicit presentation characteristics associated with them (the <EM> tag, for instance, makes the text it contains highlighted in some manner– typically by making the text italicized). Note again that these are conventional, based upon the browser – HTML does not explicitly indicate exactly what an <H1> or <EM> tag should look like.*

In other words, the HTML browser provides a built-in map that matches a given tag with an associated **rule** for describing how this tag is rendered. That rule contains a great deal of information about the element, from the font characteristics of the text in the tag to whether the contents of the tag are displayed as separate rectangular regions (a **block**) or are incorporated into the flow of the paragraph they are found in (**inline**), the amount of space between the element and surrounding elements (or within the element), background and foreground colors and images, and so forth.

In web browsers prior to the implementation of HTML 4.0, these qualities were largely built into the browser and were essentially immutable – although you could change some of these characteristics on a local basis with judicious application of the <FONT> tag. However, this came with a hidden cost. Consider this bit of HTML 3.2 code:

```
<BODY>
    <DIV><FONT family="Times New Roman" color="red" size="18">
        A New Chapter
    </FONT></DIV>
</BODY>
```

When this is displayed, the user sees a large red font in Times New Roman, and would probably be easily excused for believing that this was a first level heading. Unfortunately, there's no indication to the browser that the contents contained within the <FONT> element are any more important than if the text was in fact made up of normal paragraphs. Put another way, the <FONT> tag has no **context** – there is no information that can be extracted from the document about the nature of its contents. If the size attribute had been set to 6, the same element becomes practically invisible, but again there is no real way to *interpret* the contents.

The History of Styling HTML

This problem with context has been one of the most insidious problems that HTML has faced, and is in fact a prime motivator for the development of XML. It's insidious because many people, especially those new to working with HTML, don't understand the primary purpose of HTML (at least in the minds of those who created it). This is not to position elements on the page, set their fonts, change the colors and so forth, but instead to create a document with a **logical structure**. Of course, many HTML authors now consider the primary purpose to be the positioning and presentation of page elements.

HTML started out as a way of describing physics abstracts, documents that summarized the contents of articles that physicists had written. It was a logical structure with a head and a body, primary, secondary and tertiary headlines, definitions, quotations, and so forth – in other words, a structure that described the logical partitioning of an abstract. (However, it should be pointed out that even then there wasn't much organization – if it had been properly structured there would have been sections and title heading and a much stronger container/contained relationship.) There was nothing in the original specifications that described font or color, or any of the other elements that most web designers see as indispensable. Because it didn't have much in the way of structure to begin with, the language began to pick up other tags in a fairly haphazard fashion, and even early on the distinction between markup code that described the underlying structure of the web page and markup code that indicated presentation information had become far too intertwined. It would take the advent of XML, and a significant rethinking on how documents should be structured, for the web to unravel the skein.

The Origins of Markup

For a while, I worked as a typesetter on a Linotronics typesetting machine in 1988, about the time that a new software product called Pagemaker had begun devastating the typesetting industry. Until the emergence of What You See Is What You Get, or WYSIWYG editing, most typesetting software used specialized markup tags to indicate the visual characteristics of the page. The code was cryptic, but more to the point, it didn't tell you anything about the *content* of the document, only about *appearance* (and then only if you were highly conversant with the exact codes used).

A typical section of a document might have looked something like this:

```
.p/ffH1/fs12/lin3pi.One of the most common questions that many people new to XML
ask when they encounter XML is this: .iIf I create an arbitrary tag in XML, then
how does the browser know what that tag looks like on the screen - in other words,
how does it know what to display?.i. The answer is perhaps not terribly comforting
- it doesn't!/cr/
.p/ffH1/fs12/lin3pi.Imagine if I create a nested XML structure that looks like
this:/cr/
```

Not surprisingly, typesetters were considered highly trained computer professionals and were compensated accordingly – at least until the advent of do-it-yourself graphic design, which completely wiped them out. However, even if Pagemaker had not cut such a swath through the industry, doubtless other programs would have. The ability to change font and page characteristics was a burning demand from the earliest days of personal computers, and Pagemaker was only one in a large line of innovations that made inline markup in general disappear from people's awareness (although Pagemaker did incorporate a somewhat simplistic style sheet engine).

Markup for the Web

While proprietary products made dedicated markup language pretty much obsolete, the situation was not quite the same on the Internet. An HTML document contained structural code, which defined the page logically, but the responsibility of how a tag was rendered fell solely into the province of the web browser.

Unfortunately, this lack of specification meant that whereas one company's browser might render an H1 tag as being 24 point bold Helvetica, another could just as readily render it as 20 point plain Times Roman. As the web became fundamentally a graphical medium, this meant that graphic designers were typically stymied in their effort to produce web pages that looked even remotely good on more than one browser.

So these early web designers did what creative people typically do in such situations – they improvised. Text was replaced by images, tags were forced into formatting duty, invisible graphics were pressed into duty to properly position elements. The browser manufacturers noticed, and started adding features – but of course, given that each vendor was attempting to gain market share, the features were proprietary to the specific browser.

Loss of Contextual Information

At around the same time, the World Wide Web Consortium (the W3C) realized that the endless proliferation of tags, including many fairly spurious ones, was fragmenting the HTML standard.

One such tag, the <FONT> tag, could be used to set a font's size (at a fairly coarse degree of granularity), color, and font family. Unfortunately, this tag provides no semantic information, and tends to hide the real meaning of the tag both visually and otherwise. For example, you could use a paragraph block and an embedded FONT tag to visually create text that looked like a header tag:

```
<P>
  <FONT size="7" color="black" family="Times Roman">
    This is paragraph text
  </FONT>
</P>
```

A number of HTML editors (especially the WYSIWYG type of editors like Microsoft FrontPage) at the time took advantage of this technique to simplify their code, by making most blocks of text "paragraph text", even the ones that were obviously headers or served in other capacities. This further eroded the underlying logical structure of web pages in favor of more graphical structures, making it even harder to determine context from a web page.

Of course, many people have questioned whether this is necessarily a bad thing, but in many ways the loss of context is a crucial problem that the Internet now has to deal with daily. This is exacerbated by the fact that much more web content is now generated dynamically through server pages or CGI scripts, rather than being served up straight from existing files. As the web becomes increasingly driven from database back ends, trying to extract any meaningful information becomes harder.

As long as a document has some form of consistent logical structure, a computer program can simply treat the document as a container that holds other pieces of information. For example, a report may contain a sales chart. With the current state of HTML, in order to retrieve that chart you would have to load the entire report, strip out everything but those structures that look chart-like, determine which of those chart-like chunks are the correct one (which means knowing a great deal about the structure of the specific document), then load that chart, correcting for any changes that may have resulted by pulling it out of the page.

On the other hand, in a more logically structured document (one that deliberately attempts to incorporate meaning and context), you could retrieve the same chart simply by knowing its name. The structures assist in that retrieval process. In a more mundane example, by knowing the logical structure of a document you can display it in any number of different ways, but if you only know the visual structure of the document, then extracting the structure and doing anything with it is a considerably more customized (hence, expensive) operation.

Style Sheets and HTML

The biggest costs associated with building web sites don't come from the initial design – they come from the maintenance of that site over time and incorporating new content. Internet development in general has migrated to a model where (at least in more productive IT departments) the actual content of the site is stored in a database then integrated in using a server pages language such as Active Server Pages (ASP) or Java Server Pages (JSP). XML will take this one step further by abstracting out the process of retrieving data from the process of presenting it, in time assuming much of the responsibility that the older ASP and JSP languages do now.

This is a common paradigm in programming, but it may not necessarily be familiar to you if you haven't had to deal with the complexities of writing a lot of procedural code.

> **In essence, this pattern is called the** Content/Presentation paradigm, **and is one of the most pervasive patterns in XML. At its root, the concept means that you separate data from the way that the data is displayed.**

In this light, the H1 tag goes back to being simply the primary header, and contains no information about how the browser should display text wrapped in the H1 tag. A browser can assign a style to it, of course, but so can we, and that style need not necessarily even be a visual one.

65

For example, the latest specifications include support for aural or spoken styles, so we could specify to the aural browser that whenever an H1 tag is encountered by the "renderer" then the voice would be spoken as if by the actor James Earl Jones (full of stentorian authority), while a paragraph tag might be spoken as if by British actress Kelly McGillis (who can make even a book of legal drafts sound stimulating).

The beauty of separating out content from style is that we (as the user) could change the way that the information is presented. Thus, you may prefer to have both styles read as if by Sean Connery, displayed in a visual browser with a Garamond type face, rendered into Braille, or (although the tags to do this don't yet support this capability) spoken while scents of different types are wafted into the air.

> **The important thing is that by separating the content – the logical structure – from the presentation, you can target your message to any number of different viewers without having to worry about whether the message gets mangled in the medium.**

This led to an effort – still ongoing – to remake the web with a little bit more attention paid to structure rather than style. One of the first efforts of this was the creation of cascading style sheets (or CSS) in 1995 by the W3C. The concept of a style sheet goes back to the 1960s, and the principle is not all that different from the markup on those old Linotronics machines.

In essence, a **style** – a set of (mostly) visual characteristics – can be applied to an HTML tag to change the visual appearance of the tag. Unlike the aforementioned <FONT> element, however, the style is not an intrinsic part of the structure – we can remove the style and the visual appearance of the element may change, but we're not adding or removing information to/from the document itself, simply the *visualization* of that information.

The W3C set up a Style Sheet Working Group to handle the specific problems of building presentation layer architectures. In addition to the first CSS specification, there are in fact two other CSS specs at varying levels. CSS1 defined the association between specific CSS property names and their visual appearance. CSS2, approved in May of 1998, clarified a number of ambiguities from the first specification, and also incorporated support for sound and non-traditional media.

The CSS standards are maintained by the Style sheets Group of the W3C, and for all the benefits that other forms of XML presentation offer, it's likely that CSS will not disappear any time soon. Currently, the most recent formal recommendation (the closest thing to an "approved standard" in the W3C lexicon) for CSS is the Cascading Style Sheets level 2 CSS2 Specification *(located at http://www.w3.org/TR/1998/REC-CSS2).*

Creating Styles in HTML

A style consists of a collection of CSS properties assigned to specific values, of the form property:value; where you can have one style following the preceding one.

Thus, if we wanted to create a style that consisted of a James Earl Jones voice spoken at the loudest possible volume, we could do this with the style:

```
voice-family:JamesEarlJones;volume:x-loud;
```

Styles can be assigned in one of three ways in HTML, using:

❑ the `style` attribute of the element you want to apply the style to

❑ the `<STYLE>` element

❑ an external style sheet

The style Attribute

In the first case, the style would look much like:

```
<H1 style="voice-family:JamesEarlJones;volume:x-loud;">
  Welcome To My Site
</H1>
<P style="voice-family:KellyMcGillis;volume:medium;">
  This is the aural website, where everything is read to you.
</P>
```

This works well when you only need to assign styles to change a few elements from their default display, but has some serious limitations when applied to the document as a whole.

For starters, in most documents we're likely to want all elements of a given type to have the same style – we want Kelly to read *all* of the paragraphs that the browser encounters, not just one. Yet `style` attributes apply only to the elements on which they're added, and any elements that are contained within them, not on all elements of the same type outside of that one element.

Furthermore, this isn't all that much different from applying the `<FONT>` tag – there's too close a dependency between a given element or attribute and its external representation.

The <STYLE> Element

Fortunately, there are other options, which also become important when dealing with XML. The first of these, the `<STYLE>` element, allows you to associate a given style with a specific type of element.

For example, the following `<STYLE>` declaration ensures that whenever an H1 tag is encountered, it's rendered to speak in its James Earl Jones voice, while a paragraph tag will speak with Ms. McGillis' voice:

```
<STYLE>
  H1 {voice-family:JamesEarlJones;volume:x-loud;}
  P {voice-family:KellyMcGillis;volume:medium;}
</STYLE>

<H1>This will be read as if by James Earl Jones</H1>
<P>This would be read as if by Kelly McGillis</P>
<P>So will this.</P>
<H2>This won't be spoken by the language interpreter, as there is no association
with a specific rule here.</H2>
```

In this case, the actual CSS style declaration for each type of tag is called a **rule**, and the collection of all rules within the `<STYLE>` tag are together known as a **style sheet**.

The name of the tag in turn is called the **selector** for the rule. Hence, `P {voice-family:KellyMcGillis;volume:medium;}` is a rule, `P` is the selector for the rule and the block:

```
H1 {voice-family:JamesEarlJones;volume:x-loud;}
P {voice-family:KellyMcGillis;volume:medium;}
```

in total makes up a style sheet. So a style sheet consists of a collection of rules, each of which are associated with a given HTML or XML tag through a selector:

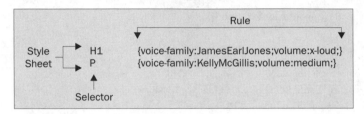

Cascading Styles

So what about the "cascading" part? Visions of lovely mountain brooks come to mind, but that's not quite the case – although it is in fact a useful metaphor.

A cascade implies a falling, moving from one level down to the next. It's sometimes useful to visualize a well formed HTML document (in other words, one where elements are always explicitly terminated) as being a plateau with steps carved into it. Each step represents a child element, and can be said to contain all of the elements that are lower in altitude than it is. So what you end up with is something like an inverted topographic map.

A style applied to a given step thus also affects everything within the step. In other words a style applies not only to the element that it's defined on, but also to all children of that element:

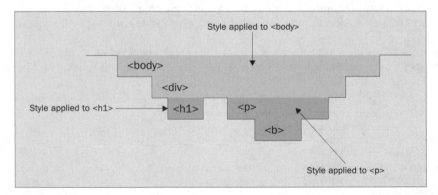

Whenever a style is applied to an element, many of the properties cascade to all child elements within that element. That is, unless those children specifically override the styles with the same CSS properties in their own styles.

It's high time we got our hands dirty and looked at some code. So let's demonstrate the effects of cascading with a practical exercise.

1. Open up Notepad and create an HTML document (showcascades.html) as follows:

```
<HTML>
<HEAD>
<TITLE>Showing Cascades</TITLE>
</HEAD>
<BODY>
<H1>Showing Cascades</H1>
<DIV style="background-color:red;color:white;">
  This text will be shown with white text on a red background.
  <DIV>So will this text, which is in a DIV contained in the first.</DIV>
  <DIV style="background-color:blue">
    This text has a blue background, and inherits (or cascades)
    the white text.
    <DIV style="color:black;">
      Meanwhile, this inherits the blue background, from the most
      immediate parent element, but sets the text color to black.
    </DIV>
  </DIV>
  This text is back to red on white, because it inherits the topmost style.
</DIV>
<DIV>
  This has no styles associated with it, so should appear as black on white
  (or gray, if viewed in certain Netscape browsers)
</DIV>
</BODY>
</HTML>
```

2. View the document in your browser (Internet Explorer 4.0, Opera 3.0 and above, or Netscape Navigator 6.0 Beta or above). The result should be as follows (but in color!):

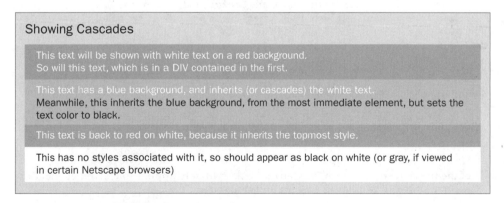

How It Works

The HTML DIV elements are useful as block content containers – anything within a DIV will be displayed as if in its own rectangle.

We've used the `background-color` property to set the color of the background, and the `color` property to set the color of the foreground (the text). So in the first, top-most `DIV`, we've assigned a red background, and this applies to the text that's contained only in this `DIV`, and to first child, as does the foreground color assignment to white:

```
<DIV style="background-color:red;color:white;">
   This text will be shown with white text on a red background.
   <DIV>So will this text, which is in a DIV contained in the first.</DIV>

   ...

   This text is back to red on white, because it inherits the topmost style.
</DIV>
```

With the second child, however, the background color (but not the foreground color) is changed to blue – the element still inherits the white text since the foreground color property wasn't overridden:

```
<DIV style="background-color:red;color:white;">

   ...

  <DIV style="background-color:blue">
    This text has a blue background, and inherits (or cascades)
    the white text.
```

Finally, the child of that child sets the foreground color from white to black. Note that since this element didn't override the background color – that color is still blue:

```
<DIV style="background-color:blue">
   This text has a blue background, and inherits (or cascades)
   the white text.
   <DIV style="color:black;">
     Meanwhile, this inherits the blue background, from the most
     immediate parent element, but sets the text color to black.
   </DIV>
</DIV>
```

The second top-level `DIV` element, on the other hand, has had no styles associated with it:

```
<DIV>
   This has no styles associated with it, so should appear as black on white
   (or gray, if viewed in certain Netscape browsers)
</DIV>
```

The style of the previous node doesn't cascade to it. A style only applies to a given element or children of that element, not to any siblings or parents of that element.

Overriding Styles with Style Elements

Style sheets contained in `<STYLE>` elements are, ironically, one of the few HTML elements that do not cascade. If we declare a given rule for a specific selector (such as the `DIV` element) in one style sheet, then declare a different rule for the same selector, the last rule declared will be the one used for the page – even if there were `DIV`s between the first and second `<STYLE>` sections.

In other words, in the code:

```
<STYLE>
  <!-- This defines the DIV style -->
  DIV {background-color:red;}
</STYLE>

<DIV>This may look like it will be red, but in fact will be blue</DIV>

<STYLE>
  <!-- This redefines the DIV style -->
  DIV {background-color:blue;}
</STYLE>

<DIV>This will also be blue, of course</DIV>
```

both the first and second DIV block will be blue – the second DIV rule overrides the first.

Note that one characteristic of style blocks is that rules apply in successive order. We can define a rule for a selector more than once, and the rules will be cumulative. However, if one rule defines a property, and the same selector rule in a later style sheet changes that property, then the last change in the document is the one that applies.

This concept becomes especially important when dealing with external style sheets. So far we've looked at adding style information within the HTML web page, but it's also possible to hold style information in separate files (external style sheets). That style information can then be referred to from and applied in any HTML page. If we define a selector for some base characteristics in an external style sheet, any rule in the importing document will overrule a selector property in an imported style sheet. This is covered in more depth later in this chapter.

Comments in Style Sheets

By the way, the need for comments in style sheets is just as pressing as it is in more traditional code. You can use either the delimiters <!-- and --> (HTML style comments) or /*   */ (JavaScript style comments) to mark the beginning and end of a comment.

Comments can extend for more that one line, but can't contain other comment delimiters between the brackets – the parser automatically assumes that the closing comment delimiter in an interior comment terminates the original comment as well, usually with the unintended consequence of having part of a comment treated as part of the style block (typically with less than useful results).

A Class Act in HTML

Suppose that we had a need for three different kinds of notes within a document:

❑   A tip note (in which the background color is yellow)

❑   A note that indicated some kind of resource (with a green background)

❑   A warning (in red)

71

This opens up a bit of a quandary. Under earlier versions of HTML, we would have had to specifically define a style for each element that fell into one of those three definitions. Yet clearly, if we suddenly decide that we want resources to appear in blue, rather than green, then we have to change each of those elements that have the green attribute. What's worse, there's nothing within the tags that tells us whether any given node is a tip, a resource, or a warning, other than the contents of the tag:

```
<DIV style="background-color:yellow">This is a tip.</DIV>
<DIV style="background-color:green">This is a resource.</DIV>
<DIV style="background-color:red">This is a warning.</DIV>
<DIV style="background-color:red">If this was actually a tip, you'd be very
confused by now, because it is red.</DIV>
```

Fortunately, within the CSS specification there is a mechanism that lets us actually name specific styles – the `class` attribute. A class can be declared within an HTML document in the same way as a normal element rule, with the exception that the class declaration starts with a period:

```
<STYLE>
    .tip { background-color:yellow; }
    .resource { background-color:green; }
    .warning { background-color:red; }
</STYLE>
```

Applying the new class requires just adding the `class` attribute to the element, as follows (note that the `class` attribute doesn't use the "." character at the beginning of the class name):

```
<DIV class="tip">This is a tip.</DIV>
<DIV class="resource">This is a resource.</DIV>
<DIV class="warning">This is a warning.</DIV>
<DIV class="warning">This tip is now clearly mislabeled.</DIV>
```

It's also possible to apply two classes to a single tag simultaneously, by separating each class from the next with a space character. Thus, we could create a note attribute that specifically created an offset box with a distinct border, and then apply the sub-note styles (tip, resource or warning) to differentiate between note types. The style sheet for this might be as follows:

```
<STYLE>
    .note {margin-left:-.5in;width:250;border:solid 3px
    black;position:relative;background-color:lightBlue;}
    .tip { background-color:yellow; }
    .resource { background-color:green; }
    .warning { background-color:red; }
</STYLE>
```

In our HTML markup, we'd then specify a warning note with the `class` attribute value `note warning`, in other words:

```
<BODY>
    <P>This is some text</P>
    <DIV class="note warning">
        This will display as a warning type note.
    </DIV>
</BODY>
```

This applies the styles of both the `note` and `warning` classes. In general, when we have more than one class given in a `class` attribute, the precedence moves from left to right. For example, in the style sheet given above, a note automatically sets the background color to a light blue. However, the `warning` class name also changes the background color (in this case to red) and since it occurs later in the list it takes precedence.

Try It Out – Making Class Selectors

We can combine class designations with normal tag selectors to provide rules that apply to specific combinations. For example, suppose that we had two note styles that we wanted to use: one when applied to paragraphs (`<P>` tags), the other when applied to list items (`<LI>` tags). We could then differentiate between the two in a style sheet.

1. Create the following document and save it as `classselectors.html`:

```
<HTML>
<HEAD>
<TITLE>Making Class Selectors</TITLE>
</HEAD>
<BODY>
<H1>Making Class Selectors</H1>
<STYLE>
    P.note {margin-left:-.05in;width:250;border:solid 3px
    black;position:relative;background-color:lightBlue;}
    LI.note {border:inset 3px gray;background-color:cyan;}
    .tip { background-color:yellow;border:inset 2px yellow;
    margin-bottom:.2in;}
    .resource { background-color:green;border:inset 2px green;
    margin-bottom:.2in;color:white;}
    .warning { background-color:red;border:inset 2px red;
    margin-bottom:.2in;}
</STYLE>
<BODY>
    <P class="note">This text will appear as a light blue box
    with black borders.</P>
    <UL>
        <LI class="note">This will appear as a bulleted point with a
        cyan, inset background.</LI>
    </UL>
    <DIV class="tip">This is a specialized note called a tip.</DIV>
    <DIV class="resource">A resource note, like this, might point to some
                        external resource.</DIV>
    <DIV class="warning">A warning note indicates an action that might prove
                        problematic (like causing your system to crash).
    </DIV>
</BODY>
</HTML>
```

2. View this in your browser. Despite the fact that both paragraph and list items have the same `note` class, their context (`<P>` versus `<LI>`) will end up producing two very different results:

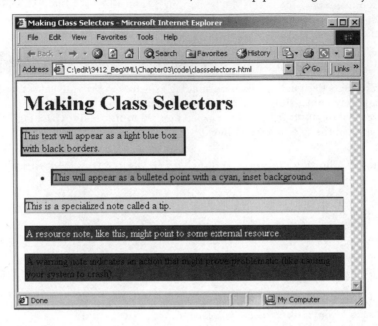

How It Works

This Try It Out demonstrates some of the ways class selectors can be used.

We can have class selectors applied as absolute tags (such as `class="tip"`, `class="resource"`, or `class="warning"`:

```
<DIV class="tip">This is a specialized note called a tip.</DIV>
<DIV class="resource">A resource note, like this, might point to some
                      external resource.</DIV>
<DIV class="warning">A warning note indicates an action that might prove
                     problematic (like causing your system to crash).
```

where the background colors and borders are set in our style sheet:

```
.tip { background-color:yellow;border:inset 2px yellow;
margin-bottom:.2in;}
.resource { background-color:green;border:inset 2px green;
margin-bottom:.2in;color:white;}
.warning { background-color:red;border:inset 2px red;
margin-bottom:.2in;}
```

However, for `class=".note"`, we have two options specified in our style sheet:

```
P.note {margin-left:-.05in;width:250;border:solid 3px
black;position:relative;background-color:lightBlue;}
LI.note {border:inset 3px gray;background-color:cyan;}
.tip { background-color:yellow;border:inset 2px yellow;
```

The first dictates how to display text in a `<P>` tag with `class="note"`:

```
<P class="note">This text will appear as a light blue box
with black borders.</P>
```

The second relates to `<LI>` tags. The `LI` item is a list item, so has a bullet, indented text, and so forth. Here, the `.note` class acting on the list item sets the border and background of the element, but doesn't change the fact that it is a bulleted list item.

```
<UL>
    <LI class="note">This will appear as a bulleted point with a
    cyan, inset background.</LI>
</UL>
```

HTML supports two types of tags for determining the nature of lists – the Ordered List tag (`<OL>`), which automatically numbers `LI` items in the tag, and the Unordered List tag (`<UL>`), which makes each `LI` element a bullet point.

> *The UL tag, for an unordered list, acts as a container for bulleted list items. <OL> does the same thing for ordered, or numbered, lists.*

Cascading Class Selectors

Similarly, you can create an ancestor/descendant relationship in CSS.

We've just been introduced to Ordered and Unordered List tags. You can differentiate between the two within a style sheet using the child operator >. In other words OL>LI will only match list items in an *ordered*, or numbered, list, while UL>LI will only match list items in an *unordered*, or bulleted, list.

> **Note that this is a CSS2 specification exclusively, and is not supported by a number of browsers that are still based primarily on CSS1 (such as Internet Explorer).**

Try It Out – Inheriting Selectors

As an application of this, suppose that you wanted to replace a simple bullet with a more fancy bulleted graphic called `bluebullet.jpg`. If you set the `LI` tag itself, you run the risk of having ordered list items (if there are any in the web page) display the graphic as well. By limiting the selection simply to unordered lists, you can be sure that your numbered entries aren't touched.

1. You can find `bluebullet.jpg` in the code download file for this book, available from the Wrox web site. Put it on your hard drive, in the same folder as the HTML file you're about to create.

2. Create the following file and save it as `inheritselector.html`:

```
<HTML>
<HEAD>
<TITLE>Inheriting Selectors</TITLE>
```

```
</HEAD>
<BODY>
<H1>Inheriting Selectors</H1>
<STYLE>
    UL>LI {list-style-image:url(bluebullet.jpg);}
</STYLE>
<UL>
    <LI>This will have a blue bulleted graphic.</LI>
    <LI>So will this</LI>
</UL>
<OL>
    <LI>However, this point will be numbered.</LI>
    <LI>So will this.
        <UL>
            <LI>But this will be bulleted again.</LI>
        </UL>
    </LI>
</OL>
</BODY>
</HTML>
```

3. Now when viewed in a CSS2 compliant browser, this will end up creating bulleted items only when they aren't numbered, as shown:

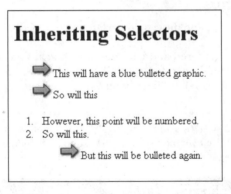

4. We can also choose to indicate that one element is contained in another element, at any depth. This is accomplished by separating the containing and contained element with a space in the selector. Make the following changes to the style sheet:

```
<H1>Inheriting Selectors</H1>
<STYLE>
    UL LI {list-style-image:url(bluebullet.jpg);}
</STYLE>
```

This will apply to any LI element that is contained in an unordered list element, regardless of how deep that element is. This means that if the unordered list contains an ordered list, any element within the ordered list will still be given the bullet instead of being numbered.

5. So change the unordered list to include an ordered list, as follows:

```
<UL>
    <LI>This will have a blue bulleted graphic.</LI>
    <LI>So will this</LI>
    <OL>
      <LI>However, even though this is in an ordered list it
      will have a graphic as well.</LI>
    </OL>
</UL>
```

6. View this in your browser (this time, you can use a CCS1 browser such as IE5):

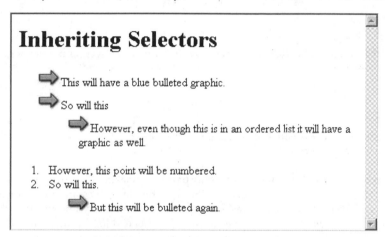

7. Finally, we might want to affect all possible tags with some style sheet. For example, we may want to make sure that all text elements are rendered in the same font-size and style (12 point Courier, say), perhaps for printed output for editing. We can do this with the * operator, which applies a style to all elements that don't otherwise override it.

```
<H1>Inheriting Selectors</H1>
<STYLE>
    UL LI {list-style-image:url(bluebullet.jpg);}
    *{font-family:Courier;font-size:12pt;font-style:plain;}
    H1 {text-decoration:underline;}
</STYLE>
<H1>Announcement</H1>
<P>There's a new technique being used for output here.</P>
<UL>
    <LI>This will have a blue bulleted graphic.</LI>
    <LI>So will this</LI>
```

This will make all output render as 12pt Courier, but heading 1 tags (<H1>) will also be underlined.

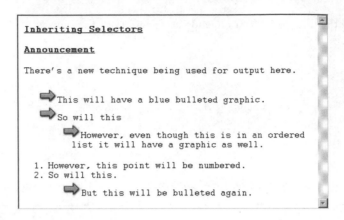

The * operator should be used with care, as it has a global effect on properties.

Pseudo-Classes

Sometimes the distinction between a presentation element and a logical one isn't terribly clear cut. Consider, for instance, drop caps.

First made fashionable nearly a millennium ago as part of monastic manuscripts, drop caps can be created through HTML <SPAN> elements and CSS, but they introduce an uncomfortable linkage between logical and presentation structures – it requires that you apply markup to a character to emphasize its appearance while the character itself has no special logical meaning. The role of **pseudo-classes** is to identify the most common of these linkages, and make them distinct "classes" of their own.

A pseudo-class always starts with a colon character (:) and is defined by CSS, not within the XML or HTML structure. There are a number of useful CSS pseudo-classes in the CSS2 specification, which we'll look at next.

> Pseudo-properties have been a feature of the specification for some time, but there hasn't been a rush to implement them in most browsers. Of all the properties, most version 4.0 or above browsers support the :link and :visited pseudo-properties, but not many of the others. Internet Explorer 5.5 currently supports :first-letter and will likely support :hover and :active. In general though, you should test your code with pseudo-properties carefully on as wide a number of browsers as possible.

:first-child

This pseudo-class applies to the first child element of the given type for a node. As an example, the rule:

```
UL>LI {list-style-type:disc}
UL>LI:first-child {list-style-image:url(bluebullet.jpg)}
```

sets all unordered list items to start with disc shaped bullets, except for the first, which uses a dedicated graphic (`bluebullet.jpg`).

> *Note that this isn't supported in Internet Explorer 5.0.*

:link and :visited

A common feature of most browsers is to display unvisited link elements in a different way to visited links. `:link` handles the unvisited case, while `:visited` obviously handles the visited state. You can use these to change the link colors or other characteristics away from the default characteristics that the browser supports.

For example:

```
A:link {background-color:blue;color:white;}
A:visited {background-color:navy;color:gray;}
```

displays unvisited links as white text on a blue background, while visited links are gray on navy blue, a lower contrast format.

> *Note that the browser has to recognize previously visited links for these to work. Fortunately, this is one of the earliest pseudo-classes and both Internet Explorer and Netscape Navigator support it.*

:hover, :active, and :focus

For interactive browsers, `:hover`, `:active`, and `:focus` can be used to better handle a number of base user-interface features that have traditionally required the use of scripting languages such as JavaScript. Each has a slightly different purpose:

- ❑   `:hover`. Applied whenever the cursor moves into the region of the element, but the element hasn't yet been clicked. For a computer screen, this usually means that the cursor has been placed over the item, but the mouse button hasn't yet been pressed. When the cursor moves off the item, `:hover` is removed.

- ❑   `:active`. Applied when the item is activated (clicked on in the computer screen context). Typically, the system maintains an active element internally, and turns off the previously active element if one exists.

- ❑   `:focus`. The distinction between the active element and the element that has the focus is not an easy one to make. Typically, a focused item is one that can receive input – thus a rectangle could be active but not focused, while a text box could have the focus (through tabbing for instance) but might not necessarily be the active item.

The following demonstrates the application of all three of these:

```
<STYLE>
  UL LI:hover {background-color:lightBlue;color:black;}
  UL LI:active {background-color:navy;color:white;}
  INPUT[type=text]:focus {border:solid 1px red;}
</STYLE>
```

79

As a user rolls over a set of items in a list, the items "light up" showing black text on a light blue background. If the user clicks an item, that item is then shown as being white against a navy background – note that if you hover over it and leave, it will briefly show the `:hover` state but revert back to the `:active` state. If you click on a text box, the box's border will turn red, indicating that it now has the focus.

:lang

HTML is intended to work for any human language. You can use the `:lang` attribute to change code output depending on the language code used (as covered in the Internet document RFC-1766, which specifies the codes used for different languages on the Internet).

You can use this to set such things as quote marks so that they properly match the convention of the language. For example:

```
<STYLE>
   HTML:lang(fr) {quotes:'« ' ' »';}
</STYLE>
```

will replace any English language double quotes with the symbols << and >> respectively.

:first-letter and :first-line

The `:first-letter` and `:first-line` pseudo-properties can be used to select the first displayed character and the first line in a given tag. The primary use for these is typographic – it allows you to create drop caps and lead-lines that are frequently shown in books and newspapers. For example:

```
<STYLE>
   P:first-letter {float:left;font-size:48pt;margin-top:20px;}
</STYLE>
<P>When in the course of human events it becomes necessary for one people to
dissolve the political bonds which have connected them to another and to assume
among the powers of the earth the equal and separate stations to which the laws of
nature and natures God belong, a decent respect for the opinions of mankind
require that we should declare the causes which impel them to the separation.<P>
```

There are a few properties used here, such as float, which we haven't covered yet. Read on ... we're just beginning!

This will output the paragraph as follows:

When in the course of human events it becomes necessary for one people to dissolve the political bonds which have connected them to another and to assume among the powers of the earth the equal and separate stations to which the laws of nature and natures God belong, a decent respect for the opinions of mankind require that we should declare the causes which impel them to the separation.

:before and :after

The `:before` and `:after` CSS attributes exist primarily to add elements prior to or after a given element. Each of these provides content of some sort that is added at the beginning or end of what the tag already contains. This property can be useful in creating bulleted elements, placing brackets around code, or defining specialized delimiters for text.

For example, you could create a set of styles corresponding to different people talking in a script:

```
<STYLE>
   P.Juliet {font-style:italic;}
   P.Juliet:before {content: "Juliet: ";color:red;}
   P.Romeo {font-weight:bold;}
   P.Romeo:before {content: "Romeo: ";color:blue;}
</STYLE>
<P class="Romeo">Hark! What light on yonder window breaks?</P>
<P class="Juliet">Romeo? Romeo? Wherefore art thou, Romeo?</P>
```

The `content` property returns content that can be included with the `:before` or `:after` pseudo-property. Thus, the above text is then rendered as:

Romeo: Hark! What light on yonder window breaks?
Juliet: Romeo? Romeo? Wherefore art thou, Romeo?

> *Unfortunately, this is not supported by Internet Explorer 5.0 – an omission that makes any number of useful effects impossible to pull off.*

External Styles in HTML

It has become typical practice to create style sheets as **external** documents rather than internal code blocks. If you're careful, you can create a site's entire look and feel and encode it in a single style sheet that can be referenced by each HTML document in turn. In HTML, this mechanism is handled in one of two ways: through the `<LINK>` tag and through the `@import` CSS directive.

<LINK>

The `<LINK>` tag is one of the more underutilized elements in HTML, which is something of a shame. Its primary purpose is to create a relationship between the current document and some other document, but the linking mechanism of the anchor tag (the `<A HREF="">` tag that binds the web together) is the only relationship that most people explicitly define.

Note that one of the limitations of `<LINK>` is that it is only supported in the `<HEAD>` of an HTML document (because the `<HEAD>` is supposed to contain references that describe the document relative to other documents).

The `<LINK>` tag can, however, be used to load style sheets. Specifically, the expression:

```
<LINK type="text/css" rel="stylesheet" href="mystylesheet.css">
```

will associate the style sheet called `mystylesheet.css` with the current page. The `type` attribute indicates the mime type of the linked document (`text/css`), while `rel` (short for relationship) tells the HTML rendering engine that the link is a type of `stylesheet` and should be applied accordingly. Finally, `href` gives the hypertext reference – the relative or absolute URL – of the document being linked.

Such a style sheet looks like the body of a `<STYLE>` element without the `<STYLE>` tags themselves – in other words, a selection of rules and nothing else. For example, the note declarations we created earlier might be given as a separate document, `notes.css`, and look something like:

```
<!-- notes.css -->
<!-- Define note classes -->
  P.note {margin-left:-.5in;width:250;border:solid 3px
  black;position:relative;background-color:lightBlue;}
  LI.note {border:inset 3px gray;background-color:lightGray;}
  .tip { background-color:yellow;}
  .resource { background-color:green;}
  .warning { background-color:red;}
```

There are a number of problems with using the `LINK` element, however. It was never really intended to handle style sheets; it just seemed to fit the current requirements. A `LINK` element can only be declared in the header of an HTML document, uses a syntax that suggests its somewhat mixed ancestry, and would be meaningless if you only had a fragment of HTML that didn't include the `<HEAD>` element.

The @import Directive

As it turns out, CSS also includes a special directive to handle importing of style sheets, called, not surprisingly, `@import`. The `@` indicates that this is a **directive**, not a property – rather than simply defining a style it performs an operation on the style sheet itself. With `@import`, you can load in a style sheet from a `<STYLE>` block, or even from a different external style sheet.

For example, you could include the directive:

```
<STYLE>
    @import url(notes.css)
</STYLE>
```

and it would apply the rules given in `notes.css` to the current document. The `url()` notation is a common one in CSS – it specifies that the content can be found at the indicated URL.

> *Unlike a function in Visual Basic or Java, the URL contained within the `url()` expression should not be enclosed in quotes – `url(myPage.css)` is the correct usage, while url('myPage.css') will cause an error and the style sheet won't load.*

One of the most intriguing things about the `@import` directive is that it can also be contained in external style sheets. When the initial style sheet is retrieved, these secondary commands will load their own style sheets into the document at the point where `@import` is found. With a few exceptions, `<STYLE>` blocks in the document will override the same selectors contained in external sheets, and the styles in a sheet that loads another sheet will override the imported sheet. Note that, as a consequence, `@import` should always be the first style in a style sheet or block, so that any rules in the current page override the imported rules (providing, of course, that you want the rules in the current page to apply).

Cascading Style Sheets and XML

Now we've had an introduction to cascading style sheets, we can go ahead and study how they are used with XML. As it turns out, the difference between CSS in HTML and in XML is small enough that if you understand how it works in HTML, you can apply it pretty readily to XML.

One of the primary differences that you'll encounter is that the `style` attribute, the `class` attribute, and the `<STYLE>` or `<LINK>` elements have no meaning in XML. (Actually, as you should be aware by now, they can have *any* meaning, but what we mean here is that they don't have *predefined* ones.) As a consequence, we have to assign styles through a different mechanism with XML – the `<?xml-stylesheet ?>` processing instruction.

> *First a comment, however – CSS is a big subject. The full CSS specification encompasses at least five distinct documents, a couple of which run into hundreds of pages. Don't panic! While the amount of content there (and here) can be a little overwhelming, CSS is meant to be fairly comprehensive. You'll find that maybe twenty properties are fairly important (and they're covered first here), while many of the other properties fall into the realm of the obscure. Like so much of HTML and XML, 10% of the specification will cover you in about 90% of the cases.*

As we saw in Chapter 1, a processing instruction is a command meant for the host application (in this case the browser) to do something with the XML. In most cases this something falls outside of the immediate scope of the XML parser, such as associating a style sheet with a given document.

External Style Sheets in XML

The `?xml-stylesheet` processing instruction works with any style sheet format that is defined for XML, but in particular applies to CSS and the Extensible Style sheet Language (which is the subject of Chapter 4). The full syntax of the xml-stylesheet command is as follows:

```
<?xml-stylesheet type=mimetype href=stylesheetURL?>
```

This actually bears a striking resemblance to the `LINK` element in HTML. *mimetype* here can reference any style sheet language that the browser supports, but will most likely have the value `"text/css"` or `"text/xsl"`. It should be included after the XML declaration (`<?xml version="1.0"…?>`) but before the first element of the XML document proper.

You may have noticed in our discussion on classes earlier in this chapter that a class seems to share some similarity to an XML element. In both cases you're dealing with a way of defining a logical meaning for a given element, rather than defining a presentation for that element. For example, our `note` object has a distinct logical meaning, and could be represented in conceivably any fashion. In HTML you might create such an object with a `class="note"` attribute, but in XML, you can actually create a `<note>` element as a separate entity.

The principal difference between the CSS generated in HTML and XML is that in XML there really is no need for the `class` attribute – the objects are already defined through the tags themselves, and the `class` attribute consequently isn't needed. Thus the dot notation (`.note`) is not supported, but other than that the characteristics are pretty close.

Let's begin by looking at an example of how we might create an external style sheet for an XML document. We'll use our `note` example again.

Try It Out – Multiple Classes in XML

Remember our problem of the multiple types of notes – let's look at how we could style this in XML.

1. We could, of course, create a different tag for each type of note. Create the following simple XML document (`notesTest1.xml`) which contains a number of different `note` notations:

```
<?xml-stylesheet type="text/css" href="notes1.css"?>
<!-- notesTest1.xml -->
<document>
    <body>
    <warning>This is a warning.</warning> On the other hand <tip>this
    is a tip</tip>, while <resource>this is a resource</resource>
    </body>
</document>
```

2. The document contains a reference to an XML style sheet, `notes1.css`, which is nearly identical to the HTML file `notes.css` that we looked at earlier. Save the following as `notes1.css`:

```
tip {margin-left:.5in;width:250px;border:solid 3px
    black;position:relative; background-color:yellow;}
resource {margin-left:.5in;width:250px;border:solid 3px
    black;position:relative; background-color:green;}
warning {margin-left:.5in;width:250px;border:solid 3px
    black;position:relative; background-color:red;}
```

3. Display the XML in your browser – you should see something like this:

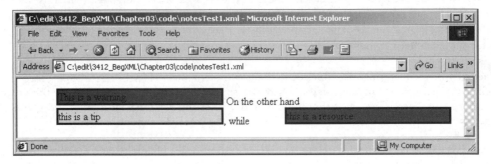

4. However, all three of these rules are essentially subclasses of `note`. It may be more advantageous to create an attribute for the `note` called something like `type`, which would codify the exact type of `note` that we are talking about.

Modify the `notesTest1.xml` code as follows (it looks a little more expansive, but is easier to work with if notes are primary objects) and save it as `notesTest2.xml`:

```
<?xml-stylesheet type="text/css" href="notes2.css"?>
<!-- notesTest2.xml -->
<document>
  <body>
```

```
        <note type="warning">This is a warning.</note> On the other hand
        <note type="tip">this is a tip</note>, while
        <note type="resource">this is a resource</note>
    </body>
</document>
```

5. The CSS for this, however, is something that can't readily be expressed using the HTML notation. Fortunately, the CSS2 specification includes a mechanism for referencing attributes – the bracket [ ] notation. With brackets you can either search to make sure that a given attribute exists for the specific element (i.e., note[type]) or can match those tokens for which the attribute has a given value. Save the following style sheet as notes2.css:

```
note {margin-left:.5in;width:250px;border-width:3px;
    border-style:outset;border-color:blue;
    position:relative;background-color;lightBlue;}
note[type="tip"]   {background-color:yellow;border-color:yellow;}
note[type="resource"] {background-color:green;
border-color:green}
note[type="warning"] {background-color:red;border-color:red;}
```

6. Display the notesTest2.xml in the browser. If your browser supports CSS2, it should look exactly the same as the previous screenshot.

How It Works

In our second style sheet, the note rule will automatically match all notes, regardless of their type, so all are guaranteed of having an indented margin, a width of 250 pixels, and a solid black border:

```
note {margin-left:.5in;width:250px;border-width:3px;
    border-style:outset;border-color:blue;
    position:relative;background-color;lightBlue;}
```

If the type is not included, or not one of those mentioned, the background for the note will also be light blue. On the other hand, if the type does match, then the CSS script will set the background color of the note to the new value (for example, warning becomes red, and so forth):

```
note[type="warning"] {background-color:red;border-color:red;}
```

Using this method can make both your XML and HTML code more robust by giving you limited inheritance. In other words, all of the types of note will be given the parent element's style, and then each sub-type can be given replacement or additional styles as required.

More on External Style Sheets

You can apply more than one bracket test. For example, if your notes also contained identifiers (in other words IDs, assuming you've defined IDs in your DTD or XML Schemas), then you could search for a specific note by name, but only apply the style if the note was a warning.

For example, if we added the CSS rule:

```
note[type="warning"][importance="primaryNote"]    {font-size:150%;}
```

after the more generic `note[type="warning"]`, we'd ensure that if the note had an `importance` attribute of `primaryNote`, then the font size would be half as large again as the standard sized note.

Similarly, you can apply styles based upon container/contained or parent/child relationships. For example, if you had an XML structure that looked like this:

```
<document>
    <head>
        <note>This shouldn't appear in the final output - it's
        an internal note for the processor.</note>
    </head>
    <body>
        <note>This is an important note, and since it belongs in
        the body it should be visible</note>
    </body>
</document>
```

Notes are used very differently here – a head note shouldn't appear in the output but a body note should. You could create a CSS style sheet that would handle this situation. Here, we've used the `head` element with a descendant `note` child:

```
head note {display:none;}
body note {
    margin-left:-.5in;
    display:block;
    width:250px;
    border:solid 3px black;
    position:relative;
    background-color;lightBlue;
    }
```

Note that style blocks don't care whether line breaks are used or not between CSS property assignments.

In this case, the notes could be children of the head or body respectively, but could also be arbitrarily deep descendants instead – either way the notes are displayed properly. If you specifically wanted to target notes that are first level children of the head or body exclusively, you could equally well use the notation `head>note` or `body>note` respectively, as we saw earlier in the chapter when we were discussing cascading class selectors.

Also notice that the `body note` selector includes an explicit `display:block` property. This is perhaps one of the most significant differences between HTML and XML from a CSS standpoint – HTML elements know whether they are block or inline elements, so this property doesn't usually need to be set. XML elements, on the other hand, must have their display attributes set explicitly. We'll come back to this later in the chapter.

Internal XML Cascading Style Sheets

While external style sheets are handy for maintaining a consistent style between XML documents, there are times where it would be more useful to work with styles *within* an XML document. Unfortunately, while the `<STYLE>` tag is meaningful for HTML documents, it's considerably less so for XML documents (where it's simply another tag). How can we incorporate a style sheet given that restriction?

It turns out that there is a way, though one that's not terribly well known. We can include style sheet rules in an element in the XML document with a named ID, then reference the style sheet by that ID in the `xml-stylesheet` processing-instruction.

For example, the following simple XML document contains its own style sheet:

```
<?xml-stylesheet type="text/css" href="#myStyleSheet"?>
<document>
    <st id="myStyleSheet">
        title {font-size:24pt;display:block;}
        p {font-size:11pt;display:block;}
        p:first-letter {float:left;font-size:36pt;}
        st {display:none;}   <!-- this means that the st element will
                                 not be displayed -->
        b {font-weight:bold;}
    </st>
    <title>CSS Style Sheets in XML Documents</title>
        <para>You can use the pound sign "#" to indicate that you want to
reference a stylesheet from within your document. In this case, the style sheet is
contained in the <b>st</b> element, and is labeled "stylesheet".</para>
</document>
```

In this particular case, the style sheet is contained in the `<st>` node, but is referenced through its ID `myStyleSheet`. The way that the # sign in the `xml-stylesheet` declaration functions with IDs is similar to the way the HTML anchor tag (A) works with the `name` attribute – it identifies that unit as being a distinct part of the document. In other words the `href` value `#myStyleSheet` indicates that somewhere within this document is an element with an `id` of `myStyleSheet`, and that's where the style sheet will be found.

The Medium is the Message

> It's worth reviewing here what exactly the role of CSS is: it provides a presentation layer that associates patterns of tags (whether HTML or XML is largely immaterial) with some kind of media representation.

As the voice examples we discussed earlier in this chapter point out, media does not simply mean output to a web page. Indeed, the ultimate direction of both CSS and other XML-related technologies such as XSL-Formatting Objects (which we'll discuss in later chapters) is to replace the way that we represent *any* sort of document structure. This is a tall order, especially in the sea of formats that currently exist to do the same thing, but if it can be pulled off the benefits would be impressive.

While CSS1 and CSS2 are similar, the primary difference between the two is the realization that CSS can potentially apply to many more media than simply web pages. Indeed, the CSS2 specification currently recognizes a number of different media types (and leaves open the door for other types as they become available):

- ❑ **all**. The style property applies to all media types
- ❑ **aural**. Intended for speech synthesizers
- ❑ **braille**. Intended for Braille tactile feedback devices
- ❑ **embossed**. Intended for paged Braille printers
- ❑ **handheld**. Intended for handheld devices which typically have a small screen, monochrome output, limited bandwidth
- ❑ **print**. Intended for printing to an opaque page, for example paper
- ❑ **projection**. Intended for projection to a screen (such as a slideshow)
- ❑ **screen**. Intended principally for color computer screens
- ❑ **tty**. Intended for fixed pitch printers and related character grid devices such as teletypes, terminals and the like
- ❑ **tv**. Intended for use on a television screen, with low definition but with known sound capabilities

The @media Directive

CSS can let you target different media through the @media directive, making the code displayed by, say, a web browser and a Palm Pilot look very different. CSS allows you to group together rules that apply to a specific type of medium, and a rule for a given tag can be given several times (as long as each applies to a different medium).

For example, let's return to our notes in an XML document, and present them to different media devices:

```
<!-- NotesMedia.css -->
@media screen, print {
   note { margin-left:-.5in;width:250px;border-width:3px;
   border-style:inset;position:relative;background-color;lightBlue;}
   note[type="tip"]  {background-color:yellow;border-color:yellow;}
   note[type="resource"] {background-color:green;
   border-color:green;color:white;}
   note[type="warning"] { background-color:red;border-color:red;}


}

@media aural {
   note[type="tip"]  {volume:medium;voice-family:FriendlyAdvice;}
   note[type="resource"] { volume:soft;voice-family:Directions;}
   note[type="warning"] { volume:loud;voice-family:WarningWillRobinson;}
}
```

```
@media tty,braille {
    note {display:block;}
    note[type="tip"]:before {content: "[TIP]";}
    note[type="tip"]:after {content: "[END TIP]"; }
    note[type="resource"]:before {content: "[RESOURCE]";}
    note[type="resource"]:after {content: "[END RESOURCE]";}
    note[type="warning"]:before {content: "[WARNING]";}
    note[type="warning"]:after {content: "[END WARNING]";}
}
```

In this case, output to the screen or printed output will draw different colored boxes containing text, output to a speech synthesizer will set the appropriate voice and volume, while output to a teletype or Braille machine will, for example, surround a tip so that it always starts with [TIP] and ends with [END TIP].

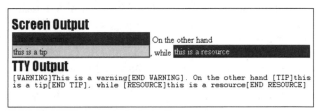

Media Groups

While this version of the @media directive works well when the specific device is known, we may also want to have our media defined using the desired **display characteristics**, not the specific **device**.

In addition to the media **type**, we can also specify **media groups**, as follows:

- ❑ **continuous** or **paged**. The medium is either one long stream of information, such as found in spoken output or a web page, or is broken into discrete pages

- ❑ **visual, aural** or **tactile**. The medium is either concentrated in a visual display (a printed page or web page, for example), an aural display (a speech synthesizer) or a tactile display (a Braille reader)

- ❑ **grid** or **bitmap**. The medium either consists of a fixed width set of characters (such as a teletype machine) or can render graphics through a painted bitmap

- ❑ **interactive** or **static**. The medium either allows interaction (such as a computer display) or doesn't (such as a printed page)

- ❑ **all**. Includes all media types

Thus you could create a new specification for some of the interactive handheld devices that are becoming ubiquitous, through the @media directive:

```
@media paged, visual, bitmap, interactive {
    note {margin-left:-.5in;
    border:solid 2px black;position:relative;}
    note[type="tip"]   {border:solid 1px black;}
    note[type="resource"] {border:dashed 1px black;}
    note[type="warning"] {border:solid 5px black;}
}
```

While this assumes a bitmap, the fact that it's working with paged media also implies that there is a possibility that it doesn't support color, so the output is generated accordingly. Note that it is the responsibility of the user agent (the browser, printer or related device) to determine whether the device actually supports the given media rules, and generate its own accordingly if there is no match.

The Box Model

Cascading style sheets make use of what's called a **"Box" Model**, which determines the way that information flows on the page. In general, the idea behind the box model is simple: the content flows into the available presentation space in specific containers (the analogy that comes to mind are water balloons that will shape themselves to best fit the available area). This container could be a page with constrained margins, the pane of a web browser, or the temporal bounds of spoken text.

There are essentially two types of such boxes – **inline** elements and **block** elements.

An inline element will fit itself into the smallest available space, and the element immediately after the inline element will fill in immediately adjacent to it (with the direction determined largely by the language that the browser uses). In theory, each character in a string of text could be considered an inline element, but for most purposes inline elements are specifically HTML or XML tags that allow other such tags to precede or follow them in a continuous line. In HTML, inline elements include such tags as <B> (bold), <I> (italic), <A> (anchor tags), <SPAN> and so forth.

A block element, on the other hand, fills all of the available space in the flow direction unless otherwise constrained. By flow direction here, we're referring to the direction that text would normally be ordered in – English text flows to the right and down, Arabic text flows to the left and down, Japanese text flows down and to the right, etc. Thus in an English language web page a block element would start at the left margin of the page, then its contents would fill all the way to the right margin before starting the next line. Vertical Japanese Kanji, on the other hand, would flow to the bottom margin of the page then loop back to the next line at the top. If another block followed the current one, that block would automatically move back to the start of the page flow. The HTML tags <P>, <LI>, <DIV>, <HR>, and so forth illustrate the principle of the block tag.

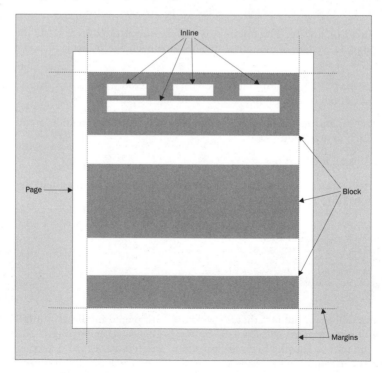

The display Property

From a CSS standpoint, one of the principle differences between HTML and XML is that the latter doesn't specifically define an element as being block or inline – and typically assumes that all elements are inline unless specified otherwise. Thus, when defining CSS tags in XML you need to explicitly declare whether the tag refers to a block or an inline element, which is done through the `display` property. For example, with a style sheet that looks like this:

```
para {display:block;color:black;}
comment {display:inline;color:gray;font-size:120%;font-family:courier;}
```

the markup text:

```
<para>I'd like to include a comment: <comment>This is an interesting way of
expressing yourself.</comment></para>
<para>Here's another line with no comment.</para>
```

will display as:

I'd like to include a comment: `This is an interesting way of expressing yourself.`
Here's another line with no comment.

Other display Values

The values of `block` and `inline` are not the only ones that `display` can hold. The full list is in fact fairly exhaustive, and is shown in the following table of `display` properties:

Property name	Property Description
inline	Content assumes the smallest possible size, with additional elements flowing automatically in line with the current element when possible.
block	Content fills the extent of the flow boundaries, and that content always starts as part of a new flow region (for example by starting on the next line of text).
none	Indicates that the contents are not rendered to the output canvas.
inherit	The element inherits the style attribute of the object's immediate container. This is the default display property.
list-item	The item is treated as an element in a list. One consequence of this is that you can use the CSS list properties (list-style-type, list-style-image, list-style-position) to determine the appearance and characteristics of bullets (see the section on Lists, later in this chapter).
run-in	The contents are essentially treated as belonging to the next block of text encountered. This can be useful for definitions.
compact	The contents are a display-type box, but occupy the smallest area possible.
marker	The contents are to be treated as a marker or bullet.

Table continued on following page

91

Property name	Property Description
table	The contents are displayed as if in a table. In order for this to work, elements within the table must have one of the table- styles mentioned later in this table. (table is equivalent to HTML's <TABLE> element).
inline-table	Indicates a table that is contained as part of the flow.
table-row-group	Equivalent to the HTML <TBODY> element, this contains all of the regular rows (those not part of the column headers) in the table.
table-column-group	Equivalent to the HTML <COL-GROUP> element. This contains a grouping of columns in the table.
table-header-group	Equivalent to the HTML <THEAD> element. This contains all of the header elements in the table (such as column heads).
table-footer-group	Equivalent to the HTML <TFOOT> element. This contains all of the footer elements in the table.
table-row	Equivalent to the HTML <TR> element. This contains a standard row in a table.
table-cell	Equivalent to the HTML <TD> element. This contains a standard cell from a row in a table.
table-caption	Equivalent to the HTML <CAPTION> element. This contains a caption that is associated with the table.

Of these display properties the bulk are dedicated to handling lists or tables, and will be covered in the next couple of sections. The one property value we need to emphasize here, however, is the none value.

This would seem to be a fairly useless state, but in fact like the number *zero* it makes some useful things possible. The value of none indicates to the rendering engine that the block in question is simply not rendered to the page – no area is taken up by it, it receives no events, so in general the element is both disabled and unseen.

This characteristic has value primarily when combined with a scripting model– by turning display on or off you can essentially create the illusion of expanding or collapsing structures such as hierarchical trees, dynamic tables, pop-up elements, and more. When display is set from none to some other value the hidden text is rendered back into the stream, pushing other elements farther down in the process to give the illusion of expansion, while going from a visual display to a display of none collapses (or hides) that same capability.

Additionally, with XML it provides a way of insuring that certain elements are simply not shown – such as an XML <style> block that contains style information but that isn't meant for public display.

The Difference Between display and visibility

CSS includes a second property called visibility. This is similar to display, but not identical, and in fact visibility is the weaker of the two properties. Visibility determines whether a given element (or set of elements) is rendered within its bounding rectangle (visibility:visible) or not (visibility:hidden).

Unlike `display:none`, `visibility:hidden` sets aside the area for the bounding rectangle of the content and, in many browsers, actually accepts mouse-clicks and similar events. This makes `visibility` good for creating a transparent area for handling events, but in general it's far less useful than `display`.

> *`visibility` also includes a third property for rendering – `visibility:collapse` – but this isn't currently supported by any browser. It performs the same action as `display:none`, and it doesn't need to know what the previous state of the element was to toggle between two collapsed and expanded states.*

By the way, the default behavior for an XML element that doesn't have a style sheet is for it to inherit the `display` property of the containing element (with the specific default for the root object being inline). What this means, however, is that if you have an element that has no style sheet rule associated with it, then the text of that element (and any sub-element) will appear in the final output of the page (though this isn't always handled consistently between browsers, not that much is). However, if you define a container element to be invisible (to have a `display` property of `none`), then no child of that element will appear, unless it's explicitly given a display property other than `none`.

Try It Out – Working With Display

Using a CSS2-compliant browser, you can see how `display` works by experimenting with `display:none` and `display:block`. For example, let's illustrate the default mechanism of `display`.

1. Enter the following code and save it as `midnightRain.xml`:

```
<?xml-stylesheet type="text/css" href="#docstyle"?>
<!-- MidnightRain.xml -->
<document>
    <style id="docstyle">
        style {display:none;}
        head {display:none;}
        title {display:block;font-size:24pt; }
        author {display:block;font-size:18pt;}
        body {display:block;font-size:10pt;}
        para {font-size:11pt; }
    </style>
    <head>
        <title>Midnight Rain</title>
        <author>Kurt Cagle</author>
        <email>cagle@olywa.net</email>
    </head>
    <body>
        <note>From the first chapter of Midnight Rain, by Kurt Cagle</note>
        <para>The rain spat against the apartment's window pane,
        torrential for this part of Los Angeles, though Gina would
        not have much noticed it at home. The rain straddled the
        boundary between being the life blessing touch that this
        valley so seldom received and the caustic depressed state
        that lately so made up her soul.</para>
        <para>"Rain, Rain, Go Away …" she sang listlessly, though
        as she doodled over the script that Stan had sent, Gina
        secretly relished the rain, as indulgent as the black mood
        she wore around herself.</para>
    </body>
</document>
```

2. View this in the browser. It will not display the email contents (since that element is a child of the element <head>, which has display set to none), but will show the <note> element, since the default display for its container is set to block:

Midnight Rain
Kurt Cagle

From the first chapter of Midnight Rain, by Kurt Cagle

The rain spat against the apartment's window pane, torrential for this part of Los Angeles, though Gina would not have much noticed it at home. The rain straddled the boundary between being the life blessing touch that this valley so seldom received and the caustic depressed state that lately so made up her soul.

"Rain, Rain, Go Away ..." she sang listlessly, though as she doodled over the script that Stan had sent, Gina secretly relished the rain, as indulgent as the black mood she wore around herself.

Note that this behavior, as with the nature of display in general, is not uniform across browsers – in Internet Explorer, for example, an element that has display set to block within another element with display set to none will simply not appear, whereas the correct behavior is to show any sub-element that has the display explicitly defined (you would use visibility:collapse to get the correct behavior). To make the story appear properly in Internet Explorer, you would need to explicitly make the <head> element visible, then hide any sub-elements that don't appear:

```
<style id="docstyle2">
    style {display:block;}
    head {display:none;}
    title {display:block;font-size:24pt; }
    author {display:block;font-size:18pt;}
    email {display:none;}
    body {display:block;font-size:10pt;}
    para {font-size:11pt;display:block; }
</style>
```

This inconsistency can be rather aggravating, especially since IE5 also doesn't inherit display properties – even though the para rule is a child of the body rule, which sets display to block, you still have to set display to block for the para child as well.

Setting Colors

In HTML or XML, the ability to control colors was one of the first customizations that web designers demanded. One consequence of this is that there are a number of different mechanisms for working with color in HTML, which have emerged as the HTML (and later the CSS) specification emerged.

At first, you could set the color of all of the text in the document (or the background of the document) to a single uniform color (from the <BODY text="color" and bgcolor="bgcolor"> tags), although you could set the colors of visited and unvisited hypertext links from the same line as well.

The introduction of the `<FONT>` tag let you apply this level at a finer granularity, as you could change the color of text elements within a given subset of the page (delineated by the `<FONT>` tag, which had the same scope as the more recent `<SPAN>` tag). However, the `<FONT>` tag is a completely decorative element – it contains no information about the underlying structure, and furthermore tended to significantly erode the logical structure that did exist.

Until CSS, though, you couldn't set the color of an element's background without resorting to Byzantine tricks with images. CSS changes that. You can create rectangular blocks that had specific colors (or background-images) within the document itself. For example, to set the color of a text block to red with the background set to white you'd make the call:

```
<P style="color:red;background-color:white;">Warning, Will Robinson!!
Warning!!</P>
```

Similarly, you can set the colors of whole tag sets in the same way by adding these attributes to style sheets:

```
<style>
H1 {color:red;background-color:white}
</style>
```

Notice here that I'm making free use of the values "red" and "white" without bothering to explain what they are. The CSS standard defines a number of standard colors, such as red, white, orange, yellow, and so forth that correspond to the numerical values of these colors (see the next section). However, many of the colors that *are* available have been defined slightly differently between Netscape and Internet Explorer, and with the exception of a handful of colors, the name of a color in one browser stands a good chance of not existing (or not meaning the same) as a color in the other browser. For this reason, you should only use color names for the eight or so primary colors.

Note: it used to be an old trick with web pages (used primarily by adult sites) to set the foreground color of the text to the background color of the page, making information that you want picked up by search engines available without showing them on the screen. This is a bad (and expensive) hack – it adds to the download and rendering time (the text is rendered, even if it isn't visible), is subject to discovery by anyone dragging on the page with the mouse, and can be done more effectively by placing the search keywords into a `<META>` tag, which is the first place that a search engine will inspect, anyway.

Hex Color Codes

Because there is a difference in the way that different browsers may display certain colors called by name, in general you should avoid representing your colors by name and instead use **hexadecimal triplets** to encode the color. Hexadecimal triplets are a standard way of representing the intensities of colors, but if you are unfamiliar with the notion of hexadecimal numbers or the way that colors are stored internally, then they can be a little confusing.

Most computer systems internally represent colors as relative percentages of the three colors: red, green and blue (usually abbreviated as RGB). Because screen pixels are actually light elements, they use the same additive model that televisions use: by varying the amount of red, green, and blue in a signal, you can approximate most of the colors that the eye can see. The exceptions are typically called the fluorescent colors (such as bright pink), which have vividnesses that are simply not possible to duplicate with three colors.

100% of all three of the colors red, green and blue will produce a completely white signal, while 0% of the colors make black. Otherwise, by varying the percentage, you can make nearly any color: 100% of red and green and 0% blue makes yellow, 100% of red and blue make magenta (a light purple), and 50% of all three colors makes gray. However, internally, representing everything as a proportion of 100 doesn't fit well with the architectures of most computers, which work best with powers of 2. By using eight bits to represent each color, you can represent 256 shades of red, 256 shades of green, and so forth, giving you a total of 16 million colors.

Again, because you're dealing with powers of two, representing each color in decimal format means that the computer has to do some time-consuming multiplication and division calculations that could slow down the speed at which the screen is refreshed. So instead, it is traditional to use base 16 or hexadecimal notation, in which you use sixteen digits (from 0 to 9, then with A to F representing the values 10 to 15 respectively).

Thus, 2F in hex notation is the same as $(2*16)+(15)$ or 47. Not coincidentally, the largest two digit number that you can write, FF, is equivalent to $(15*16)+15$ or 255. In other words, 8 bits or one base color can be specified with a two digit hexadecimal number.

The CSS specification uses three sets of two digit hex values for red, green and blue respectively. Thus to represent red, you'd use #FF0000, while green is #00FF00 and blue is #0000FF. It is conventional to include the hash mark to indicate that the expression is a hexadecimal number (although it's not strictly required).

As many (though not all) colors can be represented through a combination of red, green and blue, you can display the output by setting the intensities of the respective parts (in computer parlance, the colors red, green, and blue are said to be *orthogonal*). Thus, yellow is made up of full intensity red (#FF0000) mixed with full intensity green (#00FF00), but with no blue: in other words #FFFF00. Brown is a fairly complex color, although one shade of brown could be represented as a reddish color with a strong green component and a little bit of blue (#FFC020).

In general, you're encouraged to use the hexadecimal equivalents for most colors – they represent colors absolutely, they won't be ambiguous between browsers, and you can be sure that their use won't cause one browser to break.

Building Borders

Borders can be used to provide a number of useful special effects, if used properly. If you're working with borders in Internet Explorer, there are a number of useful CSS properties that you can call on. Each border supports three distinct properties: **style**, **width** and **color**.

Style lets you change the visual appearance of the border, with possible values including:

- ❑ **solid** (a single solid line)
- ❑ **double** (two concentric lines of at least three pixels width)
- ❑ **inset** (a border where the upper and left hand sides are darker than the bottom and right hand sides)
- ❑ **outset** (the inverse of inset)

- ❑ **groove** (a border that appears incised around the container)
- ❑ **ridge** (a border that's excised around the container)
- ❑ **dotted** (a border consisting of alternating dots and spaces)
- ❑ **dashed** (a border consisting of alternating dashes and spaces)
- ❑ **none** (turns bordering off)

Note that Internet Explorer treats dotted and dashed lines as solid lines under Windows and Unix, but recognizes those styles on the Macintosh. Certain styles, such as double, grooved and ridged, require that the width of the border be set to at least 3. Also, Internet Explorer 5.5 seems to reverse this and represent dotted and dashed lines as dotted and dashed lines, surprisingly enough.

Let's have a go at working with borders to demonstrate the different styles.

Try It Out – Building Borders

1. Create the following file (`borders.html`):

```
<HTML>
<HEAD>
   <TITLE>Borders</TITLE>
   <STYLE>
   P {border:solid 5px #C0C0C0;}
   </STYLE>
</HEAD>
<BODY>
<H3>Borders</H3>
<P style="border-style:solid">border-style:solid</P>
<P style="border-style:double">border-style:double</P>
<P style="border-style:inset">border-style:inset</P>
<P style="border-style:outset">border-style:outset</P>
<P style="border-style:groove">border-style:groove</P>
<P style="border-style:ridge">border-style:ridge</P>
<P style="border-style:dotted">border-style:dotted</P>
<P style="border-style:dashed">border-style:dashed</P>
<P style="border-style:none">border-style:none</P>
</BODY>
</HTML>
```

2. If you view this in a compliant browser, this produces a gray, 5 pixel-wide border in the various styles:

3. Create another file (`borders.xml`) as follows:

```xml
<?xml-stylesheet type="text/css" href="#internalstyles" ?>
<document>
<style id="internalstyles">
    annotation {border:solid 3px green;font-size:12pt;
                display:block;border-left:none;border-right:none;
                font-family:Arial}
    para {font-size:11pt;display:block;}
    style {display:none;}
</style>
        <para>The rain spat against the apartment's window pane,
        torrential for this part of Los Angeles, though Gina would
        not have much noticed it at home. The rain straddled the
        boundary between being the life blessing touch that this
        valley so seldom received and the the caustic depressed
        state that lately so made up her soul.</para>
        <para>"Rain, Rain, Go Away," she sang listlessly, though as
        she doodled over the script that Stan had sent, Gina secretly
        relished the rain, as indulgent as the black mood she wore
        around herself.</para>
        <annotation>
            <para>Rain is a metaphor throughout this story as an expression
            of both elemental force and chaotic emotions. </para>
        </annotation>
        <para>She didn't want to do the script, not really - the
        scripts that she received anymore were hardly star makers,
        though her star had risen fairly high once, only to be knocked
        off course by the ... ah, what was the term the publicist had
        used ... the incident, that was it.</para>
</document>
```

4. This would produce the following output:

> The rain spat against the apartment's window pane, torrential for this part of Los Angeles, though Gina would not have much noticed it at home. The rain straddled the boundary between being the life blessing touch that this valley so seldom received and the the caustic depressed state that lately so made up her soul.
> "Rain, Rain, Go Away," she sang listlessly, though as she doodled over the script that Stan had sent, Gina secretly relished the rain, as indulgent as the black mood she wore around herself.
>
> Rain is a metaphor throughout this story as an expression of both elemental force and chaotic emotions.
>
> She didn't want to do the script, not really - the scripts that she received anymore were hardly star makers, though her star had risen fairly high once, only to be knocked off course by the ... ah, what was the term the publicist had used ... the incident, that was it.

By specifying just part of a border (or in this case, by turning off those sides that you don't want to display) you can create rules and other special effects.

How It Works

From our HTML example, we can see how we could create sophisticated button and container effects just by modifying the `border-style` characteristic. The source code for this borders image demonstrates two techniques for applying attributes. We can apply them one at a time through the CSS `border` property (using the `border-style`, `border-color` and `border-width` properties respectively):

```
<P style="border-style:solid">border-style:solid</P>
```

Or we can apply them as a single triplet attribute, in the order `border:style width color`:

```
P {border:solid 5px #C0C0C0;}
```

We could also choose to set the left, right, top or bottom side of the border rectangle directly by specifying the side as `border-left`, `border-right`, etc, then appending the qualifying attribute (`style`, `width`, `color`) to the term. In our XML file, we created an annotation style in which a green border runs along the top and bottom of a paragraph:

```
<style id="internalstyles">
     annotation {border:solid 3px green;font-size:12pt;
                 display:block;border-left:none;border-right:none;
                 font-family:Arial}
```

We then use this to highlight a paragraph of annotation text:

```
relished the rain, as indulgent as the black mood she wore
around herself.</para>
<annotation>
    <para>Rain is a metaphor throughout this story as an expression
    of both elemental force and chaotic emotions. </para>
</annotation>
```

Background Images

Images are a regular staple of web pages, but incorporating images is considerably more complex in XML documents. While it is possible to use notations introduced through DTDs (a topic we'll cover in Chapter 9), this mechanism (which relies heavily on SGML to accomplish the same task) creates undue dependencies upon specific helper programs to make this work effectively for XML – in other words, your browser needs a specific piece of software to display the appropriate images. Fortunately it is possible to use CSS to accomplish the same thing, without having to specifically define the exact mechanism that the browser or viewer uses to render the image.

The `background-image` style attribute offers one way of setting such an image. To do it, you need to make use of a special **meta-function** used in CSS, the `url()` function. This converts a string expression into a URL that the style sheet can then reference.

For example, the following style samples will load a graphic called `mybackground.jpg` from the same folder as the page, from a different folder on the same server, and from a different server:

```
<style>
<!-- to load from the same folder as the source XML document -->
body {background-image:url(mybackground.jpg); }
<!-- to load from a subordinate folder called images relative to the source XML
document -->
body {background-image:url(images/mybackground.jpg);}
<!-- to load from a different web server -->
body {background-image:url(http://www.myserver.com/images/mybackground.jpg);
background-color:blue;}
</style>
```

Notice that, unlike a scripted call, the `url()` location being passed is not enclosed in quotation marks. Also, in the third `body` tag, a `background-color` is set as well. This color will be displayed either until the image loads, or will persist if the browser can't find the image. This is a good technique for making sure that text is legible even when the background hasn't completely loaded yet (anyone who has had to read light yellow text against a white background while the predominantly blue background is loading can appreciate this).

The `background-image` will occupy the extent of the element, with the image becoming cropped if the bounding rectangle of the element is smaller than the image, and with the image repeating (depending upon repeating characteristics described below) if the bounding box is larger than the image.

Limitations When Working with Images

In CSS, there is nothing that specifically lets you create an image element that will automatically size to the same size as the image itself, or that conversely will scale the image to match the boundaries, at least within straight XML. However, if you do know the dimensions of the image, you can use a `background-image` property to incorporate such an image into your document.

For example, if you know that your logo is 125 pixels wide by 110 pixels high, you can incorporate it into the flow of your document with the following style sheet:

```
logo_img {background-image:url(myLogo.jpg);width:125px;
height:110px;position:relative;}
```

which would then be referenced inside the XML document itself as:

```
<logo_img/><p>Welcome to our company.</p>
```

The other limitation with XML and CSS-based images is more serious: you can't just create an image through an `src` attribute as you would with the HTML `<IMG src="uri"/>` expression. Unfortunately, this is not a minor problem – typically XML documents will contain information internally for describing which images will be displayed, and requiring that you know ahead of time what graphics you'll be needing often renders the advantages of CSS (at least for image display) moot.

Later in this chapter we'll see some ways of working around this problem, but it is a significant constraint on how effective CSS can be when working with XML as a display language. Other possible solutions include making use of XHTML namespaces, XSL-FO, or building images with SVG and transforming the result with inline XSLT.

Positioning and Repeating Background Images

We can control the way that our backgrounds repeat, as well as where they start on the page.

Repeating

Repetition is specified by using the various `repeat` properties. These control the tiling behavior of background graphics:

`repeat`	Repeats the indicated graphic both horizontally and vertically (the default)
`repeat-x`	Repeats the indicated graphic horizontally, but not vertically
`repeat-y`	Repeats the indicated graphic vertically, but not horizontally
`no-repeat`	Doesn't repeat the graphic at all

So, if we wanted to have our strip repeat vertically along the left side of the page, we'd set the style as:

```
{background-image:url(mybackground.jpg);background-repeat:repeat-y;}
```

When you scroll, the background will typically scroll with the page. In some cases you may actually want to turn this behavior off, so that the background remains static when you scroll the page. To do this, we'd set the `background-attachment` style attribute to `fixed`. What this function does under the surface is to tie the background rendering buffer to the window, not the document. As a consequence, we can create an interesting effect with background attachment in a block element coupled with animation.

Positioning

Normally, when you load in a background image (whether tiled or not) the image is positioned so that it starts tiling from the upper left-hand corner. In some instances, you may want the image to start tiling somewhere else in the graphic. This is actually more useful when dealing with behaviors than it is with normal style sheets, but in either case the solution is simple – use the `background-position` style attribute. There are several different ways that you can position the image:

`percentage` (e.g., 40% 60%)	Sets the graphic so that it starts 40% of the width from the left and 60% of the height from the top
`length` (e.g., 50,75)	Positions the left coordinate at 50 pixels and the top at 75 pixels
`top｜center｜bottom`	Sets the graphic flush to the top, centered vertically, or flush to the bottom of the document
`left｜center｜right`	Sets the graphic flush to the left, centered horizontally, or flush to the right of the document

So, if we wanted to align the graphic so that it was centered on the web page horizontally at the top of the page, without tiling, we'd use the expression:

```
<h1 style="background-url(mybackground.jpg);background-repeat:no-repeat;
background-position:top center;">Here's a test.</h1>
```

Here we must specify both `top` and `center` in the `background-position` property, since the default is `middle` and `left` respectively.

Specifying Multiple Background Properties

Since you'll frequently perform multiple actions upon a background (either the background of the document's `BODY` or of a block tag like a `DIV` or `P` tag), CSS lets you combine multiple options in a single statement. Specifically, these are:

- ❑ `background-color` (which sets the color)
- ❑ `background-image` (sets the image)
- ❑ `background-repeat` (indicates how the background tiles)
- ❑ `background-attachment` (indicates whether the background scrolls or remains fixed)
- ❑ `background-position` (the location of the upper-left hand point of the background)

In other words, the previous expression could be rewritten as:

```
<h1 style="background:blue url(mybackground.jpg) no-repeat scroll
top center">Here's a test.</h1>
```

This is typical of several CSS attributes, such as `font`, `border`, and `margin`. Order is usually not important and the arguments are always separated by a space. This makes it especially easy to update these properties programmatically, as you can set several attributes in one fell swoop.

Creating Backgrounds

One of the more frustrating problems when dealing with XML is that certain concepts, such as that of the browser pane background, don't really exist in CSS. However, you can do the next best thing by creating a block element that is outside of the normal flow (see the next section for more details about flow), position it so that it takes up the entire window, then apply background styling to it.

Try It Out – Creating XML Web Page Backgrounds

For example, a common visual effect in HTML web pages is to run a repeating graphic along the left hand side of the page to give the impression of a visual border. This is typically done by setting the `body` attribute directly. However, with XML, you will probably want to separate the background block from the body block.

Let's look at how we can do this.

1. You'll find the file `BGTile.jpg` in the code download for this book. Put it in the same folder as the XML file you'll create next.

2. Create the following XML document and save it as `rainWithBG.xml`:

```
<?xml-stylesheet type="text/css" href="#internalstyles" ?>
<!-- rainWithBG.xml -->
<document>
<style id="internalstyles">
    annotation {border:solid 3px green;font-size:12pt;
    display:block;border-left:none;border-right:none;font-family:Arial}
    para {font-size:11pt;display:block;}
    style {display:none;}
    background {background-image:url(BGTile.jpg);
    background-repeat-x:no;background-repeat-y:yes;
    width:128px;height:100%;position:absolute;left:0px;top:0px;}
    body {margin-left:136px;position:absolute;}
</style>
    <background/>
    <body>
        <para>The rain spat against the apartment's window pane,
        torrential for this part of Los Angeles, though Gina would
        not have much noticed it at home. The rain straddled the
        boundary between being the life blessing touch that this
        valley so seldom received and the caustic depressed
        state that lately so made up her soul.</para>
        <para>"Rain, Rain, Go Away," she sang listlessly, though as
        she doodled over the script that Stan had sent, Gina secretly
        relished the rain, as indulgent as the black mood she wore
        around herself.</para>
        <annotation>
            <para>Rain is a metaphor throughout this story as an expression
            of both elemental force and chaotic emotions. </para>
        </annotation>
        <para>She didn't want to do the script, not really - the
        scripts that she received anymore were hardly star makers,
        though her star had risen fairly high once, only to be
        knocked off course by the ... ah, what was the term the
        publicist had used ... the incident, that was it.</para>
    </body>
</document>
```

By splitting the body into a `body` and `background`, we can assign background characteristics without having to worry about the effects of margins, and can then reposition the `body` element relative to the background.

3. View the above document in the browser – the result is shown:

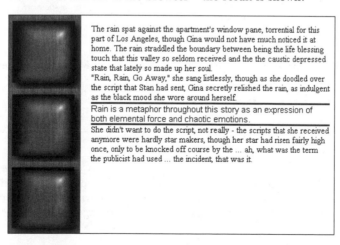

By applying absolute positioning and background repetition, we can duplicate the effects of an HTML background in XML.

Understanding Positioning Schemes

The concept of flow is a treacherous one – it seems so intuitive and obvious, but the more you examine it the more amorphous it actually becomes. CSS identifies four distinct types of positioning (which affects the flow) – static, relative, absolute and fixed – all values of the position CSS property.

Static Position

A static position is one in which the position of the content is controlled by the browser – we have no ability to specify where it should be laid out. Static content has the advantage of being quick to lay out, since the CSS rendering engine can position it without having to check user information. However, it's also content that can't be positioned by the web designer. The static position is the default – if you don't specify a position explicitly this will be the one used.

Relative Position

The relative position is similar to the static position except that the top and left values can be overridden by code or CSS properties. You would use relative content to position items that you want to set in their "natural" positions, but which will also likely change in position during the user session.

Using relative on a static page can significantly slow down rendering, since every time a relative element is encountered, the HTML renderer needs to store this information as a user defined object. (Static content, on the other hand, is maintained by the browser in a more efficient manner, since CSS properties don't have to be explicitly maintained the way they are with relative elements.)

If you do change the top and left positions of relative elements, these values are offset relative to where the output would be if the object had been positioned statically. Thus, for a paragraph within a division element in HTML, there's typically a certain amount of space from the top-left of the division to the top-left of the paragraph (called the **margin** of the paragraph).

For convenience sake, assume this default amount is 10 pixels (10px) in either direction. So the CSS document:

```
P {position:relative;}
```

will place the newly created paragraph 10 pixels to the right and down. On the other hand:

```
P {position:relative;top:10px;left:15px;}
```

will place the newly created paragraph 25 pixels to the right (10+15) and twenty pixels down (10+10).

Absolute Position

Opposite to the relative position is the absolute position. The origin (the starting position both horizontally and vertically) for a relatively positioned item is its "normal" position in the flow. For items positioned absolutely, however, the origin is located at the beginning of the flow for the page.

For example, in a web browser this position would be located at the upper left hand corner of the browser page (assuming a Western left-right top-bottom orientation), while for a printed page the position is relative to the top-left margin of the page. If an object is positioned absolutely and no origin (no `top` or `left` coordinates) is specified, then the object will be placed in the flow where it would normally be. On the other hand, if the object is given either one of these values, then it will be positioned relative to the page origin for that coordinate.

Fixed Position

The `fixed` position uses the `absolute` model, but it won't change its position if the viewport (the browser display window, for example) changes. For example, if you scroll down on a long page, the `fixed` element will always remain on the screen, regardless of any other content. This can be useful for building constructs such a menu bars that will always retain their position relative to the top of the screen.

Note that Internet Explorer 4.x and 5.x do not support the `fixed` position property.

Inherited Position

Unlike other properties, `position` is not a property that is explicitly inherited. However, you can explicitly specify that the element inherits the positioning model of its parent through the `inherit` value.

In general you're better making this association explicit – in other words declaring an element position relatively or absolutely – rather than telling the element to inherit its parent's positioning mode. Not all browsers handle subordinate inheritance terribly well.

Setting Positions and Units

Once you set up the positioning mode, you can position an element from the top, bottom, left or right. In most cases the top-left corner serves as the positioning element (and indeed in many browsers top and left are the only two coordinates recognized) but you can in fact place a box of text from any of the four directions.

What you set those positions to, however, is a little more complex. You're essentially dealing with an abstract canvas when working with CSS – in fact it doesn't have any preferred units. It does distinguish between two types of coordinate:

- ❑ **absolute** coordinates – ones where the lengths correspond to standardized lengths such as inches or centimeters

- ❑ **relative** coordinates – such as pixels or ems that are measured as part of a device specification (like the resolution of a computer screen or the height of a font character)

The units that CSS2 supports are given in the following table:

Units	Absolute or Relative	Comments
Em (em)	Relative	The font-size of the relevant font – this is typically the width of a lower case m.
X-Height (ex)	Relative	The x-height (the height of a lower case x) of the relevant font
Pixel (px)	Relative	The height of one drawing element on the computer screen
Inch (in)	Absolute	One inch is equal to 2.54 cm
Centimeter (cm)	Absolute	One centimeter is equal to 0.39 inch
Millimeter (mm)	Absolute	10 millimeters = 1 centimeter
Point (pt)	Absolute	A point is a printers' term, and is defined as being (for computer purposes) 1/72 in
Pica (pt)	Absolute	One pica = 12 points, or 1/6 of an inch

The units are appended to the end of the CSS property with no space between value and unit. For example, to specify that you want a rectangle to start two inches from the left margin, and be three inches wide, you'd use the rule:

```
rect {left:2in;width:3in;position:absolute;}
```

In general, unless you specifically know that your output will be sent exclusively to a computer screen of known width, you should get into the habit of using relative rather than absolute coordinates. This guarantees that your output will always have the same dimensions regardless of wrapping, screen density, or the like.

> *To demonstrate this, think about how long 72 pixels is in absolute terms. On a 640x480 view of a given monitor, 72 pixels is one inch (and one pixel is one point). On a 1024x768 view on the same monitor, 72 pixels is roughly half an inch, while on a printer 72 pixels may be drawn as being less than 1/5th of an inch (although most printers actually treat screen pixels as having a resolution of four printer pixels).*

If you don't specify a unit, it's assumed that the unit carries over from the previously defined unit for that property – and that if no unit is specified for the property then pixel is assumed to be the unit in question. If you set the width of a particular rule to use inches (say, by setting its value to 1in), then the next time a number is used for that property the renderer will assume that inches are still in force until explicitly changed.

Percentages and Auto

You can also choose to set a unit as a percentage value (by adding % to the end of the number). In this case, the CSS renderer will calculate the value by taking the value of the parent and multiplying by the percentage.

For example, you could specify that you want to have a pullout quote with a width that's about 75% of the width of the containing field, and moved 5% from the left of the container:

```
column {width:300 px;display:block;}
pullout {position:relative;left:5%;width:75%;background-
color:#C0C0FF;display:block;}
```

The XML fragment:

```
<column>What he said was <pullout>This is a truly remarkable way of staying busy,
although I think I would have preferred the dried frog.</pullout> We're still
trying to understand the context of that particular statement.</column>
```

will then render as:

```
What he said was
This is a truly remarkable way of
staying busy, although I think I
would have preferred the dried frog.

We're still trying to understand the context of that
particular statement.
```

The `auto` property provides the default value for the given element based upon the current flow – in essence it tells the CSS rendering engine to set the position or size to what it would normally be if no properties were specified.

Width and Height

While `width` and `height`, two other primary CSS properties, would seem not to need much explanation, they can cause some interesting complications in your layout. A major reason for this stems from the fact that if you constrain the width but not the height, its actual value may change considerably depending upon the width of the browser window, the size of fonts, the volume of text within the box and so forth.

The `width` property can, as with the positioning properties, take either a number (with or without explicit units) or can be assigned a percentage of the overall width of the container (either the element's immediate container or the browser window, depending upon the value of the `position` property). Note that if the width of the element (combined with its location) exceeds the immediate display window, then most browsers will automatically add a horizontal scrollbar to accommodate the width – it overrides the default margins.

In addition to the `width` property itself, CSS provides for the two properties `min-width` and `max-width`, which can take the same arguments that `width` itself can. `min-width` gives the minimum size that a container can be, and is useful for making sure that block elements with a small amount of text continue to be drawn with at least a minimal width. Similarly, `max-width` indicates the largest size that an element can take on the page before the text is dropped to the next line. There are similarly `min-height` and `max-height` properties that do the same thing for the `height` property.

Overflow

One of the more useful properties for trying to control height and width in applications is the `overflow` property. This property defines what happens when the contents of a given field exceed the boundaries of a given element. The `overflow` property can take one of five distinct values:

❑ `visible` – the overflow content continues to push beyond the specified height boundary. This can make for some interesting effects, especially if you clearly define a border or background for the element.

❑ `hidden` – when the overflow content reaches the boundaries of the container, it will get clipped so that no additional content will show. The content is still there, but it's essentially invisible and takes up no additional space for subsequent elements.

❑ `scroll` – the scroll value turns on a scroll bar at one edge of the element's box. The scroll bar is active if the content exceeds the height (or width) specified, but is visible even if the contents don't completely extend to the height.

❑ `auto` – when `overflow` is set to `auto`, the content will only show a scroll bar if the content exceeds the height specified in the height property, otherwise it doesn't show the bar. This can be used to good effect in DHTML with text area boxes. If you set their `overflow` property to `auto` then they will appear as ordinary blocks of text unless the contents of the box exceed the height of the container.

❑ `inherit` – the element inherits the overflow characteristics of its containing element.

Note that Internet Explorer 5.0 and above supports the two sub-properties `overflow-x` and `overflow-y`, letting you handle the overflow in each direction. However, neither of these properties is specifically defined in the CSS or CSS2 specification.

Clipping

The `clip` property can work in conjunction with the `overflow` property. You can choose to create a clip region that will expose just a small portion of the overall contents by providing a shape that describes the region to clip. The command is currently little more than a place-holder – its intent ultimately is to let you describe an irregular (i.e., non-rectangular) region to clip the contents of an element into. However, at the moment you can only specify a rectangular region.

The rectangle so defined can be a little confusing at first – it invokes a pseudo-function in CSS, in this case the `rect()` pseudo function, which takes the coordinates in the order <top> <right> <bottom> <left>, separated by spaces. Note that since most computer languages that deal with rectangles define them in the order <left> <top> <right> <bottom>, you should be especially wary when using the `rect()` function, or `clip` itself.

For example, if you wanted to create a clip region that showed the rectangle from (100,120) to (200,240) of a background image, you would set up the CSS rule:

```
ClipRegion {clip:rect(120 200 240 100);background-image:url(myImage.jpg);
width:100px;height:120px;}
```

Clip regions, while fairly high in the gee whiz factor, generally don't have a lot of specialized features yet. Ultimately, you should be able to specify a more generic path or even use text as a mask in the clip region, but this hasn't been defined in the CSS1 or CSS2 specification (although it may be a part of a future version of CSS – such capabilities are also part of the SVG specification).

Floats

Drop-caps, which we discussed earlier as part of the `first-letter` pseudo property, illustrate a fairly common scenario for both HTML and XML output – the need to have a block of text that other text can flow around. This is a concept that may be familiar to you through the `align` attribute of the HTML `IMG` property, which sets not only the alignment of an image but also how other text flows around it. To do it with text requires the use of CSS – in particular, the `float` property.

`float` can take one of three possible values – `left`, `right`, or `none` – and works by forcing the element that has this CSS property to "float" in the direction specified as far left or right as it can. Text that's outside of the float will in turn attempt to flow to the opposite side – so that if a block element had the CSS property `float:left` then it would move to the left of the object's container, with the remaining content flowed around on the right-hand side.

Text that's floated ends up outside of the normal flow – it could very well be the last element contained in a block of text, but if the `flow` value is set to `left` then it will migrate to the beginning. Once you specify that an element floats, it automatically migrates to the upper-left corner of the nearest block element (in Western scripts, anyway). At this stage, the floated item no longer contributes to the line height of the font.

Try It Out – Simple Drop Caps

Floats have a number of uses, but the two that are perhaps most common are for drop caps and sidebars.

1. Enter the HTML code shown and save it as `DropCaps.html`:

```
<HTML>
<HEAD>
    <TITLE>DropCaps</TITLE>
    <STYLE>
    P {border:solid 5px #C0C0C0;}
    </STYLE>
</HEAD>
<BODY>
<H3>Drop Caps</H3>
<STYLE>
P:first-letter {float:left;font-size:36pt;font-family:Times Roman;}
</STYLE>
<BODY>
<P>This is an example of the float element in HTML, although it works in a similar
fashion in XML. Note that the height of the initial cap includes the height of the
"ascender" length, which describes a margin above characters for handling parts of
the character glyph that extends beyond the nominal top of the line.</P>
</BODY>
</HTML>
```

2. In the browser, this will create the drop cap shown:

> his is an example of the float element in HTML, although it works in a similar fashion in XML. Note that the height of the initial cap includes the height of the "ascender" length, which describes a margin above characters for handling parts of the character glyph that extends beyond the nominal top of the line.

Drop caps work well with a combination of the `float` property and `first-letter` pseudo property.

Sidebars

You can also use floats for handling **sidebars**. A sidebar is a term used in books and magazines to indicate a box of text that's separated from the main text, often with a story that complements the main story.

Sidebars are useful to point out additional information without distracting from the flow of the original text, but they're not as common in HTML layout as they could be, because they're difficult to pull off in normal HTML. However, we can use CSS to create the appropriate sidebars in HTML (or in this case in XML) by placing the containing rectangle of the sidebar into a float.

Try It Out - Sidebars

In the following example we'll add a sidebar that will float to the right of the main text.

1. Create the following file and save it as `sidebars.xml`:

```
<?xml-stylesheet type="text/css" href="#internalstyles"?>
<!-- sidebars.xml -->
<document>
<style id="internalstyles">
style {display:none;}
document {display:block;}
heading {display:block;font-size:24pt;font-family:Times Roman;}
p {display:block;font-size:11pt;position:relative;}
sidebar {display:block;float:right;width:250px;border:inset 3pt gray;background-
color:#C0C0FF;padding:3px; }
sidebar heading {display:block;font-size:18pt;font-family:Helvetica;}
sidebar p {display:block;font-size:9pt;font-family:Times Roman;}
</style>
    <heading>CSS helps with XML Page Layout</heading>
        <sidebar>
        <heading>A Few Tips</heading>
        <p>Full support of CSS unfortunately is hard to find. Netscape 4.x doesn't
support it anywhere near as robustly as it should, for example, while Microsoft's
Internet Explorer provides an implementation that is similar, but not identical,
to the CSS 2 specification.</p>
        </sidebar>
    <p>XML is commonly used for passing data between systems, but its original
purpose, providing layout for data that doesn't necessarily fit well into the HTML
model, sometimes gets lost in the din. However, that doesn't have to be the case.
By using CSS, you can place a visual presentation layer in front of your XML that
will make it usable through any interface.
    </p>
</document>
```

2. View the file in the browser:

CSS helps with XML Page Layout

XML is commonly used for passing data between systems, but its original purpose, providing layout for data that doesn't necessarily fit well into the HTML model, sometimes gets lost in the din. However, that doesn't have to be the case. By using CSS, you can place a visual presentation layer in front of your XML that will make it usable through any interface.

A Few Tips

Full support of CSS unfortunately is hard to find. Netscape 4.x doesn't support it anywhere near as robustly as it should, for example, while Microsoft's Internet Explorer provides an implementation that is similar, but not identical, to the CSS 2 specification.

The sidebar has its own internal style characteristics. Note that it precedes the main body of text – the float is relative to the current flow, so placing it after the main text will cause it to float beneath the body, which is probably not the desired effect).

The output shown above demonstrates how you can achieve sophisticated formatting with the float object. The ability to flow around such a floating object makes it useful in situations where you need wraps, although it would be nice if there was a way to better shape the boundaries of a floating object (for example, so that it followed the contours of a partially transparent GIF).

Lists and Tables

Because a great number of XML structures are at least semi-regular, the need for lists and tables occurs frequently. In HTML, such structures are defined by a specific set of elements (such as the <LI>, <UL> and <OL> tags for lists and <TABLE>, <TR>, <TD> and so forth for tables).

However, the problem with any of these elements is that they're essentially display-oriented rather than logical structures. If you create a table in HTML, you have no knowledge of what the table is "about", only that it's presented in a specific manner. Similarly, with lists you don't know what your objects are a list "of", only that they are a list. As a consequence, it's difficult when extracting (or creating) information within an HTML document, to know with any surety that you're dealing with objects rather than just simply a table with a given name.

The CSS2 specification attempts to fix this problem somewhat. It actually defines CSS property equivalents to the HTML table and list tags, so that they can be applied to XML documents. By associating these characteristics as style sheet properties you can specify an object and display it in a number of different ways, depending upon the style sheet that you use.

Try It Out – Lists

For example, suppose that you had an XML structure that showed employees at a company.

1. We could create an XML document like this one (employees.xml):

```
<?xml-stylesheet type="text/css" href="cssemployeelist.css"?>
<employees>
    <employee id="101">
        <firstName>Jean</firstName>
        <lastName>Janus</lastName>
        <title>President</title>
        <dateStarted>1997-11-12</dateStarted>
        <salary>324021</salary>
        <department>Administration</department>
        <image>images/jjanus.jpg</image>
</employee>
<employee id="102">
        <firstName>Kitara</firstName>
        <lastName>Milleaux</lastName>
        <title>Chief Executive Officer</title>
        <dateStarted>1997-08-12</dateStarted>
        <salary>329215</salary>
        <department>Administration</department>
```

```
            <image>kmilleaux.jjpg</image>
    </employee>
    <employee id="103">
            <firstName>Shelley</firstName>
            <lastName>Janes</lastName>
            <title>Chief Financial Officer</title>
            <dateStarted>1998-03-16</dateStarted>
            <salary>232768</salary>
            <department>Finance</department>
            <image>images/sjanes.jpg</image>
    </employee>
    <employee id="104">
            <firstName>Marissa</firstName>
            <lastName>Mendez</lastName>
            <title>Chief Technical Officer</title>
            <dateStarted>1998-09-16</dateStarted>
            <salary>242768</salary>
            <department>Information Technologies</department>
            <image>images/mmendez.jpg</image>
    </employee>
    <employee id="105">
            <firstName>Kace</firstName>
            <lastName>Juriden</lastName>
            <title>Vice President, Marketing</title>
            <dateStarted>1998-11-03</dateStarted>
            <salary>210359</salary>
            <department>Marketing</department>
            <image>images/kjuriden.jpg</image>
    </employee>
    <!-- more employees, as required -->
    </employees>
```

2. We could set up an external style sheet (`cssemployeelist.css`) that will display a list of each employee, first name and last name:

```
<!-- cssemployeelist.css -->
employees {display:block;visibility:visible;}
employee {display:list-item;list-style-type:disc;}
lastName {display:inline;font-size:12pt;}
firstName {display:inline;font-size:12pt;}
title {display:none;font-size:12pt;}
dateStarted {display:none;font-size:12pt;}
salary {display:none;font-size:12pt;}
department {display:none;font-size:12pt;}
image {display:none;}
```

This will display a bulleted list of each employee by first and last name.

Note how we use the `display:list-item` property for the `<employee>` element. This indicates that the employee node marks the scope of the list item, and that any child of that element is considered to be a part of that list item in turn.

Working with Lists in XML

List items have three characteristics which define them:

- ❏ `list-style-type`
- ❏ `list-style-position`
- ❏ `list-style-image`

Any or all of these characteristics will just be set to default values if the property is not explicitly set.

Bullet Characters

`list-style-type` describes the bullet character that is used to visually indicate a list item, either with a specific bullet (like a disc or circle), or with an ordered list of numbers or letters. Some of these are shown in the following table, although the full set varies according to the character set supported:

Value of `list-style-type`	Character	Description
`Disc`	•	An unordered disc bullet character (default)
`Circle`	o	An unordered circle bullet character
`Square`		An unordered diamond bullet character
`Decimal`	1,2,3	An ordered Western digital character
`decimal-leading-zero`	01,02,03,...,97,98,99	An ordered Western digital character with a leading zero (the number of zeros is a characteristic of the number of digits in the list – 1-9, none, 10-99, one, 100-999, two, and so forth)
`lower-roman`	i,ii,iii,iv	Ordered lower case Roman numbers
`upper-roman`	I,II,III,IV	Ordered upper case Roman numbers
`lower-greek`	, , ,	Ordered lower case Greek characters
`lower-alpha`	a,b,c,d	Ordered lower case alphabetic characters
`upper-alpha`	A,B,C,D	Ordered upper case alphabetic characters

The ordered list style types will automatically increment the count of items for the given style rule.

CSS also includes a number of more sophisticated counting mechanisms that let you more precisely control the way that ordering and bullet marking is performed. This is outside the scope of our discussion here, but you can find more information on this in the CSS2 specification at http://www.w3.org/TR/REC-CSS2.

Graphical Bullets

In addition to specifying the `list-style-type`, you can also specify a specific bullet graphic to replace the system graphics. The `list-style-image` property performs this task, and it overrides the `list-style-type`.

For example, you could specify that you want to use a hand pointer graphic as a bullet point indicator, contained in the file `images/hand.gif`. A CSS style sheet rule to assign this to a bullet point (which we might have called, say, the `<point>` element in our XML document) would look like:

```
point {list-style-image:url(images/hand.gif);list-style-type:square;}
```

In this case, the browser would display the hand image as a bullet indicator if it finds the graphic, and revert to the `square` (actually a diamond) if it doesn't.

Positioning Bullets

Finally, `list-style-position` tells the browser or printer whether to display the bullet indicator offset from the block of the list element (`outside`, the default) or inline to the element (`inside`), in other words:

*   This is a list element for which
    the list-style-position is *outside*.
*   This is a list element for which
the list-style-position is *inside*.

Supporting Tables in CSS

Tables straddle the boundary between presentation elements and structural elements. In general, however, a table is a representation of a set of objects contained within an XML document, and as such, it should really be considered more in the domain of presentation. Unfortunately, most people's experiences with tables come not from XML but from HTML, where the `<TABLE>`, `<TR>`, `<TH>`, etc., tags are well known, and are embedded in the fabric of HTML editors and web pages.

The CSS2 specification has attempted to rectify that by introducing a number of table properties into the fold. These properties let you associate a given table-like characteristic to a data structure, and are listed in the following table:

Display Property	Description
table	The contents are displayed as if in a table. These require that subordinate display properties be applied to contained elements (equivalent to HTML `<TABLE>` element).
inline-table	Indicates a table that is contained as part of the flow.
table-row-group	Equivalent to the HTML `<TBODY>` element, this contains all of the regular rows (those not part of the column headers) in the table.
table-column-group	Equivalent to the HTML `<COL-GROUP>` element. This contains a grouping of columns in the table.

Display Property	Description
table-header-group	Equivalent to the HTML <THEAD> element. This contains all of the header elements in the table (such as column heads).
table-footer-group	Equivalent to the HTML <TFOOT> element. This contains all of the footer elements in the table.
table-row	Equivalent to the HTML <TR> element. This contains a standard row in a table.
table-cell	Equivalent to the HTML <TD> element. This contains a standard cell from a row in a table.
table-caption	Equivalent to the HTML <CAPTION> element. This contains a caption that's associated with the table.

The employee listing in the previous section provides a good example where table representations come in handy. You can define a table structure that shows the employees collection as a table, with each employee being a row and each employee property a cell in that row, through the following style sheet:

```
employees {display:table;}
employee {display:table-row;}
firstName {display:table-cell;}
lastName {display:table-cell;}
title {display:table-cell;}
dateStarted {display:table-cell;}
salary {display:table-cell;}
department {display:table-cell;}
image {display:none;}
```

This will end up creating a table that looks something like:

Jean	Janus	President	1997-11-12	324021	Administration
Kitara	Milleaux	Chief Executive Officer	1997-08-12	329215	Administration
Shelley	Janes	Chief Financial Officer	1998-03-16	232768	Finance
Marissa	Mendez	Chief Technical Officer	1998-09-16	242768	Information Technologies
Kace	Juriden	Vice President, Marketing	1998-11-03	210359	Marketing

The CSS2 table *property and its associated sub-properties (such as* table-row *or* table-cell*) are not supported by Internet Explorer in any version. As such, to properly display the table contents here you'd need to transform the results into HTML using XSLT rather than relying on CSS to indicate table information.*

Text and Font Manipulation

HTML is fundamentally a text medium, and so it's not surprising that a significant amount of CSS is devoted to the formatting and spacing of text. When displaying XML the same conditions apply – the need to showcase information through formatted and emphasized text is still one of the underlying reasons that the browser has the power it does. In many ways, it was because of a shortcoming of HTML (namely the FONT tag we discussed earlier) that CSS arose in the first place. As we discussed, the FONT tag was used more and more as a replacement for tags such as H1 and H2, so we lost structural information about the document.

The original purpose of cascading style sheets was to provide a better way of applying stylistic elements to a web page without the dangers of introducing new tags. By making style sheets work with fonts, it meant that tags could get back to their original purpose of describing a document in logical terms, rather than graphical ones. Since font usage had been such a significant part of this presentation problem, setting font attributes with style sheets was a natural way of doing things.

> *FONT has been deprecated in HTML 4.0. **Deprecated** simply means that future versions of HTML will not support the tag. While there's nothing to stop you using the tag, just keep in mind that using FONT is a less powerful way of manipulating fonts, corrupts the integrity of your data model, and is generally not recommended for use when designing HTML. Of course, it isn't a part of XML, but you should avoid creating a tag like it (and avoid setting the font attributes of a specific element directly in XML, rather than through style sheets).*

There are a number of CSS properties that can be used to assign font styles, in this section we'll look at each in turn.

font-size

font-size is the CSS property that, believe it or not, sets the font size. However, unlike the FONT tag's Size attribute, you can set the font size to a number of different units, set it as a percentage, or specify a named term for it (such as small, medium, large) or relative terms (such as larger or smaller):

The syntax is:

```
font-size:absolute size|length|percentage
```

font-size sets the height of the text within the element. There are several different ways that you can specify the size. The usual method is to provide a *length*, with appropriate units. For example, font-size:12pt will make the text 12 pts (or 12/72 of an inch) tall.

Absolute units such as inches (in) or centimeters (cm) will always attempt to set the size of the font to the given value regardless of the medium (two inches on the screen, two inches on the page), while relative units such as pixels (px) will draw the image so that it takes up that many units. (Also note that many high-resolution devices (such as a 600 dpi printer) will actually use several printer pixels to approximate one screen pixel.

> *Note that for the same font-size value, different font families can look radically different in size – font-size is a typographer's designation that may vary considerably from face to face and designer to designer (see the section on font-family for an example of this).*

You can also set an element's `font-size` to be a percentage of its parent's `font-size`. For example, as in the style sheet:

```
body {font-size:12pt;}
body note {font-size:75%;}
```

In this case, a `note` child of the `body` element will have a font-size 3/4 of the size specified for the `body` element, or 9pt in this case.

font-style and font-weight

The `font-style` and `font-weight` appear to give us the same capabilities as italic `<I>` or bold `<b>` respectively. Originally, the HTML specification did include both tags, but preferred instead the more logical EM and STRONG tags for emphasis (*italic*) and strong emphasis (**bold**). Of course, Netscape introduced the I and B tags as a shorthand, and they very quickly displaced the logical notation to such an extent that few web designers today have even heard of emphasis and strong.

While B and I will be around for a long time to come (they're simply too convenient for applying emphasis), CSS does have another mechanism for specifying these attributes in styles: the `font-style` and `font-weight` properties.

```
font-style:normal|italic|oblique
```

A `font-style` of `normal` indicates that no styling is applied. `italic` and `oblique` do more or less the same thing, but in slightly different manners. When you set the `font-style` to `italic`, it will attempt to use italic rendering of the font if the font supports this (and has no effect on fonts that don't). `oblique`, on the other hand, slants the font's characters in all cases, usually with disastrous results. In general, you should use `italic` in just about every situation.

Most operating systems have a fairly detailed convention concerning font usage and display, and one notion that incorporates is the concept of **font weight**. The weight is essentially a measure of how "heavily", or thickly, the characters are drawn. A weight of 100 is ultra-thin for a font, and is occasionally described on typographic terms as demi-book. On the other hand, a weight of 900 is extremely heavy, and is known by such terms as extra-bold:

```
font-weight:light|normal|bold|bolder|lighter|
            100|200|300|400|500|600|700|800|900
```

In CSS, `normal` corresponds to a weight of 400 (no units, by the way), while `bold` corresponds to a weight of 700. These two weights usually have specific faces associated with them, so they will be rendered at their best. If supported at all, intermediate `font-weight`s usually don't look as good because they have to be rendered programmatically (in Internet Explorer, for instance, font-weights aren't even supported under 400). `lighter` and `bolder` are *relative* terms, and simply indicate that the font should be made lighter or bolder than the font of the container/parent.

font-family and @font-face

When designers talk about font, they are almost invariably referring to the font *family*, which basically describes the characteristics that make a font unique. There are such divergent font families as Chancery (a calligraphic long hand), Helvetica (a work-horse sans serif font), or Byte (a stylized computerish-looking font). One of the holy grails of web designers has been the ability to use more than just the standard fonts on a web page.

117

Unfortunately, there are several problems with this, some technical, others more in the realm of copyright law.

- ❑ The first has to do with the architecture of fonts – a font is a file, just like any other, but in order for the system to know what to do with it, the file needs to be registered in the system. One way of doing this is to place the fonts in the system Fonts folder. However, this provides a major security headache, since viruses and malevolent code could likewise be placed in the Fonts folder.

- ❑ In addition to this, if every web page that you visited loaded its own custom fonts into your Fonts folder, you'd very quickly exceed the system resource limits.

- ❑ Finally, many fonts that are out there are proprietary, which means that loading them into your system from a web page is essentially an act of software piracy.

So how do we get around this problem? There are two solutions, depending upon how common your desired font is and whether you're willing to go the extra mile for your design.

The first solution is to use the `font-family` CSS property. This property lets you specify the name of one or more font families to use in displaying a given selection of text.

The general syntax for `font-family` is:

```
font-family:familyname[,familyname]
```

The *familyname* is the name that appears whenever a drop-down list of fonts is given, for example in a word processor or design package, and as such can contain spaces. If you have a name that does contain a space, you should wrap the name in single quotes:

```
style="font-family:'new century schoolbook',serif;"
```

Font names are specified from the one you most want to use to the one you least want to use but will accept if all else fails, and the browser will attempt a match in that order. This solution works especially well when you're using the browser as part of a local application – your set-up routine could install the desired fonts into the Fonts folder, and then you can reference them directly.

For example, let's say we wanted to have a calligraphic font display some text. We want to use the font Engravers script whenever possible, to use Zapf Chancery if Engravers isn't available, and to use Fantasy as default font. So we'd make the call:

```
font-family:Engravers,'Zapf Chancery',Fantasy;
```

The IE5 browser supports within CSS a standard set of "fallback" fonts that can be used if the desired font isn't available. These are supported by Netscape as well, and can work when you want some broad characteristic (like whether the font has serifs or not) and are less picky about the actual font.

One of the mechanisms that CSS provides for is a way of downloading font resources. This has been one of the most contentious aspects of CSS, since fonts, unlike images, started out as having much more stringent intellectual property restraints on them (due to the fact that until the explosion of fonts in the mid-1990s, most fonts were provided by typesetting companies that charged significant amounts of money for their use). In other words, downloading a font is relatively easy, keeping the font from being part of the font resources of the client after leaving the font's page is considerably more complicated.

At any rate, the `@font-face` directive provides a means to download font resources by providing a URL to the resource. This lets you integrate custom fonts into your web page. The syntax for this directive is as follows:

```
@font-face {font-family:familyname; src:url(url);}
```

You specify the name of the `font-family` that you wish to refer to the newly loaded font by, as well as the source `url` for that font, and the new `font-family` can consequently be used anywhere you would normally use a `font-family`.

font-variant, text-decoration, text-transform

The rest of the font-immediate specifications are fairly innocuous. `font-variant`, for example, will give you small caps, while `font-decoration` is useful for handling underlining and strikethrough. Finally, `text-transform` is actually a pretty cool function that will set a string selection to initial caps, all caps, or all lowercase characters.

```
font-variant:normal|small-caps
```

```
text-decoration:none|underline|overline|line-through|blink
```

```
text-transform:capitalize|uppercase|lowercase|none
```

I'm actually at a little bit of a loss to explain why `font-variant` exists as something separate from `text-transform`, since they both involve setting case. I would suspect that one or the other may end up becoming deprecated (not supported in future versions of CSS), but that's only a hunch.

Indentation, Padding and Margins

When web pages are printed out, they invariably stand out for the simple reason that most web pages don't support **indentation**. Instead, paragraphs are usually separated by a space between each block. As web pages move more into the print arena (see the section on Printing later in this chapter for more information on this move), having the ability to set precise margins, indentations and spacing will become increasingly important.

text-indent

`text-indent` lets you specify the amount of space that the first line **indents** (or hangs out if you use a negative value) from a paragraph:

```
text-indent:length|percentage
```

The length value must be specified in valid units (e.g., 15px, 10pt; 2cm; .5in) and can be negative, producing an outdent rather than an indent. The text-indent can also be a percentage value of the total width of the block (i.e., text-indent:80%;}.

Margins and Padding

Margins and **padding** are two related properties. If you think of the text block as being within a secondary box, then padding is the space between the inner box and the outer box, while margins are the distance between the outer box and any other container. Margins essentially control how a block element relates to its surroundings, while padding describes how the contents of a box relate to the box itself.

margin

margin provides the amount of space between a block element and the surrounding elements, and can be expressed in a variety of ways:

    margin:length|percentage|auto

If absolute numbers are provided, they must have units specified for them. You can set up a negative margin, which will cause the bounding box of the text to actually exceed the bounding box of the text's container. Likewise, you can supply 1, 2, 3 or 4 different values for the margin, with the following behavior:

❑   auto setting, the default – sets a margin of 5% of the dimensions of the container

❑   margin-left, margin-right, margin-top, and margin-bottom – specifies each side independently

You can take advantage of this by setting the general margin first, then setting one of the margin sides that differs from the basic value. Note that margins are not inherited.

padding

padding provides the amount of space between a block element and the elements that it contains, and can also be expressed in a variety of ways:

    padding:length|percentage|auto

If absolute numbers are provided, they must have units specified for them. Unlike margins, padding cannot have a negative value associated with it. However, like margins, you can supply 1, 2, 3 or 4 different values for the padding, with the following behavior:

❑   auto setting, the default – sets a padding of 5% of the dimensions of the container

❑   padding-left, padding-right, padding-top, and padding-bottom – specifies each side independently

Again, you can take advantage of this by setting the general padding first, then setting one of the padding sides that differs from the basic value. Note that paddings are not inherited, and that paddings do not apply to inline elements (such as the B element).

Kerning and Spacing

Kerning comes from an old typesetting term for placing thin strips of lead (or kerns) between letters to better space them prior to printing. With large fonts especially, letters may not look particularly good when juxtaposed together.

Consider, for example, the combination of A and V. If placed so that they are spaced a typical amount for an average letter, they seem to separate into two distinct words:

A V.

You can increase or decrease the amount of kerning (it is possible to have negative kerning) so that letters that create large gutters can be moved closer together:

AV.

In this case the top left of the V actually partially overlaps the lower right foot of the A.

letter-spacing

The level of kerning control that you have in most browsers is fairly limited, but it does exist via the `letter-spacing` CSS property. This will allow you to specify the distance between characters for any string of characters, which lets you compress or expand text to fit graphical sections.

```
letter-spacing:length|percentage
```

You can even set the kerning between individual characters by using `letter-spacing` within a span containing two or three characters. Some page layout tools give you the ability to kern individual pairs of letters – something that CSS doesn't yet have the bandwidth for.

`letter-spacing` provides broad level support for spacing between characters. A `letter-spacing` of 0 will give the default spacing, positive values will expand the text, and negative values will contract the text. You can also specify units – for example, a `letter-spacing` of 1cm will give you 1cm distance between characters, while a `letter-spacing` of –10% will decrease the `letter-spacing` by 10% of the current distance.

line-height

`line-height` gives the distance between the base line (the line where the characters rest, not counting descenders such as in the letters gpq) of one line and the next in a paragraph or other text block.

```
line-height:normal|number|length|percentage
```

The `normal` `line-height` is 120% of the font-size for the characters. You can also specify the `line-height` as a number with no units, which is translated as a multiplier (i.e., a `line-height` of 2 is twice normal size, 3 is triple normal size, 1.5 is one and a half lines, and so forth). If you do provide units, then that absolute distance will be used. `line-height` can be less than zero (a `line-height` of -1 will cause lines to appear going up instead of down – in effect, squishing the lines closer together.

We should just note the distinction between `line-height` and `margin-bottom`. `margin-bottom` sets the height between a block element and the *next* element in an HTML (or XML) page, while the `line-height` gives the distance between lines of the *same* block or paragraph.

Alignment

Alignment has been a part of the HTML specifications for a long time, but there are some kinds of alignment, like centering, that are a little harder to pull off (and vertical alignment is really horrendous, when you get right down to it). The good news is that CSS simplifies both horizontal and vertical alignment capabilities. You can create left or right aligned text, justified text, subscripts and superscripts. You can also control flow with the alignment commands.

text-align

`text-align` lets you set the alignment characteristics of a block of text (it has no effect on inline elements, but you can do this with `float`, as we discussed earlier in this chapter). Note that text-align only affects the horizontal alignment, not vertical alignment.

```
text-align:left|right|center|justify
```

vertical-align

`vertical-align` sets a block of text to be a superscript or subscript of another block of text. While this doesn't quite have the power of a full-blown vertical alignment routine, it's usually adequate for most purposes (in essence, it's the CSS-ification of the SUB and SUPER tags from earlier HTML versions).

```
vertical-align:sub|super
```

Ruby Characters

In order to accommodate the burgeoning use of browsers in many Asian countries, Microsoft introduced the notion of the **Ruby** character. This is in fact a fairly sophisticated mechanism for expressing characters that are composed of sub-characters (such as the upper and lower body of most Japanese Kanji characters).

The Ruby specifications are quite complex, and are primarily designed for expressing complex characters, but if you have a need for building integrated character sets you may very well want to check it out. You can find out more about Ruby characters in the CSS2 specification at http://www.w3.org/TR/REC-CSS2.

Printing

You know, with all of these improvements and typesetting capabilities, I bet that Internet Explorer could be a pretty effective way to lay out pages. Yet whenever I try to print something, it's always kind of hit or miss whether it'll look decent. Any suggestions?

When the CSS1 specifications were first proposed, one of the ideas that was kicked around (and to a limited extent adopted) was the notion that the browser "space" shouldn't just be seen as a vehicle for computer screens. HTML, after all, started out as a markup language based upon SGML, which forms the basis of many university and corporate documentation systems. Such documentation was meant to be printed – the computer-viewing aspects of HTML in that regard are kind of an aberration. However, because there really wasn't any standardized mechanism geared toward printing in the HTML specification, its malleability eventually became a liability in the print world.

However, with a little bit of diligence, you can make your web pages adaptable for the printed page as readily as the screen, and CSS is the appropriate vehicle to do just that. The techniques for designing the page fall into two categories – conscientious use of units, and taking advantage of some new features in IE5.

Units – Pixels versus Points

Most of the language for describing web design was borrowed from the traditional print process, and this has had to be adjusted somewhat for the newer media.

Take, for instance, the computer monitor. A monitor has characteristics consisting of a fixed number of **pixels** displayed on a screen, with a pixel's actual size more or less independent of any specific unit (think about a 640x480 screen on a 13" versus a 15" monitor, and you'll see what I mean). However, in the printed world, a pixel is a meaningless unit of measure. It's this disparity between the physical units of paper and the virtual units of a computer screen that make printing such an "exciting" activity for both regular application developers and web designers.

However, if you know that your page is going to be printed, there are a few things you can do to make the transition as smooth as possible.

Firstly, work with **points** instead of pixels. A point is defined as a constant 1/72 of an inch (a computer based point is actual smaller than a layout point, though with the rise of graphical layout tools like Quark and Pagemaker this distinction has pretty much disappeared in favor of the computer unit). If you specify everything as points, then you won't be surprised by unexpected page overflows.

Similarly, remember that most printed pages have a margin of 1 1/4" inches on each side, with a "live" area of 6 in. This translates into a page that is 432 points wide. Since it's not uncommon to have vertical table-of-contents frames take up 20% of the screen or so, making your display area fit that size will assure you of having a good "print" area. Furthermore, you can pour your columns into DIVs that are precisely that width.

Typically, browsers are perfectly able to handle themselves when it comes to flowing text. Where things break down is when graphics are thrown into the mix. In order to accommodate a graphic, the browser engine may very well expand the column, meaning that your text will get truncated on the right hand side, so keep graphics smaller than the 432pt limit if you want to guarantee good output. Note that when a page gets printed, it usually reformats itself internally to match the page width of the paper, but irregular graphics can wreak all kinds of havoc to that formula.

The resolution of a screen font is less than 1/4 of its printed counterpart. Because of that, it's harder to read text on the screen than it is in print, since the eye spends more time trying to blend the shapes together into something legible on the screen. One consequence of this is that font sizes need to be larger to be more legible. Unfortunately, what looks just fine on the screen can look huge on the printed page, and vice versa, so it's a good idea to reset the size of fonts when you're outputting to the printer. The browser's print driver reads the type specifications from the font files, not the bits on the screen, in creating its print output, which is why printed output doesn't shrink when output to a 600 dpi printer.

All of these things together add up to one interesting solution – maintain two copies of your style sheet: one for displaying the page on the screen, and a second for formatting it to text to be printed. You can then assign the appropriate style sheet using the @media processing directive that we met earlier in the chapter.

The @page Directive

Printing obviously imposes a limitation on the way that output is handled that continuous media like a web page doesn't have – you need to be able to make sure that the content easily fits within the physical boundaries of a page of paper (or other media). Since pages change size depending upon the size of the paper they're printed on, CSS provides a tool for printing out to a page of varying size – the @page directive. With this directive, you can set the physical dimensions of the page, margins, and similar delimiters. For example, to specify an 8 ½" x 11" page with one inch margins all around, you can set up a page directive in the style sheet that looks like:

```
@page {size:8.5 in 11 in;margin:1in;}
```

Left, Right and First Pages

You can specify the default characteristics for left pages and right pages separately. For example, many typesetting programs will typically create unbalanced margins so that the inner margin is 3/4 of an inch wide (1.5 in total) while the outer margin is 1 1/4 inches. The left and right pseudo-classes let you specify margins and other properties of the page separately:

```
@page:left {margin-left:1.25in;margin-right:0.75in;}
@page:right {margin-left:0.75in;margin-right:1.25in;}
```

Similarly, you can specify the first page to have different margins to subsequent pages (perhaps with much more extensive top margins for example), using the @page:first pseudo-class:

```
@page {margin-top:1.5in;}
@page:first {margin-top:3in;}
```

Order is important here – @page:first will override the general @page in this example, but only because it's defined after @page.

Page Breaks

One of the limitations that's made web printing a little more problematic has been the lack of an effective page-break mechanism. Because of this, pages would often break at the most inconvenient point when sent to the printer.

Fortunately, there are two new CSS properties that fill that void: `page-break-before` and `page-break-after`. These force a new page to feed whenever they are invoked, and they can be added as CSS properties to a `class` definition or `style` attribute.

page-break-before, page-break-after CSS Format

`page-break-before` and `page-break-after` affect where a page breaks when printing:

```
page-break-before:auto|always|never
page-break-after:auto|always|never
```

These default to `auto` (no special consideration for breaking). Setting `page-break-before` will always force a page break before the element is printed. This can come in handy if you have a header element that always appears at the top of the page. If you set `page-break-before/after` to `never`, then the page will not break at all, which can be useful if you're trying to print out a continuous scroll of material on multiple sheets.

Printing Using Scripting

Finally, the IE5.5 HTML object model introduces the `print()` method on the `window` object. This scripting method performs exactly the same calls as pressing the *PRINT* button (or selecting Print from the File menu), including bringing up the printer dialog box in order to more accurately specify the output to the target printer. This means that you can now write applications that support printing, and IE5 becomes a much more useful multi-purpose document browser.

Aural Style Sheets

The CSS2 specification was basically built around the integration of various media into the web browser. Among these was the use of sound, which up until now has been typically limited to bad MIDI sound-tracks and the occasional button special effect. However, the ability to have your web page read aurally can prove useful in any number of situations, for example:

❑   automobile and cell-phone access to your web sites

❑   sites that can be accessed by sight-impaired people

❑   kiosks that use a web page base and allow us to listen to one site in the background while viewing another in the foreground

There are a number of basic CSS2 properties that deal with sound. Note that all of these require some form of add-on to existing browsers to actually read the text, although most of the browser manufacturers are working on ways of incorporating speech rendition into their browsers, especially for such devices as kiosks and car browser systems.

Most of these properties should be placed after the visual CSS properties in style rules, since older Netscape browsers will typically ignore any properties after ones that it can't decipher.

The properties are shown in the following table:

Property Name	Possible Values	Description
volume	{number}, {percentage}, silent, x-soft, soft, medium, loud, x-loud	This gives the average volume of the aural presentation, and can range between 0 and 100 (or 0% and 100%) of the possible aural comfort levels.
speech-rate	{number}, x-slow, slow, medium, fast, x-fast, faster, slower	This provides the speed at which text is read, from x-slow (80 words per minute) to x-fast (500 words per minute).
voice-family	male, female, child, {custom}	Roughly analogous to font-family, these provide specifications to describe the voices used. A custom voice-family could conceivably be an agent with a distinct voice signature, for example a 'Spock' voice, or 'Jean Luc Picard' (not that either one of these exist, but you get the idea).
pitch	{number}[Hz|kHz]	The pitch provides the tone of the character speaking in their average vocal range. A typical male voice has a pitch of about 120 Hz, while a female voice is closer to 200 Hz.
pitch-range	0-100	The range of the voice – from 0 for a completely flat "robotic" voice to 100 for an extremely inflected voice.
azimuth	{angle}, left-side, far-left, left, center-left, center, center-right, right, far-right, right-side, behind, leftwards, rightwards	The direction that the voice is projected from. Note that you can specify multiple azimuth elements in the same line: azimuth:left-side behind will make the sound appear as if it is coming both from your left and from behind you.
pause	{time}, {percentage}	This indicates that a pause should exist before or after (or both) a given selection. For example, <p style="pause:1000ms 500ms"> will pause before the selection begins for one second, and afterwards for half a second. This is the aural equivalent of a margin.

Property Name	Possible Values	Description
cue-before, cue-after, cue	{url}	This provides an aural icon before or after a selection begins, roughly the equivalent of a bullet in a bullet point. The cue property can take a url both before and after a selection. For example: `<li style="cue-before:url(bink.au);">An important point</li>` will cause a "bink" sound to play before the reader says "An important point".
play-during	{url} mix, repeat, auto, none, inherit	Plays the selection indicated in the url() in the background as the text contained in the corresponding selection is read.
speak	normal, none, spell-out	This global property determines whether speech is enabled (normal), disabled (none), or the contents are spelled out.

Conceptually, aural style sheets take a little getting used to – you are specifying a presentation where space, in other words the physical dimensions of the browser, is replaced by time. One useful technique is to define the visual characteristics of a page first within a style sheet, then set up a separate aural section using the @media operator, for example:

```
@media visual {
    document {position:absolute;left:0px;top:0px;
    background-image(myBackground.jpg);}
    title {display:block;font-size:24pt;font-family:Helvetica;}
    author {display:block;font-size:15pt;font-family:Helvetica;}
    para {display:block;font-size:10pt;font-family:Times Roman;}
}
@media aural {
    document {play-during:url(backgroundMusic.mp3) repeat mix;}
    title {voice-family:'James Earl Jones' male;volume:medium;}
    author {voice-family:'James Earl Jones' male;volume:soft;}
    para {voice-family:'Kelly McGillis' female;volume:medium;}
}
```

An aural device will then be able to handle the appropriate output without the need to mix the two media. Note that there are frequently aural equivalents to visual properties. For example, the background image in the visual presentation is replaced by background music in the aural presentation, setting the mood while simultaneously letting other sounds emerge. Intriguingly enough, if your browser supports both a visual and an aural representation, then you'll end up with a full multimedia show – background music playing as you read the text along with James Earl Jones and Kelly McGillis (or the system supplied male and female voices if either of these two aren't present, as is likely to be the case).

Currently there aren't a large number of audio browsers out there. One that may be worth exploring is the VOXML browser, available on the Internet at http://www.voxml.com. It supports both a native XML voice format as well as support for the CSS audio properties. There are likely to be more developed in the future as the technology becomes more widespread.

127

Summary

In the first part of the chapter we concentrated on CSS with HTML and saw:

❑ Why style sheets are useful

❑ How styles are defined for HTML, using three different methods

❑ How styles are cascaded

❑ The use of HTML classes and pseudo-classes

❑ That style sheets can be internal or external

This gave us a good platform from which we moved on to look at how CSS can be used with XML documents. We have seen that their impact on XML is both more sophisticated and more complex. In developing an XML strategy for your own business, you should look upon CSS as the mechanism that maps the structural tags of XML object descriptions into media representations of those objects.

In the following chapter we're going to find out about another method of transforming XML data for display in a web browser, and beyond.

XSLT and XPath

In the last chapter we covered Cascading Style Sheets, which can be used to display XML documents in a web browser. This is a great way to put our XML documents to immediate use, but what if we need more power than CSS allows? Or what if our XML file isn't structured in a way that's readily useable by CSS? We may need some way to transform our XML document into another format that better suits our application. Enter **Extensible Style sheet Language for Transformations**, **XSLT**: a language which can transform XML documents into any text-based format, XML or otherwise.

As we'll see later, XSLT is a sub-component of a larger language called XSL. XSLT is a powerful tool for e-commerce, as well as any other place where XML might be used.

As an example, suppose we're going to be running a news-oriented web site. In addition to our site itself, we'll also want to provide a way for our readers to get individual news stories from us in XML. In other words, people can use the news stories we provide in their own applications, for whatever purposes they wish; some might want to display the stories on their own web sites, others might want to put the data into their own back-end databases for some other application.

However, when we're deciding on what structure to give the XML for our news stories, we probably won't be thinking about those other uses people have for our XML; in fact, it would be impossible to guess all of the different things that people will want to do with our data. Instead, we'll be concentrating on inventing element names and a structure that properly describe a news story.

This is where XSLT comes in. Once others have received our XML documents, they can use this transformation language to transform these documents into whatever other format they wish – HTML for display on their web sites, a different XML-based structure for other applications, or even just regular text files.

XSLT relies on finding parts of an XML document that match a series of predefined templates, and then applying transformation and formatting rules to each matched part. Another language, XPath, is used to help in finding those matching parts.

In this chapter we'll learn:

❑ What XSL and XSLT are

❑ How XSLT differs from *imperative* programming languages, like JavaScript

❑ What templates are, and how they are used

❑ How to address the innards of an XML document using XPath

Running the Examples

In order to perform an XSLT transformation, you need at least three things: an XML document to transform, an **XSLT style sheet**, and an **XSLT engine**.

❑ The style sheet contains the instructions for the transformation you want to perform; the "source code". This is the part we'll write, and it's what the next two chapters of this book are concerned with.

❑ The engine is the software which will carry out the instructions in your style sheet. There are a number of engines available, many of which are free.

XT

All of the examples in this and the following chapter were tested with the Win32 executable version of **XT**, version 19991105, written by James Clark. It is available at http://www.jclark.com/xml/xt.html. Simply download the `.zip` file and unzip the program, which consists of a single `xt.exe` file.

You run XT from the command prompt of the DOS window (available on most Windows computers under Start | Programs | MS-DOS Prompt or Start | Programs | Accessories | Command Prompt), like this:

```
C:\>xt source stylesheet result
```

where `source` is the XML file you want to transform, `stylesheet` is the XSL style sheet you're using to do the transform, and `result` is the optional output file you want to create. (All of the examples assume that XT is in the root directory on your C: drive, but you can put it anywhere you like – just remember to change the path to the one on your own computer.) In working with the samples in this chapter, you might find it useful to create a separate directory on your hard drive specifically for the examples, and copy `xt.exe` to that directory.

If you want to use the Java version of XT, or use XT as a servlet, there are instructions at the web site for running it in those ways as well.

MSXML

MSXML, the XML parser that ships with Internet Explorer 5, also includes an XSLT engine. However, IE5 shipped before the XSLT Recommendation was finished, so the preview version of XSLT that MSXML understands is different from the Recommended XSLT.

At the time of writing, Microsoft has been releasing preview versions of MSXML every couple of months, with increasing XSLT support. You can download the latest preview from http://msdn.microsoft.com/downloads/webtechnology/xml/msxml.asp. Many of the examples in this chapter will also work with these preview versions of MSXML. Along with the preview versions of the XSLT engine, Microsoft has also released a style sheet that will take a style sheet written in the old IE5-XSL language, and transform it to the current XSLT syntax – a style sheet which transforms style sheets!

Since this is a preview (meaning beta), it will not replace your existing MSXML parser unless you explicitly tell it to. If you would like to use the new version exclusively, Microsoft provides a tool to let you run the preview in **Replace Mode**, meaning that it replaces the previous version of MSXML shipped with IE5; simply double-click the file named `xmlinst.exe` in your system directory.

What is XSL?

Extensible Style sheet Language, as the name implies, is an XML-based language used to create **style sheets**. An XML engine uses style sheets to transform XML documents into other document types, and to format the output. In these style sheets you define the layout of the output document, and where to get the data from within the input document. That is, "the data you want is at this place in the input document; make it look like this in the output". In XSL parlance, the input document is called the **source tree**, and the output document the **result tree**.

There are actually two complete languages under the XSL umbrella:

❑   a transformation language, which is named **XSLT**

❑   a language used to describe XML documents for display, **XSL Formatting Objects**

Of course, the two languages can be used together, so that XSLT transforms the data, and XSL Formatting Objects then further modifies the data for display, much like Cascading Style Sheets.

> *XSLT became a W3C Recommendation in November of 1999; the specification can be found at http://www.w3.org/TR/xslt. XSL Formatting Objects was still being worked on at the time of writing, but the latest version of the specification can be found at http://www.w3.org/TR/xsl/.*

This chapter and the one that follows it will focus on XSLT. Most XSL processors only implement the XSLT half of XSL anyway: XSLT is designed to be self-standing, meaning that developers can write XSLT engines, even if they don't want to implement the XSL Formatting Objects functionality.

Note that in addition to well-formed XML, XSLT can also output HTML, or even regular text. In fact, one of the most hyped uses of XSLT is for transforming XML documents into HTML documents, for display in a browser.

The first thing we need to do before looking at the more detailed syntax of XSLT and XPath is to find out how XSLT style sheets actually work.

So How Do XSLT Style Sheets Work?

XSLT style sheets are built on structures called **templates**. A template specifies what to look for in the source tree, and what to put into the result tree.

XSLT is written in XML, meaning that there are special XSLT elements and attributes you use to create your style sheets. Let's look at a simple example:

```
<xsl:template match="first">First tag found!</xsl:template>
```

Templates are defined using the XSLT <xsl:template> element. There are two important pieces to this template: the match attribute, and the contents of the template.

The match attribute specifies a pattern in the source tree; this template will be applied for any nodes in the source tree that match that pattern. In this case, the template will be applied for any elements named first.

You specify what should go into the result tree in the contents of the template element. Here we've simply specified some text; if this template was included in a style sheet, every time the XSLT engine found a `<first>` element in the source tree, it would output the text "First tag found!".

The contents of a template can be – and almost always are – much more complex than simply outputting text. There are numerous XSLT elements you can insert into the template to perform various actions. For example, there's an `<xsl:value-of>` element, which can take information from the source tree, and add it to the result tree. The following will work the same as our previous template, but instead of outputting "First tag found!", this template will add the contents of any elements named first to the result tree:

```
<xsl:template match="first"><xsl:value-of select="."/></xsl:template>
```

In other words, if the XSLT engine finds:

```
<first>John</first>
```

it will output John, and if it finds:

```
<first>Andrea</first>
```

it will output Andrea.

Most of this chapter will concern itself with XPath, the language we'll use to specify the match patterns in our style sheets. The next chapter will get more in-depth with many of the available XSLT elements.

Associating Style Sheets Using Processing Instructions

An XSL style sheet can be associated with an XML document using the same type of style sheet processing instruction as we used for CSS in the last chapter, like this:

```
<?xml-stylesheet type="text/xsl" href="stylesheet.xsl"?>
```

However, since IE5 is currently the only major web browser that understands XML and XSL, this will only work for IE5. Your style sheets would have to use the older syntax for XSLT – newer style sheets won't be understood by IE5's XSLT engine. Or, if you wish, you can run the preview version of MSXML in Replace Mode, as described above.

Why is XSLT So Important for E-Commerce?

To get an idea of the power of XSLT, let's create a fictional example to demonstrate. Imagine that there are two companies working together, sharing information over the Internet. *Company A* is a store, which sends purchase orders to *Company B*, who fulfills those orders. Let's assume that we have already decided that XML is the best way to send that information.

Unfortunately, the chances are that *Company A* will need a different set of information for this transaction than *Company B* does. Perhaps *Company A* needs information on the salesperson who made the order for commissioning purposes, but *Company B* doesn't need it. Whereas *Company B* needs to know the part numbers, which *Company A*'s order doesn't really care about.

Company A has XML such as the following:

```
<?xml version="1.0"?>
<order>
  <salesperson>John Doe</salesperson>
  <item>Production-Class Widget</item>
  <quantity>16</quantity>
  <date>
    <month>1</month>
    <day>13</day>
    <year>2000</year>
  </date>
  <customer>Sally Finkelstein</customer>
</order>
```

Whereas *Company B* requires XML which looks more like this:

```
<?xml version="1.0"?>
<order>
  <date>2000/1/13</date>
  <customer>Company A</customer>
  <item>
    <part-number>E16-25A</part-number>
    <description>Production-Class Widget</description>
    <quantity>16</quantity>
  </item>
</order>
```

In this scenario, we have three choices:

❑   *Company A* can use the same structure for their XML that *Company B* uses. The disadvantage is that they now need a separate XML document to accompany the first one, for their own additional information. However, the business-to-business (B2B) communication is much easier, since both are using the same format.

❑   *Company B* can use the same format for their XML that *Company A* uses. This would have the same results as the previous choice.

❑   Both companies can use whatever XML format they wish internally, but transform their data to a common format whenever they need to transmit the information outside. Obviously this option provides the most flexibility for both companies, and still allows cross-company communication.

With XSLT, this kind of transformation is quite easy: it's probably one of the most important uses of XSLT, and one of the more exciting areas where XML is already making its presence felt.

Try It Out – A Simple Business-to-Business Example

I claimed the transformation would be easy, so I guess I'd better put my money where my mouth is, and create a style sheet which can do this kind of transformation!

1. Open Notepad, and type in the XML for *Company A's* data:

```
<?xml version="1.0"?>
<order>
  <salesperson>John Doe</salesperson>
  <item>Production-Class Widget</item>
  <quantity>16</quantity>
  <date>
    <month>1</month>
    <day>13</day>
    <year>2000</year>
  </date>
  <customer>Sally Finkelstein</customer>
</order>
```

Save this as `CompanyA.xml`.

2. Now open a new file and type in the following XSLT, which contains the instructions for the transformation:

```
<?xml version="1.0"?>
<xsl:stylesheet version="1.0" xmlns:xsl="http://www.w3.org/1999/XSL/Transform">
<xsl:output method="xml" indent="yes"/>

<xsl:template match="/">
  <order>
    <date>
      <xsl:value-of select="/order/date/year"/>/<xsl:value-of
      select="/order/date/month"/>/<xsl:value-of select="/order/date/day"/>
    </date>
    <customer>Company A</customer>
    <item>
      <xsl:apply-templates select="/order/item"/>
      <quantity><xsl:value-of select="/order/quantity"/></quantity>
    </item>
  </order>
</xsl:template>

<xsl:template match="item">
  <part-number>
    <xsl:choose>
      <xsl:when test=". = 'Production-Class Widget'">E16-25A</xsl:when>
      <xsl:when test=". = 'Economy-Class Widget'">E16-25B</xsl:when>
      <!--other part-numbers would go here-->
      <xsl:otherwise>00</xsl:otherwise>
    </xsl:choose>
  </part-number>
  <description><xsl:value-of select="."/></description>
</xsl:template>
</xsl:stylesheet>
```

Save this as `order.xsl`.

Looks like a big jumble of nonsense, right? Don't worry: by the end of this and the next chapter, this style sheet will look pretty simple. However, do note that, as we mentioned, this style sheet is written in XML.

3. In order to perform the transformation, we'll get our first use of XT. Go to Start | Programs | MS-DOS Prompt (or the equivalent for your system), and find the directory where you put `xt.exe`. (Again, the examples in this book assume you have XT in your root C:\ directory.)

4. Type in `xt CompanyA.xml order.xsl`, specifying the full path to the XML and XSLT files if need be. Your output should look like this:

```
C:\>xt CompanyA.xml order.xsl
<?xml version="1.0" encoding="utf-8"?>
<order>
<date>2000/1/13</date>
<customer>Company A</customer>
<item>
<part-number>E16-25A</part-number>
<description>Production-Class Widget</description>
<quantity>16</quantity>
</item>
</order>
```

which, you may notice, is the same as the *Company B* XML document we saw earlier, with the slight addition of an `encoding` attribute in the XML Declaration. *Company A* now has an XML document type which suits their business needs, but also has the ability to send the same information to *Company B* in a format which is understandable to them.

5. Now type in `xt CompanyA.xml order.xsl CompanyB.xml`, again specifying the full path to the XML and XSLT files, if need be. This time, XT won't send any output to the screen; instead, it will create a file called `CompanyB.xml`, which will contain the results of the transformation. Open it up in Notepad or in IE5 to verify that the results are the same.

Imperative versus Declarative Programming

Before we go on to study XSLT in depth, we should stop here and discuss the type of programming you'll be doing with XSLT.

There are two types of programming languages in the computing world: **imperative** and **declarative**.

Imperative Programming

Imperative programming languages are ones like JavaScript, or Java, or C++, where the programmer tells the computer exactly what to do, and how to do it. For example, if we had three strings, and wanted to create some HTML using those strings for paragraphs, we might write a function like the following in JavaScript:

```
function createHTML()
{
  //our three strings
  var aParagraphs = new Array("Para 1", "Para 2", "Para 3");
  var strOutput, strTemp, i;

  //create the opening HTML and BODY tags
  strOutput = new String("<HTML>\n<BODY>\n");

  for(i = 0; i < aParagraphs.length; i++)
  {
    //add a new paragraph with this string
    strTemp = new String("<P>" + aParagraphs[i] + "</P>\n");
    strOutput = strOutput + strTemp;
  }

  //add the closing HTML and BODY tags
  strOutput = strOutput + "</BODY>\n</HTML>";
  return strOutput;
}
```

This returns the following HTML:

```
<HTML>
<BODY>
<P>Para 1</P>
<P>Para 2</P>
<P>Para 3</P>
</BODY>
</HTML>
```

which is what we wanted. But in order to create the HTML we wanted with JavaScript, we had to instruct the computer to do all of the following:

❑   Create the <HTML> and <BODY> start-tags.

❑   Loop through all of the strings. For each string, prepend a <P> start-tag, and append a </P> end-tag. Then add this string to the main string.

❑   Create the </BODY> and </HTML> end-tags.

In between these steps we also had to tell the computer to add whatever new lines we needed (\n is a new line in JavaScript), and we had to make sure we did everything in the proper order. (We need to have the <HTML> start-tag before the <P> elements, for example.)

Declarative Programming

XSLT, however, is not an imperative programming language like JavaScript; it's **declarative**, and declarative languages don't require quite so much work from the developer. With XSLT, we don't specify to the computer *how* we want anything done, just what we want it to do. We do this using **templates,** which specify the conditions in which the process takes place and the output that's produced. How to do the work is entirely up to the processor.

For example, assuming that our three strings were in an XML file like so:

```
<?xml version="1.0"?>
<strings>
  <s>Para 1</s>
  <s>Para 2</s>
  <s>Para 3</s>
</strings>
```

we could get the same HTML as above using an XSLT style sheet like this:

```
<?xml version="1.0"?>
<xsl:stylesheet version="1.0" xmlns:xsl="http://www.w3.org/1999/XSL/Transform">
  <xsl:template match="/">
    <HTML>
    <BODY>
      <xsl:for-each select="/strings/s">
        <P><xsl:value-of select="."/></P>
      </xsl:for-each>
    </BODY>
    </HTML>
  </xsl:template>
</xsl:stylesheet>
```

Notice that this style sheet looks very much like the output, with some XSLT elements mixed in to specify where content should go – these are the elements with the `xsl:` prefix. The XSLT engine will:

❑   Find the document root of the source tree. (That is, the virtual root of the document's hierarchy – more on the document root coming up.)

❑   Match the document root against the single template in our style sheet.

❑   Output the HTML elements in the template.

❑   Process the XSLT elements in the template; in this case, it will process the `<xsl:for-each>` element.

   ❑   The `<xsl:for-each>` works like a template-in-a-template, and applies to any `<s>` elements which are children of a `<strings>` root element. The contents of this template are a `<P>` element, which will be output to the result tree, and the `<xsl:value-of>` element.

   ❑   The `<xsl:value-of>` element will output the contents of those `<s>` elements to the result tree, as the contents of the `<P>` element.

Phew. That's a lot of work the XSLT engine does for us!

If we wanted to, we could even specify the order in which we want our paragraphs sorted, by simply changing the `<xsl:for-each>` element from this:

```
<xsl:for-each select="/strings/s">
  <!--other XSLT here-->
</xsl:for-each>
```

to this:

```
<xsl:for-each select="/strings/s">
  <xsl:sort select="."/>
  <!--other XSLT here-->
</xsl:for-each>
```

We don't have to program any logic in our style sheet on how to sort the strings, we simply tell it to do it, and let the XSL processor take care of the sorting for us. (Programming this logic into our JavaScript function would have required us to know complex rules about sorting algorithms, which aren't required for sorting in XSLT.)

XSLT Has No Side Effects

Whenever people start talking about the benefits of XSLT, they usually mention the fact that it has no **side effects**. In order to understand why this might be considered a benefit, let's look at what they mean by "side effect".

Suppose you're writing a program in Java, or C++, or some other imperative language, which will take an XML document and print it out from a printer. Also suppose that we have a global variable in that program, which is keeping track of the current page number. As a global variable is available to any code in the program, we can call different functions and they can update that variable, to increment it as more pages are printed.

When we call a function and it updates our global variable, this is a side effect. If any other function accesses that variable after it has been changed, that function will see the new value. This is very important, because it means we have to call the functions in a particular order. For example, if we have one function that prints out the page number, and another function that updates the page number, calling them in the wrong order would mean that the wrong page number is printed in the output.

This means two things:

- ❑ As programmers, we have to be careful to do everything in exactly the right order. If we make all of the right calculations, but perform them in the wrong order, it's just as bad as making incorrect calculations.

- ❑ When we compile our code, the compiler has to run it exactly as we tell it to. That is, even if our code would run more efficiently in a different order, it has to run the way we wrote it.

XSLT doesn't have these side effects. We can't modify global variables at run time the way we can with other programming languages. This means:

- ❑ As programmers, we aren't as concerned with doing things in the proper order, just what we want the end result to be. This can greatly reduce the number of bugs in our code, since it's one less thing that we, as programmers, need to worry about.

- ❑ An XSLT engine can run the code in your style sheet in any order it wishes. It can even run multiple pieces of code simultaneously. (Realistically, these optimizations might not exist in current XSLT engines, or may exist only to a very limited degree. However, declarative languages are inherently easier to optimize than imperative ones, so it's only a matter of time.)

And there's another consequence to this: programmers who are familiar with imperative languages will have to learn a completely new style of programming. Working with, and changing, variables has been one of the most fundamental aspects of imperative programming, and it can take some getting used to working declaratively. If you're more used to declarative programming languages, XSLT as a declarative language makes a lot of sense, and allows great power and flexibility. However, if you're used to imperative languages like JavaScript, it might take a while to train yourself to stop thinking in imperative terms. Nevertheless, you can be sure that once you get used to XSLT's declarative nature, you'll begin to appreciate the power that's available to you.

Hopefully, you're now convinced that XSLT is something you want to know more about. But before we get into specifics, there's another language we're going to have to get to grips with: XPath.

XPath

Even in the short examples we've seen so far, it seems like we're spending a lot of time looking at pieces of the source tree; we must need a pretty flexible way of pointing to different pieces of an XML document. In fact, there's a whole separate specification from the W3C for a language called **XPath**, which does exactly that: address sections of an XML document, to allow us to get the exact pieces of information we need. XSL uses XPath extensively.

XPath version 1.0 became a W3C recommendation on 16 Nov 1999.

You use **XPath expressions** to address your documents by specifying a **location path**, which conveys to XPath, step-by-step, where you are going in the document. Of course, you can't know where you're going unless you know where you are, so XPath also needs to know the **context node**; that is, the section of the XML document from which you're starting. (We've already seen the shortcut in XPath for the starting context node, which is a simple" . ".)

> **Think of an XPath expression as giving directions through the XML document. ("Okay, you're here, so you need to go down here, turn right at the next street, and it's the first house on the left.")**

order.xml

To demonstrate some of these concepts in the next few sections, we'll be using a modified version of our order XML from the earlier Try It Out (CompanyB.xml), so you might want to save the following to your hard drive as order.xml, and keep it handy:

```xml
<?xml version="1.0"?>
<order number="312597">
  <date>2000/1/1</date>
  <customer id="216A">Company A</customer>
  <item>
    <part-number warehouse="Warehouse 11">E16-25A</part-number>
    <description>Production-Class Widget</description>
    <quantity>16</quantity>
  </item>
</order>
```

We've just added some attributes, for the sake of demonstrating how to address them with XPath.

Node? What's a Node?

Up to this point, we've been dealing with elements, attributes, comments, processing instructions, and other XML constructs. XPath adds an additional concept, called a **node**.

We covered the hierarchical nature of XML documents in Chapters 1 and 2, where we saw that XML documents can be viewed as a tree, with parents and children. But it's not just elements that form this tree; the attributes, comments, processing instructions, and anything else in the document also form parts of this tree. For this reason, it's often useful to work with the parent/child relationships of an XML document without having to worry about whether the branches and leaves are elements, attributes, pieces of text, or anything else.

> **XPath uses the term node to refer to any part of a document, whether it be element, attribute, or otherwise.**

In this chapter, we'll sometimes use the term node to refer to these items, and sometimes the terms attribute, element, etc., depending on the context.

We'll also be talking about **node-sets**, which are collections of nodes. For example, if you tell XPath to look for any elements with an `id` attribute, there might be more than one. XPath will return a node-set, which will be a collection of all of the elements in the source tree that have an `id` attribute. Node-sets can contain any type of node, not just elements.

Location Paths

The first thing to note about XPath is the concept of the **document root**, which is **not** the root element we learned about in Chapter 2. Since there can be other things at the beginning or end of an XML document before or after the root element, XPath needs a virtual document root to act as the root of the document's hierarchy. In fact, the root element is a child of the document root.

Recall our <name> example from Chapter 2, which had this XML:

```
<name>
  <first>John</first>
  <middle>Fitzgerald Johansen</middle>
  <last>Doe</last>
</name>
```

the hierarchy according to XPath would be more like this:

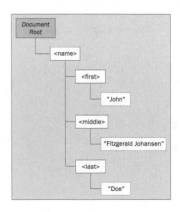

The document root doesn't point at any element in the document; it's just the conceptual root of the document. In XPath, the document root is specified by a single "/". This is why the template in our first XSLT example, which matched against "/", applied to the entire document.

```
<xsl:template match="/">
```

Building Location Paths

If we only wanted to match against the `<order>` element in our `order.xml` file, instead of the entire document, we could write the XPath expression "`/order`" instead. XPath reads expressions from left to right, so in this case it reads "start at the document root node, and return the `<order>` element, which is a child of that node".

> *Remember, the location path specifies where you are going in the document, and the context node is the section of the document that you're starting at. So in this example, our context node is the document root.*

However, it's often easier to read XPath expressions backwards, and work your way back to the context node. If we read this expression from right to left it means "select any elements named `<order>` which are children of the document root".

Removing the "/" from the expression and just specifying "`order`" for our XPath expression would instead mean "select any elements named `<order>` which are children of the context node".

> **Remember: XPath expressions can be relative, meaning that they start at the context node, or absolute, meaning that they start at the document root.**

Additional steps in instructions to XPath are separated by additional "/" characters. So we can create an expression such as "`/order/item/part-number`", which means "select any elements named `<part-number>` which are children of `<item>` elements, which are children of `<order>` elements, which are children of the document root."

XPath also lets us address attributes, using the "`@`" symbol. For example, "`@id`" means "select the id attribute of the context node".

The Recursive Descent Operator

Locating nodes based on their names, regardless of where in the document they come, is done using the "`//`" notation. So "`//customer`" selects any `<customer>` element in the document, regardless of how far down the tree it is, and "`//@id`" selects any id attribute in the document, regardless of which element it belongs to.

> **This "`//`" syntax is called the** recursive descent operator. **There are cases where it is useful. However, it can also greatly decrease the performance of your style sheets. (This is because the XSLT engine must search through the entire XML document looking for matches.) As a general rule, you shouldn't use the "`//`" syntax unless you really need to.**

But Why Doesn't XPath Use XML Syntax?

Notice that these XPath expressions are not expressed in XML, but in XPath's own syntax. This may seem strange, when so many of the other technologies surrounding XML are expressed using XML, but the decision not to use XML for XPath was quite deliberate.

Often, XML attributes will have XPath expressions as values, including many of the attributes in XSL. (For example, the match attribute of the <xsl:template> element.) If XPath were expressed using XML, we couldn't put XPath expressions into attributes, which would make XSL much more cumbersome and difficult to work with.

For example, instead of writing:

```
<xsl:template match="/name/first">
  <!--do something here-->
</xsl:template>
```

we might have had to write something like

```
<xsl:template>
  <xsl:select>
    <xsl:path>
      <xsl:element type="name"/>
      <xsl:element type="first"/>
    </xsl:path>
  </xsl:select>
  <!--do something here-->
</xsl:template>
```

Using a specialized syntax for XPath also makes it possible to return XML fragments or node-sets from a URL. For example, the following might return a node-set containing <salesperson> elements:

```
http://my.server/location/file.xml#xpointer(//order/salesperson)
```

We'll be talking much more about this type of functionality in Chapter 12, when we introduce XLink and XPointer.

More Specific Location Paths

So now that we can address pieces of our XML document, can we get more specific? Of course! Not only can we locate nodes which are in specific locations in our document, but we can match against nodes with specific values, or that meet other conditions. So, for example, instead of matching against <first> elements from the source tree, we could match only <first> elements whose text is "John".

This is done using "[]" brackets, which act like a filter on the node being selected. We can test for elements with specific child nodes by simply putting the name of the child node in the "[]" brackets. So:

- ❑ "order[customer]" matches any <order> element which is a child of the context node and which has a <customer> child element.

❑ "order[@number]" matches any <order> element which is a child of the context node and which has a number attribute.

❑ And to take it a step further, "order[customer = 'Company A']" matches any <order> element which is a child of the context node, and which has a <customer> child with a value of "Company A".

Notice that in all of the cases above we're selecting the <order> element, *not* the number attribute or the <customer> element. The "[]" brackets just act as a filter, so that only certain <order> elements will be selected.

To check for a node with a specific value, you would use "." for the comparison. For example, "customer[. = 'Company A']" matches any <customer> element with a value of "Company A".

These filters are not limited, but can be as complex as we want. For example, "//order[customer/@id = '216A']" says select any <order> elements which have a child element named <customer>, which in turn has an id attribute with a value of "216A". But again, it's the <order> element we're selecting, not the <customer> element or the id attribute.

Dealing with Complex Expressions

For more complex XPath expressions, like the following:

```
/order[@number = '312597']/item/part-number[@warehouse = 'Warehouse 11']
```

you might find it easier to break things down into steps as you go. For example, you can specify the XPath expression to the node you want to select, and then add in any filters after. In this case, we can first write the XPath expression as:

```
/order/item/part-number
```

We can then narrow this down to only select the <part-number> elements whose warehouse attribute has a value of "Warehouse 11":

```
/order/item/part-number[@warehouse = 'Warehouse 11']
```

And finally, we select these <part-number> elements only if they are descended from an <order> element whose number attribute had the value "312597":

```
/order[@number = '312597']/item/part-number[@warehouse = 'Warehouse 11']
```

Quotation Marks

Like the syntax for attributes in XML, either double or single quotes can be used in XPath expressions. However, it's best to get into the habit of using either one or the other, and making it the opposite of what you normally use for attributes. (That is, if you normally use double quotes for attributes, you should get into the habit of using single quotes in your XPath expressions.) This will make things much easier for you, since you'll be inserting these XPath expressions into attributes on a regular basis.

For example, let's assume that you always use double quotes for your attribute values, like:

```
<xsl:template match="">
```

In this case you would probably want to start using single quotes in your XPath expressions, like:

```
customer[. = 'Company A']
```

This way, when you start inserting XPath expressions into XML attribute values, you'll be prepared to use the proper quotation marks in the proper context:

```
<xsl:template match="customer[. = 'Company A']">
```

So now we know how to address specific parts of our XML documents, it's time to move on to look at how we can actually use this to extract useful information from our documents.

XPath Functions

In order to make XPath even more powerful and useful, there are a number of **functions** that can be used in XPath expressions. Some of these can be used to return nodes and node-sets that can't be matched with regular child/parent and element/attribute relationships. There are also functions that can be used to work with strings and numbers, which can be used both to retrieve information from the original document, and to format it for output.

You can recognize functions because they end with "()" brackets. Some functions need information to work; this information is passed in the form of **parameters**, which are inserted between the "()" brackets.

For example, further on we'll be introducing a function called string-length(), which returns the number of characters in a string. It might be used something like this:

```
string-length('this is a string')
```

The parameter is the string "this is a string". The function string-length() will use this information to calculate its result (which in this example is 16).

Some functions will take parameters, but will also have **default parameters**. In these cases, you can use the function without passing it any parameters, but the function will operate as if you had passed it the default parameters.

Let's look at some of these functions in more detail.

Node Functions

Node functions are used for working with nodes in general. They can return information about a node, or return specific types of nodes. The functions we'll look at here are

❑   name()

❑   node()

❑ `processing-instruction()`

❑ `comment()`

❑ `text()`

name

You'd use the `name()` function to get the name of a node. For example, `name(.)` returns the name of the context node. The context node is the default used if no node is passed to `name()`, so "`name()`" is the same as "`name(.)`".

For example, the following template will output the name of every element that's a child of a `<name>` element:

```
<xsl:template match="name">
  <xsl:for-each select="*">
    <p><xsl:value-of select="name()"/></p>
  </xsl:for-each>
</xsl:template>
```

node

The `node()` function returns the node itself. You'll almost never need to use the `node()` function – but hey, the people who write these specifications like to be thorough!

processing-instruction

To return processing instructions, we'd use the `processing-instruction()` function. This function can take an optional parameter to specify the name.

For example, the following template returns the contents of any processing instructions in your document:

```
<xsl:template match="processing-instruction()">
  <xsl:value-of select="."/>
</xsl:template>
```

and this one outputs the contents of any processing instructions in your document with a PITarget of AppName:

```
<xsl:template match="processing-instruction('AppName')">
  <xsl:value-of select="."/>
</xsl:template>
```

This returns PIs like `<?AppName stuff?>`.

comment

The `comment()` function is used to return comments. So, the following will output the text in any comment:

```
<xsl:template match="comment()">
  <xsl:value-of select="."/>
</xsl:template>
```

> **Remember that an XML parser isn't required to pass comments up to the application. That means that even if your XSLT style sheet is written to do something with comments, it may never get the chance.**

If you really need to use the comments in the source tree for your style sheet, make sure the XML parser used by your XSL processor does pass the comments up to the application. The parser used by XT, and Microsoft's MSXML, do pass comments up, so the template above will work.

text

Finally, there's a `text()` function. This returns the PCDATA content of a node, without the PCDATA of the node's children, if any. For example, consider the following XML:

```
<parent>This is some text.
  <child>And this is some more text</child>
</parent>
```

We've been using the `<xsl:value-of>` element to get at the text contents of an element. In this case, we might write a template like the following to get at the text in the `<parent>` element:

```
<xsl:template match="parent">
  <xsl:value-of select="."/>
</xsl:template>
```

However, in this case the template would return:

```
This is some text.
  And this is some more text
```

In other words, getting the contents of any element also returns the contents of any children, and their children, etc. This isn't necessarily what we want – we might not wish to include the text in the `<child>` element – in which case, we'd use `text()`:

```
<xsl:template match="parent">
  <xsl:value-of select="text()"/>
</xsl:template>
```

This would return:

```
This is some text.
```

Positional Functions

For nodes that belong to a node-set, there are functions to determine or match against the position of those nodes within the set. These functions are:

- ❑   `position()`
- ❑   `last()`
- ❑   `count()`

position

The position() function is used to get the node's position in a node-set, in document-order. For example, if we have the following XML:

```
<nodes>
    <node>a</node>
    <node>b</node>
    <node>c</node>
</nodes>
```

then we can define a template to match any <node> element, like so:

```
<xsl:template match="/nodes/node">
```

This will match any of the <node> elements in this particular document. But using position(), we can define a template which only matches the second <node> element, like so:

```
<xsl:template match="/nodes/node[position() = 2]">
```

Since this is such a common thing to do, there's a shorthand way of writing it, which is:

```
<xsl:template match="/nodes/node[2]">
```

last

There's also a function to return the position of the last node in a node-set, called last(). (There's no need for a first() function, since the node with a position() of 1 will always be the first node in the node-set.)

So to create a template that matches against the last <node> element in our previous XML, we would do the following:

```
<xsl:template match="/nodes/node[position() = last ()]">
```

count

And to return the number of nodes in the node-set, use the count() function. To get the number of <node> elements in our XML, we'd do this:

```
<xsl:value-of select="count(node)"/>
```

Numeric Functions

Any programming language provides many functions for dealing with numbers, and XPath is no exception. There are a number of numeric functions available from the language, but by far the two most common are number() and sum().

number

The number() function converts PCDATA text to a numeric value. For example, say we've got an element like this:

```
<element>256</element>
```

According to XPath, this element contains a string containing the characters "2", "5", and "6". In order to treat the PCDATA as a numeric value of 256, we would have to use number(element).

sum

The sum() function can be used to add together all of the numeric values in a node-set. If we change our previous example from:

```
<nodes>
   <node>a</node>
   <node>b</node>
   <node>c</node>
</nodes>
```

to:

```
<nodes>
   <node>1</node>
   <node>2</node>
   <node>1</node>
</nodes>
```

then:

```
<xsl:value-of select="sum(/nodes/node)"/>
```

returns the sum of all of the <node> elements.

If we left the XML as before, and tried to use the sum() function, it would return NaN, since XPath wouldn't be able to convert "a", "b", and "c" to numbers and sum them. (NaN stands for Not a Number.)

Boolean Functions

There are a number of XPath functions which can be used for Boolean mathematics. We'll be looking at:

- ❑   boolean()
- ❑   not()
- ❑   true()
- ❑   false()

150

> Boolean values can only have one of two choices: true or false, yes or no, on or off, 1 or 0, etc.

boolean

The `boolean()` function simply evaluates an XPath expression to be `true` or `false`, using the following rules:

❏ If the value is numeric, it's considered `false` if it is 0, or the special `NaN` value. If the number is any other value, positive or negative, it is `true`.

❏ If the value is a string, it is `true` if its length is longer than 0 characters.

❏ If the value is a node-set, it is `true` if it's not empty, otherwise it's `false`.

❏ Any other type of object is converted to a Boolean in a way which is dependent on the type of object.

For example, this expression would be considered `true` if there was a `<name>` element which is a child of the context node, otherwise it would be `false`:

```
boolean(name)
```

not

But sometimes we want to do the opposite of our test condition; for example, instead of doing something if there **is** a `<name>` child element, we might want to do something if there **is not** a `<name>` child element. XPath provides the `not()` function so we can do this. It simply takes whatever the result would have been, and reverses it.

We could do the opposite of the above example like so:

```
not(boolean(name))
```

or simply:

```
not(name)
```

true and false

And, just to round things out, XPath provides two other Boolean functions:

❏ `true()`, which always returns `true`

❏ `false()`, which always returns `false`

The `true()` and `false()` functions can be handy when debugging a style sheet. For example, in the next chapter we'll be studying the `<xsl:if>` element, which can be used to test for certain conditions so that we only perform some processing if those conditions are met. We could write code like the following:

```
<xsl:if test="first[.='John']">
  <!--some HTML here...-->
</xsl:if>
```

If the context node has a child `<first>` element with the value "John", the HTML inside the `<xsl:if>` will be added to the result tree. However, during the debugging stage of development, we might need a way to purposely output the HTML even when the condition isn't true, just so we can check what it looks like. In that case, we could do something like:

```
<xsl:if test="true()">         <!--first[.='John']-->
  <!--some HTML here...-->
</xsl:if>
```

Now, no matter what the value of the `<first>` element, this HTML will be added to the result tree. Similarly:

```
<xsl:if test="false()">         <!--first[.='John']-->
  <!--some HTML here...-->
</xsl:if>
```

would ensure that the HTML is never written to the result tree.

Notice that I keep the old test in an XML comment; this is good practice, to ensure that you remember to change the test back to what it should be when you're done testing.

String Functions

Since all XML is really just text, there are a number of XPath functions provided for dealing with strings. We'll be looking at:

- ❑ `string()`
- ❑ `string-length()`
- ❑ `concat()`
- ❑ `contains()`
- ❑ `starts-with()`
- ❑ `substring()`
- ❑ `substring-after()`
- ❑ `substring-before()`
- ❑ `translate()`

string

The `string()` function converts any value to a string. In most cases the `string()` function is not required when reading the data from the source tree, since the data is all text anyway. However, it can come in handy when you need to perform calculations, and then convert the results of those calculations to a string for use in other parts of a style sheet.

string-length

To get the length of a string, you would use the `string-length()` function, which returns the number of characters in the string, including spaces.

concat

Concatenation is the act of taking two (or more) strings and combining them to make one large string. So "This is" concatenated with " a string" would form "This is a string".

The `concat()` function is used to concatenate multiple strings together. It takes as many strings as you want to give it (two or more) for parameters, and simply combines them all to create one large string, which it returns. For example:

```
concat('mystring', ' ', 'more string')"
```

returns a string containing the text "mystring more string".

contains

There are also string functions that you can use to analyze the data in the source tree. The `contains()` function indicates if one string contains anywhere within it the contents of a second string. That is.

```
contains("This is a string", "is a")
```

returns `true`, because the string "This is a string" does contain the string "is a", and:

```
contains("This is a string", "not a")
```

returns `false` because the string "This is a string" does not contain the string "not a".

> Note that the `contains()` function, like all string functions in XPath, is case-sensitive.

So:

```
contains("This is a string", "is A")
```

would also return `false`, since the "A" is now capitalized.

starts-with

Similarly, there's a `starts-with()` function, which indicates whether a string starts with the contents of a second string. For example:

```
starts-with("This is a string", "This")
```

returns `true`, since the string does indeed start with "This". However:

```
starts-with("This is a string", "a string")
```

returns `false`. Even though the string contains the string "a string", it isn't right at the beginning.

substring(), substring-after() and substring-before()

Next, there are a few functions that can return a sub-string out of a larger string. (Think of this as the opposite of concatenation.)

The `substring()` function takes a specified number of characters out of a string. It takes two parameters, and an optional third:

❑ the string to pull the characters out of

❑ the position in that string at which to start taking characters

❑ (optionally) the number of characters to take

If you're used to languages like C and Java, it might be handy to note that the numbering of characters in a string in XPath starts at 1, not 0.

If no third parameter is specified, `substring()` takes the characters up until the end of the string. So:

```
substring('This is the main string', 13)
```

returns "`main string`". Since we didn't specify how many characters to take, it starts at the thirteenth character and goes on right up to the end. However, if we change the code to:

```
substring('This is the main string', 13, 4)
```

it returns "`main`", because we told it to start at the thirteenth character, but only take 4 characters.

If you know that you're going to be taking all of the characters after a certain character, or all of the characters before a certain character, you can use `substring-after()` or `substring-before()`. So:

```
substring-after('This is the main string', 'a')
```

returns all of the characters after the first occurrence of the letter "a", in other words, "`in string`". Whereas:

```
substring-before('This is the main string', 'a')
```

returns all of the characters before the first occurrence of the letter "a", or "`This is the m`".

The Translate Function

Finally, there's the `translate()` function. This can be bit more difficult to get your head around.

When I was younger, my friends and I used to invent secret codes, so that we could send notes to each other without anyone else being able to understand them. Of course, the easiest code in the world was this one:

```
ABCDEFGHIJKLMNOPQRSTUVWXYZ
ZYXWVUTSRQPONMLKJIHGFEDCBA
```

In other words, if I wanted to insert the letter "A" into my note, I would instead use the letter "Z". The person receiving the note would then have to translate what I'd written, by substituting the letters in reverse.

The `translate()` function works very much the same as this simple code; you supply it with a string to translate, a string of characters to look for (like the first line of letters above), and a string of characters to replace them with (like the second line of letters above). So:

```
translate('QLSN', 'ABCDEFGHIJKLMNOPQRSTUVWXYZ',
          'ZYXWVUTSRQPONMLKJIHGFEDCBA')
```

would return "JOHN".

This demonstrates how `translate()` works, but it isn't very realistic. (Very few style sheets will be written to convert notes between schoolchildren.) A more realistic example would be case-conversion, such as the following:

```
translate("John", "abcdefghijklmnopqrstuvwxyz",
          "ABCDEFGHIJKLMNOPQRSTUVWXYZ")
```

This will return the string "JOHN", because all of the lower-case letters have been replaced with upper-case letters. Another example might be the case where you need to replace all occurrences of a character with some other character; maybe you need to replace all spaces with plus signs, such as:

```
translate('This is a string', ' ', '+')
```

which returns "This+is+a+string".

Let's look at the case conversion example again, to see how `translate()` works:

```
translate("John", "abcdefghijklmnopqrstuvwxyz",
          "ABCDEFGHIJKLMNOPQRSTUVWXYZ")
```

The function goes through the first string, character by character. For each one, it searches for a match in the second string, and remembers its index. For example, the second character in our string is "o", which is found in the second string, at the fifteenth character.

abcdefghijklmnopqrstuvwxyz

This index is then used to find a character in the third string, which is used to replace the character in the first string. That is, when translate() searches for "o", it finds it at the fifteenth position in the second string, so it takes the fifteenth character from the third string to use as a replacement:

```
abcdefghijklmnopqrstuvwxyz
ABCDEFGHIJKLMNOPQRSTUVWXYZ
```

In this case, the fifteenth character in the third string is "O", so "o" is replaced with "O".

In some cases, a character will exist in the first string that doesn't exist in the second string. For example, the first character in our first string is "J", which isn't found in the second string. (Remember, XPath is case-sensitive, meaning that "j" is not the same as "J".) When this happens, the character is not replaced, but stays in the string as-is. So the "J" in our first string would remain "J" in the final result.

There may also be cases where the second string passed to translate() is shorter than the third string. For example,

```
    translate('+bat+', 'abc+', 'ABC')
```

Here, any occurrence of "a" will be replaced by "A", "b" will be replaced by "B", and "c" will be replaced by "C". However, there's no corresponding character for a "+"; it's the fourth character in the second string, and the third string doesn't have a fourth character. translate() will simply strip the character out of the string, so the result of the above would be "BAt".

If the third string passed to translate() were longer than the second string, it would have no effect.

Most of the time you won't be passing translate() raw strings as we've been doing; instead you'll pass it XPath expressions. For example, you could translate the value of the context node to uppercase using the following:

```
    <xsl:value-of select=
    "translate(., 'abcdefghijklmnopqrstuvwxyz', 'ABCDEFGHIJKLMNOPQRSTUVWXYZ')"/>
```

In this case, the first parameter to the function is simply ".".

Axis Names

So far we've always been dealing with children and attributes. However, there are other sections of the tree structure in XML that we could be looking at. Or, to put it another way, there are numerous directions we can travel, in addition to just moving up and down between parents and children.

The way that we move in these other directions is through different **axes**. There are 13 axes defined in XPath, which you use in XPath expressions by specifying the axis name, followed by ::, followed by the node name. Consider the following diagram:

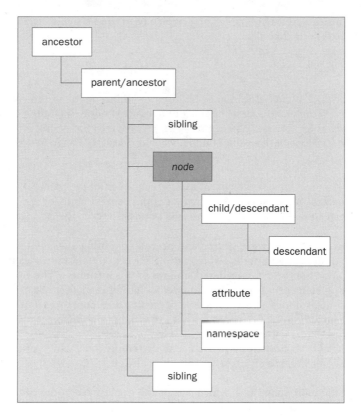

From our node, we have access to parents and ancestors, children and descendants, and siblings. If the node is an element, we also have access to any attributes that are attached to that node. And the last section of the tree we have access to is the namespace. (Namespaces will be covered in Chapter 8.)

The simplest is the **self** axis, which refers to the context node. The "." notation we've seen in some of our examples is a shortcut for self::node().

The axis we'll be using most often is the **child** axis, which contains the children of the context node. Luckily, child is the default axis, meaning that we don't need to specify it. That means that "order" gives exactly the same result as "child::order".

There are also wildcards available for child elements and child attributes:" *" selects any child elements, and "@*" selects any child attributes. For example, this template would match any element, regardless of its name:

```
<xsl:template match="*">
```

and this one would match any attribute regardless of its name:

```
<xsl:template match="@*">
```

We've already seen a simple `<xsl:for-each>`, which used the "*" wild card to process all child elements of the context node, like this:

```
<xsl:for-each select="*">
```

The **descendant** axis specifies any children, or children of children, etc. of the current node, while the **descendant-or-self** axis contains the descendants of the context node, including itself. We've been using "//", which is a shortcut for `descendant-or-self`, relative to the document root. To get the `descendant-or-self` axis of the context node, we could use ".//". So ".//description" means the same as "descendant-or-self::description".

In order to move up the tree, we use the **parent** axis, which specifies the parent of the context node (if any), and the **ancestor** axis, which specifies the parent of the context node, or the parent's parent, etc. There is also an **ancestor-or-self** axis, which works the opposite way to the `descendant-or-self` axis.

To get at siblings, we use the **following-sibling** and **preceding-sibling** axes, which together contain all of the sibling elements of the context node. (Note that these axes contain no nodes if the context node is an attribute – other attributes aren't considered siblings of this attribute.) The **following** axis contains all of the following sibling elements of the context node, including their descendants (but not including descendants of the context node). Conversely, the **preceding** axis contains all of the preceding elements of the context node, including their descendants (but not including the ancestors of the context node).

To get at the attributes of the context node, we use the **attribute** axis, which provides those nodes. The "@" notation we've been using is a shortcut for the `attribute` axis.

And finally, there is the **namespace** axis, which selects the namespace nodes of the context node, if any. We'll learn about namespaces in Chapter 8.

After all that theory, it's time to see some more working code.

Try It Out – Axes In Action

In order to try out all of the axis examples above, let's create a simple style sheet to look at our `<order>` example, and output the results of the XPath expressions.

1. Type the following into Notepad, and save it to your hard drive as `xpath.xsl`, in the same directory as our `order.xml` from earlier:

```
<?xml version="1.0"?>
<xsl:stylesheet version="1.0"
                xmlns:xsl="http://www.w3.org/1999/XSL/Transform">
<xsl:output method="text"/>

<xsl:template match="/">
  <xsl:for-each select="//description/following-sibling::quantity">
    <xsl:value-of select="name()"/>
    <xsl:text>
    </xsl:text>
  </xsl:for-each>
```

```
    </xsl:template>

    <xsl:template match="text()"/>
    </xsl:stylesheet>
```

2. Run this as usual:

```
C:\>xt order.xml xpath.xsl
```

3. And you should see the following result:

quantity

> We asked XPath to select any `<quantity>` element that's a sibling of a `<description>` node, provided it comes after the `<description>` node in the document order.

The following table lists a number of XPath expressions using axes, along with descriptions of what they do.

XPath Expression	Abbreviated Syntax	Explanation
`child::order`	`order`	Selects any `<order>` elements which are children of the context node.
	`order/*`	Selects any elements which are a child of `<order>`.
	`order/@*`	Selects any attributes which belong to `<order>`.
`descendant-or-self::description`	`.//description`	Selects any `<description>` elements which are a descendant of the context node, including the context node if applicable.
`order/attribute::number`	`order/@number`	Selects the number attribute of the `<order>` node.
`//date/parent::order`	`//date/../order`	Selects any `<order>` elements which are a parent of a `<date>` element.
`/order/descendant::description`		Selects any `<description>` elements which are descendants of the `<order>` element.
`//quantity/ancestor::order`		Selects any `<order>` element which is an ancestor of a `<quantity>` element.
`//description/following-sibling::quantity`		Selects a `<quantity>` element, if that element is a sibling of a `<description>` node, and it comes after the `<description>` node in the document order.

XPath Expression	Abbreviated Syntax	Explanation
`//quantity/preceding-sibling::description`		Select a `<description>` element, if that element is a sibling of the `<quantity>` node, and it comes before the `<quantity>` node in document order.
`/order/date/following::*`		Selects any elements which come after the `<date>` element in the document, not including descendants.
`/order/item/preceding::*`		Select any elements which come before the `<item>` element, not including ancestors.

In order to see the results, simply change the `select` attribute of the `<xsl:for-each>` element to the XPath expression you're trying out from the above table, and then run it through XT.

The template will go through each node which matches the XPath expression, and output the name of that node to the result tree. The context node for the XPath expression will be the document root. The results of the transformation will be a simple list of the selected node names.

4. For example, change the select attribute to `/order/date/following::*`:

```
<xsl:template match="/">
  <xsl:for-each select="/order/date/following::*">
    <xsl:value-of select="name()"/>
    <xsl:text>
    </xsl:text>
  </xsl:for-each>
</xsl:template>
```

5. Save `xpath.xsl`, and run it again:

```
C:\>xt order.xml xpath.xsl
```

6. This time you should get the following:

```
customer
item
part-number
description
quantity
```

Summary

This chapter has introduced the concepts behind Extensible Style sheet Language for Transformations – XSLT – a language for transforming XML documents into any text-based format. In particular, we've concentrated on a language called XPath, which we need to understand if we're going to get at the exact pieces of information we need from our XML documents.

We've seen:

❑ What XSLT is good for, and some of the ways it's already being used today

❑ How XPath is used to address pieces of an XML document

❑ How to use XPath functions to return nodes and node-sets, retrieve information from an XML document, and to format it for output

❑ How to use the axes that XPath defines

In the next chapter we're going to take a closer look at how to write XSLT style sheets, and study the syntax of XSLT's main elements.

XSLT – The Gory Details

All right, we've introduced XSLT to death. We've seen some things it can be used for, and even seen some style sheets. Now that we're all giddy with anticipation, let's start learning it properly! In this chapter we'll take a closer look at the elements which make up XSLT, and really see how to put it to good use.

This will include:

❑   Reinforcing what we learned about templates

❑   Studying the main XSLT elements and how to use them

❑   Looking at how XSLT and CSS can complement each other for transforming and displaying XML

Once again we'll be making use of James Clark's XT, which we showed how to obtain and use at the beginning of Chapter 4.

Templates

We have been introduced briefly to the concept of **templates**. These are really the heart and soul of XSLT. Style sheets are simply a collection of these templates, which are applied to the input document to create the output document. In this section, we'll take a closer look at the syntax of templates, and how they work.

Let's take another look at a previous XSLT style sheet, from the last chapter:

```
<?xml version="1.0"?>
<xsl:stylesheet version="1.0" xmlns:xsl="http://www.w3.org/1999/XSL/Transform">
  <xsl:template match="/">
    <HTML>
    <BODY>
      <xsl:for-each select="/strings/s">
        <P><xsl:value-of select="."/></P>
      </xsl:for-each>
    </BODY>
    </HTML>
  </xsl:template>
</xsl:stylesheet>
```

This style sheet has only one template, which is the highlighted section of code, but style sheets can have as many templates as are needed. There are two important pieces to this template:

❑ The section of the *source* tree to which this template applies

❑ The output that will be inserted into the *result* tree

The section of the source tree we're matching against is specified in the `match` attribute. In this case, we've specified `match="/"` which means that the template is matched against the document root.

Everything inside the template, between the start- and end-tags, is what will be output to the result tree. Any normal XML elements or text which appear inside the `<xsl:template>` element will end up in the output document as-is; any elements which are prefixed with `xsl:` are special XSLT elements, which indicate to the processor that it should do some work. In this case, we have:

❑ An element called `<xsl:for-each>`, which is, in effect, a mini-template, applying to any XML in the source tree matching its `select` attribute

❑ An element named `<xsl:value-of>`, which is used to put the value of an XML element into the result tree

Note that you could create a template which had no XSLT elements in it at all (apart from the template element itself). In this case, the output from the template would always be the same. For instance, take the following template:

```
<xsl:template match="name">
  <name>
    <first>John</first>
    <last>Doe</last>
  </name>
</xsl:template>
```

Any time the XSL processor matches a `<name>` element in the source tree with this template, it will output the XML above; so no matter what information was contained in the source `<name>`, the output will be a `<name>` element containing the information "John Doe". In most cases, this is probably not what we want.

XSLT's Order of Operations

If a style sheet can have more than one template, then how do we know which one will be instantiated first? Does the XSL processor go through each template in the style sheet one by one, and look for matches in the source tree? Or does it go through the source tree node by node, and look for matching templates in the style sheet?

Actually, it does neither. The XSL processor starts the process off by matching the document root against the template in the style sheet which best matches it; in most cases, there will be only one, but in some cases there may be multiple templates which are possible matches. For example, we could have two templates like this:

```
<xsl:template match="/[order]">
```

```
<xsl:template match="/">
```

In this case, if the root element is named "order", the first template will be used, but in any other cases the second will be used.

Default Templates

If you don't specify a template in your document which matches against the document root, XSLT provides a default one, which simply then applies any other templates which exist. The default style sheet is defined as follows:

```
<xsl:template match="*|/">
   <xsl:apply-templates/>
</xsl:template>
```

This matches against any elements in the document, or the document root, and calls `<xsl:apply-templates>`, to process any children. We'll look at `<xsl:apply-templates>` in a moment. There is also a built-in template for text and attribute nodes, which is:

```
<xsl:template match="text()|@*">
   <xsl:value-of select="."/>
</xsl:template>
```

This template simply adds the value of the text node or attribute to the result tree. The net result of combining these two default templates is that you could create a style sheet with no templates of your own, and the defaults would go through every element in the document, and print out the values.

Once the template matching the document root is finished, any further processing is controlled by the style sheet itself, by calling other templates, or getting values from the source tree, etc. This means that if you were to provide a template which matched against the document root but which did nothing, then your style sheet would also effectively do nothing.

How Do Templates Affect the Context Node?

An important point to remember in XSLT is that whatever the template uses for its match attribute becomes the **context node** for that template. This means that all XPath expressions within the template are **relative** to that node. Take the following example:

```
<xsl:template match="/order/item">
    <xsl:value-of select="part-number"/>
</xsl:template>
```

This template will be instantiated for any `<item>` element, which is a child of an `<order>` element, which is a child of the document root. That `<item>` element is now the context node for this template, meaning that the XPath expression in the `<xsl:value-of>` attribute is actually only selecting any `<part-number>` elements which are children of the `<item>` element already selected for this template.

However, we can always get at the document root using "/", so if we needed to get at an element which wasn't directly accessible from the context node we could use an XPath expression which accessed the element from the document root, like this:

```
<xsl:template match="/order/item">
    <xsl:value-of select="/order/date"/>
</xsl:template>
```

XSLT Elements and their Use

The previous chapter covered some of the reasons for using XSLT, and some of the general methodologies used, including XPath, which is used extensively in XSLT. It also teased you with some sample style sheets, with promises that all would be made clear later. Now it's time to roll up our sleeves and take a look at some of the XSLT elements we can use in our style sheets, which will do the actual work of our XSL transformations.

This chapter won't list all of the elements available with XSLT 1.0, but will introduce the more common ones that you're likely to encounter. Furthermore, not all of the attributes are listed for some of the elements, but again, only the more common ones. A comprehensive on-line XSLT reference, written by Teun Duynstee, is available at http://www.vbxml.com. Or you can keep an eye on the W3C web site for the current specifications.

<xsl:stylesheet>

The <xsl:stylesheet> element is the root element of nearly all XSLT style sheets, and is used like this:

```
<xsl:stylesheet version="version number"
    xmlns:xsl="http://www.w3.org/1999/XSL/Transform">
```

If you are following the current XSLT specification from the W3C, you should use "1.0" for the *version number*. You also must specify that strange looking xmlns:xsl attribute, and the value must be exactly as written above. This is how XSL processors can identify your XSLT elements. (It has to do with namespaces, which will be covered in Chapter 8.)

Instead of the <xsl:stylesheet> element, you could use the <xsl:transform> element. It has exactly the same meaning and syntax as <xsl:stylesheet>, and is available for those who wish to differentiate their XSLT style sheets from their XSL Formatting Objects style sheets. Most people don't use it, however, and stick to <xsl:stylesheet> exclusively, which is the practice we'll follow.

For style sheets which will only define one template, which matches against the document root, the <xsl:stylesheet> element is optional. For example, instead of this style sheet from earlier:

```
<?xml version="1.0"?>
<xsl:stylesheet version="1.0" xmlns:xsl="http://www.w3.org/1999/XSL/Transform">
  <xsl:template match="/">
    <HTML>
    <BODY>
      <xsl:for-each select="/strings/s">
        <P><xsl:value-of select="."/></P>
      </xsl:for-each>
    </BODY>
    </HTML>
  </xsl:template>
</xsl:stylesheet>
```

we could have used this instead:

```
<HTML xsl:version="1.0" xmlns:xsl="http://www.w3.org/1999/XSL/Transform">
<BODY>
  <xsl:for-each select="/strings/s">
    <P><xsl:value-of select="."/></P>
  </xsl:for-each>
</BODY>
</HTML>
```

Both of these style sheets mean exactly the same thing to an XSL processor. All you need to specify are the `xsl:version` and `xmlns:xsl` attributes in the root element, and include the rest of the XSLT elements you need as usual. This shorthand syntax comes in handy most often when transforming XML documents to HTML, but can be useful in other transformations as well.

In fact, this shorthand was developed specifically for people who already know HTML, and who want to learn XSL. It was believed that it would be easier for them to get their feet wet before jumping right into fully-fledged XSLT.

<xsl:template>

As we have seen already, `<xsl:template>` is the element used to define the templates which make up our XSLT style sheets. Although this is one of the more important elements you'll be using with XSLT, it's also one of the simplest:

```
<xsl:template match="XPath expression"
    name="template name"
    priority="number"
    mode="mode name">
```

The `match` attribute is used to indicate the **XPath pattern** which is matched against the source tree. Notice that I say "pattern", and not "expression", which is the word we've been using up to now. What we're specifying for our template is the *type* of node to select, not a *path* to a particular node. Consider the following simple XPath syntax:

```
/name/first
```

If this were treated as a full XPath *expression*, it would mean "go to the document root, then to the child element of that named <name>, and then go to the child element of that named <first>". On the other hand, if this were treated as an XPath *pattern*, as it would be in a template's `match` attribute, it would mean "match *any* <first> element which is a child of a <name> element, which is a child of the document root". A very subtle difference, to be sure.

Template Priority

In some cases, there will be more than one template in a document which matches a particular node. In these cases, XSLT has some rules which it uses to determine which template to call. For example, a more specific template has a higher priority than a less specific one. Consider the following two templates:

```
<xsl:template match="name">
```

```
<xsl:template match="name[.='John']">
```

A <name> element with any value other than "John" will match the first template, but not the second, so the first will be called. On the other hand, a <name> element with a value of "John" will match both templates, and in this case the XSLT engine will use the second one instead, because it is more specific.

If there is more than one template which could be instantiated for a node, and XSLT's rules give them the same priority, the `priority` attribute can be used to force one to be called over the other. (The XSLT engine will instantiate the template with the highest priority.)

The `name` attribute can be used to create a **named template**; that is, a template which you can explicitly call in your style sheet. Named templates will be discussed in a section of their own, later in the chapter.

The `mode` attribute can be used when the same section of the source tree must be processed more than once. Modes will also be discussed in a section of their own, later in the chapter.

<xsl:apply-templates>

The <xsl:apply-templates> element is used from within a template, to call other templates:

```
<xsl:apply-templates select="XPath expression"
    mode="mode name">
```

If the `select` attribute is specified, then the `XPath expression` specified will be evaluated, and the result will be used as the context node which other templates are then checked against. It is optional, though, so if it's not specified then the current context node will be used instead. The `mode` attribute works along with the `mode` attribute of the <xsl:template> element, so will be discussed in the section on **Modes** later on.

Try It Out – <xsl:apply-templates> in Action

We now have enough XSLT elements to create a rudimentary style sheet. For this example, we will create an XML document containing a list of names. Our style sheet will create a simple HTML document, and for each name encountered, it will output a paragraph with the text "name encountered".

This isn't really the type of processing you would probably do in the real world, but it will prepare us for some more complex transformations later in the chapter, and give us a chance to use the XSLT elements we've come across so far.

1. Here is our XML document, which you should save as `simple.xml`:

```
<?xml version="1.0"?>
<simple>
  <name>John</name>
  <name>David</name>
```

```
<name>Andrea</name>
<name>Ify</name>
<name>Chaulene</name>
<name>Cheryl</name>
<name>Shurnette</name>
<name>Mark</name>
<name>Carolyn</name>
<name>Agatha</name>
</simple>
```

2. Now, we'll create a style sheet for this XML. First, we'll need a template to create the main HTML elements. This template will match against the document root, and then call `<xsl:apply-templates>` to let other templates take care of processing the `<name>` elements:

```
<xsl:template match="/">
  <HTML>
  <HEAD><title>Sample XSLT Stylesheet</TITLE></HEAD>
  <BODY>
    <xsl:apply-templates/>
  </BODY>
  </HTML>
</xsl:template>
```

3. Then all we need is a template to process the `<name>` elements:

```
<xsl:template match="name">
  <P>Name encountered</P>
</xsl:template>
```

4. Combining these templates together, along with an `<xsl:stylesheet>` element, produces our XSLT style sheet in all its glory. Save this as `simple.xsl`:

```
<?xml version="1.0"?>
<xsl:stylesheet version="1.0" xmlns:xsl="http://www.w3.org/1999/XSL/Transform">
<xsl:template match="/">
  <HTML>
  <HEAD><TITLE>Sample XSLT Stylesheet</TITLE></HEAD>
  <BODY>
    <xsl:apply-templates/>
  </BODY>
  </HTML>
</xsl:template>

<xsl:template match="name">
  <P>Name encountered</P>
</xsl:template>
</xsl:stylesheet>
```

Okay, so it's not very exciting, and neither is the output. Running this through XT produces the following:

```
C:\>xt simple.xml simple.xsl
<HTML>
<HEAD>
<TITLE>Sample XSLT Stylesheet</TITLE>
</HEAD>
<BODY>
  <P>Name encountered</P>
  <P>Name encountered</P>
  <P>Name encountered</P>
  <P>Name encountered</P>
  <P>Name encountered</P>
  <P>Name encountered</P>
  <P>Name encountered</P>
  <P>Name encountered</P>
  <P>Name encountered</P>
  <P>Name encountered</P>
</BODY>
</HTML>
```

5. Remember that you can add a third parameter to XT to specify the output file. So running this again like so:

```
C:\>xt simple.xml simple.xsl simple.html
```

would produce a `simple.html` file, which would contain the result of the XSLT transformation.

XT doesn't care what you name the file; it doesn't affect the processing, so the file doesn't have to have an `html` extension. We could just as easily name the file `simple.xyz`.

6. Viewing this HTML in a browser will look something like this:

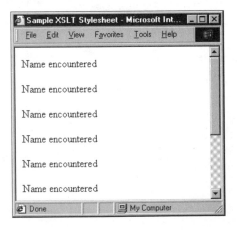

How It Works

After the XSL processor has loaded the XML document and the XSLT style sheet, it instantiates the template which matches the document root. This template outputs the `<HTML>`, `<HEAD>`, and `<BODY>` start-tags, and the `<TITLE>` element, and then comes across the `<xsl:apply-templates>`.

It then searches the source tree for further templates which can be run, and for each `<name>` element instantiates the second template. The second template simply outputs `"<P>Name encountered</P>"`. Once the XSLT processor has finished scanning for matching elements, it finishes outputting the `</BODY>` and `</HTML>` end-tags, and exits.

`<xsl:value-of>`

Okay, so the last style sheet was kind of boring. Now that we've got the basics for creating XSLT style sheets, it would be great if we could actually get them to do something useful with the information in our source tree. The `<xsl:value-of>` element is a good first-step in accomplishing this:

```
<xsl:value-of select="XPath expression"
    disable-output-escaping="yes or no"/>
```

The element is quite simple. It searches the context node for the value specified in the `select` attribute's *XPath expression*, and inserts it into the result tree. For example:

```
<xsl:value-of select=".">
```

inserts the PCDATA from the context node into the output, and:

```
<xsl:value-of select="customer/@id">
```

inserts the text from the `id` attribute of the `<customer>` element.

The `disable-output-escaping` attribute causes the XSLT processor to output "&" and "<" characters, instead of "`&amp;`" and "`&lt;`" escape sequences. Normally, the XSLT processor automatically escapes these characters for you if they make it into the output, but if you specify `disable-output-escaping` as "yes", then they won't. (The default is "no".) For example, if we have the following XML element:

```
<name>&amp;</name>
```

we have two options. This:

```
<xsl:value-of select="name" disable-output-escaping="no"/>
```

which produces:

&

and this:

```
<xsl:value-of select="name" disable-output-escaping="yes"/>
```

171

which produces:

&

Now that we can access the information in our source tree, let's make better use of our list of names. We'll modify the style sheet from the last Try It Out, so that in the second template each paragraph will contain the text from the <name> elements, instead of a simple string.

1. Open up `simple.xsl`, and change the second template to this:

```
<xsl:template match="name">
  <p><xsl:value-of select="."/></p>
</xsl:template>
```

2. Running the modified style sheet through XT produces the following:

```
C:\ >xt simple.xml simple.xsl
<HTML>
<HEAD>
<TITLE>Sample XSLT Stylesheet</TITLE>
</HEAD>
<BODY>
  <P>John</P>
  <P>David</P>
  <P>Andrea</P>
  <P>Ify</P>
  <P>Chaulene</P>
  <P>Cheryl</P>
  <P>Shurnette</P>
  <P>Mark</P>
  <P>Carolyn</P>
  <P>Agatha</P>
</BODY>
</HTML>
```

3. Viewing this in a browser will look something like this:

We've mentioned that XSLT can output XML, or HTML, or even plain text. The <xsl:output> element allows us to specify the method we'll be using, and also gives us much more control over the way our output is created. If it is included in a style sheet, it must be a direct child of the <xsl:stylesheet> element. In XSLT, elements which must be direct children of <xsl:stylesheet> are called **top-level** elements. The syntax of <xsl:output> is as follows:

```
<xsl:output method="xml or html or text"
    version="version"
    encoding="encoding"
    omit-xml-declaration="yes or no"
    standalone="yes or no"
    cdata-section-elements="CDATA sections"
    indent="yes or no"/>
```

The method attribute specifies which type of output is being produced:

❑ XML

❑ HTML

❑ Text

❑ Some other method (the XSLT specification says that XSL processors are free to define other types for the method attribute, which they can use for other output methods)

If the <xsl:output> element is not included, and the root element in the result tree is <HTML> (in upper or lowercase), then the default output method is "html"; otherwise, the default output method is "xml". When the method attribute is specified as "html", the XSL processor can do things like changing "<BR/>" in the style sheet to "<BR>" in the result tree, since HTML browsers expect the <BR> tag to be written like that.

The version, encoding, and standalone attributes can be used when the output method is "xml". Values specified for these attributes will be used to create the XML declaration for the result tree. However, the XSLT specification states that the value used for the encoding attribute is the *preferred* encoding to use for the result tree; the XSL processor is free to ignore this attribute if it doesn't understand the desired encoding. For example, if the following is used in XT:

```
<xsl:output method="xml" version="1.0" encoding="windows-1252" standalone="yes"/>
```

the actual XML declaration will end up looking like this instead:

```
<?xml version="1.0" encoding="utf-8" standalone="yes"?>
```

since XT ignores the encoding, and all documents are output from XT in UTF-8.

omit-xml-declaration, as its name implies, can be used when outputting XML if the XML declaration is or is not wanted, for whatever reason. (For example, if you knew that the output of your transformation was going to be inserted as part of a larger XML document, you would want to make sure you didn't output the XML declaration, so that you wouldn't end up with two XML declarations in the final document.) The default is "no" when the output method is "xml", meaning that the XML declaration *will* appear in the result tree.

173

The indent attribute can be used to specify some formatting to be used for the result tree. If it is specified with a value of "yes", the XSL processor is allowed to add extra white space to the result tree, for "pretty printing". For example, in the previous chapter we had the following XSLT style sheet, where we specified the `<xsl:output>` element with indent set to "yes".

```xml
<?xml version="1.0"?>
<xsl:stylesheet version="1.0" xmlns:xsl="http://www.w3.org/1999/XSL/Transform">
<xsl:output method="xml" indent="yes"/>

<xsl:template match="/">
  <order>
    <date>
      <xsl:value-of select="/order/date/year"/>/<xsl:value-of
      select="/order/date/month"/>/<xsl:value-of select="/order/date/day"/>
    </date>
    <customer>Company A</customer>
    <item>
      <xsl:apply-templates select="/order/item"/>
      <quantity><xsl:value-of select="/order/quantity"/></quantity>
    </item>
  </order>
</xsl:template>

<xsl:template match="item">
  <part-number>
    <xsl:choose>
      <xsl:when test=". = 'Production-Class Widget'">E16-25A</xsl:when>
      <xsl:when test=". = 'Economy-Class Widget'">E16-25B</xsl:when>
      <!--other part-numbers would go here-->
      <xsl:otherwise>00</xsl:otherwise>
    </xsl:choose>
  </part-number>
  <description><xsl:value-of select="."/></description>
</xsl:template>
</xsl:stylesheet>
```

The result of that transformation was:

```xml
<?xml version="1.0" encoding="utf-8"?>
<order>
<date>2000/1/13</date>
<customer>Company A</customer>
<item>
<part-number>E16-25A</part-number>
<description>Production-Class Widget</description>
<quantity>16</quantity>
</item>
</order>
```

If we had left out the `<xsl:output>` element or set indent to "no", our output would have looked like this instead:

```
C:\>xt order.xml order.xsl
<?xml version="1.0" encoding="utf-8"?>
<order><date>2000/1/13</date><customer>Company A</customer><item><part-number>E16
-25A</part-number><description>Production-Class Widget</description><quantity>16
</quantity></item></order>
```

As far as any application is concerned these documents are the same. However, if a human will be reading the output, then the extra new lines are very helpful. The XSLT specification gives a lot of leeway when it comes to the `indent` attribute, so different XSL processors may output the result tree differently when it is set to `"yes"`, but in most cases, if not all, it will still be easier to read by a human.

The `cdata-section-elements` attribute specifies any elements in the result tree which should be output using CDATA sections. For example, if `cdata-section-elements` has a value of `"customer"`, and the style sheet contains an element like this:

```
<customer>A&amp;P</customer>
```

or like this:

```
<customer><![CDATA[A&P]]></customer>
```

then the output will always look like this:

```
<customer><![CDATA[A&P]]></customer>
```

Note that the version of XT used for this book (version 19991105) ignored the `cdata-section-element` attribute, so if you are using XT to try the examples out, you may not get the results expected. However, the output will always be escaped somehow, so that the XML created is well-formed.

<xsl:element>

We've already seen how to insert elements directly into the result tree, but what if we don't know ahead of time what elements we're creating? That is, what if the names of the elements which go into the result tree depend on the contents of the source tree?

The `<xsl:element>` element allows us to dynamically create elements:

```
<xsl:element name="element name"
    use-attribute-sets="attribute set names">
```

The `name` attribute specifies the name of the element. So the following:

```
<xsl:element name="blah">My text</xsl:element>
```

will produce an element like this in the result tree:

```
<blah>My text</blah>
```

Of course, this isn't very exciting, nor dynamic. We could have done the same thing by simply writing that `<blah>` element into the style sheet manually, and with less typing. The exciting and dynamic part comes into play when we change the `name` attribute like so:

```
<xsl:element name="{.}">My text</xsl:element>
```

Anything inserted into those curly braces gets evaluated as an XPath expression! In this case, we will create an element, and give it the name from the value from the context node. That is, if we have a template like this:

```
<xsl:template match="name">
  <xsl:element name="{.}">My text</xsl:element>
</xsl:template>
```

then running it against:

```
<name>Andrea</name>
```

will produce:

\<Andrea\>My text\</Andrea\>

and running it against:

```
<name>Ify</name>
```

will produce:

\<Ify\>My text\</Ify\>

We'll revisit the `use-attribute-sets` attribute in the next section. First let's have a look at another example.

Try It Out – <xsl:element> in Action

To demonstrate `<xsl:element>`, let's take an XML document which uses attributes exclusively for its information, and transform it to one which uses elements instead.

1. Save the following XML as `people.xml`:

```
<?xml version="1.0"?>
<people>
  <name first="John" middle="Fitzgerald Johansen" last="Doe"/>
  <name first="Franklin" middle="D." last="Roosevelt"/>
  <name first="Alfred" middle="E." last="Neuman"/>
  <name first="John" middle="Q." last="Public"/>
  <name first="Jane" middle="" last="Doe"/>
</people>
```

Now let's create an XSLT style sheet which can convert all of those attributes to elements.

2. The first step is our template to match against the document root. This template can output the root `<people>` element, and then call `<xsl:apply-templates>` to match any further elements:

```
<xsl:template match="/">
  <people>
    <xsl:apply-templates select="/people/name"/>
  </people>
</xsl:template>
```

3. We then need to take care of those `<name>` elements. To do this, we can create a template to output the new `<name>` element, and then call `<xsl:apply-templates>` to take care of all of the attributes:

```
<xsl:template match="name">
  <name>
    <xsl:apply-templates select="@*"/>
  </name>
</xsl:template>
```

4. And finally, we need a template to process those attributes. For each attribute encountered, an element with the same name and same value should be output. This template will do the trick:

```
<xsl:template match="@*">
  <xsl:element name="{name()}"><xsl:value-of select="."/></xsl:element>
</xsl:template>
```

5. Combining these templates together produces the following style sheet, which you should save as `people.xsl`:

```
<?xml version="1.0"?>
<xsl:stylesheet version="1.0" xmlns:xsl="http://www.w3.org/1999/XSL/Transform">
<xsl:output method="xml" indent="yes"/>

<xsl:template match="/">
  <people>
    <xsl:apply-templates select="/people/name"/>
  </people>
</xsl:template>

<xsl:template match="name">
  <name>
    <xsl:apply-templates select="@*"/>
  </name>
</xsl:template>

<xsl:template match="@*">
  <xsl:element name="{name()}"><xsl:value-of select="."/></xsl:element>
</xsl:template>
</xsl:stylesheet>
```

6. Running it through XT produces the following:

```
C:\>xt people.xml people.xsl
<?xml version="1.0" encoding="utf-8"?>
<people>
<name>
<first>John</first>
<middle>Fitzgerald Johansen</middle>
<last>Doe</last>
</name>
<name>
<first>Franklin</first>
<middle>D.</middle>
<last>Roosevelt</last>
</name>
<name>
<first>Alfred</first>
<middle>E.</middle>
<last>Neuman</last>
</name>
<name>
<first>John</first>
<middle>Q.</middle>
<last>Public</last>
</name>
<name>
<first>Jane</first>
<middle/>
<last>Doe</last>
</name>
</people>
```

<xsl:attribute> and <xsl:attribute-set>

Similar to `<xsl:element>`, `<xsl:attribute>` can be used to dynamically add an attribute to an element in the result tree:

```
<xsl:attribute name="attribute name">
```

It works in exactly the same way, with the `name` attribute specifying the name of the attribute, and the text inside the `<xsl:attribute>` element specifying its value. For example:

```
<name><xsl:attribute name="id">213</xsl:attribute>Chaulene</name>
```

will produce the following in the result tree:

```
<name id="213">Chaulene</name>
```

and:

```
<name><xsl:attribute name="{.}">213</xsl:attribute>Chaulene</name>
```

will do the same, but the name of the attribute will be the text of the context node.

Note that <xsl:attribute> must come before any PCDATA of the element to which it is being appended. So if we rewrote the above XSLT like this:

```
<name>Chaulene<xsl:attribute name="{.}">213</xsl:attribute></name>
```

the attribute wouldn't get appended to the <name> element. (XT simply ignores the attribute in this case. Other processors may treat the error differently.) In fact, what we are trying to do in this case is to create an attribute on the PCDATA, not on the <name> element, which is not possible.

Related Groups of Attributes

An <xsl:attribute-set> is a handy shortcut for a related group of attributes that always go together:

```
<xsl:attribute-set name="name of att set"
    use-attribute-sets="att set names">
```

For example, if we have an id attribute and a size attribute, we can define an attribute set as follows:

```
<xsl:attribute-set name="IdSize">
  <xsl:attribute name="id">213</xsl:attribute>
  <xsl:attribute name="size">123</xsl:attribute>
</xsl:attribute-set>
```

which will append an id with a value of "213" and a size with a value of "123" to any element which uses this attribute set. Or we can define the attribute set like this:

```
<xsl:attribute-set name="IdSize">
  <xsl:attribute name="{.}">123</xsl:attribute>
  <xsl:attribute name="size"><xsl:value-of select="."/></xsl:attribute>
</xsl:attribute-set>
```

which will append one attribute with the same name as the text of the context node, and a value of "123", and another value with the name size, and the value of the text of the context node.

This attribute set can then be appended to elements in the result tree by using the use-attribute-sets attribute of <xsl:element>. Notice also that attribute sets can use other attribute sets, since <xsl:attribute-set> also has a use-attribute-sets attribute!

Try It Out – Attributes and Attribute Sets in Action

Just for fun, let's take an XML document which uses no attributes, and transform it back to a format which uses attributes exclusively for its information.

1. Save the following document as `people.xml`:

```xml
<?xml version="1.0"?>
<people>
  <name>
    <first>John</first>
    <middle>Fitzgerald Johansen</middle>
    <last>Doe</last>
  </name>
  <name>
    <first>Franklin</first>
    <middle>D.</middle>
    <last>Roosevelt</last>
  </name>
  <name>
    <first>Alfred</first>
    <middle>E.</middle>
    <last>Neuman</last>
  </name>
  <name>
    <first>John</first>
    <middle>Q.</middle>
    <last>Public</last>
  </name>
  <name>
    <first>Jane</first>
    <middle></middle>
    <last>Doe</last>
  </name>
</people>
```

2. For our style sheet, the first template will simply match against the document root and output the `<people>` tag, like our previous templates. But our second template, to take care of the `<name>` elements, is different:

```xml
<xsl:template match="//name">
  <xsl:element name="name" use-attribute-sets="NameAttributes"/>
</xsl:template>
```

It creates a `<name>` element, and then uses an attribute set for the rest of the information.

3. The last piece we need is that attribute set:

```xml
<xsl:attribute-set name="NameAttributes">
  <xsl:attribute name="first"><xsl:value-of select="first"/></xsl:attribute>
  <xsl:attribute name="middle"><xsl:value-of select="middle"/></xsl:attribute>
  <xsl:attribute name="last"><xsl:value-of select="last"/></xsl:attribute>
</xsl:attribute-set>
```

4. And here is the whole XSLT style sheet, which you should save as `people.xsl`, that will do the transformation for us:

```
<?xml version="1.0"?>
<xsl:stylesheet version="1.0" xmlns:xsl="http://www.w3.org/1999/XSL/Transform">
  <xsl:template match="/">
    <people>
      <xsl:apply-templates/>
    </people>
  </xsl:template>

  <xsl:template match="//name">
    <xsl:element name="name" use-attribute-sets="NameAttributes"/>
  </xsl:template>

  <xsl:attribute-set name="NameAttributes">
    <xsl:attribute name="first"><xsl:value-of select="first"/></xsl:attribute>
    <xsl:attribute name="middle"><xsl:value-of select="middle"/></xsl:attribute>
    <xsl:attribute name="last"><xsl:value-of select="last"/></xsl:attribute>
  </xsl:attribute-set>
</xsl:stylesheet>
```

5. Running that through XT produces the following:

```
C:\>xt people.xml people.xsl
<?xml version="1.0" encoding="utf-8"?>
<people>
  <name first="John" middle="Fitzgerald Johansen" last="Doe"/>
  <name first="Franklin" middle="D." last="Roosevelt"/>
  <name first="Alfred" middle="E." last="Neuman"/>
  <name first="John" middle="Q." last="Public"/>
  <name first="Jane" middle="" last="Doe"/>
</people>
```

<xsl:text>

The `<xsl:text>` element, as its name implies, simply inserts some text (PCDATA) into the result tree.

```
<xsl:text disable-output-escaping="yes or no">
```

Much of the time the `<xsl:text>` element isn't needed, since you can just insert text directly, but there are two reasons you may sometimes want to use it: it preserves all white space, and you can disable output escaping.

We've already seen the `disable-output-escaping` attribute, in the `<xsl:value-of>` element. We do the same when inserting normal text into the document by using `<xsl:text>` like this:

```
<xsl:text disable-output-escaping="yes">6 is &lt; 7 &amp; 7 > 6</xsl:text>
```

The text which is inserted into the result tree will look like this:

6 is < 7 & 7 > 6

(Notice that we still had to escape the characters in the XSLT style sheet. Remember, no matter what you want the output to look like, your style sheet is XML, and must be well-formed.)

The other advantage is that all white space in the `<xsl:text>` element is preserved. To see why this is important, consider the following:

```
<xsl:value-of select="'John'"/> <xsl:value-of select="'Fitzgerald Johansen'"/>
<xsl:value-of select="'Doe'"/>
```

You might expect that to produce:

John Fitzgerald Johansen Doe

However, it will actually produce:

JohnFitzgerald JohansenDoe

because the spaces between the `<xsl:value-of>` elements are stripped out by the XSLT processor. (The space in the text "Fitzgerald Johansen" is preserved, however.) If we were to insert something like this in between each one:

```
<xsl:text> </xsl:text>
```

then a space would be inserted, since the space in `<xsl:text>` is preserved.

`<xsl:text>` can only have PCDATA for its content; it can not contain other XSLT elements.

Conditional Processing with `<xsl:if>` and `<xsl:choose>`

Every programming language in the world has to let you make choices in your code, or else it wouldn't be very useful. XSLT is no exception, and it allows us a couple of ways to make choices: `<xsl:if>` and `<xsl:choose>`:

```
<xsl:if test="Boolean expression">
```

```
<xsl:choose>
  <xsl:when test="Boolean expression">
  <xsl:when test="Boolean expression">
  <xsl:otherwise>
</xsl:choose>
```

For both `<xsl:if>` and `<xsl:choose>`, the Boolean expression is simply an XPath expression which is converted to a Boolean value. (It is converted using the same rules as the `boolean()` function, discussed in Chapter 4.)

`<xsl:if>` is the simpler of the two conditional processing constructs. It evaluates the expression in the `test` attribute, and if it is true the contents of the `<xsl:if>` element are evaluated. If the test expression is not true, the contents of `<xsl:if>` are not evaluated. For example, consider the following:

```
<xsl:if test="name">Name encountered.</xsl:if>
```

If there is a `<name>` element which is a child of the context node, then the text "`Name encountered.`" will be inserted into the result tree. If there is no `<name>` child of the context node, then nothing will happen.

> *Note that `<xsl:if>` does not change the context node, the way a template `match` does. That is, even though the `test` expression evaluated as `true`, and we entered the `<xsl:if>` element, `<name>` is not the context node; the context node is still whatever it was before we evaluated the `test` expression.*

`<xsl:choose>` provides a bit more flexibility than `<xsl:if>`. It allows us to make any one of a number of choices, and even allows for a "default" choice, if desired. For example:

```
<xsl:choose>
    <xsl:when test="number[. &gt; 2000]">A big number</xsl:when>
    <xsl:when test="number[. &gt; 1000]">A medium number</xsl:when>
    <xsl:otherwise>A small number</xsl:otherwise>
</xsl:choose>
```

If the `<number>` element contains a numeric value which is greater than 2,000, then the string "`A big number`" will be inserted into the result tree. If the number is greater than 1,000, the string "`A medium number`" will be inserted, and in any other case the string "`A small number`" will be inserted.

> *Notice that we escaped the "`>`" signs using "`&gt;`". This isn't strictly necessary, since "`>`" characters are allowed in XML; however, "`<`" characters are not, and this often trips people up when writing style sheets. Many people consider it a good practice to always escape both "`>`" and "`<`" characters, just to be consistent.*

Note that for the `<xsl:otherwise>` to be evaluated, any of the following could be true:

❑ `<number>` could contain a numeric value, which is less than 1,000

❑ `<number>` could contain text, instead of a numeric value

❑ There could be no `<number>` node where we specified it in our test expression

That is, none of the other tests in the style sheet can pass the `test` attribute, for any reason.

In an `<xsl:choose>`, as soon as one of the test expressions evaluates to `true`, control leaves the `<xsl:choose>`. So if two of the `<xsl:when>` test expressions evaluate to `true`, then only the first one will be evaluated, and control will leave the `<xsl:choose>` without evaluating the second `<xsl:when>`. If we had written our example like this instead:

```
<xsl:choose>
  <xsl:when test="/numbers/number[. > 1000]">A medium number</xsl:when>
  <xsl:when test="/numbers/number[. > 2000]">A big number</xsl:when>
  <xsl:otherwise>A small number</xsl:otherwise>
</xsl:choose>
```

then the second `<xsl:when>` would never get called, since any numbers which are greater than 1,000 would cause the first `<xsl:when>` to be true.

The `<xsl:otherwise>` is not mandatory in an `<xsl:choose>`. If it is not included, and none of the `<xsl:when>` test expressions evaluate to true, then control will leave the `<xsl:choose>` without inserting anything into the result tree.

Try It Out – Conditional Processing in Action

Let's imagine that we have a database of a company's employee information. The database can return the information in XML form, like so:

```
<?xml version="1.0"?>
<employee FullSecurity="1">
  <name>John Doe</name>
  <department>Widget Sales</department>
  <phone>(555)555-5555<extension>2974</extension></phone>
  <salary>62,000</salary>
  <area>3</area>
</employee>
```

The FullSecurity attribute is determined by the ID of the user requesting the information: "1" indicates a member of H.R., who has access to the salary information, and "0" indicates someone who has no such access. (A truly poor use of security, but very helpful for demonstrating conditional processing.)

The company is broken down into various physical locations, so the `<area>` element tells us which physical location this employee is stationed at.

1. We don't have an actual database, so we'll just save the above XML as employee.xml, and pretend that it came from a database; (we'll be looking at this for real in Chapter 13).

2. Now let's create an HTML document which can display this employee's information. Our first template will do most of the work in creating this document; it will create the HTML layout, and insert the values for all of our information except for the phone number and the area. It will also determine if it is allowed to insert the salary, depending on the security.

```
<xsl:template match="/">
  <HTML>
  <HEAD>
  <TITLE><xsl:value-of select="/employee/name"/></TITLE>
  </HEAD>
  <BODY>
  <H1>Employee: <xsl:value-of select="/employee/name"/></H1>
```

```
    <P>Department: <xsl:value-of select="/employee/department"/></P>
    <P><xsl:apply-templates select="/employee/phone"/></P>
    <xsl:if test="number(/employee/@FullSecurity)">
      <P>Salary: <xsl:value-of select="/employee/salary"/></P>
    </xsl:if>
    <P>Location: <xsl:apply-templates select="/employee/area"/></P>
    </BODY>
    </HTML>
  </xsl:template>
```

Most of this is pretty easy to us by now, so the only portion of the code we've highlighted is the section that determines whether we can output the salary. The value of the FullSecurity attribute is just text, so we have to first convert it to a number, using the number() XPath function. (If we didn't, and XPath treated the value of this attribute like a string, then *any* value with one character or more would cause it to evaluate to true. And that's not what we want.) Then, since the test attribute expects a Boolean value, it converts that number to true or false. In our case, we have decided to set FullSecurity to either 1 (which evaluates to true in XPath), or 0 (which evaluates to false).

3. Because the phone number is a little more complex, we'll create a simple template to process just that:

```
<xsl:template match="phone">
  Phone: <xsl:value-of select="text()"/> x<xsl:value-of select="extension"/>
</xsl:template>
```

Notice that the first <xsl:value-of> must have its select attribute set to "text()", instead of ".". Otherwise, the extension would have been printed out twice; once from the first <xsl:value-of>, and again from the second, since it is a child of <phone>.

4. And finally, we need a template to take care of that <area> element. It needs to decide where this employee is located, based on the value in the XML document. We can use <xsl:choose> to do that, like this:

```
<xsl:template match="area">
  <xsl:choose>
    <xsl:when test=". = '1'">Toronto</xsl:when>
    <xsl:when test=". = '2'">London</xsl:when>
    <xsl:when test=". = '3'">New York</xsl:when>
    <xsl:when test=". = '4'">Tokyo</xsl:when>
    <xsl:otherwise>Unknown Location</xsl:otherwise>
  </xsl:choose>
</xsl:template>
```

5. Save the final style sheet as employee.xsl, which will look like this:

```
<?xml version="1.0"?>
<xsl:stylesheet version="1.0" xmlns:xsl="http://www.w3.org/1999/XSL/Transform">
<xsl:template match="/">
  <HTML>
  <HEAD>
```

```
        <TITLE><xsl:value-of select="/employee/name"/></TITLE>
        </HEAD>
        <BODY>
        <H1>Employee: <xsl:value-of select="/employee/name"/></H1>
        <P>Department: <xsl:value-of select="/employee/department"/></P>
        <P><xsl:apply-templates select="/employee/phone"/></P>
        <xsl:if test="number(/employee/@FullSecurity)">
          <P>Salary: <xsl:value-of select="/employee/salary"/></P>
        </xsl:if>
        <P>Location: <xsl:apply-templates select="/employee/area"/></P>
        </BODY>
        </HTML>
      </xsl:template>

      <xsl:template match="phone">
        Phone: <xsl:value-of select="text()"/> x<xsl:value-of select="extension"/>
      </xsl:template>

      <xsl:template match="area">
        <xsl:choose>
          <xsl:when test="number(.) = 1">Toronto</xsl:when>
          <xsl:when test="number(.) = 2">London</xsl:when>
          <xsl:when test="number(.) = 3">New York</xsl:when>
          <xsl:when test="number(.) = 4">Tokyo</xsl:when>
          <xsl:otherwise>Unknown Location</xsl:otherwise>
        </xsl:choose>
      </xsl:template>
    </xsl:stylesheet>
```

6. When XT is run against the XML above, this style sheet produces the following HTML:

```
C:\>xt employee.xml employee.xsl
<HTML>
<HEAD>
<TITLE>John Doe</TITLE>
</HEAD>
<BODY>
<H1>Employee: John Doe</H1>
<P>Department: Widget Sales</P>
<P>
  Phone: (555)555-5555 x2974</P>
<P>Salary: 62,000</P>
<P>Location: New York</P>
</BODY>
</HTML>
```

which looks like this in a web browser:

7. Now change the FullSecurity attribute to "0", and the <area> element to "1", and re-run the transformation. The HTML will be changed to this:

```
C:\>xt employee.xml employee.xsl
<HTML>
<HEAD>
<TITLE>John Doe</TITLE>
</HEAD>
<BODY>
<H1>Employee: John Doe</H1>
<P>Department: Widget Sales</P>
<P>
  Phone: (555)555-5555 x2974</P>
<P>Location: Toronto</P>
</BODY>
</HTML>
```

which looks like this in a browser:

<xsl:for-each>

In many cases there is some specific processing that we want to do for a number of nodes in the source tree. For example, in the Try It Out section which demonstrated <xsl:element>, we had processing that we needed to do for every <name> element.

So far we've been handling this by creating a new template to do that processing, and then inserting an <xsl:apply-templates> element where we wanted that template instantiated from. But there is an alternative way to do this kind of processing, using <xsl:for-each>:

```
<xsl:for-each select="XPath expression">
```

The contents of <xsl:for-each> form a template-within-a-template; it is instantiated for any node matching the XPath expression in the select attribute. For example, consider the following:

```
<xsl:for-each select="name">
  This is a name element.
</xsl:for-each>
```

This "template" will be instantiated for every <name> element which is a child of the context node. In this case, all the template does is output the text "This is a name element.".

Because <xsl:for-each> is a template, it also changes the context node, as does a regular template. For example, consider the following XML:

```
<names>
  <name>
    <first>John</first>
    <last>Doe</last>
  </name>
  <name>
    <first>Jane</first>
    <last>Smith</last>
  </name>
</names>
```

We could create HTML paragraphs for each <first> element, using a template like this:

```
<xsl:template match="names">
  <xsl:for-each select="name">
    <P><xsl:value-of select="first"/></P>
  </xsl:for-each>
</xsl:template>
```

When the template is instantiated, the context node is changed to the <names> element. So our <xsl:for-each> element need only specify <name> in the select attribute, as it's a child of this new context node. Then, inside the <xsl:for-each>, the context node is changed again, to <name>. So the select attribute of the <xsl:value-of> only needs to specify the <first> element, as it's a child of this new context node.

Try It Out – <xsl:for-each> in Action

To demonstrate <xsl:for-each>, let's re-write the earlier style sheet which transformed an attributes-only document to an elements-only document. The original style sheet was this:

```
<?xml version="1.0"?>
<xsl:stylesheet version="1.0" xmlns:xsl="http://www.w3.org/1999/XSL/Transform">
<xsl:output method="xml" indent="yes"/>

<xsl:template match="/">
  <people>
    <xsl:apply-templates select="/people/name"/>
  </people>
</xsl:template>

<xsl:template match="name">
  <name>
    <xsl:apply-templates select="@*"/>
  </name>
</xsl:template>
```

```
<xsl:template match="@*">
  <xsl:element name="{name()}"><xsl:value-of select="."/></xsl:element>
</xsl:template>
</xsl:stylesheet>
```

1. And here it is again, with the changes highlighted. Save this as `people2.xsl`:

```
<?xml version="1.0"?>
<xsl:stylesheet version="1.0" xmlns:xsl="http://www.w3.org/1999/XSL/Transform">
<xsl:template match="/">
  <people>
    <xsl:for-each select="/people/name">
      <name>
        <xsl:apply-templates select="@*"/>
      </name>
    </xsl:for-each>
  </people>
</xsl:template>

<xsl:template match="@*">
  <xsl:element name="{name()}"><xsl:value-of select="."/></xsl:element>
</xsl:template>
</xsl:stylesheet>
```

2. Running this style sheet through XT produces the same results as the previous version:

```
C:\>xt people.xml people2.xsl
<?xml version="1.0" encoding="utf-8"?>
<people>
<name>
<first>John</first>
<middle>Fitzgerald Johansen</middle>
<last>Doe</last>
</name>
<name>
<first>Franklin</first>
<middle>D.</middle>
<last>Roosevelt</last>
</name>
<name>
<first>Alfred</first>
<middle>E.</middle>
<last>Neuman</last>
</name>
<name>
<first>John</first>
<middle>Q.</middle>
<last>Public</last>
</name>
<name>
<first>Jane</first>
```

```
<middle/>
<last>Doe</last>
</name>
</people>
```

How It Works

This style sheet seems a lot simpler than the first one. For one thing, we now only have two templates, instead of three, since the template which was used for <name> elements has now been moved up into the first template.

If we look closely at the <xsl:for-each>, which is highlighted in the code, we might notice that the contents are exactly the same as the template we replaced.

Remember, for all intents and purposes <xsl:for-each> is a template. The only difference between using <xsl:for-each> and <xsl:template> is that <xsl:for-each> can be inserted into other templates, whereas <xsl:template> must stand on its own.

<xsl:copy-of>

In many cases the result tree from our XSLT style sheets will be very similar to the source tree. Perhaps there will even be large sections which are exactly the same.

The <xsl:copy-of> element allows us to take sections of the source tree and copy them to the result tree. This is much easier than having to create all of the elements/attributes manually, and then copying the values using <xsl:value-of>, especially if we don't know ahead of time what the source tree will look like. The syntax is as shown:

```
<xsl:copy-of select="XPath expression"/>
```

The element is quite easy to use. The select attribute simply specifies an XPath expression pointing to the node or node-set required, and that node or node-set is inserted directly into the result tree, along with any attributes or child elements.

Try It Out – <xsl:copy-of> in Action

As a simple example of <xsl:copy-of>, let's re-examine our employee XML. We've already seen how to use the FullSecurity attribute to specify when to include the information from our <salary> element when creating HTML output. But what if we have another application that needs to use the raw XML, and we can't trust it to do the right thing with our security? It would be better to create an XSLT style sheet which will remove <salary>, under the right conditions. So let's create one.

1. If you don't still have it, recreate the original employee XML, and save it as employee.xml:

```
<?xml version="1.0"?>
<employee FullSecurity="1">
  <name>John Doe</name>
  <department>Widget Sales</department>
  <phone>(555)555-5555<extension>2974</extension></phone>
  <salary>62,000</salary>
  <area>3</area>
</employee>
```

2. Now enter the following, and save it as `employee2.xsl`:

```
<?xml version="1.0"?>
<xsl:stylesheet version="1.0" xmlns:xsl="http://www.w3.org/1999/XSL/Transform">
<xsl:output method="xml" indent="yes"/>

<xsl:template match="/">
  <xsl:choose>
    <xsl:when test="number(/employee/@FullSecurity)">
      <xsl:copy-of select="/"/>
    </xsl:when>
    <xsl:otherwise>
      <employee FullSecurity="{/employee/@FullSecurity}">
        <xsl:for-each select="employee/*[not(self::salary)]">
          <xsl:copy-of select="."/>
        </xsl:for-each>
      </employee>
    </xsl:otherwise>
  </xsl:choose>
</xsl:template>
</xsl:stylesheet>
```

3. When `FullSecurity` is "1", as above, the output is as follows:

```
C:\>xt employee.xml employee.xsl
<?xml version="1.0" encoding="utf-8"?>
<employee FullSecurity="1">
 <name>John Doe</name>
 <department>Widget Sales</department>
 <phone>(555)555-5555<extension>2974</extension></phone>
 <salary>62,000</salary>
 <area>3</area>
</employee>
```

4. Now change `FullSecurity` to "0", and resave the XML. The new result is as follows:

```
C:\>xt employee.xml employee2.xsl
<?xml version="1.0" encoding="utf-8"?>
<employee FullSecurity="0">
<name>John Doe</name>
<department>Widget Sales</department>
<phone>(555)555-5555<extension>2974</extension>
</phone>
<area>3</area>
</employee>
```

How It Works

The first thing our template does is to check the `FullSecurity` attribute. If it's `true`, we call
`<xsl:copy-of>` with the `select` attribute set to "/". This copies the entire document root, including
all of its children and attributes, to the result tree.

However, if the attribute is `false`, we need to copy all of the nodes except for the `<salary>` element to the result tree. This is done using the `<xsl:for-each>` element, to loop through all of the child elements of the `<employee>` element that are not the `<salary>` element. (If you look at the `select` attribute, it selects all children of the `<employee>` element, using "employee/*". But it then further filters that, to select only the ones that aren't `<salary>`, using "[not(self::salary)]".)

Each of these nodes is then copied to the result tree using `<xsl:copy-of>`.

`<xsl:copy>`

Similar to `<xsl:copy-of>` is the `<xsl:copy>` element. It allows much more flexibility when copying sections of the source tree to the result tree:

```
<xsl:copy use-attribute-sets="att set names">
```

Instead of providing a `select` attribute, to indicate which section of the source tree to copy, `<xsl:copy>` simply copies the context node. And, unlike the `<xsl:copy-of>` construct, children and attributes of the context node are not automatically copied to the result tree. However, the contents of the `<xsl:copy>` element provide a template where you specify the attributes and children of the node which will go into the result tree. For example, if we have our good old `<name>` XML:

```
<name>
  <first>John</first>
  <middle>Fitzgerald Johansen</middle>
  <last>Doe</last>
</name>
```

We could create a template that looked like this:

```
<xsl:template match="name">
  <xsl:copy/>
</xsl:template>
```

The output of this, from XT, would be:

```
<name/>
```

since none of the children would be copied. However, we could modify the template to look like this:

```
<xsl:template match="name">
  <xsl:copy>
    <blah><xsl:value-of select="."/></blah>
  </xsl:copy>
</xsl:template>
```

in which case the output would look like this:

```
<name><blah>
 John
 Fitzgerald Johansen
 Doe
</blah></name>
```

Remember, when you use ". "for the `select` *attribute in* `<xsl:value-of>`, *you get the contents of the context node* plus *any descendants.*

What we have done in the second example is to copy the context node, which in this case is the `<name>` element, created a child element called `<blah>`, and populated it with the text from `<name>` and its children.

Try It Out – <xsl:copy> in Action

Let's redo the style sheet from the last Try It Out, using `<xsl:copy>` instead of `<xsl:copy-of>`, and using a fancy methodology called **recursion**.

Recursion is a method whereby a function can call itself, which can then call itself again, etc. Of course, in the case of XSLT, instead of creating a recursive *function*, we would create recursive *templates*. These recursive templates are used quite a lot in XSLT, so it would be a good idea to start learning about them.

1. Since the best way to understand recursion is to see it in action, let's create the main template for this style sheet:

```
<xsl:template match="/ | * | @*">
  <xsl:copy>
    <xsl:apply-templates select="* | @* | text()"/>
  </xsl:copy>
</xsl:template>
```

This template applies to the document root, as well as any elements, and any attributes. When an XSL processor starts going through the source tree, it will match the document root against this template. It will then be copied to the result tree, from the `<xsl:copy>`, and `<xsl:apply-templates>` will be called.

The XSL processor will then look through the source tree for further nodes, and when it finds any element or attribute, it will match against this template again. The new node will also be copied to the result tree, `<xsl:apply-templates>` will be called again, and any elements and attributes which are found will once more match against this template.

The template will keep getting called until it processes a node which doesn't have any child elements or attributes. Then it will return up the recursion tree and find further nodes to process, until it has processed all elements and attributes. (Because of the built-in template for text nodes we mentioned earlier, the XSLT engine will automatically add the text nodes' contents to the result tree.)

2. As we can see, if we were to just put this one template in our style sheet, all elements and attributes would be copied to the result tree, as is, every time. However, we need to keep that `<salary>` element from being copied when FullSecurity is false. In order to do that, we can create a second template, which will match against this specific case:

```
<xsl:template match="employee[not(number(@FullSecurity))]/salary">
  <!--do not process this node-->
</xsl:template>
```

To explain that `match` attribute further, the template matches any `<salary>` element, if the `FullSecurity` attribute of the `<employee>` element is `false`. And, since the template doesn't do anything, the node is not processed. We could also have accomplished this by simply using an empty element, like this:

```
<xsl:template match="employee[not(number(@FullSecurity))]/salary"/>
```

However, with the comment included in our version things are clearer.

In the case where `FullSecurity` is `false`, the `<salary>` element matches both templates. However, one of the rules we mentioned earlier is that the most explicit match wins. In this case, our first template matches against any element, whereas the second matches against this specific element, so the second one wins.

3. Putting it all together produces the following style sheet, which you should save as `employee3.xsl`:

```
<?xml version="1.0"?>
<xsl:stylesheet version="1.0" xmlns:xsl="http://www.w3.org/1999/XSL/Transform">
<xsl:template match="/ | * | @*">
  <xsl:copy>
    <xsl:apply-templates select="* | @* | text()"/>
</xsl:copy>
</xsl:template>

<xsl:template match="employee[not(number(@FullSecurity))]/salary">
  <!--do not process this node-->
</xsl:template>
</xsl:stylesheet>
```

4. Make sure the `FullSecurity` attribute in your XML is "1", and then run it through XT. The results should look like this:

```
C:\>xt employee.xml employee3.xsl
<?xml version="1.0" encoding="utf-8"?>
<employee FullSecurity="1">
 <name>John Doe</name>
 <department>Widget Sales</department>
 <phone>(555)555-5555<extension>2974</extension></phone>
 <salary>62,000</salary>
 <area>3</area>
</employee>
```

5. Now change `FullSecurity` to "0" and re-run it. The results will look like this:

```
C:\>xt employee.xml employee2.xsl
<?xml version="1.0" encoding="utf-8"?>
<employee FullSecurity="0">
 <name>John Doe</name>
 <department>Widget Sales</department>
 <phone>(555)555-5555<extension>2974</extension></phone>

 <area>3</area>
</employee>
```

194

<xsl:sort>

Sorting in XSLT is accomplished by adding one or more <xsl:sort> children to an <xsl:apply-templates> element, or an <xsl:for-each> element:

```
<xsl:sort select="XPath expression"
    lang="lang"
    data-type="text or number"
    order="ascending or descending"
    case-order="upper-first or lower-first"/>
```

The select attribute chooses the element/attribute/etc. by which you want the XSL processor to sort. If more than one <xsl:sort> child is added, then the output is sorted first by the element/attribute/etc. in the first <xsl:sort>, and if there are any duplicates they are sorted by the element/attribute/etc. in the second, and so on.

If the XSL processor goes through all of the <xsl:sort> elements, and there are still two or more items with identical results, they are inserted into the result tree in the order they appear in the source tree.

The data-type attribute specifies whether the data you are sorting is numeric or textual in nature. For example, consider the numbers 1, 10, 5, and 11. If we sort these with data-type specified as "text", the result will be 1, 10, 11, 5. But if we sort numerically, the result will be 1, 5, 10, 11. The default is "text".

The order attribute specifies whether the result should be sorted in ascending or descending order. The default is ascending.

The case-order attribute specifies whether uppercase letters should come first, or lowercase letters should come first. For example, if case-order is "upper-first", then "A B a b" would be sorted as "A a B b", and if case-order is "lower-first", it would be sorted as "a A b B". The default value for case-order depends on the lang attribute, which specifies the language this document is in. When lang is set to "en", the default case-order is upper-first.

Note that XT has a bug in this area, and will sort using lower-first, even if you specify "en" for the lang attribute.

Try It Out – <xsl:sort> in Action

To demonstrate sorting with <xsl:sort>, let's sort our simple names XML.

1. If you don't still have it, recreate people.xml, using the following XML:

```
<?xml version="1.0"?>
<people>
  <name>
    <first>John</first>
    <middle>Fitzgerald Johansen</middle>
    <last>Doe</last>
  </name>
```

195

```
    <name>
      <first>Franklin</first>
      <middle>D.</middle>
      <last>Roosevelt</last>
    </name>
    <name>
      <first>Alfred</first>
      <middle>E.</middle>
      <last>Neuman</last>
    </name>
    <name>
      <first>John</first>
      <middle>Q.</middle>
      <last>Public</last>
    </name>
    <name>
      <first>Jane</first>
      <middle></middle>
      <last>Doe</last>
    </name>
  </people>
```

2. The following XSLT style sheet will take that XML and sort it, first by last name, then by first. Save it as `sort.xsl`:

```
<?xml version="1.0"?>
<xsl:stylesheet version="1.0" xmlns:xsl="http://www.w3.org/1999/XSL/Transform">
<xsl:output method="xml" indent="yes"/>

<xsl:template match="/">
  <people>
    <xsl:for-each select="/people/name">
      <xsl:sort select="last"/>
      <xsl:sort select="first"/>
      <xsl:copy-of select="."/>
    </xsl:for-each>
  </people>
</xsl:template>
</xsl:stylesheet>
```

Since ascending order is the default, we didn't bother to specify it.

3. Running this through XT produces the following:

```
C:\>xt people.xml people.xsl
<?xml version="1.0" encoding="utf-8"?>
<people>
<name>
  <first>Jane</first>
  <middle/>
  <last>Doe</last>
</name>
```

```
<name>
   <first>John</first>
   <middle>Fitzgerald Johansen</middle>
   <last>Doe</last>
</name>
<name>
   <first>Alfred</first>
   <middle>E.</middle>
   <last>Neuman</last>
</name>
<name>
   <first>John</first>
   <middle>Q.</middle>
   <last>Public</last>
</name>
<name>
   <first>Franklin</first>
   <middle>D.</middle>
   <last>Roosevelt</last>
</name>
</people>
```

Modes

The `<xsl:template>` and `<xsl:apply-templates>` elements both had a mode attribute, which we conveniently ignored. What does that attribute do?

Modes are convenient when you need to have templates which match the same section of XML, but do different things with it. It allows you to create these templates and only call the one you want.

Using modes is pretty trivial. When you create the template, you specify the mode attribute, giving it a name to describe this mode. To call the template, use `<xsl:apply-templates>` as before, but with the addition of the mode attribute, specifying the same mode. Now, in addition to matching the templates against the source tree, the XSL processor will also make sure that the only templates called are ones which are part of this mode. For example, if we have the following XSLT:

```
<xsl:apply-templates select="name" mode="TOC"/>
```

and the following templates:

```
<xsl:template match="name" mode="TOC"/>
<xsl:template match="name" mode="body"/>
```

only the first template will be instantiated, even though both templates match against the same section of the source tree.

Try It Out – Modes in Action

One common example given for modes is transforming an XML document to a web page. A template running under one mode can be used for a table of contents, and a template matching against the same section of the document can be run under another mode for the actual body of the document.

To demonstrate this, we'll use some XML to represent a chapter from one of the most brilliant XML books ever written.

1. Type in the following, and save it as `chapter.xml`:

```
<?xml version="1.0"?>
<XSL>
  <title>XSLT - The Gory Details</title>
  <section>Templates
    <paragraph> We have been introduced briefly to the concept of
<important>templates</important>. These are really the heart and soul of XSLT.
Style sheets are simply a collection of these templates, which are applied to the
input document to create the output document. In this section, we'll take a closer
look at the syntax of templates, and how they work. </paragraph>
      <paragraph> Let's take another look at a previous...</paragraph>
  </section>
  <section> XSLT's Order of Operations
    <paragraph> If a style sheet can have...</paragraph>
    <paragraph>Actually...</paragraph>
  </section>
</XSL>
```

This is a bit shorter than the text of the actual chapter, but it's enough to demonstrate what we're doing. We want to take this and transform it to HTML, with a table of contents we can use to navigate to any section.

2. Our first step is to set up the template to match against the document root, which will output the main structure of the HTML file:

```
<xsl:template match="/">
  <HTML>
  <HEAD><TITLE><xsl:value-of select="/XSL/title"/></TITLE></HEAD>
  <BODY>
  <H1><xsl:value-of select="/XSL/title"/></H1>

  <H2>Table of Contents</H2>
  <OL>
    <xsl:apply-templates select="/XSL/section" mode="TOC"/>
  </OL>

  <xsl:apply-templates select="/XSL/section" mode="body"/>

  </BODY>
  </HTML>
</xsl:template>
```

The two important pieces of code are the ones where we call <xsl:apply-templates> to process the main body of our document. The same portion of the source tree will be processed twice by two separate templates, once for each mode.

3. Next we need to create those two templates. The first will output our table of contents:

```
<xsl:template match="section" mode="TOC">
    <LI><A href="{concat('#section', position())}">
        <xsl:value-of select="text()"/></A>
    </LI>
</xsl:template>
```

It simply creates an HTML list item for each section in the body, using the position() function to make sure that every section is uniquely identified. Notice that the <xsl:value-of> is using text() for the value of each item, instead of ".", because we only want the title of each section, not the entire text. We could have made this more explicit, and used a separate child element for the name of the section, but we didn't.

4. The second template will output the main body of the document:

```
<xsl:template match="section" mode="body">
  <A name="{concat('section', position())}"><H2>
      <xsl:value-of select="text()"/></H2>
  </A>
  <xsl:apply-templates/>
</xsl:template>
```

It matches against the <section> elements again, but works in "body" mode. This template creates an <H2> heading, with the title of the section, and wraps it in an <A> to identify it, so that the links from the table of contents will work. Then <xsl:apply-templates> is called, to take care of the rest of the work in creating this section.

5. The two following templates are very simple ones, which just transform the <paragraph> elements to HTML <P> elements, and the <important> elements to HTML <STRONG> elements:

```
<xsl:template match="paragraph">
  <P><xsl:apply-templates/></P>
</xsl:template>

<xsl:template match="important">
  <STRONG><xsl:apply-templates/></STRONG>
</xsl:template>
```

6. And finally, we come to the last template in the style sheet, which matches against any PCDATA which is a direct child of a <section> element; that is, its title. This is done so that these titles won't make it into the body of the section itself.

The problem is those default templates, which all XSL processors implement. Remember that one of these default templates matches against any text which isn't matched against any other templates, and outputs that text to the result tree. This means that when we call <xsl:apply-templates> from within the body template, we would get the PCDATA which is a direct child of a <section> element inserted into the result tree as well, because of this default template. The template to hide these titles is as follows:

```
<xsl:template match="/XSL/section/text()"/>
```

This time, to save space, we simply used an empty element, instead of including a comment.

7. Putting all of this together produces the following style sheet:

```xml
<?xml version="1.0"?>
<xsl:stylesheet version="1.0" xmlns:xsl="http://www.w3.org/1999/XSL/Transform">
<xsl:template match="/">
  <HTML>
  <HEAD><TITLE><xsl:value-of select="/XSL/title"/></TITLE></HEAD>
  <BODY>
  <H1><xsl:value-of select="/XSL/title"/></H1>

  <H2>Table of Contents</H2>
  <OL>
    <xsl:apply-templates select="/XSL/section" mode="TOC"/>
  </OL>

  <xsl:apply-templates select="/XSL/section" mode="body"/>

  </BODY>
  </HTML>
</xsl:template>

<xsl:template match="section" mode="TOC">
    <LI><A href="{concat('#section', position())}"><xsl:value-of
select="text()"/></A></LI>
</xsl:template>

<xsl:template match="section" mode="body">
  <A name="{concat('section', position())}"><H2><xsl:value-of
select="text()"/></H2></A>
  <xsl:apply-templates/>
</xsl:template>

<xsl:template match="paragraph">
  <P><xsl:apply-templates/></P>
</xsl:template>

<xsl:template match="important">
  <STRONG><xsl:apply-templates/></STRONG>
</xsl:template>

<xsl:template match="/XSL/section/text()"/>
</xsl:stylesheet>
```

8. Save this as `chapter.xsl`, and run it through XT like this:

xt chapter.xml chapter.xsl chapter.html

You will get an HTML file called `chapter.html`, which contains the information from this chapter. In a browser, it will look similar to this:

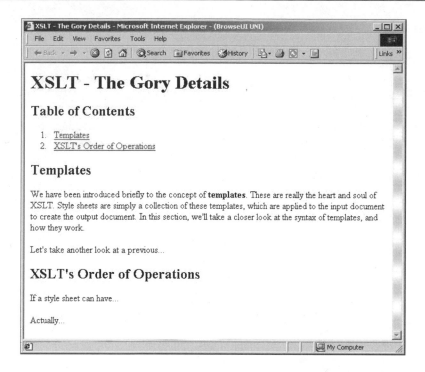

Variables, Constants, and Named Templates

Anyone who has worked with programming languages is familiar with **variables** and **constants**. Variables are places in your program where you store information, while constants are values which are predetermined when the program is written, and can never be changed. For example, in Java we could create a variable to store a person's age and a constant to store the value of pi like this:

```
int intAge = 30;
final int csngPI = 3.14;
```

The `intAge` variable can then be changed any time we need to in our application, whereas `csngPI` can never be changed, but will always be 3.14:

```
intAge = 42;   //this is allowed
csngPI = 42;   //this is not allowed
```

Constants can be useful in a variety of situations. For example, if you were designing an application to print out reports to a printer, you might need to know throughout the application how many lines per page you're outputting, or what fonts to use. You could just manually put the values in wherever you need them, or you could define constants to store the values, and then use those. The usefulness of constants would become immediately apparent the first time you needed to change one of those values: instead of searching through all of the code for your application, and manually replacing each occurrence of the value, you would simply need to change the value of your constant, in one place. XSLT also provides us with mechanisms for adding constants and variables to style sheets, using `<xsl:variable>` and named templates.

<xsl:variable>

The `<xsl:variable>` element allows us to add simple constants to style sheets. For example, we could define a constant for pi like so:

```
<xsl:variable name="csngPI">3.14</xsl:variable>
```

This constant can then be accessed anywhere you would use a regular XPath expression, using a dollar sign followed by the variable name. For example:

```
<math pi="{$csngPI}"/>
```

or:

```
<xsl:value-of select="$csngPI"/>
```

But wait, there's more! `<xsl:variable>` can also contain XML markup, and even XSLT elements! For example:

```
<xsl:variable name="space">
  <xsl:text> </xsl:text>
</xsl:variable>

<xsl:variable name="name">
  <name>
    <xsl:value-of select="/name/first"/>
    <xsl:value-of select="$space"/>
    <xsl:value-of select="/name/last"/>
  </name>
</xsl:variable>

<!--this gets the value of the $name variable, including any XML markup-->
<xsl:copy-of select="$name"/>
```

Notice that $name is allowed to reference $space. One important note, however, is that constants are not allowed to reference themselves, and neither are circular references allowed. (These would both be the XSLT equivalent of infinite loops. An XSL engine should catch this for you, to prevent your machine from crashing.) For example, neither of the following is allowed:

```
<!--variables are not allowed to reference themselves-->
<xsl:variable name="name">
  <name><xsl:value-of select="$name"/></name>
</xsl:variable>

<!--circular references are not allowed either-->
<xsl:variable name="A">
  <B><xsl:value-of select="$B"/></B>
</xsl:variable>

<xsl:variable name="B">
  <A><xsl:value-of select="$A"/></A>
</xsl:variable>
```

As an alternative syntax, `<xsl:variable>` can have a `select` attribute. In this case, the value of the constant is the result from the XPath expression supplied. When `<xsl:variable>` has a `select` attribute, it is not allowed to have any content. For example:

```
<xsl:variable name="name" select="/people/name"/>
```

In all cases, whether the constant contains straight text or gets its value from the source tree, the value of the constant is fixed. This means that you can't change the value of a constant after it has been declared. (Refer back to the "*XSLT Has No Side Effects*" section in the last chapter, for the reasons behind this.) This is why I keep calling them "constants", instead of "variables"; programmers who are used to imperative languages will have a much easier time if they don't think in terms of variables when programming with XSLT.

When working with constants, it's important to remember the **binding**. That is, *where* in our style sheet the constant can be referenced. (In other programming languages, this is often called the *scope*.) Consider the following example:

```
<?xml version="1.0"?>
<xsl:stylesheet version="1.0" xmlns:xsl="http://www.w3.org/1999/XSL/Transform">
  <xsl:output method="text"/>

  <xsl:variable name="age">30</xsl:variable>

  <xsl:template match="/">
    <xsl:variable name="name">Fred</xsl:variable>
    <xsl:value-of select="concat($name, ' is ', $age)"/>
  </xsl:template>
</xsl:stylesheet>
```

When run, this produces the following:

```
C:\>xt blah.xml scope.xsl
Fred is 30
```

The `$age` constant is called a **global** constant, because it is defined outside of any templates, which makes it accessible anywhere in the style sheet. `$name`, on the other hand, is a **local** constant, because it is defined inside a template, and therefore only accessible inside that template. It is also possible to create constants in different bindings with the same name. For example:

```
<xsl:stylesheet version="1.0" xmlns:xsl="http://www.w3.org/1999/XSL/Transform">
<xsl:output method="text"/>

<xsl:variable name="name">Fred</xsl:variable>

<xsl:template match="/">
  <xsl:variable name="name">Barney</xsl:variable>
  <xsl:value-of select="$name"/>
</xsl:template>
</xsl:stylesheet>
```

In that `<xsl:value-of>`, which $name are we selecting? The answer is that the constant with the most restrictive binding is used. In this instance, the $name of "Fred" is global, and the $name of "Barney" is local, so the second one is used. Running this in XT produces the following:

```
C:\ >xt blah.xml blah.xsl
Barney
```

Named Templates

Constants can be a powerful tool in XSLT style sheets, but sometimes we need a bit more flexibility. Perhaps we need the functionality of a constant, but we also need to change the value of that constant, similar to a template.

The problem with templates, though, is that they work by matching against the source tree, so we can't just explicitly call a template whenever we want it. Furthermore, if we had one particular template which we wanted to instantiate for a number of different nodes in the source tree, we would have to define separate, identical, templates for each node we match against, or else create a complex XPath expression for the template's `select` attribute, saying "match against this node, or that node, or this other node...".

Luckily, XSLT introduced the concept of **named templates**, which makes both of the above statements untrue. We create them using the same `<xsl:template>` element we have been using, but instead of using the `select` attribute, we specify the `name` attribute. These templates are then called with the simple `<xsl:call-template>` element. For example, consider the following XSLT:

```
<xsl:template match="/">
  <xsl:for-each select="name">
    <xsl:call-template name="bold"/>
  </xsl:for-each>

  <xsl:for-each select="not-name">
    <xsl:call-template name="bold"/>
  </xsl:for-each>
</xsl:template>

<xsl:template name="bold">
  <B><xsl:value-of select="."/></B>
</xsl:template>
```

We have a simple template, which just outputs the contents of the current node, wrapped in HTML `<B>` tags. But this template is called both for `<name>` elements and for `<not-name>` elements in the source tree; in fact, the bold template in this case doesn't care what elements it is operating on.

If you wish, you can create templates with both the `match` and the `name` attributes; this will create a normal template which is instantiated through `<xsl:apply-templates>`, but that can also be called explicitly if desired.

Parameters

At times we may not be able to make our templates generic enough for every case. For example, consider a template for outputting a name into the result tree:

```
<xsl:template name="name">
  First name:  <xsl:value-of select="first"/>
  Last name:  <xsl:value-of select="last"/>
</xsl:template>
```

In this case, we're assuming that the first name will always be in a `<first>` element, and the last name will always be in a `<last>` element. But what if we have an input document with names represented in different places in different ways? It might be better if we could specify to the template which elements to use for the first name, and which elements to use for the last.

The `<xsl:param>` element allows us to give our templates parameters, just like we give functions parameters. We could rewrite the previous template like this:

```
<xsl:template name="name">
  <xsl:param name="first"><xsl:value-of select="first"/></xsl:param>
  <xsl:param name="last"><xsl:value-of select="last"/></xsl:param>

  First name:  <xsl:value-of select="$first"/>
  Last name:  <xsl:value-of select="$last"/>
</xsl:template>
```

Now we're getting the values from our parameters. But, since those parameters are just getting their information from the `<first>` and `<last>` elements like before, how have we bought ourselves any benefits? The answer is that the information put inside the `<xsl:param>` element is only the default value for that parameter. So if we call our name template, without giving it any parameters, it will use the values from the `<first>` and `<last>` elements; if we call it with parameters, it will use the values we give it, instead of the defaults.

We pass parameters to the templates using the `<xsl:with-param>` element.

Style sheets can also have parameters, by specifying top-level `<xsl:param>` elements. However, the XSLT specification doesn't specify how those parameters should be passed to the XSL processor, so the mechanics will vary from processor to processor.

Try It Out – Parameters in Action

Just to verify that this parameter stuff really works, let's put the above name template into an actual style sheet, and see it in action.

1. For our XML, we'll use the following format, which you should save (if you haven't already) as `name.xml`:

```
<?xml version="1.0"?>
<person>
  <name>
```

```
      <first>John</first>
      <last>Doe</last>
   </name>
</person>
```

2. And here is our style sheet, which you should save as `name.xsl`:

```xml
<?xml version="1.0"?>
<xsl:stylesheet version="1.0" xmlns:xsl="http://www.w3.org/1999/XSL/Transform">
<xsl:output method="text"/>

<xsl:template match="/">
  <xsl:for-each select="/person/name">
    <xsl:call-template name="name"/>
  </xsl:for-each>
</xsl:template>

<xsl:template name="name">
  <xsl:param name="first"><xsl:value-of select="first"/></xsl:param>
  <xsl:param name="last"><xsl:value-of select="last"/></xsl:param>

  First:  <xsl:value-of select="$first"/>
  Last:  <xsl:value-of select="$last"/>
</xsl:template>
</xsl:stylesheet>
```

Because the first and last names are contained in the `<first>` and `<last>` elements, just like our named template is expecting, we don't need to supply it any parameters.

3. Running this through XT produces the following:

```
C:\>xt name.xml name.xsl

First: John
Last: Doe
```

4. Now let's change our XML document slightly:

```xml
<?xml version="1.0"?>
<person>
  <name>
    <given>John</given>
    <family>Doe</family>
  </name>
</person>
```

5. And also change our style sheet just a bit:

```xml
<?xml version="1.0"?>
<xsl:stylesheet version="1.0" xmlns:xsl="http://www.w3.org/1999/XSL/Transform">
<xsl:output method="text"/>
```

```
<xsl:template match="/">
  <xsl:for-each select="/person/name">
    <xsl:call-template name="name">
      <xsl:with-param name="first"><xsl:value-of select="given"/></xsl:with-param>
      <xsl:with-param name="last"><xsl:value-of select="family"/></xsl:with-param>
    </xsl:call-template>
  </xsl:for-each>
</xsl:template>

<xsl:template name="name">
  <xsl:param name="first"><xsl:value-of select="first"/></xsl:param>
  <xsl:param name="last"><xsl:value-of select="last"/></xsl:param>

  First:  <xsl:value-of select="$first"/>
  Last:   <xsl:value-of select="$last"/>
</xsl:template>
</xsl:stylesheet>
```

Since the first and last names aren't where the template expects to find them anymore, we pass it the parameters instead.

6. Running this through XT produces the following:

C:\>xt name.xml name.xsl

First: John
Last: Doe

Which, you may notice, is the same output as last time.

7. Finally, let's modify our style sheet one last time:

```
<?xml version="1.0"?>
<xsl:stylesheet version="1.0" xmlns:xsl="http://www.w3.org/1999/XSL/Transform">
<xsl:output method="text"/>

<xsl:template match="/">
  <xsl:for-each select="/person/name">
    <xsl:call-template name="name">
      <xsl:with-param name="first">Fred</xsl:with-param>
      <xsl:with-param name="last">Garvin</xsl:with-param>
    </xsl:call-template>
  </xsl:for-each>
</xsl:template>

<xsl:template name="name">
  <xsl:param name="first"><xsl:value-of select="first"/></xsl:param>
  <xsl:param name="last"><xsl:value-of select="last"/></xsl:param>

  First:  <xsl:value-of select="$first"/>
  Last:   <xsl:value-of select="$last"/>
</xsl:template>
</xsl:stylesheet>
```

This is just to demonstrate that the values passed to the parameters don't have to come from the source tree at all; in this case, we just pass it the strings "Fred" and "Garvin", and it uses those for its values.

8. Running this through XT produces the following:

```
C:\>xt name.xml name.xsl

First:  Fred
Last:  Garvin
```

Using XSLT with CSS

So now we know about XSLT, and have seen it used to add style to our XML documents – will we ever use cascading style sheets? As we saw in Chapter 3, cascading style sheets provide a rich environment for presenting the contents of an HTML or XML document to the reader, but the technology has a number of significant limitations that limit its utility as a general presentation language for XML:

❑ **Content Blind.** There is no way, using just CSS, to pull information from an XML document. This limitation is most devastating with media sources, such as graphics, that are dependent upon information within the XML structure to display properly.

❑ **Sensitive to Order.** The output of a CSS-formatted XML document is strongly reliant upon the order of the XML data in the first place. If you had two tags: <first_name> and <last_name> in that order, it's not possible to output the result as last_name, first_name.

❑ **Indifferent Browser Support.** This point, brought up frequently in the CSS chapter, is a major problem in terms of working with CSS. The Mozilla 6.0 browser (formerly the Netscape 5 Build 13) will likely offer complete or near complete support for CSS, but the support for CSS at the 4.0 level is hideously insufficient. On the other hand, Microsoft's Internet Explorer 5.5 is about 90% compliant, but has some idiosyncrasies to it that differ widely enough from the CSS2 specification (the lack of support for content(), the strange implementation of display:none, the collection of about six distinct coordinate systems, etc.) that the results of formatting with IE5 can be unpredictable. However, the Opera browser, written in Java and increasingly incorporated into Personal Digital Assistants (PDAs) and other handheld devices, boasts a 99% compliance rate with CSS.

❑ **Limited Interactivity.** CSS is not a programming language, or even (technically speaking) a set of interfaces. One of the nice features of both IE and Netscape implementations of style sheets is that they do offer a number of mechanisms for making them interactive, from the style object of IE to the introduction of behaviors and dynamic properties.

As it turns out, none of these issues are sufficiently severe to declare that cascading style sheets are a failure. Indeed, it turns out that CSS should be considered an integral part of any web developer's use of XML, because it handles the task of media presentation very well. One of the common questions when dealing with XML is the distinction between XSL and CSS for presentation purposes, and the answer highlights both the power of CSS and the role that it plays in the formal processes of XML.

An XML document (or more properly, an XML stream) contains a set of structured data, but should know nothing about how it needs to be presented. In this respect it is much like an object with specific characteristics (a hardwood table, for example).

The way that the table appears is completely separate from the reality of the table. The table itself has four legs, a wide table surface, and is made of a specific type of wood attached with a certain type of screw. These are the characteristic properties of the table, and are essentially immutable. However, how you view the table can change radically depending upon circumstances such as where you are located relative to the table, the level (and color) of light in the room, whether you're concentrating on it or just noting it in passing, etc. Furthermore, you can abstract the table out to a drawing or photograph of the table, which loses depth information, you can describe the table in words, you can shoot radar at it to determine its characteristics from a sonogram. Each of these are different views of the table, and while they differ radically in their medium they share the concept that they only show an aspect or presentation of the table object.

An XML document can be thought of as a view of an object in relationship to other objects, one that concentrates on usable characteristics of the object relative to the problem at hand. Thus by itself an XML document is a view, but it is media independent.

XSL, as mentioned in the previous chapter, is broken up into two distinct areas – XSL-Transformation (or XSLT), and XSL-Formatting Objects (XSL-FO). As we have just seen in this chapter, an XSL transformation takes an XML structure and maps it into a different structure – typically an XML structure, but this isn't a strict requirement. While it is possible that the transformation can in fact create the presentation layer (it was for this purpose that XSLT emerged, after all) in fact XSLT makes for a fairly limited formatting option. It can change the *structure* of an XML document, but by attempting to put all of your *formatting* code within an XSLT document you will frequently discover that you lose the flexibility of the transformation.

What is preferable is to use XSLT to determine the output characteristics of the browser or medium that the XML is targeted to and then set the CSS formatting up in such a way as to best suit this output. This works especially well when working with internal CSS style sheets.

Try It Out – Styling Business Cards with XSLT and CSS

For example, suppose that you wanted to present a "business card" for each employee in a company, complete with a picture of that employee (contained in the image field). The employee list would contain a reference to the XSLT style sheet that will do the initial transformation.

1. Let's first create the XML document (which has only one line different to `employees.xml` from Chapter 3):

```
<?xml-stylesheet type="text/xsl" href="bizcard.xsl"?>
<employees>
    <employee id="101">
        <firstName>Jean</firstName>
        <lastName>Janus</lastName>
        <title>President</title>
        <dateStarted>1997-11-12</dateStarted>
        <salary>324021</salary>
        <department>Administration</department>
        <image>images/jjanus.jpg</image>
```

```
        </employee>
        <employee id="102">
                <firstName>Kitara</firstName>
                <lastName>Milleaux</lastName>
                <title>Chief Executive Officer</title>
                <dateStarted>1997-08-12</dateStarted>
                <salary>329215</salary>
                <department>Administration</department>
                <image>kmilleaux.jpg</image>
        </employee>
        <employee id="103">
                <firstName>Shelley</firstName>
                <lastName>Janes</lastName>
                <title>Chief Financial Officer</title>
                <dateStarted>1998-03-16</dateStarted>
                <salary>232768</salary>
                <department>Finance</department>
                <image>images/sjanes.jpg</image>
        </employee>
        <employee id="104">
                <firstName>Marissa</firstName>
                <lastName>Mendez</lastName>
                <title>Chief Technical Officer</title>
                <dateStarted>1998-09-16</dateStarted>
                <salary>242768</salary>
                <department>Information Technologies</department>
                <image>images/mmendez.jpg</image>
        </employee>
        <employee id="105">
                <firstName>Kace</firstName>
                <lastName>Juriden</lastName>
                <title>Vice President, Marketing</title>
                <dateStarted>1998-11-03</dateStarted>
                <salary>210359</salary>
                <department>Marketing</department>
                <image>images/kjuriden.jpg</image>
        </employee>
        <!-- more employees, as required -->
        </employees>
```

2. The XSLT to handle this is a little convoluted, but in essence it creates a new document that is almost identical to the first but that now includes a style sheet. This style sheet has both the element definitions and declarations for linking the images to external graphical resources. Here is the XSLT style sheet, `bizcard.xsl`. First we have the style sheet declaration and the `<xsl:template>` element for the root element:

```
<?xml version="1.0"?>
<xsl:stylesheet version="1.0" xmlns:xsl="http://www.w3.org/1999/XSL/Transform">

    <xsl:template match="/">
      <xsl:processing-instruction name="xml-stylesheet">
        type="text/css" href="#bcards"
      </xsl:processing-instruction>
      <xsl:apply-templates select="employees"/>
    </xsl:template>
```

3. This template adds a processing instruction to the output, then calls another template, to apply styles to the employees elements, which we'll see in a moment. There is also a template to copy the employee elements and their children into the output:

```
<xsl:template match=".">
    <xsl:copy><xsl:value-of select="."/></xsl:copy>
</xsl:template>
```

4. The template which applies styles to each of the elements comes next; essentially this contains the CSS style sheet, writes out the image file information and then calls the template above to copy all employee elements and their children:

```
<xsl:template match="employees">
  <style id="bcards">

    employee
    {
      display:block;position:relative;width:350px;height:225px;border:inset
      3px gray;
    }
    firstName {display:inline;font-size:14pt;}
    lastName {display:inline;font-size:14pt;)
    title {display:block;font-size:11pt;}
    dateStarted {display:none;}
    salary {display:none;}
    department {display:block;}
    image
    {
      width:120px;height:160px;position:relative;display:block;float:right;
    }

    <xsl:for-each select="//employee">
      image[img<xsl:value-of select="@id" />]
      {background-image:url(<xsl:value-of select="image"/>); }
    </xsl:for-each>
  </style>

  <xsl:apply-templates select="employee"/>
</xsl:template>
```

5. Next we have the final template and close the style sheet:

```
<xsl:template match="image">
    <image id="{concat('img', ancestor::employee/@id)}"
    href="{ancestor::employee/image}"/>
</xsl:template>
</xsl:stylesheet>
```

6. We can process this through XT using the following command line:

C:\>xt employees.xml bizcard.xsl employeeresult.xml

Once processed through the XSLT style sheet, this actually creates a document with a reference to an internal CSS style sheet looking something like this:

```
<?xml-stylesheet type="text/css" href="bcard"?>

<employees>
  <style id="bcards">
    employee {display:block;position:relative;width:350px;height:225px;
    border:inset 3px gray;}
    firstName {display:inline;font-size:14pt;}
    lastName {display:inline;font-size:14pt;)
    title {display:block;font-size:11pt;}
    dateStarted {display:none;}
    salary {display:none;}
    department {display:block;}
    image {float:right;width:120px;height:160px;display:block;}

<!--The square brackets serve to identify the specific ID elements in the output
that are generated by the XSLT. -->
    image[img101] {background-image:url(images/jjanus.jpg); }
    image[img102] {background-image:url(images/kmilleaux.jpg); }
    image[img103] {background-image:url(images/kjuriden.jpg); }
    image[img104] {background-image:url(images/mmendez.jpg); }
    image[img105] {background-image:url(images/sjanes.jpg); }
  </style>

  <employee id="101">
    <firstName>Jean</firstName>
    <lastName>Janus</lastName>
    <title>President</title>
    <dateStarted>1997-11-12</dateStarted>
    <salary>324021</salary>
    <department>Administration</department>
    <image id="img101" href="jjanus.jpg"/>
  </employee>
  <employee id="102">
    <firstName>Kitara</firstName>
    <lastName>Milleaux</lastName>
    <title>Chief Executive Officer</title>
    <dateStarted>1997-08-12</dateStarted>
    <salary>329215</salary>
    <department>Administration</department>
    <image id="img102" href="kmilleaux.jpg"/>
  </employee>

<!-- more employees, as available -->
</employees>
```

The document is similar to what it was before but not identical – the <image> tag, for instance, now contains an identifier instead of a path to an image, and the paths are now generated automatically as part of the style sheet.

7. The output of this (at least on CSS2 compliant browsers), is shown:

How It Works

It is worth noting here that the actual presentation – the rendering of the data to the browser or page – is still not reflected in the XML. Instead, the XML retains its underlying structure (with the exception of the image tag, where the contents of the tag are moved inside the element as the href attribute, in case the calling document needs to retrieve the image for some other purpose). The CSS block within the XML document handles the actual presentation, and most of that style block could easily have come from part of an external file that contained switchable blocks of style elements.

CSS and XSL-Formatting Objects

One of the most recent XML specifications (still in review at the time of writing) concerns the XSL-Formatting Objects technology (XSL-FO). This specification provides a browser neutral, non-HTML way of specifying blocks of content for publishing information. While it is far too complex to cover in this book, it's worth noting that most of XSL-FO is a mechanism to encapsulate CSS in a completely XML related way. In other words, XSL-FO takes the property:value model that CSS uses and recasts it into a more XML-centric metaphor. Thus, if you are looking at working with formatting objects in the future, you should take some time to get a better understanding of the CSS standard.

XSLT in the Real World

As an interesting example of XSL in action, readers with Internet Explorer 5 who have been viewing the XML samples in their browser have already been using XSL all along. IE uses a default XSL style sheet, which is used to render XML documents into HTML for the browser, if no other style sheet is specified. If you have IE5 you can see the style sheet by typing res://msxml.dll/defaultss.xsl into the address bar. Since all XSL style sheets are XML, and since you aren't supplying any style sheet, IE5 will render the style sheet with itself! But again, since IE5 came out before the XSLT specification was finalized, some of the syntax of the language has changed since then, so if you borrow code for your own style sheets, you may have to change some things around to get them to work right for any XSL processor other than IE5.

Summary

This chapter has completed our introduction to XSLT, and provided you with almost all of the expertise needed to create some fairly complex transformations. You've seen descriptions of the most-used XSLT elements, and examples of each in use.

We also saw how XSLT and CSS provide *complementary* functionality – XSLT can help you structure your pages in a wide number of formats, and CSS can then balance this with easily modifiable media representations for those browsers that support it.

XSLT doesn't replace CSS, despite claims to the contrary – XSLT's primary domain is to provide transformation (i.e., programming) services to XML, while CSS takes the results of such transformations and paints pictures or speaks words or wafts smells with them; it makes XML into multimedia.

Now that we have covered some ways to view XML in the browser, and some ways to transform our XML from one format to another, the next couple of chapters will focus on some ways that we can access the information in an XML document from code.

The Document Object Model (DOM)

Now that we've got our information in XML format, we want to be able to do things with that information in the applications we write. We need not only to access it, but to change it and add to it. The **Document Object Model (DOM)** provides a means for working with XML documents (and other types of documents) through the use of code, and a way to interface with that code in the programs we write.

For example, the DOM enables us to create documents and parts of documents, navigate through the document, move, copy and remove parts of the document, add or modify attributes. In this chapter you will learn how to work with the DOM to achieve such tasks, as well as seeing:

- ❑ What the DOM is, and why it was created
- ❑ What interfaces are, and how they differ from objects
- ❑ What XML-related interfaces exist in the DOM, and what they can do
- ❑ What exceptions are

The DOM specification is being built level by level. That is, when the W3C produced the first DOM Recommendation, it was **DOM Level 1**. Level 1 was then added to, producing **Level 2**. At the time of writing, DOM Level 2 was the currently released Candidate Recommendation, and DOM Level 3 was in its beginning stages, so in this chapter we'll be discussing the DOM Level 2. Keep in mind that because the DOM Level 2 was a Candidate Recommendation, there could be minor changes from what is discussed in this chapter.

You can find the DOM Level 2 specification at http://www.w3.org/TR/DOM-Level-2/, and there's more information at http://www.w3.org/TR/1999/CR-DOM-Level-2-19991210/core.html

Since the DOM is really for programmers, some programming experience is assumed for this chapter; Object Oriented Programming experience would be helpful but isn't essential.

What is the DOM?

In Chapter 1 we looked at the concept of an object model, and how using one can make working with information easier. We also noted the fact that an XML document is structured very much like an object model: it is hierarchical, with nodes potentially having other nodes as children.

XML as an Object Model

For example, we could take our `<order>` XML, which looked like this:

```
<?xml version="1.0"?>
<order number="312597">
  <date>2000/1/1</date>
  <customer id="216A">Company A</customer>
  <item>
    <part-number warehouse="Warehouse 11">E16-25A</part-number>
    <description>Production-Class Widget</description>
    <quantity>16</quantity>
  </item>
</order>
```

and structure it as an object model, such as the following:

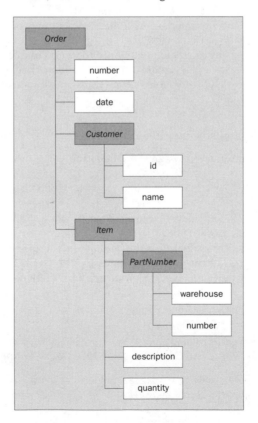

Some of the elements have been made into *objects*, as shown by the shaded boxes, and some have been made into *properties* of those objects, as shown by the white boxes. If we were writing code to deal with an order, this object model would make it easier to process that information, and would probably even include *methods* to provide some functionality for us.

For example, we might provide a method on the object model called `fulfill()`, which would fulfill the order, or `saveToDatabase()`, which could take all of the information and save it to our database.

The XML DOM

You may have noticed that the object model above would only work for this specific document type. To work with other document types, we would have to create a new object model for each one. While these proprietary object models will be useful in many situations, there are also situations where a more generic approach is needed. That is, we need an object model that can model *any* XML document, regardless of how it is structured. The **Document Object Model (DOM)** takes this generic approach.

The DOM is usually added as a layer between the XML parser and the application that needs the information in the document, meaning that the parser reads the data from the XML document and then feeds that data into a DOM. The DOM is then used by a higher-level application. The application can do whatever it wants with this information, including putting it into another proprietary object model, if so desired.

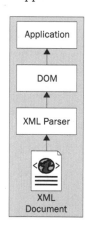

So, in order to write an application which will be accessing an XML document through the DOM, you need to have an XML parser and a DOM implementation installed on your machine. (There is an alternative, which we'll look at in the following chapter, but for now we'll concentrate on using the DOM.) Some DOM implementations, such as the one that ships with Internet Explorer, have the parser built right in, while others can be configured to sit on top of one of many parsers.

We'll be using some of IE5's built-in XML capabilities for the Try It Outs in this chapter; IE5 ships with a library called **MSXML** which includes a DOM implementation (Level 1 plus some extensions). The same code should also work with the ActiveDOM product from Vivid Creation at http://www.vivid-creations.com and CueXML from http://www.cuesoft.com. Also check out http://www.xmlsoftware.com/parsers/ for others.

Most of the time, when working with the DOM, the developer will never even have to know that an XML parser is involved, because the parser is at a lower level than the DOM, and will be hidden away.

DOMString

In order to ensure that all DOM implementations work the same, the DOM specifies the `DOMString` data type. This is a sequence of 16-bit units (characters) which is used anywhere that a string is expected.

In other words, the DOM specifies that all strings must be UTF-16 (refer back to Chapter 2 if you need a reminder of what this is). Although the DOM specification uses this `DOMString` type anywhere it's talking about strings, this is just for the sake of convenience; a DOM implementation doesn't actually need to make any type of `DOMString` object available.

Many programming languages, such as Java, JavaScript, and Visual Basic, work with strings in 16-bit units natively, so anywhere a `DOMString` is specified these programming languages could use their native string types. On the other hand, C and C++ can work with strings in 8-bit units or in 16-bit units, so care must be taken to ensure that you are always using the 16-bit units in these languages.

DOM Interfaces

Although the name "Document Object Model" has the word "object" in it, the DOM doesn't really deal with objects very much; it mostly deals with **interfaces**. Since that's the case, we'd better take a look at what these interfaces are, and what they're good for.

To get an idea of what interfaces are involved in the DOM, let's take a very simple XML document, such as this one:

```
<parent>
  <child id="123">text goes here</child>
</parent>
```

and see how it would look as represented by the DOM:

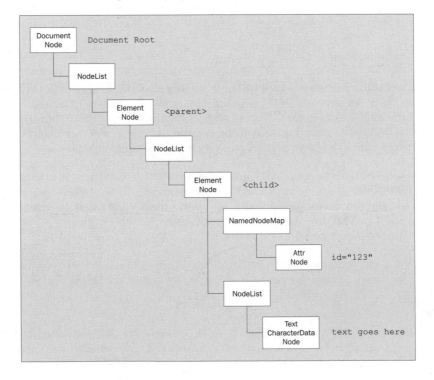

Each box represents an object that will be created; the names in the boxes are the interfaces that will be implemented by each object. For example, we have an object to represent the whole document, and objects to represent each of the elements and nodes. Each object implements a number of appropriate interfaces, such as `Text`, `CharacterData` and `Node` for the object which represents the "`text goes here`" character data.

So What are Interfaces?

We already know what objects are. They encapsulate our data, and the code to work with that data. But sometimes, when we're modeling our data, we don't want to create a specific object, but a *type* of object, in other words a collection of methods and properties that one or more objects may support. For example, I might want to create an object type for a musician, which I would call `Musician` (I'm nothing if not boring and predictable). This type would have a property for the type of instrument the musician plays (maybe `instrument`, which would return a string containing the name of the instrument), and methods to play the music (maybe `startSong()`, `crescendo()`, `improvise()`, etc.).

But, the thing about musicians is, anyone can be a musician. There are people who devote their lives to being musicians, and there are people who play music as a hobby. Someone can be a musician and, at the same time, be a teacher, or a bank teller, or the President of the United States. What we need is a way to apply our object types to any object. That's what an interface does. It's a contract to support certain properties and methods, which can be applied to an object.

> *Different programming languages may or may not use the word "interface", or have a specific mechanism for providing interfaces, but the same concept can be applied in any language.*

Implementing Interfaces

If we were to create an object called `Person`, we could program that object to **implement** the `Musician` interface. This means that we're declaring our `Person` object to provide all of the properties and methods of the `Musician` interface. Anyone using our `Person` object would then know that the object had an `instruments` property, and a `startSong()` method, in addition to whatever other properties and methods the `Person` object supports.

> *Normally, in Object Oriented Programming, we talk about writing **classes**, not objects. A class is the definition for an object, whereas an object is an instantiation of a class. By analogy, Person might be a class, whereas David Hunter would be an object. For this book, we'll be using the terms "object" and "class" pretty interchangeably.*

Of course, we would still have to write all of the needed code for the `Person` object's implementation of `Musician`; it's not enough to say that `Person` implements `Musician`, we have to then write the code for all of the methods and all of the properties. This has the added benefit that the way our `Person` object implements `startSong()` might be entirely different from the way an `OtherPerson` object implements `startSong()`, although both will deliver the same behavior/semantics.

Implementing Multiple Interfaces

But we aren't just limited to one interface per object. I could also create a SoftwareDeveloper interface, with a writeCode() method, and have the Person object implement that interface in addition to the Musician interface. People using our Person object would then know that it is not only a musician, but a software developer as well, and with all of the functionality of both.

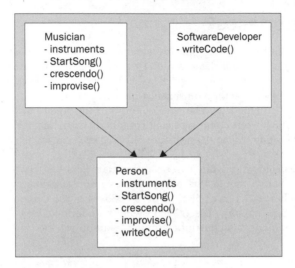

If had written these interfaces and objects in Java, we could write code like the following:

```
//create a Person object
Person myObject = new Person();

//call methods of the Musician and Software Developer interfaces
myObject.improvise();
myObject.writeCode();
```

This declares a Person object, and calls various methods from both of the interfaces that Person implements. Since we know that Person implements these interfaces, we know that these methods will be present, as will all of the other methods and properties available from a Person object. (In Java, if an object declares that it implements an interface, the Java compiler won't let the program compile until we write code for *all* of the properties and methods of the interface.)

We could also write code like the following:

```
//create a Musician variable, which references a Person object
Musician myObject = new Person();

//call Musician methods
myObject.improvise();

//this won't work
myObject.writeCode();
```

This may be a bit confusing if you haven't programmed with interfaces before. We have created a variable of type `Musician`, and that variable is referencing a `Person` object. Or, to put it another way, we have created a `Person` object, but when accessing the object through this variable, we are only allowed to access the methods and properties available from the `Musician` interface. (That's why we can't call the `writeCode()` method.) We can't access any methods or properties of the other interfaces associated with the `Person` object. This `Musician` variable doesn't have to reference a `Person` object, but can reference *any* type of object that implements the `Musician` interface.

The point is: a `Person` object isn't *just* a `Person` object. It is also a `Musician` object, and a `SoftwareDeveloper` object. If I were to write a function in Java, which took a `Musician` object as a parameter, then I could pass it a `Person` object, because a `Person` object is a `Musician` object.

> *Taking an object of one type, such as our `Person` object, and treating it as if it were another type of object, such as a `Musician`, is called **casting**.*

Because the DOM uses interfaces exclusively for defining its Application Programming Interface (API), a lot of flexibility is provided for people creating DOM implementations; they can use any programming language they wish, and still create W3C-DOM-compliant implementations.

DOM Implementations

The Document Object Model is not just an API for working with XML documents; it can also be used for working with HTML documents, CSS style sheets, and a variety of other documents. In fact, DOM implementations can be specialized to work only with XML documents or only with HTML documents, or they can be built to work with a number of types of documents. For example, a DOM which is shipped as part of an XML parser would probably only have the XML-specific APIs implemented, whereas a DOM which is shipped as part of a web browser would probably have the HTML and CSS-specific APIs included, to allow programmatic access to those types of documents.

The combination of the DOM (with the HTML API) scripting languages and HTML is what makes **Dynamic HTML** (or **DHTML**) possible, because the contents of an HTML document are exposed through the object model. When a web page is loaded into a DHTML-aware web browser, objects are created for each and every element on the page. This allows the web page writer to insert script on the page, to call methods and properties on those objects.

For example, if we have an HTML form like this:

```
<FORM id="frmScratchForm" name="frmScratchForm">
  <INPUT name="myRadio" type="radio" checked>First <BR>
  <INPUT name="myRadio" type="radio">Second
</FORM>
```

we can write JavaScript code to select the second radio button (the index is zero-based so 0 refers to the first item , 1 to the second, etc.) like this:

```
document.frmScratchForm.myRadio[1].checked = true;
```

So even though the first radio button will be selected when the page loads, we can change it programmatically.

Because there are different types of DOM implementation, the DOM provides the **DOM Core**, a core set of interfaces for working with basic documents, and a number of optional modules for working with other documents: **DOM HTML, DOM CSS**, etc. These modules are sets of additional interfaces that can be implemented. The DHTML example above used objects from the DOM HTML module.

For the rest of this chapter, we're going to be concentrating on the DOM Core.

The DOM Core

The DOM Core provides the following interfaces:

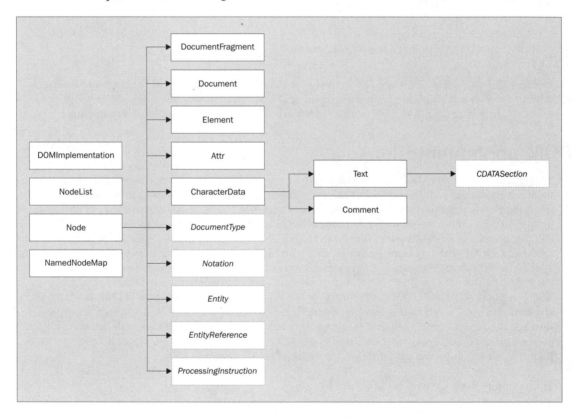

These core interfaces are further broken down into **Fundamental Interfaces** and **Extended Interfaces**.

❑ The Fundamental Interfaces must be implemented by all DOM implementations, even ones which will only be working with non-XML documents

❑ The Extended Interfaces only need to be implemented by DOM implementations that will be working with XML

This begs the question why the Extended Interfaces were included in the DOM Core, instead of being in a separate DOM XML, but that's the way it is. Since this is a book on XML, we will only study the DOM Core interfaces, but many of the concepts you learn will be useful if you ever need to learn one of the optional modules.

Extending Interfaces

As you're reading through the interface descriptions in this chapter, keep in mind that the properties and methods listed for each interface are just the *minimum* required in any DOM implementation. That means someone writing an implementation of the DOM can **extend** these interfaces with their own properties and methods, and most DOM implementations do extend the basic interface.

What Do We Mean By Extending Interfaces?

With our interfaces we can define generic types of objects, and by implementing the interfaces any object can be of that type.

Let's go back to our `Musician` example. The more I think about it, the more I realize that there are a lot of different types of musicians out there. What if we wanted an interface for a specific type of musician, like a `JazzMusician` interface? Jazz musicians might do things other musicians might not, like free-form solos, but they will also do anything that a regular musician would do.

In this case, what we want to do is *extend* the `Musician` interface. (Again, the terminology may differ from language to language.) When we create our `JazzMusician` interface, we declare that it does everything a `Musician` does, plus whatever extra properties and methods we choose to add, like maybe a `freeFormSolo()` method. Like all other aspects of interfaces, the way we extend an interface is entirely language-dependent, meaning that it would work differently in C++ than in Java or Visual Basic.

But in all cases, the net result is the same: if an object is implementing the `JazzMusician` interface, it must implement all of the properties and methods of that interface, plus all of the properties and methods of `Musician`. That object would not only be a `JazzMusician` object, but also a `Musician` object.

Extending Interfaces in the DOM

The most fundamental interface we'll meet with the DOM is the `Node` interface. This interface represents a single node in the document tree. Since most of the objects in the DOM are nodes, most of the interfaces extend the `Node` interface. This means that the objects implementing these interfaces have all of the properties and methods of `Node`, plus whatever additional properties and methods are needed.

There's no limit to how many levels deep your extensions can go. For example, you can see from our diagram of the DOM interfaces that there's a `CDATASection` interface, which extends the `Text` interface, which in turn extends the `CharacterData` interface, which in turn extends the `Node` interface. So any object which implements `CDATASection` is also by definition a `Text` object, a `CharacterData` object, and a `Node` object.

A good example of extensions provided for DOM implementations is the ability to load and save XML documents. The DOM specification doesn't specify any way to do this, so it is completely implementation-specific as to how you would load an XML document into the DOM, or save it to disk. The MSXML DOM, which we'll be using in this chapter, provides three extensions for this purpose:

❑ The `load()` method will load an XML document from a URL

❑ The `loadXML()` method will load an XML document from a string

❑ The `save()` method will save an XML document as a Unicode string to your hard drive, in the location you specify

225

The DOM Core in Detail

So let's take a closer look at some of the more important core interfaces.

In the next few sections, not all of the properties and methods will be listed for every interface. For some of the more complex interfaces, only the most commonly used ones will be listed here.

Many of the methods listed have equivalent namespace-aware versions, for working with namespaces. In most cases, the namespace-aware function has the same name, with "NS" added to it, such as the `createElement()` and `createElementNS()` methods of the `Document` interface. As these two methods are used in pretty much the same way, we don't cover the namespace-aware versions here.

> **There is a complete listing of all the properties and methods of every interface in DOM Level 2, including these namespace-aware methods, in Appendix A.**

Exceptions

There is one concept that you should be aware of, before you work with the DOM: that of **exceptions**. These are a way to signal that a problem has occurred, and they're used very heavily by the DOM.

Exceptions are defined by creating a special type of object. When a situation arises which will cause an exception, this object is **thrown**, and then **caught** by an **exception handler**.

Different programming languages deal with exceptions differently. For example, in Java exception handling would look like this:

```
try
{
    //code here that might raise an exception

    //OR, raise one ourselves
    throw objException;
}
catch(ObjectType e)
{
    //deal with the exception
}
```

Any code that might raise an exception is included in a `try` block, and the code to handle the exception is in a `catch` block.

Exception handling in Visual Basic looks quite different:

```
On Error Resume Next
'code which might raise an exception goes here
If Err.Number <> 0 Then
    'an error occurred; deal with it
End If
On Error GoTo 0
```

Visual Basic uses a special object, called `Err`, which holds an error. There are some default actions that VB performs when an error occurs, so `On Error Resume Next` tells VB not to handle the error, because we want to do it ourselves, and to keep on going with the processing. We then check the `Err` object's `number` property, to see if there is indeed an error, and if so deal with it. Finally, `On Error GoTo 0` tells VB to go ahead and start handling errors in its own way again.

So, as you can see, exception handling can differ greatly from language to language. Also, not all languages have this kind of exception handling; this makes working with the DOM a little bit different.

For our examples, we'll be working with JavaScript on a web page in IE5. Earlier versions of the JavaScript language have no specified exception handling capabilities, while later versions support exception handling through the same `try ... catch` syntax as Java.

DOMException

The DOM defines an interface that is implemented by any exception objects that are thrown: the `DOMException` interface. This is actually a very simple interface; it has only one property, `code`, which is a number indicating what type of error has occurred.

In the DOM Level 2 Recommendation there are 15 possible values for `code`, with other codes reserved by the W3C for future use. (For a full list of the codes and their meanings, see Appendix A.)

Node

`Node` is the fundamental interface in the DOM. Almost all of the objects you will be dealing with will extend this interface, which makes sense, since any part of an XML document is a node.

However, though `Node` is implemented in all DOM objects, it has some properties and methods which may not be appropriate for certain node types. These are just included for the sake of convenience, so that if you're working with a variable of type `Node`, you will have access to some of the functionality of the other interfaces, without having to cast to one of those types.

Getting Node Information

The `Node` interface has several properties that let us get information about the node in question.

The nodeType Property

If you're ever not sure what type of node you're dealing with, the `nodeType` property can tell you (all of the possible values for `nodeType` are listed in Appendix A). For example, you could check to see if you're working with an `Element` like:

```
if(objNode.nodeType == 1)
```

Luckily for us, most DOM implementations will include pre-defined constants for these node types. For example, a constant might be defined called NODE_ELEMENT, with the value of 1, meaning that we could write code like this:

```
if(objNode.nodeType == NODE_ELEMENT)
```

This makes it easier to tell what we are checking for, without having to remember that `nodeType` returns "1" for an element.

The attributes Property

A good example of a property of `Node` that doesn't apply to every node type is the `attributes` property, which is *only* applicable if the node is an element. The `attributes` property returns a `NamedNodeMap`, which we'll be discussing later, containing any attributes of the node. If the node is not an element, or is an element with no attributes, the `attributes` property returns `null`.

The nodeName and nodeValue Properties

Two pieces if information that you will probably want from any type of node are its name and its value, and `Node` provides the `nodeName` and `nodeValue` attributes to retrieve this information. `nodeName` is **read-only**, meaning that you can get the value from the property but not change it, and `nodeValue` is **read-write**, meaning that you can change the value of a node if desired.

The values returned from these properties differ from node-type to node-type (this is covered in more detail in Appendix A). For example, for an element, `nodeName` will return the name of the element, but for a text node, `nodeName` will return the string "`#text`", since PCDATA nodes don't really have a name.

If we have a variable named `objNode` referencing an element like `<name>John</name>`, then we can write code like this:

```
alert(objNode.nodeName);
//pops up a message box saying "name"

objNode.nodeName = "FirstName";
//will raise an exception!  nodeName is read-only

alert(objNode.nodeValue);
//pops up a message box saying "null"
```

The result of that second alert may surprise you; why does it return "null", instead of "John"? The answer is that the text inside an element is not part of the element itself; it actually belongs to a text node, which is a child of the element node.

If we have a variable named `objText`, which points to the text node child of this element, we can write code like this:

```
alert(objText.nodeName);
//pops up a message box saying "#text"

alert(objText.nodeValue);
//pops up a message box saying "John"

objText.nodeValue = "Bill";
//this is allowed, the element is now <name>Bill</name>
```

Try It Out – Accessing Element Information with Node

To demonstrate some of these concepts, we'll create a simple XML document, and access it from a web page in IE5.

1. First, create the following XML document, and save it to your hard drive, as `domnode.xml`:

```
<root>
  <DemoElement DemoAttribute="stuff">This is the PCDATA</DemoElement>
</root>
```

2. Now we'll create our web page, with the following HTML and JavaScript:

```
<HTML>
<HEAD><TITLE>DOM Demo</TITLE>

<SCRIPT language="JavaScript">

  var objDOM;
  objDOM = new ActiveXObject("MSXML.DOMDocument");
  objDOM.async = false;
  objDOM.load("domnode.xml");

  //our code will go here...

</SCRIPT>

</HEAD>
<BODY>
  <P>This page demos some of the DOM capabilities.</P>
</BODY>
</HTML>
```

3. Save this page as `dom.htm`, in the same directory as you saved the `domnode.xml` file. We'll use this HTML page as the basis for our examples throughout the rest of the chapter, to demonstrate our DOM concepts.

4. After the comment, add the following code:

```
//our code will go here...
var objMainNode;
objMainNode = objDOM.documentElement.firstChild;
alert(objMainNode.nodeName);
```

5. Now save the file as `domnode.htm`, and open it in IE5. The result will be a message box, with the name of the node: in this case DemoElement:

6. Now change the last line of the previous code to print the node's value, instead of its name, like this:

```
//our code will go here...
  var objMainNode;
  objMainNode = objDOM.documentElement.firstChild;
  alert(objMainNode.nodeValue);
```

7. Save the HTML again, and refresh the page in the browser. This pops up a message box with the word null; why is that?

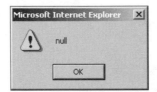

Remember that this is an element we're talking about. The text in that element is contained not in the element itself, but in a `Text` child. Therefore, an element doesn't have any values of its own, only children.

How It Works

The HTML page itself doesn't actually do anything, except display the text This page demos some of the DOM capabilities. All of the work is actually done in that `<SCRIPT>` block, and any results we want to see are displayed in message boxes.

In our second step, when we created the initial HTML file, we had to load our XML document into Microsoft's DOM implementation, MSXML. We did this using two of the extensions Microsoft added to the DOM: the `async` property, and the `load()` method. The `load()` method takes in a URL to an XML file, and loads it. The `async` property tells the parser whether it should load the file **synchronously**, or **asynchronously**.

> *If we load the file synchronously, `load()` won't return until the file is finished loading. Loading the file asynchronously would allow our code to do other things while the document is loading, which isn't necessary in this case.*

And finally, we access the nodes in the tree, in this case using the `documentElement` and `firstChild` properties (which will be discussed in the next section), and give the `nodeName` and `nodeValue` properties a try as well.

Traversing the Tree

As you'll recall from previous chapters, XML documents are trees of information, and the relationships between nodes are expressed as parent/child, ancestor/descendent etc. The DOM allows access to the nodes in a tree by exposing properties which work with these concepts.

These properties are the `parentNode`, `firstChild`, `lastChild`, `previousSibling`, and `nextSibling` properties, all of which return a `Node`, or the `childNodes` property, which returns a `NodeList`. (The `NodeList` interface is discussed in an upcoming section.)

Not all nodes can have children (attributes, for example), and even if a node can have children it might not, but when that happens any properties which are supposed to return children will just return `null`. (Or, in the case of `childNodes`, will return a `NodeList` with no nodes.)

The following diagram shows a node, and the node which would be returned from each of these properties:

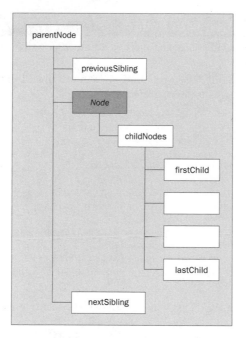

To get at the children of the node, we access the `childNodes` property. Or, if we want the first or the last child, there are properties which directly return these nodes, which is easier than having to navigate through the `childNodes` property. (If a node has only one child, `firstChild` and `lastChild` will both return that node.)

The `parentNode` property returns the node to which this node belongs in the tree, and `previousSibling` and `nextSibling` return the two nodes which are children of that parent node, and on either side of the node we're working with.

The hasChildNodes Method

If you just want to check if the node has children at all, there is a method named `hasChildNodes()`, which returns a Boolean value indicating whether there are any. (Note that this includes text nodes, so even if an element has only text for a child, `hasChildNodes()` will return `true`.) For example, we could write code like the following, so that if a node has any children, a message box will pop up with the name of the first one:

```
if(objNode.hasChildNodes())
{
   alert(objNode.firstChild.nodeName);
}
```

The ownerDocument Property

Since every node must belong to a document, there's also a property called `ownerDocument`, which returns an object implementing the `Document` interface to which this node belongs. Almost all of the objects in the DOM implement the `Node` interface, so this allows you to find the owner document from any object in the DOM.

Try It Out – Navigating the Tree with Node

Now let's modify our previous HTML page, and use it to navigate through our document.

1. Since this element has only one text child, we can use the `firstChild` property to access it. Modify `domnode.htm` as follows, and save it as `domtree.htm`:

```
<SCRIPT language="JavaScript">

  var objDOM;
  objDOM = new ActiveXObject("MSXML.DOMDocument");
  objDOM.load("dom.xml");

  //our code will go here...
  var objMainNode;
  objMainNode = objDOM.selectSingleNode("/root/DemoElement");
  alert(objMainNode.firstChild.nodeName);
  alert(objMainNode.firstChild.nodeValue);
</SCRIPT>
```

2. Then view the page in IE5. This will pop up two consecutive message boxes:

How It Works

As we mentioned before, `Text` nodes always return **#text** from `nodeName`, since PCDATA nodes don't have names. `nodeValue` returns the value of the PCDATA in the element.

Adding and Removing Nodes

All of the above properties for traversing the tree are read-only, meaning that you can get at the existing children, but not add new ones or remove old ones. To do that, there are a number of methods exposed from the `Node` interface.

The appendChild Method

The simplest is the `appendChild()` method, which takes an object implementing `Node` as a parameter, and just appends it to the end of the list of children. You might append one node to another like this:

```
objParentNode.appendChild(objChildNode);
```

The `objChildNode` node is now the last child node of `objParentNode`, regardless of what type of node it is.

The insertBefore Method

To have more control over where the node is inserted, you could call `insertBefore()`. This takes two parameters: the node to insert, and the "reference node", or the one before which you want the new child inserted. The following will add the same `objChildNode` to the same `objParentNode`, but the child will be added as the second last child:

```
objParentNode.insertBefore(objChildNode, objParentNode.lastChild);
```

The removeChild Method

To remove a child, you would call the `removeChild()` method, which takes a reference to the child you want to remove, and returns that object back to you, in case you want to use it somewhere else. Even though the node is removed from the tree, it still belongs to the document, although if we were to remove the child and then save the document, it would be lost. So we could remove the last child of any node, and keep it in a variable, like this:

```
objOldChild = objParent.removeChild(objParent.lastChild);
```

The replaceChild Method

There is also a time-saving method, `replaceChild()`, which can remove one node, and replace it with another. This is quicker than calling `removeChild()`, and then `appendChild()` or `insertBefore()`. Again, the child that's removed is returned from the method, in case you want to use it somewhere else. To replace the first child of a node with another node, you would do this:

```
objOldChild = objParent.replaceChild(objNewChild, objParent.firstChild);
```

The cloneNode Method

Finally, there is a method to create a copy of the node, which is `cloneNode()`. `cloneNode()` takes a Boolean parameter, indicating if this should be a **deep clone** (`true`), or a **shallow clone** (`false`). If it's a deep clone, the method will recursively clone the sub-tree under the node (in other words all of the children will also be cloned), otherwise only the node itself will be copied.

Note that if the node is an element, a shallow clone will not copy the PCDATA content of the node, since the PCDATA is a child, although attributes and their values will be copied. So if we have a node object, called `objNode`, which contains an element like `<name id="1">John</name>`, we could do this:

```
objNewNode = objNode.cloneNode(false);
//objNewNode is now <name id="1"/>

objNewNode = objNode.cloneNode(true);
//objNewNode is now <name id="1">John</name>
```

Again, notice that the attribute is copied, even when we do a shallow clone.

Note that nodes which are created using the `cloneNode()` can only be used in the same document as the original node; you can't clone a node from one document and insert it into another one. For this functionality, you'll need the `importNode()` method of the `Document` interface, which is discussed in a later section.

Try It Out – Modifying the Tree with Node

Now that we're able to get our information out of the document, let's start modifying it.

1. We'll start by cloning our node, then adding the new cloned node back in the document. Modify `domnode.htm` as follows:

```
//our code will go here...

var objMainNode;
objMainNode = objDOM.documentElement.firstChild;

var objNewNode;
objNewNode = objMainNode.cloneNode(false);
objMainNode.appendChild(objNewNode);

alert(objDOM.xml);
```

This will copy our node, and then append it back into the XML tree. We've done a shallow clone, meaning that none of the children of the node were copied. The `xml` property we call in that last line is a Microsoft-specific extension to the DOM, which returns the entire XML document as a string.

2. When you save and display this (`domtreenode.htm`), the message box will show the XML in our document, which now looks like this:

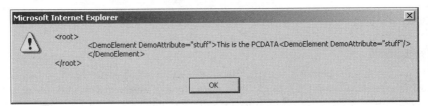

Notice that although none of the child elements of `<DemoElement>` get cloned, the attribute and its value does.

3. We can also attach that element before our text, by modifying our code:

```
//our code will go here...
var objMainNode;
objMainNode = objDOM.selectSingleNode("/root/DemoElement");

var objNewNode;
objNewNode = objMainNode.cloneNode(false);
objMainNode.insertBefore(objNewNode, objMainNode.firstChild);

alert(objDOM.xml);
```

For the reference node, we just use the `firstChild` property. The XML now looks like this:

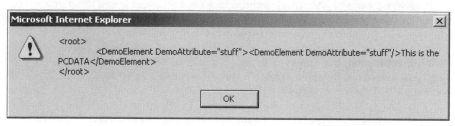

4. By simply changing the parameter to `cloneNode()` to `true`, we can copy all of the node's children:

```
var objNewNode;
objNewNode = objMainNode.cloneNode(true);
objMainNode.insertBefore(objNewNode, objMainNode.firstChild);

alert(objDOM.xml);
```

In this case, that's just the one `Text` node. Our XML now looks like this:

Document

The `Document` interface represents an entire XML document. It extends the `Node` interface, so any `Node` properties and methods will also be available from a `Document` object. For `Document`, the node will be the document root – not the root element. (Remember that for an XML document, the document root is a conceptual entity which contains everything else in the document, including the root element.)

All nodes must belong to one, and only one, document. Even if a node is not currently part of the tree-structure of the document, such as one which has been created but not yet added, it still belongs to the document. That is, if we use one of the `Document` interface's methods to create a node, which we'll be studying in the next few sections, the node won't immediately be a part of the document's tree. However, that node will belong to the document which created it.

In addition to the properties and methods provided by `Node` for navigating the tree, the `Document` interface provides some additional navigational functionality. The most often used is the `documentElement` property, which returns an `Element` object corresponding to the root element.

Another handy function is provided to find elements in the document based on their name: `getElementsByTagName()`. As a parameter, it takes a string specifying the name of the elements you're looking for, and it returns a `NodeList` containing all of the matching elements. (We'll be studying the `NodeList` interface in a later section.)

A `Document` object is often the only type of object you can create yourself. That is, if you were starting from scratch, you would not be able to create a `Node` object or a `DOMException` object, but you would be able to create a `Document` object.

The `Document` interface provides **factory methods** that can be used to create other objects. These methods are named `createNodeType()`, where *NodeType* is the type of node you want to create, for example `createElement` or `createAttribute`. This makes adding nodes to an XML document a two-step process:

❏ First, create the node using one of the `Document` factory methods

❏ Second, append the child in the appropriate spot

Try It Out – Creating an XML Document from Scratch

Let's see how to create an XML document programmatically.

1. To start, we'll go back to our original `dom.htm` document, which looked like this:

```
<HTML>
<HEAD><TITLE>DOM Demo</TITLE>

<SCRIPT language="JavaScript">
  var objDOM;
  objDOM = new ActiveXObject("MSXML.DOMDocument");
  objDOM.async = false;
  objDOM.load("domnode.xml");

  //our code will go here...

</SCRIPT>

</HEAD>
<BODY>
  <P>This page demos some of the DOM capabilities.</P>
</BODY>
</HTML>
```

Delete the lines:

```
objDOM.async = false;
objDOM.load("domnode.xml");
```

2. We're creating a `Document` object called `objDom`. We'll use that object to create an element and a text node. Insert the following lines of code right after the comment:

```
//our code will go here...
var objNode, objText;
objNode = objDOM.createElement("root");
objText = objDOM.createTextNode("root PCDATA");
```

The `createElement()` method takes the name of the element to be created as its parameter, and `createTextNode()` takes as its parameter the text we want to go into the node.

3. With these objects created, we can now add the element to our document. We will make it the root element, and add the text node to that element. Add the following code right after the code you've already entered:

```
objDOM.appendChild(objNode);
objNode.appendChild(objText);
alert(objDOM.xml);
```

The first command adds the tags and the second the PCDATA.

4. Save the HTML as `domdocument.htm` and view it with IE5. The following message box will appear:

5. Now let's add an attribute to that node. Add the following lines of code right before the alert, as shown:

```
objDOM.appendChild(objNode);
objNode.appendChild(objText);

var objAttr;
objAttr = objDOM.createAttribute("id");

//set the attribute's value
objAttr.nodeValue = "123";

//append the attribute to the element
objNode.attributes.setNamedItem(objAttr);

alert(objDOM.xml);
```

237

The createAttribute() method takes the name of the attribute as its parameter, so we've created an attribute named id, given it the value 123, then added that attribute to the node. (Later we'll see an easier way of doing this, using the setAttribute method. The setNamedItem() method is part of the NamedNodeMap interface, which we'll also be studying in a later section.)

Our XML now looks like this:

Thus, we have created an entire XML document, all from code.

DOMImplementation

The DOMImplementation interface provides methods which apply to any document from this DOM implementation. Just like most of the other types of DOM objects, you can't directly create a DOMImplementation object. Instead, you retrieve it from the implementation property of the Document interface.

The first method we'll look at is createDocument(), which works just like the createNodeType() methods of the Document interface. You probably won't use createDocument() very often, however, since you can't directly create a DOMImplementation object; you would first have to create a Document and access its implementation property to get a DOMImplementation object before you could even use this method! However, if you're creating multiple documents, meaning that you already have one or more Document objects in existence, it might come in handy.

A more important method is the hasFeature() method, which you can use to find out if this DOM implementation supports a certain feature. The method takes two parameters, a string representing the feature you're looking for, and a string representing the version of the feature you need. If you don't pass the second parameter, then hasFeature() will indicate if this DOM supports *any* version of the feature. This can be useful for finding out whether a particular browser supports certain features – so you can run different code for different browsers, for example.

For example, hasFeature("XML", "2.0") would return true if this DOM implementation implements the Extended Interfaces, and is based on version 2.0 or later of the DOM specification (rather than XML version 2.0).

hasFeature("XML") would return true if this DOM implementation implements the Extended Interfaces from *any* version of the DOM specification.

Most of the time you won't need to create a separate DOMImplementation object, but will instead just call its methods directly from the Document interface's implementation property, like this:

```
objDoc.implementation.hasFeature("XML", "2.0")
```

DocumentFragment

As we all know by now, an XML document can have only one root element. However, when working with XML information, it might be handy sometimes to have a few not-so-well-formed fragments of XML gathered together, in a temporary holding place. For example, you might want to create a number of nodes, and then insert them into the document tree in one bunch. Or, you might want to remove a number of nodes from the document and keep them around to be inserted back in later, like a cut and paste type of operation. This is what the DocumentFragment interface provides.

As for the interface itself, there are no properties or methods added to those provided by the Node interface.

For its children, a DocumentFragment has zero or more nodes. These are usually element nodes, but a DocumentFragment could even contain just a text node. DocumentFragment objects can be passed to methods which are used to insert nodes into a tree; for example, the appendChild() method of Node. In this case, all of the children of the DocumentFragment are copied to the destination Node, but the DocumentFragment itself is not.

Try It Out – Document Fragments in Action

To demonstrate the DocumentFragment interface in action, we'll write some quick code, which will use one as a temporary holding place.

1. First, we'll create our root element as usual. Modify dom.htm as follows:

```
<HTML>
<HEAD><TITLE>DOM Demo</TITLE>

<SCRIPT language="JavaScript">
  var objDOM;
  objDOM = new ActiveXObject("MSXML.DOMDocument");

  var objNode;
  objNode = objDOM.createElement("root");
  objDOM.appendChild(objNode);

</SCRIPT>

</HEAD>
<BODY>
  <P>This page demos some of the DOM capabilities.</P>
</BODY>
</HTML>
```

2. We'll then create a DocumentFragment, and store a couple of elements in it:

```
  var objFrag;
  objFrag = objDOM.createDocumentFragment();

  objNode = objDOM.createElement("child1");
  objFrag.appendChild(objNode);
  objNode = objDOM.createElement("child2");
  objFrag.appendChild(objNode);
```

239

Notice that we are reusing our objNode variable, instead of creating variables for all of the nodes we're dealing with; this just makes it easier to code. Note that the nodes in this fragment have no root element; this isn't a well-formed XML document, it's just a number of nodes, which we want to keep together for the moment.

3. Since our elements aren't much fun without any text in them, let's add a text child node to each one:

```
objFrag.firstChild.appendChild(objDOM.createTextNode("First child node"));
objFrag.lastChild.appendChild(objDOM.createTextNode("Second child node"));
```

In this case, we don't bother to create a variable to hold the Text node, we just create and immediately append it to the element.

4. Finally, we'll add the elements in our DocumentFragment to the root element of our document:

```
objDOM.documentElement.appendChild(objFrag);
alert(objDOM.xml);
```

As we mentioned earlier, this appends the *children* of the DocumentFragment, not the DocumentFragment itself.

5. Save the file as domfragment.htm. Our final XML looks like this:

NodeList

We've already mentioned it a couple of times, so let's talk about the NodeList interface. Many of the properties and methods in the DOM will return an ordered collection of Nodes, instead of just one, which is why the NodeList interface was created.

It's actually a very simple interface; there is only one property and one method:

❑   The length property returns the number of items in the NodeList.

❑   The item() method returns a particular item from the list. As a parameter, it takes the **index** of the Node you want.

Items in a NodeList are numbered starting at 0, not at 1. That means that if there are five items in a NodeList, the length property will return 5, but to get at the first item you would call item(0), and to get the fifth item you would call item(4). So the last Node in the NodeList is always at position (length – 1). If you call item() with a number that's out of the range of this NodeList, it will return null.

A node list is always "live"; that means that if you add and remove nodes to the document, a node list will always reflect those changes. For example, if we got a node list of all elements in the document with a name of "first", then appended an element named "first", the node list would automatically contain this new element, without us having to ask it to recalculate itself.

Try It Out – Accessing Items in a NodeList

To see how a `NodeList` works, we'll first need a group of nodes.

1. Save the following XML to your hard drive as `domnodelist.xml`:

```xml
<?xml version="1.0"?>
<root>
  <child>First child</child>
  <child>Second child</child>
  <child>Third child</child>
  <child>Fourth child</child>
  <child>Fifth child</child>
</root>
```

2. We can load this XML into MSXML as in our previous examples. Modify `dom.htm` as follows:

```html
<HTML>
<HEAD><TITLE>DOM Demo</TITLE>

<SCRIPT language="JavaScript">

  var objDOM;
  objDOM = new ActiveXObject("MSXML.DOMDocument");
  objDOM.load("domnodelist.xml");

</SCRIPT>

</HEAD>
<BODY>
  <P>This page demos some of the DOM capabilities.</P>
</BODY>
</HTML>
```

3. Now we can get a list of all of the nodes named `child` by using this code:

```javascript
  var objNodeList;
  objNodeList = objDOM.getElementsByTagName("child");
```

4. And we can then get the text from the second `<child>` element like so:

```javascript
  alert(objNodeList.item(1).firstChild.nodeValue);
```

5. Save the file as `domnodelist.htm` and view it in IE5. This produces a message box like this:

If you are puzzled why `item(1)` returns the second child remember that it is a five member list numbered from 0 to 4, so `item(1)` is the second list member.

Element

When you're not just referring to every item in an XML document as a "node", the pieces you're going to be accessing most will be elements, so of course the DOM provides an `Element` interface.

In addition to the properties and methods available from the `Node` interface, `Element` also provides a `tagName` property, and a `getElementsByTagName()` method. The `tagName` property returns exactly the same results as the `nodeName` property of `Node`, and `getElementsByTagName()` works exactly the same as the method of the same name on the `Document` interface.

However, note that `getElementsByTagName()` on the `Element` interface will only return elements which are descended from this one. Of course, that applies to the `getElementsByTagName()` on the `Document` interface as well, but the `Document` happens to include all of the elements in the document.

All of the rest of the methods on the `Element` interface are concerned with attributes.

To start, there are `getAttribute()` and `getAttributeNode()` methods. Both methods take the name of the attribute you want as a parameter, but `getAttribute()` returns the value of that attribute in a string, whereas `getAttributeNode()` returns an object implementing the `Attr` interface (which we'll cover later).

If that isn't bad enough, there is also a `setAttribute()` method, and a `setAttributeNode()` method. `setAttribute()` takes two string parameters: the name of the attribute you want to set, and the value you want to give it. If an attribute of that name doesn't exist, it is created, but if the attribute already exists, it is replaced. `setAttributeNode()` takes one parameter, an object implementing the `Attr` interface. Again, if an attribute with the same name already exists, it is replaced by the new attribute, but in this case, the old attribute is returned from the method, in case you need it for something else.

And finally, there's a `removeAttribute()` method, and a `removeAttributeNode()` method. `removeAttribute()` takes a string parameter, specifying the name of the attribute you wish to remove, and `removeAttributeNode()` takes as a parameter an `Attr` object, which is the attribute you want to remove. `removeAttributeNode()` returns the `Attr` object that was removed.

Try It Out – Using the Element Interface

Since most of the functionality of the `Element` interface revolves around attributes, all we'll really need to use to demonstrate it is a small XML document.

1. Save the following to your hard drive as `domelement.xml`:

```
<?xml version="1.0"?>
<root first='John' last='Doe'/>
```

2. Then use the following modification to `dom.htm` to load the document into MSXML, and create an `Element` variable to point to the `documentElement`:

```
<HTML>
<HEAD><TITLE>DOM Demo</TITLE>

<SCRIPT language="JavaScript">

  var objDOM;
  objDOM = new ActiveXObject("MSXML.DOMDocument");
  objDOM.load("domelement.xml");

  var objElement;
  objElement = objDOM.documentElement;

</SCRIPT>

</HEAD>
<BODY>
  <P>This page demos some of the DOM capabilities.</P>
</BODY>
</HTML>
```

3. Getting the value of an attribute is easy. Add the following to the end of your script code:

```
  alert(objElement.getAttribute("first"));
```

This gets the value of the `first` attribute

4. Save the page as `domelement.htm` and view it: the resulting message box contains the word John:

5. We can change the value of the first attribute by adding the following line of code:

```
var objElement;
objElement = objDOM.documentElement;

objElement.setAttribute("first", "Bill");

alert(objElement.getAttribute("first"));
```

Our message box will then read:

6. But, as we learned earlier, we can also do this using an `Attr` object. Try replacing the previous line of code with the following:

```
objElement = objDOM.documentElement;

var objAttr;
objAttr = objElement.getAttributeNode("first");
objAttr.nodeValue = "Bill";

alert(objElement.getAttribute("first"));var objAttr;
```

Or we can use the `Element` object like this:

```
objElement.getAttributeNode("first").nodeValue = "Bill";
```

Both of these methods will return the same message box containing the name Bill.

7. And finally, we have two ways to add a `middle` attribute to our element. Add the following code to append an `Attr` object:

```
objElement.getAttributeNode("first").nodeValue = "Bill";

alert(objElement.getAttribute("first"));

var objAttr;
objAttr = objDOM.createAttribute("middle");
objAttr.nodeValue = "Fitzgerald Johansen";
objElement.setAttributeNode(objAttr);

alert(objDOM.xml);
```

The resulting XML looks like this:

We can get exactly the same result by just using the `setAttribute()` method, like this:

```
objElement.getAttributeNode("first").nodeValue = "Bill";

alert(objElement.getAttribute("first"));

objElement.setAttribute("middle", "Fitzgerald Johansen");

alert(objDOM.xml);
```

There isn't any way to arrange the `middle` attribute between the `first` and `last` attributes, but we don't really mind, since the order of attributes on an XML element is insignificant. This is because attributes are usually accessed by name.

NamedNodeMap

In addition to the `NodeList` interface, there's also a `NamedNodeMap` interface, which is used to represent an unordered collection of nodes. Items in a `NamedNodeMap` are usually retrieved by name.

It should come as no surprise that there is a `getNamedItem()` method, which takes a string parameter specifying the name of the node, and returns a `Node` object. There is also a `removeNamedItem()` method, which takes a string parameter specifying the name of the item you wish to remove, and returns the `Node` that was removed. And, to round out the functionality, there's a `setNamedItem()` method, which takes a parameter for the `Node` you want to insert into the `NamedNodeMap`.

Even though the items in a `NamedNodeMap` are not ordered, you still might want to iterate through them one by one. For this reason, `NamedNodeMap` provides a `length` property and an `item()` method, which work the same as `length` and `item()` on the `NodeList` interface. But the DOM specification is clear that this "does not imply that the DOM specifies an order to these Nodes". (You can see this for yourself at http://www.w3.org/TR/1999/CR-DOM-Level-2-19991210/core.html#ID-1780488922).

Try It Out – Accessing Nodes in a NamedNodeMap

We saw before that the `attributes` property of `Node` returns a `NamedNodeMap`, so let's reuse our XML document from the last Try It Out, and write some simple JavaScript code to work with the map:

1. Save the following as `nodemap.xml`:

```
<root first="John" last="Doe" middle="Fitzgerald Johansen"/>
```

2. Next open up the `dom.htm` web page we've been working with, and change it to load the new XML file, like so:

```
<HTML>
<HEAD><TITLE>DOM Demo</TITLE>

<SCRIPT language="JavaScript">

  var objDOM;
  objDOM = new ActiveXObject("MSXML.DOMDocument");
  objDOM.async = false;
  objDOM.load("nodemap.xml");

  //our code will go here...
</SCRIPT>

</HEAD>
<BODY>
  <P>This page demos some of the DOM capabilities.</P>
</BODY>
</HTML>
```

3. First of all, we'll get our `NamedNodeMap` to contain the attributes of this node, which happens to be the root element. Add the following code right after the comment:

```
var objMap;
objMap = objDOM.documentElement.attributes;
```

4. We could then get the value of the first attribute like so:

```
alert(objMap.getNamedItem("first").nodeValue);
```

5. Or, we could change the last name to `Smith` like so:

```
var objNode;
objNode = objMap.removeNamedItem("last");
objNode.nodeValue = "Smith";
objMap.setNamedItem(objNode);
```

Notice that we have to remove the `last` attribute, before modifying and re-adding it. `NamedNodeMap` uses the name of the item to keep track of it in the list, and won't let us try to add an item with a name it already has. But because `removeNamedItem()` returns the `Node` which was removed, we can use it and then just re-add it.

6. Finally, we'll pop up another message box, to show the final state of the XML document. The final HTML document should look like this:

```
<HTML>
<HEAD><TITLE>DOM Demo</TITLE>
```

```
<SCRIPT language="JavaScript">

  var objDOM;
  objDOM = new ActiveXObject("MSXML.DOMDocument");
  objDOM.async = false;
  //objDOM.load("C:\nodemap.xml");
  objDOM.loadXML("<root first='John' last='Doe' middle='Fitzgerald Johansen'/>");

  //our code will go here...
  var objMap;
  objMap = objDOM.documentElement.attributes;

  alert(objMap.getNamedItem("first").nodeValue);

  var objNode;
  objNode = objMap.removeNamedItem("last");
  objNode.nodeValue = "Smith";
  objMap.setNamedItem(objNode);

  alert(objDOM.xml);
</SCRIPT>

</HEAD>
<BODY>
  <P>This page demos some of the DOM capabilities.</P>
</BODY>
</HTML>
```

7. If you open this in IE5 you will see the following two messages:

Attr

Although most of the interfaces in the DOM are spelled out in full, in some bizarre moment of nomenclature weakness, the interface for attributes was abbreviated to `Attr`.

The `Attr` interface extends the `Node` interface, but it is good to keep in mind the differences between attributes and other items in the XML document. For one thing, attributes are not directly part of the tree structure in a document; that is, attributes are not children of elements, they are just properties of the elements to which they are attached. That means that the `parentNode`, `previousSibling`, and `nextSibling` properties for an attribute will always return `null`. But, since `parentNode` returns `null`, `Attr` provides instead an `ownerElement` property, which returns the `Element` to which this attribute belongs.

`Attr` also supplies `name` and `value` attributes, which return the name and value of the attribute. These properties have the same values as the `nodeName` and `nodeValue` properties of `Node`.

The final property supplied by the `Attr` interface is the `specified` property. In Chapter 9 we'll learn about a way that we can give attributes in an XML document default and fixed values. The `specified` property indicates whether this attribute is really a physical attribute on the element, with a real value, or whether it is just an *implied* attribute, with the default value supplied.

Try It Out – Attr in Action

The `Attr` interface is a simple one, so this will be a simple Try It Out.

1. We'll use our `domelement.xml` document from our earlier Try It Out:

```
<?xml version="1.0"?>
<root first='John' last='Doe'/>
```

2. And we'll use our usual initial HTML page (`dom.htm`) to load it:

```
<HTML>
<HEAD><TITLE>DOM Demo</TITLE>

<SCRIPT language="JavaScript">

  var objDOM;
  objDOM = new ActiveXObject("MSXML.DOMDocument");
  objDOM.load("domelement.xml");

  //our code will go here...

</SCRIPT>

</HEAD>
<BODY>
  <P>This page demos some of the DOM capabilities.</P>
</BODY>
</HTML>
```

3. We'll now create an `Attr` object, to point to our first attribute. Insert the following code after the comment:

```
  //our code will go here...
  var objAttr;
  objAttr = objDOM.documentElement.attributes.getNamedItem("first");
```

4. We'll now get the names of this object, first using the `name` property of the `Attr` interface, and then using the `nodeName` property of the `Node` interface:

```
  alert (objAttr.name);
  alert(objAttr.nodeName);
```

This is possible because the objAttr object implements both interfaces. Both of these will pop up a message box with the value "first".

We can get the value in a similar way: once via the value property of the Attr interface, and once via nodeValue property of the Node interface:

```
alert(objAttr.value);
alert(objAttr.nodeValue);
```

This produces two message boxes, both displaying the text John.

CharacterData and Text

As you're well aware, working with XML documents involves a lot of work with text: sometimes in PCDATA in the XML document, and sometimes in other places, like attribute values, or comments. The DOM defines two interfaces for this purpose:

❑ A CharacterData interface, which has a number of properties and methods for working with text

❑ A Text interface, which extends CharacterData, and is used specifically for PCDATA in the XML document

Because CharacterData extends Node, both CharacterData objects and Text objects are also Node objects. CharacterData nodes, like Attr nodes, can't have children, so the same rules for Attr's handling of child properties also apply to CharacterData objects.

Handling Complete Strings

The simplest way to get or set the PCDATA in a CharacterData object is simply to get it from the data property. This sets or returns the whole string in one chunk.

There is also a length property, which returns the number of Unicode characters in the string.

When dealing with strings in CharacterData objects, note that the characters in the string are numbered starting at 0, not 1. So in the string "Hi", "H" would be letter 0, and "i" would be letter 1.

So, if we have a Text node object named objText containing the string "John", then:

```
alert(objText.length);
```

pops up a message box saying 4, and :

```
alert(objText.data);
```

pops up a message box saying John.

Handling Sub-Strings

If you only want a part of the string, there is a `substringData()` method, which takes two parameters:

❑ The offset at which to start taking characters

❑ The number of characters to take

If you specify more characters than are available in the string, `substringData()` just returns the number of characters up until the end and stops.

For example, if we have a `CharacterData` object named `objText`, and the contents of that object are "This is the main string", then:

```
alert(objText.substring(12, 4));
```

would pop up a message box saying main, and:

```
alert(objText.substringData(12, 2000));
```

would pop up a message box saying main string.

Modifying Strings

Adding text to the end of a string is done with the `appendData()` function, which takes a single string parameter, containing the text to add to the end of the existing text.

If we used the same `objText` node as above, then:

```
objText.appendData(".");
```

would change the contents to "This is the main string." with the period added.

But since we sometimes need to add data to the middle of a string, there is also the `insertData()` method, which takes two parameters:

❑ The offset at which to start inserting characters

❑ The string you wish to insert

The following code would change the data to "This is the groovy main string.":

```
objText.insertData(12, "groovy ");
```

Deleting characters from the string is done via the `deleteData()` method, which you use exactly the same as the `substringData()` method. So calling:

```
objText.deleteData(12, 7);
```

on the `CharacterData` node we've been working with would change the string back to `"This is the main string."` removing the text `"groovy"`.

And finally, if you want to replace characters in a string with other characters, instead of calling `deleteData()` and then `insertData()`, you could simply use `replaceData()`. This method takes three arguments:

- ❏ The offset position at which to start replacing
- ❏ The number of characters to replace
- ❏ The string to replace them with

Note that the number of characters you're inserting doesn't have to be the same as the number of characters you're replacing.

If we still have the same `objText` node containing `"This is the main string."`, we could do the following:

```
objText.replaceData(8, 8, "a");
```

which would replace `"the main"` with `"a"`, thus changing the string to `"This is a string."`.

Splitting Text

The `Text` interface only adds one method to the ones inherited from `CharacterData`, which is the `splitText()` method. This takes one `Text` object and splits it into two, which are siblings of each other. The method takes one parameter, which is the offset at which to make the split.

The result is that the first `Text` node will contain the text from the old node until (but not including) the offset point, and the second `Text` node will contain the rest of the text from the old node. If the offset is equal to the length of the string, the first `Text` node will contain the old string as it was, and the new node will be empty; and if the offset is greater than the string's length, a `DOMException` will be raised.

We could, therefore, write code like this:

```
objText.splitText(11);
```

And the result would look something like this:

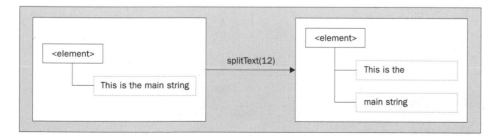

Of course, if we were to save this XML document like that, our change would be lost, since the PCDATA would then just become one string again. `splitText()` comes in most handy when you are going to be inserting other elements in the middle of the text.

Try It Out – Putting splitText() to Practical Use

To demonstrate this, let's take the following HTML paragraph:

```
<p>This is the main string</p>
```

and make that word "main" bold.

1. Save the following as `domtext.xml`:

```
<?xml version="1.0"?>
<p>This is the main string</p>
```

2. Extend our usual HTML document as follows, to create a `Node` object to hold this paragraph:

```
<HTML>
<HEAD><TITLE>DOM Demo</TITLE>

<SCRIPT language="JavaScript">

  var objDOM;
  objDOM = new ActiveXObject("MSXML.DOMDocument");
  objDOM.load("domtext.xml");

  var objNode;
  objNode = objDOM.documentElement;

</SCRIPT>

</HEAD>
<BODY>
  <P>This page demos some of the DOM capabilities.</P>
</BODY>
</HTML>
```

We're going to take this one `Text` node, and change it into three nodes:

❑ A `Text` node

❑ A child `<b>` node

❑ Another `Text` node

3. Our first step is to break the node into two separate text nodes. Add the following to the HTML file:

```
  var objNode;
  objNode = objDOM.documentElement;
```

```
var objText;
objText = objNode.firstChild;
objText.splitText(12);
```

Our <p> node now looks like this:

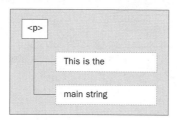

4. Next, we'll create the <b> element, and insert it as a child:

```
var objBElement;
objBElement = objDOM.createElement("b");
objNode.insertBefore(objBElement, objNode.lastChild);
```

Now our <p> node looks like this:

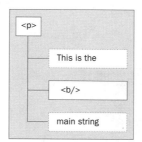

5. We now want to split the second Text node, so that we can strip the word "main" out and insert it as a child of the <b> element:

```
objText = objNode.lastChild;
objText.splitText(4);
```

Which makes our <p> node look like this:

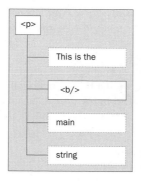

6. And, finally, we want to remove the second `Text` node, and append it to the `<b>` element:

```
objText = objNode.removeChild(objNode.childNodes.item(2));
objNode.childNodes.item(1).appendChild(objText);

alert(objNode.xml);
```

Our final result looks like this:

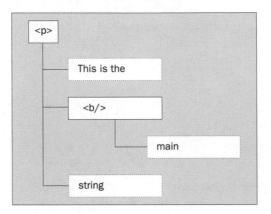

7. Now save the file as `domsplit.htm`, and run the HTML. The message box contains the following XML:

And you thought `splitText()` would be difficult!

Comment and CDATASection

The `Comment` and `CDATASection` interfaces are the two easiest interfaces we'll be studying in this chapter. `Comment` extends the `CharacterData` interface, and `CDATASection` extends `Text`, but neither interface adds any properties or methods! Working with a comment or a CDATA section in the DOM is just like working with any other text.

In fact, the only benefit you get from working with these interfaces is that when you create a `Comment` object and append it to the document, the DOM automatically adds the `"<!-- -->"` markup, and when you create a `CDATASection` and append it, the DOM automatically adds the `"<![CDATA[ ]]>"` markup.

Try It Out – Adding Comments and CDATA Sections

For our easy interfaces, we'll have an easy Try It Out. First, we'll make an extremely simple XML document.

1. Save the following as `domcomment.xml`:

```
<?xml version="1.0"?>
<root/>
```

2. Load that into MSXML in the usual way:

```
<HTML>
<HEAD><TITLE>DOM Demo</TITLE>

<SCRIPT language="JavaScript">

  var objDOM;
  objDOM = new ActiveXObject("MSXML.DOMDocument");
  objDOM.load("domcomment.xml");;

  //our code will go here...

</SCRIPT>

</HEAD>
<BODY>
  <P>This page demos some of the DOM capabilities.</P>
</BODY>
</HTML>
```

3. And then we'll just add a comment and a CDATA section. (Remember back in Chapter 2, we discussed that for well-formed XML, > and & characters can't be included except in CDATA sections.)

```
  var objComment, objCDATA;
  objComment = objDOM.createComment("This is my comment");
  objCDATA = objDOM.createCDATASection("6 < 7 & 7 > 6");

  objDOM.documentElement.appendChild(objComment);
  objDOM.documentElement.appendChild(objCDATA);

  alert(objDOM.xml);
```

4. Save as `domcomment.htm`, and run the HTML in IE5. The XML in our message box looks like this:

ProcessingInstruction

Finally, no DOM would be complete without a method for adding processing instructions. The `ProcessingInstruction` interface extends `Node`, and adds two properties of its own: `target`, and `data`.

In Chapter 2 we saw that the `target` property is the name of the application to which we want to pass the PI, and the `data` is the instruction itself. The `data` property can be changed, but `target` is read-only.

Try It Out – Accessing Processing Instructions

To demonstrate our new processing instruction capabilities, we'll add one to some simple XML.

1. Save the following as `dompi.xml`:

```
<?xml version="1.0"?>
<root>
  <child/>
  <?MyApp MessageBox("This is a Processing Instruction!")?>
</root>
```

2. Load this into MSXML as usual:

```
<HTML>
<HEAD><TITLE>DOM Demo</TITLE>

<SCRIPT language="JavaScript">

  var objDOM;
  objDOM = new ActiveXObject("MSXML.DOMDocument");
  objDOM.load("dompi.xml");

  //our code will go here...

</SCRIPT>

</HEAD>
<BODY>
  <P>This page demos some of the DOM capabilities.</P>
</BODY>
</HTML>
```

Instead of targeting the `MyApp` application, we'll change our PI to target the `YourApp` application. However, we can't just change the target on the existing PI, because the `target` property is read-only. So, in order to do this, we must first create a new PI, with the target we want.

The way we'll accomplish this is to cycle through each of the `<root>` element's child nodes. If that node is a PI, we'll create a new one with the desired target, copy the data from the old PI, add the new PI, and remove the old one. Sounds simple? It is!

3. Our first step is to create a `NodeList` object, to point to the `documentElement`'s child nodes, just for convenience. Add the following code after the comment:

```
//our code will go here...
var objNodeList;
objNodeList = objDOM.documentElement.childNodes;
```

4. Next, we want to loop through all of the nodes in our `NodeList`, with a JavaScript `for` loop:

```
var i;
for(i = 0; i < objNodeList.length; i++)
{
}
```

5. For each item, we want to check and see if the `nodeType` of the node is that of a processing instruction. Most DOM implementations will provide constants for this information, but from script we have to look for the value itself. A PI has a `nodeType` of 7, so add the following:

```
var i, objNode;
for(i = 0; i < objNodeList.length; i++)
{
  objNode = objNodeList.item(i);
  if(objNode.nodeType == 7)
  {
  }
}
```

6. If the condition is true, we'll create a new PI and copy the data from the old one. We get the old one by creating a variable of type `ProcessingInstruction`, and pointing it to the `objNode` object, which we know is our processing instruction:

```
var i, objNode;
for(i = 0; i < objNodeList.length; i++)
{
  objNode = objNodeList.item(i);
  if(objNode.nodeType == 7)
  {
    var objNewPI;
    objNewPI = objDOM.createProcessingInstruction("YourApp", "");
    objNewPI.data = objNode.data;
  }
}
```

7. And now we'll insert the new PI into the tree, and remove the old one:

```
for(i = 0; i < objNodeList.length; i++)
{
  objNode = objNodeList.item(i);
  if(objNode.nodeType == 7)
  {
    var objNewPI;
```

```
        objNewPI = objDOM.createProcessingInstruction("YourApp", "");
        objNewPI.data = objNode.data;

        objNode.parentNode.replaceChild(objNewPI, objNode);
    }
  }
```

8. Finally, we'll just add an alert to give us the new XML. The final HTML document should look like this:

```
<HTML>
<HEAD><TITLE>DOM Demo</TITLE>

<SCRIPT language="JavaScript">

  var objDOM;
  objDOM = new ActiveXObject("MSXML.DOMDocument");
  objDOM.load("dom.xml");

  //our code will go here...
  var objNodeList;
  objNodeList = objDOM.documentElement.childNodes;

  var i, objNode;
  for(i = 0; i < objNodeList.length; i++)
  {
    objNode = objNodeList.item(i);
    if(objNode.nodeType == 7)
    {
      var objNewPI;
      objNewPI = objDOM.createProcessingInstruction("YourApp", "");
      objNewPI.data = objNode.data;

      objNode.parentNode.replaceChild(objNewPI, objNode);
    }
  }

  alert(objDOM.xml);

</SCRIPT>

</HEAD>
<BODY>
  <P>This page demos some of the DOM capabilities.</P>
</BODY>
</HTML>
```

9. Save and view the HTML page (`dompi.htm`). The message box contains the following XML:

Summary

The DOM is one of the more widely-recognized and easiest to use specifications to come out of the W3C concerning XML. Many, if not most, programmers who will be working with XML will be using the DOM to get at the data, or to create new XML documents.

In this chapter we have learned all we need to use the DOM to process XML documents, including:

- ❏ The interfaces that are provided for us
- ❏ How to handle exceptions arising from those interfaces
- ❏ How to use the DOM to get data out of our XML documents, add data to our documents, and even create documents from scratch

Because the DOM is creating all of these objects in memory, one for each and every node in the XML document, DOM implementations can be quite large, and processing XML documents via the DOM can take up a lot of memory. In the next chapter, we'll be studying another way that we can get information out of our documents. If the DOM is too slow, or takes up too much memory, we can use the Simple API for XML (SAX) instead.

The Simple API for XML (SAX)

And now for something *slightly* different. When it comes to analyzing XML documents and extracting information out of them, the DOM isn't the only game in town. There's another API called **SAX**, which turns out to be very good at the things that the DOM isn't so good at (although, as you might expect, it's not so good at the things the DOM is good at). The two approaches should be regarded as complementary, and any XML programmer should be conversant with both of them.

In this chapter you will learn:

- ❑ What the SAX is, and why it was created
- ❑ Where you can get SAX
- ❑ How to use the two main SAX 1.0 interfaces: `DocumentHandler` and `ErrorHandler`
- ❑ When to use SAX
- ❑ What's new in SAX 2.0

I'm duty bound at this point to issue a programming warning. This chapter contains explicit illustrations of programming – using Java in particular – and anyone who is uncomfortable with this may like to skip to another chapter now. (In fact, unless you plan to use XML with Java, you'll probably never come across SAX.) As with the last chapter (in fact more so) we're going to have to assume some programming experience, although I promise I'll steer clear of the weird stuff. If you want to try any of the examples, you're also going to need some kind of Java development environment – JavaSoft's free JDK is perfectly adequate for our purposes. (We'll talk about getting hold of this later.) You won't, however, be needing a browser.

What is SAX, and Why Was it Invented?

The **Simple API for XML**, or **SAX**, was developed in order to enable more efficient analysis of large XML documents. The problem with the DOM is that before you can use it to traverse a document, it has to build up a massive in-memory map of it. This takes up space, and – more importantly – time. If you're trying to extract a small amount of information from the document, this can be extremely inefficient.

Let's illustrate this by a simple analogy.

The Fabulous Lost Treasure of the Xenics

Imagine that you're an archaeologist searching a labyrinth of catacombs somewhere to find the Fabulous Lost Treasure Of The Xenics (FLTOTX). Unfortunately, in recent years, you've spent more time on the interview circuit than in the field, and, as a result, you're no longer in good enough shape to go rummaging around in damp tunnels with low ceilings. (Although you'd like to be able to stroll in and pick up the treasure for the benefit of the world's cameras, of course.) Instead, you send in your athletic young assistant, Indy. Or is it Lara? All these kids look the same to you ...

We have two approaches here to locating the FLTOTX. Firstly, Indy/Lara could map out the entire catacombs and contents for you. Once you've got such a map, you could find your way to the treasure without any trouble. However, this is a process that could, frankly, take years, and our evil arch-rival (there's always one) may well get to the treasure before us. Instead, what we could do is fit our assistants with a radio mike, and send them off, telling them to map everything as they go, but also to report back to us on everything they find.

On our headset, we'd probably hear something like:

"Er ... pile of flints ... spear ... ornamental vase ... small votive bust ... Fabulous Lost Treasure Of The Xenics ..."

"STOP!"

So What Does That Have to Do with SAX?

If only life was always that simple. Well, maybe XML can be. Let's interpret the analogy. The catacombs are, of course, supposed to represent an XML document. Indy/Lara is our parser, and the map that they are writing is the in-memory image of the XML document.

In the first instance, they were providing us with a DOM view of the document. As we saw, this can be time-consuming, although if we need that complete map (for instance, if we wished to build a copy of the catacombs for our new theme-park venture, or if we also wanted to find the Amazing Missing Treasure Of The Vrmls) it's the best way to proceed.

However, if all we want to do is locate specific parts of the document, the second approach is more appropriate. This is the way SAX works, and we call it **event-driven**. Rather than parse the document into the DOM and then use the DOM to navigate around the document, we tell the parser to raise **events** whenever it finds something, just like Indy/Lara giving us a running commentary over the headset.

If we were to show the two approaches diagrammatically, DOM would look something like this:

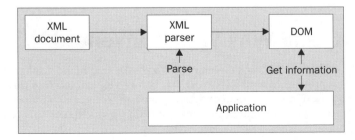

Whereas the SAX approach is more like this:

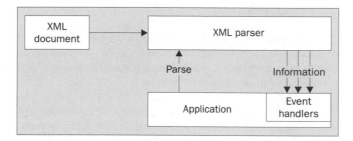

Now anyone who has done user-interface work will be familiar with this kind of "tell me when something happens" approach. After all, the best way to deal with a user clicking on buttons is to have a bit of code that's triggered whenever the user does something, rather than having it in a constant loop saying "What are you doing now?" over and over again. However, it's a little different from the run of the mill for document analysis. The good news is that it's not rocket science, either, and once you've got used to the idea of event-driven programming, you'll be doing it all the time, I promise you.

Where to Get SAX

I don't know about you, but I'm itching to try all this out. But before we can do anything, we need to get hold of some software. There are two things that we need in order to get this show on the road: a SAX-aware parser and the SAX Java classes. These classes are what we build on in our application in order to be able to receive SAX events. The bad news is that, at the time of writing, standard browsers do not contain a parser that supports SAX. The good news is that many public domain parsers do. So we're going to have to do some downloading:

❑   For our parser, we're going to follow the lead set by that excellent book *Professional XML* (*Wrox Press, ISBN 1-861003-11-0*), and use xp, the parser developed by James Clark. This is available from http://www.jclark.com/xml/xp/.

❑   Some parsers come with the SAX classes bundled in; however, xp doesn't, so we'll need to get them from http://www.megginson.com/SAX/.

❑   Finally, if we don't already have it, we'll need our Java development kit: we can get this from http://java.sun.com/products/jdk/1.1/download-jdk-windows.html.

   Warning: the first two downloads are nice and quick, but the JDK download is 8Mbytes, so you might want to get this ready well in advance. Don't worry about installing the downloads yet – we'll go through the process step by step before we start programming.

If you're interested in trying out some other SAX-aware parsers, you might be interested in getting hold of IBM xml4j (from http://alphaworks.ibm.com/tech/xml4j) or Sun Project X (from http://java.sun.com/products/xml/). The IBM parser is particularly interesting in that this is the one that the Xerces parser from the Apache project is based on (for more on that, see http://xml.apache.org). A full list of SAX-aware parsers can be found on http://www.megginson.com/SAX/.

SAX is specified in terms of Java interfaces, and as such is not supported to a large extent under other languages. For up-to-date information on support for other languages, see http://www.megginson.com/SAX/.

Who is this Megginson Guy Anyway?

A quick word about SAX's chief progenitor.

The extraordinary thing about SAX is that it isn't owned by anyone. It doesn't belong to any consortium, standards body, company or individual. So it doesn't survive because so-and-so says that you must use it in order to comply with standard X, or because company Y is dominant in the marketplace. It survives because it's simple and it works.

SAX arose out of discussions on the XML-DEV mailing list (now hosted by OASIS at http://www.oasis-open.org/) aimed at resolving incompatibilities between different XML parsers (this was back in the infancy of XML in late 1997). David Megginson took on the job of coordinating the process of specifying a new API, and then declared the specification frozen on 11 May 1998. This was SAX 1.0. If you're interested in reading more about the history of SAX, you can find it at http://www.megginson.com/SAX/history.html.

To this day, David Megginson continues to coordinate SAX development, and (at the time of writing) is just about to release SAX 2.0: of which more later in this chapter.

Using the SAX Interfaces

It's time to get to work and actually try some of this out.

Preparing the Ground

Before we launch into some programming, we'll need to do a little preparation work. Let's go through it step by step.

Try It Out – Step 1: Install JDK

This is the easy bit! JDK pretty much installs itself. Under Windows, for example, it comes as a self-extracting executable, and all you have to do is follow the instructions on screen.

Try It Out – Step 2: Install SAX

1. We should create a self-contained area for our experiments, so create a new directory somewhere convenient, called something like XML. Create another directory underneath this, called SAX.

2. Under Windows, SAX 1.0 comes as a zip file. Simply extract all the files in it into the SAX directory.

    You'll find that it creates its own directory structure underneath this, so that it looks something like this:

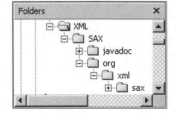

3. You may find that the top-level SAX directory contains a whole load of .java files; you should remove these, as they may confuse the compiler. They're actually the Java source for the SAX classes, in case you're interested in taking a look.

You should find a set of .html files in the javadoc folder – this is the official documentation, so don't lose it! In the org\xml\sax folder you should find a set of .class files. These are the SAX Java class files.

Try It Out – Step 3: Install xp

1. Now create another directory under XML, called xp. Our structure now looks like this:

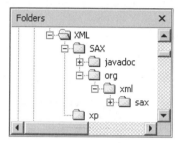

2. Again, the xp kit comes in the form of a zip file, and – again – all you need to do is extract all the files in it into our top-level directory: xp in this case. Your directory structure should now look like this:

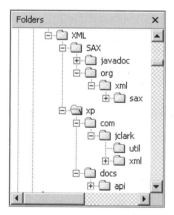

I've simplified this slightly. In actual fact, the only parts of it that are of any interest to us are the .html files in the docs subdirectory, and a file called xp.jar in the top-level directory. The .html files are, not surprisingly, the documentation. The xp.jar file is a Java archive, containing all the class files that we're going to need. Most of the rest of the download is the source that goes into creating these classes, and unless you're really interested, I'd leave it alone for the time being.

Try It Out – Step 4: Modifying the Class Path

The big question that we need to resolve now is how to tell our Java compiler where to find these classes. We do this by amending the value of an environment variable called CLASSPATH.

1. Under Windows, you can do this via the **System** icon on the control panel. In Windows NT, the relevant tab is the one labeled **Environment**. In Windows 2000, you'll find it by clicking on **Environment Variables** under the **Advanced** tab.

2. CLASSPATH should be in the **User Variables** section. You'll need to amend it (or create a new variable) so that it includes both the top-level SAX directory and the full pathname of the xp Java archive. You should also check that the path contains the current directory, " . ".

So, for instance, if your XML tree is on your c: drive, you'll need to add the following:

```
.;c:\XML\SAX;c:\XML\xp\xp.jar
```

This is how it looks in the Windows NT 4.0 control panel:

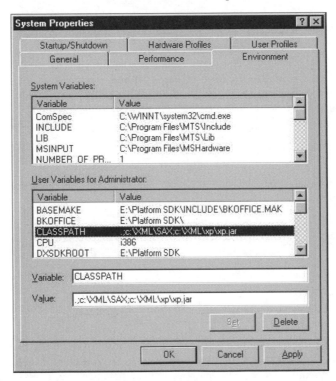

And this is how it looks in Windows 2000 (you'll need to click on **New...** or **Edit...** to create or alter **CLASSPATH**):

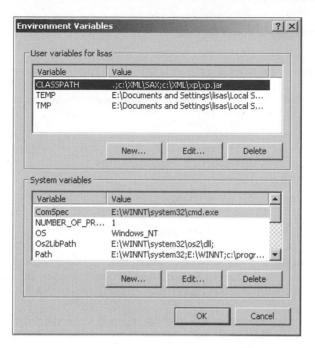

3. To execute the JDK tools, you need to specify the path to the tool from the command prompt. For example, if the JDK software is installed at `c:\jdk`, to run the compiler on a file called `myfile.java` you'd need to type the following:

```
c:\jdk\bin\javac myfile.java
```

If you'd rather simply type:

```
javac myfile.java
```

at the command prompt from any directory, you can change the PATH statement. This enables Windows to find the java executables from any current directory.

You'll find **PATH** under the **System Variables** section (shown in the previous screenshots). Select it and click on **Edit**. For example, if you have the JDK installed at the absolute path `C:\jdk`, you can edit your **PATH** variable by adding the following to the end of the **PATH** statement:

```
;C:\JDK\BIN
```

as follows:

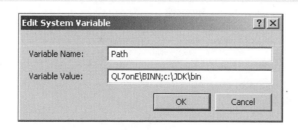

How to Receive SAX Events

One final thing before we get stuck in. You may be wondering how we're going to be receiving these events. Remember the discussion on **interfaces** in the last chapter? If not, it might be a good time to take a look again to refresh your memory. What we're going to do is write a Java class that **implements** one of the SAX interfaces. If we pass a reference to an instance of that class into our parser, the parser can then use that interface to talk back to us.

> *Imagine that the archaeologist in our example was actually French. In order for Indy/Lara to tell her what they had found, the archaeologist would have to learn English.*

We specify that a class implements an interface by declaring it like this:

```
public class MyClass implements DocumentHandler
```

`MyClass` is the name of my new class, and `DocumentHandler` is the name of the interface. Actually, this is the most important interface in SAX, as it's the one that it uses to call back to us with events. So what we're doing here is creating a class that contains methods that a SAX-aware parser knows about.

The `DocumentHandler` interface contains a whole series of methods, most of which in the normal course of events we don't really want to be bothered with. Fortunately, SAX provides us with a standard implementation of most of them, called `HandlerBase`. So rather than *implement* `DocumentHandler`, we can instead *extend* `HandlerBase`, like this:

```
public class MyClass extends HandlerBase
```

We can then pick and choose which methods we want to provide our own implementations, in order to trap specific events. This is called **overriding** the methods, and it works like this.

If we leave things as they are, the base class (`HandlerBase` in this case) provides its own implementation of them for use by `MyClass`. So if, for instance, there's a method in the `DocumentHandler` interface called `doSomething`, whenever another piece of code invokes the `doSomething` method of `MyClass`'s implementation of `DocumentHandler`, the method invoked is actually `HandlerBase.doSomething`. This is because `HandlerBase` is providing a default implementation of `doSomething`.

However, if we provide our own implementations of the methods, then they are used instead. In our example above, the method invoked would now be `MyClass.doSomething`. This might do something totally different from `HandlerBase`'s implementation.

The first pair of methods that we might want to override are `startDocument` and `endDocument`. There are no prizes for guessing that these are invoked at the start and end of the document, respectively. I think we're ready for a small Try It Out.

Try It Out – Minimal Parsing Using SAX

1. In order to do this example, we'll need an XML document. Create one as follows:

```
<?xml version="1.0"?>
<bands>
    <band type="progressive">
        <name>King Crimson</name>
        <guitar>Robert Fripp</guitar>
        <saxophone>Mel Collins</saxophone >
        <bass>Boz</bass>
        <drums>Ian Wallace</drums>
    </band>
    <band type="punk">
        <name>X-Ray Spex</name>
        <vocals>Poly Styrene</vocals>
        <saxophone >Laura Logic</saxophone >
        <guitar>Someone else</guitar>
    </band>
    <band type="classical">
        <name>Hilliard Ensemble</name>
        <saxophone >Jan Garbarek</saxophone >
    </band>
    <band type="progressive">
        <name>Soft Machine</name>
        <organ>Mike Ratledge</organ>
        <bass>Hugh Hopper</bass>
        <drums>Robert Wyatt</drums>
        <saxophone >Elton Dean</saxophone >
    </band>
</bands>
```

A motley bunch, if ever there was one. Save this as bands.xml, in a convenient directory. We're going to start by writing a piece of software that will print out the name of every element found.

2. Now let's create our Java class, in a separate document. The class will be called BandReader. In order to be able to use names like HandlerBase, rather than org.xml.sax.HandlerBase, we need to add the following line at the start of our code:

```
import org.xml.sax.*;
```

This will ensure that the Java compiler will know where to look for classes that it can't find locally.

3. Now here comes our class declaration and main method:

```
public class BandReader extends HandlerBase
{
    public static void main(String[] args) throws Exception
    {
        System.out.println("Here we go ...");
        BandReader readerObj = new BandReader();
        readerObj.read();
    }
```

The `main` method declaration is standard Java: this is the piece of code that will be executed when we start the class. It prints out a message, creates a new instance of itself, and invokes a method called `read`.

The `void` part of the declaration, incidentally, means that the method doesn't return a value to its caller, and the `throws Exception` part means that if anything happens that it can't cope with, it passes the exception back so the caller can deal with it. We'll see more of exceptions later.

4. The `read` method is where things get interesting:

```
public void read () throws Exception
{
    Parser parserObj = new com.jclark.xml.sax.Driver();
    parserObj.setDocumentHandler (this);
    parserObj.parse ("file:///e:/code/chapter06/bands.xml");
}
```

The first line of this method creates an object of type `Parser`. This is a SAX interface (so it's actually `org.sax.xml.Parser`, but the `import` statement at the top of the code allows us to use shorthand). Anything that wishes to call itself a SAX parser must implement this interface. Fortunately for us, our chosen parser, XP, does just that. The parser class for xp is called `Driver`.

Having created our parser, we need to tell it who we are, and we do this by passing a reference to the current object (known – not unreasonably – as `this`) into the `setDocumentHandler` method (remember that we're actually implementing a class called `DocumentHandler`?).

Finally, we need to tell xp which document to parse, by invoking the `parse` method. Notice that we're passing the file name as a URL; you'll probably want to change it to point to wherever your copy of `bands.xml` is.

5. All that's left to do is to write the methods that will catch the events coming back from the parser. These are pretty simple (even if it may not feel that way just now if you're new to Java). There's one to catch the "start of document" event:

```
public void startDocument() throws SAXException
{
    System.out.println("Starting ...");
}
```

There's one to catch the "end of document" event:

```
public void endDocument() throws SAXException
{
    System.out.println("... Finished");
}
```

And there's one to catch the start of each element:

```
public void startElement(String name, AttributeList atts)
            throws SAXException
{
    System.out.println("Element is " + name);
}
}
```

So here's our entire BandReader class:

```
import org.xml.sax.*;

public class BandReader extends HandlerBase
{
    public static void main(String[] args) throws Exception
    {
        System.out.println("Here we go ...");
        BandReader readerObj = new BandReader();
        readerObj.read();
    }

    public void read () throws Exception
    {
        Parser parserObj = new com.jclark.xml.sax.Driver();
        parserObj.setDocumentHandler (this);
        parserObj.parse ("file:///e:/code/chapter06/bands.xml");
    }

    public void startDocument() throws SAXException
    {
        System.out.println("Starting ...");
    }

    public void endDocument() throws SAXException
    {
        System.out.println("... Finished");
    }

    public void startElement(String name, AttributeList atts)
                throws SAXException
    {
        System.out.println("Element is " + name);
    }
}
```

6. Save this as file BandReader.java, in the same directory as bands.xml. As you will have probably realized by now, this program doesn't have one of those clever flashy user interfaces, so we'll need to run it from a terminal session. In Windows, we can do this by opening a DOS box and changing the directory to the one where we've saved our files. Now let's compile it. (Incidentally, I'm assuming from here on that we're using the JavaSoft JDK that I described earlier on in the chapter. And remember, if you haven't changed your PATH variable, you may have to type the absolute path to the java executable javac.)

```
javac BandReader.java
```

7. Now let's run it:

```
java BandReader
```

8. Here's what we see:

```
Here we go ...
Starting ...
Element is bands
Element is band
Element is name
Element is guitar
Element is saxophone
Element is bass
Element is drums
Element is band
Element is name
Element is vocals
Element is saxophone
Element is guitar
Element is band
Element is name
Element is saxophone
Element is band
Element is name
Element is organ
Element is bass
Element is drums
Element is saxophone
... Finished
```

How It Works

We instantiated an xp `Driver` object, with the SAX `Parser` interface:

```
Parser parserObj = new com.jclark.xml.sax.Driver();
```

Then we told it which object to raise the events with via the `DocumentHandler` interface, and which file to parse:

```
parserObj.setDocumentHandler (this);
parserObj.parse ("file:///e:/code/chapter06/bands.xml");
```

Then it simply scanned through the document, raising the appropriate events at the start and end of the document:

```
public void startDocument() throws SAXException
{
    System.out.println("Starting ...");
}

public void endDocument() throws SAXException
{
    System.out.println("... Finished");
}
```

and at the start of each element:

```
public void startElement(String name, AttributeList atts)
            throws SAXException
{
    System.out.println("Element is " + name);
}
```

Extracting Character Data

Believe it or not, at this point we've actually covered most of the principles of SAX. However, it would be fair to say that we haven't actually used it for anything remotely interesting or useful. As you may have noticed, all we've managed to extract so far are the names of the tags. What would be more interesting is extracting the actual *character data* between those tags.

To do that, we need to implement a further method in the DocumentHandler interface: characters. The declaration of characters looks like:

```
public void characters(char[] chars, int start, int len) throws SAXException
```

This method gets fired whenever the parser encounters a chunk of character data. That's not quite as straightforward as it might seem, as there's no obligation on the parser writer to deliver all the character data between two tags as a single block. (If you think about it, this is actually quite reasonable – after all, the string might turn out to be extremely long, and it could make for a very clumsy parser implementation.) From an application point of view, this just means that you may need to build up your string over a number of character events.

Let's see how this might work in practice.

Try It Out – Extracting Characters Using SAX

For this example, we'll stick with the same XML file as last time, bands.xml. This time, however, we're going to extract the names of all the saxophonists that we come across. (It's like using SAX to find sax, if you see what I mean.)

1. Let's start off by copying BandReader.java to a new file, SaxFinder.java. We'll also need to change every occurrence of BandReader in the file to SaxFinder.

2. Next, we need to add a couple of private member variables to our SaxFinder class, just before the declaration of the main method:

```
public class SaxFinder extends HandlerBase
{
    private StringBuffer saxophonist = new StringBuffer();
    private boolean isSaxophone = false;
    public static void main(String[] args) throws Exception
```

273

The first one is the string buffer that's going to hold the name of each saxophone player as we receive character events from SAX. The second one is a flag that we're going to use to keep track of whether or not we're currently inside <saxophone> ... </saxophone> tags.

3. We need to make some changes to the startElement method:

```
public void startElement(String name, AttributeList atts)
            throws SAXException
{
    if (name.equals("saxophone"))
    {
        isSaxophone = true;
        saxophonist.setLength(0);
    }

    else
        isSaxophone = false;
}
```

What we're doing here is checking to see if we're at the start of a <saxophone> element. If we are, then we set our flag, and clear out anything left behind in our string buffer, so that it's ready to hold our saxophonist's name as we build up the string.

4. We also need to add an endElement method. We didn't need one previously, because we were only interested in the *start* of each element. Here's the new method:

```
public void endElement(String name) throws SAXException
{
    if (isSaxophone)
    {
        System.out.println("Saxophonist is " + saxophonist.toString());
        isSaxophone = false;
    }
}
```

This simply checks to see if we've just finished a <saxophone> element. If we have, it outputs the saxophonist's name from our string buffer, and then clears down the flag.

5. The last change that we need to make is to add a characters method:

```
public void characters(char[] chars, int start, int len)
            throws SAXException
{
    if (isSaxophone)
        saxophonist.append(chars, start, len);
}
```

This method checks to see if we're currently looking at a saxophonist, and, if we are, appends the incoming characters to the end of our string buffer. Remember that we can't rely on SAX to give us the complete string in one go. There's no reason why we shouldn't get three events with characters like this, for example:

```
        Andy S
        hep
        pard
```

instead of a single one with `Andy Sheppard`.

Just to recap, here's the full code of `SaxFinder`:

```java
import org.xml.sax.*;

public class SaxFinder extends HandlerBase
{
    private StringBuffer saxophonist = new StringBuffer();
    private boolean isSaxophone = false;

    public static void main(String[] args) throws Exception
    {
        System.out.println("Here we go ...");
        SaxFinder readerObj = new SaxFinder();
        readerObj.read();
    }

    public void read () throws Exception
    {
        Parser parserObj = new com.jclark.xml.sax.Driver();
        parserObj.setDocumentHandler (this);
        parserObj.parse ("file:///e:/code/chapter06/bands.xml");
    }

    public void startDocument() throws SAXException
    {
        System.out.println("Starting ...");
    }

    public void endDocument() throws SAXException
    {
        System.out.println("... Finished");
    }

    public void startElement(String name, AttributeList atts)
                throws SAXException
    {
        if (name.equals("saxophone"))
        {
            isSaxophone = true;
            saxophonist.setLength(0);
        }

        else
            isSaxophone = false;

    }
```

```
public void endElement(String name) throws SAXException
{
   if (isSaxophone)
   {
      System.out.println("Saxophonist is " + saxophonist.toString());
      isSaxophone = false;
   }
}

public void characters(char[] chars, int start, int len)
         throws SAXException
{
   if (isSaxophone)
      saxophonist.append(chars, start, len);
}

}
```

6. Save the file and compile it in the same way as before:

```
javac SaxFinder.java
```

7. Let's see what happens when we run it:

```
Here we go ...
Starting ...
Saxophonist is Mel Collins
Saxophonist is Laura Logic
Saxophonist is Jan Garbarek
Saxophonist is Elton Dean
... Finished
```

How It Works

The SAX parser searches through our document, finding our elements. The only thing that we're interested in are the elements enclosed in <saxophone> ... </saxophone> tags. We collect any character data that SAX throws at us between these tags and concatenate it into a string:

```
if (isSaxophone)
   saxophonist.append(chars, start, len);
```

Then we output it once we've received the closing tag:

```
System.out.println("Saxophonist is " + saxophonist.toString());
```

Extracting Attributes

By this point, I would imagine that you're beginning to get more than a little curious about a couple of aspects of the startElement declaration that we've so far glossed over. Just to remind ourselves, this is what it looks like:

```
public void startElement(String name, AttributeList atts)
            throws SAXException
```

The two things lurking in this declaration that we haven't mentioned yet are that `AttributeList` parameter, and that `SAXException` thing. We'll take a look at `SAXException` in a little while, when we discuss error handling, but for the time being we'll concentrate on `AttributeList`.

There are four methods available on this object:

❑   `getLength` returns an integer giving the number of attributes in the list.

❑   `getName` returns the name of the attribute at a specified position in the list (starting from 0).

❑   `getValue` returns the value of an attribute; we can either specify which attribute by giving it a string containing the attribute name, or by specifying its position in the list (starting from 0).

❑   `getType` returns the type of an attribute; again we can either specify which attribute by name or by position. The various types are described in Appendix B.

Let's see if we can make good use of these in developing our application still further.

Try It Out – Extracting Attributes

In this example, we're going to take the example from the last Try It Out, and extend it to list the names of all the bands that our saxophone players in `bands.xml` belong to, and what type of band they are. Here's how we do it.

1. Copy the Java class `SaxFinder.java` to `BandFinder.java`. Don't forget to change all the instances of `SaxFinder` to `BandFinder`.

2. Add three more member variables to our class:

```
public class BandFinder extends HandlerBase
{
    private StringBuffer saxophonist = new StringBuffer();
    private boolean isSaxophone = false;
    private StringBuffer bandName = new StringBuffer();
    private boolean isName = false;
    private String bandType = new String();
```

bandName and `isName` are exact analogues of `saxophonist` and `isSaxophonist`, and we're going to use them to extract the name of the band from between the `<name>…</name>` tags. We're going to use `bandType` to hold the type of the band, as extracted from the attribute associated with the `<band>` tag.

3. Our `startElement` method needs a little work doing to it. First of all, let's add a couple of lines to the beginning:

```
public void startElement(String name, AttributeList atts)
            throws SAXException
{
```

277

```
    if (name.equals("band"))
        bandType = atts.getValue("type");
```

Here, we're checking to see if we've got a `<band>` tag. If so, we know that we can extract its type from the `type` attribute, so this is what we do, using the `getValue` method. (You might be wondering what would happen if there wasn't a `type` attribute. As it happens, the next section is devoted to just this topic.)

Next, we need to add some code to handle `<name>` tags. We can pretty much clone this from the code for `<saxophone>`:

```
public void startElement(String name, AttributeList atts)
            throws SAXException
{
    if (name.equals("band"))
        bandType = atts.getValue("type");

        else if (name.equals("name"))
        {
            isName = true;
            isSaxophone = false;
            bandName.setLength(0);
        }

        else if (name.equals("saxophone"))
        {
            isName = false;
            isSaxophone = true;
            saxophonist.setLength(0);
        }

        else
        {
            isName = false;
            isSaxophone = false;
        }
}
```

4. There's also a small change to `endElement`, to output the name of the band as well as the saxophonist. Then we clear out the flag that's used to keep track of the fact that we're in the middle of the band name element:

```
public void endElement(String name) throws SAXException
{
    if (isSaxophone)
    {
        System.out.println("The saxophonist in " + bandName.toString()
            + " (" + bandType + ") is " + saxophonist.toString());
        isSaxophone = false;
    }
```

```
        if (isName)
            isName = false;
    }
```

5. Finally, there's some more cloning to be done in characters:

```
    public void characters(char[] chars, int start, int len)
                throws SAXException
    {
        if (isName)
            bandName.append(chars, start, len);

        if (isSaxophone)
            saxophonist.append(chars, start, len);
    }
```

Here's the complete BandFinder code:

```
import org.xml.sax.*;

public class BandFinder extends HandlerBase
{
    private StringBuffer saxophonist = new StringBuffer();
    private boolean isSaxophone = false;
    private StringBuffer bandName = new StringBuffer();
    private boolean isName = false;
    private String bandType = new String();

    public static void main(String[] args) throws Exception
    {
        System.out.println("Here we go ...");
        BandFinder readerObj = new BandFinder();
        readerObj.read();
    }

    public void read () throws Exception
    {
        Parser parserObj = new com.jclark.xml.sax.Driver();
        parserObj.setDocumentHandler (this);
        parserObj.parse ("file:///e:/code/chapter06/bands.xml");
    }

    public void startDocument() throws SAXException
    {
        System.out.println("Starting ...");
    }

    public void endDocument() throws SAXException
    {
        System.out.println("... Finished");
    }
```

```java
    public void startElement(String name, AttributeList atts)
            throws SAXException
    {
        if (name.equals("band"))
            bandType = atts.getValue("type");

        else if (name.equals("name"))
        {
            isName = true;
            isSaxophone = false;
            bandName.setLength(0);
        }

        else if (name.equals("saxophone"))
        {
            isName = false;
            isSaxophone = true;
            saxophonist.setLength(0);
        }

        else
        {
            isName = false;
            isSaxophone = false;
        }

    }

    public void endElement(String name) throws SAXException
    {
        if (isSaxophone)
        {
            System.out.println("The saxophonist in " + bandName.toString()
                    + " (" + bandType + ") is " + saxophonist.toString());
            isSaxophone = false;
        }

        if (isName)
            isName = false;
    }


    public void characters(char[] chars, int start, int len)
            throws SAXException
    {
        if (isName)
            bandName.append(chars, start, len);


        if (isSaxophone)
            saxophonist.append(chars, start, len);
    }

}
```

6. Save and compile the file as before. Then all that's left to do is to take it for a drive:

```
Here we go ...
Starting ...
The saxophonist in King Crimson (progressive) is Mel Collins
The saxophonist in X-Ray Spex (punk) is Laura Logic
The saxophonist in Hilliard Ensemble (classical) is Jan Garbarek
The saxophonist in Soft Machine (progressive) is Elton Dean
... Finished
```

How It Works

We can extract the data for band names in the same way as we extract the names of their saxophonists:

```
if (isName)
    bandName.append(chars, start, len);
```

We can extract the attribute type from the attribute list passed in to `startElement`:

```
public void startElement(String name, AttributeList atts)
        throws SAXException
{
    if (name.equals("band"))
        bandType = atts.getValue("type");
```

Error Handling

By now you'll have noticed that all the methods in the `DocumentHandler` interface throw exceptions of type `SAXException` if anything goes wrong that can't be handled locally. If one of these exceptions gets thrown, it gets caught by the parser, which reports the error and shuts down. The same mechanism is used for reporting errors in parsing the XML.

So if, for example, we were to supply it with an incorrect `bands.xml` file, like this:

```
<?xml version="1.0"?>
<bands>
    <band type="progressive">
        <name>King Crimson</name>
        <guitar>Robert Fripp
        <saxophone>Mel Collins</saxophone>
        <bass>Boz</bass>
        <drums>Ian Wallace</drums>
    </band>
    <band type="punk">
        <name>X-Ray Spex</name>
        <vocals>Poly Styrene</vocals>
        <saxophone>Laura Logic</saxophone>
        <guitar>Someone else</guitar>
    </band>
    <band type="classical">
        <name>Hilliard Ensemble</name>
```

```
            <saxophone>Jan Garbarek</saxophone>
        </band>
        <band type="progressive">
            <name>Soft Machine</name>
            <organ>Mike Ratledge</organ>
            <bass>Hugh Hopper</bass>
            <drums>Robert Wyatt</drums>
            <saxophone>Elton Dean</saxophone>
        </band>
    </bands>
```

we'd see something like this (because we missed off the closing `guitar` tag):

```
Here we go ...
Starting ...
The saxophonist in King Crimson (progressive) is Mel Collins
mismatched end tag: expected "guitar" but got "band"
        at com.jclark.xml.sax.Driver.parse(Driver.java:95)
        at com.jclark.xml.sax.Driver.parse(Driver.java:80)
        at BandFinder.read(BandFinder.java:22)
        at BandFinder.main(BandFinder.java:15)
```

We can make use of this mechanism ourselves, by explicitly throwing a SAXException when something has gone wrong:

```
if (something bad happened)
    throw new SAXException ("Something bad happened");
```

Let's see how this works in practice.

Try It Out – Throwing Exceptions

For this example, let's say that we are particularly obsessive, and we want to insist that each of the bands described in our XML must have a category attribute.

We could actually do this using Document Type Definitions (DTDs) or schemas, but as we haven't learned these yet, we'll have to find some other mechanism. For more on DTDs and schemas, see Chapters 9 and 10.

1. Copy `BandFinder.java` to `BandValidator.java`, and change every occurrence of `BandFinder` to `BandValidator`.

2. Let's make a small change to our `startElement` method, so that it checks to see if the `type` attribute is non-null:

```
public void startElement(String name, AttributeList atts)
            throws SAXException
{
    if (name.equals("band"))
```

```
        {
            bandType = atts.getValue("type");

            if (bandType == null)
                throw new SAXException("Band type not specified");
        }

        else if (name.equals("name"))
```

So as soon as a band with a null `type` attribute is encountered, the exception is thrown and the execution of the method ceases. The parser will catch the exception, report the error and stop.

Incidentally, if you're not familiar with Java, take care with the double "=" in the line where we're checking to see if the band type is null. Java uses this to denote a comparison, rather than an assignment (which just uses one "=").

3. Now let's repair the damage we did to `bands.xml` last time, and then change it so that one of the bands has no category:

```xml
<?xml version="1.0"?>
<bands>
    <band>
        <name>King Crimson</name>
        <guitar>Robert Fripp</guitar>
        <saxophone>Mel Collins</saxophone>
        <bass>Boz</bass>
        <drums>Ian Wallace</drums>
    </band>
    <band type="punk">
        <name>X-Ray Spex</name>
        <vocals>Poly Styrene</vocals>
        <saxophone>Laura Logic</saxophone>
        <guitar>Someone else</guitar>
    </band>
    <band type="classical">
        <name>Hilliard Ensemble</name>
        <saxophone>Jan Garbarek</saxophone>
    </band>
    <band type="progressive">
        <name>Soft Machine</name>
        <organ>Mike Ratledge</organ>
        <bass>Hugh Hopper</bass>
        <drums>Robert Wyatt</drums>
        <saxophone>Elton Dean</saxophone>
    </band>
</bands>
```

Well, after all, the Crims *are* pretty hard to categorize …

4. Save both files and compile `BandValidator.java`. This is what we see if we now run it:

```
Here we go ...
Starting ...
Band type not specified
  at BandFinder.startElement(BandFinder.java:42)
  at com.jclark.xml.sax.Driver.startElement(Driver.java:118)
  at com.jclark.xml.parse.EntityParser.parseContent(Compiled Code)
  at com.jclark.xml.parse.EntityParser.parseDocumentEntity(EntityParser.java)
  at com.jclark.xml.parse.DocumentParser.parse(DocumentParser.java)
  at com.jclark.xml.parse.base.ParserImpl.parseDocument(ParserImpl.java)
  at com.jclark.xml.sax.Driver.parse(Driver.java:87)
  at com.jclark.xml.sax.Driver.parse(Driver.java:80)
  at BandFinder.read(BandFinder.java:22)
  at BandFinder.main(BandFinder.java:15)
```

So the XML is rejected as being incorrect. We've used the parser's existing error-catching mechanism by throwing a `SAXException` at it. It's worth noting that we could use this kind of mechanism to do some extremely sophisticated validity checking, in fact more so than if we used DTDs.

More About Errors – Using the Locator Object

In the last Try It Out, we raised the possibility of using SAX to provide sophisticated validation of an XML document. However, our last effort, whilst it did report the error to us, didn't give us much in the way of information about *where* it had actually occurred. For the validation to be at all meaningful, we need to tell the user where the problem occurred. This is where the `Locator` object comes in.

The parser may provide the `Locator` object, so that we can use it in our event methods to find out where we are in the document. I use the word "may" because, according to the SAX specification, the parser isn't obliged to provide a locator. However, in practice most of them do, although the results from different parsers aren't entirely consistent.

> *For instance, just for fun, I did the next Try It Out with a couple of other parsers. Whereas* xp *reports the problem occurring at line 3, column 5, IBM* xml4j *reports it occurring at line 3, column 11. I can understand the logic behind both, although Sun Project X's line 3, column -1 leaves me slightly confused, as this value technically means that the column number is unavailable!*

How do we get hold of this `Locator` object? What we do is implement yet another method of the `DocumentHandler` interface (we'll have implemented the lot by the time we've finished, at which point the `HandlerBase` implementation is going to be a waste of time ...). This new method is called `setDocumentLocator`, and it's declared like this:

```
public void setDocumentLocator(Locator loc)
```

All we need to do in our implementation is copy the reference to the object to a local member variable. We can then use it whenever we want to find out where we are. So what methods can we use on `Locator`?

❑ We can use the method `getPublicId` to get the public identifier of the current document event: generally speaking, this will be `null`

❑ The method `getSystemId` gets us the system identifier: this is usually the file name of the XML document that we're parsing

❑ The method `getLineNumber` returns us the current line number

❑ The method `getColumnNumber` returns us the current column number

I think we should try this out.

Try It Out – Using the Locator

In this example, we'll be using the `Locator` to refine our reporting of the validation error that we found in the last example. We'll stick with our `BandValidator` class.

1. First of all, let's add a member variable to hold our reference to the `Locator`:

```
public class BandValidator extends HandlerBase
{
    private StringBuffer saxophonist = new StringBuffer();
    private boolean isSaxophone = false;
    private StringBuffer bandName = new StringBuffer();
    private boolean isName = false;
    private String bandType = new String();
    private Locator locatorObj;
```

2. Next, let's add that implementation of `setDocumentLocator` to the end of the document:

```
public void setDocumentLocator(Locator loc)
{
    locatorObj = loc;
}
```

(I told you there wasn't much to it.)

3. All we need to do now is put it to use, in our implementation of `startElement`:

```
public void startElement(String name, AttributeList atts)
            throws SAXException
{
    if (name.equals("band"))
    {
        bandType = atts.getValue("type");

        if (bandType == null)
        {
            if (locatorObj != null)
                System.err.println ("Error in " +
                            locatorObj.getSystemId() + " at line " +
                            locatorObj.getLineNumber() + ", column " +
                            locatorObj.getColumnNumber());
```

```
                     throw new SAXException("Band type not specified");
        }
    }
```

Notice that we check to see that the Locator object is non-null, in case we've picked an inferior parser that doesn't support Locator.

4. Fortunately, xp does. Save and compile BandValidator.java, and this is what you should see when it's run:

```
Here we go ...
Starting ...
Error in file:///e:/file:///e:/code/chapter06/bands.xml at line 3, column 5
Band type not specified
 at BandValidator.startElement(BandValidator.java:47)
 at com.jclark.xml.sax.Driver.startElement(Driver.java)
 at com.jclark.xml.parse.EntityParser.parseContent(Compiled Code)
 at com.jclark.xml.parse.EntityParser.parseDocumentEntity(EntityParser.java)
 at com.jclark.xml.parse.DocumentParser.parse(DocumentParser.java)
 at com.jclark.xml.parse.base.ParserImpl.parseDocument(ParserImpl.java)
 at com.jclark.xml.sax.Driver.parse(Driver.java)
 at com.jclark.xml.sax.Driver.parse(Driver.java)
 at BandValidator.read(BandValidator.java:23)
 at BandValidator.main(BandValidator.java:16)
```

The Locator object tells us where we currently are in the parsing process. Provided that the parser supports this, we can get hold of a reference to a Locator object by implementing the setLocatorObject method.

Even More About Errors – Catching Parsing Errors

We still haven't finished with errors, because we need to consider the other side of the coin. What if we want to do our own handling of parser errors?

It probably won't come as a great surprise to find out that what we do is implement some methods of an interface. However, these new methods aren't part of DocumentHandler, they're part of another interface altogether, called ErrorHandler. As it happens, HandlerBase provides us with a rudimentary implementation of this one as well, although it doesn't actually do anything apart from throw a SAXException to print out a trace of the call stack, like the one we saw in the last example.

The new methods are as follows:

❑ warning – this gives us a warning that something untoward has happened

❑ error – this reports a recoverable error

❑ fatal – this reports a non-recoverable error

In order to make use of this, we need to pass a reference to the main object to a method on the Parser interface called setErrorHandler. This is the exact analogue of the call to setDocumentHandler that we used to tell the parser who to send parsing events to.

Try It Out – Catching Parsing Errors

In this example, we'll extend our `BandValidator` class so that we catch parser errors and report their location. So, as well as overriding some of `HandlerBase`'s implementation of `DocumentHandler`, we're going to be overriding some of its implementation of `ErrorHandler`.

1. First of all, let's tell the parser who to send the error events to:

```
public void read () throws Exception
{
    Parser parserObj = new com.jclark.xml.sax.Driver();
    parserObj.setDocumentHandler (this);
    parserObj.setErrorHandler (this);
    parserObj.parse ("file:///e:/code/chapter06/bands.xml");
}
```

2. Next, we need to add the three new methods to catch the errors. These will override the minimal implementations provided by `HandlerBase`:

```
public void warning(SAXParseException exception) throws SAXException
{
    System.err.println("Warning in " + exception.getSystemId() +
            " at line " + exception.getLineNumber() + ", column " +
            exception.getColumnNumber());
    throw exception;
}
```

```
public void error(SAXParseException exception) throws SAXException
{
    System.err.println("Error in " + exception.getSystemId() +
            " at line " + exception.getLineNumber() + ", column " +
            exception.getColumnNumber());
    throw exception;
}
```

```
public void fatalError(SAXParseException exception) throws SAXException
{
    System.err.println("Fatal error in " + exception.getSystemId() +
        " at line " + exception.getLineNumber() + ", column " +
        exception.getColumnNumber());
    throw exception;
}
```

All we're doing here is printing out the location of the error, taken from the incoming `Exception` object, and then rethrowing the error back to the parser. It's worth noting that if the parser doesn't support `Locator`, it's not going to provide us with anything meaningful in these methods on `SAXParseException`.

3. Let's go back to our badly-formed XML:

```
<?xml version="1.0"?>
<bands>
    <band type="progressive">
        <name>King Crimson</name>
```

```
            <guitar>Robert Fripp
            <saxophone>Mel Collins</saxophone>
            <bass>Boz</bass>
            <drums>Ian Wallace</drums>
        </band>
        <band type="punk">
            <name>X-Ray Spex</name>
            <vocals>Poly Styrene</vocals>
            <saxophone>Laura Logic</saxophone>
            <guitar>Someone else</guitar>
        </band>
        <band type="classical">
            <name>Hilliard Ensemble</name>
            <saxophone>Jan Garbarek</saxophone>
        </band>
        <band type="progressive">
            <name>Soft Machine</name>
            <organ>Mike Ratledge</organ>
            <bass>Hugh Hopper</bass>
            <drums>Robert Wyatt</drums>
            <saxophone>Elton Dean</saxophone>
        </band>
    </bands>
```

4. If we run `BandValidator`, what we see is this:

```
Here we go ...
Starting ...
The saxophonist in King Crimson (progressive) is Mel Collins
Fatal error in file:///e:/code/chapter06/bands.xml at line 9, column 4
mismatched end tag: expected "guitar" but got "band"
        at com.jclark.xml.sax.Driver.parse(Driver.java)
        at com.jclark.xml.sax.Driver.parse(Driver.java)
        at BandValidator.read(BandValidator.java:24)
        at BandValidator.main(BandValidator.java:16)
```

which is a little more informative than the previous version.

The parser uses the `ErrorHandler` interface to inform applications of error events. We can therefore catch parser errors by implementing the methods in this interface.

Other Methods in DocumentHandler

There are one or two other methods in the `DocumentHandler` interface that we should look at briefly.

ignorableWhitespace

The first one is `ignorableWhitespace`, and for the most part, yes, you can ignore this one. This method has the following definition:

```
public void ignorableWhitespace(char[] chars, int start, int len)
        throws SAXException
```

The sharper-eyed amongst you will spot that this is very similar to our old friend `characters`. Unfortunately, any explanation of this method won't make an awful lot of sense without some knowledge of DTDs, and seeing as we're not explaining these until Chapter 9, we're a bit stuck.

For the time being, think of it this way:

- ❑   A **DTD**, or **Document Type Definition** basically defines a structure that a valid XML document has to stick to

- ❑   This definition can state that an element can only contain children and not PCDATA

- ❑   However, the element can still contain white spaces (spaces, tabs and newlines) for readability

- ❑   If it does, a validating parser (i.e. one that makes use of the DTD) will report these characters by means of an `ignorableWhiteSpace` event rather than a `characters` one

- ❑   A non-validating parser, on the other hand, won't be able to tell whether the characters are ignorable white space or PCDATA, so it will report all characters by means of `characters` events

The upshot of this is that, unless you are particularly interested in reproducing the structure of the document exactly, you can safely ignore `ignorableWhiteSpace` events.

processingInstruction

The only other event method in `DocumentHandler` is `processingInstruction`. Unsurprisingly, this method is used to catch processing instructions, which you'll probably remember from Chapter 2. These are things like:

```
<?someApplication someParam?>
```

that act as instructions for some application processing the XML. The declaration of `processingInstruction` is as follows:

```
public abstract void processingInstruction(String target, String data)
                throws SAXException
```

In this case, `target` would be `someApplication`, and `data` would be `someParam`.

I'm sure I don't need to remind you at this point that the XML declaration at the start of an XML document is *not* really a processing instruction, and as such it won't cause you to receive a `processingInstruction` event. Or at least, if it does, then switch to another parser, quick.

Good SAX and Bad SAX

Now that we're thoroughly familiar with SAX, this is a good point to review what SAX is good at and what it isn't so good at, so that we can decide when to use it and when to use another approach, such as the DOM.

> *The discussion in this section refers only to SAX 1.0, as several of the restrictions of SAX are being addressed in SAX 2.0. However, these restrictions will only be addressed in practice if SAX 2.0 starts to be implemented on a wide basis by standard parsers.*

As we've seen, SAX is great for analyzing and extracting content from XML documents. Let's look at what makes it so good:

❑ It's simple: you only need to implement three or perhaps four interfaces to get going.

❑ It doesn't load the whole document into memory, so it doesn't take up vast amounts of space. Of course, if your application is using SAX to build up its own in-memory image of the document, it's likely to end up taking a similar amount of space as the DOM would have done (unless your image is a lot more efficient than the DOM!).

❑ It's quick, because it doesn't need to read in the whole document before you start work on it.

❑ It focuses on the real content rather than the way that it's laid out.

❑ It's great at filtering data, and letting you concentrate on the subset that you're interested in.

So why don't we use it for everything, then? Here are a few drawbacks:

❑ You get the data in the order that SAX gives it to you. You have absolutely no control over the order in which the parser searches. As we have seen in our Try It Outs, this means that you may need to build up the data that you need over several event invocations. This can be a problem if you're doing particularly complex searches.

❑ There's no **lexical information** given to you in SAX. In other words, SAX will give you everything you need to know about the active content of the document, but it won't guarantee to tell you exactly how the document's original author went about it. For instance, it won't give you any of the comments, or the order in which the attributes were specified. So you won't be able to produce an exact copy of the original document using SAX. In fact, much of this is fixed in SAX 2.0, as we will see in a moment.

❑ Despite the fact that there is an interface defined in SAX 1.0 called DTDHandler (which is beyond the scope of this book), it doesn't provide you with any real information about Document Type Definitions. Again, this is only really important if you're in the business of re-creating or editing an XML document, and – again – it's been dealt with in SAX 2.0.

❑ It's read-only: you can't adjust elements of the document. The only way to generate a new document is to catch all the events and then re-create the document yourself, with changes, by writing it all out again as text. This isn't actually quite as hard as it sounds, and there are examples of this in Chapter 6 of Professional XML, if you're interested in pursuing the subject further.

The only other disadvantage is the minor inconvenience that it isn't actually supported in current browsers, so for practical purposes, large-scale SAX is limited to server-side operation.

SAX 2.0

We authors often use the phrase "at the time of writing" in order to avoid having to speculate too much on what is going to happen in the inevitable hiatus between the point at which we are actually typing the words in and the publication date of the book. However, the phrase has just taken on a rather more literal meaning, because SAX 2.0 has actually been released during the time that I've been finishing this chapter. The list of parsers that currently support the new interface is currently small, but we should at least devote some time to looking at it in order to be prepared for future changes.

As it turns out, as far as the concepts we've been discussing in this chapter are concerned, SAX 2.0 doesn't introduce many changes, apart from the fact that many of the existing interfaces have been replaced by similar ones with different names. For instance, `DocumentHandler` becomes `ContentHandler`. Some new methods have been added here or there as well. However, as I have alluded in my discussion above on the merits and demerits of SAX, most of the changes in SAX 2.0 involve the introduction of new interfaces to address known shortcomings in SAX 1.0.

One of the more interesting aspects of this is that SAX 2.0-compliant parsers can be interrogated to find out if they currently have certain optional features operational. This is done by means of the `getFeature` method in the new `XMLReader` interface (which replaces the old `Parser` interface). The application may then switch the feature on or off by means of the `setFeature` method. One example of such a feature might be whether or not the parser is currently validating against a DTD.

> *More information on the changes from SAX 1.0 to SAX 2.0 can be found at*
> *http://www.megginson.com/SAX/Java/index.html*

Summary

SAX is an excellent API for analyzing and extracting information from large XML documents without incurring the time and space overheads associated with the DOM.

In this chapter, we learnt how to use SAX to catch events passed to us by a parser, by implementing a known SAX interface, `DocumentHandler`. We used this to extract some simple information from an XML document.

We also looked at error handling, and found out how to implement sophisticated intelligent parsing, reporting errors as we did so. In addition we looked at how to supplement the error handling mechanisms in the parser by using the `Locator` object.

Finally, we discussed the strengths and weaknesses of SAX, and took a brief peek at SAX 2.0.

In the next chapter, we're leaving programming behind in order to take a look at the problem of managing all the names of our XML elements. Stay with us as we find out about Namespaces ...

Namespaces

We can now create well-formed XML documents, view them in a browser, transform them to other formats, and even access the information they contain from either the DOM or SAX. But the time is going to come when our applications get more complex, and we'll need to combine elements from various document types into one XML document.

This chapter will introduce **namespaces**, the means by which we can differentiate elements (and sometimes attributes) of different XML document types from each other when combining them together into other documents, or even when processing multiple documents simultaneously.

In this chapter you will learn:

- ❑   Why the information we have learned so far about XML is not enough to accomplish this
- ❑   What namespaces are, conceptually, and how they solve the problem
- ❑   The syntax for using namespaces in XML documents
- ❑   What a URI is, what a URL is, and what a URN is

We will also reexamine XSLT, to better understand some of the concepts which rely on an understanding of namespaces.

Why Do We Need Namespaces?

Because of the nature of XML, it is possible for any company or individual to create XML document types which describe the world in their own terms. If my company feels that an `<order>` should contain a certain set of information, and you feel that it should contain a different set of information, we can both go ahead and create different document types to describe that information. We can even both use the name `<order>` for entirely different uses, if we wish.

However, if everyone is creating personalized XML vocabularies, we'll soon run into a problem: there are only so many words available in human languages, and a lot of them are going to get snapped up by people defining document types. How can I define a `<title>` element, to be used to denote the title in a person's name, when XHTML already has a `<title>` element, which is used to describe the title of an HTML document? How can I then further distinguish those two `<title>` elements from the title of a book?

If all of these documents were to be kept separate, this still might not be a problem. If we saw a `<title>` element in an XHTML document, we'd know what kind of title we were talking about, and if we saw one in our own proprietary XML document type, we'd know what that meant too. Unfortunately, life isn't always that simple, and eventually we're going to need to combine various XML elements from different document types into one XML document. For example, we might create an XML document type containing information about a person, including that person's title, but also containing the person's résumé, in XHTML form. Such a document may look similar to this:

```
<?xml version="1.0" encoding="windows-1252"?>
<person>
  <name>
    <title>Sir</title>
    <first>John</first>
    <middle>Fitzgerald Johansen</middle>
    <last>Doe</last>
  </name>
  <position>Vice President of Marketing</position>
  <résumé>
    <html>
    <head><title>Resume of John Doe</title></head>
    <body>
      <h1>John Doe</h1>
      <p>John's a great guy, you know?</p>
    </body>
    </html>
  </résumé>
</person>
```

To an XML parser, there isn't any difference between the two `<title>` elements in this document. If we do a simple search of the document to find John Doe's title, we might accidentally get "Resume of John Doe", instead of "Sir". Even in our application, we can't know which elements are XHTML elements and which aren't, without knowing in advance the structure of the document. That is, we'd have to know that there is a `<résumé>` element, which is a direct child of `<person>`, and that all of the descendents of `<résumé>` are a separate type of element from the others in our document. If our structure ever changed, all of our assumptions would be lost. In the document above it looks like anything inside the `<résumé>` element is XHTML, but in other documents it might not be so obvious, and to an XML parser it isn't obvious at all.

Using Prefixes

The best way to solve this problem is for every element in a document to have a completely distinct name. For example, we might come up with a naming convention whereby every element for my proprietary XML document type gets my own prefix, and every XHTML element gets another prefix.

We could rewrite our XML document from above something like this:

```
<?xml version="1.0" encoding="windows-1252"?>
<pers:person>
  <pers:name>
    <pers:title>Sir</pers:title>
    <pers:first>John</pers:first>
```

```
      <pers:middle>Fitzgerald Johansen</pers:middle>
      <pers:last>Doe</pers:last>
   </pers:name>
   <pers:position>Vice President of Marketing</pers:position>
   <pers:résumé>
      <xhtml:html>
      <xhtml:head><xhtml:title>Resume of John Doe
      </xhtml:title></xhtml:head>
      <xhtml:body>
      <xhtml:h1>John Doe</xhtml:h1>
      <xhtml:p>John's a great guy, you know?</xhtml:p>
      </xhtml:body>
      </xhtml:html>
   </pers:résumé>
</pers:person>
```

This is a lot uglier, but at least we (and our XML parser) can immediately tell what kind of title we're talking about: a `<pers:title>` or an `<xhtml:title>`. And doing a search for `<pers:title>` will always return "Sir". We can always immediately tell which elements are XHTML elements, without having to know in advance the structure of our document.

By separating these elements using a prefix, we have effectively created two kinds of elements in our document: pers types of elements, and xhtml types of elements. So any elements with the pers prefix belong in the same "category" as each other, just as any elements with the xhtml prefix belong in another "category". These "categories" are called **namespaces**.

These two namespaces could be illustrated by the following diagram:

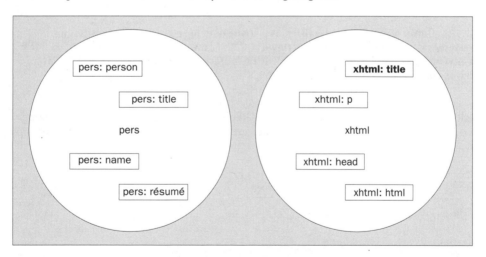

Note that namespaces are concerned with a *vocabulary*, not a *document type*. That is, the namespace distinguishes which names are in the namespace, but not what they mean or how they fit together.

> **A namespace is a purely abstract entity; it's nothing more than a group of names that belong with each other conceptually.**

295

The concept of namespaces also exists in certain programming languages, such as Java, where the same problem exists. How can I name my Java variables whatever I want, and not have those names conflict with names already defined by others, or even by the Java library itself? The answer is that Java code is broken up into packages, where the names within a package must be unique, but the same name can be used in any package.

For example, there is an object defined in Java named `java.applet.Applet`*. The actual name of the object is just* `Applet`*;* `java.applet` *is the package which contains that object. This means that I can create my own package, and in that package I could define an object of my own named* `Applet`*. I can even use* `java.applet.Applet` *from within my package, as long as I specify the package in which it resides, so that Java always knows which* `Applet` *I'm referring to.*

So Why Doesn't XML Just Use These Prefixes?

Unfortunately, there is a drawback to the prefix approach to namespaces used in the previous XML: who will monitor the prefixes? The whole reason for using them is to distinguish names from different document types, but if it is going to work, the prefixes themselves also have to be unique. If one company chose the prefix `pers` and another company also chose that same prefix, the original problem would still exist.

In fact, this prefix administration would have to work a lot like it works now for domain names on the Internet: a company or individual would go to the "prefix administrators" with the prefix they would like to use; if that prefix wasn't already being used, they could use it, otherwise they would have to pick another one.

In order to solve this problem, we could take advantage of the already unambiguous Internet domain names in existence, and specify that **URI**s must be used for the prefix names.

> **A URI (Uniform Resource Identifier) is a string of characters which identifies a resource. It can come in one of two flavors: URL (Uniform Resource Locator), or URN (Universal Resource Name). We'll look at the differences between URLs and URNs later in this chapter.**

For example, if I work for a company called Serna Ferna Inc., which owns the domain name `sernaferna.com`, I could incorporate that into my prefix. Perhaps the document might end up looking like this:

```
<?xml version="1.0" encoding="windows-1252"?>
<{http://sernaferna.com/pers}person>
  <{http://sernaferna.com/pers}name>
  <{http://sernaferna.com/pers}title>
    Sir
  </{http://sernaferna.com/pers}title>
<!--etc...-->
```

Voila! We have solved our problem of uniqueness. Since our company owns the `sernaferna.com` domain name, we know that nobody else will be using that `http://sernaferna.com/pers` prefix in their XML documents, and if we want to create any additional document types, we can just keep using our domain name, and add the new namespace name to the end, such as `http://sernaferna.com/other-namespace`.

It's important to note that we need more than just the `sernaferna.com` part of the URI; we need the whole thing. Otherwise there would be a further problem: different people could have control of different sections on that domain, and they might all want to create namespaces. For example, the company's HR department could be in charge of `http://sernaferna.com/hr`, and might need to create a namespace for `names` (of employees), and the sales department could be in charge of `http://sernaferna.com/sales`, and also need to create a namespace for `names` (of customers). As long as we're using the whole URI, we're fine – we can both create our namespaces (in this case `http://sernaferna.com/hr/names` and `http://sernaferna.com/sales/names` respectively). We also need the protocol (`http`) in there because there could be yet another department which is in charge of, for example, `ftp://sernaferna.com/hr` and `ftp://sernaferna.com/sales`.

The only drawback to this solution is that our XML is no longer well-formed. Our names can now include a myriad of characters that are allowed in URIs but not in XML names: `/` characters, for example and for the sake of this example we used `{}` characters to separate the URL from the name, neither of which is allowed in XML.

What we really need, to solve all of our namespace-related problems, is a way to create two-part names in XML: one part would be the name we are giving this element, and the other part would be an arbitrarily chosen prefix that *refers* to a URI, which specifies which namespace this element belongs to. And, in fact, this is what **XML Namespaces** provide.

How XML Namespaces Work

To use XML Namespaces in your documents, elements are given **qualified names**. (In most W3C specifications "qualified name" is abbreviated to **QName**.) These qualified names consist of two parts: the **local part**, which is the same as the names we have been giving elements all along, and the **namespace prefix**, which specifies to which namespace this name belongs.

The XML Namespaces specification is located at: http://www.w3.org/TR/1999/REC-xml-names.

For example, to declare a namespace called `http://sernaferna.com/pers`, and associate a `<person>` element with that namespace, we would do something like the following:

```
<pers:person xmlns:pers="http://sernaferna.com/pers"/>
```

The key is the `xmlns` attribute. Here we are declaring the `pers` namespace prefix, and the name of the namespace which it represents (`http://sernaferna.com/pers`). We can then use the namespace prefix with our elements, as in `pers:person`. As opposed to our previous prefixed version, the prefix itself (`pers`) doesn't have any meaning – its only purpose is to point to the namespace name. For this reason, we could replace our prefix (`pers`) with any other prefix, and this document would have exactly the same meaning.

This prefix can be used for any descendents of the `<pers:person>` element, to denote that they also belong to the `http://sernaferna.com/pers` namespace. For example:

```
<pers:person xmlns:pers="http://sernaferna.com/pers">
  <pers:name>
    <pers:title>Sir</pers:title>
  </pers:name>
</pers:person>
```

Notice that the prefix is needed on both the start and end tags of the elements. They are no longer simply being identified by their names, but by their QNames.

By now you have probably realized the reason that colons in element names are so strongly discouraged in the XML 1.0 specification (and in this book). If you were to use a name that happened to have a colon in it with a namespace-aware XML parser, the parser might get confused, thinking that you were specifying a namespace prefix.

Internally, when this document is parsed, the parser simply replaces any namespace prefixes with the namespace itself, creating a name much like the names we used earlier in the chapter. That is, internally a parser might consider `<pers:person>` to be similar to `<{http://sernaferna.com/pers}` `person>`. For this reason, the `{http://sernaferna.com/pers}person` notation is often used in namespace discussions to talk about **fully-qualified names**. Just remember that this is only for the benefit of easily discussing namespace issues, and is not valid XML syntax.

Try It Out – Adding Namespaces to Our Document

Let's see what our document would look like with proper XML Namespaces. Luckily for us, there is already a namespace defined for XHTML, which is `http://www.w3.org/1999/xhtml`. We can use this namespace for the HTML we're embedding in our document.

1. Open Notepad, and type in the following XML:

```
<?xml version="1.0" encoding="windows-1252"?>
<pers:person xmlns:pers="http://sernaferna.com/pers"
             xmlns:html="http://www.w3.org/1999/xhtml">
  <pers:name>
    <pers:title>Sir</pers:title>
    <pers:first>John</pers:first>
    <pers:middle>Fitzgerald Johansen</pers:middle>
    <pers:last>Doe</pers:last>
  </pers:name>
  <pers:position>Vice President of Marketing</pers:position>
  <pers:résumé>
    <html:html>
      <html:head><html:title>Resume of John Doe</html:title></html:head>
      <html:body>
      <html:h1>John Doe</html:h1>
      <html:p>John's a great guy, you know?</html:p>
      </html:body>
    </html:html>
  </pers:résumé>
</pers:person>
```

2. Save this document to your hard drive as `namespace.xml`.

3. Open `namespace.xml` in IE5. You should get the normal colour-coded view of your XML document, the same as you do for any other XML document in IE5. (If you don't, go back and make sure you haven't made any mistakes!)

How It Works

We now have a document with elements from two separate namespaces, which we defined in the highlighted code, and any namespace-aware XML parser will be able to tell them apart. (The fact that the file opens up fine in IE5 indicates that the parser bundled with this browser understands namespaces properly; if it didn't, the document might raise errors instead.) The two namespaces now look more like this:

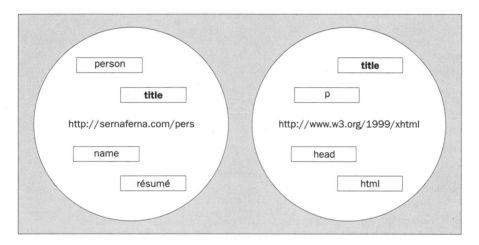

The `xmlns` attributes specify the namespace prefixes we are using to point to our two namespaces:

```
<pers:person xmlns:pers="http://sernaferna.com/pers"
             xmlns:html="http://www.w3.org/1999/xhtml">
```

That is, we declare the `pers` prefix, which will be used to specify elements which belong to the `pers` namespace, and the `html` prefix, which will be used to specify elements which belong to the XHTML namespace. But remember that the prefixes themselves mean nothing to the XML parser, they get replaced with the URI internally; we could have used `pers` or `myprefix` or `blah` or any other legal string of characters for the prefix; it's only the URI to which they point that the parser cares about.

Because we have a way of identifying which namespace each element belongs to, we don't have to give them special, unique names. We have two vocabularies, each containing a `<title>` element, and we can mix both of these `<title>` elements in the same document. If I ever need a person's title, I can easily find any `<{http://sernaferna.com/pers}title>` elements I need, and ignore the `<{http://www.w3.org/1999/xhtml}title>` elements.

However, even though my `<title>` element is prefixed with a namespace prefix, the name of the element is still `<title>`. It's just that we have now declared what namespace that `<title>` belongs to, so that it won't be confused with other `<title>` elements which belong to other namespaces.

Default Namespaces

Although the previous document solves all of our namespace-related problems, it's just a little bit ugly. We have to give every element in the document a prefix to specify which namespace this element belongs to, which makes the document look very similar to our first prefixed version. Luckily, we have the option of creating **default namespaces**.

> **A default namespace works much like a regular namespace, except that you don't have to specify a prefix for all of the elements that use it.**

It looks like this:

```
<person xmlns="http://sernaferna.com/pers">
  <name>
    <title>Sir</title>
  </name>
</person>
```

Notice that the `xmlns` attribute no longer specifies a prefix name to use for this namespace. As this is a default namespace, this element, and any elements descended from it, belongs to this namespace, unless they explicitly specify another namespace by using a prefix. So the `<name>` and `<title>` elements both belong to this namespace.

You can declare more than one namespace for an element, but only one can be the default. This allows us to set up XML like this:

```
<person xmlns="http://sernaferna.com/pers"
        xmlns:xhtml="http://www.w3.org/1999/xhtml">
  <name/>
  <xhtml:p>This is XHTML</xhtml:p>
</person>
```

In this case all of the elements belong to the `http://sernaferna.com/pers` namespace, except for the `<p>` element, which is part of the XHTML namespace. (We've declared the namespaces and their prefixes (if applicable) in the root element so that all elements in the document can use these prefixes.) However, we can't write XML like this:

```
<person xmlns="http://sernaferna.com/pers"
        xmlns="http://www.w3.org/1999/xhtml">
```

This tries to declare two default namespaces. In this case, the XML parser wouldn't be able to figure out to what namespace the `<person>` element belongs. (Not to mention that this is a duplicate attribute which, as we saw in Chapter 2, is not allowed in XML.)

Try It Out – Default Namespaces in Action

Let's rewrite our previous document, but use a default namespace to make it cleaner.

Make the following changes to `namespace.xml` and save it as `namespace2.xml`:

```
<?xml version="1.0" encoding="windows-1252"?>
<person xmlns="http://sernaferna.com/pers"
        xmlns:html="http://www.w3.org/1999/xhtml">
  <name>
    <title>Sir</title>
    <first>John</first>
    <middle>Fitzgerald Johansen</middle>
    <last>Doe</last>
  </name>
  <position>Vice President of Marketing</position>
  <résumé>
    <html:html>
      <html:head><html:title>Resume of John Doe</html:title></html:head>
      <html:body>
      <html:h1>John Doe</html:h1>
      <html:p>John's a great guy, you know?</html:p>
      </html:body>
    </html:html>
  </résumé>
</person>
```

How It Works

In the `<person>` start tag, the first `xmlns` attribute doesn't specify a prefix to associate with this namespace, so this becomes the default namespace for the element, along with any of its descendents, which is why we don't need any namespace prefixes in many of the elements, such as `<name>`, `<title>`, etc.

But, since the XHTML elements are in a different namespace, we do need to specify the prefix for them, for example:

```
<html:head><html:title>Resume of John Doe</html:title></html:head>
```

Namespaces of Descendents

So far, when we have had multiple namespaces in a document, we've been declaring them all in the root element, so that the prefixes are available throughout the document. So, in our previous Try It Out, we declared a default namespace, as well as a namespace prefix for our HTML elements, all on the `<person>` element.

This means that when we have a default namespace mixed with other namespaces, we would create a document like this:

```
<person xmlns="http://sernaferna.com/pers"
        xmlns:xhtml="http://www.w3.org/1999/xhtml">
  <name/>
  <xhtml:p>This is XHTML</xhtml:p>
</person>
```

However, we don't have to declare all of our namespace prefixes on the root element; in fact, a namespace prefix can be declared on any element in the document. We could also have written the above like this:

```
<person xmlns="http://sernaferna.com/pers">
  <name/>
  <xhtml:p xmlns:xhtml="http://www.w3.org/1999/xhtml">
  This is XHTML</xhtml:p>
</person>
```

In some cases this might make our documents more readable, because we're declaring the namespaces closer to where they'll actually be used. The downside to writing our documents like this is that the xhtml prefix is only available on the <p> element and its descendents; we couldn't use it on our <name> element, for example, or any other element that wasn't a descendent of <p>.

But we can take things even further, and declare the XHTML namespace to be the *default* namespace for our <p> element, like this:

```
<person xmlns="http://sernaferna.com/pers">
  <name/>
  <p xmlns="http://www.w3.org/1999/xhtml">This is XHTML</p>
</person>
```

Although http://sernaferna.com/pers is the default namespace for the document as a whole, http://www.w3.org/1999/xhtml is the default namespace for the <p> element, and any of its descendents. Again, in some cases this can make our documents more readable, since we are declaring the namespaces closer to where they are used.

Try It Out – Default Namespaces for Children

In the interest of readability, let's write the XML from our previous Try It Out again, to declare the default namespace for the <html> tag and its descendants.

Here are the changes to be made to namespace2.xml:

```
<?xml version="1.0" encoding="windows-1252"?>
<person xmlns="http://sernaferna.com/pers">
  <name>
    <title>Sir</title>
    <first>John</first>
    <middle>Fitzgerald Johansen</middle>
    <last>Doe</last>
  </name>
  <position>Vice President of Marketing</position>
  <résumé>
    <html xmlns="http://www.w3.org/1999/xhtml">
      <head><title>Resume of John Doe</title></head>
      <body>
      <h1>John Doe</h1>
      <p>John's a great guy, you know?</p>
      </body>
    </html>
  </résumé>
</person>
```

This looks a lot tidier than the previous version, and represents the same thing.

Canceling Default Namespaces

Sometimes you might be working with XML documents in which not all of the elements belong to a namespace. For example, you might be creating XML documents to describe employees in your organization, and those documents might include occasional HTML comments about the employees, such as in the following short fragment:

```
<employee>
  <name>Jane Doe</name>
  <notes>
    <p xmlns="http://www.w3.org/1999/xhtml">I've worked
    with <name>Jane Doe</name> for over a <em>year</em>
    now.</p>
  </notes>
</employee>
```

In this case, we have decided that anywhere the employee's name is included in the document it should be in a <name> element, in case the employee changes his/her name in the future, such as if Jane Doe ever gets married. (In this case changing the document would then be a simple matter of looking for all <name> elements which aren't in a namespace, and changing the values.) Also, since these XML documents will only ever be used by our own application, we don't have to create a namespace for it.

However, as you see above, one of the <name> elements occurs under the <p> element, which declares a default namespace, meaning that the <name> element also falls under that namespace. So if we searched for <name> elements which had no associated namespace, we wouldn't pick this one up. The way to get around this is to use the xmlns attribute to *cancel* the default namespace, by setting the value to an empty string. For example:

```
<employee>
  <name>Jane Doe</name>
  <notes>
    <p xmlns="http://www.w3.org/1999/xhtml">I've worked
    with <name xmlns="">Jane Doe</name> for over a <em>year</em>
    now.</p>
  </notes>
</employee>
```

Now the second <name> element is not in any namespace. Of course, if we had a namespace specifically for our <employee> document, this would become a non-issue, because we could just use the ways we've already learned to declare that an element is part of that namespace (using a namespace prefix, or a default namespace). But, in this case, we're not declaring that the element is part of a namespace – we're trying to declare that it's not part of *any* namespace, which is the opposite of what we've been doing so far.

Do Different Notations Make Any Difference?

We've now seen three different ways to combine elements from different namespaces. We can fully qualify every name, like this:

```
<pers:person xmlns:pers="http://sernaferna.com/pers"
             xmlns:xhtml="http://www.w3.org/1999/xhtml">
  <pers:name/>
  <xhtml:p>This is XHTML</xhtml:p>
</pers:person>
```

Or, we can use one namespace as the default, and just qualify any names from other namespaces, like this:

```
<person xmlns="http://sernaferna.com/pers"
        xmlns:xhtml="http://www.w3.org/1999/xhtml">
  <name/>
  <xhtml:p>This is XHTML</xhtml:p>
</person>
```

Or, we can just use defaults everywhere, like this:

```
<person xmlns="http://sernaferna.com/pers">
  <name/>
  <p xmlns="http://www.w3.org/1999/xhtml">This is XHTML</p>
</person>
```

This begs the question: do these three fragments of XML really mean exactly the same thing?

From the pure namespaces point of view, yes, these documents mean exactly the same thing. All three documents have the same three elements, and in each instance, each element still belongs to the same namespace as it does in the other two instances.

From the point of view of most applications, these fragments also mean the same thing. When you're doing work with an XML document, you usually only care what elements you're dealing with; you don't care whether the element's namespace was declared using a default declaration or an explicit prefix, any more than you care if an element with no data was written as a start-tag and an end-tag pair or as an empty element.

There are, however, some applications that actually do differentiate between the three examples above, such as an application that reads in XML and displays the source code to a user. As you may have noticed if you used IE5 to view the XML from the previous Try It Outs, IE5 does display each one differently. Let's look at the three examples above:

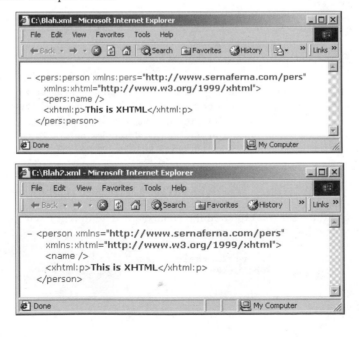

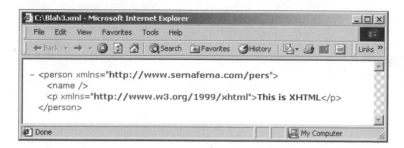

As you can see, the browser displays the documents exactly as they were written; so if we declared our namespaces using defaults; the browser displays them using defaults; if we declare them with prefixes, the browser displays them with prefixes.

Both the DOM and SAX provide methods which allow you to get not only the namespace URI for a QName, but also the prefix, for just such applications, which need the prefix. This means that you can not only find the fully-qualified namespace names for these elements, but you can go so far as to see *how* the XML author wrote those names. In real life, however, you will hardly ever need the namespace prefix, unless you are writing applications to display the XML as entered to a user. IE5's default XSL style sheet can differentiate between the above cases because it pulls this information from the DOM implementation shipped with the browser.

Namespaces and Attributes

So far all of our discussions have been centered on elements, and we've been pretty much ignoring attributes. Do namespaces work the same for attributes as they do for elements?

The answer is no, they don't. In fact, attributes usually don't have namespaces, the way that elements do. They are just "associated" with the elements to which they belong. Consider the following fragment:

```
<person xmlns="http://sernaferna.com/pers">
  <name id="25">
    <title>Sir</title>
  </name>
</person>
```

We know that the `<person>`, `<name>`, and `<title>` elements all belong to the same namespace, which is declared in the `<person>` start-tag. The `id` attribute, on the other hand, is not part of this namespace; it's simply associated with the `<name>` element, which itself is part of that default namespace. We could use a notation like this to identify it, for discussion:

```
"{http://sernaferna.com/pers}name:id"
```

However, if we used prefixes, we could specify that `id` is in the namespace like so:

```
<a:person xmlns:a="http://sernaferna.com/pers">
  <a:name a:id="25">
    <a:title>Sir</a:title>
  </a:name>
</a:person>
```

Unfortunately, there is a bit of a gray area left by the Namespaces specification concerning attributes. For example, consider the following two fragments:

```
<a:name id="25">
```

```
<a:name a:id="25">
```

Are these two fragments identical? Or are they different? Well, actually, applications can make up their own minds whether these two cases are the same or different. (In XSLT, for example, the two cases would be considered different.) For this reason, if you need to be sure that the XML processor will realize that your attributes are part of the same namespace as your element, you should include the prefix. On the other hand, most applications will treat the two situations identically.

Consider the case where you want to perform some processing on every attribute in the http://sernaferna.com/pers namespace. If an application considers both of the above cases to be the same, then in both cases the id attribute will get processed. On the other hand, if the application doesn't consider both of the above to be the same, you'll only get the second id attribute, because it is specifically declared to be in the namespace we're looking for, whereas the first one isn't.

Is this purely theoretical? Well, yes, it is. In most cases, applications don't look for attributes on their own; they look for particular elements, and then process the attributes on those elements. Whether or not those attributes belong to any particular namespace doesn't usually matter.

However, attributes from a particular namespace can also be attached to elements from a different namespace. Attributes that are specifically declared to be in a namespace are called **global attributes**. A common example of a global attribute is the XHTML class attribute, which might be used on any XML element, XHTML or not. This would make things easier when using CSS to display an XML document.

As another example of a global attribute, we could define a locator attribute, which is simply to be used to locate elements in an XML document. We'll put it in the http://sernaferna.com/locator namespace. This allows us to create an XML document like the following:

```
<person xmlns="http://sernaferna.com/pers"
        xmlns:loc="http://sernaferna.com/locator"
        loc:locator="1">
  <name id="25" loc:locator="2">
    <title loc:locator="3">Sir</title>
  </name>
</person>
```

Although all of those loc:locator attributes are associated with the elements to which they are attached, they have their own namespaces as well.

To see this in action, let's add an `id` attribute to our `<name>` element, as well as adding a `style` attribute to the HTML paragraph portion of our résumé.

Change `namespace2.xml` to this:

```
<?xml version="1.0" encoding="windows-1252"?>
<person xmlns="http://sernaferna.com/pers">
  <name id="1">
    <title>Sir</title>
    <first>John</first>
    <middle>Fitzgerald Johansen</middle>
    <last>Doe</last>
  </name>
  <position>Vice President of Marketing</position>
  <résumé>
    <html:html xmlns:html="http://www.w3.org/1999/xhtml">
    <html:head><html:title>Resume of John Doe</html:title></html:head>
    <html:body>
    <html:h1>John Doe</html:h1>
    <html:p html:style="FONT-FAMILY: Arial">
      John's a great guy, you know?
    </html:p>
    </html:body>
    </html:html>
  </résumé>
</person>
```

Because we want the `style` attribute to be specifically in the XHTML namespace, we have gone back to using prefixes on our XHTML elements, instead of a default namespace. Another alternative would have been to declare the XHTML namespace twice: once as the default, for `<html>` and all of its descendents, and once with a prefix, which could be attached to the attribute.

How It Works

The `id` attribute that we added is associated with the `<name>` element, but it doesn't actually have a namespace.

Similarly, the `style` attribute is associated with the `<p>` element, but in this case the attribute is specifically in the XHTML namespace.

Again, applications may or may not treat both of these the same, and consider them to be in the same namespace as the elements to which they are attached. All applications will treat the `style` attribute as being in the XHTML namespace, because we have specifically said so, but some will think `id` is in the same namespace as `<name>`, and some won't.

XSLT from a Namespace Point of View

Now that we understand what XML namespaces are and how they work, let's take another look at one of our simpler XSLT style sheets from Chapter 5:

```
<?xml version="1.0"?>
<xsl:stylesheet version="1.0" xmlns:xsl="http://www.w3.org/1999/XSL/Transform">
<xsl:template match="/">
<HTML>
<BODY>
<xsl:for-each select="/strings/s">
<P><xsl:value-of select="."/></P>
</xsl:for-each>
</BODY>
</HTML>
</xsl:template>
</xsl:stylesheet>
```

We said this could also be written in short-form like this:

```
<?xml version="1.0"?>
<HTML xsl:version="1.0" xmlns:xsl="http://www.w3.org/1999/XSL/Transform">
<BODY>
<xsl:for-each select="/strings/s">
<P><xsl:value-of select="."/></P>
</xsl:for-each>
</BODY>
</HTML>
```

How do XSL processors use XML namespaces when processing XSLT style sheets? The answer is that XSL processors only act on XML elements that are in the XSLT namespace, which is specified as http://www.w3.org/1999/XSL/Transform. Any other elements in the document, regardless of their namespace, are added to the result tree as-is.

So we declare our xsl prefix, which points at that URI, and we then stick it in front of any XSLT elements we want to add to the style sheet – it's as simple as that. Of course, using xsl as the prefix is only a convention; as long as you declare the namespace properly, you can use any prefix you want. (Another commonly used prefix for XSLT elements is x, since it is shorter to type.)

Notice that none of the attributes in the XSLT elements specify the namespace. This is because XSL processors specifically *do* consider all attributes of the XSLT elements to be part of the XSLT namespace, unless declared otherwise. (And if they were declared otherwise, the XSL processor would ignore them.)

Notice also that in the second, shorthand, version of our style sheet, we needed to append the xsl prefix to the version attribute, even though we didn't need to in the first style sheet. In the first style sheet, the version attribute is associated with the <xsl:stylesheet> element. In the second, the version attribute is associated with the <HTML> element, which is not in the XSLT namespace, and so it must be specified that it belongs to the XSLT namespace.

Try It Out – Using Namespaces in XSLT

Not only does XSL use namespaces to separate XSLT elements from other elements in style sheets, but we can go even further and use XSLT to make use of the namespaces in the source tree, and even output different namespaces to the result tree. For this Try It Out, we'll make use of our original `<name>` example.

1. If you haven't already got a copy of this, type the following into Notepad, and save it to your hard drive as `name.xml`:

```
<?xml version="1.0"?>
<name>
  <first>John</first>
  <middle>Fitzgerald Johansen</middle>
  <last>Doe</last>
</name>
```

2. We can then write a simple style sheet to output just the `<middle>` element, like so. Type the following into Notepad, and save it to your hard drive as `middle.xsl`:

```
<?xml version="1.0"?>
<xsl:stylesheet version="1.0"
                xmlns:xsl="http://www.w3.org/1999/XSL/Transform">
<xsl:output method="text"/>

<xsl:template match="//middle">
  <xsl:value-of select="text()"/>
</xsl:template>

<xsl:template match="text()"/>
</xsl:stylesheet>
```

For simplicity's sake, we are just searching for any `<middle>` elements, no matter where they exist in the document, by using the "`//`" notation.

3. Now, using XT which we discussed in Chapter 4, type xt name.xml middle.xsl resultfile.xml at the command prompt. The result will be a file containing the following text:

Fitzgerald Johansen

which is what we expected.

4. Now change `name.xml` to this:

```
<?xml version="1.0"?>
<name xmlns="http://sernaferna.com/name">
  <first>John</first>
  <middle>Fitzgerald Johansen</middle>
  <last>Doe</last>
</name>
```

309

5. Again, type xt name.xml middle.xsl resultfile.xml at the command prompt.

When we run the style sheet against this version of name.xml, we get no output. Why is this? Well, our style sheet, although it isn't obvious, only matches against elements that are not in any namespace, and our <middle> element is now in the http://sernaferna.com/name namespace.

6. Now we'll modify the style sheet to match against <middle> elements in that particular namespace. Change middle.xsl to look like this:

```
<?xml version="1.0"?>
<xsl:stylesheet version="1.0"
                xmlns:xsl="http://www.w3.org/1999/XSL/Transform"
                xmlns:name="http://sernaferna.com/name">

<xsl:output method="text"/>

<xsl:template match="//name:middle">
  <xsl:value-of select="text()"/>
</xsl:template>

<xsl:template match="text()"/>
</xsl:stylesheet>
```

7. Again, type in xt name.xml middle.xsl resultfile.xml at the command prompt.

This will give the same results as in step 3, since we're explicitly matching against <middle> elements from the http://sernaferna.com/name namespace. And, once again, it doesn't matter what prefix we use in our XSLT style sheet, as long as we get the URI right.

How It Works

Our first example should seem fairly straightforward by now: we simply search for all <middle> elements in the document, and print out their contents. Also, we have a template to take care of any other text in the document, and ignore it. (This ensures that we'll only get the text from the <middle> element, and not the text from other elements, through XSLT's default templates.)

In our second example, we modify our source tree slightly, so that we no longer have a <middle> element; instead, we have a <{http://sernaferna.com/name}middle> element. Thus, when we run the style sheet against this document, it doesn't find any regular <middle> elements, and so outputs nothing.

Finally, in our third example, we modify the style sheet to look for <middle> elements in the http://sernaferna.com/name namespace, and so get the correct results. Notice that this works even though the source document used the default namespace, and the XSLT style sheet used a namespace prefix; as far as XSLT is concerned, both elements are <{http://sernaferna.com/name}middle> elements, regardless of how they are declared.

There are also XPath functions that can be used with namespaces. For example, there is a namespace-uri() function which returns the namespace URI of a node, if any. For more information, see the XPath and XSLT specifications, at http://www.w3.org/TR/xpath and http://www.w3.org/TR/xslt respectively.

Try It Out – Outputting Namespaces with XSLT

Of course, not only can XSL deal with namespaces in the source tree, but we can also output elements in different namespaces to the result tree.

1. Create the following simple style sheet, and save it as `namespaceoutput.xsl`:

```
<xsl:stylesheet version="1.0"
    xmlns:xsl="http://www.w3.org/1999/XSL/Transform"
    xmlns:blah="http://sernaferna.com/blah">

<xsl:output method="xml" indent="yes"/>
<xsl:template match="/">
  <root>
    <blah:name>Hi there</blah:name>
  </root>
</xsl:template>
</xsl:stylesheet>
```

Here we declare an `http://sernaferna.com/blah` namespace, and use it for one of our elements.

2. XT, like many XSLT tools, needs an XML file for its input in order to operate. However, since this style sheet doesn't make use of any input, you can use any XML file.

Type **XT anyxmlfile.xml namespaceoutput.xsl resultfile.xml** at the command prompt. The output will be an XML document like this:

```
<?xml version="1.0" encoding="utf-8"?>
<root xmlns:blah="http://sernaferna.com/blah">
  <blah:name>Hi there</blah:name>
</root>
```

Notice that the XSL processor automatically inserts the namespace declaration for us.

3. Now modify the `<xsl:stylesheet>` start tag slightly, to include a default namespace:

```
<xsl:stylesheet version="1.0"
    xmlns:xsl="http://www.w3.org/1999/XSL/Transform"
    xmlns:blah="http://www.sernaferna.com/blah"
    xmlns="http://sernaferna.com/default">
```

4. In this case, the output would look like this:

```
<?xml version="1.0" encoding="utf-8"?>
<root xmlns:blah="http://www.sernaferna.com/blah"
    xmlns="http://sernaferna.com/default">
  <blah:name>Hi there</blah:name>
</root>
```

How It Works

The XSL processor really doesn't care what namespace your elements are in, so whatever extra namespaces are specified will be included in the result tree, including any defaults you might declare.

In the first style sheet, we declared a namespace prefix of `blah`, and applied it to the `<name>` element, which XT faithfully reproduced in our result tree.

In the second style sheet, we declared a default namespace; any elements which are not specifically in the XSLT namespace, or in our `blah` namespace, will be in this default one. So, when XT produces the output, this namespace is copied to the result tree.

What Exactly are URIs?

We have mentioned that namespaces are specified using URIs, and most of the examples shown so far have been URLs. To really understand namespaces, we'll have to look at this concept a little further.

Because so much of the work done on the Internet somehow involves finding and retrieving **resources**, much thought has been put into this process. So what is a resource? Well, simply put, a resource is anything that has identity. It could be a tangible item, such as a `.gif` file or a book, or it could be a conceptual item, like the current state of the traffic in Toronto. It could be an item which is retrievable over the Internet, such as an HTML document, or an item which is not retrievable over the Internet, such as the actual person who wrote that HTML document.

Recall our earlier definition of a URI:

> A URI (Uniform Resource Identifier) is a string of characters which identifies a resource. It can come in one of two flavors: URL (Uniform Resource Locator), or URN (Universal Resource Name).

A URI is kind of like a bank account; you can have a checking account, or a savings account, but there's no such thing as "just a bank account", it has to be one or the other. Similarly, a URI can be either a URL or a URN, but there is no such thing as "just a URI".

URLs

If you have been on the Internet for any length of time, you are probably already familiar with URLs – and most Internet-savvy people understand how URLs work. The first part of the URL specifies the **protocol**; `http` being the most common, with `mailto` and `ftp` also being used frequently, and others (such as `gopher`, `news`, `telnet`, `file`, etc.) being used on occasion. (Officially, the protocol part of the URL is called a **scheme**.)

The protocol is followed by a colon, and after the colon comes a path to the resource being identified. For example, here's a URL to a web page on the Internet:

```
http://sernaferna.com/default/home.htm
```

This URL contains information which can be used to retrieve a file named `home.htm` from a server on the Internet named `sernaferna.com`. It specifies that the file is in the `default` directory (or virtual directory), and that the file should be retrieved via the HTTP protocol.

We can also create a URL to an e-mail account, like so:

```
mailto:someone@somewhere.com
```

Of course, there is a limitation on the resources that can be retrieved via URLs: obviously they must be resources of a type that is retrievable from a computer!

URNs

URNs are not as commonly seen as URLs. In fact, most people, even those who have been on the Internet for years, have never seen a URN. They exist to provide a persistent, location-independent name for a resource.

For example, a person's name is similar to a URN, because the person has the same name, no matter where they are. Even after a person dies, the name still refers to the person who used to have it when they were alive. A name is different from a URN, though, because more than one person can have the same name, whereas URNs are unique.

A URN looks something like this:

```
urn:foo:a123,456
```

First comes the string `urn`, upper or lower-case, and a colon. After the first colon comes the **Namespace Identifier**, or **NID**, (`foo` in this case) followed by another colon. And finally comes the **Namespace Specific String**, or **NSS** (`a123,456` for example). As you can see from the terminology, URNs were designed with namespaces already in mind.

The NID portion of the URN declares what type of URN this is. For example, to create URNs for Canadian citizens, we might declare an NID of `Canadian-Citizen`.

The NSS portion of the URN is the part that must be unique, and persistent. In Canada, all citizens are assigned unique Social Insurance Numbers. So, a URN for a Canadian citizen with a Social Insurance Number of 000-000-000 might look like this:

```
urn:Canadian-Citizen:000-000-000
```

Why Use URLs for Namespaces, Not URNs?

The XML Namespace specification states that namespaces are identified with URIs, which leaves us the possibility of using either URLs or URNs. But it seems that URNs are better suited for naming namespaces than URLs – after all, a namespace is a *conceptual* resource, not one that can be retrieved via the Internet. So why are most namespaces named using URLs instead?

The answer is that using URNs instead of URLs would still leave us with one of the problems we discovered earlier: how would we guarantee that the URNs were unique? The purpose of namespaces is that element names from different document types won't accidentally overlap; they must be unique. But if two companies accidentally create the same URN to use as the name of a namespace, then the problem isn't solved. URLs, on the other hand, are already unique.

As we mentioned earlier, if Serna Ferna Inc. owns the `http://sernaferna.com` web site, then it can be sure that nobody else is using that URL, or any URLs mentioning the `sernaferna.com` domain name. Of course, this is still by convention; nothing stops someone at Ferna Serna Inc. from stealing Serna Ferna Inc.'s domain name and maliciously using it as the name for a namespace. But if everyone follows the convention then we can be sure that there won't be accidental collisions, which is good enough for our purposes. You could still construct a URN like `urn:SernaFernaHR:name`, but things are just simpler if you use URLs.

And there can also be side benefits to using URLs as namespace names. If we wanted to, we could put a document at the end of the URL that describes the elements in that namespace. For example, XSLT uses `http://www.w3.org/1999/XSL/Transform` as its namespace. If you were to point your web browser at that location, you would get an HTML page stating that the address you just entered is the Namespace for XSLT, with the appropriate hyperlink to that specification, along with links to the XML 1.0 specification, and the Namespaces specification, as shown:

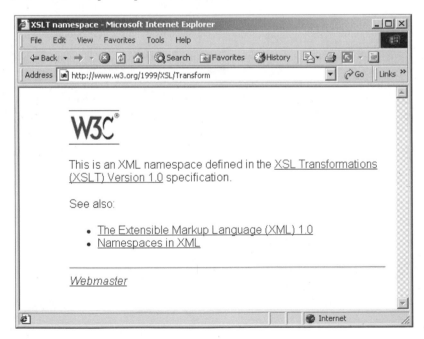

We have also been using `http://sernaferna.com/pers` as a fictional namespace. If Serna Ferna Inc. wanted to make the `pers` namespace public, for use in public document types, they might put a document at that location which describes the various XML elements and attributes in that namespace.

But regardless of what people are doing, the possibility of using a URN as a namespace identifier still exists, so if you have a system of URNs which you feel is unique, it is perfectly legal. URNs provide no benefits over URLs, except for the conceptual idea that they're a closer fit to what namespace names are trying to do. (That is, *name* something, not *point to* something.)

What Do Namespace URIs Really Mean?

Now that we know how to use namespaces to keep our element names unique, what exactly do those namespace URIs mean: in other words what does `http://sernaferna.com/pers` really represent?

The answer, according to the XML Namespaces specification, is that it doesn't mean anything. The URI is simply used to give the namespace a name, but doesn't mean anything on its own. In the same way the words "John Doe" don't mean anything on their own – they are just used to identify a particular person.

Many people feel that this isn't enough for XML. In addition to keeping element names distinct, they would also like to give those elements meaning – that is, not just distinguish `<my:element>` from `<your:element>`, but also define what `<my:element>` means. What is it used for? What are the legal values for it? If we could create some kind of "schema" which would define our document type, the namespace URI might be the logical place to declare this document as adhering to that schema.

The XML Namespaces specification (http://www.w3.org/TR/1999/REC-xml-names/#ns-decl) states that "it is not a goal that [the namespace URI] be directly useable for retrieval of a schema (if any exists)." In other words, as we've been saying, the URI is just a name or identifier: it doesn't have any kind of meaning. However, it is not strictly forbidden for it to have a meaning. For this reason, someone creating an application could legally decide that the URI used in a namespace actually does indicate some type of documentation, whether that be a prose document describing this particular document type, or a technical schema document of some sort. But, in this case, the URI still wouldn't mean anything to the XML parser; it would be up to the higher-level application to read the URI and do something with it.

As an example of where this might be useful, consider a corporate information processing system where users are entering information to be stored in XML format. If different namespaces are defined for different types of documents, and those namespaces are named with URLs, then you could put a help file at the end of each URL. If users are viewing a particular type of XML document in the special application you have written for them, all they have to do is hit *F1* to get help, and find out about this particular type of document. All your application has to do is open a web browser, and point it to the URL which defines the namespace.

> *There is a document which formally describes the syntax for URIs at the IETF (Internet Engineering Task Force) web site, located at http://www.ietf.org/rfc/rfc2396.txt; one which describes the syntax for URNs, located at http://www.ietf.org/rfc/rfc2141.txt; and one which describes the syntax for URLs, located at http://www.ietf.org/rfc/rfc1738.txt.*

When Should I Use Namespaces?

By this point in the chapter, we've covered everything that we need to know about namespaces from a technical standpoint. We know what they mean, how to use them, and how to combine them. So let's sit back for a while, put our feet up, and talk philosophy. When should we create a new namespace, and when should we add new elements to an existing one?

In the course of this chapter, we have created three namespaces:

- ❏   `http://sernaferna.com/pers`
- ❏   `http://sernaferna.com/locator`
- ❏   `http://sernaferna.com/name`

All of these namespaces were for use by our fictional company called Serna Ferna Inc. We could instead have created one namespace, which the company would use for all of its XML document types. Or, conversely, we could have broken down our namespaces further, perhaps splitting the `<person>` document type into multiple namespaces. Why did we choose three?

Remember that a namespace is just a "bag of names": that is, it's a group of element names which all belong together, and which are distinct from element names in other namespaces. This is shown in the following diagram:

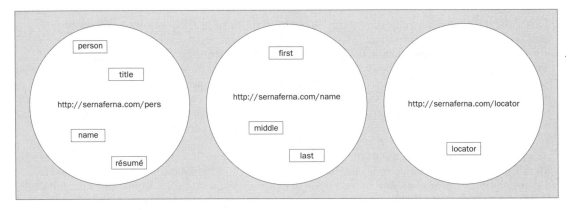

The key is the phrase "belong together". You might think of the elements in a namespace as being the vocabulary for a language, the same way that English words are in the English vocabulary. Any words that belong to that language would go in that namespace, and words from other languages would go into other namespaces. It's up to you to decide which elements belong in the same vocabulary, and which ones should go in different vocabularies.

> *The W3C went through this process when creating XHTML, the HTML language "redone" in XML. The problem is that XHTML is based on HTML4, which has three flavors:* **Frameset** *(which includes support for HTML frames),* **Strict** *(which is designed for clean structural markup, free from all layout tags), and* **Transitional** *(which allows formatting markup for older browsers, such as a* `bgcolor` *attribute on the* `<BODY>` *tag). Some HTML elements, such as* `<P>`, *appear in all three flavors, while others, such as* `<FRAMESET>`, *may only appear in certain flavors.*

This led the W3C, in the initial specifications for XHTML, to indicate that there would be three different namespaces used, one for each flavor. However, the web community strongly disagreed with this approach. Most people consider HTML (or XHTML) to be one language – even though there may be more than one "flavor" or "dialect" of that language – so they argued that XHTML should only have one namespace associated with it. In the end, the W3C decided to go with the one-namespace approach (the namespace they chose is `http://www.w3.org/1999/xhtml`, *which is why we've been using it for our XHTML examples).*

Summary

This chapter introduced the concept of namespaces, along with their implementation in XML. We've seen:

❑ What benefit namespaces can potentially give us in our documents

❑ How to declare and use namespaces

❑ How to effectively use a URI as the name of a namespace

❑ A brief recap of XSLT, with namespaces in mind

The idea behind namespaces may not seem all that relevant, unless you're combining elements from various vocabularies into one XML document. You may be thinking "If I'm just going to create XML documents to describe my data, why mess around with all of this namespace stuff?"

However, when you remember that you will be using other XML vocabularies, such as XSLT to transform your documents, or perhaps the Resource Definition Format (RDF) which is discussed in Chapter 14 and which can be used to describe documents, or even XHTML to display your data, namespaces become much more relevant. Learning the concepts behind namespaces will help you combine your documents with these other document types, in addition to any further document types you may create yourself.

Basic Valid XML: DTDs

In Chapter 2, we discussed the basic rules of the XML 1.0 syntax, and how to construct properly nested, *well-formed* XML documents. As we've seen in earlier chapters, XML data can be exchanged, processed, and displayed using only this minimal set of syntax rules, along with some related standards: CSS or XSLT for display transformation in a browser, DOM or SAX for manipulating XML data using standardized programming APIs, and namespaces as a method of identifying individual XML vocabularies.

We're now going to look at how we can specify a set of rules to define the way XML documents should be structured – using **Document Type Definitions** (**DTD**s). Being able to define such rules will become more important as we exchange, process, and display XML in a wider environment, such as in a business-to-business or e-commerce scenario. Using DTDs will allow us not only to determine that XML documents follow the syntax rules of the XML specification, but also that they follow our own rules regarding content and structure.

In this chapter we will learn:

- ❑ Why we might need DTDs, and the benefits of using them
- ❑ How to write simple DTDs
- ❑ How to use DTDs

To illustrate the various declarations and concepts in this and the following two chapters, we'll create a BookCatalog vocabulary and documents. This BookCatalog is something that publishers, bookstores, and consumers could use to describe themselves and the books that they buy or sell. We'll start by using DTDs, and in the next chapter we'll use another method – XML Schemas – to describe the same vocabulary.

Why Do We Need DTDs?

Well-formed XML data is guaranteed to use proper XML syntax, and have the properly nested (hierarchical) tree structure that's common to all XML data. This may be sufficient information for relatively static internal applications, particularly if the XML data is computer-generated and computer-consumed. In this case, it's the responsibility of the applications using the data to perform any structural or content verification, error handling, and interpretation of the data. The XML structural information and the logic to do this are usually hard-coded separately within the sending and receiving applications, from a common specification. Thus, any change to the XML data structure must be made in three places: the specification, and the sending and receiving applications.

> *An example of the "hard-coded logic" approach would be the use of the* `startElement` *and* `characters` *handlers in a SAX application. The* `startElement` *handler would be used to navigate the structure of the document, using the start-tags to maintain context within the data, and perhaps keeping a stack of element parents for additional context. The* `characters` *handler would be where the actual data (the content of the elements) would be manipulated. See Chapter 7 for more about SAX.*

This *can* be an efficient, high-performance approach to handling XML data in certain limited circumstances. For example, an internal corporate application might use well-formed XML as a data transfer mechanism between two different database management systems (DBMSs). Using XML as a transfer syntax would decouple the two DBMSs from each other, so that the transfer could just as easily be directed to a third DBMS, without needing to create yet another point-to-point transfer program. The sending DBMS would be assumed to generate good data, so the XML parser needn't be responsible for validation at that point. At the other end, the receiving DBMS is likely already to have an input data verification feature, so any data validation could occur during the XML-to-DBMS translation step. There'd be no need to validate the data whilst it was within the XML domain – well-formed XML would be sufficient to ensure the data transfer.

However, when there's no formal description of the XML data, it's difficult to describe or modify the structure of that data, since its structure and content constraints are buried within the application code. Any changes to the data structure must be made simultaneously in both the sending and receiving applications, and in the separate technical documentation as well. This might be a viable approach for applications like our DBMS example, but it can be difficult to maintain these applications, and we'd only be using a fraction of the power of XML.

XML Application Requirements

In addition to ensuring that XML data is simply well-formed, most XML applications will also need to:

- ❑ Describe document structure, preferably in a rigorous and formal manner
- ❑ Communicate document structure to other applications and people
- ❑ Check that the required elements are present – and prompt the author for their inclusion if they aren't
- ❑ Check that no disallowed elements are included – and prevent the author from using them
- ❑ Enforce element content, tree structure, and element attribute values
- ❑ Provide default values for unspecified attribute values
- ❑ Use standard document formats and data structures

All of these functions *could* be handled by specific code within a pair of cooperating applications and their accompanying documentation. However, in cases where the XML data is more widely shared – say between multiple applications – maintaining these functions in each and every application becomes an exponential nightmare. This is a problem common to most XML applications, so ideally we'd like to take a more standardized approach.

Document Type Definitions

Separating the XML data description from individual applications allows all cooperating applications to share a single description of the data, known as the **XML vocabulary**. A group of XML documents that share a common XML vocabulary is known as a **document type**, and each individual document that conforms to a document type is a **document instance**.

> *This is similar to the basic principle of object oriented ("OO") programming: objects are grouped and described as an object **class** (compare to a document type); each individual object conforming to that class description is known as an **instance** of that object (compare to the document instance).*

The XML 1.0 specification provides a standardized means of describing XML document types: the **Document Type Definition (DTD)**.

> **As we'll see throughout this chapter, DTDs are XML documents which can either be incorporated within the XML document containing the data, or exist as a separate document. They define the rules that set out how a document should be structured, what elements should be included, what kind of data may be included and what default values to use.**

Furthermore, the rules of the vocabulary description in the DTD, and how those rules are applied by a validating parser, are well-defined and standardized. This alone can go a long way toward a more reliable data exchange, particularly between diverse business partners. It's no longer necessary for each partner to create personalized custom tools – both partners can use the same standard XML tools and technologies to handle their shared data vocabulary.

Valid XML

As we've already seen, we can use an XML parser (also known more formally as an XML Processor) to ensure that an XML document is well-formed. Many parsers, known as **validating parsers**, can also provide a more rigorous verification option to check that the content of the XML document is **valid**. This means that the parser itself can verify that the document conforms to the rules of a specific XML vocabulary. This validation is accomplished by comparing the content of the document with an associated template in the form of a DTD.

> *Well-formed* **XML documents are those that comply with the basic syntax and structural rules of the XML 1.0 specification.** *Valid* **XML documents are well-formed documents that also comply with syntax, structural, and other rules as defined in a DTD.**

Simple well-formed XML data may be sufficient for applications where the data is machine-generated. Then the program creating the data can easily ensure that the data is valid. However, any program receiving the data needs either to trust the sender's data implicitly, or provide validation of its own.

Although it's possible for an XML application to handle validation, there are some real advantages to using a validating parser and a DTD to handle this task. The most significant advantage is that DTDs and validation rules are codified in the XML 1.0 specification.

Multiple documents and applications can *share* DTDs. Having a central description of the XML data and a standardized validation method lets us move both data description and validation code out of numerous individual applications. The data description code becomes the DTD, and the validation code is already present (and optimized) in the validating XML parser. This greatly simplifies our application code, and thus improves both performance and reliability.

Valid XML is also preferable to simple well-formed XML for most document-oriented data. Human authors can be guided (and restricted) by the constraints on structure and syntax that the DTD and validating parser impose. This prevents authors from creating documents that don't conform to exchange standards (the DTD). It's also possible to provide default values and structures to simplify the authoring process.

Validating Parsers

We've already discussed XML parsers (also known as XML Processors) in Chapter 2. Now let's take a look at a special kind of parser, the **validating parser**. All XML parsers must be able to process well-formed XML and report any problems encountered with the basic syntax and structure of a document. However, as we've discussed in this chapter, there are often times when we want to ensure that an XML document is not just well-formed, but valid, as well. To accomplish this, we need to use a validating parser in conjunction with a DTD.

The following table shows a sample of the currently available XML validating parsers:

Parser Name	Company / Organization	Release Date	Language
fxp	CS Dept, Univ. of Trier (DEU)	1999-06-19	SML
Java Project X TR2	Sun Microsystems	1999-09-27	Java
MSXML ("preview")	Microsoft Corp.	2000-05-17	C/C++ ???
RXP	University of Edinburgh (GBR)	1999-02-17	C
STG Validator	Brown University (USA)	1998-10-07	* (see below)
XJParser	Datachannel, Inc.	1999-06-21	Java
XML4C 3.1.0	IBM	2000-03-08	C++
XML4J 3.0.1	IBM	2000-03-13	Java
XML Parser for Java v2	Oracle	1999-10-17	Java
Xerces-C++	The Apache XML Project	1999-11-09	C++
Xerces-J	The Apache XML Project	1999-11-10	Java

Although Microsoft was one of the earliest supporters of XML, it chose to follow its own path for several related technologies (such as XSL, XML Schema). As a result of this approach, the other parsers shown here may be a better choice for those readers who are most interested in conformance to the W3C recommendations and pending standards such as XML Schema.

As the inventor of Java, it's no surprise that Sun Microsystems chose to develop its XML parser in Java. It does, however, appear that this parser is available to JDC subscribers only.

IBM and Oracle have both been involved with XML for quite a long time as well. IBM has been a particularly aggressive developer of XML parsers and other tools. Current (v3) IBM parsers are now based upon the Apache Xerces parsers, but IBM had previously developed highly-regarded parsers on their own, in both C++ and Java.

The Apache Foundation is well-known for its widely-used OpenSource web server software. It is not surprising, therefore, that Apache has also embarked upon a pair of OpenSource XML parser projects. As noted above, IBM has adopted the Xerces parser and is a major supporter of Apaches's XML efforts.

There are three offerings from the academic community that are of interest to those of us who want to validate XML documents using DTDs. The first (fxp) is one of the earliest XML 1.0 validating parsers to have been developed. The second (rxp) is another early validating parser. The third (STG Validator) is not even a parser *per se* – it is an online XML document validation service. Anyone with a browser can go to the STG website and have a document validated, and receive an HTML report describing any validation errors or warnings.

Links

fxp
http://www.informatik.uni-trier.de/~neumann/Fxp

IE 5.5
http://msdn.microsoft.com/downloads/webtechnology/ie/iepreview.asp

Java Project X TR2
http://developer.java.sun.com/developer/products/xml [JDC subscribers only!]

MSXML "preview"
http://msdn.microsoft.com/downloads/webtechnology/xml/msxml.asp

rxp
http://www.cogsci.ed.ac.uk/~richard/rxp.html

STG Validator
http://www.stg.brown.edu/service/xmlvalid

XJParser
http://xdev.datachannel.com/downloads/xjparser

XML4C / XML4J
http://www.alphaworks.ibm.com/formula/xml

XML for Java v2
http://technet.oracle.com/tech/xml/parser_java2

Xerces-C++
http://xml.apache.org/xerces-c/index.html

Xerces-J
http://xml.apache.org/xerces-j/index.html

Sharing DTDs

Shared DTDs are the basis for many XML vocabularies. Using a shared data description greatly simplifies the process of creating and maintaining an XML vocabulary. As we've already seen, it can also make any application code simpler, and thus more reliable and easier to maintain. With a shared DTD, there's only one place where we need to make modifications to the vocabulary's data description, instead of three (the specification, sending application, and receiving application).

Having standardized XML vocabularies for common things (such as bibliographic information, for example) allows developers to reuse existing DTDs, saving the cost of developing custom DTDs. Custom DTDs isolate their users and applications from others that might otherwise be able to share commonly formatted documents and data. Shared DTDs are the foundation of XML data interchange and reuse.

> *For example, there is already a common bibliographic standard known as the **Dublin Core standard** (which we'll look at further in Chapter 14). It describes the metadata used to refer to books, including title, author, ISBN (International Standard Book Number), and the like. Originally developed using SGML, it's now also available as an XML vocabulary. Our* BookCatalog *DTD could have used this standard, but it requires some extensions to XML 1.0 that we haven't yet discussed (and besides, a self-contained example is better for the purpose of this book).*

A Simple Example

So let's introduce our BookCatalog vocabulary. The BookCatalog DTD is an example of a shared XML vocabulary that can be used by a publisher to communicate with its distributors, retailers, and other interested parties. An XML-aware browser will allow users to learn about future publications, read reviews of existing books, or even order books directly from the catalog.

Why Use XML to Do This?

Of course, we could do this with existing HTML-based e-commerce applications, but we can use XML to make a much more powerful e-commerce application – allowing searches by title, author, ISBN, and other specially tagged fields. Existing Internet search engines don't provide a standard way of describing and searching for such fields. For example, a search for "Professional XML" would not only provide links to Wrox's and Amazon.com's catalogs for the book of that name, but could also return links to numerous job offerings for XML professionals, and so on.

XML also enables direct business-to-business (B2B) data exchanges. For example, when Barnes & Noble wants to order books from Wrox, an application running at B&N could query the Wrox website using the BookCatalog DTD to select specific fields needed for the order. The B&N application might then copy some of the bibliographic information to its own catalog, reformat some of the data into a purchase order ("PO") to be sent back to Wrox, and perhaps transform the XML data into some internal accounting format, as well. While it's already possible to exchange this information using standards such as Electronic Data Interchange (EDI), these cryptic binary data formats are very costly to implement and aren't universally supported.

Some of the advantages XML provides are:

- ❑   A single common standard syntax
- ❑   Easily shared vocabularies
- ❑   Standard methods and tools for transforming data
- ❑   Utilization of existing Internet protocols such as HTTP

The Basic BookCatalog Data Model

Before we can create a DTD, we first need to develop a data model that describes our BookCatalog vocabulary and its grammar. We'll consider a hierarchical tree of elements that implement our data model, and construct an example document instance that illustrates this model. We'll then return to this example later in the chapter, to show the declarations that can be used to describe formally the data model in a DTD.

We've already discussed the hypothetical purpose of the BookCatalog vocabulary. So now let's look at a simple structure that implements the basic data objects we need for a simple B2B/B2C (business-to-business/business-to-customer) book catalog.

We can describe all the data we require using just four major elements:

- ❑   Catalog – A document header describing the rest of the document
- ❑   Publisher – Vendor of Books, employer of Authors
- ❑   Author – Creator of Books, employee of Publisher
- ❑   Book – Creation of Author and Publisher

We'll begin creating our BookCatalog vocabulary with name and address information for the publishers, and a simple bibliographic description of books. For the moment, we'll treat <Author> as a child of <Book>. (Later we'll expand the structure of books and their authors, and add review threads.)

Like all well-formed XML, these elements form a hierarchical tree. This diagram illustrates the parent-child relationships of various elements comprising the basic BookCatalog vocabulary:

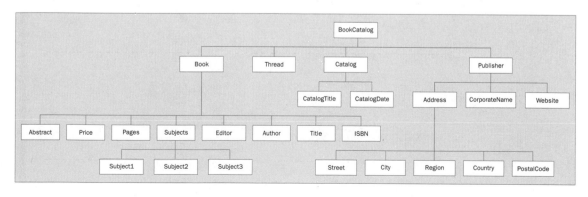

Try It Out – Basic BookCatalog Data Model and Document

At first, we'll keep things simple and just look at the `<Catalog>`, `<Publisher>`, and `<Book>` elements and their children. We're going to create an example XML document instance that conforms to this structure.

> *We'll use local file system references in all our examples so that you can experiment with documents and DTDs on your own system, without requiring an active Internet connection. When you want to display a file in your browser, simply prepend "`file://`" to your local filename and path, and use it as you would any other URL.*

> *Simply replace the "`mypath`" string with the actual path to your examples directory. It's important here to keep all your examples (DTDs and documents) together in one directory.*

1. Create a file named *mypath*/`BookCatalogBasic.xml` containing the following:

```xml
<?xml version="1.0" encoding="UTF-8" standalone="yes"?>

<BookCatalog>

  <Catalog>
    <CatalogTitle>The Wrox BookCatalog ('Basic' version)</CatalogTitle>
    <CatalogDate>2000-05-23</CatalogDate>
  </Catalog>

  <Publisher>
    <CorpName>Wrox Press Ltd.</CorpName>
    <Website>www.wrox.com</Website>
    <Address>
      <Street>Arden House</Street>
      <Street>1102 Warwick Road</Street>
      <Street>Acocks Green</Street>
      <City>Birmingham</City>
      <Region>England</Region>
      <PostalCode>B27 .6BH</PostalCode>
      <Country>UK</Country>
    </Address>
  </Publisher>

  <Publisher>
    <CorpName>Wrox Press Inc.</CorpName>
    <Website>www.wrox.com</Website>
    <Address>
      <Street>29 S LaSalle St, Suite 520</Street>
      <City>Chicago</City>
      <Region>IL</Region>
      <Country>USA</Country>
      <PostalCode>60603</PostalCode>
    </Address>
  </Publisher>
```

```
<Book>
  <ISBN>1-861003-11-0</ISBN>
  <Title>Professional XML</Title>
  <Author>Didier Martin</Author>
  <Author>Mark Birbeck</Author>
  <Author>Michael Kay</Author>
  <Author>Brian Loesgen</Author>
  <Author>Jon Pinnock</Author>
  <Author>Steven Livingstone</Author>
  <Author>Peter Stark</Author>
  <Author>Kevin Williams</Author>
  <Author>Richard Anderson</Author>
  <Author>Stephen Mohr</Author>
  <Author>David Baliles</Author>
  <Author>Bruce Peat</Author>
  <Author>Nikola Ozu</Author>
  <Editor>Jon Duckett</Editor>
  <Editor>Peter Jones</Editor>
  <Editor>Karli Watson</Editor>
  <Abstract>The complete practical encyclopedia for XML today.</Abstract>
  <Pages>1169</Pages>
  <Price>$49.99</Price>
  <Subjects>
    <Subject1>Internet</Subject1>
    <Subject2>Internet Programming</Subject2>
    <Subject3>XML</Subject3>
  </Subjects>
</Book>

</BookCatalog>
```

2. You can display this example in any XML-aware browser, such as Microsoft IE5, IE4 with MSXML, or Netscape Communicator 5 (Mozilla). Without a style sheet, the document will be shown as a simple tree structure of elements:

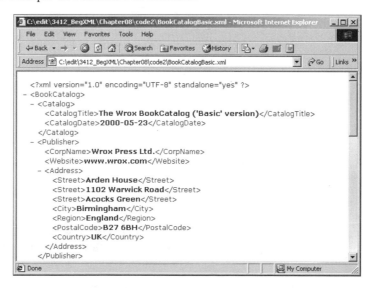

3. Do save this file, as we'll revisit it later in the chapter.

How It Works

The first line is the optional, but highly recommended, XML declaration. The XML 1.0 recommendation does permit documents to be considered well-formed without this declaration. However, its presence prevents problems with the interpretation of the document encoding, "future-proofs" the document against later versions of XML, and provides an internal statement that the document is indeed XML. This last reason is compelling even within the Internet MIME environment, since MIME types and envelopes are external to the document and are likely to be stripped before any XML processing.

By setting the `standalone` attribute to `"yes"` we're indicating to the XML parser and application that there are no external entity references.

> *We'll cover entity references in more detail in Chapter 11. And we'll be coming back to the XML declaration a little later in this chapter.*

The `<Catalog>` element is comprised of two children that simply describe this document: its title and date of creation:

```
<Catalog>
  <CatalogTitle>The Wrox BookCatalog ('Basic' version)</CatalogTitle>
  <CatalogDate>2000-05-23</CatalogDate>
</Catalog>
```

The `<CatalogTitle>` child element is simply a description of the entire document. Its significance is mostly for the reader – we'll create `'Advanced'` and `'Complete'` versions of this DTD later, as well as a corresponding XML Schema description. The `<CatalogDate>` child element uses an ISO standard date format that is probably the best compromise between compact representation and interoperability – without the infamous "Y2K" problem, though it does create a potential "Y10K" bug.

We've included two example `<Publisher>` elements – for the publisher of this book and its U.S. affiliate. The children of these elements provide a simple name and address, plus a web site URL:

```
<Publisher>
  <CorpName>Wrox Press Inc.</CorpName>
  <Website>www.wrox.com</Website>
  <Address>
    <Street>29 S LaSalle St, Suite 520</Street>
    <City>Chicago</City>
    <Region>IL</Region>
    <PostalCode>60603</PostalCode>
    <Country>USA</Country>
  </Address>
</Publisher>
```

The `<Book>` element contains the usual bibliographic metadata: ISBN, title, author(s), editor(s), an abstract, the number of pages, the price, and three subject classifications (that are provided by the publisher to help bookstores to physically organize their stock):

```
<Book>
  <ISBN>1-861003-11-0</ISBN>
  <Title>Professional XML</Title>
  <Author>Didier Martin</Author>
.....
  <Author>Nikola Ozu</Author>
  <Editor>Jon Duckett</Editor>
  <Editor>Peter Jones</Editor>
  <Editor>Karli Watson</Editor>
  <Abstract>The complete practical encyclopedia for XML today.</Abstract>
  <Pages>1169</Pages>
  <Price>$49.99</Price>
  <Subjects>
    <Subject1>Internet</Subject1>
    <Subject2>Internet Programming</Subject2>
    <Subject3>XML</Subject3>
  </Subjects>
</Book>
```

We'll refer to, and expand upon, this example throughout this chapter. You'll see it again when we discuss some of the specific DTD declarations that we'll use to describe this document. We'll also reuse it in subsequent chapters.

But first, let's find out how we can describe this hierarchy and other such constraints in a DTD.

DTDs

XML DTDs are derived from the much more complex versions that were designed and used in SGML (XML's parent markup language). DTDs use a formal grammar to describe the structure and syntax of an XML document, including the permissible values for much of that document's content. Since DTDs are part of the XML 1.0 specification, there's already widespread support for this method of data description and validation in XML parsers.

To recap what we said earlier, DTDs:

❑   Provide a formal and complete definition of an XML vocabulary

❑   Are sharable descriptions of the structure of an XML document

❑   Are a way to validate specific instances of XML documents and constrain their content

❑   Are restricted to one DTD per document instance

There *are* some proposed alternatives to DTDs, including **XML Schema**, **XML-Data** and its simpler relative, **XML-Data Reduced** (also called **XML-DR**). Schemas are well on their way to becoming a formal W3C recommendation. The XML-DR subset of XML-Data is currently integrated into Microsoft's IE5, the MSXML parser (including a version to retrofit IE4), the XML portions of Windows 2000, and has also been used as the basis for the BizTalk e-commerce initiative.

See Chapters 10 (Valid XML: Schemas), 11 (Advanced Valid XML), and 14 (Other Uses for XML) for more about the various alternatives to DTDs.

The XML 1.0 recommendation fully defines DTD syntax, as well as how XML documents may be associated with a DTD.

Internal versus External DTDs

Although only one DTD can be associated with a given XML document, that DTD may be divided into two parts: the **internal subset**; and the **external subset**. These subsets are relative to the document instance:

❑ The internal subset is a portion of the DTD included within the document

❑ The external subset is a set of declarations that are located in a separate document (which might be a database record or a file, typically using the `.dtd` filename extension)

There's no requirement that a DTD uses a particular subset, though without any DTD we can't validate the document (though we can still ensure that it's well-formed). A DTD might be contained entirely within the document (an internal subset), with no external subset, or a document may simply refer to an external subset and contain no DTD declarations of its own. In many cases, the DTD will use a combination of both of these subsets. So, there are three possible forms of DTD:

❑ An internal subset DTD

❑ An external subset DTD

❑ A combined DTD, using both the internal and external subsets

The external component is often referred to as "the DTD", even though, in the "combined" case, the DTD is actually comprised of both internal *and* external subsets.

DTD declarations in the internal subset have priority over those in the external subset.

When to Use Internal and External Subsets

You should generally use a separate document (that is, an external subset) for DTD declarations that will be shared by multiple documents. In this case, using only the internal subset would require copies of the declarations in all document instances – an obvious maintenance nightmare!

It's much easier to update shared declarations if they're kept in a single separate document. Keeping a separate DTD also provides a description of all the documents that refer to that DTD.

Often, a DTD is shared by multiple organizations, where a working group maintains the DTD and publishes copies to each of the participants. The DTD could also be maintained and stored in some form of central repository (though copies of the DTD might still be cached in multiple locations for performance reasons). Shared DTDs are a very powerful aspect of XML.

One of the best uses of the internal subset is when we want to use an existing standard DTD, but make some minor changes for our own purposes. The external subset can provide the bulk of the description and validation information. Any additional declarations could be added in the internal subset, perhaps to add some new elements and/or attributes. We may also choose to override some existing declarations (remember that the internal subset always takes priority).

This example illustrates why the priority of the internal subset of the DTD can be a blessing or a curse. Using internal subset declarations to override an external DTD can be the only way to use an existing DTD that doesn't match our needs exactly. Of course, there are also drawbacks. For example, someone who shares documents and DTDs with you might choose to override some of the constraints in your original DTD, and this might cause problems if the document is then sent back without its newly modified internal subset.

The internal subset can also be useful during the development of the DTD, or for single documents, but it's less useful if many documents are exchanged with other persons or applications.

Associating a DTD with an XML Document

It's about time we got round to experimenting with some DTDs. But since that's impossible without knowing how to associate a DTD with an XML document, let's first discuss how to do this.

In a confusing clash of names, DTDs are linked to XML documents using markup called the **Document Type Declaration** (which is *never* abbreviated as "DTD"). This declaration is commonly referred to as "the DOCTYPE declaration" to differentiate it from a DTD.

> **"DTD" refers only to the *definition* of a document type – *not* the DOCTYPE declaration that associates a DTD with an XML document instance.**

Each XML document can be associated with one, and only one, DTD using a single DOCTYPE declaration. Validating parsers use this declaration to retrieve the DTD (if it exists) and validate the document according to the DTD's rules. If the DTD isn't found, the parser will send an error message, and will be unable to validate the document.

The limit of one DTD per document can be an unfortunate restriction. For example, our BookCatalog vocabulary contains information about publishers (i.e. businesses or corporations) and books. The former might best be described using a standard industry vocabulary that describes a generic business. And the latter could be described using the Dublin Core vocabulary that we mentioned earlier. It would be nice if we could include references to three DTDs in our BookCatalog documents: two representing these standard vocabularies, plus one of our own. Unfortunately, this is not easy to do in XML.

There are some workarounds to this limitation that we'll discuss later (in Chapter 11 –Advanced Valid XML).

So let's start by taking a closer look at the syntax of the XML and DOCTYPE declarations.

The XML Declaration (a Refresher)

In our last Try It Out, we had the following XML declaration:

```
<?xml version="1.0" encoding="UTF-8" standalone="yes"?>
```

As we discussed in Chapter 2, the XML declaration has three specific attributes: version (required), and encoding and standalone (both optional). The third of these pertains to the use of DTDs, and how the XML processor or parser will interpret the DOCTYPE declaration. There are only two legal values for this attribute:

❑   yes, which means that the document is self-contained, and no other data is required

❑   no, which means that the document uses markup contained in an external DTD

> *We'll discuss the* standalone *attribute, and its implications for DTDs and validating parsers, in more detail in Chapter 11 – Advanced Valid XML.*

In our example, we've declared that the document conforms to XML 1.0 syntax (version="1.0"), it uses the UTF-8 character encoding (encoding="UTF-8"), and that *no* external entities are required (standalone="yes").

The Document Type (DOCTYPE) Declaration

This optional declaration may appear only once in an XML document. It must follow the document's XML declaration (if any) and precede any elements or character data content: only comments and/or PIs can be inserted between the xml declaration and the DOCTYPE declaration. Although this declaration is optional for simple well-formed XML documents, any document that needs to be validated using a DTD must have a DOCTYPE declaration!

> **Remember – only *one* DOCTYPE declaration (and therefore only *one* DTD) may appear in any single document. However, this one DTD *may* be divided into internal and external subsets.**

The basic structure of the DOCTYPE declaration is as follows:

```
<!DOCTYPE document_element source location1 location2 [ internal subset of DTD ]>
```

The DOCTYPE declaration consists of:

❑   The usual XML tag delimiters ("<" and ">").

❑   The exclamation mark ("!") that signifies a special XML declaration.

❑   The DOCTYPE keyword.

❑   The name of the document element (document_element).

❑   One of two legal source keywords (PUBLIC or SYSTEM – we'll see what these mean shortly).

❑   One or two DTD locations, to associate an external DTD subset with a document. The locations we need to specify depend on the value of source.

❑   Some additional declarations (those within the square brackets) referring to the internal subset of the DTD. (Of course, the internal subset might even comprise the entire DTD.)

In this section, we'll only look at the declaration that associates the external subset of the DTD with a document. We'll be covering the declarations that can be included in either subset of the DTD in the "Basic DTD Markup Tags" section later in this chapter.

The Document Element Name

The first variable parameter of any DOCTYPE declaration is the name of the document element. This name is required and connects the DTD to the entire element tree:

```
<?xml version="1.0" encoding="UTF-8" standalone="yes"?>
<!DOCTYPE BookCatalog ... >
...
<BookCatalog>
...
</BookCatalog>
```

Since all XML documents must be well-formed, there can only be one <BookCatalog> element in the document. If the DOCTYPE declaration and the document element don't match, a validating parser will report this as an error and will stop further processing of the document.

> **DTDs are always associated with the document element (the root of the element tree), so all of its children (all other elements in the tree) will inherit the association from this point.**

The DTD Source

When we want to associate an external DTD subset with a document, we need to declare at least the *source* (SYSTEM or PUBLIC) and primary location (*location1*) of that DTD.

When the SYSTEM keyword is used, we need to specify the location using either a **Uniform Resource Locator** (**URL**), or the more general **Uniform Resource Identifier** (**URI**). Remember from our discussion in Chapter 8 that URIs can either be a simple URL, or another unique name of some sort.

When the source parameter is PUBLIC, the primary location is used in some application-specific way (which we'll discuss a little later in this section). We can also optionally specify a secondary location for the same DTD. In this case, the secondary location (*location2*) is implicitly a SYSTEM location (a URI), which provides a fall-back location if the PUBLIC location can't be found.

Let's take a look at both methods of locating an external DTD.

Using SYSTEM Locations

The following example shows how we can use the SYSTEM keyword with a URL to locate the DTD:

```
<!DOCTYPE BookCatalog SYSTEM "http://www.wrox.com/DTDs/BookCatalog.dtd" >
```

In this case, the parser will attempt to retrieve the DTD from the specified URL at Wrox's website. If the DTD isn't found, an error will be reported and the parser won't be able to validate the document.

Of course, a document residing on the same web server as the DTD could also access the DTD directly, without using an external address:

```
<!DOCTYPE BookCatalog SYSTEM "file:///DTDs/BookCatalog.dtd" >
```

Although general-purpose URLs may use the number sign (#) character as a **URL fragment identifier**, you shouldn't use these in the location of a DTD. XML parsers might report such URLs as errors, so they won't be able to locate or process the DTD. The following example is an illegal DTD location, since it uses a URL fragment:

```
<!DOCTYPE BookCatalog SYSTEM
"http://www.wrox.com/DTDs/BookCatalog.dtd#Part1" >
```

In all of these examples, the declarations needed to validate a document are found in the external subset DTD file named `BookCatalog.dtd`. This approach is most useful when the DTD and all of its related document instances reside in a single system or group of systems, usually within a single organization.

However, when DTDs are shared by multiple organizations, it might be preferable to have multiple copies of the same DTD available on various geographically dispersed servers. Or, in a production environment, the DTD might reside on the local production system for performance reasons. In either of these cases, using a specific URL would unnecessarily restrict the DTD to a specific source and location. It would be better if the application processing the document could retrieve the associated DTD using its own DTD catalog or search algorithm. This is the kind of situation where we need to use `PUBLIC` locations.

Using PUBLIC Locations

Using the `PUBLIC` keyword allows a non-specific reference to the DTD via a URI, even perhaps via a secondary (specific) URI.

For example, the `BookCatalog` DTD could become a well-known publishing industry standard, in which case we might refer to it using the following declaration:

```
<!DOCTYPE BookCatalog PUBLIC "PublishingConsortium/BookCatalog" >
```

In this example, the XML application would have more flexibility in locating the DTD – a local copy of the DTD might be used, a shared DTD might be available via a private network to the "Publishing Consortium", or the declarations could even be stored in a non-XML database server. This means that finding the DTD at a `PUBLIC` location and handling its possible absence is left to the application, rather than the XML parser.

Of course there are circumstances (e.g. no active Internet connection, the DTD's server is down, the DTD has been withdrawn from public use by its author) where the "well-known" DTD might not be available using the URI and the application-specific search algorithm. Therefore, when using the `PUBLIC` source keyword, it's common practice to include both primary and secondary locations:

```
<!DOCTYPE BookCatalog PUBLIC
        "PublishingConsortium/BookCatalog"
        "http://www.wrox.com/DTDs/BookCatalog.dtd" >
```

If the parser or application cannot locate the DTD using the primary (PUBLIC) location, the second (SYSTEM) location is used. Note that the SYSTEM keyword is *implied* in this example, and that the SYSTEM keyword is never included in a declaration in combination with the PUBLIC keyword.

Any one of these forms of the DOCTYPE declaration is all that we need to associate a DTD with a document. The last form we looked at is probably the most valuable, since it allows for the efficient caching of multiple copies of a shared DTD, and doesn't require that every document knows the exact location of the DTD. At the same time, including a specific SYSTEM location provides a fallback URL for the DTD.

Despite the potential advantages of a PUBLIC location for the DTD, most of the examples in this book will use the much simpler SYSTEM location. You'll probably find this to be a better option for your own experiments with DTDs as well.

Additional DTD declarations may also be included in the internal subset. In most cases, however, we will want to separate the DTD from the document using the DOCTYPE declaration.

Try It Out — DOCTYPE Declaration (Linking a DTD to a Document)

Let's create and use a trivial DTD and demonstrate linking it to two different document instances, both using the same DOCTYPE declaration. The contents of the DTD can be ignored for the moment, since we'll discuss basic DTD markup later in this chapter.

For the time being, let's just stipulate that this DTD requires a conforming document to have exactly three empty elements, named X, Y, Z, with the elements appearing in XYZ order.

Once again, we'll use local file system references so that you can experiment with this document and its associated DTD on your own system – simply replace the mypath string in the example with the actual path to the directory where you want to put your example files.

1. Create the following example DTD as a text file named *mypath*/BookCatalogTrivial.dtd:

```
<!ELEMENT BookCatalog (X,Y,Z) >
<!ELEMENT X EMPTY >
<!ELEMENT Y EMPTY >
<!ELEMENT Z EMPTY >
```

You needn't worry about the specifics of these ELEMENT declarations for the moment. They simply mean that any BookCatalog-conforming document must have exactly three empty elements, named X, Y, and Z, that appear in exactly that order.

2. Now, we'll create the three example documents. First, create a text file named *mypath*/BookCatalogTrivial.xml containing the following:

```
<?xml version="1.0"?>
<!DOCTYPE BookCatalog SYSTEM "file:///mypath/BookCatalogTrivial.dtd" >
<BookCatalog>
  <X/>
  <Y/>
  <Z/>
</BookCatalog>
```

3. Create another text file named *mypath*/BookCatalogAbsentDTD.xml containing the following:

```
<?xml version="1.0"?>
<!DOCTYPE BookCatalog SYSTEM "file:///mypath/MissingDTD.dtd" >
<BookCatalog>
    <X/>
    <Y/>
    <Z/>
</BookCatalog>
```

4. You can view these XML documents in an XML-enabled browser. The valid document should be displayed in your browser's default XML style:

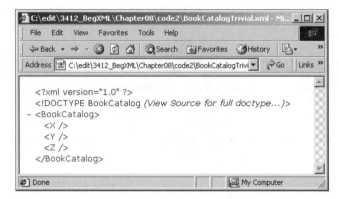

5. The "bad" document (BookCatalogAbsentDTD.xml) includes a reference to a non-existent DTD. Depending on the parser, this document may be fully displayed (without any validity checking), or might show an error message instead:

Now that we've seen the basic structure of a DTD, and the method of linking that DTD to an XML document, let's look at a few of the declarations that are common to almost all DTDs.

Basic DTD Markup

DTD declarations are delimited with the usual XML tag delimiters ("<" and ">"). Like the DOCTYPE declaration, all DTD declarations are indicated by the use of the exclamation mark ("!") followed by a keyword, and its specific parameters:

```
<!keyword parameter1 parameter2 ..parameterN >
```

Although we've only used single spaces between the parameters in the above example, any amount of white space is permitted – as with most XML declarations and content, white space is *not* significant, and tabs or spaces may be used to align text for greater clarity. However, this general rule doesn't apply to the initial keyword strings of a declaration, which must appear exactly as shown above.

For example, the following element type declaration is *illegal*, due to the two spaces around the ! character (all the other extra white space *is* legal):

```
< ! keyword    parameter1
    parameter2
      ..
    parameterN
  >
```

Assuming the two illegal spaces are removed, this example shows an otherwise valid and very useful format for DTD declarations. Multi-line declarations are commonly used to clarify element structure, sequence, and other constraints.

There are four basic keywords used in DTD declarations:

Keyword	Description
ELEMENT	Declares an XML element type name and its permissible sub-elements ("children")
ATTLIST	Declares XML element attribute names, plus permissible and/or default attribute values
ENTITY	Declares special character references, text macros (much like a C/C++ #define statement), and other repetitive content from external sources (like a C/C++ #include)
NOTATION	Declares external non-XML content (for example, binary image data) and the external application that handles that content

The first two keywords are essential for describing any XML content or data model (elements and their attributes). The latter two provide useful shortcuts for creating documents with reusable content, plus methods for handling non-XML data.

Advanced DTD syntax, including the ENTITY and NOTATION declarations, will be discussed in Chapter 11.

First, let's look at the two basic DTD declarations that are required to describe most XML documents.

Element Type (ELEMENT) Declarations

Elements are the fundamental building blocks of XML data. Any useful document will include several element types, some nested within others (perhaps many levels deep). Many documents will also use element attributes, but we'll discuss those in the next section.

> **The only mandatory component of an XML document is an element – even the most trivial XML document must have at least the document element. None of the other components, including the xml and DOCTYPE declarations, comments, PIs, or element attributes, are *required* to create a well-formed XML document.**

Elements are described using the **element type declaration**. This declaration can have one of two different forms, depending on the value of the category parameter (which is implied in the latter form):

```
<!ELEMENT name category >
<!ELEMENT name (content_model) >
```

The *name* parameter is the **element type name** that is being described – it must be a legal XML name.

Remember, XML names must comprise letters (not just ASCII letters; these can be any Unicode letter, including extenders and combining characters), numeric digits (ditto), and/or any of four punctuation characters: underscore (_), colon (:), hyphen (-), and period / full stop (.). These are known as the XML NameChar characters.

The first character of an XML name (known as the Name1 character) must be a letter, underscore, or colon (though colons should not be used in XML names, except as the XML Namespace delimiter character).

The *category* (**content category**) and *content_model* (**content model**) parameters describe what kind of content (if any) may appear within elements of the given name.

Let's now look into the details of these other two parameters.

Element Content Categories

There are five categories of element content:

Content category	Description
ANY	Element type may contain any well-formed XML data
EMPTY	Element type may *not* contain any text or child elements – only element attributes are permitted
element	Element type contains only child elements – no additional text is permitted within this element type
mixed	Element type may contain text and/or child elements
PCDATA	Element type may contain text (character data) only

In addition to content as described in the above table, all of these categories of element content allow the use of attributes within the element start-tag. These attributes are defined using an Attribute (`ATTLIST`) declaration, which will be covered later in this chapter.

The simplest of these categories are ANY and EMPTY.

The ANY Category

As the name implies, elements defined in the ANY category may contain any well-formed XML. This could include character data, other elements, comments, PIs, CDATA sections – anything goes, as long as it's well-formed.

The following is an example of the element type declaration for the ANY category:

```
<!ELEMENT AnythingGoesInHere ANY >
```

This sort of element should be used very sparingly, as we lose almost all validity checking if we only use this permissive category. We're left with little more then a simple well-formed document, and probably won't need to use a DTD at all!

The EMPTY Category

At the other end of the element spectrum are elements that can't contain anything except attributes. These are known as **empty elements**, and they're defined using the EMPTY keyword. Examples of empty elements include HTML's line-break tag or a hypothetical end-of-file (EOF) marker tag:

```
<BR/>
<EOF/>
```

Empty elements can also be used for configuration files that use name-value pairs (element attributes), organized in named sections (the element type name):

```
<ParserConfig validate="yes" externalEntity="no" keepComments="no"/>
<BrowserConfig showtags="yes" showcomments="no" showPIs="no"/>
```

The above examples all use the abbreviated empty element form. While this form is commonly used, it is also acceptable to use explicit start and end-tags, as long as nothing appears between those tags.

So, the previously shown `<EOF/>` empty element could also be represented as:

```
<EOF></EOF>
```

The two EOF element examples above are equivalent, and both forms would be considered valid empty elements. However, using the longer form isn't recommended, since it might imply that it was possible to insert content into what is supposed to be an empty element. The abbreviated form directly implies that no such content is allowed, and it's also more compact.

Some browsers and other applications (such as older versions of MSXML and IE5) will change the abbreviated form into its longer start-tag plus end-tag form, but it's still an empty element.

The element type declarations describing the above empty elements are:

```
<!ELEMENT BR EMPTY >
<!ELEMENT EOF EMPTY >
<!ELEMENT ParserConfig EMPTY >
<!ELEMENT BrowserConfig EMPTY >
```

Other Categories

The other content categories (`element`, `mixed` and `PCDATA`) are used to restrict an element's content to data of a certain type. These all use the second form in our basic syntax example, and thus require the use of a content model and maybe **cardinality operators** (which we'll discuss a few sections from now) within the element declaration.

So let's look at the syntax and grammar of content models and these other three content categories.

Content Models

Content models are used to describe the structure and content of a given element type. This content may be:

❑   Character data (PCDATA content)

❑   One or more child element types (element-only content)

❑   A combination of the two (mixed content)

If a content model is present, the content category is implied to be `element`, `mixed`, or `PCDATA` – element types that are declared as `ANY` or `EMPTY` may never use content models.

The basic syntax of a content model is a list of child element type names and/or the `#PCDATA` keyword contained within a pair of parentheses:

```
<!ELEMENT name ( ..content_model.. ) >
```

Additional pairs of parentheses may be used to nest various sub-expressions, but they must always be matched pairs (proper nesting of DTD declarations is analogous to the proper nesting of elements in well-formed XML).

> The key difference between element content and mixed content is the use of the **#PCDATA** keyword. If present, the content model is either **mixed** or **PCDATA**. The absence of this keyword indicates element-only content.

PCDATA Content

The following document excerpt shows an element with **PCDATA content**:

```
<name>
  Character data can include entity references (e.g. &amp; or &lt;).
</name>
```

Elements in the PCDATA content category only allow character data, and the #PCDATA keyword is the only parameter allowed in such a content model:

```
<!ELEMENT name (#PCDATA) >
```

Element Content

As the name suggests, elements that are defined as having **element content** may only contain other (child) elements. An example document fragment that would conform to this category might be:

```
<name>
   <a_child_element>Some elemental content..</a_child_element>
   <another_child_element>
     ..some other childish content..
   </another_child_element>
   <a_third_element>..yet another child's content...</a_third_element>
</name>
```

You've probably noticed that no text (other than some insignificant white space) appears outside of any element tags. This is the essence of element content – the only data that may appear within a <name> element are three child elements named <a_child_element>, <another_child_element>, and <a_third_element>.

This <name> element example would be declared as having only element content, like so:

```
<!ELEMENT name (a_child_element, another_child_element, a_third_element) >
```

Element content is both the most versatile and yet potentially most restrictive content model. It allows the most control over the presence and/or absence of child elements, and their sequence of appearance. It also allows the possibility of alternative children. The only drawback to this content model is that all text (character data) must be contained within one of the child elements. There are, however, some advantages to this restriction, particularly when trying to construct an XSL style sheet to display the content.

The comma-separated list of child element names within the parentheses in a declaration is known as a **sequence list**. In the example above, there may only be three child elements, and they must always appear in the sequence shown in the declaration. However, all element content models may use combinations of sequence lists and **choice lists** (which we'll discuss shortly) to limit the appearance of child elements. We can also exert additional control upon the child element structure using cardinality operators.

> **Child elements may be constrained to appear in a specific sequence (*sequence list*) and/or limited to a list of several mutually exclusive choices (*choice list*). The number of occurrences of a given child element may be specified using a single character *cardinality operator*.**

Combinations of these two types of lists are also permitted, which provides for very powerful and complex content models. These combinations can be nested using additional pairs of parentheses – but of course the parentheses must always be *matched* pairs. We'll look at these lists and cardinality operators in greater detail right after we take a quick look at the last kind of content model – mixed content.

Mixed Content

The following example shows a document excerpt with **mixed content**:

```
<name>Mixed content element types can include other elements, as well as character
data, and/or entity references. <a_child_element>More text..</a_child_element>
<another_child_element>Its text.</another_child_element> And some more character
data in the &lt;name&gt; element.
</name>
```

The four child elements and the text outside of the children are all contents of the `<name>` element.

If both character data and elements are allowed, the element must be declared as having mixed content by using the `#PCDATA` keyword as the first item in the content model's element list:

```
<!ELEMENT name (#PCDATA, a_child_element, another_child_element) >
```

Child element sequence, choices, and cardinality can't be specified for mixed content models – which is a major drawback to the use of this content category. This means that the list of valid child elements above doesn't imply that there's any required sequence of those elements. Therefore, the previous declaration is equivalent to this one:

```
<!ELEMENT name (#PCDATA, another_child_element, a_child_element) >
```

> **In a mixed content model, child elements are constrained to character data plus a simple list of valid child element types, without any sequence or choice specifications.**

However, whenever the `#PCDATA` keyword is used, it must always be the first item in the content model (followed by the child element type names, if any). Thus, the following is *illegal*, since a child element type name appears before the `#PCDATA` keyword:

```
<!ELEMENT name (a_child_element, #PCDATA, another_child_element) >
```

A very common example of XML's mixed content model is the body of an HTML web page. The entire web page may well be contained within <html>, <head>, and <body> elements. However, the rest of the body is clearly mixed content, since it's usually a mixture of text, entity references, empty elements (e.g.
, <p/>), and regular non-empty elements (e.g. ..).

For example:

```
<html>
   <body>This is some text that is part of the &lt;body&gt; element's content. It
may also contain other child elements that tell the browser to <em>emphasize</em>
the text, or make it <b>bold</b> or <i>italic</i>.<br/>Empty elements may appear
anywhere within the mixed content, usually to indicate the end of a line or
paragraph.<p/>Other empty elements provide links to external data, such as images:
<img src="someImage.jpg"/><br/>
   </body>
</html>
```

In this example, the value of mixed content becomes apparent: we'd be very hard-pressed to construct a content model that handled all the variations of text and child element sequences. There's really no reason that we would even want to try to limit the sequence of child elements – it's enough simply to list the element types that *may* appear within the <body> element – no other constraints are needed.

> *The above example uses XHTML syntax. This more rigorous version of HTML must always be well-formed XML, hence the slashes that indicate empty elements, e.g.
 and <p/> instead of the more commonly used <br> and <p>. Although HTML is case-INsensitive, XHTML (like XML) is case-sensitive. By specification, all XHTML element and attribute names must use only lower case. This is an important markup language option for those who are interested in using HTML within an XML environment. It also provides a compatible version of HTML that can be embedded within XML documents for display in existing HTML browsers.*

There are times when it's desirable to be more restrictive about the content of an element. This does require the use of element content and is implemented using choice and/or sequence lists, and cardinality operators.

Using Sequence and Choice Lists

These lists are comprised of the child element type names separated by one of two **list operator** characters (and the enclosing parentheses). Each child element type name in a list may have a cardinality operator appended, and/or the list as a whole may also include a cardinality operator.

There are two content model list operators:

List Operator	Description
, (comma)	Sequence – child elements must appear in the specified order
| (vertical bar)	Choice – only one of several child elements is permitted

These operators are used to separate the child element type names within the content model. Parentheses are used to enclose the entire content model, as well as for grouping individual lists. This simple grammar allows the construction of some fairly powerful expressions to describe an element's children.

Let's look at an example. A simple, five-element sequence list for a person's name could be declared as:

```
<!ELEMENT  PersonName  (Title, FirstName, MiddleName, LastName, Suffix) >

<!ELEMENT  Title       (#PCDATA) >
<!ELEMENT  FirstName   (#PCDATA) >
<!ELEMENT  MiddleName  (#PCDATA) >
<!ELEMENT  LastName    (#PCDATA) >
<!ELEMENT  Suffix      (#PCDATA) >
```

By declaring <PersonName> to have element content, we are restricting this element to these five child elements in the specified order, and no other data. The child elements only contain character data, so they're declared to use the PCDATA content model.

A document instance that conforms to this declaration might be:

```
<PersonName>
  <Title>Mr</Title>
  <FirstName>John</FirstName>
  <MiddleName>Q</MiddleName>
  <LastName>Public</LastName>
  <Suffix>Jr</Suffix>
</PersonName>
```

In common practice, neither the `<Title>` nor `<Suffix>` element is a free-form text element – there are a limited number of commonly used titles and suffixes (though we won't clutter our examples with an attempt to include all of them).

We could use choice lists of specific empty elements to replace these two text-containing elements:

```
<!ELEMENT   PersonName
    (
        (Mr | Ms | Dr | Rev), FirstName, MiddleName, LastName, (Jr | Sr | III)
    )
>

<!ELEMENT   Mr     EMPTY >
<!ELEMENT   Ms     EMPTY >
<!ELEMENT   Dr     EMPTY >
<!ELEMENT   Rev    EMPTY >

<!ELEMENT   FirstName    (#PCDATA) >
<!ELEMENT   MiddleName   (#PCDATA) >
<!ELEMENT   LastName     (#PCDATA) >

<!ELEMENT   Jr     EMPTY >
<!ELEMENT   Sr     EMPTY >
<!ELEMENT   III    EMPTY >
```

In this example, a name is still comprises five child elements in a specific sequence. But now, two of the child elements are derived from a list of mutually exclusive choices. Instead of `<Title>` or `<Suffix>` elements that contain text, specific empty elements are used. Whichever child element is chosen from a choice list, that element still must appear in the same place in the child element sequence, as specified in the sequence list.

> *This example used extra white space in the declaration to clarify both the structure of*
> `<PersonName>` *and the two choice lists. Remember that most white space is ignored in XML*
> *declarations.*

The conforming document instance would now become:

```
<PersonName>
  <Mr/>
  <FirstName>John</FirstName>
  <MiddleName>Q</MiddleName>
  <LastName>Public</LastName>
  <Jr/>
</PersonName>
```

There's an unspoken problem with all of the examples we've shown so far – we've had no way of indicating *optional* elements, or otherwise constraining the number of *occurrences* of child elements (cardinality). Let's look at how we can dictate these constraints.

Content Models – Cardinality

> **Cardinality operators define how many child elements may appear in a content model.**

As we mentioned in our basic syntax description, any content model may have a cardinality operator appended, and any child element within a content model will also have an indication of how many times it may occur.

There are four cardinality operators:

Cardinality Operator	Description
[none]	The absence of a cardinality operator character indicates that one, and only one, instance of the child element is allowed (required)
?	Zero or one child element – optional singular element
*	Zero or more child elements – optional element(s)
+	One or more child elements – required element(s)

In all the content model examples we've seen so far, the absence of any explicit cardinality operators means that each child element must occur only once. This is a problem for our personal name example – not everyone has a middle name, and most people don't have any suffix attached to their name.

So let's revise that example to use some cardinality operators:

```
<!ELEMENT PersonName
  (
    (Mr|Ms|Dr|Rev)?, FirstName, MiddleName*, LastName, (Jr|Sr|III)?
  )
>
```

The absence of cardinality operators for `<FirstName>` and `<LastName>` means that there must always be exactly one of each of these child elements in every `<PersonName>`. This also applies to the empty elements in the choice lists – if anything is chosen from the list, it must be singular. Both choice lists are declared as singular, but optional (the ? operator). For the sake of many Latinos (or my own son), the `<MiddleName>` element type is declared to be optional, but with multiple occurrences permitted (the * operator). Thus we've declared that `<FirstName>` and `<LastName>` are the only required children of the `<PersonName>` element type: all other children are optional.

Many people use only a single name (this may be cultural, as in Brazil or Indonesia; or affected, as in Balthus or Ice-T). So, let's make one more revision to allow this other form of a personal name, and also illustrate an even more complex nested declaration:

```
<!ELEMENT PersonName
  (
    SingleName |
    ( (Mr|Ms|Dr|Rev)?, FirstName, MiddleName*, LastName, (Jr|Sr|III)? )
  )
>
```

You'll notice that we've kept the existing content model for the two to five child <PersonName>, but we've now wrapped this in another pair of parentheses and included it in a new choice list. With these additions, <PersonName> may contain either a single child (<SingleName>), or two to five children that conform to the sequence and choice lists from the previous example.

> *Remember that "**internationalization**" (commonly abbreviated as "**I18N**", as in "I" + 18 other letters + "N") is one of the design goals of XML – it is very important to leave any Anglo-centric (or any other-centric) bias out of your XML design. The old "last name first, only 20 characters for a name, and only one middle initial" data design restriction is an example of the kind of practice that's no longer acceptable. Whilst the origin of this design choice is indeed similar to the infamous Y2K "bug" (the extremely limited storage available in the 1950s and 60s), there was also a cultural bias present in this case.*

Here are some conforming instances of our revised <PersonName> element:

```
<PersonName>
  <Mr/>
  <FirstName>John</FirstName>
  <MiddleName>Q</MiddleName>
  <MiddleName>P</MiddleName>
  <LastName>User</LastName>
  <Jr/>
</PersonName>
```

```
<PersonName>
  <FirstName>Jane</FirstName>
  <LastName>Doe</LastName>
</PersonName>
```

```
<PersonName>
  <SingleName>Madonna</SingleName>
</PersonName>
```

In each of the above examples, the data conforms to the required content and sequence of child elements, and would be accepted by a validating parser. Of course, any of the examples here (above or below) would always be accepted by a non-validating parser, since all these examples are well-formed XML.

Some non-conforming ("not valid") examples include:

```
<PersonName>
  <LastName>Smith</LastName>
  <FirstName>Bob</FirstName>
</PersonName>
```

where the required elements are present, but in the wrong order. Or:

```
<PersonName>
  <Miss/>
  <FirstName>Jane</FirstName>
  <LastName>Doe</LastName>
</PersonName>
```

Here, the element structure is correct, but an invalid title (not present in the choice list) is used. Finally:

```
<PersonName>
  <SingleName>Madonna</SingleName>
  <SingleName>Ciccone</SingleName>
</PersonName>
```

In this case, the single name isn't (single).

Now that we've described the various kinds of ELEMENT declarations and content models, let's look at them again in the form of a larger example (building the 'Basic' version of the BookCatalog DTD).

Try It Out — ELEMENT Declarations

We'll revisit our simple example document from the first Try It Out section in this chapter. If you didn't create an example XML document named *mypath*/BookCatalogBasic.xml when you read that section, now's the time do so.

Once again, we'll use local file system references so that you can experiment with this document and its associated DTD on your own system – simply replace the mypath *string in the example with the actual path to the directory where you've put the example DTD.*

1. So now let's create the DTD that describes the example document (and others like it). Create a file named *mypath*/BookCatalogBasic.dtd containing these lines:

```
<!-- ======= The BookCatalog DTD ('Basic' version) ======= -->

<!ELEMENT  BookCatalog (Catalog, Publisher+, Book*) >

<!-- <Catalog> section -->

<!ELEMENT  Catalog (CatalogTitle, CatalogDate) >

<!ELEMENT  CatalogTitle  (#PCDATA) >
<!ELEMENT  CatalogDate   (#PCDATA) >

<!-- <Publisher> section -->

<!ELEMENT  Publisher (CorpName, Website*, Address) >

<!ELEMENT  CorpName  (#PCDATA) >
<!ELEMENT  Website   (#PCDATA) >
```

```
<!ELEMENT  Address (Street*, City, Region?, PostalCode?, Country) >

<!ELEMENT  Street     (#PCDATA) >
<!ELEMENT  City       (#PCDATA) >
<!ELEMENT  Region     (#PCDATA) >
<!ELEMENT  PostalCode (#PCDATA) >
<!ELEMENT  Country    (#PCDATA) >


<!-- <Book> and <Author> section -->

<!ELEMENT  Book (ISBN, Title, Author+, Editor*, Abstract?, Pages, Price,
Subjects?) >

<!ELEMENT  ISBN    (#PCDATA) >
<!ELEMENT  Title   (#PCDATA) >
<!ELEMENT  Author  (#PCDATA) >          <!-- Just a placeholder for now -->
<!ELEMENT  Editor  (#PCDATA) >            <!-- Ditto -->
<!ELEMENT  Pages   (#PCDATA) >
<!ELEMENT  Price   (#PCDATA) >


<!ELEMENT  Subjects (Subject, Subject?, Subject?) >
<!ELEMENT  Subject  (#PCDATA) >


<!-- ======= END of BookCatalog DTD ======= -->
```

2. And add the following to `BookCatalogBasic.xml`:

```
<?xml version="1.0" encoding="UTF-8" standalone="yes"?>
```

```
<!DOCTYPE BookCatalog SYSTEM "file:///mypath/BookCatalogBasic.dtd" >
```

```
<BookCatalog>
```

3. Now when you display *mypath*/`BookCatalogBasic.xml` in an XML-aware browser (one that uses a validating parser), the data will be validated before it is displayed.

How It Works

The first line of the DTD (and all others beginning with "`<!--  `") is an XML comment that describes the DTD. It's always a good idea to use comments and white space, to help yourself and others to understand your code.

The first DTD declaration is for the document element – all documents that conform to this DTD must use this container as the top-level element:

```
<!ELEMENT  BookCatalog (Catalog, Publisher+, Book*) >
```

This element always contains one `<Catalog>` and at least one `<Publisher>` element as its children. The `<Book>` element(s) may or may not be present, and there may be as many of these as necessary.

The `<Publisher>` element contains two or more children: one each of `<Name>` and `<Address>`, plus optional `<Website>`s:

```
<!ELEMENT  Publisher (CorpName, Website*, Address) >
```

The `<Address>` element will always contain at least one `<City>` and one `<Country>` as its children, whilst additional details (such as street address or postal code) are optional:

```
<!ELEMENT  Address (Street*, City, Region?, PostalCode?, Country) >
```

The `<Book>` element content model uses all four different cardinality operators:

```
<!ELEMENT Book (ISBN, Title, Author+, Editor*, Abstract?, Pages, Price, Subjects?)
>
```

`<ISBN>`, `<Title>`, `<Pages>`, and `<Price>` must be present and singular (due to the absence of any operator character). `<Author>` is also required, but multiple occurrences are allowed (the + operator). `<Editor>` isn't required, but multiples are allowed if it's used (the * operator). And the `<Abstract>` and `<Subjects>` element types are optional, but only one of each may be present (the ? operator). These children must always appear in the sequence shown.

The `<Subjects>` element is merely a container for up to three actual subject classifications:

```
<!ELEMENT Subjects (Subject, Subject?, Subject?) >
```

If `<Subjects>` is present, there must always be at least one `<Subject>` child element, but the other two are optional, thus allowing us to have one, two, or three subjects per book.

Now that we've discussed the fundamental building blocks of XML documents and DTDs, let's turn our attention to an alternative method of data markup: the element *attribute* and its DTD declaration.

Attribute (ATTLIST) Declarations

If element types are the nouns of XML, then element attributes can be considered the adjectives. Attributes can be used to describe the metadata or properties of the associated element. Attributes are also an alternative way to markup document data.

For example, either of the following document excerpts could be used to describe a book's bibliographic metadata:

```
<Book>
  <ISBN>1-861003-11-0</ISBN>
  <Title>Professional XML</Title>
  <Author>Stephen Mohr, et al.</Author>
  <Pages>1169</Pages>
  <Price>$49.99</Price>
</Book>
```

Of course, this is derived from the `BookCatalog` examples that we've used throughout the chapter. The same data can also be represented using element attributes instead of child elements:

```
<Book isbn="1-861003-11-0" title="Professional XML"
      author="Stephen Mohr, et al." pages="1169" price="$49.99" />
```

This "attributes-only" alternative representation of the same data uses an empty element, since all the data is now in those attributes. In fact, we'll make some of these very changes when we later convert from the 'Basic' to 'Advanced' versions of our example DTDs and documents.

Throughout this book, and in keeping with the "element = noun" / "attribute = adjective" metaphor, we use a stylistic convention for element and attribute names. Element names use the proper noun form (Capitalized Names) and attribute names are shown entirely in lower-case (sometimes with an underscore to separate individual words). This is a fairly common style for both XML and SGML markup (at least in English and other cased languages), and has some obvious benefits for the reader of the markup.

Element attributes are described using the **attribute-list declaration**, also called the **ATTLIST declaration**. This declaration has the usual DTD declaration format, using the ATTLIST keyword plus zero or more attribute definitions:

```
<!ATTLIST elementName attrName attrType attrDefault defaultValue >
```

Both the *elementName* and the *attrName* parameters must be legal XML names. The former is the name of the associated element type, the latter the name of the individual attribute. Each attribute requires a separate definition, usually shown on separate lines for greater readability.

The *attrDefault* parameter dictates XML parser behavior. When a given instance of an element doesn't include the attribute name-value pair, what (if any) attribute value should be used? This parameter tells the parser whether or not the attribute's presence is required, and how to handle its absence when it's optional. The parser can use the DTD's *defaultValue* parameter to provide an attribute value to the application, even when the attribute isn't present in the document.

In the second example document excerpt at the beginning of this section, we have a <Book> element which has five named attributes: isbn, title, author, pages, and price. We'd describe the attributes-only version of <Book> in the following fashion:

```
<!ELEMENT  Book   EMPTY >
<!ATTLIST  Book
     isbn    CDATA  #REQUIRED
     title   CDATA  #REQUIRED
     author  CDATA  #REQUIRED
     pages   CDATA  #IMPLIED
     price   CDATA  #IMPLIED
>
```

Because we've replaced all the child elements of <Book> with attributes, the content model has also been changed to disallow any content (it's now an EMPTY element). The five attributes are all declared to be normal character data (CDATA), three of them are required always to be present (#REQUIRED), and the other two are optional (#IMPLIED).

In the next few sections, we'll describe the ATTLIST declaration in detail. First, let's look at the various parameters of this declaration.

Attribute Types

There are ten different types of attributes defined in the XML 1.0 recommendation:

Attribute Type	Description
CDATA	Character data (simple text string).
enumerated value(s) (choice list)	Attribute value must be one of a series that is explicitly defined in the DTD.
ID	Attribute value is the unique identifier for this element instance. This must be a text string that conforms to all XML name rules – the first character may only be a letter or an underscore (_) or colon (:) character.
IDREF	A reference to the element with an ID attribute that has the same value as that of the IDREF.
IDREFS	A list of IDREFs delimited by white space.
NMTOKEN	A **name token** – a text string that conforms to the XML name rules, except that the first character of the name may be any valid name character.
NMTOKENS	A list of NMTOKENs delimited by white space.
ENTITY	The name of a pre-defined **entity**.
ENTITIES	A list of ENTITY names delimited by white space.
NOTATION	Attribute value must be a **notation type** that is explicitly declared elsewhere in the DTD.

We'll look at details of the first seven of these here – the remainder (ENTITY, ENTITIES, and NOTATION) will be discussed in Chapter 11.

CDATA Attribute Type

Most attribute values are nothing more than plain text. These attributes are declared using the CDATA type. For example:

```
<!ATTLIST AnElement its_attr CDATA #REQUIRED >
```

This states that the element type AnElement has a single, required attribute named its_attr that has a text string for its value. When an attribute is required, it must be present in every instance of that element type, or the document will not be considered valid.

You can ignore the #REQUIRED default value parameter for the moment (other than its obvious meaning, as stated above) – we'll discuss it, and the related #IMPLIED parameter, in the next section.

An example document excerpt that conforms to the above declaration might be:

```
<AnElement its_attr="some text string"> ... </AnElement>
```

As long as the attribute value is nothing but text, it will be considered valid by a validating parser. And since XML uses Unicode, such values are not constrained to be only plain ASCII text – another valid instance of this element type might use a Greek acronym:

```
<AnElement its_attr="    "> ... </AnElement>
```

However, some entity references are not allowed in CDATA attribute values, so the following version of the Greek acronym using the equivalent ISO entity references, would be *illegal*:

```
<AnElement its_attr="&Alpha;&Gamma;&Delta;"> ... </AnElement>
```

The entity references above are an example of something called **external** entity references. This restriction does not apply to **internally-defined** entities (such as the five built-in entities: <, >, &, ', and ") or character references (such as &#x1A; or *). We'll clarify these distinctions when we describe the different kinds of entities and entity references in Chapter 11.

In fact, another related restriction on all attribute values involves the beginning element-tag delimiter, the less-than sign (<). No well-formed XML document is allowed to use this character within an attribute value: it must always be escaped using the < entity reference. For example, an attribute value that needs to represent the mathematical expression "A < B < C" must use text modified to appear like this:

```
<AnElement its_attr="A &lt; B &lt; C"> ... </AnElement>
```

The following example is also *illegal*, since it doesn't have the required attribute:

```
<AnElement> ... </AnElement>
```

Let's now look at the other commonly used attribute types.

Enumerated Values Attribute Type

We'll often want to use one of a set of specific text strings for an attribute value.

In the <PersonName> element that we defined earlier in this chapter, we confined the honorific title and name suffix to a limited set of valid element types using choice lists in the element content model. A similar mechanism exists for attribute values, using a nearly identical syntax. Valid choices are one or more name tokens in a list separated by vertical bar (|) characters, with the list enclosed in parentheses.

> **All enumerated values must be legal XML name tokens.**

So let's redefine the <PersonName> element, using two new attributes instead of the two child-element choice lists (the child elements remain defined as before):

```
<!ELEMENT  PersonName  (FirstName, MiddleName, LastName) >
<!ATTLIST  PersonName
    honorific  (Mr | Ms | Dr | Rev)  #IMPLIED
    suffix  (Jr | Sr | III)  #IMPLIED
>
<!ELEMENT  FirstName   (#PCDATA) >
<!ELEMENT  MiddleName  (#PCDATA) >
<!ELEMENT  LastName    (#PCDATA) >
```

Both attributes are text strings, but each must have a value that exactly matches one of the values shown in the above declaration. Once again, you can ignore the meaning of #IMPLIED for the moment – we'll discuss it in a later section.

A document excerpt that conforms to this new definition of <PersonName> might be:

```
<PersonName honorific="Mr" suffix="Jr">
  <FirstName>John</FirstName>
  <MiddleName>Q</MiddleName>
  <LastName>Public</LastName>
</PersonName>
```

Remember that since XML is case-sensitive, "Ms" is *not* equivalent to "MS" or "ms" or "mS" – so none of these other forms would be valid for this attribute value. If you're creating a DTD for documents that will be manually entered, you might want to allow for all the various case-insensitive permutations of such strings (though this quickly becomes ridiculous in practice). A better practice is to establish a convention for attribute values – always use UPPERCASE or always use lowercase, and then use the DTD and a validating XML editor to enforce this rule.

ID / IDREF / IDREFS Attribute Types (Relationships Between Elements)

Attributes using the ID type provide a unique identifying name for a given element instance. The *value* of an ID attribute must conform to the rules for XML names, and this value must also be unique within a document. This also means that all-numeric IDs, such as the U.S. Social Security Number (SSN) or a database record number, cannot be used as an ID attribute value in XML (unless we prepend the number with a legal Name1 character).

Each element type may use only one ID attribute, and thus every instance of that element can be referred to using a single unique identifier. One more rule: any attribute of this type must be declared as #IMPLIED (optional) or #REQUIRED – it would make no sense to use a constant or even a default value for what is supposed to be a unique identifier for each element.

> The one-ID-per-element restriction is another rule inherited from SGML. The ID attribute type is intended to be the unique name for an instance of an element – not the equivalent of a database record key (which often allows for the use of both primary and secondary keys).

Let's create a new <Person> element type that has a required ID attribute, and a content model that includes a few familiar children:

```
<!ELEMENT  Person (PersonName, FirstName, MiddleName, LastName, CorpName?, Email*,
Biography?) >
<!ATTLIST  Person
    perID  ID  #REQUIRED
>
```

We always want this element to have an ID, so we've declared perID to be #REQUIRED.

> *You may notice that all our example attributes of the "ID" type have that string in the attribute*
> *name – a common and suggested style of markup (and another SGML practice). At the same time,*
> *using any variation of "id" or "ID" for any non-ID attributes is strongly discouraged.*

This new element type's content model includes one (and only one each) of our previously defined
<PersonName>, <FirstName>, <MiddleName> and <LastName> element types. We've also added
three simple PCDATA child elements for the person's corporate affiliation and biography (zero or one
of each of these), and e-mail address (zero or more).

A document excerpt that conforms to this definition of <Person> might be:

```
<Person perID="JHN_Q_PBLC">
  <PersonName honorific="Mr." suffix="Jr.">
    <FirstName>John</FirstName>
    <MiddleName>Q</MiddleName>
    <LastName>Public</LastName>
  </PersonName>
<CorpName>Acme XML Writers</CorpName>
<Email>jqpublic@notmail.com</Email>
<Biography>John, Jr. is a swell fellow, son of John, Sr.</Biography>
</Person>
```

Remember that an ID attribute is not only case-sensitive (like all XML names and content), it must also
be a valid XML name that is unique within a given document instance. In this example, no other
element in the same document could have an ID of "JHN_Q_PBLC", though the string "jhn_q_pblc"
would be acceptable (since it uses a different case for the same letters, it's *not* the same ID value).

Thus, the following is an example of an *illegal* ID attribute (the *value* is not a legal XML name because it
begins with a numeric digit):

```
<Person perID="2Pac" .. >
```

> The *value* of an **ID** attribute must be a legal XML name, unique within a document,
> and use the **#IMPLIED** or **#REQUIRED** default value. There may only be one **ID**
> attribute for each element type.

To establish a one-to-one link to a Person from another element, we can use an IDREF attribute in that
other element to define the **link source** (the ID attribute is the **link target**). Although the target must
always be unique, we can have many different elements (link sources) that refer to a single ID attribute.

> The *value* of an **IDREF** attribute must be a legal XML name, and must match the
> *value* of an **ID** attribute within the same document. Multiple **IDREF**s to the same **ID**
> are permitted.

For example, a `<Book>` element might link to an author in this way:

```
<Book author="JHN_Q_PBLC" .. >
```

This would be declared in the DTD as follows:

```
<!ATTLIST Book author IDREF #REQUIRED >
```

Of course, many books have multiple authors (a one-to-many relationship). We might try to use multiple instances of the IDREF attribute to represent these links, but since a well-formed element may only have one attribute of a given name, the following example is *illegal* syntax:

```
<Book author="JHN_Q_PBLC" author="JN_D" .. >
```

Fortunately, XML does have a way to handle multiple IDREF attributes in a single element. Instead of trying to use multiple instances of the author attribute, we re-declare this attribute to use the IDREF<u>S</u> type:

```
<!ATTLIST Book author IDREFS #REQUIRED >
```

and use a space-delimited list of the IDREFs within a single author attribute value:

```
<Book author="JHN_Q_PBLC JN_D TW_PC" .. >
```

The XML parser will present the application with a single value for the author attribute – and it will be up to that application to separate each individual IDREF value from the list. In this case, we'd end up with three such values: "JHN_Q_PBLC", "JN_D", and "TW_PC".

> **An IDREFs attribute is a white space-delimited list of individual IDREF attributes, each of which must conform to all the rules of the IDREF type of attribute.**

These attribute types allow us to express both one-to-one and one-to-many relationships between elements. This can be very useful when using XML as an exchange format for data from a relational database management system (RDBMS).

> *You might be tempted to use a database record number (maybe a numeric primary key) as the value of an ID attribute. However, don't forget that an ID attribute's value must be a legal XML name (which cannot begin with a numeric digit), so you must precede this with a letter or some other legal XML* Name1 *character.*

Attribute Type – NMTOKEN / NMTOKENS (Name Tokens)

Sometimes, it's desirable to restrict the syntax of an attribute value, but still allow the use of unspecified values. The CDATA attribute type allows any string of characters without any restrictions. At the other end of the spectrum we have enumerated values – only those strings specified in the DTD are permitted. The XML 1.0 recommendation does, however, provide a middle ground in the form of the NMTOKEN and NMTOKENS attribute types.

These types restrict the attribute values to use of only XML NameChar characters. Unlike ID values, any of these characters may be used at the beginning of the string – there is no Name1 character restriction. Unlike enumerated values, the value of an NMTOKEN is not limited to a finite set of specific values.

As with the IDREFs type, there is a plural form (NMTOKENS) that allows a white space-delimited list of multiple NMTOKEN values.

> *These attribute types are another part of XML that was inherited from SGML, and are mostly useful for interoperability with SGML tools and DTDs. Another possibility is the direct use of numeric keys as attribute values, though the parser would not be able to enforce unique values within a document (as with the ID and IDREF attribute types).*

We could change the declarations of <PersonName>'s honorific and suffix attributes to use the NMTOKEN and NMTOKENS types instead of limiting these to a set of enumerated values:

```
<!ATTLIST  PersonName
    honorific  NMTOKENS  #IMPLIED
    suffix     NMTOKEN   #IMPLIED
>
```

An example use of this in a document might be:

```
<PersonName honorific="Rev. Dr." suffix="Jr."> .. </PersonName>
```

There are two advantages to this approach:

❏ We aren't constrained to pre-specified short lists of valid honorific titles and suffixes

❏ We can now use multiple titles ("Rev. Dr.") without having to specify every possible combination

Of course, these can also be seen as disadvantages – without the constraints of enumerated values, an author could use "Mr Ms", "blah", or some other nonsensical title or suffix.

There is another major drawback to these attribute types. Since their legal values aren't specified in the DTD, a validating parser can only enforce the simple NameChar syntax rule – all further validation must now be handled by the application. As with IDREFs, an NMTOKENS list must also be processed by the application – the parser will simply pass the entire list as a single attribute value.

The only real difference between a CDATA and NMTOKEN attribute is that the latter prevents the inclusion of white space and some punctuation characters. While the NMTOKEN and NMTOKENS attribute types may be useful in certain limited circumstances, in most cases a CDATA or enumerated value attribute will work as well, or better.

> *These seven attribute types are the simple types that are commonly used in XML documents. The other, more complex, attribute types (ENTITY, ENTITIES, and NOTATION) will be discussed in Chapter 11.*

Now, let's look at the attribute default parameter.

Attribute Defaults

The ATTLIST declaration uses the **attribute default** parameter to dictate whether or not an attribute's presence is required, and if it is not required, how a validating parser should handle its absence from a document.

There are four different attribute defaults:

Attribute Default	Description
#REQUIRED	The attribute *must* appear in every instance of the element.
#IMPLIED	The attribute is optional.
#FIXED (plus default value)	The attribute may or may not appear in the document. If the attribute does appear, it *must* match the default value; if it doesn't, the parser *may* supply the default value.
default value(s)	The attribute may or may not appear in the document. If the attribute does appear, it may be any value that matches those in the ATTLIST declaration; if it doesn't appear, the parser *may* supply the default value.

You may have noticed the phrase "the parser may *supply" in several of the above examples and descriptions. This is merely to alert you to the fact that, per the XML 1.0 Recommendation, a non-validating parser is* not *required to supply default values for attributes. However, validating parsers* are *required to provide defaults from a DTD (and usually do so even if the validation option is turned off).*

#IMPLIED

We've already shown examples using the #REQUIRED keyword, so let's see a similar declaration with the #IMPLIED keyword:

```
<!ATTLIST AnElement its_attr CDATA #IMPLIED >
```

All of the previous <AnElement> examples would be valid according to the above declaration:

```
<AnElement its_attr=" some text "> ... </AnElement>
<AnElement its_attr="    "> ... </AnElement>
<AnElement> ... </AnElement>
```

except for this one (remember, external entity references are never legal in any CDATA attribute):

```
<AnElement its_attr="&Alpha;&Gamma;&Delta;"> ... </AnElement>
```

#FIXED

Attributes may be optional, yet still be constrained to a specific value or values. If only one value is allowed, we use the #FIXED attribute default to restrict that value, whilst allowing the parser to supply the value if the attribute is absent.

For example, a document might have a version number that, like XML, is currently limited to a single valid value:

```
<Document version="1.00"> ... </Document>
```

This would be declared in the DTD using the #FIXED keyword with a default value:

```
<!ELEMENT   Document   (#PCDATA) >
<!ATTLIST   Document   version  CDATA   #FIXED "1.00" >
```

If a `<Document>` element appeared without a version number of "1.00", a validating parser would report an error. This form of the `ATTLIST` declaration is relatively uncommon, because if the attribute value is truly fixed and yet is required, it might just as well be hard-coded into the application (unless our application is intended to work with several versions of `<Document>`, using a different DTD for each).

Default Values

If we wanted to be more liberal with our document versions, we could let the parser supply this default value, without requiring it to be present in every instance of the element type (though that does mean we lose the capacity to restrict the attribute to a single value):

```
<!ELEMENT  Document  (#PCDATA) >
<!ATTLIST  Document  version  CDATA  "1.00" >
```

This illustrates the fourth kind of attribute default: default value(s), where the parser *may* supply the attribute value if it isn't present in the document.

For example, our document could contain elements with or without the `version` attribute:

```
<Document version="1.00"> ... </Document>
<Document> ... </Document>
<Document version="6.66"> ... </Document>
```

A validating parser would present the second instance of the `<Document>` element to the application as if the element had an explicit `version="1.00"` attribute (the first two examples would be functionally equivalent as far as the application was concerned). However, since we've lost the ability to force a singular attribute value, the third line would also be valid.

> *SAX and the DOM, do tell the application whether the attribute value was actually in the document or supplied as the default value from the DTD. This is not required by the XML 1.0 Recommendation, but could be useful for some applications.*

If we wanted to require the `version` attribute to be constrained to a single value, yet not require the attribute to be present in every instance of the element, we could use an enumerated attribute type with the `#IMPLIED` keyword instead:

```
<!ELEMENT  Document  (#PCDATA) >
<!ATTLIST  Document  version  "1.00"  #IMPLIED >
```

Now that we've looked at the various forms of the `ATTLIST` declaration, let's modify our ongoing `BookCatalog` DTD.

Extending the BookCatalog Data Model

Let's revise the definition of the `<Book>` element type by changing some child elements to attributes, add a few attributes to some other element types, and do a little data model restructuring.

The following diagram illustrates the revised parent-child relationships of the various elements in our expanded `BookCatalog` vocabulary. The numbers in the square brackets indicate how many instances of each element type are allowed, the names in square brackets are the element's identifier (`ID` attribute), and the double-line arrows show links to other elements (via `IDREF`/`ID` pairs):

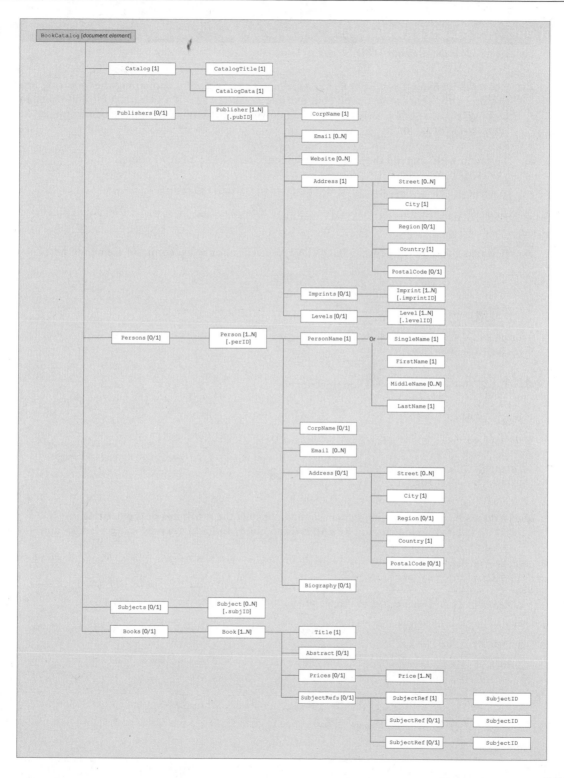

Try It Out – ATTLIST Declarations

So, let's set about changing our DTD.

1. Create a file named *mypath*/`BookCatalogExpanded.dtd` containing the following lines (it's probably easier to just copy your existing `BookCatalogBasic.dtd` file and change the highlighted lines as necessary, or you can download the complete source code from http://www.wrox.com).

2. To begin with, expand the document element (`<BookCatalog>`) content model:

```
<!-- ======= The BookCatalog DTD ('Expanded' version) ======= -->

<!ELEMENT  BookCatalog (Catalog, Publishers?, Persons?, Subjects?, Books?) >
```

3. Following this, add a generic PCDATA type section for a few common element types:

```
<!-- Generic PCDATA element types section -->

<!ELEMENT  Biography (#PCDATA) >
<!ELEMENT  CorpName  (#PCDATA) >
<!ELEMENT  Email     (#PCDATA) >
<!ELEMENT  Website   (#PCDATA) >
```

4. Leave the `<Catalog>` section unchanged:

```
<!-- <Catalog> section -->

<!ELEMENT  Catalog (CatalogTitle, CatalogDate) >

<!ELEMENT  CatalogTitle (#PCDATA) >
<!ELEMENT  CatalogDate  (#PCDATA) >
```

5. Add a `<Publishers>` container element, change the attributes of the existing `<Publisher>` element and its `<Address>` child, and add the new `<Imprints>` and `<Levels>` element types:

```
<!-- <Publishers> section -->

<!ELEMENT  Publishers (Publisher+) >

<!ELEMENT  Publisher (CorpName, Email*, Website*, Address, Imprints?, Levels?) >
<!ATTLIST  Publisher
     pubID  ID      #REQUIRED
     isbn   CDATA   "??????"
>

<!ELEMENT  Address (Street*, City, Region?, PostalCode?, Country) >
<!ATTLIST  Address  hq  (yes | no)  "yes" >
```

```
<!ELEMENT  Street      (#PCDATA) >
<!ELEMENT  City        (#PCDATA) >
<!ELEMENT  Region      (#PCDATA) >
<!ELEMENT  PostalCode  (#PCDATA) >
<!ELEMENT  Country     (#PCDATA) >
```

```
<!ELEMENT  Imprints (Imprint+) >
<!ELEMENT  Imprint (#PCDATA) >
<!ATTLIST  Imprint  imprintID  ID  #REQUIRED >
```

```
<!ELEMENT  Levels (Level+) >
<!ELEMENT  Level (#PCDATA) >
<!ATTLIST  Level  levelID  ID  #REQUIRED >
```

6. Add `<Persons>` and `<Person>` element types (with attributes) as follows:

```
<!-- <Persons> section -->

<!ELEMENT  Persons (Person*) >

<!ELEMENT  Person (PersonName, CorpName?, Email*, Address?, Biography?) >
<!ATTLIST  Person
     perID  ID  #REQUIRED
     role  (AU | ED | AE | IL | RV | unknown)  #REQUIRED
>

<!ELEMENT  PersonName (SingleName | (FirstName, MiddleName*, LastName)) >
<!ATTLIST  PersonName
     honorific  (Mr. | Ms. | Dr. | Rev.)  #IMPLIED
     suffix  (Jr. | Sr. | I | II | III | IV | V | VI | VII | VIII)  #IMPLIED
>
```

```
<!ELEMENT  FirstName   (#PCDATA) >
<!ELEMENT  MiddleName  (#PCDATA) >
<!ELEMENT  LastName    (#PCDATA) >
<!ELEMENT  SingleName  (#PCDATA) >
```

Note that this includes an expanded version of the `<PersonName>` type we've used in various examples throughout this chapter.

7. Next, add the `<Subjects>` elements:

```
<!-- <Subjects> section -->

<!ELEMENT  Subjects (Subject*) >
<!ELEMENT  Subject (#PCDATA) >
<!ATTLIST  Subject  subjectID  ID  #REQUIRED >
```

8. Add a `<Books>` container element, and modify the `<Book>` element as follows:

- ❑ Change the `<ISBN>` and `<Pages>` children of `<Book>` to be attributes of `<Book>` instead

- ❑ Add some additional attributes to `<Book>`

- ❑ Change the `<Author>` and `<Editor>` children of `<Book>` to instead use `IDREFS` attributes referencing `<Person>`

- ❑ Add a `currency` attribute to `<Price>`

- ❑ Wrap that element in the new `<Prices>` element type

```
<!-- <Books> section -->

<!ELEMENT  Books (Book+) >

<!ELEMENT  Book (Title, Abstract?, Prices?, SubjectRefs?) >
<!ATTLIST  Book
      bookID      ID       #REQUIRED
      isbn        CDATA    #REQUIRED
      publisher   IDREF    #REQUIRED
      authors     IDREFS   #REQUIRED
      editors     IDREFS   #REQUIRED
      imprint     IDREF    #IMPLIED
      pubDate     CDATA    "2000"
      pages       CDATA    "????"
      level       IDREF    #IMPLIED
>

<!ELEMENT  Title (#PCDATA) >

<!ELEMENT  Abstract (#PCDATA) >

<!ELEMENT  Prices (Price+) >
<!ELEMENT  Price (#PCDATA) >
<!ATTLIST  Price  currency  (USD | GBP | CDN) "USD" >

<!ELEMENT  SubjectRefs (SubjectRef, SubjectRef?, SubjectRef?) >
<!ELEMENT  SubjectRef  EMPTY >
<!ATTLIST  SubjectRef  subject  IDREF  #REQUIRED >

<!-- ======= END of 'Expanded' BookCatalog DTD ======= -->
```

This last sort of "wrapper element" has also been used for publishers, persons, books, and subjects. Such wrappers make it easier to process and display the document, though there are some philosophical arguments against this approach. You'll see one of the advantages here when the XML document that conforms to this DTD is displayed in IE5 – it allows quick and easy collapse of the tree structure, so you can focus upon a particular subset of the document.

How It Works

The lines we've added to our DTD illustrate some of the attribute concepts that we've just introduced in this chapter. Let's explain the expanded DTD in more detail.

We added two attributes to `<Publisher>`: a required and unique ID (`pubID`) that can be used to refer to a specific publisher from other elements (*e.g.* `<Book>`), and an ISBN that is defined as some text that may or may not be present in all instances of `<Publisher>`:

```
<!ATTLIST  Publisher
     pubID  ID      #REQUIRED
     isbn   CDATA   "??????"
>
```

If the `isbn` attribute isn't present, a validating parser (and even many non-validating parsers) will insert the default value (`"??????"`) as if the attribute were present.

We then added an attribute to `<Address>` that's just a simple flag stating whether or not this address is the publisher's headquarters location:

```
<!ATTLIST  Address  hq  (yes | no)  "yes" >
```

Unlike the `isbn` attribute, which allows any sort of text content, there are only two valid values for this attribute – `yes` or `no` – that are declared in an attribute value choice list. Since the vast majority of publisher addresses are likely to be the headquarters (or sole) address, we made the common value (`yes`) the default, so that it need not be included in every instance of `<Address>` in every document.

We added new element types and children for `<Imprints>` (publisher's imprint) and `<Levels>` (the book's intended audience level):

```
<!ELEMENT  Imprints (Imprint+) >
<!ELEMENT  Imprint (#PCDATA) >
<!ATTLIST  Imprint  imprintID  ID  #REQUIRED >

<!ELEMENT  Levels (Level+) >
<!ELEMENT  Level (#PCDATA) >
<!ATTLIST  Level  levelID  ID  #REQUIRED >
```

These will prevent duplication of data. Since many `<Book>` elements will use the same imprint and/or level, it is better to *refer* to these using an IDREF attribute (in `<Book>`), rather than *embedding* the literal text everywhere it's needed. We've also used a similar ID+IDREF approach to refer to `<Person>`, `<Publisher>`, and `<Subject>` elements from attributes in the `<Book>` and `<SubjectRef>` elements.

This classic relational/OO approach greatly reduces document sizes, and makes it easier to maintain the various "objects" within our vocabulary. For this to work, all of these target elements *must* have a unique ID attribute, which is why we've used the #REQUIRED parameter. When the pending XLink and XPointer standards are established, we'll have even more powerful mechanisms for linking XML elements and attributes to each other – this will be discussed in Chapter 12.

We added a `<Person>` element type to prevent duplication of data when the same person writes, edits, and/or reviews multiple books:

```
<!ELEMENT  Person (PersonName, CorpName?, Email*, Address?, Biography?) >
<!ATTLIST  Person
      perID  ID  #REQUIRED
      role   (AU | ED | AE | IL | RV | unknown)  #REQUIRED
>
```

We've also added another required attribute – `role` – that's used to classify each person, using a simple, limited, and completely arbitrary choice list of attribute values ("AU" for author, "ED" for editor, "AE" for author/editor, etc.).

> *The last value in the list – unknown– shows another good practice involving choice lists in shared DTDs: always allow for the "unknown" option, especially when the list could be considered open-ended and the choices aren't strictly limited to a finite set. If your DTD is for internal use and/or updates are feasible, a better practice is to omit the unknown type and simply update the list, perhaps incrementing a version number, as well.*

We also added the new `<Subjects>` and `<Subject>` element types:

```
<!ELEMENT  Subjects (Subject*) >
<!ELEMENT  Subject (#PCDATA) >
<!ATTLIST  Subject  subjectID  ID  #REQUIRED >
```

Like the `<Imprint>` and `<Level>` element types we discussed earlier, these allow us to put commonly used text in one place, and then *refer* to the text from other elements, instead of *repeating* the text everywhere that it's needed.

We also modified our `<Book>` element:

```
<!ELEMENT  Book (Title, Abstract?, Prices?, SubjectRefs?) >
<!ATTLIST  Book
      bookID      ID       #REQUIRED
      isbn        CDATA    #REQUIRED
      publisher   IDREF    #REQUIRED
      authors     IDREFS   #REQUIRED
      editors     IDREFS   #REQUIRED
      imprint     IDREF    #IMPLIED
      pubDate     CDATA    "2000"
      pages       CDATA    "????"
      level       IDREF    #IMPLIED
>
```

As with other elements in our example, we'd like to be able to refer to a specific `<Book>` using its ID. For this to be reliable, `bookID` must be a `#REQUIRED` attribute.

The `publisher` attribute is used to connect a book to its publisher (via an `IDREF` link), and since this is always necessary, this attribute is declared as `#REQUIRED` as well.

Instead of *embedding* all of this personal data in each and every instance of a <Book> element, we'll use IDREFs within the new authors and editors attributes to *reference* the ID attribute of a specific element.

We also allow optional IDREF links to the imprint and level. We could just include these as CDATA attributes in every <Book>, but keeping them separate does reduce storage and maintenance (and also further illustrates the ID/IDREF mechanism).

The pubDate and Pages attributes aren't required (any string would be acceptable), but if they are omitted a default value will be inserted by the parser. The audience level (level) is another optional attribute, but if it's used, it must have one of three enumerated values (we'll see these in the next Try It Out).

> *Remember all attributes using the ID type must be declared as either #REQUIRED or #IMPLIED.*
>
> *Also, all attributes with ID, IDREF, IDREFS, NMTOKEN, or NMTOKENS types must be valid XML names (though the latter two don't have to follow the "first character of a name" rules).*

The former <ISBN> and <Pages> elements are now included as attributes of <Book>, and we've added a pubDate attribute for good measure. Whilst an ISBN is always required, we've set default values for the latter two, so they needn't appear in every document. As with the isbn attribute in <Publisher>, these default values are just placeholders – real values *should* be included in every document instance, we're just not *requiring* them to always be present.

We've expanded the DTD, so we'll also want to create another document instance that conforms to this new DTD.

Try It Out – Using Our Attributes

1. Create a file named *mypath*/BookCatalogExpanded.xml containing the following lines. (Again, if you're not using the downloaded files, it's probably easiest to modify a copy of your existing BookCatalogBasic.xml file.)

2. Modify the DOCTYPE declaration and Catalog element as follows:

```
<?xml version="1.0" encoding="UTF-8" standalone="yes"?>

<!DOCTYPE BookCatalog SYSTEM "file:///mypath/BookCatalogExpanded.dtd" >

<BookCatalog>

<Catalog>
  <CatalogTitle>The Wrox BookCatalog ('Expanded' version)</CatalogTitle>
  <CatalogDate>2000-05-23</CatalogDate>
</Catalog>
```

3. Now add a `Publishers` element, and modify the existing `Publisher` elements:

```
<Publishers>

  <Publisher pubID="WRX_PRS_LTD" isbn="861003">
    <CorpName>Wrox Press Ltd.</CorpName>
    <Email>feedback@wrox.com</Email>
    <Website>www.wrox.com</Website>
    <Address>
      <Street>Arden House</Street>
      <Street>1102 Warwick Road</Street>
      <Street>Acocks Green</Street>
      <City>Birmingham</City>
      <Region>England</Region>
      <PostalCode>B27 6BH</PostalCode>
      <Country>UK</Country>
    </Address>
    <Imprints>
      <Imprint imprintID="PRG2PRG">Programmer to Programmer</Imprint>
    </Imprints>
    <Levels>
      <Level levelID="BEG">Beginning</Level>
      <Level levelID="INS">Instant</Level>
      <Level levelID="PRO">Professional</Level>
    </Levels>
  </Publisher>

  <Publisher pubID="WRX_PRS_INC">
    <CorpName>Wrox Press Inc.</CorpName>
    <Address hq="no">
      <Street>29 S LaSalle St, Suite 520</Street>
      <City>Chicago</City>
      <Region>IL</Region>
      <PostalCode>60603</PostalCode>
      <Country>USA</Country>
    </Address>
  </Publisher>

</Publishers>
```

4. Next, we need to add some `Persons`:

```
<Persons>

  <Person perID="DDR_MRTN" role="AU">
    <PersonName>
      <FirstName>Didier</FirstName>
      <MiddleName>P</MiddleName>
      <MiddleName>H</MiddleName>
      <LastName>Martin</LastName>
    </PersonName>
    <CorpName>Talva Corp.</CorpName>
```

```
   <Biography>Didier PH Martin has worked with computers for 21
   years.</Biography>
</Person>

<Person perID="DN_PRKR" role="ED">
  <PersonName>
    <FirstName>Dianne</FirstName>
    <LastName>Parker</LastName>
  </PersonName>
  <CorpName>Wrox Press Ltd.</CorpName>
</Person>

<Person perID="DVD_HNTR" role="AU">
  <PersonName>
    <FirstName>David</FirstName>
    <LastName>Hunter</LastName>
  </PersonName>
</Person>

<Person perID="JN_DCKT" role="ED">
  <PersonName>
    <FirstName>Jon</FirstName>
    <LastName>Duckett</LastName>
  </PersonName>
  <CorpName>Wrox Press Ltd.</CorpName>
</Person>

<Person perID="JNTHN_PNCK" role="AU">
  <PersonName>
    <FirstName>Jonathan</FirstName>
    <LastName>Pinnock</LastName>
  </PersonName>
  <Email>jon@jpassoc.co.uk</Email>
  <Address>
    <City>Hertfordshire</City>
    <Region>England</Region>
    <Country>UK</Country>
  </Address>
</Person>

<Person perID="KRL_WTSN" role="ED">
  <PersonName>
    <FirstName>Karli</FirstName>
    <LastName>Watson</LastName>
  </PersonName>
  <CorpName>Wrox Press Ltd.</CorpName>
</Person>

<Person perID="LS_STPHNSN" role="ED">
  <PersonName>
    <FirstName>Lisa</FirstName>
    <LastName>Stephenson</LastName>
  </PersonName>
```

```
      <CorpName>Wrox Press Ltd.</CorpName>
   </Person>

   <Person perID="MRK_BRBCK" role="AU">
     <PersonName>
       <FirstName>Mark</FirstName>
       <LastName>Birbeck</LastName>
     </PersonName>
     <Biography>Mark has been a professional programmer for 18
     years.</Biography>
   </Person>

   <Person perID="NKL_OZ" role="AU">
     <PersonName>
       <FirstName>Nikola</FirstName>
       <LastName>Ozu</LastName>
     </PersonName>
     <Biography>Nikola Ozu is a consultant who lives in Wyoming.</Biography>
   </Person>

   <Person perID="PTR_JNS" role="ED">
     <PersonName>
       <FirstName>Peter</FirstName>
       <LastName>Jones</LastName>
     </PersonName>
     <CorpName>Wrox Press Ltd.</CorpName>
   </Person>

   <Person perID="STPHN_MHR" role="AE">
     <PersonName>
       <FirstName>Stephen</FirstName>
       <LastName>Mohr</LastName>
     </PersonName>
     <CorpName>Omicron Consulting</CorpName>
   </Person>

   <Person perID="STVN_LVNGSTN" role="AU">
     <PersonName>
       <FirstName>Steven</FirstName>
       <LastName>Livingstone</LastName>
     </PersonName>
   </Person>

</Persons>
```

5. Following these, we'll add some `Subjects`:

```
<Subjects>
  <Subject subjectID="INTRNT">Internet</Subject>
  <Subject subjectID="INTRNT_PRGRMNG">Internet Programming</Subject>
  <Subject subjectID="XML">XML (eXtensible Markup Language)</Subject>
</Subjects>
```

6. Finally, add the `Books` element and change our existing `Book` elements as follows:

```
<Books>

  <Book bookID="PRFSNL_XML" isbn="1-861003-11-0" publisher="WRX_PRS_LTD"
      authors="DDR_MRTN JNTHN_PNCK MRK_BRBCK STPHN_MHR NKL_OZ"
      editors="JN_DCKT PTR_JNS KRL_WTSN"
      imprint="PRG2PRG" pubDate="2000-01" pages="1169" level="PRO">
    <Title>Professional XML</Title>
    <Abstract>The complete practical encyclopedia for XML today.</Abstract>
    <Prices>
      <Price currency="USD">49.99</Price>
      <Price currency="GBP">35.99</Price>
      <Price currency="CDN">74.95</Price>
    </Prices>
    <SubjectRefs>
      <SubjectRef subject="INTRNT" />
      <SubjectRef subject="INTRNT_PRGRMNG" />
      <SubjectRef subject="XML" />
    </SubjectRefs>
  </Book>

  <Book bookID="BEGNNG_XML" isbn="1-861003-41-2" publisher="WRX_PRS_LTD"
      authors="DVD_HNTR JNTHN_PNCK NKL_OZ"
      editors="DN_PRKR LS_STPHNSN"
      imprint="PRG2PRG" level="BEG">
    <Title>Beginning XML</Title>
    <Abstract>The best practical tutorial for XML.</Abstract>
    <Prices>
      <Price>39.99</Price>
      <Price currency="GBP">28.99</Price>
      <Price currency="CDN">59.95</Price>
    </Prices>
    <SubjectRefs>
      <SubjectRef subject="INTRNT" />
      <SubjectRef subject="INTRNT_PRGRMNG" />
      <SubjectRef subject="XML" />
    </SubjectRefs>
  </Book>

</Books>

</BookCatalog>
```

I trust that both my Beginning XML *and* Professional XML *co-authors aren't offended if I've omitted some of their names from these examples for the sake of a more concise presentation. Those that remain were selected to illustrate some of the concepts we've been covering, such as optional child elements, multiple* IDREFs *that point to the same ID, and so on – no value judgments are implied!*

7. Display this in IE5, and you'll see something like this (note how we can collapse the tree structure to focus upon a particular subset of the document):

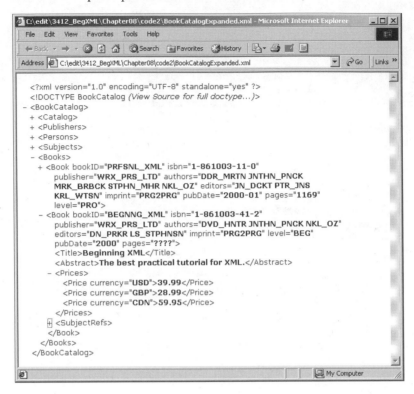

How It Works

This example conforms to the 'Expanded' DTD. We've added several ID and IDREF attributes to various element types, moved the authors and editors to their own elements (instead of being children of <Book>), and have finally fleshed-out <Book> and some of the other element types.

The highlighted lines in this XML document show the changes from the 'Basic' version to the new 'Expanded' version, to accommodate the changes we made to the DTD above. Now let's look at some of the more interesting aspects of these changes:

The <Publisher> element is our first example of an element that now has an associated ID attribute:

```
<Publisher pubID="WRX_PRS_LTD" isbn="861003">
  <CorpName>Wrox Press Ltd.</CorpName>
  <Email>feedback@wrox.com</Email>
  <Website>www.wrox.com</Website>
  <Address>
```

In this case, we've given the publisher an ID of "WRX_PRS_LTD" which can then be used in any element that needs to refer to the publisher – for example, in both of our <Book> elements:

```
        <Book bookID="PRFSNL_XML" isbn="1-861003-11-0" publisher="WRX_PRS_LTD" ..>
   ...
        <Book bookID="BEGNNG_XML" isbn="1-861003-41-2" publisher="WRX_PRS_LTD" ..>
```

<Imprint> and <Level> are other examples of elements with an associated ID attribute:

```
    <Imprints>
      <Imprint imprintID="PRG2PRG">Programmer to Programmer</Imprint>
    </Imprints>
    <Levels>
      <Level levelID="BEG">Beginning</Imprint>
      <Level levelID="INS">Instant</Imprint>
      <Level levelID="PRO">Professional</Imprint>
    </Levels>
```

Here again, the goal is to reduce redundant copies of the same data in different elements. For example, instead of including the string "Programmer to Programmer" in every instance of <Book> that has this imprint, we can have the application refer to the imprint via an IDREF.

In our second <Publisher> element, we've included the hq attribute used in the <Address> child element:

```
    <Publisher pubID="WRX_PRS_INC">
     <CorpName>Wrox Press Inc.</CorpName>
     <Address hq="no">
```

We omitted this attribute the first time we used the <Publisher> element, because we were assuming the default value (yes) from the DTD. We used it in the second instance because we want to give a value (no) that's different from the default value in the DTD.

The <Person> element also has an associated ID attribute:

```
    <Person perID="JNTHN_PNCK" role="AU">
```

In this case, we've given a person an ID of "JNTHN_PNCK", which we then used in both <Book> examples. This illustrates the main reason we separated the authors and editors from the <Book> element – the same person will often work on more than one book, but we'd rather not repeat all that person's information in every instance of every such book.

This first instance of a <Book> element is now expanded to use the new attributes, including the IDREF attributes that provide links to the book's publisher, authors, editors, imprint and audience level:

```
    <Book bookID="PRFSNL_XML" isbn="1-861003-11-0" publisher="WRX_PRS_LTD"
         authors="DDR_MRTN JNTHN_PNCK MRK_BRBCK STPHN_MHR NKL_OZ"
         editors="JN_DCKT PTR_JNS KRL_WTSN"
         imprint="PRG2PRG" pubDate="2000-01" pages="1169" level="PRO">
      <Title>Professional XML</Title>
      <Abstract>The complete practical encyclopedia for XML today.</Abstract>
```

Also note how we've made use of the default value for the `currency` attribute of the `<Price>` child of our second instance of the `<Book>` element:

```
<Prices>
  <Price>39.99</Price>
  <Price currency="GBP">28.99</Price>
  <Price currency="CDN">59.95</Price>
</Prices>
```

The omission of the `currency` attribute here is intentional – when this document is viewed in IE5, you'll see that the parser has inserted the default value for this attribute ("USD") from its definition in the DTD:

```
<!ATTLIST Price currency (USD | GBP | CDN) "USD" >
```

We also use `IDREF` attributes to link the book to its subject:

```
<SubjectRefs>
  <SubjectRef subject="INTRNT" />
  <SubjectRef subject="INTRNT_PRGRMNG" />
  <SubjectRef subject="XML" />
</SubjectRefs>
```

You may be wondering why we didn't just declare `<SubjectRefs>` to use a single `IDREF` attribute, instead of three child elements. This slightly more verbose form has one significant advantage – we can constrain the document to allow only one, two, or three subjects. There could be no such limit using an `IDREF` attribute. When we revisit this example in the next chapter, you'll see how an XML Schema can be used to specify this restriction exactly – one of the many ways that schemas can be more descriptive than DTDs.

Try It Out Summary

This Try It Out greatly expanded upon our 'Basic' DTD in two ways:

❑ First, we left simple elements-only XML behind with the addition of numerous attributes that supplemented, and in some cases replaced, elements we originally used as data containers.

❑ Secondly, and much more significantly, we've made use of `ID`/`IDREF` attributes to reduce redundancy greatly in our data representation.

Although the advantages of this second design change may not be readily apparent in such a small example, there *are* real storage and maintenance savings. Imagine a `BookCatalog` of thousands of `<Book>` elements, each with several authors and editors.

The example data for each `<Person>` was really a small portion of what we'd likely include in a real-world environment. Biographies and abstracts are typically at least a paragraph, rather than just a single sentence. Addresses (e-mail and physical) are likewise more verbose than what we included in our example. Given that our more prolific people might be involved in dozens of different books, if we had kept our original ('Basic') data model there would have been dozens of repetitions of their personal information. Imagine trying to maintain even simple things like current addresses in these redundant locations.

Granted, a global search-and-replace does work on a single or even multiple files, but it has its own possible problems. Most common text tools (e.g. rgrep, perl) don't know about XML syntax, and therefore we wouldn't be able easily and reliably to change a single person's country from say "United States" to "Ireland". Trying to make this sort of change using the cut-and-paste method is even more trouble-prone.

The other places we used ID/IDREF attributes have similar advantages. Keeping naturally separate objects separate is one of the basic principles of good OO design – "say something once, why say it again?" – it is much better to *refer* to objects, than to *copy* them everywhere they're needed.

Limitations of DTDs

Like XML itself, XML DTDs are a subset of SGML. Although DTDs are one of the most complex aspects of SGML, they are essential for describing documents and their markup. Many existing SGML tools could be used immediately with XML, thus easing the usual adoption pains of a new technology. However, it's important to remember that SGML was always intended for complex documents (for example, aircraft technical manuals, government regulations, etc.), and is not usually used for more general data exchange.

> *The abstract of the XML 1.0 recommendation explicitly states: "XML is a subset of SGML... to enable... SGML... on the Web... XML has been designed for... interoperability with both SGML and HTML".*

Whilst XML (and early HTML) shared a similar origin, these markup languages have been used for much more than technical documents. HTML began as a way to represent hypertext, but quickly became a way to present multimedia and, with the addition of JavaScript, also became the programming environment for the WWW's client-side. XML is now touted as the foundation of new e-commerce applications, a replacement for HTML (via XHTML), and a generic data exchange format for connecting disparate RDBMS and other corporate databases. XML is even being used within embedded systems, such as cellular phones and other wireless devices.

Since XML came from the SGML community, the stated design goals and even the choice of terms (for example "document") reflect a focus on technical documentation and monolithic document/DTD units. However, XML has rapidly become more than a document markup language, and the limitations of DTDs for more generic data description have become all too apparent. The speed of adoption of XML owes a lot to IBM and Microsoft's tools for XML, and the latter's use of XML in Windows 2000, as well as its early implementation of XML in MSXML and IE5. These tools have been the basis for considerable experimentation and even production use on the server-side of WWW and Internet applications. E-commerce initiatives, such as BizTalk (a central repository for document types, which we'll see more of in later chapters), have spurred widespread interest in XML as a messaging format, with no connection to the document-centric model of yore.

Some limitations of DTDs include:

❑   DTDs are not extensible (unlike XML itself!)

❑   Only one DTD may be associated with each document

❑   DTDs do not work well with XML namespaces

❑   Very weak data typing

Chapter 9

- ❑ Limited content model descriptions

- ❑ No OO-type object inheritance

- ❑ A document can override/ignore an external DTD using the internal subset

- ❑ Non-XML syntax

- ❑ No DOM support

- ❑ Relatively few older, more expensive tools

Let's take a look at these limitations in a little more detail.

DTDs Are Not Extensible

When a DTD is used to describe the rules of an XML vocabulary, all those rules must be present in that single DTD. There *is* an **external entity** mechanism that allows inclusion of declarations from multiple sources. However, this document-centric approach is limited and rather complex, and it can greatly reduce processing performance (particularly in the network environment for which XML is intended).

Only One DTD Per Document

The restriction of one DTD per document may also be evaded using external entities, but otherwise it's impossible to validate a document against multiple descriptions.

For example, in the ideal world our `BookCatalog` vocabulary would draw from a generic name & address DTD, a bibliographic DTD, and perhaps some e-commerce DTD – but the result would be very difficult to read, and isn't really possible without a great deal of work, and cooperation between the creators of the different DTDs.

Limited Support of Namespaces

Two of the advantages of XML namespaces are the ability to:

- ❑ Prevent conflicting element type names

- ❑ Resolve different name strings that are intended to mean the same thing

If namespaces are used, every element type from each namespace must be included in the DTD – which somewhat defeats the purpose of using multiple namespaces from various independent sources.

Weak Data Typing

DTDs really work with only one data type – the text string. Whilst it is true that some constraints may be applied to some strings (for example `ID`, `NMTOKEN`, and related attribute types), these are very weak and limited checks. There is no provision for numeric data types, let alone more complex (but very common) structures like dates, times, encoded numbers or strings, or URLs.

XML's use of text-only data *does* have advantages for debugging, transmission over ancient 7-bit networks, and handling incompatible binary storage formats. However, there are no standardized provisions for including binary data or requiring properly formatted data, numeric or otherwise.

No Inheritance

Modern OO systems are based on the idea that it's very often more reliable and efficient to describe new objects in terms of existing ones. Given that element types are analogous to object classes, it would be very powerful to be able to describe one element type in terms of another – but DTDs cannot really do this.

Document Can Override an External DTD

Isn't it ironic that an external DTD may be completely ignored or overridden by the internal DTD subset within a document instance (given the lack of DTD support for inheritance)? Since the internal subset has precedence over the external subset, there is no assurance that the rules of a DTD will be followed by the documents with which it is associated!

This becomes a significant problem when XML data is used for e-commerce, and other critical applications where data validation is important. The internal DTD subset could actually become something of a "Trojan Horse", used to subvert the intentions of the DTD's designer and misrepresent data in the XML document.

Non-XML Syntax

Despite the use of angle brackets to delimit declarations, DTDs do not use well-formed XML syntax. Most of the DTD is represented in **Extended Backus Naur Form** (**EBNF**), a formal language for syntax description. Although EBNF is widely used amongst computer scientists, many people find it difficult to read and use.

Its use also makes automated processing of XML and DTDs more difficult. Every validating parser must include two different parsers: one for XML and one for the EBNF. Most such parsers keep the EBNF information hidden from the application and user, even though it would often be useful to view or manipulate this data.

No DOM Support

The DOM is a commonly used way to manipulate XML data, but it doesn't handle EBNF and provides no access to the rules of the document model in the DTD. Given the investment in applications based on the DOM, it would be a great advantage to be able use this to view/modify not just an XML document, but its metadata also.

Limited Tools

The rapid adoption of XML was due, in some part, to its design goal of interoperability with SGML and HTML. Early users and developers of XML documents and vocabularies could use existing SGML tools; and with the advent of MSXML, a standard HTML browser (IE5). However, most SGML tools are both complex and expensive, and have always been targeted on a rather esoteric and specialized market. Recent HTML browsers have provided some support for XML, but very little support for DTDs.

If DTDs were written in XML, we could use any of the multitude of available XML tools to view the DTD, extract content models, or even provide dynamic selection of validation information.

Summary

In this chapter, we've seen how we can use Document Type Definitions (DTDs) to define and enforce the content and structure of our XML documents.

We've learned:

❑   The difference between **well-formed** XML – that complies with the syntax and structural rules of the XML 1.0 specification – and **valid** XML – XML that complies with syntax, structural, and other rules as defined in a DTD

❑   The difference between internal and external DTDs

❑   How to associate a DTD with an XML document

❑   How to declare element types

❑   How to declare attribute types

This chapter has concentrated on what we can do with DTDs, but as we saw in the last section, there are some things that we *can't* do with them. In the next chapter, we're going to look at an alternative way to validate our documents – using **schemas**.

Valid XML: Schemas

In Chapter 9 we discussed how to construct **valid** XML documents using DTDs. Although DTDs are the method of validating documents defined in the XML 1.0 recommendation, other methods have also been proposed for this purpose. Most of these proposals involve some sort of **schema**.

> **A schema is generally defined as: "the organization or structure of a database, usually derived from data modelling". This structure is typically described using some sort of controlled vocabulary that names items of the data, and lists any constraints that may apply (datatype, legal/illegal values, special formatting, etc.). The relationships between data items (the object of data models) are also an important part of any schema.**

Strictly speaking, a DTD is a form of a schema, and so are many of the data dictionaries and schemas used with existing relational database management systems (RDBMS) and object-oriented database management systems (OO-DBMS). In the context of XML, references to "schemas" usually mean the pending W3C proposal for an **XML Schema** standard (the Last Call Working Draft of 10 April 2000), which uses XML syntax for all of its data descriptions. This chapter focuses on the W3C's XML Schema proposal, so whenever you see the word "Schema" you can assume that we're referring to XML Schema, unless we say otherwise.

There are three W3C documents of interest: **XML Schema Part 0: Primer**, **XML Schema Part 1: Structures**, *and* **XML Schema Part 2: Datatypes** *[all 7 April 2000], at http://www.w3.org/TR/xmlschema-0, http://www.w3.org/TR/xmlschema-1, and http://www.w3.org/TR/xmlschema-2, respectively. Together, these comprise the Last Call Working Draft of XML Schema, for which the comment period ended on 12 May 2000.*

XML Schema is based on XML 1.0, but also requires the use of **Namespaces in XML** *[14 January 1999], available at http://www.w3.org/TR/REC-xml-names.html.*

A quick aside on W3C nomenclature: a "NOTE" is an informational document, which is not necessarily intended to become a standard, but is useful for background reading. A "Recommendation" (often abbreviated as "REC") is the W3C equivalent of a "standard" (though it dislikes this word in the context of its documents, preferring to defer to ISO and other such "official" standards organizations). A "Proposed Recommendation" is the last step before a Recommendation, which is in turn preceded by a "Candidate Recommendation", a "Last Call Working Draft", and earlier "Working Draft(s)". XML Schema: Part 0 is labeled "non-normative" document, which is W3C-speak for supporting documents that are informational, but aren't part of the formal specification.

Microsoft's non-W3C-compliant implementation is **XML-Data Reduced** (**XDR**). Although XDR has been implemented in MSXML 2.0 and IE5 (and is the basis of Microsoft's BizTalk e-commerce initiative), once the W3C's proposal becomes a Final Recommendation, XDR will likely become obsolete. However, until then, IE5 does give us an easy way to show (non-standard) schemas in action in that browser. There are some differences in syntax, and even slight structural differences, between XDR and the XML Schema proposal.

The W3C has also published a requirements document for XML Schema, based on the various schema proposals that have been made since the XML 1.0 recommendation was published in 1998. This document states that XML Schemas are required to:

❑ Provide a rich set of primitive datatypes (e.g. string, Boolean, float)

❑ Provide a datatype system that allows built-in and user-defined datatypes to be created (with various constraining properties), and that's adequate to support import/export from any RDBMS or OODBMS

❑ Distinguish lexical data representation from an underlying information set (more about this later)

> *The W3C requirements document is a NOTE named* **XML Schema Requirements** *(15 February1999), and is available at http://www.w3.org/TR/NOTE-xml-schema-req.*

Before we discuss the details of XML Schema, let's look back at some of the limitations of DTDs. The XML Schema proposal addresses these concerns, and provides a more robust method of data description and validation.

Schemas versus DTDs

The XML Schema Working Drafts and related proposals seek to address various limitations of DTDs, particularly in the context of XML data exchange and use with modern programming languages and networked systems.

The following table illustrates the differences between using DTDs and XML Schema to validate XML data:

	DTD	XML Schema
Syntax	EBNF + pseudo XML.	Good ol' XML 1.0.
Tools	Mature (use existing SGML tools) but these are expensive and complex.	Use almost any XML tool, including the DOM, XSLT and XML-aware browsers.
DOM support	None.	Can be displayed and manipulated with the DOM (since it's XML).

	DTD	XML Schema
Content models	Weak – simple sequence or choice lists, can't use these with mixed content; can only specify zero, one, or many occurrences of an element. No named element or attribute groups.	Strong – more detailed content model is not mutually exclusive with mixed content; can specify exact number of occurrences; named model groups.
Data typing	Weak – strings, name tokens, IDs, and little else.	Strong – all commonly used modern datatypes including: string, numeric, date/time, and structures.
Name scope	Global names only.	Global and local names.
Inheritance	No.	Yes.
Extensibility	Limited – must change XML 1.0 recommendation (and probably SGML) to extend.	Unlimited – based upon XML with its extensibility and internationalization ("I18N") features.
Legacy constraints	Yes – many less than ideal aspects of XML are due to the goal of remaining backward compatible with SGML.	No – even though some datatypes have been retained from DTDs, most of XML schema is based upon modern technology and programming languages.
Multiple vocabulary support	No – one DTD per document.	Yes – as many as needed, based upon Namespaces in XML.
Dynamic schemas	No – DTDs are read-only for all practical purposes.	Yes – schemas can be selected and even modified at runtime, perhaps as a result of user interaction.

Let's take a look at some of these in a bit more detail.

Syntax

The very first of these differences is perhaps the most significant advantage of XML Schema – it *is* XML. This allows us to use any XML tools (including the DOM) for both displaying and manipulating the schema, and opens the possibility of using related standards like XInclude, XPath, and XLink with schemas. And this in turn is likely to increase the acceptance of XML for non-document uses, such as data exchange, messaging, remote procedures, and OO class hierarchy and program representations.

Content Models

As listed in the table, DTD content models have several limitations. XML Schema provides more detailed and robust content models, and these are valuable for both traditional document-oriented XML data and the newer applications of XML.

Applications such as e-commerce, database exchange, and RPC (remote procedure call) all depend upon the advanced features of XML Schema, including its ability to create complex content models. In particular, applications that need to mix structured and free-form text (e.g. an e-commerce web page) benefit greatly from the superior description and validation of mixed content.

Data Typing

Unlike DTDs, XML Schema supports just about all of the datatypes that you're likely to want to use, which is essential for most of XML's newer uses.

Applications can now use most of the traditional programming language datatypes, along with the conceptual and maintenance benefits of OO inheritance of datatypes and structures. One of the great benefits of XML is that it gives us the ability to describe our own vocabulary, and this is greatly enhanced by XML Schema's ability to ensure that, say, a number is really a number. Other XML Schema datatypes provide for various forms of commonly-used values such as dates, times, URI references, and complex data structures.

But the ability to use strong data-typing has advantages beyond the description and validation of documents and web pages. Once web sites begin marking-up their data with XML, web spiders will be able to extract much more meaningful information about these sites.

❑ For example, the addition of numeric datatypes will allow robots to provide price comparison services that can calculate currency conversions, taxes, and/or multi-item costs.

❑ Users searching for date-sensitive items (like newspaper articles or a specific event) will benefit from standardized dates, and the ability to search on specific dates or ranges of dates.

❑ The enhanced searching capability also applies to other specific datatypes, such as URIs, and standard user-derived datatypes like ISBNs, UPCs, and part numbers.

All of these will permit much more focused searching, without needing to wade through huge lists of online search engine results. Existing free-text searches can't differentiate between the May Company, May Day, the merry month of May, or a woman's name (much less ignore the many appearances of the permissive verb – which is rarely the target of a search). Type-specific searching is an awesome benefit of XML Schema's strong data typing.

Extensibility

Isn't it ironic that a markup language that's intended to be extensible (it's even right there in the name!) doesn't have an extensible description language? Even though the EBNF syntax of a DTD uses an open-ended regular grammar, the implementation of DTDs is constrained by the XML 1.0 REC – there is no means of adding new declarations or features, without revising the specification.

XML Schema eliminates this limitation of DTDs, as well as many of the SGML-based constraints on the description and validation of XML data. XML Schema's user-derived datatypes, complex data structures, and OO inheritance all provide an open-ended way to extend schemas in tune with the demands of real-world applications. That's one reason why, despite its origin as a subset of SGML, XML is rapidly outgrowing the document-centric focus of SGML and is becoming an enabling technology for a wide range of data exchange, the WWW, and even remote computing (XML-RPC and SOAP).

The ability to reference multiple schemas from a single document allows much greater use of shared and standard XML vocabularies. Instead of everyone "inventing" their own DTD or schema for a physical address, eventually we might just use the official Post Office schema for mailing addresses. If we were to combine this with an ITU schema for telephone numbers, an IETF schema for Internet and e-mail addresses, and perhaps an ebXML business schema, we'd have the basis for shared XML-based e-commerce and communications – much more powerful than any individual corporate effort.

> *The ebXML schema (http://www.ebxml.org) doesn't quite exist yet, but it's a joint effort of the UN/CEFACT and Oasis, so there is both international and widespread commercial support for this pending e-commerce standard. The involvement of the United Nations and a non-profit industry consortium assures that ebXML will be focused upon ISO and W3C standards, including SGML, Unicode, DTDs, and XML Schema.*

> *Another similar effort initiated by Microsoft, is BizTalk. Whilst this initiative is somewhat further ahead in terms of implementation, much of it is based upon non-standard, and even proprietary components, such as XML-Data. It remains to be seen if BizTalk will embrace open standards like XML Schema.*

Dynamic Schemas

XML Schemas lets us use dynamic subsets of standardized schemas, that is, schema portions that are selected in response to some user input. This is a truly exciting possibility for schemas.

> *We'll be looking at a real-life e-commerce implementation of dynamic schemas in the last of our case studies, at the end of this book.*

For example, after conducting a bibliographic search that's governed by an appropriate schema (perhaps one like our `BookCatalog` example), a user could then be able to purchase a book online – using a completely different schema for the purchase order. Depending on the user's home country, an appropriate shipping schema (i.e. an official Post Office or ebXML schema) could be selected to ensure correct handling of the customer's order.

Even though this might be theoretically possible using only DTDs and external entities, this is a hideously complex and error-prone approach, and it's even more complicated when multiple organizations are involved. CALS (an SGML vocabulary) documents are one example, and only the U.S. government and its large corporate suppliers have been able to make use of this approach. On the other hand, with XML Schema this can be a relatively straightforward process.

So now that we know why we'd want to use XML Schema, let's begin with some background and basic structural principles.

Basic Schema Principles

XML Schema is comprised of two basic parts, which are defined in two separate documents:

❑ **datatypes** – the "atoms" and "sub-atomic particles" of XML Schema, which are used as the basis of all the larger components in a schema (http://www.w3.org/TR/xmlschema-2)

❑ **structures** – the "compounds" that can be constructed from datatypes, and are used to describe the element, attribute, and validation structure of a document type (http://www.w3.org/TR/xmlschema-1)

And there are two distinct types of markup in XML Schema that loosely correspond to these two parts of the specification:

❑ **definitions** – which create new types (both simple and complex)

❑ **declarations** – which describe the content models of elements and attributes in document instances

We saw in the last chapter how content models describe the structure of an XML vocabulary and its conformant document instances. A content model can restrict a document to a certain set of element types and attributes, describe and constrain the relationships between these different components, and uniquely identify specific elements. Sharing a content model (via a DTD or other kind of schema) allows business partners to exchange structured information and bridge the differences between their disparate internal database systems. The declarations which describe a content model in an XML Schema are a bit more complex than those in a DTD, but are also much more powerful.

XML Parsers with Schema Support

At the present time, very few XML parsers and tools support the XML Schema Working Drafts. Microsoft chose to implement their own proprietary schema language (XDR), but has promised to conform to XML Schema once it becomes a formal W3C Recommendation. IBM and Oracle have both chosen to support the open standards effort, and typically updated their parsers soon after each Working Draft was published. Several commercial XML editors have also been developed, including a few that support schemas.

❑ IBM has produced two XML parsers, **XML4C** (C++) and **XML4J** (Java) that can use XML Schema to validate documents. Information and downloads are available at http://www.alphaworks.ibm.com/formula/xml. IBM has also begun to provide XML support in its flagship **DB2** product, as well as other applications.

❑ Information about Oracle's **XML Parser for Java v2** can be found online at http://technet.oracle.com/tech/xml/parser_java2. It is integrated into the **Oracle 8i** DBMS, and thus provides XML support on the multitude of systems that can run this popular DBMS.

❑ **XML Spy 3.0** from Icon Informations-Systeme GmbH (Icon Information-Systems) supports several types of schema, including XML 1.0 DTDs, the 7 April 2000 draft of XML Schema, XDR (plus its BizTalk flavor), and even DCD. This product began as a structured XML editor and has grown into a full-blown IDE for XML. Product info can be found at http://new.xmlspy.com/features_intro.html, and the company's general web site is at http://www.icon-is.com.

❑ **XML Authority 1.2** is Extensibility's XML schema design environment that offers support for DTDs, XDR, a subset of XML Schema, Software AG's Tamino Server, and BizTalk. It also offers an editor (**XML Instance**), and a new conversion tool (**XML Console**). The company's web site is at www.extensibility.com..

Once the XML Schema becomes a W3C REC, there will likely be a flood of parsers and other tools that support this one "official" XML schema language.

Structures and Datatypes, or Chickens and Eggs

Although the W3C has chosen to specify datatypes in the second part of its schema draft (structures being the first part), we'll look at datatypes first, since schema structures (and our practical examples) are built upon these datatypes.

The next section does delve into quite a lot of rather dry details, but these will be necessary when we want to build complex datatypes and structures later in the chapter. You'll also find a more comprehensive set of dry details on datatypes in Appendix E at the end of the book.

It's a bit like the old chicken-and-egg conundrum – in this case the W3C chose to tell us about the chicken (structures) first, and then the egg whence it came. I've opted to describe the egg (datatypes) first, since structures are grown from them. I suppose you could blame my approach on my having learned physics before chemistry. So, let's look at the details of datatypes, the atomic (and sub-atomic) particles of XML Schema – then we'll build some molecules, in the form of structures.

Datatypes

As we've already seen, one of the greatest advantages of schemas over DTDs is its rich set of datatypes. These types are based upon those in XML 1.0 DTDs, Java, SQL, the ISO 11404 standard on language-independent datatypes, and existing Internet standards.

It would be nice to have a link to a web page that showed the ISO 11404 standard, but like most of its documents, this one is not available online. You can find ordering information for a paper version at http://www.iso.ch/cate/d19346.html

Much like any modern programming language, XML Schema provides two basic kinds of datatypes:

❑   **primitive datatypes** – those that are not defined in terms of other types

❑   **derived datatypes** – those that are defined in terms of existing types

And also like most programming languages, there are predefined datatypes, known as **built-in types**, which can be used in any instance of a schema that is based upon XML Schema. By definition, all primitive types are also built-in types – only the W3C can add these types by amending the XML Schema specification. The W3C has also defined a set of built-in *derived* types, which were believed to be so universal that they would end up being reinvented by most schema designers.

There are also **user-derived types** that are not a part of the specification, but are derived from existing datatypes. Derived types are created using the OO principles of **datatype extension** and **datatype restriction** (more about these later in this chapter).

Primitive Datatypes

Primitive datatypes can be thought of as the subatomic particles of XML Schema – they are the basis for all other types, and cannot themselves be defined from smaller components. By definition, primitive types can never have element content or attributes, since they are the **base types** from which all other types are derived.

> **Primitive types can be used for element or attribute *values*, but cannot *contain* child elements or attributes. Primitive types are always built-in,**

For example, floating-point numbers are based upon the well-known mathematical concept of real numbers, which correspond to the XML Schema primitive type named `float`. A string of characters is another common primitive type, known as the `string` datatype (what a surprise!).

It's worth noting that the distinction between primitive and derived types can be a little bit arbitrary, so the XML Schema classifications don't necessarily correspond to those of any particular programming language. Just as the exact definition of a string or a float is different in Java and C/C++, so too is the definition of these types in XML Schema. The entire set of built-in primitive datatypes will be described later in this section, and in much greater detail in an appendix to this book.

Primitive Types for XML Schema

The following are the primitive datatypes that are built-in to XML Schema:

❑   `string` – a finite-length sequence of UCS characters

❑   `boolean` – a two-state "true" or "false" flag

❑   `float` – a 32-bit single-precision IEEE 754-1985 floating-point number

❑   `double` – a 64-bit double-precision IEEE 754-1985 floating-point number

❑   `decimal` – a decimal number of arbitrary precision (number of significant digits)

❑   `timeDuration` – a duration of time

❑   `recurringDuration` – a recurring duration of time

❑   `binary` – text-encoded binary data

❑   `uriReference` – a standard Internet URI

❑   `ID` – equivalent to the XML 1.0 `ID` attribute type

❑   `IDREF` – equivalent to the XML 1.0 `IDREF` attribute type

❑   `ENTITY` – equivalent to the XML 1.0 `ENTITY` attribute type

❑   `NOTATION` – equivalent to the XML 1.0 `NOTATION` attribute type

❑   `QName` – a legal `QName` string (name with qualifier), as defined in ***Namespaces in XML***

See Appendix E for a comprehensive discussion of these datatypes.

Derived Datatypes

A derived datatype is one that's defined in terms of an existing datatype (known as its base type). Derived types may have attributes, and may have element or mixed content.

> **Derived types can contain any well-formed XML that is valid according to their datatype definition. They may be built-in or user-derived.**

New types may be derived from either a primitive type or another derived type.

For example, integers are a subset of real numbers. Therefore, the XML Schema integer type is derived from the floating-point number type, which is its base type. We can in turn derive an even more restricted type of integer:

```
<simpleType name="negativeInteger" base="xsi:integer">
  <minInclusive value="unbounded" />
  <maxInclusive value="-1" />
</simpleType>
```

This is an example of an XML Schema structure known as a **Simple Type Definition**. It uses the `<simpleType>` element to describe a derived integer datatype that's limited to negative values.

> *Don't worry too much about the specifics of the code in this excerpt – we'll look at the `<simpleType>` element and its companion, the `<complexType>` element (the **Complex Type Definition**), in the Structures section later in this chapter.*

As with the primitive types, the W3C has defined a set of built-in derived datatypes. These types are so common that it was felt they should be an integral part of the XML Schema specification.

Built-in Derived Types for XML Schema

These are some of the derived datatypes that are built in to XML Schema:

❑   `language` – a natural language identifier, as defined by RFC 1766

❑   `Name` – a legal XML 1.0 name

❑   `NCName` – a legal XML 1.0 "non-colonized" name, as defined in **Namespaces in XML**

❑   `integer` – an integer number

❑   `date` – a Gregorian calendar date (a single day)

❑   `time` – an instant of time that recurs every day

> *See Appendix E for a complete list of these datatypes, and a discussion of the more important ones.*

Atomic and List Datatypes

There is one last dichotomy of XML Schema datatypes:

❑ **atomic datatypes** – types that have *values* that are defined to be indivisible

❑ **list datatypes** – types that have are defined in terms of existing types

It's important to distinguish atomic types from primitive types – they are not the same thing! List types are merely a special sort of derived datatype.

Atomic Datatypes

An atomic type is one that has a *value* that cannot be divided, at least not within the context of XML Schema.

For example, numbers and strings are atomic types since their values cannot be described using any smaller pieces. The former is pretty obvious, but can't a string be defined in terms of a smaller component, namely characters? Whilst this is true in the abstract sense, XML Schema has no concept of a character as a datatype – and thus a string is atomic.

```
<atom>This string is as fine as we can slice textual data - there are no character
'atoms' in XML Schema.</atom>
<another_atom>1927-01-16</another_atom>
<yet_another_atom>469557</yet_another_atom>
```

Atomic types may be either primitive or derived types. Again, note that atomic is *not* analogous to primitive. In the above example elements, the first is an atomic primitive type (a string). The second is an atomic derived type (dates *could* be derived from the string primitive type, though in XML Schema they are derived indirectly from three other types). The third example is also an atomic derived type (an integer is derived from the float primitive type).

List Datatypes

A list type has a *value* that's comprised of a finite-length sequence of atomic values. Unlike most programming languages, an XML Schema list type cannot be made from other lists. This type can be considered a special case of the more general aggregate or collection datatypes, such as those described in ISO 11404.

List types are *always* derived types, which *must* be delimited by white space character(s), just like the IDREFS or NMTOKENS attribute types defined in XML 1.0 recommendation. Thus, a list type must allow the presence of white space, but can't use any white space within the individual values of list items.

An important consideration about a list type is its length – this descriptive value is always the number of items in the list, and has no relation to the number of characters that represent the items.

For example, we can define a simple user-derived list type for generic sizes:

```
<simpleType name='sizes' base='decimal' derivedBy='list' />
```

This new datatype might then be used within a more specific element in a document:

```
<ShoeSizes type='sizes'>8 8.5 9 9.5 10 10.5 11 12 13</ShoeSizes>
```

On the other hand, using white space as a delimiter causes problems when we want to create lists of strings. In this context, the following example is not true – it's a list of *six* items.

```
<bad_list>this is a single list item</bad_list>
```

List types can be a very useful way to represent collections of numbers, or standard XML 1.0 attribute types like IDREFs or NMTOKENS. On the other hand, they are all but worthless for manipulation of textual data that involves anything more than words – sentences and larger groupings of text cannot be represented with a list type.

Aspects of Datatypes

All XML Schema datatypes are comprised of three parts:

❑   A **value space** (the set of distinct values where each of the values is denoted by one or more literals in the datatype's lexical space)

❑   A **lexical space** (the set of lexical representations, in other words a set of valid literal strings *representing* values)

❑   A set of **facets** (properties of the value space, its individual values, and/or lexical items)

To illustrate the difference between lexical and value spaces, we'll look at a snippet of a document. We'll assume that the <Name> element is a string datatype, and that the <Population> element is defined as an integer type:

```
<State>
  <Name>Wyoming</Name>
  <Population census="1980">469557</Population>
</State>
```

In the <Name> element, the value and lexical spaces are the same thing – the lexical representation of a string is also its value.

The <Population> element on the other hand, is *represented* in XML as a string, but its value is the mathematical concept of "four hundred sixty-nine thousand, five hundred fifty-seven". Any comparison of <Population> elements would use their numeric values, not their lexical (string) representations. This means that the three different forms "469557", "469557.00", and "4695.57E2" all have the same value, even though they are lexically different.

Let's take a look closer look at these concepts.

Value Spaces

Each schema datatype has a range of possible values. These value spaces are implicit in the definition of a primitive datatype. For example, the built-in `float` datatype has a value space that ranges from negative to positive infinity. The `string` datatype is comprised of values that correspond to any of the legal XML characters.

> **Derived types inherit their value space from their base type, and may also constrain that value space to an explicit subset of the base type's value space.**

A derived datatype such as `integer` would allow any positive or negative whole number value, but wouldn't allow decimal fractions. Another integer type could be derived from `integer`, but this type might limit the range of acceptable values to only positive numbers, or to only 3-digit numbers. Value spaces may also have a set of explicitly enumerated values, or be derived from the members of a list of types.

Values spaces always have certain facets (or abstract properties), such as **equality**, **order**, **bounds**, **cardinality**, and the age-old **numeric / non-numeric** dichotomy.

Lexical Spaces

A lexical space is the set of string literals that *represent* the values of a datatype. These literals always comprise "text" characters, which may be any of the XML-legal subset of the Unicode character set.

For example,

```
<a_string>The name of the sorority was     , and their motto was "plus ça change,
plus c'est la même chose"</a_string>
```

By definition, string literals only have one lexical representation (see the discussion of the Equality facet in the next section). On the other hand, numeric values may have several equivalent and equally valid lexical representations. For example, the string literals "100", "1.0E2", and "10²" obviously have different lexical values, but they have identical numeric values in the floating-point number value space.

Facets

A facet is one of the defining properties of a datatype which distinguish that datatype from others. Facets include properties such as a string's length, or the bounds of a numeric datatype.

The abstract properties that define the semantic characteristics of a value space are known as the **fundamental facets** of the datatype. There is another kind of facet: **constraining facets**, which are optional limits on the permissible values of a datatype's value space. We'll discuss both of these here.

Fundamental Facets

There are five fundamental facets:

❏ equality – different values can be compared and determined to be equal or not

❏ order – for some datatypes, defined relationships exist between values (for example, numbers may have ordered values)

❑ bounds – ordered datatypes may be constrained to a range of values

❑ cardinality– the number of values within the value space

❑ numeric/non-numeric

Let's look at some of the details of these fundamental facets. (And see Appendix E for even more detail.)

Equality

This property applies to all types, whether numeric or not. Given two values **A** and **B**, the following rules apply:

❑ it is always true that "**A** = **A**" (identity)

❑ if "**A** = **B**" then "**A**   **B**" is never possible

❑ if "**A** = **B**" then "**B** = **A**" (value equality is commutative, or independent of order)

❑ if "**A** = **B**" and "**B** = **C**" then "**A** = **C**" (value equality is transitive)

❑ the operation "**Equal(A,B)**" is true if "**A** = **B**"

When dealing with non-numeric types, remember that XML is case-sensitive, so the string "YES" is *not* equal to "yes" or "Yes".

Many accented and ideographic characters can have multiple representations. For example, the letter "n" with a tilde accent can be represented in ASCII (or for an input device like a keyboard) as the two-letter sequence: "~n". An alternate representation, using the Latin-1 encoding would be a single accented letter: "ñ". By definition, these are equal only if they are of the same form ("~n" is *not* equal to "ñ").

Order

A datatype is ordered if a defined relationship (known as an **order-relation**) exists between values. This property also applies to both numeric and non-numeric values. An order relation has these rules:

❑ for every value "**A**", then "**A** < **A**" and "**A** > **A**" are never true

❑ for every two values "(**A**, **B**)", then one of the following must be true: "**A** = **B**", "**A** < **B**", or "**A** > **B**"

❑ for every three values "(**A**, **B**, **C**)" then it is true that: if "**A** < **B**" and "**B** < **C**", then "**A** < **C**"

Numeric order is intrinsic to the mathematical definition of numbers. On the other hand, the order of characters, or strings of characters, depends on the *encoded* numeric value (in other words the UCS code point) of the characters: "0" (ASCII zero) is less than "a", "a" is less than "b", "e" is less than "è", and so on.

Be careful not to assume that upper-case letters are always less than lower-case letters. Whilst this is true for the ASCII and Latin-1 encodings, the Latin Extended-A and -B encodings mix the two cases together. Also remember that the concept of case doesn't even exist in many non-Latin alphabets.

Bounds

Datatype values may have either lower or upper bounds, or both.

- ❑ An upper bound is the unique value **U** where for all values **v** in the value space, the statement "**v** U" is true. Such a value space is said to be **bounded above**.

- ❑ A lower bound is the unique value **L**, where it is always true that "**v** L". In this case, the value space is said to be **bounded below**.

If a value space has both upper and lower bounds, its datatype is simply considered to be **bounded**, with an assumption that the bounding is both "above" and "below".

These may be inclusive or exclusive, as we saw a while back in a Simple Type Definition example:

```
<simpleType name="negativeInteger" base="xsi:integer">
  <minInclusive value="unbounded" />
  <maxExclusive value="0" />
</simpleType>
```

This example shows a value space that is **bounded above** (has a finite maximum value), but is not **bounded below** (there is no minimum).

Cardinality

All value spaces have an associated concept of cardinality – the number of values within the value space. A value space may be:

- ❑ finite – such as a list of enumerated values

- ❑ countably infinite

- ❑ uncountably infinite

The first two of these are the categories of cardinality that are significant (we'll leave the last one to the mathematicians, eh?).

Numeric / Non-numeric

A datatype and its associated value space is classified as numeric if the values can be considered numeric quantities in some number system. Contrariwise, any datatype with values that aren't represented by numbers is, of course, considered non-numeric.

> *Remember that XML isn't limited to ASCII digits – any of the several sets of Unicode "Number" characters can be used to represent numeric values. For example, the familiar so-called Arabic numerals used in the ASCII character set are* not *actually Arabic. Unicode does have the ten Arabic digits, as well as those of many other languages.*

Constraining Facets

Constraining facets are those that limit the value space of a *derived* datatype, which in turn limits that datatype's lexical space. Strictly speaking, *primitive* types don't have constraining facets, but these may be added by creating a derived datatype that's **derived by restriction** (see the section on this later).

There are several constraining facets that may be applied to any appropriate derived datatype:

❑   length, minLength, maxLength

❑   pattern

❑   enumeration

❑   minExclusive, maxExclusive, minInclusive, maxInclusive

❑   precision, scale

❑   encoding

❑   duration, period

Let's look at the details of these constraining facets.

length, minLength, maxLength

These three facets all deal with the number of units of length of a datatype, the value of which must always be a non-negative integer. The nature of the units will vary, depending on the base datatype:

❑   For those derived from the **string type**, length is the number of Unicode code points ("characters") – and it's important to remember that each Unicode characters may be 8, 16, or 32-bits long, or even variable-length sequences of 8-bit values.

❑   Types that are derived from the **binary type** measure length as the number of octets (8-bit bytes) of the binary data.

❑   **List types** define length as the number of items in the list.

The minLength and maxLength facets are the minimum and maximum number of units permitted for the datatype respectively. For example, we could use these if we wanted to constrain some datatype (such as an Area Code) to always be a 3-digit number:

```
<simpleType name="AreaCode" base="xsi:string">
  <minLength value="3" />
  <maxLength value="3" />
</simpleType>
```

pattern

This facet is a constraint on the datatype's *lexical* space, which indirectly constrains the value space. A pattern is a regular expression (**regex**) that a datatype's lexical representation must match for that latter literal to be considered valid. The regex language used in XML Schema is similar to the one defined for the Perl programming language.

*For more about the use of regular expressions, see the main website for Perl at http://www.perl.com/pub or **Appendix E** of **XML Schema Part 2: Datatypes** at http://www.w3.org/TR/xmlschema-2/#regexs*

enumeration

This facet is very much like a DTD's specification of an element type choice list or the enumerated values of an attribute. Enumeration limits a value space to a specific set of values – if the value isn't specified in the schema, it isn't valid.

Using this facet does not impose an additional or different order relation on the value space due to the order of the enumerated values – any ordered property of the derived datatype remains the same as that of its base type.

minExclusive, maxExclusive, minInclusive, maxInclusive

All of these facets can only apply to a datatype that has an order relation (see the earlier description of the Order fundamental facet).

❑   The two "min" facets define the minimum (lower bound) of a value space

❑   The two "max" facets define its maximum (upper bound)

❑   An exclusive bound means that the bounding value is *not* included in the value space (meaning that for all values **V** in the value space, **minExclusive** < **V** < **maxExclusive**)

❑   An inclusive bound is one that *is* included within the value space (**minInclusive**   **V** **maxInclusive**)

Of course, these two types of bounds are not coupled – a lower bound might be *ex*clusive, whilst the upper bound is *in*clusive. Obviously, you must choose between the two types of bounds for each end of the spectrum – it's never possible for a bound to be both *in*clusive and *ex*clusive!

precision, scale

These two facets apply to all datatypes derived from the **decimal type**. Like the `printf` specification in the C/C++ programming languages, `precision` is the maximum number of decimal digits allowed for the entire number (which must always be a positive integer), and `scale` is the maximum number of digits (always a non-negative integer) in the fractional portion of the number.

encoding

This facet is a constraint on the *lexical* space of datatypes that are derived from the `binary` base type. The value of this facet must either be `hex` or `base64`.

If the value is `hex`, then each binary byte is encoded as a 2-digit hexadecimal number, using the ten ASCII digits and the letters A through F (either upper or lower-case letters are permitted). For example, the hex-encoded string "312D322D33" is the encoded version of the ASCII string "1-2-3" ("2D" being the hex encoding of the hyphen character, and "3x" are the ASCII representation of the digits "x").

If the value is `base64`, then the entire binary stream is encoded using the widely used Internet standard Base64 Content-Transfer-Encoding method.

> *Base64 encoding is defined in **RFC 2045: Multipurpose Internet Mail Extensions (MIME)** Part One: Format of Internet Message Bodies (1996) at http://www.ietf.org/rfc/rfc2045.txt.*

duration, period

These facets only apply to the `recurringDuration` datatype and its derived datatypes. The value must always be a `timeDuration`.

❑   The `duration` facet is the duration of `recurringDuration` values

❑   The `period` facet is the frequency of recurrence for these values

> *See the discussion of `recurringDuration` in Appendix E for more about the meaning of these two facets.*

That's all the detail we'll go into about datatypes – if you need to know about any specific types in more detail, remember that you can refer to Appendix E.

But now, it's time we discussed how to associate an XML Schema with a document instance.

Associating Schemas with XML Documents

As with DTDs, it's hard to experiment with XML Schema without first discussing how to connect a schema with an XML document.

There are some significant differences between the official XML Schema draft and Microsoft's XDR in this context. However, since support for the pending W3C Working Draft is not yet widespread, we'll look first at the official version and later at the version that's currently implemented in MSXML.

XML Schema Preamble – The <schema> Element

An XML Schema consists of a **preamble**, followed by zero or more declarations (though an empty schema isn't very useful, of course). The preamble is a group of at least three attributes within the <schema> element. This need not be the schema's document element – a schema may be embedded within another XML document. In fact, there is no requirement that a schema even be a discrete text document – it could be constructed via the DOM, for example.

The following is an example of the all-encompassing <schema> element, with references to some commonly-used XML vocabularies:

```
<xsd:schema
    xmlns:xsd="http://www.w3.org/1999/XMLSchema"
    xmlns:xsi="http://www.w3.org/1999/XMLSchema-instance"
    version="1.42.57" >
  ...
</xsd:schema>
```

The <schema> element uses its attributes to identify any external schemas that are to be used by this <schema> and all of its child elements.

Specifying the Namespaces

The first two attributes use XML namespaces to identify the two W3C schemas that are used in almost every XML Schema. The first includes the basic XML Schema elements such as `<element>`, `<attribute>`, `<group>`, `<simpleType>`, `<complexType>`, and so on. The latter is used to define the standard XML Schema datatypes, such as `string`, `float`, `integer`, etc.

You don't have to use `xsd` or `xsi` as the namespace identifiers (they could just as easily be `foo`, `bar`, or anything that didn't conflict with your own namespaces), but `xsd` and `xsi` *are* the recommended conventions.

We could also make the most widely-used namespace our default, instead of using the "xsd" prefix:

```
<schema xmlns="http://www.w3.org/1999/XMLSchema" ...
```

This way, we don't need to include the "xsd" prefix in every XML Schema declaration, and can use unqualified names:

```
<schema ...>
  ...
</schema>
```

This can greatly improve the readability of our schemas.

Specifying the Version

The `version` attribute is strictly informational, and represents the version number of the schema in which it is located. Our XML application might want to ensure that a specific version number is used to validate our documents. We could also use multiple versions: one for development, another for testing, and yet another for production purposes.

XDR Preamble – the <Schema> Element

The same preamble in XDR would be:

```
<xdr:Schema
    name="MySchemaInXDR"
    xmlns:xdr="urn:schemas-microsoft-com:xml-data"
    xmlns:dt="urn:schemas-microsoft-com:datatypes">
    version="1.42.57" >
  ...
</xdr:Schema>
```

There are a few differences:

❑   Where XML Schema uses `<schema>`, XDR uses `<Schema>`

❑   Microsoft has chosen to supply its schemas using the URN mechanism, whilst the W3C uses URIs

❑   XDR wants its schemas to be named using the `name` attribute

This discussion of XDR is based upon Microsoft's so-called **XML Schema Reference** *[undated, now labeled © 2000, but previously shown as © 1999] at http://msdn.microsoft.com/xml/reference/schema/start.asp and its* **XML Schema Developer's Guide** *[ditto] and its related web pages, available at http://msdn.microsoft.com/xml/xmlguide/schema-overview.asp*

See also **XML-Data** *[5 January 1998] at http://www.w3.org/TR/NOTE-XML-data and* **Document Content Description for XML** *[31 July 1998, also known as DCD] available at http://www.w3.org/TR/NOTE-dcd*

Microsoft has promised to reimplement the schema support in MSXML and IE5 (or will it be IE6 by then?) to conform to the W3C's XML Schema standard – once it reaches the Final Recommendation status. For better or worse, there are already products shipping that use Microsoft's proprietary implementation – and it's uncertain how soon or how conformant this promised implementation will be, or what will then become of any existing products that depend upon the proprietary schemas.

Structures

Now that we've looked at datatypes and their defining components, let's look at the other part of XML Schema – structures. These declarations will let us describe datatypes, element types, element attributes, and **content models**.

As with DTDs, content models are a means of explicitly specifying the valid structure of elements and other components as a **document type**. This document type description, now called a schema (in part to differentiate it from a DTD), can then be used to validate document instances using a validating parser that supports XML Schema.

Datatype Definitions

XML Schema provides two types of datatype definitions: simple and complex (though there is a single exception to this dichotomy, as we'll see in a moment).

❑ **Simple** definitions are how we can create derived datatypes, including those that were built in to the schema specification

❑ **Complex** definitions are primarily used to describe content models, and will be discussed in great detail later in this section

The set of type definitions for a schema form a hierarchical tree with a single root (sound familiar?), known as the **Type Definition Hierarchy**. The root of this tree is called the **ur-type definition**, and is unique in that it can function as either a complex or a Simple Type Definition, according to its context. It can also be treated as the base type of some derived datatype. All other type definitions are constructed from some other datatype (the base type), using either **datatype extension** or **datatype restriction**.

Simple Type Definitions

> **A Simple Type Definition is a set of constraints on the value space *and* the lexical space of a datatype.**

These constraints are either a **restriction** on the base type, or the specification of a **list** type that's constrained by some other Simple Type Definition.

By definition, Simple Type Definitions for all the built-in primitive and derived datatypes are present in every schema. All of these are in the XML Schema target namespace (http://www.w3.org/1999/XMLSchema).

The <simpleType> Element

A Simple Type Definition uses the <simpleType> element, its attributes, and any valid constraining facet(s). The attribute names, and the attribute value's primitive datatype or enumerated values, are:

- ❑ name – NCName
- ❑ base – QName – OPTIONAL
- ❑ abstract – boolean – OPTIONAL
- ❑ derivedBy – (list | restriction) – OPTIONAL (default is restriction)

The meaning of the name attribute should be fairly obvious – it's the name of the datatype we are describing. Like all names in XML Schema, this must conform to the XML 1.0 name rules, and in this case the name must be a simple unqualified ("non-colonized") name.

The base attribute is the name of the base datatype. It must use a qualified name, in other words a name with a namespace identifier. If this is omitted, the ur-type is assumed to be the base type.

If abstract's value is true, then this type cannot appear as the type definition in an element declaration, and cannot be referenced as an xsi:type attribute in a document (see the definition of this attribute later in the chapter). This attribute is optional, and its default value is false.

The derivedBy attribute is used to declare whether the new <simpleType> is an atomic type (derived from another type, and restricting some facet of that base type), or a list type.

Simple types are identified by name and target namespace, and must be unique within a schema. No Simple Type Definition can have the same name as any other Simple or Complex Type Definition – the scope of type names includes both simple and complex types. However, datatype names can be the same as the name of an element or attribute.

The content of <simpleType> is comprised of one or more constraining facets (which we listed and described in the Datatypes section), which are represented as empty child elements. We can also include an annotation element with the content (more about annotation elements later in the chapter – basically, we can use them to add comments to our schemas). As we've seen, the list of legal constraining facets depends on the base datatype.

Derivation by Restriction

The built-in derived type `negativeInteger` is one example of a type derived by restriction:

```
<simpleType name="negativeInteger" base="xsi:integer">
  <maxInclusive value="-1" />
</simpleType>
```

In this definition, we've named the new simple datatype `negativeInteger`, and defined it as being derived from the built-in `integer` type. Remember that restriction is the default of the `derivedBy` attribute, so it can be omitted here.

Since integers are infinite, we wouldn't want to define a lower bound, but the upper bound is the very essence of this definition. This one constraining facet could just as easily have been expressed as:

```
<maxExclusive value="0" />
```

Let's look at a more complicated simple datatype, which uses the `pattern` facet. All telephone numbers in North America are 10-digit numbers comprised of a 3-digit Area Code, a 3-digit local exchange, and a 4-digit local number. The area code and exchange have some additional restrictions. The first digit of these can never be 0 or 1, since these numbers are used to signal operator and direct-dial long-distance dialing.

At one time, area codes also required the second digit of the area code to be limited to only 0 and 1, as a way of distinguishing between calls that were local (7 digits) and long distance (10 digits). This original style of area code could be specified as follows:

```
<simpleType name="AreaCode" base="xsi:string">
  <minLength value="3" />
  <maxLength value="3" />
  <pattern value="[2-9][0-1][0-9]" />
</simpleType>
```

An example of this derived datatype in a document instance might be:

```
<TelephoneNumber>
  <AreaCode>312</AreaCode>
  <Exchange>555</Exchange>
  <Number>1212</Number>
</TelephoneNumber>
```

Since hard-wired relay switching matrices have been replaced with solid-state electronics, this restriction is no longer needed. Therefore, we could define this less-restricted area code more simply as any integer in the range from 200 to 999, inclusive:

```
<simpleType name="AreaCode" base="xsi:integer">
  <minInclusive value="200" />
  <maxInclusive value="999" />
</simpleType>
```

This newer style would allow an area code that was formerly invalid, such as:

```
<AreaCode>925</AreaCode>
```

Because new style area codes are *less* restrictive than the original ones, we cannot derive the new type from the old – derivation by extension is limited to complex datatypes. And another reason why we can't derive the new from the old is that we've changed the base type.

Derivation by List

Datatypes derived by `list` contain a white space-delimited list of values that conform to the base type. A list datatype *must* be derived from an atomic datatype: it cannot be derived from another list type. The atomic type must also be suitable for inclusion in a list – remember that unconstrained strings containing white space cause problems when we attempt to make a list of strings.

For example, we might create a simple unbounded list of floating-point numbers:

```
<simpleType name="ListOfFloats" base="xsi:float" derivedBy="list" />
```

An example of this list datatype in a document instance might be:

```
<ListOfFloats>-INF -1.02E01 -0.42e1 0</ListOfFloats>
```

This example has a length of four (remember that the units of length depend on the datatype, and list types count the number of items in the list). If we wanted to further constrain our datatype to require a length of four, we can do so using the `length` facet. The new type definition would look something like this:

```
<simpleType name="ListOfFloats" base="xsi:float" derivedBy="list">
  <length value="4" />
</simpleType>
```

This limits our type to being a list of exactly four items. If we wanted the list to be of variable-length, but restricted to a specific finite length, we could specify a range instead:

```
<simpleType name="ListOfFloats" base="xsi:float" derivedBy="list">
  <minLength value="1" />
  <maxLength value="100" />
</simpleType>
```

This re-definition allows any list of one to 100 floating-point numbers.

Complex Type Definitions

> **A Complex Type Definition is a set of attribute declarations and a content type that respectively pertain to the attributes and children of the element type that's being specified.**

The content type describes the element's content model, just like content models in DTDs. Of course, XML Schema has much better content modeling than a DTD, as we'll see in the rest of this chapter.

Like Simple Type Definitions, a Complex Type Definition may be a restriction on a base type definition. In addition, a Complex Type Definition can be an extension of a simple or complex base type, or a restriction of the ur-type definition.

A complex type extends another type by appending additional content model declarations and/or additional attribute declarations. At the present time, no other kind of extension is allowed (to simplify application processing of derived types), although future versions of XML Schema may allow other kinds.

Complex type definitions will, for the given complex type:

❑   Provide a mechanism to validate a document instance containing the type

❑   Describe element attribute existence and content

❑   Describe content of an element type, which may be element-only, text-only, mixed, or empty

❑   Derive its definition from another simple or complex type, in accordance with the Type Definition Hierarchy

❑   Control the ability to derive additional types

The first three of these are similar to, but more powerful than, the comparable features of an XML 1.0 DTD. The latter two are the OO features that really make XML Schema shine.

The <complexType> Element

A Complex Type Definition uses the <complexType> element, its attributes, and any valid constraining facet(s). The attribute names, and the attribute value's primitive datatype or enumerated values, are:

❑   name – NCName – OPTIONAL

❑   base – QName – OPTIONAL

❑   abstract – boolean – OPTIONAL

❑   derivedBy – (extension | restriction)

❑   content – (elementOnly | empty | mixed | textOnly)

❑   block – "" or (#all | (extension | restriction)) – OPTIONAL

❑   final – "" or (#all | (extension | restriction)) – OPTIONAL

The first three of these attributes are the same as those used in the Simple Type Definition. The derivedBy attribute is similar, but it must be explicitly set to one of the enumerated values.

The content attribute is comparable to the DTD's content choices of #PCDATA, EMPTY, or an implied element-only or mixed content model. We'll see more about the differences between schema and DTD content later in the chapter.

The last of these attributes control the OO inheritance features of schema type definitions.

The `block` attribute value determines whether an element declaration in a content model is prevented from validating particular elements. This can be useful when we only need to validate a portion of a document– if we don't care about the other parts, we can write our schema accordingly. We can specify elements with an `xsi:type` attribute that's derived by `extension` or `restriction`, or any similarly-derived elements in an equivalence class (more about these later). If the `block` value is empty or absent, there are no restrictions on these substitutions.

The `final` attribute specifies whether or not the complex type may be used as the base type for another datatype (and if so, how). This is similar to a final variable in Java. If its value is `#all` then no further type derivation is allowed. If the value is `extension` or `restriction`, then another type can be derived, but not by the method specified.

As with `<simpleType>`, the content of `<complexType>` is comprised of one or more constraining facets, which are represented as empty child elements. There are also a number of additional children, such as `<element>` and `<attribute>`, that are used to describe the content model of the complex datatype. As before, annotation elements may also be included in the content.

Before we discuss these additional children of `<complexType>`, let's just show an example of how one of our familiar element types from the last chapter might be represented in XML Schema.

Revisiting Our `<PersonName>` DTD

In the last chapter, we finally settled upon the following DTD definition of the `<PersonName>` element type:

```
<!ELEMENT  FirstName   (#PCDATA) >
<!ELEMENT  MiddleName  (#PCDATA) >
<!ELEMENT  LastName    (#PCDATA) >
<!ELEMENT  SingleName  (#PCDATA) >

<!ELEMENT  PersonName (SingleName | (FirstName, MiddleName*, LastName)) >
<!ATTLIST  PersonName
  honorific  (Mr. | Ms. | Dr. | Rev.)  #IMPLIED
  suffix  (Jr. | Sr. | I | II | III | IV | V | VI | VII | VIII)  #IMPLIED
>
```

As you'll probably remember, there are five element types (`<PersonName>` and its four children), and two optional attributes for `<PersonName>`, each of which uses an enumerated attribute type. The content model of `<PersonName>` is fairly simple: a sequence list (for a full name) nested within a choice list that allows for the `<SingleName>` alternate name form.

All of the children of `<PersonName>` are restricted to be simple `#PCDATA` (character data only), and all except one are required to be present and singular. The exception, `<MiddleName>`, is optional, with zero or more occurrences allowed (as indicated by the * cardinality operator). An example document instance that conforms to this definition is:

```
<PersonName honorific="Mr." suffix="Jr.">
  <FirstName>John</FirstName>
  <MiddleName>Q</MiddleName>
  <LastName>Public</LastName>
</PersonName>
```

1. The following is an XML Schema representation of these element type and attribute definitions:

```
<?xml version="1.0">

<xsd:schema xmlns:xsd="http://www.w3.org/1999/XMLSchema">

 <xsd:simpleType name="PersonTitle" base="xsd:string">
  <xsd:enumeration value="Mr." />
  <xsd:enumeration value="Ms." />
  <xsd:enumeration value="Dr." />
  <xsd:enumeration value="Rev." />
 </xsd:simpleType>

 <xsd:complexType name="Text" content="textOnly" base="xsd:string"
                  derivedBy="restriction" />

 <xsd:element name="PersonName">
  <xsd:complexType content="element">

   <xsd:choice>
    <xsd:element name="SingleName" type="Text" minOccurs="1"
                 maxOccurs="1" />
    <xsd:sequence>
     <xsd:element name="FirstName" type="Text" minOccurs="1"
                  maxOccurs="1" />
     <xsd:element name="MiddleName" type="Text" minOccurs="0"
                  maxOccurs="unbounded" />
     <xsd:element name="LastName" type="Text" minOccurs="1" maxOccurs="1" />
    </xsd:sequence>
   </xsd:choice>

   <xsd:attribute name="honorific" type="PersonTitle" />

   <xsd:attribute name="suffix">
    <xsd:simpleType base="xsd:string">
     <xsd:enumeration value="Jr." />
     <xsd:enumeration value="Sr." />
     <xsd:enumeration value="I" />
     <xsd:enumeration value="II" />
     <xsd:enumeration value="III" />              <!-- ..and so on... -->
    </xsd:simpleType>
   </xsd:attribute>

  </xsd:complexType>
 </xsd:element>

</xsd:schema>
```

2. Our document instance from above also conforms to this schema:

```
<PersonName honorific="Mr." suffix="Jr.">
  <FirstName>John</FirstName>
  <MiddleName>Q</MiddleName>
  <LastName>Public</LastName>
</PersonName>
```

How It Works

Most of these names and values are common to both the DTD and the schema, but what are these new declarations all about?

The first line is the XML declaration which *should* begin all XML files, schema or otherwise:

```
<?xml version="1.0">
```

We've omitted the `encoding` attribute since we're using the default value (UTF-8) for most of the examples in this book. However, this can be any valid XML encoding (*e.g.* UTF-16, ISO-8859-1) – an XML schema can be written in any language that can be represented with Unicode characters.

The second line probably looks familiar since we saw one just like it earlier in the chapter:

```
<xsd:schema xmlns:xsd="http://www.w3.org/1999/XMLSchema">
```

This is a critical aspect of XML Schema – the ability to include schemas from various sources (and one of the biggest problems with DTDs is the inability to do this easily). Remember, you don't have to use `xsd` as the namespace identifier, but `xsd` *is* the recommended convention.

> **For the sake of clarity, after this section we'll omit this prefix in the text, and just use unqualified names (for example `<simpleType>`). We'll also assume that we've designated the W3C's XML Schema as the default namespace, so we can omit the prefix in our examples, as well.**

The next definition uses a `<simpleType>` definition:

```
<xsd:simpleType name="PersonTitle" base="xsd:string">
  <xsd:enumeration value="Mr." />
  <xsd:enumeration value="Ms." />
  <xsd:enumeration value="Dr." />
  <xsd:enumeration value="Rev." />
</xsd:simpleType>
```

We've used the `<enumeration>` constraining facet to limit this datatype to a small list of legal string values, just as we did with an enumerated attribute type in the DTD. Later, we'll use this newly derived type *by reference* in an `<attribute>` declaration.

Our first `<complexType>` definition illustrates a simple form of this schema component:

```
<xsd:complexType name="Text" content="textOnly" base="xsd:string"
                 derivedBy="restriction" />
```

This will be useful shorthand when we use it later in some `<element>` declarations. The key issue here is the `content` attribute – any element that's declared to be of the `Text` type may only contain character data, no child elements are permitted. This is the equivalent of the `#PCDATA` attribute type in the DTD.

We can now declare the `<PersonName>` element type, with element-only content:

```
<xsd:element name="PersonName">
 <xsd:complexType content="element">

  <xsd:choice>
   <xsd:element name="SingleName" type="Text" minOccurs="1"
                maxOccurs="1" />
   <xsd:sequence>
    <xsd:element name="FirstName" type="Text" minOccurs="1"
                 maxOccurs="1" />
    <xsd:element name="MiddleName" type="Text" minOccurs="0"
                 maxOccurs="unbounded" />
    <xsd:element name="LastName" type="Text" minOccurs="1" maxOccurs="1" />
   </xsd:sequence>
  </xsd:choice>
```

The `<element>` element is analogous to a part of the `<!ELEMENT..>` declaration in a DTD. We'll look at this in much more detail later in this chapter.

The `<choice>` element is analogous to the `|` operator in a DTD. So this allows a choice between a single `<SingleName>` element and a sequence list (like the comma-separated list in a DTD) that gives a person's full name. We'll look at `<choice>` in more detail shortly.

Like all such datatypes and declarations in XML Schema, `<PersonName>` will inherit its properties from other components of the schema (such as our `Text` user-derived datatype, which in turn inherits properties from the `string` built-in primitive datatype).

The `<complexType>` without any name attribute shows the use of an **anonymous type**. This intermediary is necessary because an `<element>` cannot use the `content` attribute to specify the element-only content model. In XML Schema, `<element>` is used for naming the element type, but content models need to be described with a `<complexType>`, either named or anonymous.

We've declared the `<PersonName>` element at the **global** level (it's a direct child of `<schema>`), so this element definition can be used anywhere within the schema, and could be shared with another external schema. On the other hand, the children of `<PersonName>` are declared within an anonymous `<complexType>` and therefore only have a **local** scope.

We also declare two attributes of `<PersonName>` here. The first uses the named `<simpleType>` that we defined earlier in this example:

```
<xsd:simpleType name="PersonTitle" base="xsd:string">
 ...
<xsd:attribute name="honorific" type="PersonTitle" />
```

The second uses an anonymous type to connect a series of enumerated values to the enclosing `<attribute>` declaration. This declaration is similar to the `<!ATTLIST..>` declaration in a DTD, and, again, we'll be discussing it later in this chapter.

```
<xsd:attribute name="suffix">
 <xsd:simpleType base="xsd:string">
  <xsd:enumeration value="Jr." />
  <xsd:enumeration value="Sr." />
  <xsd:enumeration value="I" />
  <xsd:enumeration value="II" />
  <xsd:enumeration value="III" />                 <!-- ..and so on... -->
 </xsd:simpleType>
</xsd:attribute>
```

Lastly, we need to close the `<schema>` element to indicate the end of the schema. Although in this example `<schema>` is the document element, it could have been contained instead within some other element. This allows us to include a schema within another XML document – which can of course be another schema, or perhaps a text document that describes the schema embedded within.

> A **`<schema>`** element is the "root" of that schema's element tree, but it need not be the overall document element.

Now that we've had a quick overview of a simple schema, let's look at content models and their various related declarations in greater detail.

Content Models

As we saw in the last chapter, a content model is the formal description of the structure and permissible content of an element, which may be used to validate a document instance. In other words, the content model of our `<PersonName>` element is described in DTD syntax as:

```
<!ELEMENT PersonName (SingleName | (FirstName, MiddleName*, LastName)) >
```

whilst the following is the comparable schema syntax (attribute declarations have been omitted):

```
<element name="PersonName">
  <complexType content="elementOnly">
    <choice>
      <element name="SingleName" type="Text" minOccurs="1" maxOccurs="1" />
      <sequence>
        <element name="FirstName" type="Text" minOccurs="1" maxOccurs="1" />
```

```
        <element name="MiddleName" type="Text" minOccurs="0"
                maxOccurs="unbounded" />
        <element name="LastName" type="Text" minOccurs="1" maxOccurs="1" />
    </sequence>
</choice>

...

    </complexType>
</element>
```

Although this form of the content model is much more verbose, it allows us much finer control of child element occurrences (though we aren't using this ability just yet). If we'd chosen to name the `<complexType>`, we could reuse the element description in this and other schemas – this is one of the big advantages of XML Schema over DTDs. We'll see more of the enhanced content model descriptions in the next section, and in the rest of this chapter.

Element Content Categories

We used the `content` attribute in the unnamed `<complexType>` element above to explicitly categorize the content model of this datatype (instead of using the half explicit, half implicit categories in a DTD). As we've already seen, this optional attribute has four legal values – `elementOnly`, `textOnly`, `empty`, or `mixed` – and if it's omitted, its default value is `elementOnly`.

One major difference between DTDs and XML Schema involves the `mixed` content model. With a DTD, when we specify mixed content (in other words the first item in the content model is #PCDATA), we lose the ability to dictate the sequence of child elements within their parent. So, despite the *appearance* of a sequence list that could be validated using the DTD, the children may actually appear in any order in the document instance. In a schema, the sequence of the children within an `<element>` declaration is respected, and thus the order of the children in a document instance *can* be validated against the schema.

> **Unlike the XML 1.0 DTD, XML Schema may be used to validate mixed content.**

The `textOnly` attribute value is comparable to the DTD's #PCDATA declaration. As such, no child elements are allowed within an element that carries this type of content description. As you probably assumed, the `empty` value is essentially identical to the DTD's ELEMENT declaration.

The richness of XML Schema content models lies below this broader surface. In addition to the significantly different mixed content model, most of the other declarations have additional capabilities, as we'll see in the next few sections.

Cardinality – minOccurs and maxOccurs

XML Schema is a more powerful superset of a DTD when describing the possible or permitted occurrences of an element's children. The following table shows the mapping of DTD cardinality operators to the equivalent values of `minOccurs` and `maxOccurs` schema attributes:

Cardinality Operator	minOccurs Value	maxOccurs Value	Number of Child Element(s)
[none]	1	1	One and only one
?	0	1	Zero or one
*	0	unbounded	Zero or more
+	1	unbounded	One or more

These attributes determine the minimum and maximum number of times an element may occur, and both of them are optional. The default value for minOccurs is 1, but there is no single default for maxOccurs *per se*. If minOccurs is present and maxOccurs is omitted, its value is assumed to be equal to the value of minOccurs. If both attributes are omitted, there may only be one occurrence of the element and it is required (just like the absence of a cardinality operator in a DTD). The value of unbounded, which is allowed only for maxOccurs, is just the formal way of saying "..or more [without a limit]" in a schema.

You may remember that our BookCatalog DTD example in Chapter 9 used a rather clunky method of specifying that a <Book> could have only one, two, or three subject classifications:

```
<!ELEMENT SubjectRefs (SubjectRef, SubjectRef?, SubjectRef?) >
```

Whilst this worked for a small set of children, imagine how cumbersome it becomes when we want to constrain an element to have, say, one to fifty children! This is one of the times where a schema representation can actually be much more compact than that of a DTD. In schema form, this example would be:

```
<element name="SubjectRefs">
  <complexType>
    <element name="SubjectRef" minOccurs="1" maxOccurs="3" />
  </complexType>
</element>
```

Both of these attributes may also have any non-negative integer value, which allows us constraints that aren't possible in DTDs. This removes the DTD limitation of a lower bound that can only be zero or one. The DTD's upper bound can only be one or (infinitely) many – with XML Schema this bound can be restricted to any number between one and infinity (inclusive).

Choice and Sequence Groups – <choice> and <sequence>

These two elements are pretty much self-describing – they correspond to the choice (|) and sequence (,) list operators in a DTD.

Although the schema representation is more verbose than that of the DTD, it is arguably easier to read and understand a schema content model, especially if we use an XML-aware editor or browser. This is another time where XML syntax is a great advantage – the content model can be revealed and manipulated as XML, using a nice GUI tree-structure tool that can collapse/expand the content model's element tree structure. A very complex DTD content model often has lotsa inane stupefying parentheses, which can confound even the most careful reader.

One of our early, non-attribute versions of `<PersonName>` used child elements for the honorific and name suffix. These children were to appear as specified in a sequence list that contained two choice lists:

```
<!ELEMENT PersonName
    ((Mr.|Ms.|Dr.|Rev.)?, FirstName, MiddleName*, LastName, (Jr.|Sr.|III)?) >
```

The comparable XML Schema would be:

```
<element name="PersonName">
  <complexType>
    <sequence>
      <choice minOccurs="0" maxOccurs="1">
        <element name="Mr." />
        <element name="Ms." />
        <element name="Dr." />
        <element name="Rev." />
      </choice>
      <element name="FirstName" minOccurs="1" />
      <element name="MiddleName" minOccurs="0" maxOccurs="unbounded" />
      <element name="LastName" minOccurs="1" />
      <choice minOccurs="0" maxOccurs="1">
        <element name="Jr." />
        <element name="Sr." />
        <element name="III" />
      </choice>
    <sequence>
  </complexType>
</element>
```

Notice that we've applied the cardinality attributes to an entire choice list, just like in the DTD. Since the `<element>` declaration could also use these attributes, we could create a much more complex variety of choices with a schema.

Mixed Content (Unsequenced Group) – <all>

This element can be used to specify which child elements can be present, without requiring them to appear in any specific sequence. Each child element is optional, and none may appear more than once. This grouping element is also limited to the top level of the content model, and none of the children may be any kind of element group.

> *SGML note: <all> is a simplified version of the SGML &-Connector.*

For example, to allow the child elements of a more limited version of our `<PersonName>` element to appear in any order, we could redefine it as:

```
<element name="PersonName">
  <complexType>
    <all>
      <element name="FirstName" minOccurs="1" />
      <element name="MiddleName" minOccurs="0" maxOccurs="1" />
```

```
        <element name="LastName" minOccurs="1" />
      </all>
    </complexType>
  </element>
```

Due to one of the restrictions of the `<all>` declaration, we've had to change our `<MiddleName>` child element to occur once or not at all, instead of allowing multiple middle names as before.

Two examples of equally valid (albeit somewhat silly) documents using this content model are:

```
<PersonName>
  <LastName>Doe</LastName>
  <FirstName>Jane</FirstName>
</PersonName>
```

and:

```
<PersonName>
  <MiddleName>Q</MiddleName>
  <FirstName>John</FirstName>
  <LastName>Public</LastName>
</PersonName>
```

Whilst there is no need for a `name` attribute for the `<all>` element (due to its defined limits), it may have a unique identifier (`ID` attribute) for reference purposes.

Content From Another Schema – <any>

This element can be used to provide something similar to a DTD's `ANY` content model, but only in conjunction with namespaces. This allows inclusion of any well-formed XML, such as an HTML web page that conforms to XHTML 1.0 syntax.

For example:

```
<element name="SomeWebpage">
  <complexType>
    <any
      namespace="http://www.w3.org/1999/xhtml"
      minOccurs="0" maxOccurs="unbounded"
      processContents="skip" />
  </complexType>
</element>
```

This schema fragment allows a `<SomeWebpage>` element to contain any well-formed XHTML data that appears in the specified namespace.

The `processContents` attribute value of `"skip"` tells the XML parser that it doesn't need to validate the XHTML content. If this attribute is set to `"strict"` (the default value), the parser needs to obtain the schema associated with the namespace and validate the XHTML data – and if it can't find the schema, it reports an error. The middle ground is the `"lax"` value – if the parser can find the schema, it will validate the data as much as possible, but if the schema isn't found, no error is reported.

Model Groups – <group>

A **model group** is the portion of a Complex Type Definition that describes an element's content. A model group consists of element declarations, wildcards, and other model groups. In our recurring <PersonName> example above, there's an implicit group of elements, but it's also possible to create named model groups that can then be used by reference elsewhere in a schema.

For example, we can create a model group for our 1-to-3 book subjects:

```
<group name="SubjectRefs">
  <sequence>
    <element name="SubjectRef" minOccurs="1" maxOccurs="3" />
  </sequence>
</group>
```

Later in the schema, we can simply refer to the group by name, and it will inherit this description, as if it were inline within the choice list below:

```
<element name="Book">
  <complexType>
...
    <choice>
      <group ref="SubjectRefs" minOccurs="0" maxOccurs="1" />
      <element name="SomeOtherRefs" minOccurs="1" />
    </choice>
  </complexType>
</element>
```

Notice the <group> element is used for both the definition of a group and any reference to a named group. In the first fragment of this section (which must be at the top level of the schema) the group is defined, using <group name="SubjectRefs"..>. In the second fragment, it's used by reference within a Complex Type Definition (i.e. <group ref="SubjectRefs"..>).

Now that we've looked at the method of representing content models in XML Schema, it's time to find out how to describe child elements and attributes for a given element type.

Element Declarations

As we've seen in our earlier examples, the schema element declaration (<element>) is very similar to the <!ELEMENT..> declaration in a DTD. This definition of the fundamental building block of XML is more powerful, albeit more verbose, in XML Schema than it is in a DTD. In particular, strong data-typing and more comprehensive content modeling provide ways to describe complex data models that are not feasible with a DTD.

Element declarations:

❑   Provide a description that can be used for validation

❑   Provide value constraints, including default values

❑   Establish constraining relationships between related elements and attributes

❑   Control substitution of elements (using element equivalence classes)

In XML Schema, an element declaration may have a global scope, or be limited to the scope of a containing complex datatype. Like the DTD, a schema element declaration may be used to validate the structure and content of the defined element type in a document instance. In addition, since schemas were designed to work with XML namespaces, multiple vocabularies, from a variety of sources, can be supported within a single document.

> *There are also some advanced features unique to XML Schema (e.g. **element equivalence classes**, **wildcards**) that are beyond the scope of this book. Element equivalence classes provide a more powerful content model, where it's possible to substitute one named element for another. Any global element declaration can be the defining element of an element equivalence class. Other global element declarations can then declare themselves as members of this class, and they'll be validated according to the rules they inherit from it. Wildcards are a mechanism whereby we can match element and attribute names based on their namespace URI, and independently of their local names.*

Let's revisit a portion of our recurring `<PersonName>` example from the last section, and look at it in more detail as expressed in XML Schema form (we're assuming that XML Schema is the default namespace, so that we can omit the `xsd:` namespace prefix everywhere, and we've also omitted the `<attribute>` declarations for now):

```
<choice>
  <element name="SingleName" type="Text" minOccurs="1" maxOccurs="1"/>
  <sequence>
    <element name="FirstName" type="Text" minOccurs="1" maxOccurs="1"/>
    <element name="MiddleName" type="Text" minOccurs="0"
             maxOccurs="unbounded"/>
    <element name="LastName" type="Text" minOccurs="1" maxOccurs="1"/>
  </sequence>
</choice>
```

Since we've already discussed the similarities between the DTD and schema representations, let's focus on the details of the schema `<element>`, `<choice>`, and `<sequence>` declarations.

First of all, it's important to distinguish between the *definition* of datatypes (via the `<complexType>` declaration) and the *declarations* that describe the element's content (child elements and attributes). The former describes a datatype, whilst the latter are used to describe the structure of the document type for validation. Hopefully, this distinction will become clearer in a moment, when we use the complex `<PersonName>` datatype within a `<Person>` element.

Element Constraints – `<element>`

An `<element>` element may contain: zero or one `<annotation>` elements, zero or one datatype declarations (either `simpleType` or `complexType`), and zero or more key-related child elements (don't worry about these last children, they're outside the scope of this discussion) – in the order presented here.

`<element>` has 14 different possible attributes, about half of which we won't discuss here since they pertain to advanced aspects of XML Schema. A few more are mutually exclusive, as we'll see in a moment. There are eight attributes that are worth looking at now:

Attribute Name	Valid Datatype	Default Value (if any)	Description
name	NCName	none	The name of the element being declared
ref	QName	none	The name of a previously defined `<element>`
type	QName	none	Any valid built-in or user-derived datatype
minOccurs	non NegativeInteger	1	Minimum number of occurrences allowed
maxOccurs	string	minOccurs	Maximum number of occurrences allowed (if not specified, default value will be same as value of minOccurs)
default	string	none	Define element's default value
fixed	string	none	Define element's constant (default) value
id	ID	none	A unique identifier for the element

The other attributes that may be used for `<element>` *are:* `abstract`, `block`, `equivClass`, `final`, `form`, *and* `nullable`.

The `name` attribute must be a simple XML-legal unqualified name (an `NCName`, or "non-colonized name") that is unique within the scope of the schema. No `name` attribute can have a value of `xmlns`, since this value is reserved for use with namespaces.

The `ref` attribute must be a qualified name (as specified in ***Namespaces in XML***) that is unique within the scope of the namespace. This attribute is used to refer to an existing element description – and an element using this attribute inherits the constraints of the element that's being referenced.

The `type` attribute is used to constrain the content of the named element. In our Try It Out above, we created the `Text` datatype primarily as an illustrative example, but it's really just another way of saying that these elements may only contain character data – `Text` was defined as being derived from the `string` type, with `content="textOnly"`:

```
<xsd:complexType name="Text" content="textOnly" base="xsd:string"
                 derivedBy="restriction" />
```

The `minOccurs` and `maxOccurs` attributes describe the cardinality of the child elements. If `maxOccurs` is not explicitly specified, it will assume the value of `minOccurs` as its default.

Attribute Declarations

Again, it's no surprise that the `<attribute>` schema declaration is similar to an `<!ATTLIST..>` declaration in a DTD. An `<attribute>` declaration associates an attribute name with a specific simple datatype.

Attribute declarations:

❑ Provide a description that can be used for validation

❑ Constrain attribute values to a specific simple datatype

❑ Require/prevent the appearance of an attribute

❑ Provide default (or fixed) attribute values

Attribute declarations may appear in two places within a schema:

❑ As a globally scoped ("top-level") declaration within the `<schema>` element

❑ Within a `<complexType>` declaration, either as a local declaration or as a reference to a global declaration.

The namespace declarations within our example `<schema>` element are globally scoped – they apply to all elements within the schema. The local version (within the `<complexType>` declaration) is used for all of our BookCatalog attributes, as we shall see shortly.

When an attribute is declared, its type can be constrained to one of the built-in or user-declared simple types, or it can be included as an anonymous `<simpleType>` declaration within the content of the `<attribute>` element. If no type definition is referenced or included, the attribute type is unconstrained.

Top-level attribute names have their own symbol space. Locally-scoped names are a part of the symbol space of their containing type definition, unless the form attribute is "qualified", in which case they must be namespace-qualified.

Attribute Constraints – <attribute>

An `<attribute>` element may only contain:

❑ zero or one `<annotation>` elements

❑ zero or one `<simpleType>` elements

in that order.

This element has seven different possible attributes, a few of which are mutually exclusive (see below):

Attribute Name	Valid Datatype	Default Value (if any)	Description
name	NCName	none	The name of the attribute being declared
ref	QName	none	The name of a previously defined <attribute>
type	QName	none	Any valid built-in or user-derived simple datatype
use	enumerated (see below)	optional	Attribute value constraint
value	string	none	Defines the attribute's default value
id	ID	none	A unique identifier for the attribute
form	enumerated (see below)	none	Specifies whether or not the name attribute must be a qualified name

As with elements, the name attribute must be a simple XML-legal unqualified name (an NCName, or "non-colonized name") that is unique within the scope of the schema. And again, no name attribute may have a value of xmlns.

```
<attribute name="anything_goes" />
```

This example is unconstrained, so only default validity and structural constraints will be applied. The ref attribute also follows the same rules as the ref attribute of <element>.

The type attribute constrains the content of the named attribute. It must be a simple type, whether built-in or user-defined.

The use attribute is used to dictate how (and if) attributes may appear within elements described by the containing <element> declaration (the attribute's "parent element"). The legal values for this attribute are:

❑ default – the attribute being declared has a default value (as specified with the value attribute)

❑ fixed – the attribute has a constant value (specified with the value attribute)

❑ optional – the attribute is optional (the default value of the use attribute)

❑ required – the attribute is required, and must always be used with the parent element

❑ prohibited – no attribute may be present for the parent element

So we'd declare a required attribute that must be an `integer` (one of the built-in simple datatypes) like this:

```
<attribute name="quantity" type="dt:integer" use="required" />
```

We can also define a relatively rare "constant value" attribute, where the attribute value must always be "`Bonjour!`":

```
<attribute name="greeting" type="dt:string" use="fixed" value="Bonjour!" />
```

An alternate way to declare the type of an attribute is inline, using a `<simpleType>` child element within the `<attribute>`. If this alternative is used, the `type` attribute may not appear:

```
<attribute name="us_state_rank" use="default" value="50" >
  <simpleType base="positiveInteger">
    <minInclusive value="1" />
    <maxInclusive value="50" />
  </simpleType>
</attribute>
```

This example shows a complex form of declaration, where the `type` of the attribute is explicitly defined within the declaration as a positive integer in the range 1 to 50 (inclusive). There's also a default value specified.

The `form` attribute may have a value of either `qualified` or `unqualified`. This attribute is used to define the `name` or `ref` attribute's interaction with namespaces.

If the `<attribute>` is not global (in other words if its parent isn't `<schema>`), then either a `name` or `ref` attribute must be present. If `ref` is present, then both the `type` attribute and the `<simpleType>` element content must be absent. In any case, the `type` attribute and the `<simpleType>` content are mutually exclusive.

Now that we've looked at the specification of a single attribute, we'll look at how we can create groups of attribute declarations, for use within multiple element type declarations.

Attribute Groups – <attributeGroup>

Named groups of attribute declarations can greatly facilitate the maintenance and reuse of common attribute declarations in an XML Schema. The `<attributeGroup>` declaration is for attributes what the `<group>` declaration is for elements. An attribute group can be used by reference within an `<attribute>` or other `<attributeGroup>` elements.

An `<attributeGroup>` element may only contain: zero or one `<annotation>` elements, zero or more `<attribute>` or `<attributeGroup>` elements, and zero or one `<anyAttribute>` elements – in that order.

This element has three different possible attributes:

Attribute Name	Valid Datatype	Default Value (if any)	Description
name	NCName	none	The name of the attribute group being declared
ref	QName	none	The name of a previously defined `<attribute>` or `<attributeGroup>`
id	ID	none	A unique identifier for the attribute group

These `name` and `ref` attributes have the same rules as the `<element>` and `<attribute>` declarations that we've already discussed. The `ref` attribute is used to refer an existing attribute group description, and any attribute using this inherits the constraints of the attribute group that's being referenced.

Using `<attributeGroup>` Declaration

The following example shows the definition of an `<attributeGroup>` declaration and its later use by reference (the by-now familiar `<PersonName>` content model has been omitted for clarity):

```
<attributeGroup name="PersonNameExtras">
  <attribute name="honorific" type="PersonTitle" />
    <simpleType base="string">
      <enumeration value="Mr." />
      <enumeration value="Ms." />
      <enumeration value="Dr." />
      <enumeration value="Rev." />
    </simpleType>
  </attribute>
  <attribute name="suffix">
    <simpleType base="string">
      <enumeration value="Jr." />
      <enumeration value="Sr." />
      <enumeration value="I" />
      <enumeration value="II" />
      <enumeration value="III" />
    </simpleType>
  </attribute>
</attributeGroup>

<element name="PersonName">
  <complexType content="elementOnly">
    <choice>
      :
    </choice>
    <attributeGroup ref="PersonNameExtras" />
  </complexType>
</element>
```

The empty `<attributeGroup>` element within the `<PersonName>` element declaration is functionally equivalent to our earlier examples where the `<attribute>` declarations were included inline.

Annotations

Since an XML schema is just regular well-formed XML, it may include comments using the XML comment syntax:

```
<!-- This is an inane XML comment! -->
```

However, due to the XML 1.0 parser rules, an XML parser doesn't need to pass comments on to the application – any comments that appear in an XML document instance may just be discarded. Whilst this design decision makes sense in view of the widespread (and problematic) practice of embedding scripting languages within HTML comments, we do sometimes need to be able to annotate a schema and have these annotations preserved.

XML Schema has provided three elements for schema metadata, for both applications and human readers:

❑ `<annotation>` – the parent of the other two, it can appear almost anywhere in a schema, usually as the first child of some other element

❑ `<appInfo>` – this element is designated for schema information that's useful to external applications

❑ `<documentation>` – this element is the place for "comments" that are intended for people using the schema, such as an abstract, copyright and other legal information

> It is important to remember that the `<appInfo>` and `<documentation>` elements cannot be used alone – they must be children of the `<annotation>` element.

An interesting example of the use of the `<appInfo>` element is within the XML Schema specification itself. The schema that describes the constraining facets of simple datatypes included this annotation element. An application then used these elements to generate additional text for the Datatypes part of the specification.

Try It Out – Using Annotation Elements

We can add several of these elements in various places within our ongoing example schema.

1. Make the following changes to our earlier example:

```
<?xml version="1.0">
<schema xmlns="http://www.w3.org/1999/XMLSchema">
  <annotation>
    <appInfo>Wrox Schema - Annotations example</appInfo>
    <documentation>Schema is Copyright 2000 by Wrox Press Ltd.
    </documentation>
  </annotation>

  . . .
```

```
<element name="PersonName">
  <complexType content="elementOnly">
    <annotation>
      <documentation>
        The use of the &lt;SingleName&gt; element solves the 'Cher'
        problem.
      </documentation>
    </annotation>
    <choice>

...

    </choice>

...

  </complexType>
</element>
</schema>
```

You may have noticed that we made the XML Schema our default namespace, so we don't need to prefix every element type name with "xsd:".

The <appInfo> element provides a title for this schema that could be used by our XML application for display, or some other purpose. The <documentation> elements all provide information for the author and other readers of this schema.

Summary

In this chapter, we've introduced XML schemas – an alternative way to constrain the structure and nature of data items in our XML, as well as the relationships between those data items. In particular we've discussed XML Schema – the W3C's proposal for an XML schema standard.

We've seen:

- ❏   The advantages that schemas offer us over DTDs

- ❏   How to associate schemas with XML documents

- ❏   The basic datatypes available in XML Schema

- ❏   What structures are, and how we can define them

> **In the code download for this book, available from the Wrox web site (http://www.wrox.com), you'll find an example of how we can rework our `BookCatalog` example using schemas.**

Now that we've covered all the basic principles behind DTDs and schemas, we'll move on in the next chapter to look at some more advanced topics involving data validation.

Advanced Valid XML

In Chapter 9 (Basic Valid XML: DTDs), we discussed the basic rules of the XML 1.0 DTD syntax, and how to construct a simple DTD for our `BookCatalog` XML document. In this chapter, we'll address the more advanced features of DTDs that we didn't discuss in depth in that chapter.

We can categorize these roughly as:

- ❏ Replaceable content (internal/external entities and the `<!ENTITY>` declaration)
- ❏ Standardized content (ISO and other character entity sets)
- ❏ Handling non-XML data (the two `ENTITY` attribute types and the `<!NOTATION>` declaration)
- ❏ Conditional sections

We'll also revisit the topic of internal versus external subsets of the DTD and the `standalone` attribute.

Replaceable content is a key maintenance and time-saving concept. Instead of using the same text over and over again in multiple documents, we can put this boiler-plate text in a separate file, and then include it *by reference* in our documents. We can also use symbolic names for special characters in our documents, by including references to pre-defined character entity sets. Many of these are standardized by international organizations such as the ISO, whilst others have been created for specific industries or purposes.

XML is based upon text data, but not all data is textual. We need some way to include in our XML documents *references* to external data, such as images, spreadsheet files, and other binary data formats. This is done in a similar, but more general, way to HTML's `<IMG>` element type. We describe the non-XML data in the DTD, including some reference to the external application that can handle this data (since the XML parser can't do it for us). Then, when we refer to external data, like an image, within our document, the XML application will have this information available to either use itself, or pass on to a helper application.

Lastly, we'll look at another commonly-used programming technique: conditional code (in this case, it's conditional *markup*, of course). Often when developing a new DTD, or adding a new section to an existing DTD, it is useful to be able to include different declarations in the DTD, depending upon different situations. Especially in the case of additions to an existing DTD, we may need to preserve an existing content model for production purposes, but also want to test changes without using a completely separate DTD.

Entities

All XML documents are comprised of units of storage called **entities**. For example, the **document entity** serves as the entry point for an XML parser, and contains the entire document (including the document element and its tree of children, and any other declarations that precede or follow the document element). The internal and external subsets of the DTD are also entities, albeit unnamed ones. Other types of entities are always identified and referred to by name. These are the key to replaceable content in both DTDs and documents, so we will look at several different forms of entities in this chapter.

The two main categories of entities are:

❑   **General entities**, usable within any XML document

❑   **Parameter entities**, which may only be used in DTDs

Not only do these two types use different syntax, they also occupy different symbol spaces (namespaces). It's therefore possible (though perhaps inadvisable) to have a general entity and a parameter entity use the same name without any conflict.

General entities may be either **internal** or **external**, in other words within the DTD or located in an external file. There are two kinds of general entities:

❑   **Parsed entities** (can be either internal or external)

❑   **Unparsed entities** (are always external)

Parameter entities are always parsed entities.

Parsed Entities

A parsed entity can include any well-formed content, which is known as its **replacement text**. This text can be considered part of the document in which it is referenced – as if it had simply been included everywhere it was referenced. Parsed entities are always referenced by name using either a general or parameter **entity reference**:

```
<!ENTITY  TheName  "The replacement text" >
  ...
&TheName;
```

The above document fragment first shows the definition of a simple text entity using an **entity declaration** (the first line), and then its use by means of an entity reference. This would result in The replacement text being inserted in place of &TheName;. We'll look more closely at the syntax in a while.

An unparsed entity is something that may or may not be text, and if it is, need not be XML text. These general entities are always named, and can only be used as the value of an attribute having the ENTITY or ENTITIES type. All unparsed entities must have an associated **notation**, which is also identified by name:

```
<!NOTATION  png  SYSTEM "http://www.wrox.com/Programs/PNG_Viewer.exe" >
<!ENTITY  TheImageRef  SYSTEM "image.png" NDATA png >
  ...
<foo img="TheImageRef" />
```

The above document fragment shows the definition of a notation (the first line), the definition of an unparsed entity referring to that notation (the second line), and then an empty element that refers to the unparsed entity (as an attribute value).

We will address the details of entity and notation declarations later in this chapter, but first we'll look at the entity references that cause an entity's replacement text to be inserted into a document.

Entity References

All parsed entities are included in a document or DTD by means of an entity reference, as we saw in the "*Escaping Characters*" section of Chapter 2.

Parsed general entities use the ampersand (&) and semi-colon (;) as the beginning and end delimiters, respectively:

```
&name;
```

Parameter entities use the per cent sign (%) as the beginning delimiter, and the semi-colon for the end:

```
%name;
```

Unparsed general entity references can only be used as an attribute value, so they require no special reference syntax. In fact, entity references are not allowed to contain the name of an unparsed entity.

In both cases, the *name* must conform to the general rules for XML names, just like element type or attribute names. This *name* must also match the name of an entity declaration, otherwise the document containing the entity reference won't be well-formed.

In general, the defining declaration *should* precede any references to the entity. A parameter entity declaration *must* precede any references to that declaration. Any general entity that's used as the default value of an attribute must also be defined before such use.

We've already seen how we can use the five built-in general entities to avoid conflicts with special markup characters, particularly the ampersand (&) and less-than sign (<). It's not necessary to explicitly define any of these in a DTD for use with well-formed documents. However, for any would-be valid documents with a DTD, they *should* be defined for the sake of interoperability with existing SGML-based tools.

So, the strings on the left are all legal XML *general* entity references:

```
&amp;                  <!-- built-in general entity - ampersand -->
&lt;                   <!-- built-in general entity - less-than sign -->
&copy;                 <!-- symbolic entity for copyright (©) character -->
&ProductDisclaimer;    <!-- some boiler-plate legal text -->
```

and these two are legal *parameter* entity references:

```
%ISO_Latin1;           <!-- include an ISO entity set in the DTD -->
%BookCatalogElements;  <!-- the <!ELEMENT..>s for BookCatalog DTD -->
```

Later in this chapter, we'll look at how these are interpreted by an XML parser, how the referenced entity was originally declared, and how the replacement text might appear in an XML application. But first, we'll consider character references.

Character References

XML, like SGML before it, has a reference mechanism for any non-ASCII characters that don't have a direct input method (say, on an ASCII keyboard). Any XML-legal character in Unicode (or ISO 10646) may be the target of a **character reference**, using syntax similar to parsed general entities. These characters are referred to by the assigned integer value of the character.

> *Contrary to common belief (perhaps re-inforced by Microsoft's so-called Unicode support in Windows NT), these values are not limited to 16-bit integers – there are several encodings that use 32-bit numbers or variable-length multi-byte formats.*

Like general entity references, character references are delimited with an ampersand and semi-colon. The numeric value is further delimited with a preceding hash mark (#) – this is how an XML parser can easily differentiate a character reference from a general entity reference. There are two forms of numbers that may be used in these references – decimal and hexadecimal – and these are distinguished by using a lower-case x to precede all hex numbers.

For example, here are two Unicode character references:

```
&#2014;   <!-- decimal value - refers to em-dash (—) character -->
&#x199;   <!-- hexadecimal value - refers to capital C with cedilla (Ç) -->
```

There's no requirement that either one or the other of these formats be used. For most XML applications, hex is preferred since that's how the Unicode standards documents present character values.

This method of including special characters doesn't require a DTD or any other definition of the character value – as long as its numeric value is that of a legal XML character, the parser will pass it on to the application for display or other handling.

Of course, remembering ~16,000 character values for the world's letters, numbers, and symbols is both unfeasible and somewhat ludicrous. Symbolic names have been created for the most common Unicode characters, using general entities, as we'll see in the next and later sections.

> *The Unicode Standard – Version 3.0 (ISBN 0-201-61633-5) is the current version of the specification. It can be viewed or ordered online at www.unicode.org.*

General Entities

As we've already mentioned, general entities may be either parsed or unparsed, they can include any well-formed content (the replacement text), and are always referenced by name. A by-product of this well-formedness is that all XML structures remain properly nested – no XML component (for example tags, elements, PIs) can begin in one entity and end in another.

Any of the following would cause fatal XML parser errors:

- ❏ Any reference to an unparsed entity
- ❏ Any character or general-entity reference in the DTD, except within an entity or attribute value
- ❏ Any reference to an external entity from within an attribute value

We've seen how to refer to entities, so let's look at how they're defined.

Parsed Entities

A parsed general entity is defined in the DTD, in either the internal or external subset. No entity can refer to itself by its own name, directly or indirectly (in other words no recursion is allowed in definitions).

> **A parsed entity's replacement text must always be well-formed XML.**

There are two forms of parsed entities:

- ❏ **Internal**, where the actual replacement text is included in the declaration
- ❏ **External**, where the replacement text is located in an external file or other resource

Internal Parsed Entities

The basic format of an **internal parsed entity** declaration is:

```
<!ENTITY name "..replacement_text.." >
```

The *name* must conform to the general rules for XML names, whilst the *..replacement_text..* may be any well-formed XML content (as long as it doesn't include any entity references to the same entity that is being defined).

Try It Out – Using Internal Parsed Entities

For example, we could define two parsed general entities for a publisher's name and a boiler-plate copyright message in the internal DTD subset of the same document that will use the entities.

1. Save the following as BX_entity1.xml:

```
<?xml version="1.0"?>
<!DOCTYPE Book
[
  <!ENTITY copy "&#169;">
  <!ENTITY PubName "Wrox Press Ltd.">
  <!ENTITY CopyrightText "Copyright &copy; 2000 &PubName; All Rights..">
]>
```

425

```
<Book>
  <Publisher>
    <CorpName>&PubName;</CorpName>
    <Copyright>&CopyrightText;</Copyright>
  </Publisher>
</Book>
```

2. This will appear in the IE5 browser as:

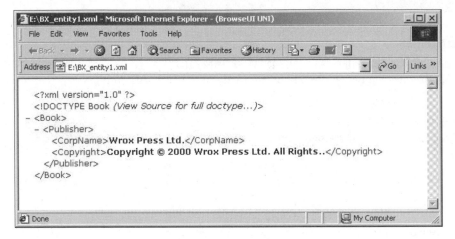

Limitations

There are two important limitations to the use of entities. We've already mentioned the prohibition against recursive references, which means that the following simple circular references are not well-formed:

```
<!ENTITY BadSelfRef "This is a &BadSelfRef; to one's own self" >
<!ENTITY BadRefToA "This is a &BadRefToB; because B refers back to A" >
<!ENTITY BadRefToB "This is a &BadRefToA; because A refers back to B" >
```

The first of the above declarations is the prohibited direct self-recursion; the other two illustrate an indirect, but still illegal, self-reference.

The other limitation involves the XML parser's handling of the attribute value delimiters (the single or double quotation marks).

Although the parser treats entity reference delimiters as such when they appear within the replacement text (as in our previous example), the quotation marks are treated as nothing more than normal data characters. Thus, the following would not be well-formed:

```
<!ENTITY ValueWithQuote "The End'" >
...
<an_element an_attribute='Some text, then &ValueWithQuote; />
```

An XML parser fully expands the &ValueWithQuote; entity reference (to The End'), and *then* starts looking for the attribute value's closing apostrophe (') *after* the closing semi-colon of the entity reference. Therefore, this attribute value is not well-formed.

Not all parsed entities need their replacement text to be included in an `<!ENTITY>` declaration within the DTD. It's also possible to refer to parsed entities that are external to the XML document.

External Parsed Entities

The same replacement text that we used in the last Try It Out section could instead be included using an **external parsed entity**. Instead of putting the copyright message directly in the DTD, we could instead store the message text in an external text file. Like the `<!DOCTYPE>` declaration and any other external reference, we can use either a `PUBLIC` location, a `SYSTEM` location, or both, to refer to this external resource.

Try It Out – Using External Parsed Entities

We will simply move the definition of our copyright message from the internal subset of the DTD to an external file. Everything else remains unchanged.

1. Save the following as `BX_copyright.dtd`:

```
<!ENTITY CopyrightText "Copyright &copy; 2000 &PubName; All Rights..">
```

2. Save the following as `BX_entity2.xml` (it's probably easiest to modify a copy of `BX_entity1.xml`) in the same directory as the DTD you just created:

```
<?xml version="1.0"?>
<!DOCTYPE Book
[
  <!ENTITY copy "&#169;">
  <!ENTITY PubName "Wrox Press Ltd.">
  <!ENTITY CopyrightText SYSTEM "BX_copyright.dtd">
]>
<Book>
  <Publisher>
     <CorpName>&PubName;</CorpName>
     <Copyright>&CopyrightText;</Copyright>
  </Publisher>
</Book>
```

3. This will appear in the IE5 browser just as it did in the previous Try It Out.

How It Works

When the XML parser encounters the external entity reference (`&CopyrightText;`), it will refer back to the earlier `<!ENTITY CopyrightText..>` declaration, read the named file (at the `SYSTEM` location), process the declaration therein, and then pass its replacement text to the application, just as if the entity were declared in the document itself (as before).

This method has the advantage of completely segregating the definitions of the boiler-plate text from the DTD – any publisher could use the exact same DTD, with custom text for the publisher's name and legalese coming from an external entity.

The downside of this approach is most significant in an Internet environment. The multiple reads and data transfers implied by a document that's comprised of multiple entities can greatly degrade performance when every piece is another HTTP transfer. This is less of a problem for an internal network application, where it can be a powerful method of sharing and reusing DTDs for multiple documents and applications.

In fact, the text of a whole book could be included into a "master" XML document with the use of external parsed entities:

```
<?xml version="1.0">
<!DOCTYPE Book
[
  <!ENTITY textFront SYSTEM "file:///mypath/BookFront.txt">
  <!ENTITY textChapter1 SYSTEM "file:///mypath/BookChapter1.txt">
  <!ENTITY textChapter2 SYSTEM "file:///mypath/BookChapter2.txt">
  <!ENTITY textChapter3 SYSTEM "file:///mypath/BookChapter3.txt">
  <!ENTITY textChapter4 SYSTEM "file:///mypath/BookChapter4.txt">
]>
<Book>
&textFront;
&textChapter1;
&textChapter2;
&textChapter3;
&textChapter4;
</Book>
```

This method is commonly used to construct a number of documents that share the same basic structure – the DTD and most of the master XML document can remain unchanged, but the contents can vary depending upon the content of the external entities.

External Parsed Entities – Text Declaration

Any *external* parsed entity can begin with a **text declaration**. This is a truncated version of the XML declaration, which may include the version and/or encoding attributes (but unlike the XML declaration, the version attribute may be omitted). This declaration must be a string literal – entity references aren't allowed within it. If this declaration is included, it may only appear at the very beginning of the entity (and nowhere else).

The following are both legal text declarations (assume that each is at the beginning of its own external entity). The first declares that the entity uses a mythic version of XML, encoded as UTF-16 characters:

```
<?xml version="1.x" encoding="UTF-16"?>
<foo>Some text in the UTF-16 encoding...
</foo>
```

And this one just declares that the entity contains text in a common Japanese encoding:

```
<?xml encoding="Shift_JIS"?>
```

The scope of these declarations is just the external entity itself – there's no effect on other document content. In the first example above, the contents of <foo> would be UTF-16 text, but the rest of the document which refers to this external entity could be in ASCII or UTF-8, or some other encoding.

This mechanism allows us to construct XML documents from data with different character encodings, or even from multiple versions of XML. Remember, by specification, all XML parsers must be able to handle at least the UTF-8 and UTF-16 encodings.

> **Any external parsed entity that is not stored in UTF-16 or UTF-8 (the default encoding) must always include a text declaration with the `encoding` attribute set to the appropriate value. It is a fatal error if the parser cannot handle a particular encoding in the external entity.**

It is an error for an external entity to declare an incorrect encoding value. If there is no `encoding` attribute and no Byte-Order-Mark (BOM) at the beginning of the entity, the data *must* be encoded in UTF-8. This implies that plain 7-bit ASCII documents don't need to use the text declaration, since ASCII is a subset of UTF-8 and all ASCII characters would be properly recognized.

Unparsed Entities

By definition, unparsed entities are always external entities. As such, the entity declaration for these entities will always reference an external location (`PUBLIC` or `SYSTEM`), and must always supplement the location with the `NDATA` keyword and the associated notation type name. There are no constraints on the contents of unparsed entities – they need not even be text, much less XML text.

The basic format of an **external unparsed entity** declaration is either of the following:

```
<!ENTITY name SYSTEM "..location.." NDATA notation_type >
<!ENTITY name PUBLIC "..location1.." "..location2.." NDATA notation_type >
```

The `NDATA` keyword is how the XML parser differentiates parsed and unparsed external entities. The parser's only obligation for processing these declarations is to provide the `name`, `location`, and `notation_type` values to the application for its own use.

Every `name` must match the name of a `<!NOTATION>` declaration for the document to be considered valid.

> **An unparsed external entity is a *reference to an external resource* (for example, an image file). The entity's associated notation is a *reference to the handler or application that will process the external resource* (for example, an image viewer).**

The following is an example of an unparsed entity being used to refer to a PNG (Portable Network Graphics format) image file:

```
<!ENTITY WroxLogo SYSTEM "http://www.wrox.com/Images/Logo.png" NDATA png >
```

Whenever a reference is made to `WroxLogo` within an attribute value, the location of the image file and the notation for the `png` type will be associated with this entity and passed on to the application for further handling. See the "Non-XML Data" section of this chapter for more about notations.

Now that we've looked at the various forms of general entities that may be used in XML documents, let's look at a similar mechanism for DTDs.

Parameter Entities

As we've noted before, parameter entities are used exclusively in DTDs and must always be parsed entities. This also means that the replacement text must be well-formed in the context of DTD syntax. These entities are a very powerful way to reuse groups of DTD declarations, include entity sets for non-ASCII characters, and/or include entire DTDs within an internal subset DTD.

The basic format of a **parameter entity** declaration is:

```
<!ENTITY % name "replacement_text" >
```

This declaration is nearly identical to a general parsed internal entity declaration – the only difference is the percent sign (%) that must appear between the "!<ENTITY" string literal and the *name* parameter. Of course, the parameter entity reference syntax is also slightly different from that of general entity references.

As before, the *name* must conform to the general rules for XML names, whilst *replacement_text* may be any well-formed XML content that would be legal within a DTD. As with external parsed entity declarations, the replacement text may be stored in an external resource that's located using the usual external reference form (a URI that may be a PUBLIC and/or SYSTEM identifier). The constraint against using recursive references also applies to this type of entity declaration.

Uses

Parameter entities are a convenient shorthand for repetitive DTD declarations, or portions of such declarations. For example, we could save some typing by defining two parameter entities called IDREF_Req and IDREF_Opt. These would be declared like this:

```
<!ENTITY % IDREF_Req "IDREF #REQUIRED">
<!ENTITY % IDREF_Opt "IDREF #IMPLIED">
```

When we later declare an element's attributes that use the IDREF type, we could use either of these parameter entities, instead of explicitly typing the latter portions of each attribute description:

```
<!ATTLIST   Book
      bookID      ID      #REQUIRED
      publisher   %IDREF_Req;
      imprint     %IDREF_Opt;
      level       %IDREF_Opt;
      isbn        CDATA   #REQUIRED
      pubDate     CDATA   "2000-??"
      pages       CDATA   "????"
   >
```

These parameter entity references would be expanded, and the appropriate replacement text would be inserted within each line of the attribute declaration. The end result would be identical to our earlier version of this <!ATTLIST> declaration:

```
<!ATTLIST   Book
      bookID      ID      #REQUIRED
      publisher   IDREF   #REQUIRED
      imprint     IDREF   #IMPLIED
```

```
        level     IDREF   #IMPLIED
        isbn      CDATA   #REQUIRED
        pubDate   CDATA   "2000-??"
        pages     CDATA   "????"
>
```

Limitations

This potentially powerful use of parameter entities has two major drawbacks. First of all, when these are used everywhere in a DTD, it quickly becomes impossible to read the DTD without much flipping of pages (or the use of many windows in an integrated development environment (IDE)). Unless the parameter entity names are quite descriptive, we've greatly reduced the readability of the DTD, in an effort to save some typing and/or reuse some previously defined declarations. Extensive use of such parameter entities in SGML is one of the main reasons that SGML documents, DTDs, and tools are so expensive and complex.

The other drawback depends upon how we provide the parameter entity declarations. If we are using entities from many different sources, in many different files over a network, our document processing performance would be greatly reduced. This is because each time an external entity is used, the parser will need to fetch the entity declaration and expand it at the point of reference (caching can help, but won't eliminate all of the additional network traffic).

A reasonable rule of thumb would be to severely restrict the use of any such parameter entities in XML data that will be used in a dynamic network environment. The use of this feature of XML is best reserved for more traditional documents.

Let's revisit our ongoing `BookCatalog` example, and see how to use a parameter entity to permit the creation of some new types of `<Book>` that reuse the same set of common attributes. We'll ignore the element's content model and just look at its attribute declaration.

Our original attribute declaration was:

```
<!ATTLIST  Book
        bookID      ID      #REQUIRED
        publisher   IDREF   #REQUIRED
        imprint     IDREF   #IMPLIED
        level       IDREF   #IMPLIED
        isbn        CDATA   #REQUIRED
        pubDate     CDATA   "2000-??"
        pages       CDATA   "????"
>
```

We'll create a parameter entity that includes all seven of these attributes:

```
<!ENTITY % BookAttrs
'
        bookID      ID      #REQUIRED
        publisher   IDREF   #REQUIRED
        imprint     IDREF   #IMPLIED
        level       IDREF   #IMPLIED
        isbn        CDATA   #REQUIRED
        pubDate     CDATA   "2000-??"
        pages       CDATA   "????"
'>
```

Then when we declare the attributes for our different kinds of book element types, we can use a reference to this parameter entity instead of repeating the seven lines of attribute descriptions:

```
<!ATTLIST  Book   %BookAttrs; >

<!ATTLIST  CookBook
     %BookAttrs;
     recipes  IDREFS  #REQUIRED >

<!ATTLIST  TravelBook
     %BookAttrs;
     travelogues  IDREFS     #REQUIRED
     maps         ENTITIES   #IMPLIED>
```

All three of these book elements share seven attributes in common, and the two new element types have added some more attributes that are specific to those types of books. Each time we use the `%BookAttrs;` parameter entity reference, it is as if we had repeated the seven attribute descriptions within each of the above three `<!ATTLIST>` declarations. The first declaration (`<!ATTLIST Book..>`), once expanded, would be functionally equivalent to the original declaration shown earlier.

The parameter entity mechanism is a powerful way to reuse DTD declarations. It is especially useful for including entity sets that have been standardized by the ISO and other organizations, as we'll see in the next section.

ISO and Other Standard Entity Sets

Both character and general entities have been used for many years in SGML. As a result, numerous standard sets of entity definitions were created, and it's been very simple to convert these SGML resources to XML. SGML's status as an international standard (ISO 8879) means that many of these components are also truly international standards.

Try It Out – Using an ISO Entity Set

1. A typical portion from the ISO Latin1 entity set looks like this. Save the following as the file `BX_Latin1.dtd`:

```
<!ENTITY  Agrave   "&#192;" > <!-- capital A, grave accent -->
<!ENTITY  Aacute   "&#193;" > <!-- capital A, acute accent -->
<!ENTITY  Acirc    "&#194;" > <!-- capital A, circumflex accent -->
<!ENTITY  Atilde   "&#195;" > <!-- capital A, tilde -->
<!ENTITY  Auml     "&#196;" > <!-- capital A, dieresis or umlaut mark -->
<!ENTITY  Aring    "&#197;" > <!-- capital A, ring over -->
<!ENTITY  AElig    "&#198;" > <!-- capital AE ligature (dipthong) -->
<!ENTITY  Ccedil   "&#199;" > <!-- capital C, cedilla -->
<!--   :   -->
<!ENTITY  egrave   "&#236;" > <!-- small e, grave accent -->
<!ENTITY  eacute   "&#237;" > <!-- small e, acute accent -->
<!--   :   -->
<!ENTITY  yuml     "&#255;" > <!-- small y, dieresis or umlaut mark -->
```

2. Now create a document named `BX_iso.xml`, that will include this entity set (changing the path name to suit your set up):

```
<?xml version="1.0" encoding="utf-8" standalone="no"?>

<!DOCTYPE foo
[
 <!ENTITY % ISO_Latin1 PUBLIC
     "ISO 8879-1986//ENTITIES Added Latin 1//EN//XML"
     "BX_Latin1.dtd" >

%ISO_Latin1;

 <!ENTITY  alpha   "&#x3B1;"  >  <!-- small alpha -->
 <!ENTITY  Omega   "&#x3a9;"  >  <!-- Capital omega -->
 <!ENTITY  mdash   "&#x2014;" >  <!-- em dash -->
]>

<foo>
&alpha; to &Omega; looks like Greek to me &mdash; and so it's d&eacute;ja-vu all
over again!
</foo>
```

The `<!ENTITY>` declarations create a parameter entity (external parsed entity) that declares both `PUBLIC` and `SYSTEM` locations for the entity set. As with the `DOCTYPE` declaration, the former of these is an "official" URN; and the latter is the "fall-back" location (the `SYSTEM` keyword is implied).

The parameter entity reference (`%ISO_Latin1`) is what causes the content of the entity set to be included within our example document's DTD (either in the form of the official ISO file, or alternatively, from our file named `BX_Latin1.dtd`). There should only be one such parameter entity reference in a given DTD, since any additional inclusions of the entity set's declarations would simply be ignored.

We can either include the appropriate parameter entities for all three necessary ISO entity sets (Latin1 – for `eacute`, Greek3 – for `alpha`/`Omega`, and PubSymbol – for `mdash`), or just copy the entity declarations into our internal subset DTD. Since we only included a single reference (to the ISO Latin1 set), the other character references will use the `<!ENTITY>` declarations from the internal subset. Then, we can use these symbolic general entity references for special characters, instead of the cryptic numeric character references.

The above `DOCTYPE` declaration shows an example where we're using both the external subset (the `SYSTEM` reference to `BX_Latin1.dtd`) and the internal subset of the DTD (the four `<!ENTITY>` declarations). The last declaration in the internal subset (for the `eacute` character) will override the same declaration in `BX_Latin1.dtd`.

3. When we view `BX_iso.xml` in IE5, it looks like this:

Despite the fact that the ISO character entities have existed for a long time (the sets we've looked at were created in mid-1997), browser support for these much-needed special characters is not widespread! For example, Netscape Navigator 4.5 can display Latin1 characters (Western European accented letters), but still can't handle simple publishing symbols (like the em-dash) or Greek letters using the symbolic references. In this respect, Microsoft's Internet Explorer 5 is much more capable – there are only a few standard character general entities that IE5 can't display properly.

Since XML 1.0 is based upon Unicode, the use of entity references for non-ASCII characters is no longer necessary. However, Unicode tools are yet to become ubiquitous, so these entity sets will remain useful for those documents that continue to use the UTF-8 encoding (or its ASCII subset).

Non-XML Data (Notations)

A **notation** is used by the XML application as a hint about handling an unparsed entity or some other non-XML data. The XML parser need only provide the names of the unparsed entity and its associated notation declaration to the application. Any further processing is strictly within the application's domain. An XML document can include unparsed entities and notations without necessarily having any means to process them – no error is reported for unknown notation types, or those for which no handler is available.

Notations can be used to identify (by name):

❑ The format of unparsed entities

❑ The format of element attributes of the ENTITY and ENTITIES types

❑ The application associated with a processing instruction (PI)

These declarations have a very similar effect to the HTML <IMG> element. Images are included in web pages with a statement like:

```
<IMG src="some_image.png"/>
```

This tells a browser to find an image named some_image.png, and display it within the web page. It is up to the browser to determine what kind of image format is being used, often based upon the filename extension (which is .png in this case, for the Portable Network Graphics format). This means that a browser that doesn't understand the PNG format can't display the image.

Since XML parsers and applications don't have any such built-in behavior associated with tags like <IMG>, we must explicitly notify the application of the kind of image format(s) we're using and how to handle this non-XML data. To do this, we need to use a combination of XML's ENTITY and NOTATION attribute types and the <!NOTATION> declaration, all of which we are about to discuss.

The <!NOTATION> Declaration

The basic syntax of this declaration is:

```
<!NOTATION name SYSTEM "..location.." >
<!NOTATION name PUBLIC "..location1.." "..location2.." >
```

The *name* is the identifier for a particular notation type. Any <!ENTITY> declaration, NOTATION attribute, or PI that pertains to this notation type will also use this exact *name* as the means of associating an external resource with its handler.

> **All notation *names* that are used in a document must be declared with a <!NOTATION>.**

For example, the handler for PNG images might be declared like this:

```
<!NOTATION png SYSTEM "http://www.wrox.com/Programs/PNG_Viewer.exe" >
```

When the XML parser encounters our earlier unparsed external entity example, it will extract the *notation_type* value (which is png) and look for a matching name amongst the notation declarations. If the name is matched, the URI from the above declaration will be passed on to the application for further processing.

In Chapter 9 we discussed most of the attribute types that may be used in an <!ATTLIST> declaration – in the next two sections, we'll look at the rest.

The NOTATION Attribute Type

For example, a simple version of the HTML <IMG> element type that permitted three different types of images could be defined as:

```
<!ELEMENT  img  EMPTY >
<!ATTLIST  img
     src  CDATA  #REQUIRED
     type NOTATION (png | gif | jpg)  #IMPLIED
>
```

This special form of an enumerated attribute value can be used by a validating parser to ensure that a proper <!NOTATION> declaration exists for each of the three notation types, as well as validating the element attribute in a conforming document instance.

The ENTITY and ENTITIES Attribute Types

These two related attribute types are used to allow a reference to an unparsed external entity to appear within a document. Like the IDREF/IDREFS pair, these two provide a singular and plural form of the same basic attribute type. The attribute value must always be a legal XML name, and the plural form uses a white space-delimited list of names.

Let's look at an example of using an external unparsed entity and notation. We might modify the definition of `<Person>` in our `BookCatalog` DTD to allow an associated author/editor photograph. Of course, the photo will be present on our server in some binary image file format, so we need to provide both an external unparsed entity (for the photo's image file) and a notation for the associated image format (the image viewer).

First we'd need to copy the `BookCatalog.expanded.dtd` file we created in Chapter 9 and save it as `BookCatalog.complete.dtd`. We'd then add the new attribute for `<Person>`, and add two more related declarations. Here is the change to the attribute declaration for the `<Person>` element:

```
<!ATTLIST  Person
    perID  ID  #REQUIRED
    role  (AU | ED | AE | RV | IL | unknown)  #REQUIRED
    photo  ENTITY  #IMPLIED
>
```

These declarations would be added immediately after `<Person>`:

```
<!NOTATION png SYSTEM "http://www.wrox.com/Programs/PNG_Viewer.exe" >

<!ENTITY picEd1 SYSTEM "http://www.wrox.com/Images/WroxEd1.png" NDATA png >
<!ENTITY picEd2 SYSTEM "http://www.wrox.com/Images/WroxEd2.png" NDATA png >
<!ENTITY picEd3 SYSTEM "http://www.wrox.com/Images/WroxEd3.png" NDATA png >
<!ENTITY picEd4 SYSTEM "http://www.wrox.com/Images/WroxEd4.png" NDATA png >
```

The `<!NOTATION>` declaration associates a specific helper application for any data of the `png` type, whilst the `<!ENTITY>` declarations define the names of four external unparsed entities (four PNG image files) and provide their locations and types.

A conforming document instance would now include a third attribute for `<Person>`. We'd use a copy of the `BookCatalog.expanded.xml` file we created in Chapter 9, and name it `BookCatalog.complete.xml`. The `DOCTYPE` declaration would be modified to refer to our new DTD:

```
<!DOCTYPE BookCatalog SYSTEM "BookCatalog.complete.dtd" >
```

We could then add the new attribute to each of the four instances of the `<Person>` element where the `role="ED"` attribute is present:

```
<Person perID="DN_PRKR" role="ED" photo="picEd1">
  <PersonName>
    <FirstName>Dianne</FirstName>
    <LastName>Parker</LastName>
  </PersonName>
  <CorpName>Wrox Press Ltd.</CorpName>
</Person>

<Person perID="JN_DCKT" role="ED" photo="picEd2">
  <PersonName>
    <FirstName>Jon</FirstName>
    <LastName>Duckett</LastName>
  </PersonName>
  <CorpName>Wrox Press Ltd.</CorpName>
</Person>

<Person perID="KRL_WTSN" role="ED" photo="picEd3">
  <PersonName>
    <FirstName>Karli</FirstName>
```

```
      <LastName>Watson</LastName>
    </PersonName>
    <CorpName>Wrox Press Ltd.</CorpName>
  </Person>

  <Person perID="LS_STPHNSN" role="ED" photo="picEd4">
    <PersonName>
      <FirstName>Lisa</FirstName>
      <LastName>Stephenson</LastName>
    </PersonName>
    <CorpName>Wrox Press Ltd.</CorpName>
  </Person>
```

Because the photo attribute has been defined as an ENTITY type, there must be a matching
<!ENTITY> declaration for each named photo. At this point in the document, we don't care what type
of thing this attribute represents – the <!NOTATION> declaration for the png type provides a reference
to the helper application.

When viewed in IE5, this document looks like this (only part shown):

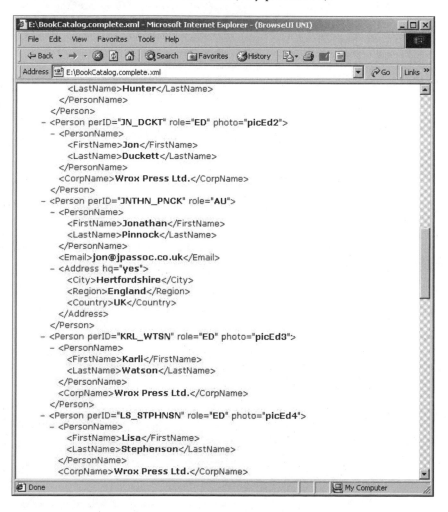

We could change this to allow multiple photos for each person. To do this, we'd modify the photo attribute so that it's now declared to be the ENTITIES type:

```
<!ATTLIST  Person
     perID  ID  #REQUIRED
     role  (AU | ED | AE | RV | IL | unknown)  #REQUIRED
     photo  ENTITIES  #IMPLIED
>
```

We could then change our document to use multiple photo references like so:

```
<Person perID="DN_PRKR" role="ED" photo="picEd1a picEd1b">..</Person>
```

Of course this implies that we've also added the necessary <!ENTITY> declarations:

```
<!ENTITY picEd1a SYSTEM "http://www.wrox.com/Images/WroxEd1.png" NDATA png >
<!ENTITY picEd1b SYSTEM "http://www.wrox.com/Images/WroxEd1.png" NDATA png >
```

As with the IDREFS attribute type, it will be up to the XML application to separate the multiple entity references and provide for their display or other handling – the parser will merely verify that the attribute value is a correctly delimited list of legal XML names. (A validating parser will also ensure that these names have been previously defined using the appropriate <!ENTITY> declaration.)

Internal versus External DTD Subsets

As we saw in Chapter 9, a DTD may be divided into internal and external subsets. These two parts are used together to describe and validate an XML document instance.

The internal subset is the portion within the document instance, and any duplicate declarations in the internal subset take precedence over those in the external subset. This internal subset priority can be very useful, especially in combination with conditional sections. However, there is a down side – we cannot completely rely on an external subset of the DTD for validation, since a document could override it using internal subset declarations.

Regardless of this consideration (and ignoring the possible use of XML Schemas), it's necessary to use shared (external subset) DTDs in order to implement shared XML vocabularies.

There are many common XML vocabularies that are represented by DTDs. Quite often, these are simplified versions of DTDs that were previously implemented using SGML. One common example is the bibliographic vocabulary known as the "Dublin Core", which as we mentioned in Chapter 9 provides a standard vocabulary for describing books.

As we discussed in Chapter 9, a DOCTYPE declaration may also include one or more DTD declarations. These declarations are delimited by square brackets ("[...]"), and must appear after all the other parameters of the DOCTYPE declaration.

For example, our `BookCatalog` DTD with both internal and external subsets would use the following framework:

```
<?xml version="1.0" encoding="UTF-8" standalone="no"?>

<!-- The external subset of the DTD is referenced by the PUBLIC keyword -->
<!-- The internal subset of the DTD is included between the "[ ]" below -->

<!DOCTYPE  BookCatalog  PUBLIC "PublishingConsortium/BookCatalog"
                        "http://www.wrox.com/DTDs/BookCatalog.dtd"
[
 ...DTD declaration...
 ...another DTD declaration...
]
>
<BookCatalog>
  ...
</BookCatalog>
```

It's a common markup style to put the delimiters on separate lines to visually separate these declarations from the other parts of the `DOCTYPE` declaration.

The standalone Attribute

You may have noticed in the previous example that we set the `standalone` attribute of the XML declaration to `"no"`. This indicates to the XML parser that the DTD contains references to external resources that may be needed to validate the document instance, and/or resolve external entities. In our earlier examples and Try It Out sections, we always used the external subset only, and so we always declared that `standalone="no"`.

It's important to remember that this attribute is primarily a *hint* to the XML parser, not an absolute command. A non-validating parser is allowed to ignore external entity references completely, though it must report an error if the document has `standalone="yes"` and an undeclared entity is encountered.

Conditional Sections

If you've ever done any programming, you've probably used compiler directives to create **conditional sections** of code, in other words, code that may or may not be used based upon some run-time condition or compiler flag. Many standard code libraries (particularly those used with Microsoft Windows) are a maze of these conditional sections, which can depend on the CPU, the target operating system (OS), the locale (for internationalization), and a whole bunch of other variables.

DTDs have a similar feature, albeit one with much more limited capabilities. In fact, without using parameter entities, the DTD conditional sections are almost useless. However, *with* parameter entities, we can construct quite elaborate multi-purpose DTDs, which use entities defined in the internal subset to modify the conditional section directives in the external subset. We can then use this to allow documents to select their own "level" of validation, or even allow radically different element structures, depending on a few carefully designed declaration structures.

There are two declarations that are used to create conditional sections in a DTD. These use syntax that is virtually identical to the CDATA declaration we saw in Chapter 2.

The basic syntax of these declarations is:

```
<![keyword
[
   ...the conditional DTD declarations go here...
]]>
```

The two possible values for *keyword* are INCLUDE and IGNORE. As the names suggest, any declarations within an INCLUDE section are to be used for validation, and declarations within an IGNORE section are read, but not processed, by the parser. Neither of these declarations can be used within the internal subset of the DTD – they may only be present in the external subset.

Unlike most programming languages, there is no "if..else" grammar to control the inclusion or exclusion of conditional sections in a DTD. So at first glance, the INCLUDE and IGNORE declarations seem pretty useless.

For example, what is the functional difference between:

```
<!ELEMENT BookCatalog (Catalog, Publishers+, Persons*, Subjects*, Books+)>
```

and:

```
<![INCLUDE
[
   <!ELEMENT BookCatalog (Catalog, Publishers+, Persons*, Subjects*, Books+)>
]]>
```

In a word – there is *no* difference! The element declaration for <BookCatalog> will always be included in the DTD in both these cases. By the same token, there's no significant difference between simply omitting a declaration, and enclosing the same declaration within an IGNORE section (except perhaps as a means of documenting the deletion of a formerly useful declaration from the current DTD).

Of course, there is a way to make these declarations quite useful – we just use a parameter entity reference in place of the *keyword* in our basic syntax example above. This little trick allows us to change our conditional section to be either an INCLUDE or IGNORE section, as we'll see in the following Try It Out.

Try It Out – Conditional Sections

For example, let's assume that the Subjects element of our BookCatalog is still in the process of being developed. We want to be able to use these elements within some internal development documents, but we don't want to allow any of these elements in any of our public documents.

1. To accomplish this, we'll need two versions of the <BookCatalog> element declaration within the external subset of the DTD, enclosed within conditional section directive delimiters. We'll use a minimized version of our BookCatalog DTD for the sake of clarity in this example. Create a file named BX_conditional.dtd:

```
<!-- BX_conditional.dtd -->

<!ENTITY % useSubjects    "IGNORE">
<!ENTITY % useNoSubjects "INCLUDE">

<![%useSubjects;
[
 <!ELEMENT BookCatalog (Catalog, Publishers+, Persons+, Subjects+, Books+)>

 <!ELEMENT Subjects (Subject, Subject+, Subject+)>
 <!ELEMENT Subject (#PCDATA)>
]]>
<![%useNoSubjects;
[
 <!ELEMENT BookCatalog (Catalog, Publishers+, Persons+, Books+)>
]]>

<!ELEMENT Catalog    (#PCDATA)>
<!ELEMENT Publishers (#PCDATA)>
<!ELEMENT Persons    (#PCDATA)>
<!ELEMENT Books      (#PCDATA)>
```

The above two parameter entities (useSubjects and useNoSubjects) must be defined in this DTD, since a parameter entity must always be defined before it is used anywhere.

We've set these two default values in such a way that the production version (no Subjects) won't need to include any additional declarations. We will need to redefine both useSubjects and useNoSubjects in the internal subset of all development version documents that need to use the <Subjects> element and its children.

2. Create a document named BX_conditional.xml, that uses Subjects elements, like this (make sure this file is in the same directory as the DTD):

```
<?xml version="1.0" encoding="UTF-8" standalone="no"?>
<!-- BX_conditional.xml -->

<!DOCTYPE BookCatalog SYSTEM "BX_conditional.dtd"
[
 <!ENTITY % useSubjects    "INCLUDE">
 <!ENTITY % useNoSubjects "IGNORE">
]>

<BookCatalog>
  <Catalog>..</Catalog>
  <Publishers>..</Publishers>
  <Persons>..</Persons>
  <Subjects>
    <Subject>subject #1</Subject>
    <Subject>subject #2</Subject>
  </Subjects>
  <Books>..</Books>
</BookCatalog>
```

3. This will appear in the IE5 browser as:

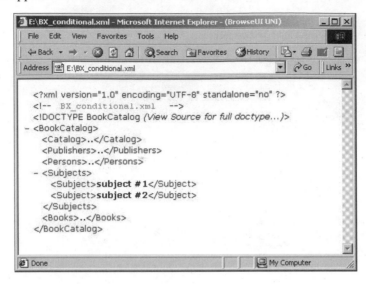

How It Works

The internal subset of the DTD has priority, so it's read and processed before the external subset. All declarations in the external subset that duplicate those in the internal subset are ignored. Thus, when the two parameter entities are expanded within the external DTD, the resulting conditional declarations would be:

```
<![INCLUDE
[
 <!ELEMENT BookCatalog (Catalog, Publishers+, Persons*, Subjects*, Books+)>
]]>
<![IGNORE
[
 <!ELEMENT BookCatalog (Catalog, Publishers+, Persons*, Books+)>
]]>
```

This accomplishes our desired goal – the document can use `Subjects` elements, and still be considered valid.

Any documents that don't need to include any `Subjects` would simply never use the two parameter entity redefinitions in the internal subset. A validating parser would report an error if the document without these redefinitions included any of the now-prohibited `Subjects` elements.

Once we've completed the development process, it's a simple matter to remove the conditional section declarations from the shared DTD. It would *not* be necessary to delete the two parameter entity declarations from any of the documents they've already been defined in – these declarations would just be ignored. All subsequent documents could just omit them, as they'd no longer be needed.

Nesting Conditional Sections

Conditional sections may be nested within each other, with the outermost directive controlling the rest. This situation might occur during DTD development, but otherwise nested conditionals only make sense if we're using the parameter entity trick we just discussed.

The following example illustrates some nested conditional sections, all of which will be ignored:

```
<![IGNORE
[
  <!-- Any declaration in this section will be bypassed. -->
  <![INCLUDE
  [
    <!-- Despite the INCLUDE, anything herein will also be ignored, -->
    <!--  due to the presence of the outermost IGNORE directive.  -->
    <![IGNORE
    [
      <!-- This section is always ignored. -->
    ]]>
  ]]>
]]>
```

While we can use the combination of parameter entities and conditional sections to create very complex DTDs from multiple sources, it's probably easier to use external parsed entities in most cases where you need variable content.

Summary

This chapter rounded off our look at valid XML – we revisited the topic of DTDs and saw how to include sections of text and other data in our XML documents and DTDs using entities. In summary we saw that there are three types of entities:

❑   Parsed general entities (internal or external) – used for including text data

❑   Unparsed general entities (external) – which can incorporate text or non-XML data, and are used with an associated NOTATION declaration to help the XML application interpret the entity

❑   Parsed parameter entities (internal or external) – used exclusively in DTDs and particularly useful for sharing DTDS or reusing sections of DTDs

We also looked at how traditional conditional sections can also be included in DTDs, albeit in a limited sense.

In the next chapter we'll be taking a break from XML validation and looking at another exciting new development, which can also provide means of incorporating external material into an XML document – the concept of linking.

Linking XML

One of the reasons for the phenomenal growth of the Internet is the ability for documents to **link** to other documents. If I create a web page about guitars, for example, I can include links on my page which point to my favorite guitar makers, my favorite musicians, etc. Even if the sites that I'm linking to have nothing to do with me, or are halfway around the world, I am able to create these links, because HTML provides a mechanism for doing so (called hyperlinks).

In this chapter, we'll be looking at similar ways to link XML documents together, using technologies called **XLink** and **XPointer**. We'll be covering:

- ❑ HTML hyperlinks, and their limitations

- ❑ How to create the same type of links that HTML provides using XLink **simple links**

- ❑ How to create links which point to multiple resources, along with rules for traversing those links, using XLink **extended links**

- ❑ How to create links which only reference certain sections of an XML document, instead of the entire document, using XPointer

As you probably knew even before you picked up this book, XML is a cutting edge technology. Some specifications, like the XML specification itself, have been "recommended" by the W3C, meaning that they are ready to be implemented, whereas others are still in various stages of revision. The latter is the case with the technologies we'll be covering in this chapter; unfortunately this means that we can't see how things work, but only how they *might work* in the future. So the sample code and 'try it outs' in this chapter are for example only.

At the time of writing the XLink specification was in "Last Call" status (meaning close to, but not at, Recommendation status), and XPointer was still only in Working Draft status. This means that the syntax shown may not be correct according to the final, recommended specifications.

> **Therefore, if you are going to be using XLink and XPointer in your own applications, you should periodically check the specifications from the W3C.**

HTML Linking

Let's start by looking at how we can link documents in HTML and the limitations of HTML linking. We can then look at how XLink and XPointer avoid these limitations.

One of the reasons for the phenomenal growth of the World Wide Web is the ability for any HTML page to link to another page via a **hyperlink**. This is what makes the web a "web", since all web pages can theoretically be connected to all other web pages. (The same applies to local intranets, in fact anywhere there is a large amount of information to be presented, where it makes sense to sub-divide the information into discrete chunks, with links connecting to detailed or related information.)

These hyperlinks work very simply: a user sees the hyperlink on a web page, clicks it, and the current page is replaced by a new one. Or, as variations on this theme, perhaps the new document opens up a new window, or just replaces the page in one of the frames on the current page. The action performed when the user selects the link is also configurable to a certain degree. For example, in some browsers you can right-click a link and choose specifically to open the link in a new window, instead of having the link replace the current page in the current window.

HTML hyperlinks are constrained in a couple of ways:

❑ A link only involves *two* resources: the resource which is initiating the link, and the resource to which the link points. (Remember, a resource is anything which has identity; in this case, the initiating resource will always be an HTML document.)

❑ These HTML hyperlinks are always *one-way* (although most web browsers provide a Back button, to provide the appearance of a two-way link).

❑ HTML links are embedded in HTML documents, meaning that the source has to be a markup document.

The diagram below illustrates the two resources involved: the string link in the originating page, and the page being retrieved (blah2.html):

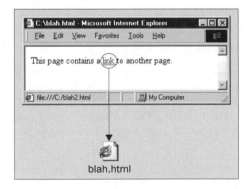

The code to do this in HTML would look something like this:

```
<P>This page contains a <A href="C:\blah2.html">link</A> to
another page.</P>
```

In this case, the resource being pointed to is an *entire* HTML page, but sometimes a link points to just a *section* of an HTML page. In this case, we might modify our link above to this:

```
<P>This page contains a <A href="C:\blah2.html#some-section">link</A> to another
page.</P>
```

This points the web browser not only to a certain page, but to a certain section of that page. Of course, even though the link points to that one section, the whole page is loaded into the browser. In the HTML world, this is much more intuitive than just having a little piece of a document showing up, since it allows the user to scroll back and forth through the entire document if they want to do so.

However, in order for this to work, the page which we are linking to must also be an HTML document. Furthermore, it must contain special markup to identify the section we want to point to, similar to this:

```
<A name="some-section">The link will point to here</A>
```

XML Linking

The **XML Linking Working Group** at the W3C is working on two specifications to provide these kinds of linking capabilities in XML, and even extend them to allow links in XML to do things that HTML links can't:

❏   **XLink** provides functionality for defining links, even links which involve multiple resources, and multiple traversal directions between those resources

❏   **XPointer** provides functionality for pointing to document fragments from XML documents

Using XLink and XPointer together, we can create much more complex links, like the following:

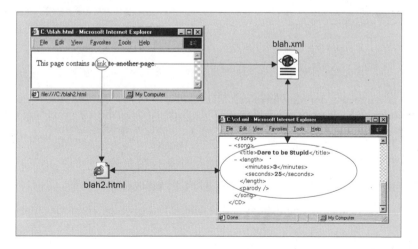

Here we have a link involving four resources instead of two; XLink would be used to link each file together, while XPointer would be used to point to just a section of, for example, the cd.xml file. As you can see from the arrows, not all of the resources are related in one-way relationships. There are a couple of resources that are two-way: for example, not only can we traverse from blah.xml to the portion of XML in cd.xml, but we can also traverse from that portion of XML back to the blah.xml file. In fact, we can do any of the following:

❑ Traverse from the link in blah.html to blah2.html

❑ Traverse from the link in blah.html to blah.xml

❑ Traverse from blah2.html to a section of cd.xml, or from the section of cd.xml to blah2.html

❑ Traverse from blah.xml to a section of cd.xml, or from the section of cd.xml to blah.xml

What's important to realize, though, is that we're just talking about *one* link – these aren't separate links in each file pointing to each other. In fact, the information about this link doesn't necessarily have to reside in *any* of these files; with XLink, we can define all of this information in a completely separate XML file, if we wish.

The XML Linking Working Group is mainly designing links for use in hypertext applications – that is, displaying XML documents in browser-type applications, the way that HTML documents are displayed today. However, both XLink and XPointer could also be used in other, non-browser-oriented, applications. For example, word processing applications could use XLink to link related documents together, or an order processing system could use XLink to link customers with the orders those customers have placed.

> *The latest version of the XLink specification can be found at http://www.w3.org/TR/xlink/, and the latest version of the XPointer specification can be found at http://www.w3.org/TR/xptr.*

XLink

XLink provides a syntax for defining links in XML, similar to the HTML links we've seen so far, but with some added functionality not available in HTML links. It does this by providing a number of **global attributes**, which can be attached to any XML element, to define the link.

In this section, we'll study:

❑ The global attributes provided by XLink, and how they work

❑ The XLink concepts of **simple links** and **extended links**, which are not available in HTML links

❑ What an **arc** is, and how it works

As a demonstration, let's consider our familiar `<name>` example:

```
<name xmlns="http://sernaferna.com/name">
  <first>John</first>
  <middle>Fitzgerald Johansen</middle>
  <last>Doe</last>
</name>
```

We might create an application which could return XML in this format, for display in a browser. A user could search for information on an employee, and get back information in this format. Now let's suppose that John Doe has a home page, located at http://sernaferna.com/homepages/doe, which we want to link to from our XML. We could do so by adding some XLink attributes to the `<last>` element, like this:

```
<name xmlns="http://sernaferna.com/name"
      xmlns:xlink="http://www.w3.org/1999/xlink">
  <first>John</first>
  <middle>Fitzgerald Johansen</middle>
  <last xlink:type="simple"
        xlink:href="http://sernaferna.com/homepages/doe">Doe</last>
</name>
```

Even though the `<last>` element is in the `http://sernaferna.com/name` namespace, we can make it an XLink linking element by adding the `type` and `href` attributes from the XLink namespace.

In the next couple of sections, we'll examine these XLink attributes, and how they work.

XLink Attributes

In order to provide the functionality mentioned above, XLink provides a number of global attributes that can be added to elements that are in any arbitrary namespace. This means that any element can be a linking element: by contrast, in HTML only a restricted few elements serve as links (such as `<A>` and `<IMG>`).

> *The namespace used for these global attributes is* `http://www.w3.org/1999/xlink/`. *For the purposes of this chapter, however, we will usually only use the* `xlink:` *prefix to denote XLink attributes; the namespace declaration will be assumed.*

The attributes are as follows:

❑ `type` specifies the type of XLink element being created

❑ `href` specifies the URI used to retrieve a resource

❑ `role` is used in extended links, to specify the function of a link's resource in a machine-readable fashion

❑ `title` is used in extended links, to specify the function of a link's resource in a human-readable fashion

❑ `show` specifies how the resource should be displayed, when retrieved

❑ actuate specifies when the specified resource should be retrieved

❑ The from and to attributes specify link directions, since XLink links are not necessarily one-way links

The type Attribute

Which attributes can be used on an element depends on the value of type, which is mandatory on any XML element being used to define a link. There are six types:

❑ simple

❑ extended

❑ locator

❑ arc

❑ resource

❑ title

The XLink specification (http://www.w3.org/TR/xlink/) provides a handy table, that summarizes which attributes are mandatory (R), which are optional (O), and which are not allowed (X) for each XLink type:

	simple	extended	locator	arc	resource	title
type	R	R	R	R	R	R
href	O	X	R	X	X	X
role	O	O	O	O	O	X
title	O	O	O	O	O	X
show	O	X	X	O	X	X
actuate	O	X	X	O	X	X
from	X	X	X	O	X	X
to	X	X	X	O	X	X

Because this attribute defines the type of XLink element being created, its value is used to refer to that type of element. That is, we refer to an element with xlink:type="simple" as a "simple-type element", and to an element with xlink:type="title" as a "title-type element".

Simple and extended-type elements are used to define an entire link. (Simple and extended links, and the differences between the two, will be covered later.) The locator, arc, resource, and title-type elements are all used in the context of an extended link, to provide more information about the link:

❑ Locator-type elements are used to indicate remote resources taking part in the link

❑ Arc-type elements are used to indicate the rules for traversing from one resource to another within the link

❑ Resource-type elements define the various resources taking part in the link

❑ Title-type elements can provide human-readable titles for a link

The href Attribute

The `href` XLink attribute is called the **locator attribute**, and it does exactly what its name implies: provides a URI where a resource can be located. Since there can be multiple resources involved in an XLink link, there can also be multiple locator attributes (on multiple elements) to provide the URIs to those resources.

The syntax for the `href` attribute is the same as that for the `href` attribute in HTML's `<A>` element. For example:

```
<A href="http://sernaferna.com/home.htm">
```

```
<myelement xlink:href="http://sernaferna.com/home.htm">
```

For each of these `href` attributes a simple URL is provided, which points to the resource being identified.

Semantic Attributes (role and title)

The `role` and `title` attributes are used to label the functions of the various resources in the link: `role` in a machine-readable way, and `title` in a human-readable way.

The role Attribute

The `role` attribute provides a machine-readable label for a resource. In other words, `role` is used to give a resource a name which is easily understandable by a computer program.

The value for the `role` attribute must be a QName, thus allowing you to distinguish roles you define from roles others define, by means of namespaces. For example:

```
<customer xmlns:order="http://www.sernaferna.com/order"
          xlink:type="resource"
          xlink:role="order:customer">
    John Doe
</customer>
```

In this example, we have a `<customer>` element, which is also a resource-type XLink element. We have given it the role of `order:customer`, so that any other XLink elements which need to refer to this resource can do so. Also, since we use QNames for the `role` attribute's value, we don't have to worry about collisions with others defining a role of `customer`, since our `customer` role is differentiated by the `order:` namespace prefix.

The title Attribute

The value for the `title` attribute is just a string that describes this link. The XLink specification doesn't stipulate any functionality that an application should perform with the information in `title`; it might not even be used at all.

One possible use for it is to create a **tool tip**, which appears if a user hovers their mouse over the link. Consider the following link:

```
<element xmlns:name="http://www.sernaferna.com/name"
         xlink:type="simple"
         xlink:href="http://www.somewhere.com"
         xlink:role="name:first"
         xlink:title="Retrieve first name">
  Click here!
</element>
```

If this were being shown in a browser and the mouse was hovered over the link, it might look something like this:

This example is, of course, contrived, since at the time of writing the Internet Explorer browser does not support XLink, but it demonstrates what could be done.

Behavior Attributes (actuate and show)

XLink allows you some flexibility in defining exactly how links work; that is, *when* the link is traversed, and *how* to treat the resource when it is retrieved.

The actuate Attribute

The `actuate` attribute specifies when the resource should be retrieved. XLink provides three possible values for this attribute – `onLoad`, `onRequest`, and `undefined` – but you are allowed to provide other values using a Qname:

❑ `onLoad` works in a similar way to the HTML `<IMG>` tag, in that the resource is retrieved as soon as the document is loaded

❑ `onRequest` works more like the HTML `<A>` tag, in that the resource is not retrieved until the user requests it

❑ If `undefined` is specified, the application is free to deal with the link in any way it feels appropriate

Applications can define other behaviors for `actuate` using a QName. For example, we might define an application which does order processing for our company, and displays a list of outstanding orders to each user. Since this list is dynamic, we could decide that we need the list to be refreshed every five minutes, which could be done with syntax similar to the following:

```
<JobList xmlns:op="http://sernaferna.com/OrderProcessing"
         xlink:type="simple"
         xlink:show="replace"
         xlink:actuate="op:EveryFiveMinutes"
         />
```

Of course, this example depends on us writing the order processing application to understand and recognize the `op:EveryFiveMinutes` value for the `actuate` attribute. If a QName is specified that the application doesn't recognize, it must treat it as if it was `undefined`.

The show Attribute

The `show` attribute specifies how to display the resource when it is loaded. XLink provides four possible values for the attribute:

❑ `new` indicates that the resource should be displayed in a separate window; this is like indicating `target="_blank"` in HTML's `<A>` element

❑ `replace` indicates that the current document should be replaced by the new document, just like the default action for an HTML `<A>` element

❑ `embed` indicates that the XLink element should be replaced by the resource, just like an image replaces the `<IMG>` element's contents in HTML

❑ `undefined` – again the application is free to deal with the link in any way it feels appropriate

As with the `actuate` attribute, you can supply your own QName for this attribute, and if the application doesn't recognize it, it must be treated the same as `undefined`. For example, you might define your own value for `show` which would cause the resource to be popped up in a little window of its own, for example to display a definition for a term.

The from and to Attributes

We mentioned earlier that XLink links can contain multiple resources, and that links can be traversed in multiple directions (For example from ResourceA to ResourceB, or from ResourceB to ResourceA). The `from` and `to` attributes are used to define the directionality for a link.

Consider the following:

```
<ExampleElement
   xlink:from="myapp:first"
   xlink:to="myapp:last"
   >
```

This element would be part of a larger link, which could traverse from `myapp:first` to `myapp:last`. The values of the `from` and `to` attributes are QNames, and correspond to the values in the `role` attributes of resources in the link.

Link Types

Now that we've looked at the various attributes, let's put them into practice. XLink defines two main types of links: a **simple link**, and an **extended link**.

A simple link is what we've been working with all along in HTML. It deals with only two resources, and is unidirectional. (That is, it goes from the "FromResource" to the "ToResource", but not the other way around.)

Extended links, on the other hand, provide extra functionality that HTML links didn't; for example they can involve more than two resources, and they allow you to specify complex traversal rules between the various resources. While simple links usually only involve a single XML element, with the XLink attributes added, extended links consist of a number of elements, which are all children or descendents of an extended-type link element.

The next sections will go into more detail about simple and extended links, including all of the elements which are available (or mandatory) for an extended link.

Simple Links

> **Simple links provide the same functionality as the hyperlinks provided in HTML: they are one-way links, involving only two resources (the source and the destination).**

To specify a simple link, we set the `type` attribute's value to `simple`. The only other XLink attribute that is really useful is `href`, to specify where to get the destination resource (although the semantic and behavior attributes are allowed as well).

The following two links, in HTML and in XML using XLink, provide the same basic functionality, which is to replace the current document with the one being linked to:

```
<A href="http://somewhere.com">Click me!</A>
<SomeElement xlink:type="simple" xlink:href="http://somewhere.com">
  Click me!
</SomeElement>
```

The following two links also provide the same basic functionality, which is to open up a document, in a new window, and to provide a tool tip for the user if the mouse is hovered over the link. First the HTML version:

```
<A href="http://somewhere.com"
   title="Click to go somewhere"
   target="_blank">
  Click me!
</A>
```

The XML version is as follows:

```
<SomeElement xlink:type="simple"
             xlink:href="http://somewhere.com"
             xlink:title="Click to go somewhere"
             xlink:show="new">
  Click me!
</SomeElement>
```

Simple links are called **inline** links, because the link's own content (in this case the `Click me!` PCDATA) serves as one of the resources. As we will see in the next section, not all XLink links have to be inline, but all *simple* ones do.

Try It Out – Creating Simple Links

1. To try out our knowledge of simple links, let's create a quick XML document that can provide some information about a person:

```
<?xml version="1.0"?>
<person>
  <name>???</name>
  <picture>???</picture>
  <homepage>???</homepage>
</person>
```

We'll assume that we would have some kind of CSS style sheet to display this document in an XLink-aware browser. As you can see, there are placeholders (???) in here, where the actual information will go, so let's start to fill them in.

2. For the `<picture>` element, we'll assume that there is a JPEG picture in this directory, called `picture.jpg`, which is a picture of the person we're describing; we can easily pull that into the document. However, the people looking at our XML document might be on slow modems; they shouldn't have to download our picture unless they really want to see it. So we'll set the picture to only load when they request it, and instead display some text to let them know that this is the case:

```
<?xml version="1.0"?>
<person xmlns:xlink="http://www.w3.org/1999/xlink/namespace/">
  <name>???</name>
  <picture xlink:type="simple"
           xlink:href="picture.jpg"
           xlink:actuate="onRequest"
           xlink:show="embed"
           xlink:title="Click to see picture!">
    Click here to see a picture!
  </picture>
  <homepage>???</homepage>
</person>
```

This will display the text Click here to see a picture!, but when the user clicks that text it will be replaced with the picture itself.

455

3. Since so many people have home pages, we'll also include a spot in here to point to this person's home page. This link will function just like an HTML <A> element:

```
<?xml version="1.0"?>
<person xmlns:xlink="http://www.w3.org/1999/xlink/namespace/">
  <name>???</name>
  <picture xlink:type="simple"
           xlink:href="picture.jpg"
           xlink:actuate="onRequest"
           xlink:show="embed"
           xlink:title="Click to see picture!">
    Click here to see a picture!
  </picture>
  <homepage xlink:type="simple"
            xlink:href="http://www.sernaferna.com/homepages/personal.htm"
            xlink:actuate="onRequest"
            xlink:show="replace">
    Click here for the homepage.
  </homepage>
</person>
```

4. Finally, we need to take care of the <name> element. For this example, let's say we happen to know there's an XML file, name.xml, which is in the same directory as our XML document, and which contains all of the information we need. So, let's pull that information in as well:

```
<?xml version="1.0"?>
<person xmlns:xlink="http://www.w3.org/1999/xlink/namespace/">
  <name xlink:type="simple"
        xlink:href="name.xml"
        xlink:actuate="onLoad"
        xlink:show="embed"/>
  <picture xlink:type="simple"
           xlink:href="picture.jpg"
           xlink:actuate="onRequest"
           xlink:show="embed"
           xlink:title="Click to see picture!">
    Click here to see a picture!
  </picture>
  <homepage xlink:type="simple"
            xlink:href="http://www.sernaferna.com/homepages/personal.htm"
            xlink:actuate="onRequest"
            xlink:show="replace">
    Click here for the homepage.
  </homepage>
</person>
```

This pulls the information right into our document; it's similar to specifying an external file in HTML's src attribute on the <SCRIPT> element. In other words, as far as the browser is concerned this is one big document, as if the contents of name.xml had been typed into this document, instead of the <name> element. (For readers familiar with C or C++, this is very much the same as using the #include directive.)

Extended Links

> **An extended link is one that associates any number of resources.**

An extended link can be inline (like a simple link) if the link's own content serves as one of the resources, or it can be **out of line**, meaning that all of the link's resources are remote. This out of line functionality allows us to define links in separate, external files, without having to make any modifications to the documents which serve as our resources. So, for example, you could create a link for your application from **Document A** to **Document B**, even if you don't have access to modify either document!

As an example of where this might be useful, consider a corporate web site. If you decided to include a simple footer at the bottom of each page, saying something like "Copyright   2000 My Company Inc.", you could create an XML file with an extended link to include that file in all of the others on the site, without having to change any of those other files.

Extended links are defined in an extended-type element:

```
xlink:type="extended"
```

They have one or more child elements, which define the local and remote resources participating in the link, traversal rules for those resources, and human-readable labels for the link.

Extended-type elements can also have the semantic attributes (`role` and `title`), in which case they apply to the *whole* link. However, as we'll see, we can apply these attributes to *specific* resources within our link as well.

Try It Out – Creating an Extended Link

For this example, we'll look at a fictitious application that can display information about a part number to a user. The user can then navigate to the last order that was placed for that part number, and to the salesperson who made that order.

Unfortunately, we don't yet have enough information to create a whole extended link – we'll pick up that information in the next few sections. So for now, we'll just have to content ourselves with the extended-type element itself.

1. First, we'll create the XML document, `parts.xml`, which will contain the link:

```
<PartNumber>
  <item>
    <part-number>E16-25A</part-number>
    <description>Production-Class Widget</description>
  </item>
</PartNumber>
```

2. Next, we'll change the `<PartNumber>` element, to be an extended-type link element:

```
<PartNumber xmlns:xlink="http://www.w3.org/1999/xlink/"
            xlink:type="extended">
  <item>
    <part-number>E16-25A</part-number>
    <description>Production-Class Widget</description>
  </item>
</PartNumber>
```

How It Works

We have declared `<PartNumber>` to be an extended-type element. Our link doesn't yet have any functionality, or even any resources, but we'll add those as we expand this example.

Locator-type Elements

> **Locator-type elements are child elements of extended-type elements, used to indicate the remote (out-of-line) resources taking part in an extended link.**

Along with the `type` attribute, locator-type elements must also include the locator attribute (`href`), which specifies the URI pointing to the resource in question. If desired, it can also include the `role` and `title` attributes, but they are not required.

The following is an example of a locator-type element, with all of the available XLink attributes specified:

```
<salesperson xlink:type="locator"
             xlink:href="http://sernaferna.com/JohnDoe.xml"
             xlink:role="op:salesperson"
             xlink:title="Salesperson"/>
```

Try It Out – Adding Remote Resources to the Extended Link

With this new information, we can now add a couple of resources to our extended link. We'll add links to the salesperson who placed the order, and the order itself:

```
<PartNumber xmlns:xlink="http://www.w3.org/1999/xlink/"
            xmlns:op="http://sernaferna.com/OrderProcessingSystem"
            xlink:type="extended">
  <item>
    <part-number>E16-25A</part-number>
    <description>Production-Class Widget</description>
  </item>
  <salesperson xlink:type="locator"
               xlink:href="http://sernaferna.com/JohnDoe.xml"
               xlink:role="op:salesperson"
               xlink:title="Salesperson"/>
  <order xlink:type="locator"
```

```
        xlink:href="http://sernaferna.com/order256.xml"
        xlink:role="op:order"
        xlink:title="Order"/>
</PartNumber>
```

How It Works

Our link now has two external resources, and specifies the URIs where these resources can be found, for example:

```
<salesperson xlink:type="locator"
             xlink:href="http://sernaferna.com/JohnDoe.xml"
```

Because we have given them `roles`, we need to declare the namespace being used for our QNames:

```
    xmlns:op="http://sernaferna.com/OrderProcessingSystem"
```

We still don't know the relationship between these resources, but we'll take care of that next.

Arcs

> **The rules for traversing from one resource to another in a link are grouped together into an entity called an** arc, **which is provided by an arc-type element.**

Arc-type elements define the direction in which the link must traverse, using the `from` and `to` attributes, and the behavior the link will follow when it retrieves these resources, using the `show` and `actuate` attributes.

Arc-type elements can even define the `role` and `title` attributes, which will define not the resource being retrieved, but the resource *in the context of this arc.* For example, in our previous example we have a resource with a title of `Salesperson`, and one with a title of `Order`. So, if we defined an arc going from the `Order` resource to this `Salesperson` resource, we might title the arc `Salesperson's name`. However, if the arc was defined as going the other way, we might call it `Last order processed`, as that makes more sense for this arc.

> **Every available XLink attribute is allowed to be used with an arc-type element, except for `href`. An arc-type element is the only place where the XLink `from` and `to` attributes are used.**

The following is an example of an arc-type element, specifying all of the available attributes:

```
<GetPhoto xlink:type="arc"
    xlink:from="myapp:name"
    xlink:to="myapp:photo"
    xlink:show="replace"
    xlink:actuate="onRequest"
    xlink:role="myapp:GetPhoto"
    xlink:title="Show photo"/>
```

This specifies that the GetPhoto element acts as a link, and "Show photo" should be displayed when the link is hovered over. When the link is activated, the link element with role myapp:name should be replaced with the link element with role myapp:photo. This link is identified as myapp:GetPhoto. The myapp:name and myapp:photo link elements will be defined elsewhere.

Try It Out – Adding Arcs to the Extended Link

So far we have two resources in our extended link, but we haven't defined how our application is allowed to traverse between these resources. For our purposes, it's OK to go either way, so we'll define two arcs, one for each direction:

```
<PartNumber xmlns:xlink="http://www.w3.org/1999/xlink/"
            xmlns:op="http://sernaferna.com/OrderProcessingSystem"
            xlink:type="extended">
  <item>
    <part-number>E16-25A</part-number>
    <description>Production-Class Widget</description>
  </item>
  <salesperson xlink:type="locator"
               xlink:href="http://sernaferna.com/JohnDoe.xml"
               xlink:role="op:salesperson"
               xlink:title="Salesperson"/>
  <order xlink:type="locator"
         xlink:href="http://sernaferna.com/order256.xml"
         xlink:role="op:order"
         xlink:title="Order"/>
  <GetOrder xlink:type="arc"
            xlink:from="op:salesperson"
            xlink:to="op:order"
            xlink:show="replace"
            xlink:actuate="onRequest"
            xlink:role="op:GetOrder"
            xlink:title="Last order processed."/>
  <GetSalesperson xlink:type="arc"
                  xlink:from="op:order"
                  xlink:to="op:salesperson"
                  xlink:show="replace"
                  xlink:actuate="onRequest"
                  xlink:role="op:GetSalesperson"
                  xlink:title="Salesperson's name"/>
</PartNumber>
```

How It Works

With these arcs defined, we can go from an order to a salesperson's name, and from a salesperson's name to an order. In both cases, the new resource will replace the current one, since we have specified replace for the show attribute, and the link won't be traversed until the user requests it, because we've specified onRequest for the actuate attribute.

Resource-type Elements

As we mentioned earlier, extended links can be inline if at least one of the resources specified is local.

> **Resource-type elements are used to create local resources, by putting an element declared as a resource-type under the extended-type element.**

Resource-type elements can only have the `role` and `title` attributes, both of which are optional. (The `href`, `show`, and `actuate` attributes wouldn't really make sense for a local resource.)

This makes resource-type elements very simple:

```
<item xlink:type="resource"
      xlink:role="order:item"
      xlink:title="Item">
  <part-number>E16-25A</part-number>
  <description>Production-Class Widget</description>
</item>
```

Everything in the `<item>` element, including its children, is part of the resource.

Try It Out – Adding a Local Resource to the Extended Link

For our example, we'll create a local resource to describe a part number. We'll then have that part number link to the `op:order` resource, leaving in place the links between the `op:order` resource and the `op:name` resource:

```
<PartNumber xmlns:xlink="http://www.w3.org/1999/xlink/"
            xmlns:op="http://sernaferna.com/OrderProcessingSystem"
            xlink:type="extended">
  <item xlink:type="resource"
        xlink:role="op:item"
        xlink:title="Item">
    <part-number>E16-25A</part-number>
    <description>Production-Class Widget</description>
  </item>
  <salesperson xlink:type="locator"
               xlink:href="http://sernaferna.com/JohnDoe.xml"
               xlink:role="op:salesperson"
               xlink:title="Salesperson"/>
  <order xlink:type="locator"
         xlink:href="http://sernaferna.com/order256.xml"
         xlink:role="op:order"
         xlink:title="Order"/>
  <GetOrder xlink:type="arc"
            xlink:from="op:salesperson"
            xlink:to="op:order"
            xlink:show="replace"
            xlink:actuate="onRequest"
            xlink:role="op:GetOrder"
            xlink:title="Last order processed."/>
  <GetSalesperson xlink:type="arc"
                  xlink:from="op:order"
                  xlink:to="op:salesperson"
```

```
                       xlink:show="replace"
                       xlink:actuate="onRequest"
                       xlink:role="op:GetSalesperson"
                       xlink:title="Salesperson's name"/>
    <GetItemOrder xlink:type="arc"
                  xlink:from="op:item"
                  xlink:to="op:order"
                  xlink:show="new"
                  xlink:actuate="onRequest"
                  xlink:role="op:GetItemOrder"
                  xlink:title="Last order placed for this item"/>
</PartNumber>
```

How It Works

What we've effectively done is create a local resource, which will go on the main page in the user's browser, and which describes a part number.

We have defined not only a local resource, but also an arc to open up an order from that resource. If the user clicks on that part number, a new window will open up, with the order information, and the user can then navigate back and forth in that new window between the order and the salesperson's name XML documents.

The end result might look something like this:

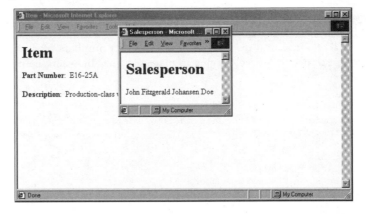

Or like this:

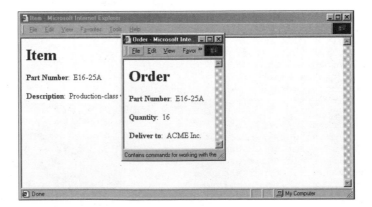

Title-type Elements

> Title-type elements are simple elements which can be used in lieu of the `title` attribute if so desired.

The benefit of using title-type elements instead of the `title` attribute is that elements can include other elements as children. One common example might be to add HTML markup to the title. This means we could rewrite:

```
<GetItemOrder xlink:type="arc"
              xlink:title="Last order placed for this item"/>
```

as:

```
<GetItemOrder xlink:type="arc">
  <description xlink:type="title">
    Last <B>order</B> placed for this <I>item</I>.
  </description>
</GetItemOrder>
```

By using a title-type element (`<description>`) we can include `B` and `I` child elements to make the link title more attractive.

Defaulting XLink Attributes

Because there are so many XLink global attributes, the XLink specification assumes that you will be using DTDs to provide default values for them. This can prove to be a great time-saver, and also makes your documents more readable.

For example, suppose you have a `<definition>` element that you will always be using in your documents to point to a definition somewhere. The link will be simple, and will just pop up the definition in a little window. You might create a `<definition>` element like this:

```
<definition xmlns:show="http://www.sernaferna.com/show"
            xlink:type="simple"
            xlink:href="definition1.xml"
            xlink:actuate="onRequest"
            xlink:show="show:popup"
            xlink:title="Click for definition">
   widget
</definition>
```

This defines a link from the word `widget` to the definition of that word. But, as you can see, most of the attributes will be exactly the same for every instance of the `<definition>` element. For this reason, we could give them all defaults in our DTD, such as the following:

```
<!ELEMENT definition ANY>
<!ATTLIST definition
  xmlns:show     CDATA          #FIXED "http://www.sernaferna.com/show"
  xmlns:xlink    CDATA          #FIXED "http://www.w3.org/1999/xlink"
  xlink:type     (simple)       #FIXED "simple"
  xlink:href     CDATA          #IMPLIED
  xlink:title    CDATA          #FIXED "Click for definition"
  xlink:show     (show:popup)   #FIXED "show:popup"
  xlink:actuate  (onLoad
                 |onRequest
                 |undefined)    #FIXED "onRequest"
>
```

This makes creating an instance of `<definition>` as easy as this:

```
<definition xlink:href="definition1.xml">widget</definition>
```

which is much easier to read.

Pointing to Document Fragments with XPointer

So far we've covered how we can create links that involve numerous resources, with varying arcs to and from those resources, and even how we can control the behavior of those arcs. But we're still dealing with entire documents. What about those times when we only need part of a document: a few elements, or even a few characters, from an XML document?

The **XPointer** specification provides a method for pointing to pieces of an XML document. These XPointer expressions can then be appended to URIs, making them useful in the context of links. For example, instead of creating a link to the names.xml document, you might create a link that points to the first `<name>` element in names.xml, or to all `<name>` elements where the child `<first>` element contains the value "John", etc.

This may seem very similar to the types of expressions you learned how to write in Chapter 4, using XPath. In fact, XPointer is built on XPath, so everything you learned before will still apply, but it also adds some extensions to basic XPath expressions. These extensions to XPath allow XPointer expressions to:

❑ Locate information by string matching

❑ Be appended to URIs, to expand the power and flexibility of links

❑ Address not only entire nodes in an XML document, but pieces of nodes

As an example of the last point, we can write an XPath expression to return the `<name>` element, but we could write an XPointer expression to return the first few characters of the text in the `<name>` element. Or we could define a spot in the document before the first `<name>` element, and another spot after the first `<middle>` element, and take everything in between these two spots.

Because of this extended functionality, XPointer no longer refers to "nodes"; instead, the specification generalizes the term further to be called a **location**. These locations can be of any node type which was allowed in XPath, but can also be one of two new types: **points** and **ranges**. Accordingly, instead of dealing in node-sets, XPointer deals in **location sets**. (More on these terms coming up.)

Most importantly, XPointer provides a syntax for appending an XPointer expression to the end of a URI, where this expression specifies the piece of the document you want. So not only can we say "get this document from this location", but we can go even further and say "get this *piece* of this document from this location".

> *When working with XPointer, you will always be dealing with XML documents: by contrast, XLink can create links to any types of documents, XML or otherwise.*

Appending XPointer Expressions to URIs

As we mentioned earlier, we can currently create hyperlinks to particular sections of HTML documents by specifying a URI like this:

```
http://www.sernaferna.com/default/page.htm#section-one
```

In order for this to work, the HTML document, page.htm, has to have an **anchor** in it, like this:

```
<A name="section-one">
```

XPointer uses a similar syntax to return pointers to parts of an XML document. For example, consider the following:

```
http://www.sernaferna.com/default/page.xml#xpointer(//section-one)
```

This URI points to a file called page.xml, but an XPointer expression is appended to the end, enclosed between the beginning xpointer(string and the closing). This expression is really just an XPath expression with a few XPointer extensions. When the XML document is retrieved, the XPointer-aware application would only be concerned with <section-one> elements, just as if we had used the following in XSLT:

```
<xsl:value-of select="//section-one"/>
```

Of course, the key difference between this XPointer expression and the URL to the HTML document above is that the HTML document needed an anchor; for XPointers to work, we don't need to modify the XML document at all.

Using Multiple XPointer Expressions

In cases where we want to use multiple XPointer expressions, we can chain them together. XPointer reads the expressions from left to right; if one expression fails (for example the specified element can't be found), the next one is evaluated. The results from the first expression to be evaluated are taken, and the rest ignored (note that an expression returning an empty location set is not the same as failing).

Consider the following example:

```
xpointer(id("section-one"))xpointer(//*[@id="section-one"])
```

If there is a DTD associated with this XML document, which defines an ID attribute, then the first XPointer expression (id("section-one")) will be evaluated and the results will be returned. However, if there is no DTD associated with this XML document, the expression will fail. The reason for this is that we can't have ID attributes without a DTD, because without the DTD the processor does not know which attributes are IDs. In that case, the second expression would be evaluated, which would return a location set of any elements with an attribute *named* id that has a value of section-one. Again, that location set could possibly be empty, which is not the same as failing.

Try It Out – Retrieving a Piece of a Document

In our extended link Try It Outs, we had separate XML documents containing the information for an order and the name of the salesperson who completed that order. Let's modify that example.

1. Suppose our order XML (order256.xml) was structured like this:

```
<?xml version="1.0"?>
<order>
  <name>
    <first>John</first>
    <middle/>
    <last>Doe</last>
  </name>
  <item>Production-Class Widget</item>
  <quantity>16</quantity>
  <date>
    <m>1</m>
    <d>1</d>
    <y>2000</y>
  </date>
  <customer>Sally Finkelstein</customer>
</order>
```

Why, it includes the salesperson's name right in it! There's no need to get a separate document for it.

2. We can then restructure our extended link like the following:

```
<PartNumber xmlns:xlink="http://www.w3.org/1999/xlink/"
            xmlns:op="http://sernaferna.com/OrderProcessingSystem"
            xlink:type="extended">
  <item xlink:type="resource"
        xlink:role="op:item"
        xlink:title="Item">
    <part-number>E16-25A</part-number>
    <description>Production-Class Widget</description>
  </item>
  <salesperson xlink:type="locator"

xlink:href="http://sernaferna.com/order256.xml#xpointer(/order/name)"
               xlink:role="op:salesperson"
               xlink:title="Salesperson"/>
```

```
<order xlink:type="locator"
       xlink:href="http://sernaferna.com/order256.xml"
       xlink:role="op:order"
       xlink:title="Order"/>
<GetOrder xlink:type="arc"
          xlink:from="op:salesperson"
          xlink:to="op:order"
          xlink:show="replace"
          xlink:actuate="onRequest"
          xlink:role="op:GetOrder"
          xlink:title="Last order processed."/>
<GetSalesperson xlink:type="arc"
                xlink:from="op:order"
                xlink:to="op:salesperson"
                xlink:show="replace"
                xlink:actuate="onRequest"
                xlink:role="op:GetSalesperson"
                xlink:title="Salesperson's name"/>
<GetItemOrder xlink:type="arc"
                xlink:from="op:item"
                xlink:to="op:order"
                xlink:show="new"
                xlink:actuate="onRequest"
                xlink:role="op:GetItemOrder"
                xlink:title="Last order placed for this item"/>
</PartNumber>
```

How It Works

What we have done, in effect, is create two resources (`Salesperson` and `Order`) which point to the same document; traversing from one resource to the other would really just be hiding most of the document (only showing the salesperson's name), or un-hiding it again (and showing the entire order document).

XPointer Schemes

In our URL, we specified a syntax like this for our XPointers:

```
#xpointer(expression)
```

The expression is easy – it's just XPath with some XPointer additions – but what does the `xpointer` really mean? It's actually called a **scheme**.

> **A scheme identifies what type of XML document we are getting our information from.**

The only scheme included in the XPointer specification is the `xpointer` scheme we've been using; it applies to any XML document.

We could create schemes for other specific document types. For example, there is an XML format for describing graphics, called SVG, and a scheme could be developed explicitly for retrieving parts of an SVG document. We could also create schemes for our own, proprietary, XML document types.

However, in order to use any scheme other than xpointer, you would need software that not only understood XPointers, but also understood your particular scheme.

XPointer Shorthand Syntaxes

In addition to the full XPointer syntax, there are also a couple of shorthand syntaxes available:

❑ The bare names syntax

❑ The child sequence syntax

For these examples, we'll create a simple XML document, with an ID attribute:

```xml
<?xml version="1.0"?>
<!DOCTYPE XPointerSample [
  <!ELEMENT XPointerSample (first, middle, last)>
  <!ELEMENT first (#PCDATA)>
  <!ELEMENT middle (#PCDATA)>
  <!ELEMENT last (#PCDATA)>
  <!ATTLIST first id ID #REQUIRED>
]>
<XPointerSample>
  <name>
    <first id="section-one">John</first>
    <middle>Fitzgerald Johansen</middle>
    <last>Doe</last>
  </name>
</XPointerSample>
```

We'll assume this file is stored on a web server, in the location http://www.sernaferna.com/default/page.xml.

Full Syntax

One common usage of XPointer will be retrieving an element from an XML document based on its ID. The full syntax for the href attribute would be like this:

```
http://www.sernaferna.com/default/page.xml#xpointer(id("section-one"))
```

This will retrieve an element which has an id attribute, with a value of "section-one"; in this case, the <first> element.

Bare Names Syntax

The **bare names** syntax allows us to retrieve an element by its ID like this:

```
http://www.sernaferna.com/default/page.xml#section-one
```

which has the same effect as the XPointer expression above. You may notice that this syntax is the same as the earlier URI we saw for retrieving an HTML document. Part of the reason that XPointer provides this shorthand syntax is to provide a mechanism which is analogous to HTML's method of retrieving a document. (The other reason for providing this shorthand is to encourage the use of IDs.)

Child Sequence Syntax

The third way we can specify XPointer expressions at the end of a URI is to use a **child sequence**:

```
http://www.sernaferna.com/default/page.xml#/1/1/2
```

The numbers after the "/" characters are child element numbers of the previously selected elements. In other words, this expression means "the second child element of the first child element of the first child element". When used right at the beginning of the child sequence, /1 means the root element. This XPointer expression is equivalent to:

```
http://www.sernaferna.com/default/page.xml#xpointer(/*[1]/*[1]/*[2])
```

which says to select the second child of the first child of the document root or, in this case, the `<middle>` element.

Instead of specifying /1 as the starting point of a child sequence, we can also append a child sequence to a bare name expression, such as in the following:

```
http://www.sernaferna.com/default/page.xml#section-one/3
```

This will take the third child element of the element with an ID of `section-one`.

> The child sequence and bare names syntaxes can only retrieve *elements* from the XML document; for other node-types, you need to use the full XPointer syntax.

An obvious drawback to ordinal references (in other words, using numbers as in the examples above) is that if the structure of the XML file changes, any links into it will be made invalid. This would not be the case had the links used an actual XPath expression. There are actually very few cases where you would want to use the child sequence syntax, rather than referring to elements and attributes by name.

Try It Out – Using the Shorthand Syntaxes

Because we know the element structure of our order XML, we can modify our last Try It Out with a child sequence, instead of the full XPointer syntax. Our link will now look more like this:

```
<PartNumber xmlns:xlink="http://www.w3.org/1999/xlink/"
            xmlns:op="http://sernaferna.com/OrderProcessingSystem"
            xlink:type="extended">
```

```
<salesperson xlink:type="locator"
             xlink:href="http://sernaferna.com/order256.xml#/1/1"
             xlink:role="op:salesperson"
             xlink:title="Salesperson"/>
</PartNumber>
```

This works because we know that the `<name>` element is always the first child of the document element for our XML document type. But again, this is a very brittle approach; if we were ever to modify our document structure, our XPointer expression would stop working, whereas the previous XPath expression has a better chance of surviving the changes.

Locations, Points and Ranges

We're already used to the idea of nodes; these represent elements, attributes, PIs, etc. We're also familiar with node-sets, which are collections of nodes. However, as mentioned earlier, XPointer adds the concepts of a **location** and a **location set**.

> **A location can be any node type that was allowed in XPath, or one of the positional declarations known as** points **and** ranges. **A location set is an ordered list of locations.**

XPointer allows us even greater flexibility than XPath, because we don't have to retrieve whole nodes, but can retrieve pieces of nodes (for example, the first few characters of a text node, or the last few characters of the text node in one element and the first few characters of the text node from the next element.) The way we can do this is by selecting ranges, which is a part of the document between two points. Let's look at the concepts of points and ranges.

Points

> **A point is simply a spot in the XML document. It is defined using the usual XPointer expressions.**

There are two pieces of information needed to define a point: a **container node** and an **index**. Points are located between bits of XML; that is between two elements or between two characters in a CDATA section. Whether the point refers to characters or elements depends on the nature of the container node. An index of zero indicates the point before any child nodes, and a non-zero index n indicates the point immediately after the nth child node. (So an index of 5 indicates the point right after the 5th child node.)

When the container node is an element (or the document root), the index becomes an index of the child elements, and the point is called a **node-point**. In the following diagram, the container node is the `<name>` element, and the index is 2. This means the point indicates a spot right after the second child element of `<name>`, which is the `<middle>` element:

The XPointer expression for this would be:

```
#xpointer(/name[2])
```

If the container is any other node-type, the index refers to the characters of the string value of that node, and the point is called a **character-point**. In the following diagram, the container node is the PCDATA child of <middle>, and the index is 2, indicating a point right after the i and right before the t of Fitzgerald:

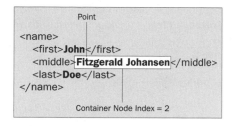

The XPointer expression for this would be:

```
#xpointer(/name/middle/text()[2])
```

Ranges

A range **is defined by two points – a** start point **and an** end point **– and consists of all of the XML structure and content between those two points.**

The start point and end point must both be in the same document. If the start point and the end point are equal, the range is a **collapsed range**. However, a range can't have a start point that is *later* in the document than the end point.

If the container node of either point is anything other than an element node, text node, or document root node, then the container node of the other point must be the same. For example, the following range is valid, because both the start point and the end point are in the same PI:

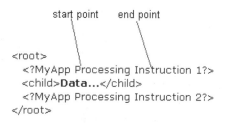

whereas this one is not, because the start point and end point are in different PIs:

```
                                 start point
          <root>                    |
              <?MyApp Processing Instruction 1?>
              <child>Data...</child>
              <?MyApp Processing Instruction 2?>
          </root>
                            end point
```

The concept of a range is the reason that the XPath usage of nodes and node-sets weren't good enough for XPointer; the information contained in a range might include only parts of nodes, which XPath can't handle.

How Do We Select Ranges?

XPointer adds the keyword `to`, which we can insert in our XPointer expressions to specify a range. It's used as follows:

```
xpointer(/order/name to /order/item)
```

This selects a range where the start point is just before the <name> element, and the end point is just after the <item> element:

```
                        <?xml version="1.0" ?>
                        <order>
    Start point ————▶   <name>
                            <first>John</first>
                            <middle />
                            <last>Doe</last>
                        </name>
    End point  ————▶    <item>Production-Class Widget</item>
                        <quantity>16</quantity>
                        <date>
                            <m>1</m>
                            <d>1</d>
                            <y>2000</y>
                        </date>
                        <customer>Sally Finkelstein</customer>
                        </order>
```

In other words, the <name> and <item> elements would both be part of this range, which would be the only member in the location set.

Ranges with Multiple Locations

This is pretty easy when the expressions on either side of the `to` keyword return a single location, but what about when the expressions return multiple locations in their location sets? Well then things get a bit more complicated. Let's create an example, and work our way through it.

Consider the following XML:

```
<people>
  <person name="John">
    <phone>(555)555-1212</phone>
    <phone>(555)555-1213</phone>
  </person>
  <person name="David">
    <phone>(555)555-1214</phone>
  </person>
  <person name="Andrea">
    <phone>(555)555-1215</phone>
    <phone>(555)555-1216</phone>
    <phone>(555)555-1217</phone>
  </person>
  <person name="Ify">
    <phone>(555)555-1218</phone>
    <phone>(555)555-1219</phone>
  </person>
  <!--more people could follow-->
</people>
```

We have a list of people, and each person can have one or more phone numbers. Now consider the following XPointer:

```
xpointer(//person to phone[1])
```

As you can see, the first expression will return a number of <person> elements, and the second expression will return the first <phone> element. XPointer tackles this as follows:

3. It evaluates the expression on the left side of the `to` keyword, and saves the returned location set. In this case, it will be a location set of all of the <person> elements.

```
<person name="John"/>
<person name="David"/>
<person name="Andrea"/>
<person name="Ify"/>
```

4. Using the first location in that set as the context location, XPath then evaluates the expression on the right side of the `to` keyword. In this case, it will select the first <phone> child of the first <person> element in the location set on the left.

```
<person name="John"/> ————— <phone>(555)555-1212</phone>
<person name="David"/>
<person name="Andrea"/>
<person name="Ify"/>
```

5. For each location in this second location set, XPointer adds a range to the result, with the start point at the beginning of the location in the first location set, and the end point at the end of the location in the second location set. In this case, only one range will be created, since the second expression only returned one location.

6. Steps 2 and 3 are then repeated for each location in the first location set, with all of the additional ranges being added to the result. So, as a result of the XPointer above, we would end up with the following pieces of XML selected in our document:

```
<person name="John">
    <phone>(555)555-1212</phone>
  <person name="David">
    <phone>(555)555-1214</phone>
  <person name="Andrea">
    <phone>(555)555-1215</phone>
  <person name="Ify">
    <phone>(555)555-1218</phone>
```

XPointer Function Extensions to XPath

Of course, to deal with these new concepts, XPointer adds a few functions to the ones supplied by XPath. We won't go into their details here, but the following is a brief description of the new functions:

❑ The start-point() function takes a location set as a parameter, and returns a location set containing the start points of all of the locations in the location set. For example, start-point(//child[1]) would return the start point of the first <child> element in the document, and start-point(//child) would return a set containing the start points of all of the <child> elements in the document.

❑ The end-point() function works exactly the same, but returns end points.

❑ The range() and range-inside() functions return ranges. range() takes a location set as a parameter, and returns another location set. For each location in the input, it creates a range for that location which it adds to the output. range-inside() works similarly, taking in and returning location sets, except that the range it creates for each location is only for the *contents* of the location, not the entire thing.

❑ The here() function returns the element which contains the XPointer. That is, if we define an XPointer which points to a specific piece of an XML document, here() returns the element which contains that piece.

❑ The origin() function returns the element from which a user or program initiated traversal of a link. It is used in the context of out-of-line XLink links.

Querying

Along with XLink and XPointer, there is also an **XML Query Working Group** in place at the W3C, which will be providing a means of creating queries that can retrieve data from XML documents across the web.

At the moment, there are no publicly accessible XML Query Working Group pages at the W3C, except for a Requirements Document, at http://www.w3.org/TR/xmlquery-req, which outlines what the XML Query data model, algebra, and language should do. Check back at http://www.w3.org/XML occasionally, for updates.

Summary

This chapter has introduced you to two technologies that will be available in the near future – or may already be available by the time you read this book. XLink and XPointer provide some powerful capabilities for linking together XML documents: especially for use in browser-type applications, although there is functionality here that could be used in any XML application that deals with multiple documents.

We've seen:

- ❑ How to create simple links in XLink, which mirror the functionality provided by HTML
- ❑ How to create complex (extended) links using XLink, even when you don't have access to modify the documents in question
- ❑ How default attribute values in a DTD can greatly simplify XML documents that use XLink
- ❑ How XPointer can be used to retrieve only those portions of an XML document that are really needed
- ❑ How different types of XML documents can be specified for XPointer using different schemes (when they become available)

We're going to move on now and take a look at how XML can be used to enhance applications which incorporate data from traditional databases.

XML and Databases

By now, it should be painfully obvious that XML is all about data. XML provides a near perfect way to communicate data, to people and to computers. For example, XML data is structured, there are ways of ensuring that the structure is adhered to, and it can easily be transmitted and transformed into other formats. So how does XML fit in with traditional databases?

In the world of computer science, you can rarely throw a proverbial rock without hitting such a database. It's inevitable that at some point or another, you're probably going to be dealing with one.

This chapter will discuss some of the issues involved in integrating XML into existing database-oriented applications or, conversely, integrating databases into your new applications. It will cover:

- ❑ An overview of what a relational database is, including the concept of normalization
- ❑ Some ideas for building an application to take advantage of your existing databases
- ❑ Some ideas for potentially building XML right into a database
- ❑ A look at what a couple of the major database vendors are doing to incorporate XML into their products

Because it's a bit unrealistic to ask all of our readers to install specific database software, this chapter will not have any hands on Try It Outs, but we will show code examples of how you could use XML with databases in general. You should then be able to apply this to whatever database you are familiar with.

You're probably already somewhat familiar with the concept of a database: they were invented as a way to store large amounts of information, and quickly retrieve it. Since decades have gone into database design and best practices, a thorough discussion of databases is not within the scope of this chapter, and indeed, this book. The chapter starts out with an explanation of relational databases; if you are already familiar with them you can skip this first part of the chapter if you wish, and move straight on to Making Use of What You've Got section.

Databases, Yesterday and Today

There are a number of database types, such as **relational**, **hierarchical**, and **object oriented**, but the most common type in use is the relational database. In a relational database, information is structured in tables which are arranged in a similar way to spreadsheets, in other words in **rows** and **columns**.

The key when arranging a relational database is to concentrate on the *data* itself, not on the *applications* that will be using that data. This makes the database much more flexible and open to changes. Arranging the data according to the application might make that application run more smoothly, but it could hinder the data from growing into other areas, and indeed, hinder the application from changing out of its initial design.

The best way to understand is to see an example, so let's see some relational tables. We'll take the following information:

Order Number:	123587
Account Number:	125692
First Name:	John
Middle Name:	Fitzgerald Johansen
Last Name:	Doe
Home Phone:	(555)555-1212
Work Phone:	(555)555-2121
Item:	E16-25A
Description:	Production Class Widget
Quantity:	16
Date:	2000/1/1

and arrange it into some tables like so:

Parts Table

item	description
E16-25A	Production Class Widget
B25-25A	Automatic Farstle Maker
E16-25B	Economy Class Widget

Customer Table

account_number	first_name	middle_name	last_name	home_phone	work_phone
125692	John	Fitzgerald Johansen	Doe	(555)555-1212	(555)555-2121
125693	Jane		Smith	(555)555-1111	(555)555-1112
125694	Alfred	E.	Neuman	(555)555-9999	(555)555-0000

Order Table

order_number	account_number	item	quantity	date
123587	125692	E16-25A	16	2000/1/1
123588	125692	E16-25A	1	2000/2/1
123589	125694	E16-25A	20	2000/2/1
123589	125693	B25-25A	5	2000/2/1

Our information is laid out in a grid, with rows and columns. The information for one "part", or for one "customer", or for one "order", gets grouped together in a *row*, which is often called a **record** in database terms. Each individual piece of data in that record, such as an "account number" or a "middle name", gets its own *column*, which is also sometimes called a **field**.

As you can see, although the information has been split into multiple tables, we still have enough information in each table to combine it back together if necessary. For example, we could ask for the information for order 123587 from the Order table; then we could use the account_number column in that table to go to the Customer table, and get our customer information, and the item column to get the information from the Parts table.

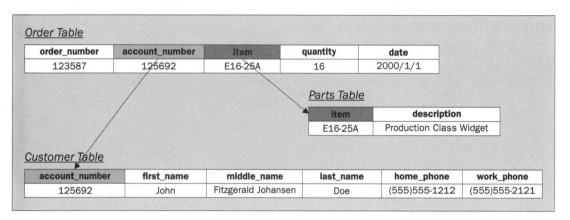

SQL

To facilitate working with relational databases, a programming language was invented to talk to them: **Structured Query Language**, or **SQL**. (Depending on who you talk to, this might be pronounced "S-Q-L", "sequel", "squeal", or any number of other variations.)

SQL is a standardized language, meaning that a basic SQL statement that works in one relational database will work with any other relational database. However, most database vendors also add their own extensions to the language. (Also, like XSL, SQL is a *declarative* language, not a *procedural* one.)

A typical SQL statement looks like this:

```
SELECT first_name FROM Customer WHERE account_number = '125692'
```

This statement will return the value from the first_name column in the Customer table, in the row where the account number is 125692. If there were more than one row with this value for the account number, the SELECT statement would return more than one value. The results from a SELECT statement are in a tabular form, just like relational tables, so in this case the statement would only return one column and one row.

One of the problems we often encounter when working with databases is that of **uniqueness**. If we ask for the information from account number 125692, we should only get at most one record returned. If there were multiple accounts with an account number of 125692, it would potentially cause confusion, and we would no longer be able to trust the data in our database. Another way to phrase this is that we would lose **database integrity**.

For this reason, databases have a special type of column called the **primary key**, which is a column whose value must be unique from record to record within the table. That is, if one record in the table has a value of "1" in its primary key, no other record in the table can have that value. Databases enforce this primary key functionality for you, so if you try to insert a new record into the database, with a value in the primary key which is already used, it will not allow the insert.

If we specified the `account_number` column in the `Customer` table to be the primary key, and tried to insert another row into the table with the value of 125692 for that column, the database would reject it. This means that we would attain our uniqueness goal, and our SQL statement would only ever return at most one record, no more.

Retrieving Data from Multiple Tables

We can also gather information for order number 123587 from across multiple tables.

```
SELECT Order.order_number, Order.account_number, Customer.first_name,
       Customer.middle_name, Customer.last_name, Customer.home_phone,
       Customer.work_phone, Order.item, Parts.description, Order.quantity,
       Order.date
FROM Order, Customer, Parts
WHERE Order.order_number = '123587'
      AND Customer.account_number = Order.account_number
      AND Parts.item = Order.item
```

The query gets data from all three tables, and the result is a tabular structure containing all of the information from the three tables. Many technologies that are capable of capturing the results of a SQL query, such as Microsoft's **ActiveX Data Objects**, or **ADO**, also capture the name of each column in the result set, to make the programmer's life easier. This result set might look something like this (only the first five fields are shown):

Customer Table					
account_number	**first_name**	**middle_name**	**last_name**	**home_phone**	**work_phone**
125692	John	Fitzgerald Johansen	Doe	(555)555-1212	(555)555-2121

However, getting data from more than one table at a time is such a common occurrence that there is a special SQL syntax you can use for that purpose, called a **join** (because it conceptually joins multiple tables together and treats them as one for the query). Using this join syntax, we could rewrite the above SQL statement like this:

```
SELECT o.order_number, o.account_number, c.first_name, c.middle_name,
       c.last_name, c.home_phone, c.work_phone, o.item, p.description,
       o.quantity, o.date
FROM Parts p INNER JOIN Order o ON p.item = o.item
     INNER JOIN Customer c ON o.account_number = c.account_number
WHERE o.order_number = '123587'
```

If you want to learn more about SQL, a good introductory text is "SQL for Dummies", and for a more comprehensive look try "An Introduction to Database Systems" by C. J. Date.

Normalization

We had to put that last SQL statement through a lot of hoops to gather data from across all three tables. Why did we bother to break the information up like that, instead of just putting it all in one table? The reason is that we don't want to have to enter all of a customer's information into the database every time that customer places an order. With our method, all we have to do in the `Order` table is refer to an existing record in the `Customer` table. If we were to enter all of the information every time, we would not only get a lot of duplication in our database, but we would also increase the likelihood that information would be entered incorrectly. (If John Doe places five different orders, and we have to enter John Doe's information for each of those orders, then it's five times as likely that we might make a mistake when entering that information.)

This **normalization** also makes it easier to write other applications to make use of this data in the future. Because we have designed our database with the data in mind, not the application, it's easier to write applications to make use of that data, in ways we had never anticipated. For example, we might write applications to create mailing lists, based on all of the customers in our `Customer` table, and another to take care of inventory, based on our `Parts` table, etc., even though neither of these applications would care about the orders in our `Order` table.

In addition to normalization, there is also a technique called **denormalization**, in which we do the opposite, and bring information which should have gone into a separate table into a less generic one. For example, in our `Customer` table, we could have broken the fields for the customer's name into a separate `Name` table, or the phone numbers into a separate `Phone` table. But after so much experience working with databases, Database Analysts have realized that sometimes the extra flexibility isn't going to buy you anything, so it would be quicker to put everything into one table.

> *There are also technical considerations involved. For example, in most database systems the optimal number of tables in a multi-table join is three or four; after this, the database starts to slow down when trying to retrieve the information.*

Although there are some rules and guidelines you can follow to normalize and denormalize a database, such as putting the data into something called "third normal form", and then denormalizing any tables which need it, it really takes a lot of experience and know-how to get it just right. This is why companies with large databases often have dedicated Database Analysts, whose only job is to manage the databases, and assist software developers who need to connect to the data in those databases.

> **If your company has a DBA, and you're going to be writing software which accesses the company's database, remember what a valuable resource that DBA is! You might be surprised how well a DBA can help you optimize your SQL statements, to squeeze every ounce of speed out of your database, and thus your application.**

Making Use of What You've Got

If you're going to be integrating XML into your *existing* infrastructure, chances are you've already got a database in place somewhere, if not more than one. In fact, there was probably a lot of time and effort spent in optimizing those databases for speed, and architecting the data in such a way that it makes sense for your business and is easily retrievable.

In these cases, it's usually a good choice to take advantage of those databases, building an **n-tier** application, in which the logic for the application is broken up into logical layers.

N-Tier Architecture

The following diagram illustrates this type of architecture:

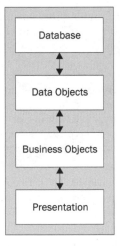

Such applications commonly have the following logical layers:

- ❑ **Data services**, where all data for the application is stored (usually a database, but not necessarily)

- ❑ **Data Objects**, which handle communication between the database and the Business Objects

- ❑ **Business Objects**, which take care of the business logic in your application, and are responsible for communications between the presentation and data tiers

- ❑ **Presentation**, which is responsible for dealing with communication between the user and the business logic tier

These logical layers don't necessarily reflect the *physical* deployment of the application. These components could be distributed across several machines, or could all be on the same machine. For large, complex applications, some or all of the layers might be broken down into further layers, giving way to more tiers, such as this:

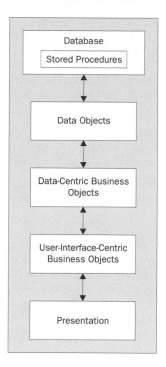

This is a common design, although different software designers may use different names for the tiers involved.

Stored procedures are a common tool used in databases. They are compiled SQL statements, bundled together like programs in the database itself. They provide much faster execution than calling the database with normal SQL statements, since they are already compiled.

The multi-tiered approach has numerous advantages:

❑ Reduced complexity for developers. For example, the developers who are writing the Data Objects need extensive knowledge about the database(s) involved, how to optimize SQL statements, etc. They need to know how to interface with the business layer but not how the business logic of the application works; the Business Objects take care of all of that. By the same token, the developers writing the Business Objects don't need to know about the complexities of the Data Objects layer, they only need to worry about their business logic and how to interface with the data layer. (Even if the same developers are writing objects in both layers, the reduced complexity will help them. It means they only have to concentrate on one task at a time, instead of having all of the logic mixed together into one component.) The complexities of one layer are hidden from other layers.

❑ Provision for change. For example, we could replace our backend database, and modify our Data Objects to make use of that new database, but our Business Objects would never have to be touched. They wouldn't know or care that the database had changed. By the same token, if the business rules ever change, we can modify the Business Object concerned, without ever having to change the Data Objects at all.

❏ More scalable than traditional client/server applications. For example, expensive database connections can be pooled and shared between Data Objects, meaning that you could potentially serve more clients than you have database connections for, as opposed to the client/server model where every client needs a dedicated connection. In addition, when an application grows, extra servers can be added to the environment, to share the load for Business Objects and Data Services objects, which is not as easy for 2-tier client/server applications.

❏ Increased re-usability. With an n-tier architecture, it's very easy to re-use components in other applications. For example, it would be possible to make use of the Data Objects tier in numerous applications, which means that code wouldn't have to be rewritten for each.

❏ Greater security. The user never accesses the data directly, always via the business tier. For example, this can help to prevent data from being corrupted inadvertently (or deliberately).

Using XML in an N-tier Application

Normally, the Data Objects tier would return information to the Business Objects tier in some kind of data-centric form. **ActiveX Data Objects** (**ADO**) are commonly used to do this. ADO provides a number of objects that can be used to retrieve data from almost any kind of database, including the **Recordset** object, which encapsulates the results of a SQL query. The Data Objects perform the SQL queries, obtain this recordset, and return it to the Business Objects, which then pull out and deal with the data they need.

So what does all of this have to do with XML? Well, if we're doing our job, that Presentation tier is going to be using XML for its data needs. (After all, this is the tier which changes the most often, making it the logical candidate to take advantage of the latest and greatest technologies.) And, if we're really on the ball, our Business Objects will also be using XML, both to communicate with the Presentation tier, and to communicate with each other. So why not go all the way, and have our Data Objects return XML as well, instead of recordsets? When updating the database, the Business Objects could pass XML to the Data Objects, which would parse the XML and pull out the appropriate data to insert into the databases.

This means that, potentially, any time one object communicates with another, it would use XML as its common language. No longer would the Business Object programmers need to know ADO, or any other data-access technology, all they would need to know is XML. The more objects you have communicating with each other, the more you'll appreciate this simplicity.

For example, consider the following diagram:

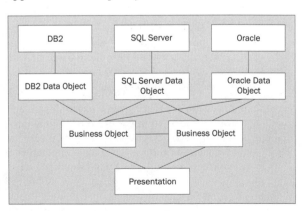

There are quite a number of objects in there! Some of these objects might be on different servers. Some might be written in different programming languages. Some might not be using compiled languages at all; the Presentation tier, for example, could be Active Server Pages or CGI scripts creating HTML pages from the server, or even DHTML, with JavaScript making use of the XML on the client. But, since we're using XML throughout the application, these differences aren't important to us; all we need to know is the format of our XML documents, and our objects can be created independently of each other.

Think about the ramifications of this. Previously, when our Data Objects were returning ADO recordsets, we would have had to write our Business Objects to understand ADO and a standard called the **Component Object Model** (**COM**), since ADO is a COM-based technology. This is great if you're already a COM developer, but if you're a Java developer, you might consider this quite a hassle!

But now, since we're just passing XML back and forth, we have gained language-independence for our objects. We could write some of our Data Objects in Visual Basic, using ADO to retrieve the data from some of the databases, and some in Java, using **JDBC** (**Java DataBase Connectivity**) to retrieve the data from other databases, but then pass XML to Business Objects which are written in completely different languages. After they've done their work, they could pass more XML on to the Presentation tier. This could be as simple as an HTML page, with an IE5 data island containing the XML and some scripting code to work with the data on the page.

Not only have we gained language-independence, but we have also gained some server-independence. Because we're just passing XML back and forth, and XML is purely text, we have a lot more freedom in putting different objects on different servers, and using lower-level protocols such as HTTP to pass the information back and forth. If we weren't using XML, we would have one of two choices:

❑ Put all of our objects on the same server. This would basically reduce us to glorified client/server computing.

❑ Lock ourselves into a particular technology for distributed computing. The two most common are **CORBA** and Microsoft's **DCOM**.

CORBA (Common Object Request Broker Architecture) is a standard for communicating between distributed objects. It can execute objects in different languages on different platforms, all over the network. DCOM (Distributed COM) is a similar standard, but it only works with Microsoft-based objects.

In either case, we would still not have the flexibility that XML allows us. For example, since CORBA implementations from different vendors don't work very well together, we would have to limit ourselves to a single CORBA vendor. Or, if we went the DCOM route, we would have to make all of our objects COM objects, which would limit us to servers running Microsoft operating systems.

Using the XML method, we can use whichever technologies make the most sense: perhaps we can use COM+ on Windows 2000 for some servers, but use Java objects on other servers running UNIX.

There are many initiatives currently under way which focus on inter-enterprise, inter-application and inter-object communications using XML. Amongst others there are the BizTalk framework, **SOAP** (Simple Object Access Protocol), and **XML-RPC** (which we'll discuss in the next chapter).

If you adopt a standard protocol you have the advantage of being able to publish interfaces for your objects that use a common, standards-based messaging system. For example, your SOAP-compliant data object could be used along with someone else's CORBA-based system without needing to negotiate all the protocol details from scratch. This would greatly reduce the time required for integration, and you would be using an accepted mechanism for critical items such as data types and error reporting.

Returning XML from a Data Object

We're going to look at some pieces of code, to see how easy it would be to create a Data Object which converts its results into XML. We'll use:

❑   Visual Basic to write the data object

❑   ADO to connect to the database

❑   Microsoft's MSXML parser to create an XML document with our results

Don't worry if you're not familiar with these technologies; the point is just to see some code doing some real work.

First of all, ADO provides an object called `Connection`, which can be used to connect to a database. So we'd set up a `Connection` object with the required details for our database (as we don't have one set up, we'll just leave out the details):

```
Dim cnnDatabaseConnection As ADODB.Connection
Set cnnDatabaseConnection = New ADODB.Connection
'here we would connect to the database...
```

We also need a `SELECT` statement to perform an operation on the database:

```
Dim strSQL As String
strSQL = "SELECT last_name FROM Customer WHERE account_number = '125692'"
```

We're now ready to execute our SQL. With ADO, that's as easy as calling the `Execute()` method on the `Connection` object, passing it the SQL statement. This returns a `Recordset` object with the results of our query:

```
Dim rsResults As ADODB.Recordset
Set rsResults = cnnDatabaseConnection.Execute(strSQL)
```

We can then create a quick XML document, and populate that object via the DOM with the values from our SQL. First of all, we'd create an initial document:

```
Dim objXML As MSXML.DOMDocument
Set objXML = New MSXML.DOMDocument

objXML.loadXML "<root><LastName/></root>"
```

Our document now contains XML like this:

```
<root>
  <LastName/>
</root>
```

The reason I did this is that I usually find it easier to create a document full of empty elements, and then just add text to those elements, rather than messing about with creating nodes and appending them back to the document.

And finally, the last step is to get the value from our `Recordset`, and add it to the XML document:

```
objXML.selectSingleNode("/root/LastName").Text = rsResults("last_name").Value
```

That's it! MSXML provides a property of the `Document` object called `xml`, which returns a string containing the XML document that this DOM is modelling. All the Data Object now has to do is return the text from that property, and we're done.

This example isn't meant to teach you how to write a Data Object; there's obviously a lot more work involved than what we've seen here. However, you can see how easy it is to take the results we got back from the database, and transform them to XML. The data we returned is easily understood by any application, regardless of the language it was written in.

Integrating XML into the Database Itself

Suppose we're creating an application from scratch. We're dealing with a lot of data, so we're probably going to need a database, but we're savvy enough to be using XML as much as possible. How can we combine the best of both worlds?

The answer might come in taking denormalization to the extreme. Perhaps we don't need every piece of information in a separate field, but can store chunks of information together, in XML form.

Storing XML in a Database

Consider a forms-based application where your users will be entering many pieces of information for every application, but most of that information only makes sense in the context of the application as a whole. For example, we might want to do a search to find the account number for the person who placed an order, but we'd never do a search to find out that customer's middle name; we only ever need to see the middle name when we're working with the whole order.

Perhaps we could store all of the information in one table in the database; any searchable fields (e.g. account number, order number) would get their own column, and then another column would be used to store all of the XML for the entire order:

Order Table		
order_number	account_number	order_xml

123587	125692	`<?xml version="1.0"?>`
		`<Order number="123587">`
		`    <Account number="125692">`
		`        <FirstName>John</FirstName>`
		`        <MiddleName>Fitzgerald Johansen</MiddleName>`
		`        <LastName>Doe</LastName>`
		`        <HomePhone>(555) 555-1212</HomePhone>`
		`        <WorkPhone>(555) 555-2121</WorkPhone>`
		`    </Account>`
		`    <Item number="E16-25A">`
		`        <Description>Production Class Widget</Description>`
		`        <Quantity>16</Quantity>`
		`    </Item>`
		`    <Date>2000/1/1</Date>`
		`</Order>`

Since we have one XML document representing each order, we can get all the information for an entire application from one field. Getting all this information might be as simple as using:

```
SELECT order_xml FROM order WHERE order_number = 123587
```

In most cases, updating an order also involves modifying just one field, since you rarely need to change the columns which are searchable.

Using the Database

Normally, this approach works best when your database is a **staging database**, or a temporary holding place for the data, until the time when it can be put into the real back-end database. This is because the requirements for a staging database are often less stringent than for other databases. As you can see from the diagram above, the data is not normalized at all, but is stored in one large chunk; making the retrieval of the data an all-or-nothing exercise. This makes it much easier to return the data for the application which is using it, eliminating joins and complex SQL statements, but makes it harder to write other applications which might want to use *parts* of the data, since those parts aren't directly exposed. (For example, a reporting application which could list all of the orders placed by a particular customer in the last month.)

> *The most common example of an application that can make use of this paradigm is a forms-based web application. A user goes through your web site, entering information on each page. Upon clicking submit at the end of each page, the data is stored in your staging database to keep it safe. When the user gets to the last page, and performs the final submit, the data from your staging database is submitted to the real database.*

When it does come time to move the data to the real database, a Data Object would read the XML from the staging database, create SQL INSERT statements with it, and insert it into the database that way. Your application gets all of the advantages of dealing with the data in an XML format it understands in the front end, and your company gets the advantages of having a fully normalized relational database in the back end.

In many cases, you don't even need to keep the data in the staging database for too long, since it will be permanently stored in your back-end databases for posterity. Not only is the database simple, it also becomes easier to maintain, since you don't have to worry too much about running out of space. Perhaps you can delete the row as soon as the data is submitted to the back-end databases, or maybe you can schedule an automatic job to run every night, and delete any data that's more than 30-days old.

Before you decide to take this drastic approach and store all your XML data in this way, you'll want to take a good hard look at what you're doing and whether this will meet your needs. Many Database Analysts would probably faint at a table like this! You might also want to consider less drastic measures, where you are only breaking certain sections of the data into their own XML fields. (Perhaps you could store an address in its own column, in XML format, for example.)

On the other hand, if this type of layout can meet your needs, you'll have all of the benefits of an n-tier architecture, but your Data Objects have one less task to perform (translating your data into XML format). It's only when we need to move the data up to a higher-level database that we need to worry about translation.

> **The less work your objects have to do, the more scalable your application becomes, and the more users you can serve.**

An Even Simpler Data Object

Following on from our last code example, where we saw how easy it would be to retrieve XML. Let's take a look at how much code we would need if our database was structured with one column that stored our information in XML form:

```
Dim cnnDatabaseConnection As ADODB.Connection
Set cnnDatabaseConnection = New ADODB.Connection
'here we would connect to the database...

Dim strSQL As String
strSQL = "SELECT order_xml FROM order WHERE order_number = '123587'"

Dim rsResults As ADODB.Recordset
Set rsResults = cnnDatabaseConnection.Execute(strSQL)

Dim strResult As String
strResult = rsResults("order_xml").Value
'return strResult
```

That was pretty easy. No more worrying about creating a DOM, or reading the values from our `Recordset`; all we have to do is perform a simple `SELECT` and return one field.

Database Vendors and XML

With both XML and databases being data-centric technologies, are they in competition with each other? Quite the contrary! XML is best used to communicate data, and a database is best used to store and retrieve data; this makes the two *complementary*, rather than *competitive*.

For this reason, database vendors are realizing the power and flexibility of XML, and are building support for XML right into their products. This potentially makes the programmer's job easier when writing Data Objects, since there is one less step to perform: instead of retrieving data from the database, and transforming it to XML, you can potentially retrieve data from the database already in XML format! In fact specialist XML databases *already* exist, such as eXcelon (http://www.exceloncorp.com/).

> **XML will never replace the database, but the two will become more closely integrated with time.**

We'll be looking at two database vendors who were quick to market with XML integration technologies: Oracle, and Microsoft. Both companies offer a suite of tools that can be used for XML development, when communicating with a database and otherwise.

Microsoft's XML Technologies

Microsoft has been big on XML since the very beginning. There is extensive documentation on XML at **MSDN** (**Microsoft Developer Network**), the online site devoted to developers working with Microsoft technologies. The XML-related information is gathered together at http://msdn.microsoft.com/xml. There's also copious amounts of sample code, just there for the, erm, "borrowing".

MSXML

The first, and most obvious, form of XML support from Microsoft is that Internet Explorer comes bundled with the **MSXML** COM-based parser, which provides a DOM interface (and, at the time of writing, a beta version which supports SAX2 as well). MSXML provides both validating and non-validating modes, as well as support for XML namespaces. It also provides support for XSL transformations. (At the time of writing, the released version of MSXML did not have full support for the XSLT standard, but was based on a very early draft; Microsoft has been releasing incremental preview versions of MSXML, with updated XSLT support.)

MSXML adds some helpful extensions to the DOM, which allow you to traverse the tree using XPath expressions. For example, in addition to the `getElementsByTagName()` method, MSXML provides the `selectSingleNode()` and `selectNodes()` methods, which take XPath expressions as their parameters, and return the node (or nodes) you specify. This can be much quicker than traversing the tree looking for nodes, as it allows you to jump directly to the node you want.

Visual Basic Code Generator

Because MSDN is big on code samples, there are a number of sample applications available for download from the site. One good example is a Visual Basic code generator, which can read XML Schema documents, and produce Visual Basic classes to match the schema (it's located at http://msdn.microsoft.com/xml/articles/generat.asp). In effect, you can build the basics of an object model, based on an XML document type, automatically. This tool isn't *supported* by Microsoft – it's only provided for convenience – but the source code is available so you can always change anything that doesn't quite work the way you want it to.

In addition, the tool is based on Microsoft's early implementation of XML Schemas, so when the final Schema syntax is published, older Microsoft-based Schemas will be out of date.

SQL Server

And finally, there's the XML support that's built into SQL Server, Microsoft's Relational Database Management System.

> **All of this is available natively in SQL Server 2000, or as a downloadable Technology Preview for SQL Server 7.**

SQL Server provides the ability to perform a SQL query through an HTTP request, via an ISAPI filter for Internet Information Server (Microsoft's web server). So we might perform a query like the following (replacing *server* and *database* with the appropriate names):

```
http://server/database?sql=SELECT+last_name+FROM+Customer+FOR+XML+RAW
```

Or, if we don't want to be passing our complex SQL statements in a URL, we can also create an **XML template** file to store the query. It would look something like this:

```
<root>
  <sql:query xmlns:sql="urn:schemas-microsoft-com:xml-sql">
    SELECT last_name FROM Customer FOR XML RAW
  </sql:query>
</root>
```

Notice the words FOR XML RAW added to the end of that SQL statement. This is a language enhancement Microsoft has added to allow SQL queries to natively return XML.

If this template were named lastname.xml, we'd execute the SQL by using the following URL:

```
http://server/database/lastname.xml
```

And this query would return XML similar to the following:

```
<?xml version="1.0" encoding="UTF-8" ?>
<root>
  <row last_name="Doe" />
  <row last_name="Smith" />
  <row last_name="Johnson" />
</root>
```

`FOR XML RAW` instructs SQL Server to format the XML in its own way. There is also a `FOR XML EXPLICIT` clause, which allows you to tell SQL Server how to format the XML. This makes the SQL queries very complex, though, because you have to tell SQL Server not only what data, and from where, but also how you want the data formatted. So if you're using `FOR XML EXPLICIT`, you will probably want to use the XML templates.

As we'll see in the upcoming example, templates can take parameters as well, to make your queries dynamic.

Not only can you get data from SQL Server in XML, you can put it in using **SQL Update Grams**. These are XML files containing the information you want to put in the database (in a certain format, of course).

Putting SQL Server to Work

For this example, let's go back to our large SQL statement, which joined together information from across all three of our tables.

Because the `SELECT` statement is so long, we're probably not going to want to pass it over in the query string, so let's create an XML template to store the results, which we'll call `order.xml`:

```
<?xml version="1.0"?>
<root>
<sql:query xmlns:sql="urn:schemas-microsoft-com:xml-sql"><![CDATA[
SELECT Order.order_number, Order.account_number, Customer.first_name,
        Customer.middle_name, Customer.last_name, Customer.home_phone,
        Customer.work_phone, Order.item, Parts.description, Order.quantity,
        Order.date
FROM Order, Customer, Parts
WHERE Order.order_number = '123587'
        AND Customer.account_number = Order.account_number
        AND Parts.item = Order.item
FOR XML RAW
]]></sql:query>
</root>
```

Notice that I have also wrapped the SQL query in a CDATA section. This isn't strictly necessary, for our query, since there are no & or < characters, but sometimes it's just better to be safe than sorry.

We would call this query something like this:

```
http://servername/databasename/order.xml
```

But wait a second: this SQL query is always going to return the same information. Why would we even bother with all of this: we could just save the result and ask for that? We need a way to choose the order number at runtime, so that we can get the information from any order. We do this like so:

```
<?xml version="1.0"?>
<root>
<sql:query ordnum='' xmlns:sql="urn:schemas-microsoft-com:xml-sql"><![CDATA[
SELECT Order.order_number, Order.account_number, Customer.first_name,
```

```
         Customer.middle_name, Customer.last_name, Customer.home_phone,
         Customer.work_phone, Order.item, Parts.description, Order.quantity,
         Order.date
   FROM Order, Customer, Parts
   WHERE Order.order_number = ?
         AND Customer.account_number = Order.account_number
         AND Parts.item = Order.item
]]></sql:query>
</root>
```

As you can see, there is an extra attribute on our `<sql:query>` element for the order number, which has no value. There is also a question mark in our WHERE clause. This will be a parameter to our template. We can then call the template like this:

```
http://servername/databasename/order.xml?ordnum='123587'
```

Next, let's ensure that the results of this query will be viewable in IE5, by adding a style sheet PI to the document (which we'll assume is stored in the same folder):

```
<?xml version="1.0"?>
<?xml-stylesheet type="text/xsl" href="html.xsl"?>
<root>
<sql:query ordnum='' xmlns:sql="urn:schemas-microsoft-com:xml-sql"><![CDATA[
SELECT Order.order_number, Order.account_number, Customer.first_name,
       Customer.middle_name, Customer.last_name, Customer.home_phone,
       Customer.work_phone, Order.item, Parts.description, Order.quantity,
       Order.date
FROM Order, Customer, Parts
WHERE Order.order_number = ?
       AND Customer.account_number = Order.account_number
       AND Parts.item = Order.item
]]></sql:query>
</root>
```

IE5 will recognize that PI, fetch the XSL style sheet (`htm.xsl`), and render the document on the client. We might end up with a web page like this:

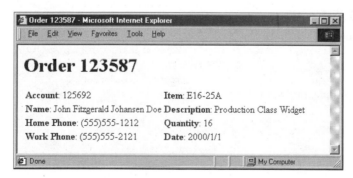

With a simple XML file, which is accessible through an ISAPI filter, we have effectively created an order-viewing system! All we need to know is the order number, and we can get the information from SQL Server formatted in XML and, once on the client, can use XSL to re-format the data as HTML.

493

Oracle's XML Technologies

Like Microsoft, Oracle provide a number of tools to work with XML, in their **XML Developer's Kit** (**XDK**). However, since Microsoft has some XML support built right into the database, it took them much longer to get their database-integration tools to market, whereas Oracle had these tools out to market very quickly indeed.

> *Oracle's Technology Network has a good web site devoted to the XML Developer's Kit, which is located at* http://technet.oracle.com/tech/xml/. *You will need to register in order to download the XDK, or see some of the documentation, but registration is free.*

XML Parsers

The first tool available from Oracle is the XML parser. Oracle provides parsers written in Java, C, C++, and PL/SQL. These parsers provide:

- ❑ A DOM interface
- ❑ A SAX interface
- ❑ Both validating and non-validating support
- ❑ Support for namespaces
- ❑ Fully compliant support for XSLT

Like MSXML, the Oracle XML parsers provide extension functions to the DOM, `selectSingleNode()` and `selectNodes()`, which function just like the Microsoft methods.

Code Generators

Oracle offers Java and C++ class generating applications, just like the Visual Basic class building application Microsoft offers. However, these generators work from DTDs, not Schemas, meaning that they are already fully conformant to the W3C specifications. Also, since these tools are part of the XDK, they are fully supported by Oracle, instead of just being sample code.

XML SQL Utility for Java

Along with these basic XML tools, the XDK also provides the **XML SQL Utility for Java**. This tool can generate an XML document from a SQL query, either in text form or in a DOM.

The XML results may differ slightly from the Microsoft SQL Server FOR XML clause, but they're just as easy to use. For example, the following SQL query:

```
SELECT last_name FROM customer
```

might return XML like the following:

```
<?xml version="1.0"?>
<ROWSET>
  <ROW id="1">
```

```
      <last_name>Doe</last_name>
    </ROW>
    <ROW id="2">
      <last_name>Smith</last_name>
    </ROW>
    <ROW id="3">
      <last_name>Johnson</last_name>
    </ROW>
  </ROWSET>
```

So, instead of including the information in attributes of the various `<row>` elements, Oracle decided to include the information in separate child elements.

And, just like Microsoft's enhancements to SQL Server 2000, Oracle's XML SQL Utility for Java can take in XML documents, and use the information to update the database.

XSQL Servlet

Microsoft decided to make SQL queries available over HTTP by providing an ISAPI filter for IIS. Oracle, on the other hand, decided to create the Java **XSQL Servlet** instead.

This servlet takes in an XML document that contains SQL Queries, like the XML templates used by SQL Server. The servlet can optionally perform an XSLT transformation on the results (if a style sheet is specified), so the results can potentially be any type of file that can be returned from an XSLT transformation, including XML and HTML. (To accomplish this, the XSQL Servlet makes use of the XML parser mentioned above.) Because it's a servlet, it will run on any web server that has a Java Virtual Machine and can host servlets.

For example, consider the following XML example document from Oracle's Technology Network web site, which might be used by the XSQL Servlet:

```
<?xml version="1.0"?>
<?xml-stylesheet type="text/xsl" href="rowcol.xsl"?>
<query connection="demo"
    find="%"
    sort="ENAME"
    null-indicator="yes" >
    SELECT *   FROM EMP
        WHERE ENAME LIKE '%{@find}%'
            ORDER BY {@sort}
</query>
```

When this query is run, the servlet will replace the `<query>` element with the results of the query. In this case, there are two variables indicated: `@find` and `@sort`, which are used to specify the search and sort criteria respectively. These variables could be specified by passing them to the servlet, for example, using the following URL:

```
http://localhost/xsql/demo/emp.xsql?find=T&sort=EMPNO
```

Notice also the `<?xml-stylesheet?>` PI. Since we have included this, the servlet will transform the results of the query, using the specified XSLT style sheet (`rowcol.xsl`).

495

Putting Oracle to Work

Just to compare the two technologies, let's redo our SQL Server example with Oracle's tools. First of all, we'll need our XSQL file, which stores the query:

```
<?xml version="1.0"?>
<?xml-stylesheet type="text/xsl" href="html.xsl"?>
<query ordnum=''><![CDATA[
SELECT Order.order_number, Order.account_number, Customer.first_name,
        Customer.middle_name, Customer.last_name, Customer.home_phone,
        Customer.work_phone, Order.item, Parts.description, Order.quantity,
        Order.date
FROM Order, Customer, Parts
WHERE Order.order_number = {@ordnum}
        AND Customer.account_number = Order.account_number
        AND Parts.item = Order.item
]]></query>
```

This is very much like the Microsoft version, except that we treat the parameter slightly differently (highlighted in the code), and we don't need a namespace for the `<query>` element. We would also call this the same way as we call the Microsoft version:

```
http://servername/databasename/order.xsql?ordnum='123587'
```

However, there is a difference between the way the Microsoft and Oracle technologies work. The XSL transformation that will take place for this XML is performed by the servlet, on the server. This means that we don't necessarily need IE5 as our client browser, but can use *any* web browser. Also, since the servlet is using Oracle's XML parser, the XSLT functionality is up to date and complete, as opposed to the XSLT preview which IE5 uses (at the time of writing).

Performing the XSL transformation on the server might slow our server down a bit, because it has one more thing to do. However, it will provide much more flexibility, both with the client browsers that can access the information, and with the power we have in our XSLT style sheets.

Who Needs a Database Anyway?

So far, most of this chapter has assumed that you are using your XML knowledge to build an "application" of some kind: an order processing application, for example. We've been talking about n-tier architecture, and building objects to do the work. But what if you're not building applications at all? Perhaps you're putting together an online magazine, for example, or a news site – something that is completely centered around content, and not around changing the content.

In this case, what you're probably most concerned with is getting that content served up to your users as quickly as possible. When they go to your site, they don't want to have to wait for the information to get to them, it should be instantaneous. This means that your web server should be doing as little as possible. When the user requests a page, the web server should be able to just give it out, and then move on to do something else.

Traditionally, web sites could get better scalability by using static HTML pages in place of dynamically generated pages, because the web server doesn't have to do any work with the page, just hand it out. With the addition of XLink and XPointer to the XML family of technologies, we could potentially do the same thing with XML-based sites: serve up static XML documents and CSS style sheets to clients, and have the clients render the XML for display. If the clients understand XLink, they would then be able to further link to the other XML documents on your site, the way that HTML pages can link to one another today with HTML hyperlinks.

However, this approach may be a little bit "pie in the sky" at this point in history – there aren't a lot of browsers that can display XML documents formatted with CSS style sheets, and even fewer (none at the time of writing) browsers which understand XLink. That brings up our other option: using XSLT to transform our XML into HTML.

When deciding how to do this, we have a few choices:

❑   We could pass the XML and XSL documents to the client, and have the browser perform the transformation. (For this to work, the client-side browser must be able to perform XSLT transformations.)

❑   We could perform the transformation server-side, using a servlet, Active Server Pages or the XSLISAPI or the SQLXML ISAPI (available for download from http://msdn.microsoft.com/xml). Writing an ASP page to call an XSL transformation only takes a few lines of code.

❑   We could perform a batch transformation of all of our XML documents to HTML, and store those static HTML documents on the web server.

Depending on your situation (including your browser-base), all of these could be viable options, so feel free to use whichever methodology works best for your application. And as we move forward, and web browsers get smarter about XML, you might find yourself leaning more and more toward the first choice, making less work for your web server.

The point is you don't always need a database. Part of the fun of software development is figuring out which technologies you need, and which you don't. And by all means, feel free to mix and match! It's not too far fetched to imagine applications with a lot of content stored in static XML documents, and other information coming from databases.

Summary

This chapter hasn't been an exhaustive look into XML and databases, but hopefully it has started to get you thinking about how the two can be used together effectively.

A more comprehensive study is included in Professional XML (ISBN 1-861003_11_0) from Wrox Press.

We have seen:

- ❑ A little bit of how normalization works, and why it is important

- ❑ Some ways that the Data Objects in an n-tier architecture can be used to keep XML as your communication format throughout the application, instead of dealing with other data-transmission technologies

- ❑ How Microsoft and Oracle have begun the work of integrating XML and the traditional database, and the tools they provide with that aim

The next chapter will also fall into that category, and present you with some ideas of other ways XML can be used in your environment. Remember, communicating data is a very broad topic, so there are inevitably lots of places it must be done!

Other Uses for XML

Finally, we get to the chapter that I've been looking forward to writing since the beginning of this book: a catch-all chapter, where we can sit back and talk about other potential uses for XML in your applications. As a developer myself, it's always exciting to play with the latest and greatest technologies, and to see how others are using those technologies. Many of the topics covered are stimulating and show some of the real potential of using XML. And, what's even more exciting to me, as a result of reading about these technologies you may find uses for XML which aren't even touched on in this chapter!

Some of the topics covered will be other XML-related technologies that you might find useful, but that didn't warrant an entire chapter on their own. Other topics are some suggestions that I've found to be very useful in my own applications, and which you might find useful as well.

In this chapter we'll cover:

❑   A way to put object models to good use in your applications

❑   Ways to call objects on other servers, even when there is a firewall in between, using **XML-RPC**

❑   How stateless objects help to enhance scalability, and how XML can help create those stateless objects

❑   A quick introduction to the **Resource Description Framework** (**RDF**), and how it will probably be used in the future on the Internet

❑   A look at a novel schema language, **Schematron**, which can provide more flexibility than normal XML Schemas and DTDs

There may not be as many Try It Out sections as in earlier chapters, but there will be a lot of practical suggestions that you can use in many of your own real-life applications.

Serializing Object Models

Yes, we're going to talk about object models yet again. We can't get away from them because they are such an all-round good idea, and here you'll learn how you can put them to good use in your applications.

A lot of functionality can be provided by a well-designed object model. Not only can it *store* your information, but it can also *validate* that information, to make sure any data you try to input is valid. For example, if you have a property for a phone number, it might have rules to indicate that the value must be a certain length, only contain numbers and certain characters, etc. So if you try to enter a value of "z!" into that property, it won't accept it.

It can also provide added functionality; for example, if I have an object which stores information for a person's name, with separate properties for first, middle, and last names, I might also provide a read-only `FullName` property, which would return the whole name. The same thing could be achieved by calling all of the separate properties individually, but `FullName` would add some convenience for the developer using the object model.

As a more concrete example, let's assume we have some kind of order-processing system. There is a client-side application written in Visual Basic, for our Windows 98 users, in which users enter data, and the data from that application will eventually be sent to the server, to be stored in the database. This client-side application is a great place to put an object model, because the object model can validate the data as it is entered.

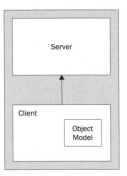

So far so good. However, remember our n-tier architecture from the last chapter: there is going to be some processing done on the server, which will also use the data. Therefore, it might be a good idea to have copies of the object model on our servers, too, something like this:

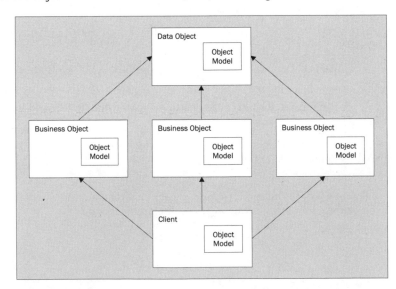

Now, *any* time we have to work with the data for our application, we can use the same object model, so we have consistent processing across all of our components. Our only problem is – how do we get the actual data into those object models?

The answer comes in a technique called **serialization**. This is a method whereby an object can write itself out as a stream of bytes, which contains all of the information stored in the object. Any object of this type is capable of then reading that stream of bytes and loading itself to the same state, or **deserializing**. For example, if our Name object is serializable, then we could serialize it, and send the stream of bytes to the server. Any Name object on that server could then deserialize, and be in the same state as the original Name object.

But a stream of bytes just isn't good enough for us, especially not in a book on XML. Why not serialize the object to XML, instead? There are a number of benefits to using XML as your serialization method:

❑ Debugging is much easier. If things go wrong, you can open the object's XML in a text editor, and see what's going on. This is difficult or impossible with a simple stream of bytes, unless you devise a special application which can read it. (And when things go wrong, that application may not be able to read the stream either!)

❑ You could store this XML in a database in a text field, as we discussed in the last chapter. Of course, you could do the same with the serialized stream of bytes, in a binary field, but again, you'd never be able to see what was in that stream without your special application to decipher it.

❑ For components which don't need the whole object model, they can just read the XML itself, and only pull out the data they need. It's a lot easier to load an XML parser than to load a whole object model (which itself would be loading the XML parser anyway).

❑ If the serialized format has a DTD or schema available, the XML parser can perform some of the type checking for you, and make sure that you have all of the required information, before you try to work with it.

But there's another benefit here, too: what if we can't put the same object model on every computer? Suppose, in addition to our initial client-base, we add some UNIX clients to the mix? They can't run a Visual Basic application, with a COM-based object model, but they can run a Java-based application, with a Java-based object model. As long as the new object model uses the same XML format to serialize and deserialize, we can then send the XML to the server, where it can be used by our server-side objects, even if they're using the COM-based object model.

Try It Out – Simulating an Object Model in JavaScript

Let's take this a step further: what if, in addition to our VB and Java clients, we also want to create a web-based front end for our application? In this case, we might not be able to use an object model at all, but we can *simulate* one, using JavaScript. For example, consider the following HTML page:

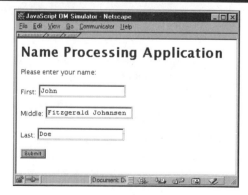

We want to be able to post the information from this page to the server, using XML. For this Try It Out you will need to have access to a web server, such as Microsoft's IIS (or PWS) on your local machine. We'll be sending the data to an ASP page on this web server, so you might also want to read the ASP Quick Start Reference in Appendix C if you're not familiar with ASP.

1. First, we'll create the HTML document itself (`OMSimulator.htm`):

```
<HTML>
<HEAD><TITLE>JavaScript OM Simulator</TITLE>
</HEAD>

<BODY><H1>Name Processing Application</H1>
```

```
<FORM id="frmScratchForm" name="frmScratchForm">
<P>Please enter your name:</P>
<P>First: <input id="txtFirst" name="txtFirst"></P>
<P>Middle: <input id="txtMiddle" name="txtMiddle"></P>
<P>Last: <input id="txtLast" name="txtLast"></P>
</FORM>
```

```
<FORM id="frmSubmitForm" name="frmSubmitForm"
action="ProcessXML.asp" method="post">
<P><INPUT id="btnSubmit" name="btnSubmit"
type="button" value="Submit" onclick="SubmitXML()"></P>
<INPUT type="hidden" id="txtSubmitText" name="txtSubmitText">
</FORM>
```

```
</BODY>
</HTML>
```

When this document is loaded into a web browser, objects will be created in the HTML DOM for each HTML element present. We have added `id` and `name` attributes to our form elements, to make it easier to work with them. For example, there is now an input box named `txtFirst`, which will contain the first name. We can get the information out of that input box using its `value` property, like this:

```
document.frmScratchForm.txtFirst.value
```

We also have two HTML forms: one called `frmScratchForm`, and one called `frmSubmitForm`. The first one will contain the information we'll be capturing, and the second one will be the form used to actually submit the information to the server.

2. Next we'll create a function in JavaScript and add it into the HEAD section of our page. This can get the information out of our form and use it to create an XML document:

```
<SCRIPT language="JavaScript">
function GetXML()
{
  var strXML = new String();
  strXML = "<?xml version='1.0'?>\n";
  strXML = strXML + "<name>\n";
  strXML = strXML + "\t<first>" +
```

```
                document.frmScratchForm.txtFirst.value + "</first>\n";
        strXML = strXML + "\t<middle>" +
                document.frmScratchForm.txtMiddle.value + "</middle>\n";
        strXML = strXML + "\t<last>" +
                document.frmScratchForm.txtLast.value + "</last>\n";
        strXML = strXML + "</name>";

        return strXML;
}
```

What this function is doing is creating a string, piece by piece, which will contain our XML. (We're also including the special "\t" and "\n" characters, which create tabs and newlines, respectively.) It will return XML in the following format:

```
<?xml version='1.0'?>
<name>
        <first>John</first>
        <middle>Fitzgerald Johansen</middle>
        <last>Doe</last>
</name>
```

Because XML is just text, it's relatively easy to write this kind of routine in JavaScript.

3. And finally, we'll add some code to send the information to the server, via the frmSubmitForm form:

```
function SubmitXML()
{
  document.frmSubmitForm.txtSubmitText.value = GetXML();
  document.frmSubmitForm.submit();
}
</SCRIPT>
```

This function calls the GetXML() function described in step 2, to return a string containing the information from our form in XML format. It assigns that string to the hidden input box txtSubmitText, which is in the frmSubmitForm HTML form. It then submits the form to the server.

Our final web page will look like this:

```
<HTML>
<HEAD><TITLE>JavaScript OM Simulator</TITLE>
<SCRIPT language="JavaScript">
function GetXML()
{
  var strXML = new String();
  strXML = "<?xml version='1.0'?>\n";
  strXML = strXML + "<name>\n";
  strXML = strXML + "\t<first>" +
      document.frmScratchForm.txtFirst.value + "</first>\n";
  strXML = strXML + "\t<middle>" +
      document.frmScratchForm.txtMiddle.value + "</middle>\n";
```

```
  strXML = strXML + "\t<last>" +
      document.frmScratchForm.txtLast.value + "</last>\n";
  strXML = strXML + "</name>";

  return strXML;
}

function SubmitXML()
{
  document.frmSubmitForm.txtSubmitText.value = GetXML();
  document.frmSubmitForm.submit();
}
</SCRIPT>
</HEAD>

<BODY><H1>Name Processing Application</H1>

<FORM id="frmScratchForm" name="frmScratchForm">
<P>Please enter your name:</P>
<P>First: <INPUT id="txtFirst" name="txtFirst"></P>
<P>Middle: <INPUT id="txtMiddle" name="txtMiddle"></P>
<P>Last: <INPUT id="txtLast" name="txtLast"></P>
</FORM>

<FORM id="frmSubmitForm" name="frmSubmitForm"
action="ProcessXML.asp" method="post">
<P><INPUT id="btnSubmit" name="btnSubmit"
type="button" value="Submit" onclick="SubmitXML()"></P>
<INPUT type="hidden" id="txtSubmitText" name="txtSubmitText">
</FORM>

</BODY>
</HTML>
```

4. In this case we need to have an ASP page on the server called `ProcessXML.asp` to do something with this data. For now let's create a simple page to acknowledge that the data has been sent. Create `ProcessXML.asp` as follows and place both files in the root directory of your web server (usually `Inetpub/wwwroot`):

```
<HTML>
<HEAD>
<%@ Language=VBScript %>
<TITLE>Confirmation</TITLE>
</HEAD>
<BODY>
<%
Dim strXML
On Error Resume Next

strXML = ""
strXML = Request.Form("txtSubmitText")
```

```
If Err.Number <> 0 Then
    WriteErrorXML Err.Description
Else
    Response.Write strXML
End If

Sub WriteErrorXML(ErrorDescription)
    Response.Write "<error>" & ErrorDescription & "</error>"
End Sub
%>
</BODY>
</HTML>
```

This ASP page contains script to take the contents of the `txtSubmitText` box (from the `frmSubmitForm` of the `OMSimulator.htm` page) and put this data into the `strXML` variable. After checking for errors it then writes a message to show the data that was received.

5. Now if you open up IE5 and type in the URL of the OMSimulator page (for example http://localhost/OMSimulator.htm), fill in some details and click submit, you will get a response from the server. If you view the source of this page you'll see that the data was passed to the server in XML format (but the IE5 parser chose to remove the XML before displaying just the raw data).

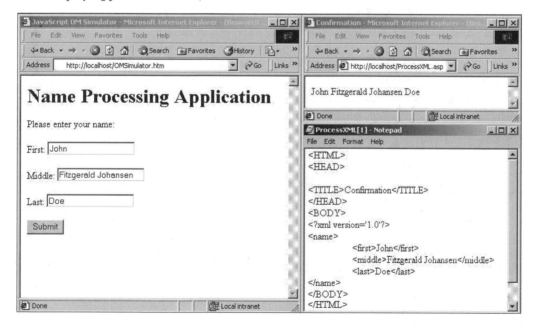

How It Works

This page simulates creating a `Name` object, setting the properties, and serializing it to XML. The information is sent to the server, where it could be deserialized into a real `Name` object, for further processing or for insertion into the database.

In a case where there was validation to perform, that would probably also be performed in JavaScript, on the client. (We might also have some further validation on the server as a final precaution against deliberately bogus data.) For example, we could set the `onChange` property of each text box to call a simple JavaScript validation function, which would make sure the information entered was sensible.

The net effect of this simulated object model is that it can be sent to the server where it can be passed to the very same Business Objects which would have taken the XML output from our Visual Basic clients, or our Java clients.

To really make use of this paradigm, we would never send the XML to the server until the application was finished; so, if there were a number of pages from start to finish, we would just save the XML on the client until we were done, and then send it all to the server in one big lump. This means less work for the server, which gives better scalability.

Suggestions for a Good Object Model

This process of serialization isn't completely theoretical; I, myself, have used object models which serialize to and from XML, some of which have been very large and complex. So, in this section, I'm sharing some of my hard-earned knowledge with you, to help you to be as productive as possible. The tips presented here include:

❑   Making the output more visually attractive

❑   'Nesting' the serialization process for hierarchical object models

❑   Allowing cancellation of user input

❑   Dealing with empty objects

❑   Tracking an object model's serialization history

Include Pretty-Printing Characters

When you're creating an object model which serializes itself to XML, you may be doing it all through string concatenation, as in the `GetXML()` example above. (That is, creating strings which contain start-tags and end-tags, and then just putting the information in between.) In this case, it's very easy to create XML that looks like this:

```
<?xml version='1.0'?><person><name><first>John</first><middle>Fitzgerald
Johansen</middle><last>Doe</last></name><phone><number>(555)555-
1212</number><extension>123</extension></phone></person>
```

or like this:

```
<?xml version='1.0'?>
<person>
<name>
<first>John</first>
<middle>Fitzgerald Johansen</middle>
<last>Doe</last>
</name>
<phone>
```

```
<number>(555)555-1212</number>
<extension>123</extension>
</phone>
</person>
```

Instead, I suggest that you always include newlines and initial spaces in your XML, to make it more like this:

```
<?xml version='1.0'?>
<person>
  <name>
    <first>John</first>
    <middle>Fitzgerald Johansen</middle>
    <last>Doe</last>
  </name>
  <phone>
    <number>(555)555-1212</number>
    <extension>123</extension>
  </phone>
</person>
```

To an XML parser, this doesn't really make a difference; the data included is the same in any case. It's mostly for the sake of debugging because, as you can see, the last version is much easier to read, and it makes it clearer which elements are children of which other elements.

We did this in our previous JavaScript Try It Out, adding "\t" and "\n" characters to our output, to make it friendlier. Even in more complex cases, where you might be using the DOM to create your XML, you can get the same effect by adding text nodes to the object model, to add in the extra white space. For example, in the case where we have XML which looks like this:

```
<name><first/></name>
```

To make this look better, we could create two text nodes. First, a text node containing a newline and a tab, which would go before the <first> element. This would make the XML look more like this:

```
<name>
      <first/></name>
```

Then we would add the second text node, after the <first> element, which contained a newline. Our final XML would look like this:

```
<name>
      <first/>
</name>
```

Allow Each Object to Serialize Itself

Object models are usually going to be arranged in a hierarchy of objects, with many objects having children. In this case, it's usually better to let each object serialize itself, rather than have the top-most object read all of the children's properties, and create the XML. This makes the objects much less dependent on each other, which makes your application easier to change and enhance in the future. (It also makes it easier for an object to serialize its own private state. More about this in the next section, entitled "Commit/Rollback Functionality".)

In the example above, we might have three objects, like this:

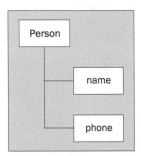

The best way to have the `person` object serialize itself is to create its initial XML like so:

```
<person>
</person>
```

Then it would serialize its `name` child, and add the XML to its own, like this:

```
<person>
  <name>
    <first>John</first>
    <middle>Fitzgerald Johansen</middle>
    <last>Doe</last>
  </name>
</person>
```

And finally, the `phone` object would be serialized, and its XML added to the overall result, like this:

```
<person>
  <name>
    <first>John</first>
    <middle>Fitzgerald Johansen</middle>
    <last>Doe</last>
  </name>
  <phone>
    <number>(555)555-1212</number>
    <extension>123</extension>
  </phone>
</person>
```

In order to make this easier, it is often handy to pass a parameter to the objects' serialization methods, indicating how far to indent the results of the serialization. So person would ask its name and phone children to each indent one level, making it immediately obvious that they belong under the person object.

I have also found it handy to create a parameter to indicate what name you want to use for the root element; that way, if person happened to have two phone child objects, one for the office and one for home, it could tell the first one to serialize itself using <OfficePhone> for its root element, and the second one using <HomePhone> for its root element, like this:

```
<person>
  <name>
    <first>John</first>
    <middle>Fitzgerald Johansen</middle>
    <last>Doe</last>
  </name>
  <OfficePhone>
    <number>(555)555-1212</number>
    <extension>123</extension>
  </OfficePhone>
  <HomePhone>
    <number>(555)555-2121</number>
    <extension/>
  </HomePhone>
</person>
```

Try It Out – Creating a Serialize Method

To demonstrate these concepts, let's create a Serialize() method, which can return an object's state in XML format. We'll stick with JavaScript as our programming language, although most of your object models will probably be written in a compiled language such as Visual Basic or Java. (For more on the differences between compiled and interpreted languages, see the JavaScript reference in Appendix D.)

1. To start off with, we'll create the Serialize() method, which will return our object's state in XML form. Make a copy of OMSimulator.htm and save it as OMSerialize.htm. Replace the GetXML() function with the following code:

```
function Serialize()
{
  var strXML = new String();

  strXML = "<name>";
  strXML = strXML + "<first>" + document.frmScratchForm.txtFirst.value +
           "</first>";
  strXML = strXML + "<middle>" + document.frmScratchForm.txtMiddle.value +
           "</middle>";
  strXML = strXML + "<last>" + document.frmScratchForm.txtLast.value +
           "</last>";
  strXML = strXML + "</name>";

  return strXML;
}
```

I purposely decided not to include the XML declaration in our output, in case this isn't the topmost object in our object model. (We don't want to generate multiple XML declarations in the same XML document.) So far our method is pretty simple; it will create the XML we need, but it will be in one long line, similar to this:

```
<name><first>John</first><middle>Fitzgerald
Johansen</middle><last>Doe</last></name>
```

2. The next step is to add some newlines to our code:

```
function Serialize()
{
  var strXML = new String();

  strXML = "<name>" + "\n";
  strXML = strXML + "<first>" + document.frmScratchForm.txtFirst.value +
          "</first>" + "\n";
  strXML = strXML + "<middle>" + document.frmScratchForm.txtMiddle.value +
          "</middle>" + "\n";
  strXML = strXML + "<last>" + document.frmScratchForm.txtLast.value +
          "</last>" + "\n";
  strXML = strXML + "</name>" + "\n";

  return strXML;
}
```

As we mentioned earlier, "\n" in JavaScript inserts a newline into our string. Our results now look more like this:

```
<name>
<first>John</first>
<middle>Fitzgerald Johansen</middle>
<last>Doe</last>
</name>
```

This is more readable, but still not quite as pretty as we'd like it. We should really indent the <first>, <middle>, and <last> elements, to visually identify them as children of the <name> element.

3. To do this, we'll create a helper function, which can generate a specific number of tabs for us:

```
function InsertTabs(NumberOfTabs)
{
  var i;
  var strTabs = new String();

  for(i = 0; i < NumberOfTabs; i++)
  {
    strTabs = strTabs + "\t";
  }

  return strTabs;
}
```

4. This helper function can then be called from our `Serialize()` method, like so:

```
function Serialize()
{
  var strXML = new String();

  strXML = "<name>" + "\n";
  strXML = strXML + InsertTabs(1) + "<first>"
           + document.frmScratchForm.txtFirst.value
           + "</first>" + "\n";
  strXML = strXML + InsertTabs(1) + "<middle>"
           + document.frmScratchForm.txtMiddle.value
           + "</middle>" + "\n";
  strXML = strXML + InsertTabs(1) + "<last>"
           + document.frmScratchForm.txtLast.value
           + "</last>" + "\n";
  strXML = strXML + "</name>" + "\n";

  return strXML;
}
```

Which will return results like this:

```
<name>
    <first>John</first>
    <middle>Fitzgerald Johansen</middle>
    <last>Doe</last>
</name>
```

This is exactly what we wanted our output to look like, however, it's still not as generic as we want. It will always return XML with the <name> start and end tags all the way to the left of the output, and the <first>, <middle>, and <last> elements indented exactly one tab to the right.

5. What we need is a way to specify to the `Serialize()` method how far to indent things. Then, if this object was a child of another object, it can be indented under that object's XML. We'll do this by adding a new parameter to our function, which indicates how far things should be indented:

```
function Serialize(Level)
{
  if(Level == null)
    Level = 0;
```

As you can see, if no value is passed to `Serialize()` for the `Level` parameter, we set it to 0.

6. We can then use this value to indent our XML, still using our `InsertTabs()` function:

```
  strXML = InsertTabs(Level) + "<name>" + "\n";
  strXML = strXML + InsertTabs(Level + 1) + "<first>"
           + document.frmScratchForm.txtFirst.value
```

```
              + "</first>" + "\n";
    strXML = strXML + InsertTabs(Level + 1) + "<middle>"
             + document.frmScratchForm.txtMiddle.value
             + "</middle>" + "\n";
    strXML = strXML + InsertTabs(Level + 1) + "<last>"
             + document.frmScratchForm.txtLast.value
             + "</last>" + "\n";
    strXML = strXML + InsertTabs(Level) + "</name>" + "\n";
```

Notice that we are now indenting the <name> start and end-tags, in addition to the other elements. This means that we now have to indent <name>'s child elements an additional time, so that they will still visually indicate that they are children of <name>. If we were to call Serialize() with no parameters, we would get the same output as before:

```
<name>
    <first>John</first>
    <middle>Fitzgerald Johansen</middle>
    <last>Doe</last>
</name>
```

but if we were to pass the method a "1" as a parameter (like "Serialize(1)"), the output would look like this:

```
    <name>
        <first>John</first>
        <middle>Fitzgerald Johansen</middle>
        <last>Doe</last>
    </name>
```

So now our output's indentation is completely generalized. The final step is to make our root element's name more generic, in case a parent object happens to contain two name objects.

7. The first step in making our root tag name generic is to add a parameter to the function. We also need to take care of the case where it is not specified, as we did for the Level parameter:

```
function Serialize(Level, RootTagName)
{
  if(RootTagName == null)
    RootTagName = "name";
```

8. We then need to insert the RootTagName parameter when we create our root element's start and end-tags:

```
    strXML = InsertTabs(Level) + "<" + RootTagName + ">" + "\n";
    strXML = strXML + InsertTabs(Level + 1) + "<first>"
             + document.frmScratchForm.txtFirst.value
             + "</first>" + "\n";
    strXML = strXML + InsertTabs(Level + 1) + "<middle>"
             + document.frmScratchForm.txtMiddle.value
             + "</middle>" + "\n";
    strXML = strXML + InsertTabs(Level + 1) + "<last>"
```

```
                + document.frmScratchForm.txtLast.value
                + "</last>" + "\n";
    strXML = strXML + InsertTabs(Level) + "</" + RootTagName + ">" + "\n";
```

Putting it all together, we now have a fully generic `Serialize()` method, with a helper function to create our tabs for us:

```
function Serialize(Level, RootTagName)
{
  var strXML = new String();
  if(Level == null)
    Level = 0;
  if(RootTagName == null)
    RootTagName = "name";

  strXML = InsertTabs(Level) + "<" + RootTagName + ">" + "\n";
  strXML = strXML + InsertTabs(Level + 1) + "<first>"
          + document.frmScratchForm.txtFirst.value
          + "</first>" + "\n";
  strXML = strXML + InsertTabs(Level + 1) + "<middle>"
          + document.frmScratchForm.txtMiddle.value
          + "</middle>" + "\n";
  strXML = strXML + InsertTabs(Level + 1) + "<last>"
          + document.frmScratchForm.txtLast.value
          + "</last>" + "\n";
  strXML = strXML + InsertTabs(Level) + "</" + RootTagName + ">" + "\n";

  return strXML;
}

function InsertTabs(NumberOfTabs)
{
  var i;
  var strTabs = new String();

  for(i = 0; i < NumberOfTabs; i++)
  {
    strTabs = strTabs + "\t";
  }

  return strTabs;
}
```

9. The final change that needs to be made is in the `SubmitXML()` function. Change `GetXML()` to `Serialize()`:

```
function SubmitXML()
{
  document.frmSubmitForm.txtSubmitText.value = Serialize();
  document.frmSubmitForm.submit();
}
```

10. Now when you view `OMSerialize.htm` in the browser, submit some details and view the source, you will get a similar result to the one shown:

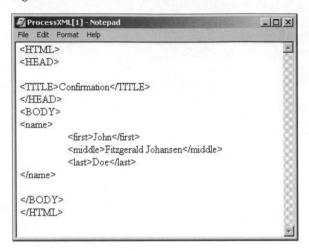

How It Works

Putting these two functions together, our object now has pretty generic serialization capabilities: we can tell it not only how far to indent itself, but even what name the resultant XML should use for its root element! For example, we could pass some parameters, like so:

```
function SubmitXML()
{
    document.frmSubmitForm.txtSubmitText.value = Serialize(1, "EmployeeName");
    document.frmSubmitForm.submit();
}
```

This would result in the following:

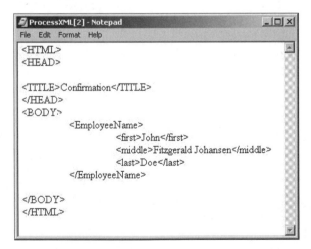

Commit/Rollback Functionality

In many instances, the user will be entering some information on the screen, and then might want to cancel the information they have just added. In this case, it would be nice to be able to "roll back" to a previously saved state. Since we're already able to serialize to XML, this would be easy to implement, by saving a "committed" state internally, in an additional XML field.

All we need is an extra variable for our object, to store the committed state of the object, and `Commit()` and `Rollback()` methods. The `Commit()` method would simply call `Serialize()`, and save it in our committed state field, like this:

```
Commit()
{
  strCommittedState = Serialize();
}
```

Similarly, the `Rollback()` method would use this private member to deserialize the object, (provided we had written a `Deserialize()` method of course), like this:

```
Rollback()
{
  Deserialize(strCommittedState);
}
```

As an example, suppose we have an application where the user is entering information in multiple screens, where each screen has a **Previous** and a **Next** button. When the user clicks **Next** we assume that everything is fine and the information will be kept, but if they click **Previous**, we want to ask them "Do you want to save the changes?". A typical scenario might look like this:

❑ The user enters information on Screen 1, and clicks **Next**. The application commits the object model, so each object will internally serialize itself, and save its XML representation.

❑ The user starts to enter information on Screen 2, then clicks **Previous**. We ask "Do you want to save your changes from Screen 2?", and the user says "no".

❑ The application then tells the object model to roll back. Each object on Screen 2 deserializes itself from the saved XML.

❑ Our object model is now at the same state it was in when we left Screen 1, meaning that Screen 2's changes have been effectively cancelled.

Not every application will require commit/roll back functionality, but it's nice to know how easy it is to implement, when needed. If you do implement it, the commit and roll back functions of any object should also call the commit and roll back methods of any children of the object; this way, your application only ever has to commit or roll back the top-level object in the object model, and all the child objects will also be committed or rolled back as well.

Don't Return Anything from an Empty Object

You may have noticed that I haven't been using DTDs or XML Schemas in my object serialization. Since knowledge of the XML structure is compiled right into my objects, I usually write my objects to produce well-formed, but not valid, XML.

517

This allows me to add an extra optimization to my serialization code: if an object has no information, instead of returning empty XML for all of the properties it could have, it just returns an empty root element. This reduces the size of the XML, meaning that it will be quicker to send it over the wire, and also makes it easier to read, since you can tell at a glance which objects are there and which are not.

Alternatively, you could return an empty string, instead of an empty root element, but then your parent objects would need logic in their deserialization methods, to see if a child object's XML exists, before it tries to deserialize it.

You might also want to get more specific, and only write out each property in the XML if there is a value in that property, but for my object models I have usually found this to be more work than it is worth. It's much easier to keep a Boolean variable internally, which indicates whether or not the object is empty, and act based on that. (When the object is first instantiated, the variable would indicate that it is empty; any time a property is set, that variable would be changed to indicate that the object is no longer empty.)

Keep Track of Historical Information, Including Errors

Since you're going to be passing the serialized version of your object model around from computer to computer and object to object, you have the perfect chance to keep track of where that object model has been, by including an object which can store this information.

For example, you might have a dynamic collection of `Event` objects. Each `Event` object will be used to store some details about events that have been carried out on the object model. For example, when you send the `Order` object model to the server, it will be sent to a Business Object. This will do some work, and then it can add an `Event` object to the collection, which says that this work has been done, and at what time it was done. The next Business Object would do the same, until your application is finished with the object model, and it is stored in the database. If an error occurs during processing of the order, that would be added to the collection of `Event` objects as well.

This is enormously helpful when debugging; if a user complains that they had trouble with a particular order, you can pull the XML for that order out of your staging database, and see exactly when and where that order has been. (We introduced the concept of a staging database in Chapter 13, but basically it's just a place where you store the data until you are ready to commit it to the real database.)

For example, suppose we had the following information from a serialized object model:

```
<order>
  <CustomerInfo>
    <!--customer info...-->
  </CustomerInfo>
  <OrderInfo>
    <!--order info...-->
  </OrderInfo>
</order>
```

If we have correctly designed our object model, we should have all of the information we need in here concerning this particular order. However, we don't know if this order has been processed or not, or whether there were any problems processing it, or where in the system it has been, and where it has not been. To solve this problem we can add some extra data to the end to give us this information, like this:

```
<order>
  <CustomerInfo>
    <!--customer info...-->
  </CustomerInfo>
  <OrderInfo>
    <!--order info...-->
  </OrderInfo>
  <events>
    <event>
      <date>May 07, 2000 09:00:00</date>
      <computer>Server1</computer>
      <description>Order received</description>
    </event>
    <event>
      <date>May 07, 2000 09:00:03</date>
      <computer>Server2</computer>
      <description>Submitted to warehouse system</description>
    </event>
    <event>
      <date>May 07, 2000 09:00:04</date>
      <computer>Server2</computer>
      <description>Error</description>
        <error>
          <number>9</number>
          <source>order processing system</source>
          <description>Invalid customer number</description>
        </error>
    </event>
  </events>
</order>
```

The format you use to capture your events is completely up to you, as is anything else when you're designing systems which use XML.

XML-RPC

In order to get truly distributed computing, objects need to call other objects which reside on different servers, across a network. This is called a **Remote Procedure Call** (**RPC**). For the last number of years, the two main ways to let objects communicate over a network were **DCOM** (**Distributed Component Object Model**), and **IIOP** (**Internet Inter-ORB Protocol**), which can provide remote procedure calls for CORBA objects. (As mentioned in Chapter 13, CORBA is a standard for communicating between different objects, regardless of the programming language or platform used.)

For example, consider the following diagram, where objects (the circles) are calling other objects, which reside on different computers (the rectangles).

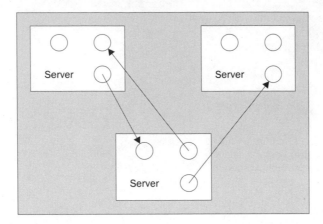

In order to use DCOM, realistically, you need all of the computers involved to be running Microsoft operating systems. With CORBA you can use any number of programming languages and platforms. (There are versions of DCOM for other operating systems, but it hasn't gained much marked penetration, or displaced CORBA.) And, in order to use IIOP, you need to lock yourself into one CORBA vendor, because they don't mix well.

But there's another problem with DCOM and IIOP: they don't work well across a **firewall**.

> *Firewalls are designed to protect a network, for example from outside hackers, by blocking certain types of network traffic. For example, many firewalls allow HTTP traffic (the type of network traffic which would be generated by browsing the web), but disallow other types of traffic.*

This may not be a problem if you're writing an application for your company, which will work within your corporate firewall, but if you're writing an Internet-based application, both DCOM and CORBA are pretty much ruled out. Many, if not most, firewalls are configured to block all types of network traffic, except for HTTP traffic:

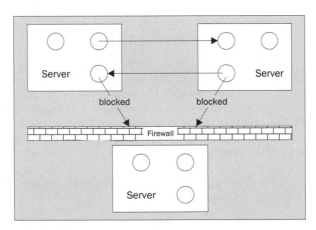

Hmm… wait a minute. If firewalls let HTTP traffic go through, why not create an RPC protocol which communicates via HTTP? This is what XML-RPC is: a standard for an RPC protocol, where procedure calls are sent via HTTP, and information is encoded in XML. Here is an example, taken from the xml-rpc.com web site:

```
POST /RPC2 HTTP/1.0
User-Agent: Frontier/5.1.2   (WinNT)
Host: betty.userland.com
Content-Type: text/xml
Content-length: 181

<?xml version="1.0"?>
<methodCall>
  <methodName>examples.getStateName</methodName>
  <params>
    <param>
      <value><i4>41</i4></value>
    </param>
  </params>
</methodCall>
```

This is a simple HTTP post, which is intended to call a method (in this case `examples.getStateName`). The lines at the top are the HTTP headers, while the XML below is the actual body of the HTTP message.

In order for this to work, the server receiving the request must understand XML-RPC, and there are a number of implementations available. XML-RPC is an advanced topic but if you want to find out more about it there is a web site devoted entirely to the protocol, at http://www.xmlrpc.com/.

SOAP

Microsoft is also pushing a technology called the **Simple Object Access Protocol**, or **SOAP**, which is built on XML-RPC. It's still at the draft stage but you can get information on SOAP from MSDN, at http://msdn.microsoft.com/xml/general/soapspec-v1.asp or DevelopMentor, at http://www.develop.com/soap/issues.htm.

The Poor Man's RPC

XML-RPC is a good idea. However, instead of finding an XML-RPC implementation, there will be times that you might be able to cheat. The reason that you might be able to cheat is that most DOM implementations allow you to load an XML document from a URL, so if you get your web server to return XML, instead of HTML, you're off to the races.

That's right, we've already been half way to XML-RPC for years, using CGI (Common Gateway Interface) and ASP and servlets on our web servers! Think about it: if you call a server which is using one of these technologies, the server is going to instantiate some objects, call methods on those objects and, based on what they return, will dynamically generate the HTML which eventually ends up in our browsers. If only we were generating XML instead of HTML, we'd be making remote procedure calls! I term these dynamic XML pages **instantiator pages**, because their only purpose in life is to instantiate objects, on behalf of the client.

The trick is to make sure that the URL you are calling will always return XML, and to agree on a convention for how the requests will be packaged. If an error occurs, your server has to catch it, package the error in XML, and send that instead. If no errors occur, then whatever information the client needs is packaged up in XML, and sent on, even if it's just a confirmation that the method was run.

521

Let's look at an example of how we might create an instantiator page, to see just how easy it can be. First, we'll create a web page, which will be used in Internet Explorer 5. Initially, it will look something like this:

When the user enters a phone number, the information will appear below, looking something like this:

This is done via a hidden `<DIV>` element, which contains the table. When the user clicks Submit, the page goes to the server, gets the appropriate information, puts it into the table using `<SPAN>`s, and un-hides the `<DIV>`.

The User Interface Page

Here's the source for the page, without the script which will call our instantiator:

```
<HTML><HEAD><TITLE>Employee Directory</TITLE>
<SCRIPT language="VBScript">
    'the GetResults() function will go here...
</SCRIPT>
</HEAD>
<BODY>
<H1>Employee Directory</H1>

<P>Phone Number:
<INPUT id="txtPhone" size="10">
<INPUT id="btnSubmit" type="button" value="Submit" onclick="GetResults()">
</P>
```

```
<DIV id="divResults" style="display:none">
<TABLE border=1 cellPadding=1 cellSpacing=1>
  <TR>
    <TD>Name:</TD>
    <TD><SPAN id="spName"> </SPAN></TD>
  </TR>
  <TR>
    <TD>Phone:</TD>
    <TD><SPAN id="spPhone"> </SPAN></TD>
  </TR>
  <TR>
    <TD>Title:</TD>
    <TD><SPAN id="spTitle"> </SPAN></TD>
  </TR>
  <TR>
    <TD>Location:</TD>
    <TD><SPAN id="spLocation"> </SPAN></TD>
  </TR>
  <TR>
    <TD>Manager:</TD>
    <TD><SPAN id="spManager"> </SPAN></TD>
  </TR>
</TABLE>
</DIV>

</BODY></HTML>
```

Now let's take a look at the GetResults() function, step by step. I used the MSXML DOM implementation, because it comes bundled with IE5, and provides a load() method, which can load an XML document from a server.

First, we need to create our URL, and call the server to get our XML results:

```
strURL = "http://servername/ServerLookup.asp?phone="
strURL = strURL & txtPhone.value

On Error Resume Next
Set objXML = CreateObject("MSXML.DOMDocument")
objXML.async = False    'blocks load operation until it is completed
objXML.Load strURL
```

We're assuming we have a page on our server (servername would need to be replaced with the actual name), called ServerLookup.asp, which we'll discuss in a while. Next we need to throw in a bit of error handling, in case something goes wrong:

```
If Err.number <> 0 Then
    MsgBox Err.description,,"Error"
    Exit Sub
ElseIf objXML.parseError.errorCode <> 0 Then
    MsgBox "Error loading XML: " & objXML.parseError.reason, , "Error"
    Exit Sub
ElseIf objXML.documentElement.nodeName = "error" Then
    MsgBox objXML.documentElement.Text, , "Error"
    Exit Sub
End If
```

Most of this is pretty standard error handling for our development environment (we probably would not want to use this in a production environment because it exposes the fact that we are using XML to the end user). MSXML provides a `parseError` object, which has an `errorCode` property. If the DOM has trouble loading the XML document, this property will have a value other than 0. The `reason` property will contain a description of the error. But in addition to the standard error handling, we also have to check to see if our XML is indicating an error; if so, we want to display that error to the user. This is the highlighted part of the code.

And finally, we want to take the information out of our XML, put it into the various `<SPAN>` elements, and unhide our `<DIV>`:

```
spName.innerText = objXML.selectSingleNode("/employee/name").Text
spPhone.innerText = objXML.selectSingleNode("/employee/phone").Text
spTitle.innerText = objXML.selectSingleNode("/employee/title").Text
spLocation.innerText = objXML.selectSingleNode("/employee/location").Text
spManager.innerText = objXML.selectSingleNode("/employee/manager").Text

divResults.style.display = ""
```

Notice that we're making use of MSXML's `selectSingleNode()` extension method, and using XPath expressions to specify which nodes to select. Putting it all together gives us our whole function:

```
<SCRIPT language="VBScript">
Sub GetResults()
    Dim strURL, objXML

    strURL = "http://servername/ServerLookup.asp?phone="
    strURL = strURL & txtPhone.value

    On Error Resume Next
    Set objXML = CreateObject("MSXML.DOMDocument")
    objXML.async = False
    objXML.Load strURL

    If Err.number <> 0 Then
        MsgBox Err.description,,"Error"
        Exit Sub
    ElseIf objXML.parseError.errorCode <> 0 Then
        MsgBox "Error loading XML: " & objXML.parseError.reason, , "Error"
        Exit Sub
    ElseIf objXML.documentElement.nodeName = "error" Then
        MsgBox objXML.documentElement.Text, , "Error"
        Exit Sub
    End If

    spName.innerText = objXML.selectSingleNode("/employee/name").Text
    spPhone.innerText = objXML.selectSingleNode("/employee/phone").Text
    spTitle.innerText = objXML.selectSingleNode("/employee/title").Text
    spLocation.innerText = objXML.selectSingleNode("/employee/location").Text
    spManager.innerText = objXML.selectSingleNode("/employee/manager").Text

    divResults.style.display = ""
End Sub
</SCRIPT>
```

The Instantiator Page

Now that's done, we need our instantiator. I wrote this one using Active Server Pages and called it
`ServerLookup.asp`. My first step was to set the page's content type to `"text/xml"`, to make sure the
client knows the page is XML, and not HTML or text:

```
Response.ContentType = "text/xml"
```

Once that task was done, I got the phone number from the request string, instantiated my
`ServerLookup.PhoneNumber` object, and called a method (`GetEmployeeInfo()`) to return the
appropriate information:

```
strPhoneNumber = Request("phone")

Set objServerLookup = Server.CreateObject("ServerLookup.PhoneNumber")
strXML = objServerLookup.GetEmployeeInfo(strPhoneNumber)
Set objServerLookup = Nothing
```

We won't be looking in detail at the `ServerLookup` object, but notice that this method will be
returning XML; it's always easier to get the object to return XML itself, rather than making the ASP
translate information into XML. In real life, the `ServerLookup` component would probably be getting
the information from a database, using the techniques we saw in Chapter 13, or perhaps even calling
other objects to do more work.

I then throw in a bit of error handling:

```
If Err.number <> 0 Then
    WriteErrorXML Err.description
```

But if everything is fine, the XML is just sent back to the client:

```
Else
    Response.Write strXML
End If
```

And finally, there is that `WriteErrorXML()` function, which handles any errors that might be
encountered:

```
Sub WriteErrorXML(ErrorDescription)
    Response.Write "<error>" & ErrorDescription & "</error>"
End Sub
```

Putting the whole thing together, we get the following ASP page:

```
<%@ Language=VBScript %>
<%
Response.ContentType = "text/xml"
Dim strPhoneNumber, strXML, objServerLookup
On Error Resume Next
```

525

```
    strPhoneNumber = Request("phone")

    Set objServerLookup = Server.CreateObject("ServerLookup.PhoneNumber")
    strXML = objServerLookup.GetEmployeeInfo(strPhoneNumber)
    Set objServerLookup = Nothing

    If Err.number <> 0 Then
        WriteErrorXML Err.description
    Else
        Response.Write strXML
    End If

    Sub WriteErrorXML(ErrorDescription)
        Response.Write "<error>" & ErrorDescription & "</error>"
    End Sub
%>
```

Benefits of this Approach

This isn't all that difficult. The trick is that we want to do as much work as possible in the compiled object, and as little work as possible in the ASP code; ASP is written in scripting code, which is inherently slower than compiled objects, meaning that it will be less scalable. Also, by putting much of the functionality into an object, we can reuse it elsewhere.

From a functionality standpoint, you may be completely and utterly unimpressed with this demonstration; after all, isn't this what forms-based processing has been doing since the beginning of the web? We click Submit, and we get the information back. The only real difference is that the page doesn't go away and get reloaded when the user clicks Submit, it just stays and deals with the new information, or displays a message box. That's better UI design, but is it worth the hassle?

The real benefit we get with this is the *flexibility* it provides. Not all of our clients might be web browsers; we might have Java applications, and Visual Basic applications, and any number of other applications. But as long as they all have access to a DOM implementation which can load itself from a URL, they can all use the same instantiator page to get this information from the server.

This methodology could also be used for things like validation; if we have a page full of information, and need the server to validate that one of the pieces of information is correct, we can use an instantiator page to return the information, but the page will never have to go away.

Stateless Objects

We've talked a bit about scalability, and some ways we could enhance the scalability of our applications. Developers of Internet applications have to be especially worried about scalability, since there could be thousands or even millions of users on the application at any one time, and the application has to be able to either handle it, or break down gracefully. (In other words, showing the users a "Sorry, the site is unavailable right now" message is much better than a "System is out of memory!" error.)

One good way to achieve scalability, or at least help, is to make all of your server-side objects **stateless**. That means that you can instantiate the object, call the method you need, and then release the object again, rather than instantiating it, keeping it around while you give it all of the information it needs, calling whatever method(s) you need, and then releasing it.

Furthermore, you want to create the object as late as possible, and release it as soon as possible. This frees up resources, such as memory, file handles, and any other resources the object might be taking up.

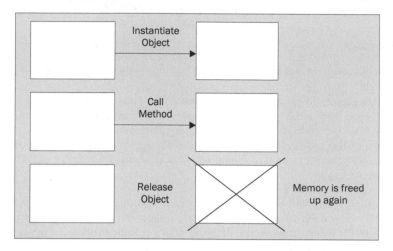

If your objects are going to be stateless, though, you're going to need to pass the object all of the information it needs in that one function call. There are a couple of reasons why setting properties on the object are a bad idea:

❑ If you need to set properties on the object *before* you call the desired method, to give it the information it needs, then it needs to remember those values; that is, maintain its state. So you need to keep the object around for a while, before you can call the method to get the object to do its work.

❑ If the object resides on a remote computer, the setting of every property will involve two trips across the network: once to set the property, and once to inform you that it has been set. Both of these trips across the network will happen for each property, before you even get to the method you need to call.

The problem is even worse if you are using something like **Microsoft Transaction Server** (**MTS**), which can help you manage the instantiation and releasing of your objects, because it doesn't guarantee that your objects will maintain state. (That is, if you call an object and set its property, you aren't guaranteed that the next time you call that object it will be the same one; it could be another copy of the object.)

So if we're writing a function that will save 50 pieces of information to the database, should we create 50 parameters? Not necessarily. There is a way that we can pass 50 pieces of information, without having to keep track of 50 parameters, and you've probably already guessed what it is: XML! What could be easier than building an XML document with all of the information needed, and passing that one document to the function? The parameter list suddenly drops from 50 parameters to one string. And since that parameter is text, we have not only made our function easier to call, but we've helped to make it more accessible through a protocol like XML-RPC.

This type of function is especially suited to applications which are using object models, as described earlier. Since all of the information is contained in your object model, many of the functions in your application will be able to just accept one parameter, representing the XML for your object model, and then deserialize the object model and work with the information from there.

An Example of a Stateless Object

Let's re-examine the `ServerLookup.asp` page we studied earlier, which called an object to lookup an employee's information based on a phone number. Specifically, let's look at these three lines of code:

```
Set objServerLookup = Server.CreateObject("ServerLookup.PhoneNumber")
strXML = objServerLookup.GetEmployeeInfo(strPhoneNumber)
Set objServerLookup = Nothing
```

This is a textbook example of calling a stateless object. We're instantiating the object (`objServerLookup`) right before we need it, and releasing it as soon as we're done, so that our server's memory will only be used up by our object for the bare minimum of time. (In Visual Basic and VBScript, setting an object to `Nothing` is how you release it.) We're only calling one function on that object (`GetEmployeeInfo`), and all of the information it needs is passed as parameters, not by assigning properties.

Although this particular function only needs one piece of information, and therefore didn't really necessitate using XML, we could easily envision a complementary `SetEmployeeInfo()` method, which could update the information in the database and would possibly have many more parameters. So the user could look up the information based on phone number, edit the data, and then send it back to the server in XML form.

Resource Description Framework (RDF)

Throughout the book we have mentioned the concept of metadata, or "information about information". Depending on your point of view, the markup in an XML document could be considered metadata, or it could be considered data. To the DOM, for example, all of the XML markup is data. To a developer pulling information out of the DOM, it would probably be considered metadata.

But metadata isn't only important in the context of a document; it is also valuable at a higher level. Not only do we need to be able to say that "this element represents a name", but "this document represents an order", and "these documents represent all of the orders for our division", and "this site represents all of the information about our division".

The **Resource Description Framework** (**RDF**), backed by the W3C, provides a means to create this kind of metadata. It allows you to create named properties for your resources, so that you can describe the data the way you want to. To give a common RDF example, if you wanted to create properties to describe a book, you might use properties like "author", "publisher", etc.

You then create RDF statements, much like you would create an English sentence. The RDF statement has three characteristics: the **Subject** (the resource you are describing), the **Predicate** (the name of the property you are creating), and the **Object** (the value of that property). Consider the following examples:

Subject	Predicate	Object	Example English
Beginning XML	Author	David Hunter	David Hunter is the author of Beginning XML The author of Beginning XML is David Hunter
Beginning XML	Contributing Authors	Nik Ozu, Kurt Cagle	Nik Ozu and Kurt Cagle are contributing authors to Beginning XML
David Hunter	Occupation	consultant, author	Consultant and author are occupations of David Hunter

The difference between this table and real RDF is that the Subject would always be a URI, such as "The MIME type of http://www.sernaferna.com/default.htm is 'text/html'". (In this case "MIME type" is the Predicate or property and "text/html" is the Object or value of the property.)

So what does all of this buy us? Well, let's take search engines as an example. Most search engines work by indexing all of the words in all of the HTML documents they can find. So if I'm looking for web pages about the television show "The Simpsons", I would go to a search engine, type in "simpsons", and it would return all of the pages which have the word "simpsons" in them. (Many search engines can be more "intelligent" than this, and return results based on how many times the word "simpsons" appears, for example.) Many search engines also return the first little bit of text on the page, so that I can get an idea of what the page is about. But these search engines don't allow me to just search for a page which is *about* "The Simpsons"; I might also get pages written by someone *named* Fred Simpson, for example.

On the other side of the coin, one of the most visited sites on the Internet is Yahoo!, which doesn't work like a regular search engine. Yahoo! shows sites based on their subject matter, not based on what words they contain. So if I'm looking for web pages on "The Simpsons", I could go to a section in Yahoo! which is devoted to TV shows, and find that there is even a section related totally to The "Simpsons" (http://dir.yahoo.com/News_and_Media/Television/Shows/Animation/Simpsons_The/). I know that any page I find in that section is going to be about the television show "The Simpsons".

There is a down-side to the Yahoo! method of indexing: it's *manual*. Someone who works for Yahoo! had to manually set up a category for TV shows, and someone who created a page about "The Simpsons" had to go to Yahoo! and register their web page under that category. There would then be a further delay while the page was added to the index. But if we created a search engine which used RDF, and there were RDF descriptions of these different sites, then we could do a search for all web sites which were about "The Simpsons", even if they hadn't registered with our search engine, just as we can do full-text searches today.

How Does It Work?

RDF works by defining **vocabularies**, with properties to describe certain types of items. For example, there is a vocabulary called **Dublin Core**, which specifies some properties which can describe web (and other) resources (like title, creator, description, etc.). If I created a web site about "The Simpsons", I might describe that web site like this:

```
<rdf:description xmlns:rdf="http://www.w3.org/1999/02/22-rdf-syntax-ns#"
                about="http://www.sernaferna.com/userpages/simpsons.htm">
  <title>Dave's Simpsons Page</title>
  <creator>dave@email.com</creator>
  <description>Everything you wanted to know about the Simpsons, but were
  too afraid to ask</description>
</rdf:description>
```

Some points on this syntax:

❑   The entire `<rdf:description>` element describes the resource in question.

❑   The `about` attribute of `<rdf:description>` is the Subject (or resource) we are describing.

❑   Each child element of `<rdf:description>` is one property for the resource; the values of those elements are the values of the properties. These child elements can also be put into a namespace, to distinguish your RDF vocabulary from other vocabularies.

There is a lot more to RDF than this simple explanation; in fact, too much to cover in a small section in a book like this. It is anticipated that RDF will be used for site maps, rating content on the web, and describing articles held in digital libraries, amongst many others. It can take a substantial effort to set up the RDF definitions, but the power they give in terms of being able to specify meaningful and expressive statements will potentially make this effort worthwhile.

The specifications related to RDF can be found at http://www.w3.org/RDF/. Information about the Dublin Core standard can also be found at the same site. There is also an introduction to "RDF and Metadata" by Tim Bray at XML.com, which you can find at http://www.xml.com/pub/98/06/rdf.html, and a PowerPoint presentation by John Cowan called "RDF Made Easy", which is available at http://www.ccil.org/~cowan/XML/rdf-made-easy.ppt.

Schematron

In Chapters 9, 10 and 11 we studied DTDs and XML Schemas, which allow us to validate our documents, but there are some limitations to both of these schema languages. For example, we can ensure that a `<name>` element has a `<first>` element, but we can't enforce that a `<first>` element has a `<name>` parent. We can create a `<CanadianCurrency>` element with `<dollars>` and `<cents>` children, but we can't enforce that if the value of `<cents>` is over 100, then we shouldn't have a `<dollar>` element.

Another schema language, called **Schematron**, has been developed, by Rick Jelliffe. Schematron is not based on grammars, but on patterns in your XML tree. Interestingly, it works on top of XSLT and XPath, which means that it can print out reports if there are problems in your XML document, or even if everything is fine. Schematron can be used instead of, or in addition to, regular DTDs and XML Schemas.

In order to use Schematron, you write an XML document (a Schematron Schema) which contains your rules, using special Schematron elements. This document is then run through the Schematron XSLT style sheet (`schematron.xsl`), which produces a second XSLT style sheet, containing your rules. This second style sheet is then run against the XML document you want to validate, to produce the results.

This is illustrated in the following diagram:

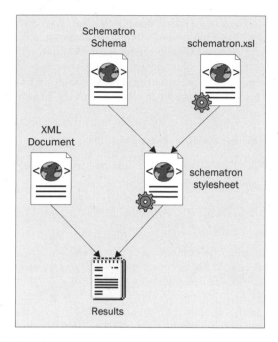

Once you have your style sheet working properly, you won't need `schematron.xsl` anymore, until the next time you need to write a schema.

Schematron schemas are only really suitable for running from the command line, and taking a look at the results. This means that an XML parser couldn't automatically validate an XML document against a Schematron schema, the way that it could validate against an XML Schema or DTD. However, Schematron is a good candidate for debugging; when things go wrong, and you pass the XML document through your Schematron schema, you will get detailed information as to what is wrong in the document.

Try It Out – Using Schematron

1. To try out Schematron, let's create an XML document which represents all of the sales for a department:

```
<?xml version="1.0"?>
<department>
  <sales>
    <salesperson name="John">50</salesperson>
    <salesperson name="Fred">20</salesperson>
    <salesperson name="David">10</salesperson>
    <salesperson name="Rebecca">30</salesperson>
  </sales>
</department>
```

Save this file as `sales.xml`. The numbers in each `<salesperson>` element represent the percentage of the sales made by that salesperson; so John made 50% of the department's sales, and Rebecca made 30%. (David didn't do so well.) But, wait a second! If we add these numbers up, we get 110%! That's obviously not an acceptable number in this situation, but a DTD or an XML Schema couldn't capture an error like that.

2. As you've probably guessed, a Schematron schema could, or I wouldn't be bothering with this example. Let's write a quick Schematron schema, and see how it works:

```
<schema>
  <pattern name="Department Sales Percentage">
    <rule context="sales">
      <assert test="sum(salesperson) = 100">The Department's sales don't
      add to 100%.</assert>
    </rule>
  </pattern>
</schema>
```

That looks pretty simple. The contents of the `<assert>` element will be printed if the test does *not* pass, in this case, if the contents of the `<salesperson>` elements don't add up to 100. Save this file as `salesschema.xml`.

3. Next, we need to run this against the Schematron XSLT style sheet, which can be downloaded from http://www.ascc.net/xml/resource/schematron/schematron.xsl. We'll use XT (as discussed in Chapter 4) and produce a style sheet named `salesschema.xsl`:

C:\>xt salesschema.xml schematron.xsl salesschema.xsl

4. And finally, we'll run our XML file, `sales.xml`, against this generated XSLT style sheet, and see what happens:

C:\>xt sales.xml salesschema.xsl
<?xml version="1.0" encoding="utf-8"?>

In pattern Department Sales Percentage:
        The Department's sales don't add to 100%.

5. As you can see, we are told exactly what's wrong with our style sheet. If we go back and ask all of the salespeople, we'll find that David was ashamed of his sales, and lied when he said he was responsible for 10%; he actually didn't make any sales at all. If we change his sales to 0 in our XML document, and rerun it against our XSLT style sheet, we'll get:

C:\>xt sales.xml salesschema.xsl
<?xml version="1.0" encoding="utf-8"?>

6. Since there were no errors, no error messages will be printed, and we know that we're all right. If we wanted to, we could re-arrange our Schematron schema to print out an error message if the sales don't add up to 100%, and print out an "everything's OK" message if they do, like this:

```
<schema>
  <pattern name="Department Sales Percentage">
    <rule context="sales">
      <assert test="sum(salesperson) = 100">The Department's sales don't
      add to 100%.</assert>
      <report test="sum(salesperson) = 100">The Department's sales add up
      to 100%.</report>
    </rule>
  </pattern>
</schema>
```

7. The `<report>` element is the opposite of the `<assert>` element, in that the contents are printed if the test *does* pass. If we re-generate the XSLT style sheet, and re-run the fixed version of the XML document against the new XSLT style sheet as in step 3, we'll get this:

C:\>xt sales.xml salesschema.xsl
<?xml version="1.0" encoding="utf-8"?>

In pattern Department Sales Percentage:
            The Department's sales add up to 100%.

And we know that everything is all right.

How It Works

Because Schematron uses the power and flexibility of XSLT and XPath, we can create powerful and flexible schemas, which can greatly aid in debugging situations.

Since you're using an XSLT style sheet to get the results, you can always edit this style sheet to make the results more readable, or format them in some other way. For example, in automated systems, you might want to make your style sheet output one of two elements for every test: an error element, with the error description, or an "everything's OK" element. Maybe you want the output to be something like this:

```
<?xml version="1.0"?>
<results>
  <test>OK</test>
  <test>OK</test>
  <test>The Department's sales don't add up to 100%</test>
</results>
```

The advantage of this is that you can easily write software to make sure that your document contains only elements with a value of "OK"; if not, then you know errors have occurred, and the values which are not "OK" will contain descriptions of those errors. In this manner, you can validate documents against Schematron schemas, the same way that you can validate against DTDs or XML Schemas, with slightly more work.

The Schematron web site also has an XSL style sheet that can be used for better formatting, in IE5. The web site is at http://www.ascc.net/xml/resource/schematron/schematron.html. There are also tutorials by Miloslav Nic, which can be found at http://zvon.vscht.cz/HTMLonly/SchematronTutorial/General/contents.html.

Summary

In this chapter we have covered some topics that, hopefully, will help you as you create your own XML-enabled applications. As an author and a developer, I had some fun writing sample applications, and you should be able to modify these easily in your own applications.

We have seen:

❑ Some helpful tips on creating well-designed object models

❑ How we can use XML to make remote procedure calls, even in cases where we don't have a server which understands XML-RPC

❑ An example of how a stateless object would be used in an application, and why

❑ What RDF is and where it might be used

❑ Schematron in action

We've now covered all of the major technologies that we're going to look at in this book.

We started by understanding what well-formed XML is, and learned how CSS can be used to apply style to our logically structured data. We covered the use of XSLT to transform the data into other formats, and used XPath to help identify specific parts of the XML documents.

The DOM and SAX were introduced as ways of accessing XML programmatically, and we also learned about using namespaces to avoid ambiguity in our element names. We saw how DTDs and Schemas provide a way to define how an XML document should be structured, and to specify default values. These technologies are particularly helpful when sharing documents with other developers.

Another area we looked at was linking between resources using XLink and XPointer. Finally we discussed how XML can be integrated with database applications, in n-tier architectures, and in this chapter discussed a few other areas where XML is being used.

Let's now move on and reinforce our new-found knowledge with a few practical case studies, which include using XML and XSLT for e-commerce and message board applications, and discussing how XML technologies were used in a particular real-life Business to Business application.

Case Study 1: Lydia's Lugnuts Web Store

Lydia is a (mythical) programmer/entrepreneur who is trying to cash in on the e-commerce boom with her own niche-oriented web site. Her chosen niche is lugnuts (nuts used to connect wheels to autos), a topic she understands thoroughly due to years of experience installing them in her family's garage.

The hands-on lugnut industry experience gave Lydia some contacts in the lugnut supply channel, some of which have web-based catalogs of their own lugnut stocks. Her main suppliers are:

- ❑ "Nuts. Nuts? Nuts!" (which supplies locking nuts)
- ❑ "The Nut Haus" (which also supplies locking nuts)
- ❑ "Nutters" (which supplies simple nuts)
- ❑ "Wild Genghis's Nuts, Bolts, and Fasteners" (which supplies very exotic lugnuts)

For obvious reasons, all have recently converted their catalogs to XML.

Lydia currently has a web-hosting account on an inexpensive Unix system, but if business goes well she might get a few NT servers and a T1 line so she can host the site from her office.

So far business *isn't* going well.

She is selling plenty of lugnuts, but she has two major business problems:

- ❑ Web customers are complaining about the web site being difficult to use
- ❑ She spends too much time updating the site manually

Complexity

The root cause of the first problem is the extensive listing Lydia gives each nut. When she first designed the site, she knew much of her traffic would come from search engines like Yahoo!, AltaVista, and HotBot. To make sure the correct pages from her site showed up in the search engines' results, she loaded (or overloaded) each part listing with:

❑ Compatibility information

❑ Alternate spellings

❑ Related keywords

The listings are so cumbersome, in fact, that customers are lucky if they can see more than two listings on each page:

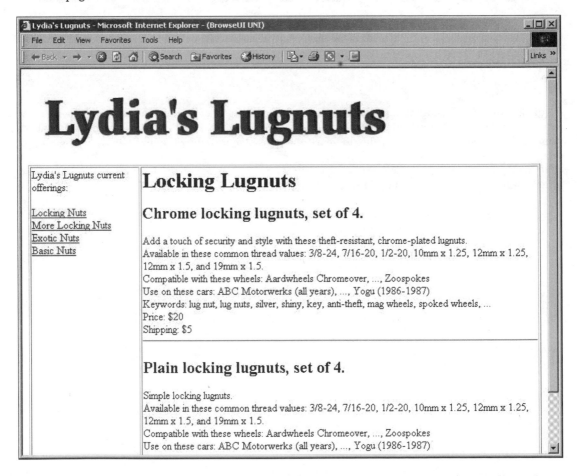

The HTML code for each of Lydia's four pages is relatively simple. Each follows this format:

❑ The logo

❑ A table which includes:

    ❑ A navigation section, with links to all the pages on the site, including the current page

    ❑ The lugnuts listing

❑ A short copyright statement (not visible in the screenshot)

This is the code for the Locking Nuts page shown (`locking.html`). The top and bottom sections are common to all four pages – the middle section contains the specific product listings:

```
<HTML>
<HEAD><TITLE>Lydia's Lugnuts</TITLE></HEAD>
<IMG src="images/logo.gif">
<TABLE border="1">
  <TR>
    <TD valign="top">
      <P>Lydia's Lugnuts current offerings:</P>
      <A href="locking.html">Locking Nuts</A><BR>
      <A href="locking2.html">More Locking Nuts</A><BR>
      <A href="exotic.html">Exotic Nuts</A><BR>
      <A href="basic.html">Basic Nuts</A><BR>
    </TD>
    <TD>


      <H1>Locking Lugnuts</H1>
      <H2>Chrome locking lugnuts, set of 4.</H2>
      Add a touch of security and style with these theft-resistant,
      chrome-plated lugnuts.<BR>
      Available in these common thread values: 3/8-24, 7/16-20, 1/2-20,
      10mm x 1.25, 12mm x 1.25, 12mm x 1.5, and 19mm x 1.5.<BR>
      Compatible with these wheels: Aardwheels Chromeover, ..., Zoospokes<BR>
      Use on these cars: ABC Motorwerks (all years), ..., Yogu (1986-1987)<BR>
      Keywords: lug nut, lug nuts, silver, shiny, key, anti-theft, mag wheels,
      spoked wheels, ...<BR>
      Price: $20<BR>
      Shipping: $5
      <HR>
      <H2>Plain locking lugnuts, set of 4.</H2>
      Simple locking lugnuts.<BR>
      Available in these common thread values: 3/8-24, 7/16-20, 1/2-20,
      10mm x 1.25, 12mm x 1.25, 12mm x 1.5, and 19mm x 1.5.<BR>
      Compatible with these wheels: Aardwheels Chromeover, ..., Zoospokes<BR>
      Use on these cars: ABC Motorwerks (all years), ..., Yogu (1986-1987)<BR>
      Keywords: lug nut, lug nuts, key, anti-theft, mag wheels, spoked wheels,
      ...<BR>
      Price: $20<BR>
      Shipping: $5


    </TD>
  </TR>
</TABLE>
Copyright MM, Lydia's Lugnuts
</HTML>
```

539

Maintenance

Maintenance on the site takes up most of Lydia's workday, because it all has to be done manually. If a supplier runs out of a particular nut, Lydia has to cut out the corresponding listing. She also has to change the navigation section on each page to reflect the change. Unexpected price changes also mean extra work for Lydia. And since she's not connected directly to the suppliers' databases, she has to verify current pricing on each lugnut herself. She tries to check the prices every week, but she's often too busy. This aspect of site maintenance has a very real cost: several orders have come in at the wrong price, and Lydia has had to make up the difference out of her own pocket.

Since you can hardly walk past a newsagent these days without seeing a headline about XML, Lydia has read a little about it. She thinks it might solve some of her problems, and she's right. Armed with a preview copy of Beginning XML from Wrox, Lydia sets about creating an XML-based version of Lydia's Lugnuts.

Her project has these goals:

- ❏ Make the site more efficient for the visitor by only displaying relevant information
- ❏ Keep all the extra data that catches the search engines' spiders, but make the site easier to read
- ❏ Make site maintenance easier by adding structure to the parts listings
- ❏ Save time and expense by linking directly to the suppliers' parts lists

She sits down on a crate of lugnuts and starts to read.

Creating Order from Chaos

Having read Chapters 1 and 2, Lydia knows XML is (among other things) a way to store similar data in well-defined structures, so she looks at ways to apply that concept to her site.

The first step in converting Lydia's Lugnuts from plain HTML to XML is to analyze the existing information and see how it might be converted into common structures.

In technical college, Lydia took some classes in database design. She's known from the start of her business venture that she was essentially working with a manually-managed database of parts. She knew how to automate many database functions on a PC or a LAN, but not on a web server. XML sounds like a relatively easy way to add this functionality, but she'll have to convert parts of the site from HTML to XML.

Designing the XML Structure

Lydia starts by identifying the pieces that make up each part listing. For example, here is a selected listing from her site:

```
Chrome locking lugnuts, set of 4.
Add a touch of security and style with these theft-resistant, chrome-plated
lugnuts.
```

Available in these common thread values: 3/8-24, 7/16-20, 1/2-20, 10mm x 1.25, 12mm x 1.25, 12mm x 1.5, and 19mm x 1.5.
Compatible with these wheels: Aardwheels Chromeover, …, Zoospokes
Use on these cars: ABC Motorwerks (all years), …, Yogu (1986-1987)
Keywords: lug nut, lug nuts, silver, shiny, key, anti-theft, mag wheels, spoked wheels, …
Price: $20
Shipping: $5

She sees several possible *elements*, some with potential *attributes*. For example, the first line could become one element called item, with attributes finish, locking, and quantity. It could alternatively be four separate elements. She decides to set up her listings with this structure:

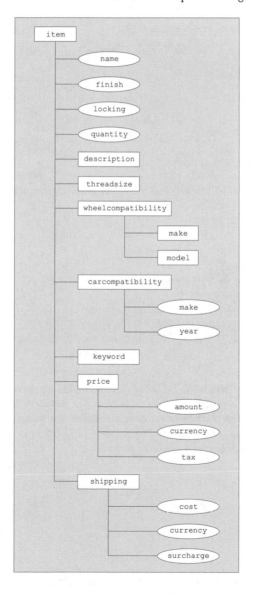

Creating XML Files

Lydia uses a text editor to create an XML file (`my_first.xml`) for one part listing:

```xml
<?xml version="1.0"?>
<item name="Wondernut Chrome" finish="chrome" locking="yes" quantity="4">
  <description>Add a touch of security and style with these theft-resistant,
  chrome-plated lugnuts.</description>
  <threadsize>3/8-24</threadsize>
  <threadsize>7/16-20</threadsize>
  <threadsize>1/2-20</threadsize>
  <threadsize>10mm x 1.25</threadsize>
  <threadsize>12mm x 1.25</threadsize>
  <threadsize>12mm x 1.5</threadsize>
  <threadsize>19mm x 1.5</threadsize>
  <wheelcompatibility>
    <make>Aardwheels</make>
    <model>Chromeover</model>
  </wheelcompatibility>
  <wheelcompatibility>
    <make>Zoospokes</make>
    <model/>
  </wheelcompatibility>
  <carcompatibility make="ABC Motorwerks" year="all"></carcompatibility>
  <carcompatibility make="Yogu" year="1986-1987"></carcompatibility>
  <keyword>lug nut</keyword>
  <keyword>lug nuts</keyword>
  <keyword>silver</keyword>
  <keyword>shiny</keyword>
  <keyword>key</keyword>
  <keyword>anti-theft</keyword>
  <keyword>mag wheels</keyword>
  <keyword>spoked wheels</keyword>
  <price amount="20" currency="$US" tax="10%"></price>
  <shipping cost="5" currency="$US" surcharge=""></shipping>
</item>
```

You might be wondering "Where is the DTD?" Lydia has looked at the structures of XML files from her suppliers, and they are very different from each other. She decides to skip the DTD and simply use well-formed XML instead. This turns out to be a wise decision as the project progresses, because DTDs and namespaces would be difficult-to-impossible to integrate in this particular case, as all the suppliers have settled on their own preferred format.

IE5 displays the XML file like this:

Lydia sees how `item` and `wheelcompatibility` collapse and expand, and she wants the same functionality in some of the more repetitive elements, such as `threadsize` and `keyword`. The current file isn't bad, but it could be a little more useful for the developer working with it. Lydia adds elements to "wrap" around the thread sizes and keywords:

```xml
<?xml version="1.0"?>
<item name="Wondernut Chrome" finish="chrome" locking="yes" quantity="4">
  <description>Add a touch of security and style with these theft-resistant,
  chrome-plated lugnuts.</description>
  <threadsizelist>
    <threadsize>3/8-24</threadsize>
    <threadsize>7/16-20</threadsize>
    <threadsize>1/2-20</threadsize>
    <threadsize>10mm x 1.25</threadsize>
    <threadsize>12mm x 1.25</threadsize>
    <threadsize>12mm x 1.5</threadsize>
    <threadsize>19mm x 1.5</threadsize>
  </threadsizelist>
```

```
    <wheelcompatibility>
      <make>Aardwheels</make>
      <model>Chromeover</model>
    </wheelcompatibility>
    <wheelcompatibility>
      <make>Zoospokes</make>
      <model/>
    </wheelcompatibility>
    <carcompatibility make="ABC Motorwerks" year="all"></carcompatibility>
    <carcompatibility make="Yogu" year="1986-1987"></carcompatibility>
    <keywordlist>
      <keyword>lug nut</keyword>
      <keyword>lug nuts</keyword>
      <keyword>silver</keyword>
      <keyword>shiny</keyword>
      <keyword>key</keyword>
      <keyword>anti-theft</keyword>
      <keyword>mag wheels</keyword>
      <keyword>spoked wheels</keyword>
    </keywordlist>
    <price amount="20" currency="$US" tax="10%"></price>
    <shipping cost="5" currency="$US" surcharge=""></shipping>
  </item>
```

These changes are strictly for readability on Lydia's side – they won't affect the way the final XML file(s) looks to Lydia's customers. IE5 shows the modified file (my_second.xml) like this (with the thread sizes and keywords collapsed):

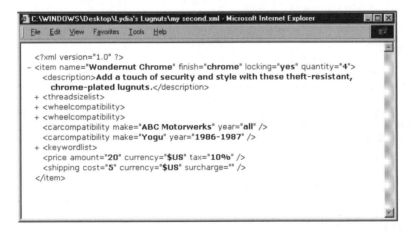

This enables Lydia to see several item listings on one screen and only expand elements she wants to see. In practice, Lydia would probably do the same thing with the extensive list of compatible cars in carcompatibility. This example uses only two cars, but a real listing could include dozens.

Grouping Products Together

The XML file now works fine in her browser, but there may be a major problem: it only works for one item. item is the root element. Lydia's site includes many lugnuts, so what does she do with the other items? She has at least two options:

- ❑ Keep the design as it is and have a separate XML file for each item
- ❑ Include several (even all) items in the same file, but redesign it with a root element like `catalog` or `partslist`

Each approach has advantages and disadvantages. If she divides the site into separate XML files for each item, she'll have to redesign the site to navigate between them. That could mean listing every nut on every page for navigation purposes, potentially making the site even less usable than it is now. On the positive side, using individual files for each nut would make search results more accurate. But that approach doesn't seem right. Visitors wouldn't be able to compare similar lugnut features or prices on the same page. The other approach, combining several similar nuts together on a page, seems more usable. But not *all* nuts on one page. In fact, the general design that the site already has (a page for each popular category) seems intuitive, it's just difficult to use at the moment because the listings are so long. But Lydia plans to remove much of the irrelevant information anyway, so this seems like a good solution.

Transforming and Displaying XML with XSL

After reading Chapters 3, 4 and 5, Lydia has now learned how to display XML in all kinds of ways. She is relieved to see she doesn't have to wipe out all of the lovely HTML she worked so hard to create. She can keep some of her existing HTML code and integrate her XML data into it using style sheets.

She makes a new test XML file (`my_third.xml`) for her site so she can try a few XSLT style sheets. The new XML file includes three of her most popular lugnuts, with the three `item` listings wrapped in a `catalog` root element:

```xml
<?xml version="1.0"?>
<catalog>
  <item name="Wondernut Chrome" finish="chrome" locking="yes" quantity="4">
    <description>Add a touch of security and style with these theft-resistant,
    chrome-plated lugnuts.</description>
    <threadsizelist>
      <threadsize>3/8-24</threadsize>
      <threadsize>7/16-20</threadsize>
      <threadsize>1/2-20</threadsize>
      <threadsize>10mm x 1.25</threadsize>
      <threadsize>12mm x 1.25</threadsize>
      <threadsize>12mm x 1.5</threadsize>
      <threadsize>19mm x 1.5</threadsize>
    </threadsizelist>
    <wheelcompatibility>
      <make>Aardwheels</make>
      <model>Chromeover</model>
    </wheelcompatibility>
    <wheelcompatibility>
      <make>Zoospokes</make>
      <model/>
    </wheelcompatibility>
    <carcompatibility make="ABC Motorwerks" year="all"></carcompatibility>
    <carcompatibility make="Yogu" year="1986-1987"></carcompatibility>
    <keywordlist>
```

```
      <keyword>lug nut</keyword>
      <keyword>lug nuts</keyword>
      <keyword>silver</keyword>
      <keyword>shiny</keyword>
      <keyword>key</keyword>
      <keyword>anti-theft</keyword>
      <keyword>mag wheels</keyword>
      <keyword>spoked wheels</keyword>
    </keywordlist>
    <price amount="20" currency="$US" tax="10%"></price>
    <shipping cost="5" currency="$US" surcharge=""></shipping>
  </item>

  <item name="Wondernut Blue Fuzzy" finish="blue fuzz" locking="no" quantity="20">
    <description>Stand out from the crowd with these blue, fuzzy lug
    nuts.</description>
    <threadsizelist>
      <threadsize>10mm x 1.25</threadsize>
      <threadsize>12mm x 1.25</threadsize>
      <threadsize>12mm x 1.5</threadsize>
      <threadsize>19mm x 1.5</threadsize>
    </threadsizelist>
    <wheelcompatibility>
      <make>Aardwheels</make>
      <model>Chromeover</model>
    </wheelcompatibility>
    <wheelcompatibility>
      <make>Zoospokes</make>
      <model/>
    </wheelcompatibility>
    <carcompatibility make="ABC Motorwerks" year="all"></carcompatibility>
    <carcompatibility make="Yogu" year="1986-1987"></carcompatibility>
    <keywordlist>
      <keyword>lug nut</keyword>
      <keyword>lug nuts</keyword>
      <keyword>fuzzy</keyword>
      <keyword>blue</keyword>
    </keywordlist>
    <price amount="40" currency="$US" tax="10%"></price>
    <shipping cost="5" currency="$US" surcharge="$5 special handling"></shipping>
  </item>

  <item name="Basic Lugnut" finish="none" locking="no" quantity="5">
    <description>When you just need a set of no-frills lugnuts, try these
    bargains.</description>
    <threadsizelist>
      <threadsize>3/8-24</threadsize>
      <threadsize>7/16-20</threadsize>
      <threadsize>1/2-20</threadsize>
      <threadsize>10mm x 1.25</threadsize>
      <threadsize>12mm x 1.25</threadsize>
      <threadsize>12mm x 1.5</threadsize>
      <threadsize>19mm x 1.5</threadsize>
    </threadsizelist>
    <wheelcompatibility>
      <make>Aardwheels</make>
      <model>Chromeover</model>
```

```
          </wheelcompatibility>
          <wheelcompatibility>
            <make>Zoospokes</make>
            <model/>
          </wheelcompatibility>
          <carcompatibility make="ABC Motorwerks" year="all"></carcompatibility>
          <carcompatibility make="Yogu" year="1986-1987"></carcompatibility>
          <keywordlist>
            <keyword>lug nut</keyword>
            <keyword>lug nuts</keyword>
          </keywordlist>
          <price amount="5" currency="$US" tax="10%"></price>
          <shipping cost="5" currency="$US" surcharge=""></shipping>
      </item>
  </catalog>
```

In IE5, it collapses down to this:

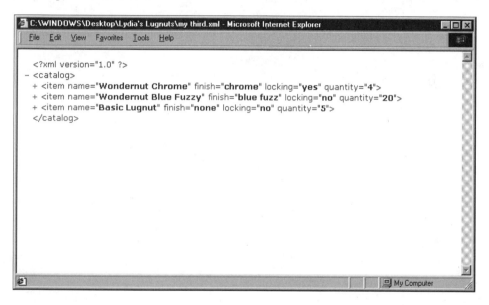

The Existing Web Page

Now she looks at the (very simple) HTML version of her home page so she can decide what to keep when she converts to XML:

```
<HTML>
<HEAD><TITLE>Lydia's Lugnuts</TITLE></HEAD>
<IMG src="images/logo.gif">
<TABLE border="1">
  <TR>
    <TD valign="top">
      <P>Lydia's Lugnuts current offerings:</P>
      <A href="locking.html">Locking Nuts</A><BR>

      <A href="locking2.html">More Locking Nuts</A><BR>
      <A href="exotic.html">Exotic Nuts</A><BR>
```

```
        <A href="basic.html">Basic Nuts</A><BR>
     </TD>
     <TD>

        <H1>Locking Lugnuts</H1>
        <H2>Chrome locking lugnuts, set of 4.</H2>
        Add a touch of security and style with these theft-resistant,
        chrome-plated lugnuts.<BR>
        Available in these common thread values: 3/8-24, 7/16-20, 1/2-20,
        10mm x 1.25, 12mm x 1.25, 12mm x 1.5, and 19mm x 1.5.<BR>
        Compatible with these wheels: Aardwheels Chromeover, ..., Zoospokes<BR>
        Use on these cars: ABC Motorwerks (all years), ..., Yogu (1986-1987)<BR>
        Keywords: lug nut, lug nuts, silver, shiny, key, anti-theft, mag wheels,
        spoked wheels, ...<BR>
        Price: $20<BR>
        Shipping: $5
        <HR>
        <H2>Plain locking lugnuts, set of 4.</H2>
        Simple locking lugnuts.<BR>
        Available in these common thread values: 3/8-24, 7/16-20, 1/2-20,
        10mm x 1.25, 12mm x 1.25, 12mm x 1.5, and 19mm x 1.5.<BR>
        Compatible with these wheels: Aardwheels Chromeover, ..., Zoospokes<BR>
        Use on these cars: ABC Motorwerks (all years), ..., Yogu (1986-1987)<BR>
        Keywords: lug nut, lug nuts, key, anti-theft, mag wheels, spoked wheels,
        ...<BR>
        Price: $20<BR>
        Shipping: $5

 ... other product listings

     </TD>
   </TR>
 </TABLE>
 Copyright MM, Lydia's Lugnuts
 </HTML>
```

The home page (with a single nut listing) looks like this:

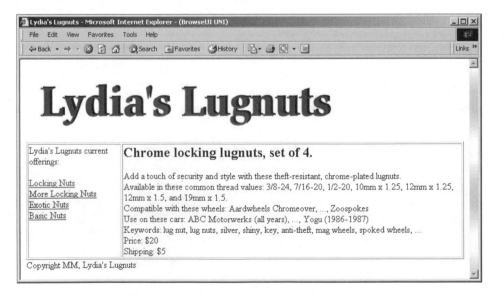

Well, for now it looks like the product listing has to go, but everything else would become part of the template. Heck, she'll have an XML site cobbled together in ten minutes! The XSLT template, like her old HTML template, will include the basic HTML elements:

❑ The HTML header, including the title

❑ The logo (the <IMG> tag)

❑ The table header (<TABLE>, <TR> and <TD> tags)

❑ The navigation section, with hyperlinks to all the pages on the site, including the current page

❑ The next part of the table section (closing the column with </TD> and opening the next column with <TD>)

❑ An XSLT section to create the lugnuts listing

❑ The last part of the table section (closing the column with </TD>, closing the row with </TR>, and closing the table with </TABLE>)

❑ A short copyright statement

The XSLT Style Sheet

Here is Lydia's first XSLT template (first.xsl), which will be used in combination with her test XML file to create an HTML file. The XSLT section grabs each item in the XML catalog and creates an HTML version of it (the template is very wrong, so rather than have you type it and get errors, we'll first explore the problem areas):

```
<?xml version="1.0"?>
<xsl:stylesheet version="1.0" xmlns:xsl="http://www.w3.org/1999/XSL/Transform">
<xsl:output method="xml"/>
<xsl:template match="/">
<HTML>
<HEAD><TITLE>Lydia's Lugnuts</TITLE></HEAD>
<BODY>
<IMG src="images/logo.gif">
<TABLE border="1">
  <TR>
    <TD valign="top">
      <P>Lydia's Lugnuts current offerings:</P>
      <A href="locking.html">Locking Nuts</A><BR>
      <A href="locking2.html">More Locking Nuts</A><BR>
      <A href="exotic.html">Exotic Nuts</A><BR>
      <A href="basic.html">Basic Nuts</A><BR>
    </TD>
    <TD>
      <xsl:for-each select=".">
        <P><xsl:value-of select="."/></P>
      </xsl:for-each>
    </TD>
  </TR>
</TABLE>
Copyright MM, Lydia's Lugnuts
</BODY>
</HTML>
</xsl:template>
</xsl:stylesheet>
```

She runs it through XT (which was introduced in Chapter 4) with this syntax:

```
xt my_third.xml first.xsl first.html
```

Whoa! She gets an error, fixes it, then gets more. Some of them are easy to diagnose, some more difficult, like the first one:

```
file:/C:/xt/first.xsl:17: mismatched end tag: expected "BR" but got "TD"
```

So line 17 is missing an end tag for
 (a commonly used line break)?
 doesn't even *have* an end tag! Lydia restrains herself from throwing a lugnut at her monitor. Wait, wait. This is XML, so *everything* has an end tag. But what about
? She tries this:

```
<BR><A href="locking.html">Locking Nuts</A></BR>
```

Same error. It looks like she'll have to rework that section. No, there was something in the chapter about <BR>. It's supposed to be <BR/> in XML. She tries this:

```
<A href="locking.html">Locking Nuts</A><BR/>
<A href="locking2.html">More Locking Nuts</A><BR/>
<A href="exotic.html">Exotic Nuts</A><BR/>
<A href="basic.html">Basic Nuts</A><BR/>
```

That works, but there's another error from XT:

```
file:/C:/xt/first.xsl:28: mismatched end tag: expected "IMG" but got "BODY"
```

Line 28? That line looks fine – it's just the closing tag </BODY>. From previous experience with compilers, Lydia knows that if one of the last lines (in a procedure, a program, or, in this case, an XSLT template) appears to cause an error, it's usually the fault of some earlier line. Here XT gives a hint: it says it expected "IMG" but found something else. Lydia looks at the <IMG> line earlier in the template:

```
<IMG src="images/logo.gif">
```

So what's wrong with that? XT says "mismatched end tag." Oh. Even IMG tags need closing tags in XML, so she changes it to this:

```
<IMG src="images/logo.gif"/>
```

That works. XT creates an HTML file (first.html) from Lydia's XML file and template. But here's what it looks like:

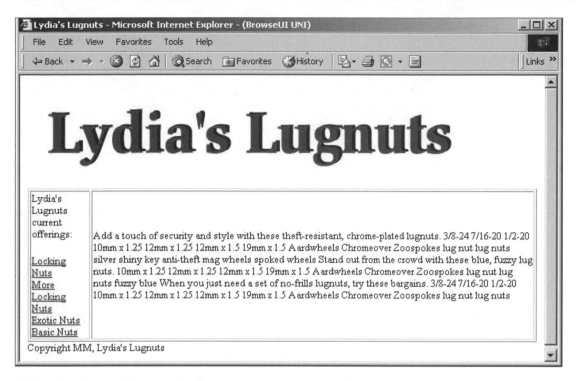

That will never do. The information all runs together, and it doesn't even give the names or prices of the products. She's pretty sure she can work out the formatting of individual elements, but Lydia also needs to spend some time working out what she wants to show in the product listings. Once she determines that, she can figure out the XSL she would use to make it happen.

Removing Unwanted Detail

First, there is too much information. One of the original problems she wanted to address was the clutter of the listings. Maybe the listings could be as simple as this:

Product
Description
Price
Shipping

The second draft of her XSLT style sheet (second.xsl) ignores the other elements and attributes outside of those she chose. Here is the basic HTML wrapper, which selects item, description, price, and shipping, adding a horizontal rule after each item:

```
<?xml version="1.0"?>
<xsl:stylesheet version="1.0" xmlns:xsl="http://www.w3.org/1999/XSL/Transform">
<xsl:output method="xml" indent="yes"/>
  <xsl:template match="/">
    <HTML>
      <HEAD><TITLE>Lydia's Lugnuts</TITLE></HEAD>
      <BODY>
```

551

```
          <IMG src="images/logo.gif"/>
          <TABLE border="1">
            <TR>
              <TD valign="top">
                <P>Lydia's Lugnuts current offerings:</P>
                <A href="locking.html">Locking Nuts</A><BR/>
                <A href="locking2.html">More Locking Nuts</A><BR/>
                <A href="exotic.html">Exotic Nuts</A><BR/>
                <A href="basic.html">Basic Nuts</A><BR/>
              </TD>
              <TD>
                <xsl:for-each select="/catalog/item">
                  <xsl:apply-templates select="."/>
                  <xsl:apply-templates select="./description"/>
                  <xsl:apply-templates select="./price"/>
                  <xsl:apply-templates select="./shipping"/>
                  <HR/>
                </xsl:for-each>
              </TD>
            </TR>
          </TABLE>
          Copyright MM, Lydia's Lugnuts
          </BODY>
        </HTML>
      </xsl:template>
```

And here are the templates for those selections. The template below matches each `item` element and applies templates to its `name` and `finish` attributes:

```
<xsl:template match="item">
    <xsl:apply-templates select="@name"/>
    <xsl:apply-templates select="@finish"/>
  </xsl:template>
```

This template adds a bold tag before and after the `name` attribute, then a line break:

```
<xsl:template match="@name">
  <B><xsl:value-of select="."/>
  </B><BR/>
</xsl:template>
```

The next template adds an italic tag before and after the `finish` attribute, then a paragraph marker. (Note: using an empty paragraph tag for padding is poor form, but very common in HTML design.)

```
<xsl:template match="@finish">
  <I>Finish: <xsl:value-of select="."/>
  </I><P/>
</xsl:template>
```

This template adds an italic tag before and after the `description` element, and makes the entire description its own paragraph:

```
<xsl:template match="description">
    <P><I><xsl:value-of select="."/></I></P>
</xsl:template>
```

This template breaks down the `price` element into its attributes: `currency`, `amount`, and `tax`:

```
<xsl:template match="price">
  Price:
    <xsl:apply-templates select="@currency"/>
    <xsl:apply-templates select="@amount"/>
    <xsl:apply-templates select="@tax"/>
    <xsl:value-of select="."/>
</xsl:template>
```

This template pretty much ignores the `currency` attribute, replacing it with a dollar sign and a space. (This is a good place for future expansion. How about using a function like `xsl:choose` to show the correct symbol based on the `currency` value?)

```
<xsl:template match="@currency">
  <xsl:text>$ </xsl:text>
</xsl:template>
```

This next template shows the value of the `amount` attribute, then adds a line break:

```
<xsl:template match="@amount">
  <xsl:value-of select="."/><BR/>
</xsl:template>
```

Then there is a template to show the value of the `tax` attribute, and add a paragraph break:

```
<xsl:template match="@tax">
  Tax: <xsl:value-of select="."/><P/>
</xsl:template>
```

A further template breaks down the `shipping` element into its attributes: `currency`, `cost`, and `surcharge`, then calls a template for each:

```
<xsl:template match="shipping">
  Shipping:
    <xsl:apply-templates select="@currency"/>
    <xsl:apply-templates select="@cost"/>
    <xsl:apply-templates select="@surcharge"/>
    <xsl:value-of select="."/>
</xsl:template>
```

This template simply shows the value of the `currency` attribute:

```
<xsl:template match="@currency">
  <xsl:value-of select="."/>
</xsl:template>
```

This template shows the value of the `cost` attribute, then adds a line break:

```
<xsl:template match="@cost">
  <xsl:value-of select="."/><BR/>
</xsl:template>
```

This template shows the text "Surcharge: ", the value of the `surcharge` attribute, and a paragraph break:

```
<xsl:template match="@surcharge">
  Surcharge: <xsl:value-of select="."/><P/>
</xsl:template>
```

And finally, this line closes our style sheet:

```
</xsl:stylesheet>
```

When she runs this file (`second.xsl`) through XT and displays the result in IE5, this is what Lydia sees:

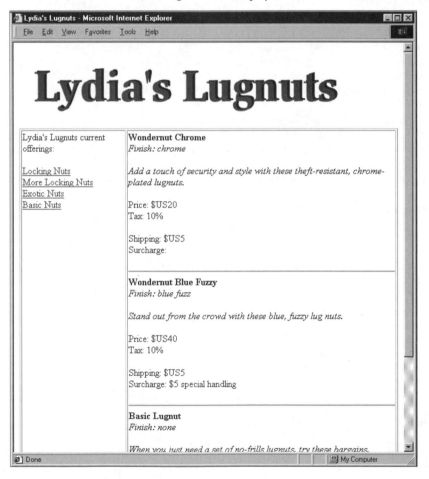

Formatting the Output

That's not quite right. The price is supposed to show a dollar sign, not $US. If you try this example, you'll also notice that the last item looks odd because it ends with a horizontal line right above the table's last line.

First things first: what's wrong with the price? There's a clue on the screen, in that both the price and shipping show the string $US, but surcharge doesn't. The XML file lists the price and shipping elements for the first item like this:

```
<price amount="20" currency="$US" tax="10%"></price>
<shipping cost="5" currency="$US" surcharge=""></shipping>
```

They both have currency attributes, so our two templates that try to process currency attributes are stepping over each other. (Actually only one gets called, and with properly-behaved processors like XT it's the last one.) Only one of the currency templates works on any or all currency attributes, no matter where the template is in the style sheet. So what does Lydia do now? She can either:

❑   Manually change the name of one of the currency attributes

❑   Handle all currency attributes the same way, and add any specific formatting to the root, price, and/or shipping templates

The second option is probably best. You may remember the note about how a template like the currency handler would be a great place for future expansion. Lydia could extend the functionality of a single currency template so it could determine what symbols to display, how or whether to use decimals, and maybe even the current conversion rate based on the value of the currency attribute of *any* element. For now, she just needs to take one out, and the second one (shown below) is probably the easier target for deletion because it's less useful.

```
<xsl:template match="@currency">
  <xsl:value-of select="."/>
</xsl:template>
```

With just one `currency` template, Lydia now sees the layout she wants:

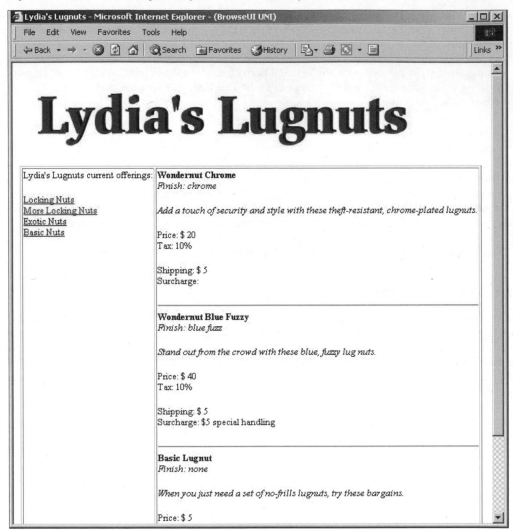

But there's still the problem of the last, unnecessary horizontal rule (not shown in the figure). This is easily dealt with by changing the `<HR/>` line in the main template to something like this:

```
<xsl:if test="not(position()=last())"><HR/></xsl:if>
```

If this is not the last `item`, the template inserts a horizontal rule. If it *is* the last `item`, the `if` condition fails and no horizontal rule is inserted.

There's just one final refinement Lydia might want to make. Rather than *delete* the extra information like `keywords`, she could put that information in metadata, such as `<META keywords>` or `<META description>` tags. This would allow search engines and utilities to find that information without cluttering up the listings. This addition to the style sheet does exactly that with the `keywordlist/keyword` elements:

```
<xsl:template match="keywordlist">
  <xsl:text disable-output-escaping="yes">&lt;META keywords="</xsl:text>
  <xsl:for-each select="//keyword">
    <xsl:value-of select="."/>
    <xsl:text> </xsl:text>
  </xsl:for-each>
  <xsl:text disable-output-escaping="yes">"&gt;</xsl:text>
</xsl:template>
```

To make this work, you need an extra line in the <HEAD> section of the template:

```
<xsl:apply-templates select="//keywordlist"/>
```

The output isn't pretty (which is all right – users won't see it unless they view the HTML source), but it serves its purpose:

```
<HEAD>
                    rwords="lug nut lug nuts silver shiny key
                  nut lug nuts fuzzy blue lug nut lug nuts
                  er shiny key anti-theft mag wheels spoked
               lu nut lug nuts "><META keywords="lug nut lug
                  eels spoked wheels lug nut lug nuts fuzzy
```

and other information that was cluttering up her

L/XSL and link to her suppliers' catalogs.

Multiple Sources

XML, but she still has an outstanding problem:
more closely with her suppliers. She already has a
transforms it into a page suitable for display by a
roduct information from her suppliers into the

ts)

uts)

h supplies very exotic lugnuts)

557

She has XML files from each supplier. She can think of a few options for using the suppliers' XML files to create HTML pages for her site:

- ❑ Leave the existing Lydia's-Lugnuts-product-file to HTML-web-browser-page transformation template alone and write new style sheets to transform each supplier file into a format similar to the Lydia's Lugnuts product file

- ❑ Modify the existing XSLT style sheet and then run it against a *combined* product file, made up of all of the information she has available

- ❑ Modify the existing XSLT style sheet to accommodate all the suppliers' formats, then run each supplier's XML file against that style sheet to create up to date HTML files

Having chosen the third option, and remembering that Chapter 7 showed how namespaces and related technologies make this possible, she is ready to try it out. Here is the process she has in mind:

1. Get an XML catalog file from a supplier (for example, a catalog of locking nuts from "Nuts. Nuts? Nuts!")

2. Use XT to create an HTML file from that file and her XSLT style sheet

For the sake of this example (and to avoid stepping on domains that are currently registered, or will be in the future) we will imagine each of these companies uses wrox.com to host their XML content.

For this simple example, we'll look at just two of her imaginary suppliers:

- ❑ "Nuts. Nuts? Nuts!" (which we'll say is at http://www.wrox.com/nnn)

- ❑ "The Nut Haus" (hypothetically at http://www.wrox.com/nh)

Product Listings

A nut from "Nuts. Nuts? Nuts!" product listings looks like this (you may notice that this structure was largely the inspiration for Lydia's own product listings):

```
<onlinecatalog xmlns="http://www.wrox.com/nnn/">
  <nut name="Wondernut Chrome" finish="chrome" locking="yes" quantity="4">
    <description>Add a touch of security and style with these theft-resistant,
    chrome-plated lugnuts.</description>
    <threadsizelist>
      <thread>3/8-24</thread>
      <thread>7/16-20</thread>
      <thread>1/2-20</thread>
      <thread>10mm x 1.25</thread>
      <thread>12mm x 1.25</thread>
      <thread>12mm x 1.5</thread>
      <thread>19mm x 1.5</thread>
    </threadsizelist>
```

```
<xsl:template match="keywordlist">
  <xsl:text disable-output-escaping="yes">&lt;META keywords="</xsl:text>
  <xsl:for-each select="//keyword">
    <xsl:value-of select="."/>
    <xsl:text> </xsl:text>
  </xsl:for-each>
  <xsl:text disable-output-escaping="yes">"&gt;</xsl:text>
</xsl:template>
```

To make this work, you need an extra line in the `<HEAD>` section of the template:

```
<xsl:apply-templates select="//keywordlist"/>
```

The output isn't pretty (which is all right – users won't see it unless they view the HTML source), but it serves its purpose:

```
<HEAD>
<TITLE>Lydia's Lugnuts</TITLE><META keywords="lug nut lug nuts silver shiny key
anti-theft mag wheels spoked wheels lug nut lug nuts fuzzy blue lug nut lug nuts
"><META keywords="lug nut lug nuts silver shiny key anti-theft mag wheels spoked
wheels lug nut lug nuts fuzzy blue lug nut lug nuts "><META keywords="lug nut lug
nuts silver shiny key anti-theft mag wheels spoked wheels lug nut lug nuts fuzzy
blue lug nut lug nuts "></HEAD>
```

Lydia could repeat this process for the thread sizes and other information that was cluttering up her listings.

Now Lydia is ready to convert her entire site to XML/XSL and link to her suppliers' catalogs.

Incorporating Content from Multiple Sources

Lydia now has her site for Lydia's Lugnuts set up in XML, but she still has an outstanding problem: maintenance will be a nightmare unless she integrates more closely with her suppliers. She already has a style sheet that takes her own product listings file and transforms it into a page suitable for display by a web browser. She now needs a way of incorporating product information from her suppliers into the web page.

As a reminder, here are Lydia's suppliers:

- ❑ "Nuts. Nuts? Nuts!" (which supplies locking nuts)
- ❑ "The Nut Haus" (which also supplies locking nuts)
- ❑ Nutters (which supplies simple nuts)
- ❑ Wild Genghis's Nuts, Bolts, and Fasteners (which supplies very exotic lugnuts)

She has XML files from each supplier. She can think of a few options for using the suppliers' XML files to create HTML pages for her site:

❑ Leave the existing Lydia's-Lugnuts-product-file to HTML-web-browser-page transformation template alone and write new style sheets to transform each supplier file into a format similar to the Lydia's Lugnuts product file

❑ Modify the existing XSLT style sheet and then run it against a *combined* product file, made up of all of the information she has available

❑ Modify the existing XSLT style sheet to accommodate all the suppliers' formats, then run each supplier's XML file against that style sheet to create up to date HTML files

Having chosen the third option, and remembering that Chapter 7 showed how namespaces and related technologies make this possible, she is ready to try it out. Here is the process she has in mind:

1. Get an XML catalog file from a supplier (for example, a catalog of locking nuts from "Nuts. Nuts? Nuts!")

2. Use XT to create an HTML file from that file and her XSLT style sheet

For the sake of this example (and to avoid stepping on domains that are currently registered, or will be in the future) we will imagine each of these companies uses wrox.com to host their XML content.

For this simple example, we'll look at just two of her imaginary suppliers:

❑ "Nuts. Nuts? Nuts!" (which we'll say is at http://www.wrox.com/nnn)

❑ "The Nut Haus" (hypothetically at http://www.wrox.com/nh)

Product Listings

A nut from "Nuts. Nuts? Nuts!" product listings looks like this (you may notice that this structure was largely the inspiration for Lydia's own product listings):

```
<onlinecatalog xmlns="http://www.wrox.com/nnn/">
  <nut name="Wondernut Chrome" finish="chrome" locking="yes" quantity="4">
    <description>Add a touch of security and style with these theft-resistant,
    chrome-plated lugnuts.</description>
    <threadsizelist>
      <thread>3/8-24</thread>
      <thread>7/16-20</thread>
      <thread>1/2-20</thread>
      <thread>10mm x 1.25</thread>
      <thread>12mm x 1.25</thread>
      <thread>12mm x 1.5</thread>
      <thread>19mm x 1.5</thread>
    </threadsizelist>
  </nut>
```

```
      <wheelcompatibility>
        <make>Aardwheels</make>
        <model>Chromeover</model>
      </wheelcompatibility>
      <wheelcompatibility>
        <make>Zoospokes</make>
        <model/>
      </wheelcompatibility>
      <price amount="18" currency="$US" tax="10%"></price>
    </nut>
  </onlinecatalog>
```

A product listing from "The Nut Haus" looks like this:

```
<nuts xmlns="http://www.wrox.com/nh/">
  <item>
    <name>
      Basic Lugnut
    </name>
    <color>
      silver
    </color>
    <locking>
      no
    </locking>
    <quantityperorder>
      5
    </quantityperorder>
    <description>
      When you just need a set of no-frills lugnuts, try these bargains.
    </description>
    <threadsizes>
      <threadsize>3/8-24</threadsize>
      <threadsize>7/16-20</threadsize>
      <threadsize>1/2-20</threadsize>
      <threadsize>10mm x 1.25</threadsize>
      <threadsize>12mm x 1.25</threadsize>
      <threadsize>12mm x 1.5</threadsize>
      <threadsize>19mm x 1.5</threadsize>
    </threadsizes>
    <wheelcompatibility>
      <make>Aardwheels</make>
      <model>Chromeover</model>
    </wheelcompatibility>
    <wheelcompatibility>
      <make>Zoospokes</make>
      <model/>
    </wheelcompatibility>
    <carcompatibility make="ABC Motorwerks" year="all"></carcompatibility>
    <carcompatibility make="Yogu" year="1986-1987"></carcompatibility>
    <price>
      <amount>
        $5
```

```
      </amount>
    </price>
    <shipping>
      <amount>
        $5
      </amount>
    </shipping>
  </item>
</nuts>
```

And, as you may remember, Lydia's Lugnut's listings are like this:

```
<catalog>
  <item name="Wondernut Chrome" finish="chrome" locking="yes" quantity="4">
    <description>Add a touch of security and style with these theft-resistant,
    chrome-plated lugnuts.</description>
    <threadsizelist>
      <threadsize>3/8-24</threadsize>
      <threadsize>7/16-20</threadsize>
      <threadsize>1/2-20</threadsize>
      <threadsize>10mm x 1.25</threadsize>
      <threadsize>12mm x 1.25</threadsize>
      <threadsize>12mm x 1.5</threadsize>
      <threadsize>19mm x 1.5</threadsize>
    </threadsizelist>
    <wheelcompatibility>
      <make>Aardwheels</make>
      <model>Chromeover</model>
    </wheelcompatibility>
    <wheelcompatibility>
      <make>Zoospokes</make>
      <model/>
    </wheelcompatibility>
    <carcompatibility make="ABC Motorwerks" year="all"></carcompatibility>
    <carcompatibility make="Yogu" year="1986-1987"></carcompatibility>
    <keywordlist>
      <keyword>lug nut</keyword>
      <keyword>lug nuts</keyword>
      <keyword>silver</keyword>
      <keyword>shiny</keyword>
      <keyword>key</keyword>
      <keyword>anti-theft</keyword>
      <keyword>mag wheels</keyword>
      <keyword>spoked wheels</keyword>
    </keywordlist>
    <price amount="20" currency="$US" tax="10%"></price>
    <shipping cost="5" currency="$US" surcharge=""></shipping>
  </item>
```

She started by comparing the differences in the product listings, and realized that she would need a slightly different set of templates for each supplier. She knew that namespaces would help here. Opening up her XSLT style sheet (second.xsl) she added the following namespace declarations:

```
<xsl:stylesheet version="1.0" xmlns:xsl="http://www.w3.org/1999/XSL/Transform"
                              xmlns:nnn="http://www.wrox.com/nnn/"
                              xmlns:nh="http://www.wrox.com/nh">
```

For now she added a section into her table for each of the product file formats, and set about working out exactly what templates would be needed:

```
<xsl:for-each select="/catalog/item">
            <xsl:apply-templates select="."/>
            <xsl:apply-templates select="./description"/>
            <xsl:apply-templates select="./price"/>
            <xsl:apply-templates select="./shipping"/>
            <HR/>
        </xsl:for-each>

<xsl:for-each select="//nnn.nut">
            … Nuts. Nuts? Nuts! template calls will go here
</xsl:for-each>

<xsl:for-each select="nh:nuts">
            … Nut Haus template calls will go here
</xsl:for-each>
```

Nuts. Nuts? Nuts! Templates

In the product listing section (the second cell of the table), these lines enable the items from "Nuts. Nuts? Nuts!" to be processed separately from other content (note that since the original catalog doesn't include any shipping information, the style sheet hardcodes an `xsl:text` value for shipping):

```
<xsl:for-each select="//nnn:nut">
        <xsl:apply-templates select="."/>
        <xsl:apply-templates select="nnn:description"/>
        <xsl:apply-templates select="nnn:price"/>
        <xsl:text>Shipping: $5</xsl:text>
        <xsl:if test="not(position()=last())"><HR/> </xsl:if>
    </xsl:for-each>
```

The template for the root element is similar to that for her own product listing, but with the name changed, to reflect the fact that the `<item>` element is called `<nnn:nut>`:

```
<xsl:template match="nnn:nut">
    <xsl:apply-templates select="@name"/>
    <xsl:apply-templates select="@finish"/>
</xsl:template>
```

The same templates are used for the name and finish attributes as are used for her own listings.

Here is the simple template for the nnn:description element:

```
<xsl:template match="nnn:description">
    <P><xsl:value-of select="."/></P>
</xsl:template>
```

This template is added for the "Nuts. Nuts? Nuts!" price elements and attributes (this example hard-codes the text "$," since all of the "Nuts. Nuts? Nuts!" prices are in US dollars):

```
<xsl:template match="nnn:price">
  Price:
    <xsl-text>$ </xsl-text>
    <xsl:apply-templates select="@amount"/>
    <xsl:apply-templates select="@tax"/>
</xsl:template>
```

This template uses the existing templates for the amount and tax attributes of the price element.

The Nut Haus Templates

To process the listings from The Nut Haus, Lydia needs a different approach throughout, because the XML structure is so different from the earlier one. The templates Lydia decides to add are shown in the highlighted section below:

```
<xsl:for-each select="nh:nuts">
        <xsl:apply-templates select="."/>
        <xsl:apply-templates select="nh:name"/>
        <xsl:apply-templates select="nh:color"/>
        <xsl:apply-templates select="nh:description"/>
        <xsl:apply-templates select="nh:price"/>
        <xsl:apply-templates select="nh:amount"/>
        <xsl:if test="not(position()=last())"><HR/> </xsl:if>
</xsl:for-each>
```

These templates are added to the style sheet:

```
<xsl:template match="nh:name">
    <P><B><xsl:value-of select="."/></B></P>
</xsl:template>

<xsl:template match="nh:color">
    <P><I><xsl:value-of select="."/></I></P>
</xsl:template>

<xsl:template match="nh:description">
    <P><xsl:value-of select="."/></P>
</xsl:template>

<xsl:template match="nh:price">
    <P>Price: <xsl:value-of select="."/></P>
</xsl:template>
```

```
<xsl:template match="nh:amount">
    <P>Shipping: <xsl:value-of select="text()"/></P>
</xsl:template>
```

The New HTML Web Pages

Lydia now has a single style sheet (`third.xsl`) which she can run against any of the product files to produce an up-to-date page. First using her own product file:

c:/> xt my_third.xml third.xsl locking.html

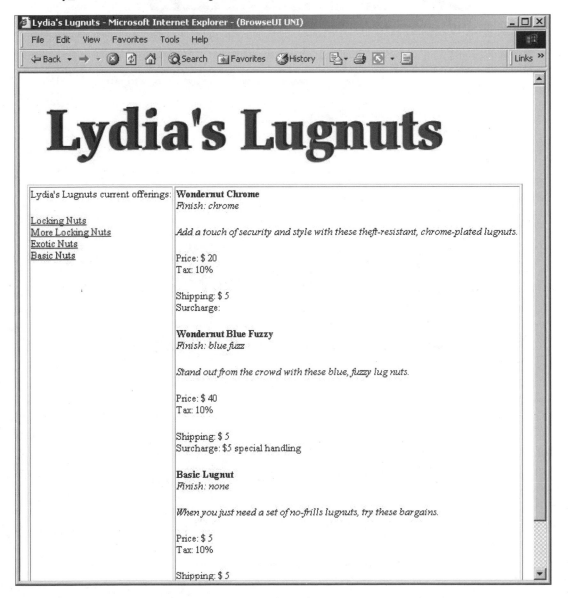

Then using the product listing from "Nuts. Nuts? Nuts!":

c:/> xt nnn.xml third.xsl locking.html

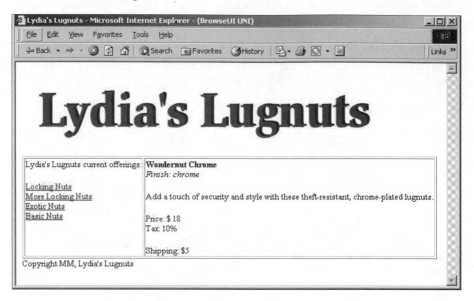

And finally using the "Nut Haus" product file:

c:/> xt nh.xml third.xsl locking.html

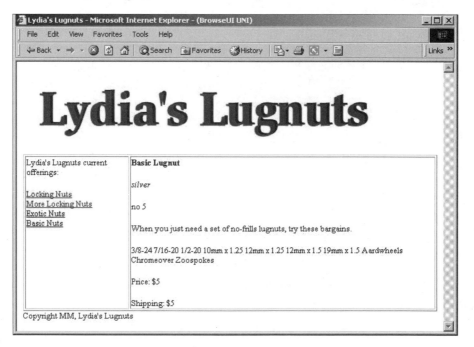

The Future of Lydia's Lugnuts

Lydia now has a functional web application which uses XML to store product information. The application comprises an XSLT style sheet to convert XML product information files into HTML pages suitable for display on a web browser. Whenever product details change, all she needs to do is regenerate the HTML page by running the new product information files against this style sheet. At regular intervals (every day or every few days, for example), she will get current XML catalogs from her suppliers and convert them to her own format.

The time she saves updating her site, and the benefits of keeping up to date with price changes, will allow Lydia to spend more time growing the business. As she does, and Lydia's Lugnuts expands, she will be able to incorporate new suppliers into her system by simply modifying her style sheet to accommodate each one. As technology progresses, she will be able to make her product information available to other customers too, by simply writing new style sheets to transform her information into pages suitable for display on, for example, a TV screen or mobile phone.

This case study has focused on creating HTML documents from XML and XSLT sources, which is useful for today's mixed-browser environment. With the advent of client-aware XML servers, server-side Java (servlets) for XML, and near-universal scripting languages like ECMAScript, Lydia's Lugnuts could be redone in an active XML model as opposed to the manual-transformation model shown here. In other words an application could automatically produce the new output pages instead of Lydia herself having to manually run files through XT.

Case Study 2:
Discussion Group System

Throughout this book, one of the common threads that has appeared is that XML is likely to replace not just HTML, but to a certain extent the way that we write server-based applications in general. In conjunction with XSLT, XML can produce a surprisingly sophisticated server environment in a relatively compact space, relying only minimally on external services such as Active Server Pages (ASP) or Java Server Pages (JSP).

The exercise presented in this case study aims to illustrate this point by showing how XML can be used to create a **discussion group** or **bulletin board system**. While it makes use of certain features that are specific to the Microsoft MSXML 3.0 parser (Technology Preview) and Microsoft's Internet Information Server (IIS) 5.0 web server package, the general principles can easily be adapted for use with a Java-based parser, as long as it supports XSLT.

> *The case study shown here is part of an open source XSLT-based framework system called XMLPipes by Kurt Cagle, which aims to create a package of XSLT modules and related components that can be used to generate XML-based web sites. The full package can be seen at the VBXML web site at* http://www.vbxml.com.

If you are not familiar with ASP and want to really understand the workings of this case study, you might find it useful to first read the ASP Quick Start tutorial in Appendix C. You may also wish to refer back to the relevant sections of Chapters 5 and 6 to refresh your memory of XSLT syntax and the objects and methods of the DOM.

Designing the Architecture

The discussion group is perhaps one of the oldest structures of community on the Internet. Indeed, it could be argued that one of the principal precursors of the Internet as we know it today, the **Bulletin Board System** (or **BBS**), paved the way for the rapid acceptance of online communities, and can be traced as a direct ancestor of everything from America Online to E-Bay's flea-market-like auctions.

The concept is simple – you place a message up on a physical message board with a thumbtack, and someone in turn can place a message up in response to it. Such boards are essentially flat – the response can be considered to exist at the same level as the initial message. There is a little ambiguity around whether or not a response following that one is in response to the *initial message* or the *first response*. Thus, one of the first innovations in dealing with online message boards is the notion of **threading**. A message thread turns the *linear* structure of a physical bulletin board into a *hierarchical* structure – a message may spawn multiple responses, each of which may have their own responses, and so on. This tree can branch repeatedly as a consequence.

Not surprisingly, such a system works surprisingly well in the context of XML. The language is, of course, intrinsically hierarchical, and the descriptions of the multithreaded messages should evoke similarities with XML elements. Moreover, if for any given message you define an *absolute* address (an id or unique name) as well as a *relative* one (where a message is compared to its parent and sibling messages), then you have a structure which allows you to retrieve messages either alone or as part of a series, that provides an intrinsic navigation mechanism, and that can be generated pretty much automatically.

Furthermore, by providing a linking mechanism in the discussion board system, the content of these pages could actually be retrieved from external sources – an existing web page, a filtered XML stream, a database – *independent* of the navigational systems. This model is especially important in the case of XML, since by abstracting the *content* of the XML as an external stream, you can effectively decouple the navigation system completely from the content. Put another way, by using the message board system as a way to identify the location of a page within a system, regardless of the contents of that page, you can cut down on the work necessary to create and maintain links in a web site, since a link to a page in the message board system would actually point to an indexed table of links to actual content. We'll look at this in a while when we design the message boards for our case study application.

> *It turns out that such a linked structure can also be used in other areas. For example, one of the most common structures on web pages is a selection of correlated links – sites that you recommend, trading partners, directory services and so forth. The* structure *for a link-based discussion group system and for a hierarchical linked list page is identical – the only substantial differences being that a discussion group* resolves *links (in other words it loads in the contents that those links point to from the web) while a linked list doesn't (necessarily), and the* presentation *of the two differs. Thus, a messaging system essentially gives you a link-list for free.*

An XHTML Framework System

XSLT is a very new technology, and people are still experimenting with how best to use it. One common technique that people have used to convert XML into HTML, for example, is to embed the HTML document (including style sheet information) directly into the XSLT document. (We saw an example of this approach in Case Study 1.) There are, however, several problems with this approach:

❑ **Confused Code**. When you place HTML and XSLT in the same document, editing such code becomes trial and error that can be maddeningly difficult. For example, simple structures get lost in conditional statements, namespace effects can produce problems and it forces the XML developer to take on much of the task of the graphic designer, usually with unfortunate results.

❑ **Limited Reuse**. A problem that is common in ASP, especially among users new to the technology, is the tendency to want to embed HTML in your ASP code and make the whole thing one long function, rather than modularizing the code and keeping the interaction between ASP and HTML down to a minimum. XSLT can easily result in the same tendency, where the functional elements become intertwined with the output code.

❑ **Lack of Modularity**. XSLT has the ability to include other XSLT scripts, a very powerful feature that XML developers are only just beginning to play with. The less interconnected the HTML source code is with the XSLT, the more generic the XSLT and the easier it is to create code frameworks – separate, easily referenced code modules that can be dropped into your application without a lot of knowledge about how these modules work internally.

❑ **Browser Differences**. One of the promises of XML is that it can free designers from the dependency of browser code, but until there is some mechanism for separating the HTML, WAP or other browser code from the XSLT code, this independence is largely a myth.

One solution to this, and the one taken in this case study, is to create what amounts to an **XHTML server** written in XSLT and ASP on the server, with the resulting output being potentially sent to any generic browser. (Remember, XHTML is a specification for XML compliant HTML.) This server effectively takes as its source an XHTML or WAP template, with specialized XML tags that give access to the ASP `Request`, `Response`, and `Server` objects as well as to custom tags that are defined by the frameworks package (and that can be extended by an XML developer). The server then reads the framework tags and matches them to XSLT templates (passing parameters through attributes on the tag), which in turn replace the contents of these tags with output generated by subordinate XSLT scripts.

A Note About the XMLPipes Framework

Simplicity in programming typically comes at some cost – to create something simple for the end user, you frequently have to compensate by making the underlying code complex. A framework, by definition, is a mechanism to simplify the creation of fairly complex systems by the end user, by encapsulating much of the code into easier to use classes, objects or other programming constructs. Unfortunately, that means that the code to pull off the development of such a framework can get very involved and complicated.

The XMLPipes framework is no exception to this rule. While the *principle* behind the frameworks is simple – the use of XSLT to act as a server, transforming XHTML into final HTML in the process – in practice there is a great deal of code that is simply way beyond the scope of a Beginning XML book. As a consequence, what I want to do in the code here is to illustrate how components could be developed around XSLT rather than using more traditional programming tools. The code that is shown in this chapter looks at the intermediate results, in other words at the XSLT that performs the operations of adding or removing messages from the appropriate queues, primarily to demonstrate how to create complex XSLT scripts for handling different situations.

We will not be looking in detail at the code behind the framework itself, in other words the user interfaces and the server routines, but most of the code in this case study is contained as part of the XML Pipes Framework, an open source XML project that I've written for use on the VBXML web site. The source code for the frameworks is available from the VBXML web site at http://www.vbxml.com and can be freely adapted for use in your own web sites.

The Framework handles a great deal of other activities besides the creation of message boards, such as maintaining page counts, creating and processing forms, providing output in a number of different formats for data structures, and simplifying the production of web pages in general through the use of XSLT. In essence, it is an attempt to build an XHTML engine.

I do want to note that as I write this the MSXML 3.0 parser, on which this is based, is still in development, and there are elements contained in this case study that will become obsolete by the time this book goes to print. As such, you should use the examples contained herein as general guidelines, but use the code at the VBXML frameworks site for your own applications.

What Does the XHTML Framework Do?

An example is definitely in order here (this is code that *could* be called within the XMLPipes framework, though it doesn't have any direct bearing on the code described later in the chapter). Suppose that you had an article written in XML, where each section was contained in a `<section>` element, and each section had a unique `<title>` node. The document you want to have sent to the browser needs to perform two tasks:

❑ Generate a table of contents that will allow users to link to the appropriate section

❑ Format each section

Both of these actions have associated style sheets: `makeTOC.xsl` and `formatSections.xsl` respectively. The framework XHTML for displaying this might look something like `articlePage.xml`:

```
<!-- articlePage.xml -->
<html    xmlns:xp="http://www.vbxml.com/xmlpipes"
         xmlns:xpo="http://www.vbxml.com/xmlpipes/objects"
         xmlns:rq="http://www.vbxml.com/request"
         xmlns="http://www.w3.org/1999/xhtml"
>
<xp:source href="rq:source"/>
<xp:store name="title" set="xp:source/document/head/title"/>
    <head>
        <title><xp:get name="xp:title"/></title>
        <xp:css_style href="rq:style"/>
    </head>
    <body>
    <h1><xp:get name="xp:title"/></h1>
    <xp:apply filter="makeTOC" section_path="section" title_path="section/title"/>
    <xp:apply filter="formatSections"/>
    <div class="datestamp">There have been <xpo:page method="getAccessCount"
    url="rq:source" increment="yes"/> accesses of this page.</div>
    </body>
</html>
```

This may look a little intimidating at first glance, but is actually pretty easy to understand (for some reason the inclusion of namespaces can render even the simplest code terrifying). Three namespaces are defined here, in addition to the default HTML namespace:

```
<html    xmlns:xp="http://www.vbxml.com/xmlpipes"
         xmlns:xpo="http://www.vbxml.com/xmlpipes/objects"
         xmlns:rq="http://www.vbxml.com/request"
         xmlns="http://www.w3.org/1999/xhtml"
>
```

The rq namespace contains IIS Request parameters from query strings or forms (among other places), converted into XML parameters, so that the expression $rq:source will retrieve the name of the source file from the HTML URL "xmlserver.asp?source=myarticle.xml". (See "Defining the Server" in the next section for more information on xmlserver.asp – for now you just need to know that it is the page calling articlePage.xml, in other words the request page.

Meanwhile, the xp namespace (for **XML P**ipes, the commercial name of the architecture) contains the functional calls that are associated with the architecture itself. For example, the xp:source element points to the location of the data that will populate this template, and it can be used in other expressions (such as the set attribute of the <xp:store name="title"> element) by referencing the document with a dollar sign ($xp:source thus contains the actual data rather than just a reference). Similarly, <xp:get> retrieves the contents of the named element in the same way that an <xsl:copy-of> may do so in XSLT.

This actually gives a clue to how the server works (and how other XHTML servers can be modelled on it). The server actually *pre-processes* this document, replacing Request (rq:) items with their corresponding values in XSLT variables, and resolving xp namespace items as XSLT templates, includes, variables, and parameters. In other words, the XHTML template is transformed by XSLT into an XSLT document, which is in turn run against the source document.

The xp:apply element shows how this strategy can be carried one step further:

```
<xp:apply filter="makeTOC" section_path="section" title_path="section/title"/>
<xp:apply filter="formatSections"/>
```

It effectively applies the style sheet named in the filter attribute to the primary data source (or to a secondary named source if the right attributes are specified) and inserts that back into the output stream. This makes it possible to modularize your XSL transformations, so that, for example, your "table of contents code" doesn't always have to go into your "document display code". The resulting code is generated through an internal script (as mentioned previously, this is not a pure XSLT solution) and this minimizes the possible conflict of namespaces.

Finally, the last line:

```
<div class="datestamp">There have been <xpo:page method="getAccessCount"
url="rq:source" increment="yes"/> accesses of this page.</div>
```

demonstrates that the framework can also invoke specially designed objects within the framework. In this case the framework defines the xpo:page object which contains a number of distinct methods, which we'll look at later. One of these, getAccessCount(), takes a URL as an argument and then returns the number of times that the particular URL was referenced.

The particular function (not shown here) reads a local file called page.xml (or creates it if it doesn't exist), then creates a page node associated with the given URL. Every time that the getAccessCount() method is called, a counter is retrieved from the node. If increment="yes" then the counter is incremented and the document resaved.

The advantage to this approach is that the pre-processor can scan the page for any elements in the xpo namespace, then include the scripts for only those objects that are specifically called. This can keep processing time down considerably.

Although the architecture will hide most of the URL calls, these pages are essentially generated and retrieved by a simple URL call. For example, if your source document is called "XMLIdeas.xml" then the page itself would be called as:

```
http://www.myserver.com/xmlserver.asp?source=xmlideas.xml&
       format=articlepage.xml
```

where the format is the original template associated with the xp namespace, and source is the name of the XML file or stream resource.

The final version of the framework will almost certainly include a SOAP-based interface, so that the server could also send out information based upon POSTed SOAP XML requests. Similarly, the server makes no distinction between GET and POST in terms of its accepted formats, so it can handle the retrieval and processing of form data from HTML-generated pages. This is an important aspect of the discussion group system, where you need to be able to send edited content up to the server itself.

Defining the Server

I've made repeated reference throughout this section to the xmlserver.asp file. This particular file lies at the heart of the framework system. The ASP script has two distinct phases – converting the XP document into an XSLT document, then applying the XSLT document to an indicated input XML stream. These achieve the following:

❑ **Namespace pre-parse**. The initial (or format) template, which contains the framework tags, is run through a specialized XSLT script to convert the namespace into an XSLT namespace instead. The purpose of this first pass is to take what is probably an attribute-driven template and convert it into the XSLT functionality.

❑ **XSLT parse**. The resulting XML is itself an XSLT document, which is in turn applied to the indicated source stream to produce the output that will be sent back to the client. It should be noted that parameter values are essentially passed into this second parse directly from the server objects, not through the first pass parse, primarily for helping with scaling issues.

This process is illustrated below:

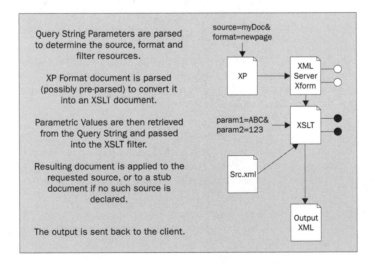

In a number of cases, once the framework format document is parsed, it essentially remains unchanged except for the assignment of parameters. Because of this, the ASP script caches any pre-parsed XP documents unless the template expressly turns this option off. In this particular case, the ASP script specifically takes advantage of the processor caching mechanism that comes with the Microsoft XML Technology Preview parser, which can maintain an XSLT style sheet as a compiled processor. In this way, the XSLT gains the speed and efficiency of working as a COM object while still working within the XSL environment.

This makes a big difference when it comes to scalability. One of the largest problems with applying a text-based XSLT script to an XML data stream is that the routine that applies it (either something like the MXSML `transformNode` method or through James Clarke's XT Java classes) must internally parse the XSLT stream into a set of instructions every time the function is called. When you have a high capacity site, the demands of constantly parsing the same stream every time can be excessive, and can bog down the performance of the code.

By compiling and storing the results from the template objects, you need only parse the templates once, then store the resulting XSLT object as a binary file. Not only does this cut down on the number of parses that need to be made (once per session per style sheet versus once per transaction) but it also means that subsequent transformations are made at the speed of a compiled object rather than an interpreted one.

The actual details of how the server works are beyond the scope of this book, but you can begin to see why XML and XSLT are so important to this project.

Defining Membership Directories

One of the aspects of an XML-based message board system is the requirement of a **membership directory**. Being able to maintain a membership list is useful for a number of reasons:

❑ **Personalization.** You can customize your content based upon characteristic interests of the person viewing the content. For example, a **citizen** (the term for a member of your membership group) can specify in her profile that she's interested in articles about personal finance and investment. Any article (or even discussion group message) that has a set of associated keywords matching these requirements would then be displayed to this citizen.

❑ **Security Access.** You can designate that a specific individual has advanced access to certain pages or boards (such as "write" privileges in a specialized board, or "create" and "delete" privileges for a board or messages on the board).

❑ **Private Content.** A membership directory makes it possible for the creation of private "mail" systems, as well as personalized web pages.

❑ **Integration with Other Services.** By creating such a membership system, you can use it outside the current web system, perhaps providing such services as virtual desktops, application environments, and so forth.

❑ **Advertising.** You gotta pay the bills. Membership lists make it possible to collate mailing lists, although as concerns about privacy continue to rise there will be mounting pressure to stop that practice. However, it also turns out that membership lists make possible *anonymous directed advertising* – the advertiser creates an advertisement to match specific profiles, and any time a page is displayed, if the member's profile correlates well with the advertisement profile then the advertisement if displayed. Advertisers get charged on the basis of the frequency of their advertisements – high match advertisements cost more, but are seen by more eyeballs.

While there are any number of different ways that you can implement a membership directory, for relatively small directories (up to a few thousand members) you can actually maintain the membership records as a relatively flat XML structure, as shown in the following listing:

Once you get beyond this point, (in other words as membership numbers increase) it may be worth moving to a database to retrieve this information, or use membership and personalization servers such as Microsoft's Site Server package.

```xml
<document idcount="">
    <record id="anonymous">
        <member>
            <user>anonymous</user>
            <password></password>
        </member>
        <access>
            <general>
                <read>1</read>
                <write>0</write>
                <admin>0</admin>
            </general>
        </access>
        <profile/>
    </record>
    <record id="cagle">
        <member>
            <first_name>Kurt</first_name>
            <last_name>Cagle</last_name>
            <email>cagle@olywa.net</email>
            <user>cagle</user>
            <password>ae19cdj6</password>
        </member>
        <access>
            <general>
                <read>yes</read>
                <write>yes</write>
                <admin>yes</admin>
            </general>
            <board idref="cagle">
                <read>yes</read>
                <write>yes</write>
                <admin>yes</admin>
            </board>
        </access>
        <profile>
            <key last_accessed="2000-05-24">xml</key>
            <key last_accessed="2000-05-24">art</key>
            <key last_accessed="2000-05-24">mermaids</key>
            <key last_accessed="2000-05-19">visual basic</key>
            <key last_accessed="2000-05-18">schema</key>
            <key last_accessed="2000-05-16">family</key>
            <key last_accessed="2000-04-30">xslt</key>
            <key last_accessed="2000-04-11">science fiction</key>
            <key last_accessed="2000-03-21">science</key>
```

```
            </profile>
        </record>
        <record id="Ashera">
            <first_name>Aleria</first_name>
            <last_name>Delamare</last_name>
            <email>aleria@wrox.com</email>
            <user>Ashera</user>
            <password>j33nfjas</password>
            <access>
                <general>
                    <read>yes</read>
                    <write>yes</write>
                    <admin>no</admin>
                </general>
                <board idref="Ashera">
                    <read>yes</read>
                    <write>yes</write>
                    <admin>yes</admin>
                </board>
                <board idref="news">
                    <read>yes</read>
                    <write>yes</write>
                    <admin>no</admin>
                </board>
            </access>
            <profile>
                <key last_accessed="2000-05-24">finance</key>
                <key last_accessed="2000-05-24">xml</key>
                <key last_accessed="2000-05-24">xslt</key>
                <key last_accessed="2000-05-19">schemas</key>
                <key last_accessed="2000-05-18">soap</key>
                <key last_accessed="2000-05-16">databases</key>
                <key last_accessed="2000-04-30">personal accounting</key>
            </profile>
        </record>
        <!-- more records -->
    </document>
```

Each member `record` is made up of three distinct sections – `member`, `access`, and `profile`. The `member` section contains personal information about the member, and can be as limited or extensive as is needed for your site. I've deliberately simplified the fields here to the requisite minimum for space considerations, but this field could possibly also include such information as mailing addresses, web site locations, links to personal images and so forth.

The `access` section handles access permissions for any given user, and is broken up into the `general` level of access that the member has, and then access levels for specific sites (`boards`) if they differ from the `general` privileges for that individual. Each member has three specific access privileges – `read`, `write`, and `admin`, where the `admin` privilege determines whether the member has the right to edit or delete messages by other users (you always have the right to delete messages that you personally have written).

Message boards similarly have three levels of access – *public*, *privileged*, and *private*, where *public* boards can be seen by anyone with a read access, *private* boards can only be seen and written to by the specific members who have the specific site's access privilege (this is useful for such services as e-mail or system administrator boards), while *privileged* boards can be read by anyone but can only be written to by people who have the board listed as part of their access privileges. The primary use for *privileged* boards is for the posting of news articles and the like – for example, the authors (or the editor of the site) would be given access to write material which could then be called up by reference in a "featured articles and stories" section. Note that the access level is something that is associated with the XML for the boards themselves, rather than for the users of those boards (which is why no access level information is given for the users).

The final section, `profile`, contains a number of `keys` that indicate topics of interest to the member, and could be generated in a number of different ways – as part of a form, in response to searches performed within the framework, a specialized resource uploaded to the system. The `keys` form a basic way of matching interests to topics in the framework itself – as a `key` enters into a `profile`, it is assigned the date it was created, with more weight being given to more recent entries. After a certain period of time (to be determined by the administrator but typically one month) the oldest `keys` are deleted. This keeps the `profile` relatively fresh with respect to current interests.

Every user has a unique `record id`, which also happens to correspond to the `user` property. This somewhat redundant information ensures that items can be retrieved from an id without the need to know the specific object type (objects other than `users`, for example, could also use both the `id` attribute and `record` element), while still providing a place to maintain validation of information and a consistent interface (people are more likely to request a `user` object than an `id`, for example).

This is a simple XML-based approach to data storage, but you should begin to see how other XML technologies would be used to, for example, create new member profiles, update the information or retrieve it for use elsewhere in the framework – using the DOM, XPath and XSLT.

Designing the Message Boards

Let's get back to the message boards themselves. There are, in fact, two ways of designing a hierarchical message board. The more obvious of the two involves mimicking the *hierarchical* structure of the board directly in an XML structure, such that a response to a given message is contained as a message within the original message block. If we had a message with three responses, one of which has a response of its own, the XML would look like this:

```
<messages>
    <message id="0">
        <title><![CDATA[Welcome to VB-XML Programming]]></title>
        <date>2/6/00 5:50:13 PM</date>
        <idate/>
        <from>Kurt Cagle</from>
        <email>cagle@olywa.net</email>
        <body><![CDATA[XML is becoming a pervasive part of web
programming. This discussion board, itself written using XML and ASP, is intended
for the working professional who has questions about XML, XSL, Schemas,
programming, and more. If you want to know more about a topic (or conversely have
an answer to a topic), feel free to ask it here.
```

```
        Also, if you have any questions about the construction or maintenance of this
        particular board, please feel free to contact me, Kurt Cagle, at cagle@olywa.net
        (or just click on the CAGLE tab in the menu bar). -- Kurt Cagle]]></body>
                    <message id="1">
                        <title><![CDATA[Re:Welcome to VB-XML Programming]]></title>
                        <date>2/6/00 11:16:26 PM</date>
                        <idate/>
                        <from>Kurt Cagle</from>
                        <email>cagle@olywa.net</email>
                        <body><![CDATA[Another message, content removed for
demonstration purposes.]]></body>
                    <message id="8">
                        <title><![CDATA[Live links and file update]]></title>
                        <date>2/7/00 4:01:49 AM</date>
                        <idate/>
                        <from>Kurt Cagle</from>
                        <email>cagle@olywa.net</email>
                        <body><![CDATA[Another message, content removed for
demonstration purposes.]]></body>
                    </message>
                </message>
            <message id="2">
                    <title><![CDATA[ASP Code for msgBoard.asp]]></title>
                    <date>2/6/00 11:17:22 PM</date>
                    <idate/>
                    <from>Kurt Cagle</from>
                    <email>cagle@olywa.net</email>
                    <body><![CDATA[Another message, content removed for
demonstration purposes.]]></body>
                </message>
            <message id="3">
                    <title><![CDATA[submitMessage.asp]]></title>
                    <date>2/6/00 11:18:34 PM</date>
                    <idate/>
                    <from>Kurt Cagle</from>
                    <email>cagle@olywa.net</email>
                    <body><![CDATA[Another message, content removed for
demonstration purposes.]]></body>
                </message>
            </message>
        </messages>
```

This would result in a message board design something like this:

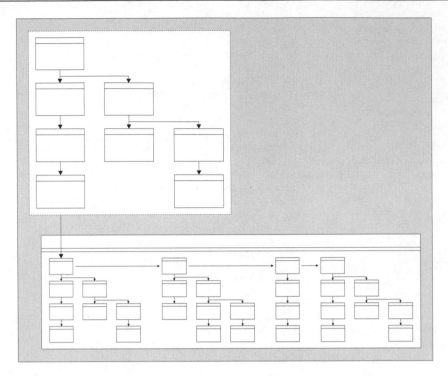

This was in fact the approach that I started with when designing the precursor to this site, but I very quickly discovered a number of problems with this approach, specifically:

❑ **Unwieldy Size**. Each message can effectively hold the contents of an entire web page (HTML is allowed in the messaging system). After a relatively small number of messages (even a few hundred) the size of such files become astonishingly large, reducing performance considerably.

❑ **Hard to Manipulate**. While it's easy to get hierarchical (or tree-view, as they're sometimes known) structures, it's much harder to use XSLT to add a new message. Removing a message can be hideously complex, and the DOM structure needed to retrieve this can become quite deep.

❑ **Difficult to Port**. As message board systems get larger, the temptation to use a more traditional database as a data provider grows as well. Unfortunately, creating a staggered hierarchy from a relational database can be difficult, and often requires knowing the depth of the hierarchy (something that can prove troublesome for such databases).

The alternative to building such a staggered system is to mimic the way that a database might treat the problem – make the list of records *linear*, but reference the parent of a given message by passing the parent's id value to find all children for those parents (as shown in the following listing and figure):

```
<messages>
    <message id="1">
        <title><![CDATA[Welcome to VB-XML Programming]]></title>
        <date>2000-06-05T5:50:13 PM</date>
```

```
        <idate/>
        <from>cagle</from>
        <content href="vbboards/vbxmlboard/vbxml_1.xml"/>
    </message>
    <message id="2">
        <title><![CDATA[Live links and file update]]></title>
        <date>2000-06-05T11:16:26 PM</date>
        <from>cagle</from>
        <content href="vbboards/vbxmlboard/vbxml_2.xml"/>
        <parent idref="1"/>
     </message>
     <message id="3">
         <title><![CDATA[Re:Live links and file update]]></title>
         <date>2000-06-05T4:01:49 AM</date>
         <from>Ashira</from>
        <content href="vbboards/vbxmlboard/vbxml_3.xml"/>
         <parent idref="2"/>
    </message>
    <message id="4">
         <title><![CDATA[Live links and file update]]></title>
         <date>2000-06-05T4:01:49 AM</date>
         <from>Ashira</from>
        <content href="vbboards/vbxmlboard/vbxml_4.xml"/>
         <parent idref="3"/>
    </message>
    <!-- more messages -->
</messages>
```

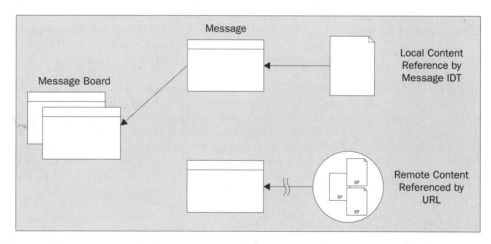

In this case, the list has been turned into a flat list rather than a hierarchy. Moreover, the content has been removed from the message and inserted into a secondary file in the file system. For example:

```
<content href="vbboards/vbxmlboard/vbxml_1.xml"/>
```

By doing this, you can essentially include HTML that is not fully-compliant-XML into your web page system (even if that HTML comes from a separate file or even a different server).

That is not to say that the hierarchy isn't still there – the `parent` attribute of each message (when it exists) acts as a pointer to the message for which the current message is a response. For any given message, the children of that message are the ones that have a `parent idref` equal to the current `id`.

Retrieving the Message Child Tree

For example, you can create a tree of all of the descendents of a given node with a fairly simple XSLT style sheet (the following creates the output in HTML):

```
<xsl:template name="get_child_tree">
    <xsl:param name="msg">
    <xsl:variable name="current_id" select="$msg/@id"/>
    <LI><SPAN id="{$current_id}"><xsl:value-of select="$msg/title"></SPAN>
    <UL>
        <xsl:for-each select="//message[@parent=$current_id]">
            <xsl:sort select="date" direction="descending"/>
            <xsl:call-template name="get_child_tree">
                <xsl:with-param name="msg" select="."/>
            </xsl:call-template>
        </xsl:for-each>
    </UL>
    </LI>
</xsl:template>
```

In this function, the variable `$current_id` is assigned the id of the current message. This is then passed as an `id` to the SPAN (a block of inline text) of a list element (`<LI>`) along with the `title` of the message as the caption of the list item. After this, a new unordered list container (`<UL>`) is created, and all messages for which the parent id is the current id are then iterated through (this makes up all of the child responses of the list). This list is sorted in `descending` order of `date`, so that the most recent response is given first – you could effectively change the nature of this list by switching the direction from `descending` (most recent dates first) to `ascending` (oldest messages first).

Each of the messages thus selected is then passed as a parameter to the `get_child_tree` named template (which by no coincidence happens to be the template that was called initially). Put another way, the `get_child_tree` function is *recursive* – the template is applied to the current message, which calls the same template on the message's children, which calls the same template on their children, and so forth. Eventually, no message thus called has children, and the template terminates. Recursion plays a big part in many of the XSLT functions used in the framework for a very simple reason – an XML tree by definition consists of a root node and one or more sub-trees, which in turn have their own sub-trees. By applying the same template to each sub-tree in turn, you are able to write very concise, compact code.

Retrieving the Message Ancestor Tree

While producing child trees is not much more difficult using this approach than it would be if the message tree was explicit, ancestor calls are a little harder to work with. For any given message node, the parent node is the `<messages>` element, not the initial message for which the current message is a response.

However, you can create a list of parent elements from the initial message to the current message in a manner similar to referencing the children. In this case, you read the current message's `parent` attribute and reference that new message, and *then* place the current tag into the output stream:

```
<xsl:template name="get_parent_list">
    <xsl:param name="msg">
    <xsl:variable name="current_id" select="$msg/@id"/>
        <xsl:for-each select="//message[@id=$msg/parent_id]">
            <xsl:call-template name="get_parent_list">
                <xsl:with-param name="msg" select="."/>
            </xsl:call-template>
        </xsl:for-each>
    <LI><SPAN id="{$current_id}"><xsl:value-of select="$msg/title"></SPAN></LI>
</xsl:template>
```

By placing the contents of the current template into the output stream *after* the recursive calls to the template, you effectively reverse the order of the output – the current message is last, the message's parent is next to last, and so forth right back to the initial message.

Retrieving the Message Sibling Tree – Next

Getting to sibling messages – other responses to the same message – relies on the date element to determine when one sibling is before another sibling. Thus, to retrieve the "next" response to a message from the current response, you need to better clarify what you mean by "next". The next message in the context of the message boards is not the response to the current message (the response is a *child* of the current message). Instead, the next message is one that was submitted more recently in response to the current message's parent message. It may have no bearing whatsoever on the current message.

A good way of thinking about this is to imagine a test in school where each student submits his or her exam in response to the questions being asked – the first test that the teacher grades is the first one she received, the next test is the second she received and so forth. How well the second student did is likely to be completely independent of how well the first student did (unless, of course, he was cheating). The teacher's grade on the first test (the response to the student's answers, if you will) will on the other hand be highly dependent upon the content of the answers – in message board parlance, it is a response.

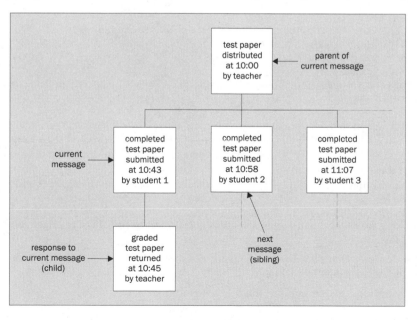

Given that, determining the next message requires a test to determine the first message that has the same parent as the current message and which has a greater `date` value:

```
<xsl:template name="getNextMessage">
    <xsl:param name="msg"/>
     <xsl:variable name="current_id" select="$msg/@id"/>
    <xsl:variable name="parent_id" select="$msg/@parent_id"/>
    <xsl:variable name="future_siblings">
        <xsl:for-each select="//message[@parent_id=$parent_id]
        [date &gt; $msg/date]">
            <xsl:sort select="date" direction="ascending"/>
            <xsl:copy-of select="."/>
        </xsl:for-each>
    </xsl:variable>
    <xsl:copy-of select="$future_siblings[1]"/>
</xsl:template>
```

Since there is no formal guarantee that the elements are ordered by date in the initial document, the variable `$future_siblings` sorts all messages that are children of the current message's parent and that have dates greater than the current date in ascending order. The requisite message is then the first message given.

Retrieving the Message Sibling Tree – Previous

The previous message test is nearly identical, the only major difference being that the dates are listed in *descending* order and the test involves ordering with the "less than" rather than "greater than" operator:

```
<xsl:template name="getPreviousMessage">
    <xsl:param name="msg"/>
     <xsl:variable name="current_id" select="$msg/@id"/>
    <xsl:variable name="parent_id" select="$msg/@parent_id"/>
    <xsl:variable name="past_siblings">
        <xsl:for-each select="//message[@parent_id=$parent_id]
        [date &lt; $msg/date]">
            <xsl:sort select="date" direction="descending"/>
            <xsl:copy-of select="."/>
        </xsl:for-each>
    </xsl:variable>
    <xsl:copy-of select="$past_siblings[1]"/>
</xsl:template>
```

The point of this is to demonstrate that programming a hierarchical tree structure by breaking it into a linear list of such structures isn't any harder (and in some cases much easier) than keeping the data in the hierarchy. It *is* less efficient – the XSLT processor has to search all nodes in the list rather than retrieving just the child messages of the current message (as would be the case with a tree structure), but there are a few optimizations that can be made to the list to ensure that information can be found as quickly as possible, such as:

❑ Making sure that the messages are ordered from last to first if the message list is built in this fashion

❑ Making sure that selection mechanisms are placed in the `select` statements rather than tested in the target templates

❑ Constraining searches to just the first items found

We've seen the templates for retrieving messages, but how do the messages get onto the message board in the first place?

Creating Messages

XSLT is curiously incomplete. If you think of XSLT as a black box for transforming XML, it would seem to have one primary source for input data (the document that is being transformed) and several secondary sources for input in the form of parameters. Yet all of this seems to be funnelled to only one output source – the default output stream that is passed back to the environment when the transformation finishes. Yet with XSLT, the output stream may in fact not be the only stream that the document needs to modify.

Suppose, for example, that you had an ASP program that received the data coming in from an HTML Request object, converted into XML (perhaps as parameters). Typically, the purpose for sending form data is not to display a new result but rather to update some internal data source – *then* display the result. If you add a new message, for example, you will want the message list to update itself internally to reflect the new message, which means sending a stream of data to some file on the server (or some database).

Using Namespaces

One of the more thoughtfully designed parts of the W3C XSLT specification was the concept of associating objects with namespaces. An object, in this sense, is a unit of encapsulated code with exposed properties, methods and events that maintains its own internal state. For example, you could create a date object that handles such tasks as converting the current system date to the W3C date representation, determining the amount of time between two such dates, and converting numeric months and days of the week into their correct named representation.

Different parsers handle the specific implementation of these features in a similar manner, although not always an identical one. James Clark's XT parser, used by the Apache Xerces XML classes, allows you to associate *Java classes* to namespaces, so that you can call Java routines from within XSLT. The Microsoft MSXML 3.0 parser allows users to associate *COM objects* with namespaces, either externally through the use of customized XSL processors, or internally through a scripting interface (that itself uses the namespace notation).

Concentrating on the MSXML parser for the moment, it is possible to create a set of internal functions via script that will let you both transform a stream of XML that's defined within an XSLT document, *and* save a stream to an external file on the server. The combination of these with the XPath document() function means that you can effectively load a secondary XML file (such as the members directory file), apply any transforms to retrieve the information that you need (the access level of the current user, for example), and then use this information to help generate a new record. This record in turn can be added to a list of messages and saved out to the server. This capability lies at the heart of the message board system, and indeed of the XMLPipes framework as a whole.

In order to create an internal component that loads or saves XML resources (using the MSXML 3.0 parser only), you must first set up the msxsl namespace, that Microsoft uses for access to the scripting engine, within the style sheet itself. This particular namespace *must* point to the urn "urn:schemas-microsoft-com:xslt" or scripting won't work. Additionally, you need to declare the namespace of the object that you're creating (here "http://www.vbxml.com/state" for the state namespace). Note that, as we discussed in Chapter 8, there is no requirement that this URN actually exists, only that it is *unique* within the collection of namespaces being declared.

```
<xsl:stylesheet
    xmlns:xsl="http://www.w3.org/1999/XSL/Transform"
    xmlns:msxsl="urn:schemas-microsoft-com:xslt"
    xmlns:state="http://www.vbxml.com/state"
    xmlns:str="http://www.vbxml.com/string"
    version="1.0">
```

Once declared, you create an internal object by adding an `msxsl:script` element. This script block *must* include the attribute `implements-prefix`, which takes the value of the namespace you're planning to define. This script block in turn defines five functions:

- ❏ `state:document()`
- ❏ `state:persistDocument()`
- ❏ `state:transformDocument()`
- ❏ `state:getCurrentDate()`
- ❏ `state:encapsulateXML()`

The namespace prefix is important here – you are not extending the scope of the XSLT namespace – instead you are creating a new namespace and defining the functionality of the implementation. For example, you are creating the `state` namespace and defining for that namespace the five functions mentioned above:

```
<msxsl:script language="VBScript" implements-prefix="state">'<![CDATA[
function document(url)
    set xmlDoc=createObject("MSXML2.DOMDocument")
    xmlDoc.async=false
    xmlDoc.load url
    set document=xmlDoc
end function

function persistDocument(url,newDoc)
    set doc=createObject("MSXML2.DOMDocument")
    doc.async=false
    set node=newDoc(0).cloneNode(true)
    doc.appendChild node
    doc.save url
    set persistDocument=doc
end function

function transformDocument(source,filter,paramsObject)
    set sourceDoc=createObject("MSXML2.FreeThreadedDOMDocument")
    set filterDoc=createObject("MSXML2.FreeThreadedDOMDocument")
    set resultDoc=createObject("MSXML2.FreeThreadedDOMDocument")
    if typename(source)="String" then
        sourceDoc.async=false
        sourceDoc.load source
    else
        set sourceDoc.documentElement=source.documentElement.cloneNode(true)
    end if
    if typename(filter)="String" then
```

```
        filterDoc.async=false
        filterDoc.load filter
    else
        set filterDoc.documentElement=filter.documentElement.cloneNode(true)
    end if

    if not typename(paramsObject)="String" then
        for each paramNode in paramsObject
            set nameNode=paramNode.selectSingleNode(".//@name")
            paramName=nameNode.text
            set valueNode=paramNode.selectSingleNode(".//@select")
            paramValue=valueNode.text
            set curParamNode=filterDoc.selectSingleNode("//xsl:param[@name='" &_
                    +paramName+"']")
            if not (curParamNode is nothing) then
                curParamNode.setAttribute "select",paramValue
            end if
        next
    end if
    sourceDoc.transformNodeToObject filterDoc,resultDoc
    set transformDocument=resultDoc
end function

    function getCurrentDate()
        dt=now
        getCurrentDate=cstr(datePart("yyyy",dt)) + "-" + &_
            right("00" +cstr(datePart("m",dt)),2) + "-" + &_
            right("00"+cstr(datePart("d",dt)),2)+"T"+ &_
            right("00"+cstr(datePart("h",dt)),2)+":"+ &_
            right("00"+cstr(datePart("n",dt)),2)+":"+ &_
            right("00"+cstr(datePart("s",dt)),2)
    end function

    function encapsulateXML(text,resourceURL)
        set xmlDoc=createObject("MSXML2.DOMDocument")
        xmlDoc.async=false
        xmlDoc.loadxml text
        errorReason=xmlDoc.parseError.reason
        if errorReason = "" then
            xmlDoc.save resourceURL
        else
            divText="<div>"+text+"</div>"
            xmlDoc.loadxml divText
            errorReason=xmlDoc.parseError.reason
            if errorReason="" then
                xmlDoc.save resourceURL
            else
                div2Text="<div><![CDATA["+text+"]]&gt;</div>"
                xmlDoc.saveXML div2Text
            end if
        end if
        set encapsulateXML=xmlDoc
    end function
```

585

```
        dim fso
        set fso=createObject("Scripting.FileSystemObject")

        function deleteFile(filepath)
            fso.deleteFile(filepath)
            deleteFile=filepath
        end function

  ']]></msxsl:script>
```

The code for defining the `state` namespace illustrates a number of useful points. For starters, it is perfectly permissible to load an object into a script block. For example, the `document()` function loads in the `MSXML2.DOMDocument` object as a local variable. This object in turn can load in other XML and XSL files, can save these same files, and can even save XML structures passed to it from the XSLT script – although with a little bit of work. If you pass a construct created solely within the XSL space to the `persistDocument()` function described above, this object is set as read-only – attempting to save it will raise an error. However, if you clone the root node and all of its children with:

```
    set node=newDoc(0).cloneNode(true)
```

you can create a new document, assign this node to the `documentElement` node of that document, then save the newly minted XML object back to the server with the `xmlDoc.save` method.

> *A brief aside here – it's worth noting in the first line of the `<msxsl:>` element the use of the VBScript comment character ('). Any text within the `msxsl` element is treated as belonging to the language specified rather than XML, which means that a `<![CDATA]]>` section will generate an error. By putting this behind a VBScript comment signal the CDATA section becomes invisible to the VBScript parser but is still visible to the XML parser (which doesn't recognize the quote character as being a comment character).*

Similarly, you can create an object to handle certain string functions (the string functions that XSLT itself provides are sufficient, but they leave a lot to be desired). A `replaceStr` function, for example, can prove especially useful for handling intermediate processing of data:

```
    <msxsl:script language="VBScript" implements-prefix="str">
      function replaceStr(baseStr,sourceStr,targetStr)
        replaceStr=replace(baseStr,sourceStr,targetStr)
      end function

      function evaluate(text)
        evaluate=eval(text)
      end function
    </msxsl:script>
```

You can then use these functions to read in a resource (such as the message list), add a message (or update an existing message), and save the resource back to server, all within a single XSLT template. This is shown below, but we'll discuss each section afterwards:

```
    <xsl:template name="add_message">
      <xsl:variable name="id" select="number(//messages/@idcounter)+1"/>
      <xsl:param name="parent"/>
```

```
<xsl:param name="title">
        <xsl:if test="@parent">
            <xsl:value-of select="concat('Re:',
                str:replaceStr(string(//message[@id=$parent]/title)),
                'Re:',''))"/>
        </xsl:if>
</xsl:param>
<xsl:param name="from" select="$user"/>
<xsl:variable name="$board" select="//messages/@board"/>
<xsl:param name="content_href"
    select=" concat('msgboards/',$board,'/',$board,'_',$id,'.xml')"/>
<xsl:param name="board_href"
    select=" concat('msgboards/',$board,'.xml')"/>
<xsl:param name="content"><stub/></xsl:param>
<xsl:param name="abstract" select="$title"/>
<xsl:param name="is_xml" select="'yes'"/>
<xsl:param name="is_external" select="'no'"/>

<!-- create new message -->
<xsl:variable name="new_message">
    <message id="{$id}">
        <xsl:if test="$parent">
            <xsl:attribute name="parent">
                <xsl:value-of select="$parent"/>
            </xsl:attribute>
        </xsl:if>
        <title><![CDATA[<xsl:value-of select="$title"/>]]></title>
        <date><xsl:value-of select= "state:getCurrentDate()"/></date>
        <from><xsl:value-of select="$from"/></from>
        <content href="{$content_href}" is_xml="{$is_xml}"/>
        <abstract><![CDATA[<xsl:value-of select="$abstract"/></abstract>
        <is_xml><xsl:value-of select="$is_xml"/></is_xml>
        <is_external><xsl:value-of select="$is_external"/></is_external>
        </message>
</xsl:variable>

<xsl:variable name="current_message_board">
    <xsl:copy-of select="state:document($board_href)"/>
</xsl:variable>

<!-- create new board with new message at the beginning of the board -->
<xsl:variable name="new_message_board">
    <messages board="{$current_message_board/@board}"
            idcounter="{number($current_message_board/@idcounter)+1}">
        <xsl:copy-of select="$new_message"/>
        <xsl:for-each select="$current_message_board //message">
            <xsl:copy-of select="."/>
        </xsl:for-each>
    </messages>
</xsl:variable>

<!-- persist the message board -->
<xsl:variable name="persist_board">
    <xsl:variable name="persist_board_internal"
```

```
            select="state:persistDocument($board_href,
            $new_message_board/messages)"/>
        <xsl:if test="$is_external='no'">
            <xsl:variable name="new_content"
            select="state:encapsulateXML($content,$content_href)"/>
        </xsl:if>
        <xsl:copy-of select="$new_message/message"/>
    </xsl:variable>
    <xsl:copy-of select="$persist_board"/>
</xsl:template>
```

Uniquely Identifying Messages

The `add_message` template actually handles a lot of different activities. The first third of the template consists of parameters to assist in creating a new message. It also uses the notion of an `idcounter` – every time a new message is added to the message queue, the `idcounter` attribute is incremented by one, but if a message is deleted, the value is *not* decremented. This effectively serves the same function as a running index in a database – it makes sure that each message is uniquely defined over time, so that `id="325"` will always point to the same message. This does mean, of course, that any given message board can never have more than about two billion records, but unless you have insanely active chat board members this is not likely to be a problem.

Dealing with a Multitude of "Re:" Characters

The `title` parameter shows some of the power of the parameter defaulting mechanism. The id of the parent must be passed when adding a new message if the message isn't at the topmost level. In a typical message board, responses to a given message are usually indicated by the characters "Re:" followed by the title of the initial message. One danger with just adding these characters is that a response to a response might end up with the title "Re:Re:My Message", the response to this might look like "Re:Re:Re:My Message" and so forth. One way around this is to remove any "Re:" characters in the title before appending a new "Re:" at the beginning. In this case, the user-defined function `str:replaceStr` that we saw previously is used to do the actual replacement. This is only used if no title is provided, and will automatically be replaced with a new title if one is given.

The actual creation of the new message is pretty straightforward:

```
<!-- create new message -->
<xsl:variable name="new_message">
    <message id="{$id}">
        <xsl:if test="$parent">
          <xsl:attribute name="parent">
            <xsl:value-of select="$parent"/>
          </xsl:attribute>
        </xsl:if>
        <title><![CDATA[<xsl:value-of select="$title"/>]]></title>
        <date><xsl:value-of select= "state:getCurrentDate()"/></date>
        <from><xsl:value-of select="$from"/></from>
        <content href="{$content_href}" is_xml="{$is_xml}"/>
        <abstract><![CDATA[<xsl:value-of select="$abstract"/></abstract>
        <is_xml><xsl:value-of select="$is_xml"/></is_xml>
        <is_external><xsl:value-of select="$is_external"/></is_external>
        </message>
</xsl:variable>
```

Dealing with Markup Characters

If a parent id is provided (which will be the case only for a response) the `parent` attribute is added to the message element being created. Because it is entirely possible for titles to contain potential markup characters (for example "I'm having problems with the `<IMG>` tag & I don't know what to do") and because this can cause endless headaches, the title (and the abstract) are contained within CDATA sections to wall them off from processing. In this environment, in particular, you need to pay special attention to such markup in any user-entered data.

Dating the Message

The `date` of the message pulls the current date and time from the user defined `state:getCurrentDate()` function relative to the server. The date is given in the W3C date notation: YYYY-MM-DDTHH:NN:SS.ddd, which has the advantage that you can order dates in this fashion alphabetically and still have them in correct time order. This `date` element is critical in this application, since dates determine the relative position of siblings.

Adding a Link from the Board to the Message

Note that the actual content of the message being added *is not* stored in the message board structure itself. Instead, a pointer is created to an external resource – either an XML file located within a folder in the message board system, or as a pointer to an external link on the web. The `is_external` attribute takes the value of 'no' if the content is stored locally, and 'yes' if it is located on the web. The display mechanisms for showing the message may then encapsulate the contents of the new message in an `IFRAME` or `ILAYER` for external resources, just to avoid namespace and schema conflicts:

```
<xsl:variable name="current_message_board">
    <xsl:copy-of select="state:document($board_href)"/>
</xsl:variable>

<!-- create new board with new message at the beginning of the board -->
<xsl:variable name="new_message_board">
    <messages board="{$current_message_board/@board}"
            idcounter="{number($current_message_board/@idcounter)+1}">
        <xsl:copy-of select="$new_message"/>
        <xsl:for-each select="$current_message_board //message">
            <xsl:copy-of select="."/>
        </xsl:for-each>
    </messages>
</xsl:variable>

<!-- persist the message board -->
<xsl:variable name="persist_board">
    <xsl:variable name="persist_board_internal"
        select="state:persistDocument($board_href,
        $new_message_board/messages)"/>
    <xsl:if test="$is_external='no'">
        <xsl:variable name="new_content"
        select="state:encapsulateXML($content,$content_href)"/>
    </xsl:if>
    <xsl:copy-of select="$new_message/message"/>
</xsl:variable>
```

XSLT is a *declarative* language – you effectively create a stream of information, and once data is written to the stream the only place you can add more information is at the end of the stream. A DOM approach to adding a new message would be to load the message board document into memory, append a pointer to the new message to the end (or in this case the beginning) of the list of messages, then save the document. The XSLT approach, on the other hand, is to create a new message board header using information from the old one, insert the `<message>` into the `<messages>` container, copy everything else into the new document, then save the new document. This is probably not as efficient, but it means that you can construct the new message in XSLT, which is much easier than trying to build the same message in the DOM.

The `persist_board` variable illustrates one of the differences between a declarative and procedural variable. In this case, the principal purpose of `persist_board` is to provide a container for persisting the message board information out to the server through both the `persistDocument()` function for updating the board itself and the `encapsulateXML()` function for saving the (potentially non-XML) content to an XML file. The body of the new message is then passed to the variable itself and from there to the outlying template. The primary difference between a template and variable has more to do with the *time* that an item is evaluated – in a variable the contents are evaluated when the variable is "defined" while with a template the contents evaluation is deferred.

Editing and Deleting Messages

Editing a message is nearly identical to creating a message. The primary difference comes in some of the parameterization (if you know the id of the message you can retrieve a significant amount of information that you don't explicitly need to pass). It should be noted that when you edit a message it retains the same position that it had in the original list, but in fact the old message is deleted and the new message replaces it.

```
<xsl:template name="edit_message">
    <xsl:param name="id"/>
    <xsl:variable name="msg" select="//message[@id=$id]"/>
    <xsl:variable name="parent" select="$msg/@parent"/>
    <xsl:param name="title" select="$msg/title"/>
    <xsl:variable name="from" select="$msg/user"/>
    <xsl:variable name="$board" select="//messages/@board"/>
    <xsl:param name="content_href" select="$msg/content/@href"/>
    <xsl:param name="board_href"
        select="concat('msgboards/',$board,'.xml')"/>
    <xsl:param name="abstract" select="$msg/abstract"/>
    <xsl:param name="is_xml" select="$msg/is_xml"/>
    <xsl:param name="is_external" select="$msg/is_external"/>
    <xsl:param name="content">
        <xsl:if test="$is_external='no'">
            <xsl:copy-of select="state:document($content_href)"/>
        </xsl:if>
    </xsl:param>

    <!-- Create replacement message -->
    <xsl:variable name="new_message">
        <message id="{$id}">
            <xsl:if test="$parent">
                <xsl:attribute name="parent">
                    <xsl:value-of select="$parent"/>
```

```
              </xsl:attribute>
            </xsl:if>
            <title><xsl:comment>
              <xsl:value-of select='$title'/>
            </xsl:comment></title>
            <date><xsl:value-of select= "$msg/date"/></date>
            <date_modified>
              <xsl:value-of select= "state:getCurrentDate()"/>
            </date_modified>
            <from><xsl:value-of select="$from"/></from>
            <content href="{$content_href}" is_xml="{$is_xml}"/>
            <abstract><xsl:comment>
              <xsl:value-of select="$abstract"/>
            </xsl:comment></abstract>
            <is_xml><xsl:value-of select="$is_xml"/></is_xml>
            <is_external><xsl:value-of select="$is_external"/></is_external>
            </message>
      </xsl:variable>

      <!-- Retrieve old board -->
      <xsl:variable name="current_message_board">
            <xsl:copy-of select="state:document($board_href)"/>
      </xsl:variable>

      <!-- Create new board with edited content -->
      <xsl:variable name="new_message_board">
            <messages board="{$current_message_board/@board}"
                      idcounter="{$current_message_board/@idcounter}">
                <xsl:for-each select="$current_message_board//message">
                    <xsl:choose>
                        <xsl:when "./@id=$msg/@id">
                            <xsl:copy-of select="$new_message"/>
                        </xsl:when>
                        <xsl:otherwise>
                            <xsl:copy-of select="."/>
                        </xsl:otherwise>
                    </xsl:choose>
                </xsl:for-each>
            </messages>
      </xsl:variable>

      <!-- Update the board in storage -->
      <xsl:variable name="persist_board">
          <xsl:variable name="persist_board_internal"
              select="state:persistDocument($board_href,
              $new_message_board/messages)"/>
          <xsl:if test="$is_external='no'">
              <xsl:variable name="new_content"
              select="state:encapsulateXML($content,$content_href)"/>
      </xsl:if>
          <xsl:copy-of select="$new_message/message"/>
      </xsl:variable>
      <xsl:copy-of select="$persist_board"/>
</xsl:template>
```

The parameterization mechanism once again comes to the fore here, since defaults can be chosen to handle most cases without requiring extensive parameter passing on the part of the calling template. By changing some parameters (such as those for user) into variables, it also means that a person who edits a message won't change the original owner – a feature that can prove helpful for handling administrative privileges.

Deleting a Message

Deleting a message sounds like it should be fairly simple. Unfortunately, the fact that a message can have both responses and external content links complicates the picture considerably. Any message that has responses must also be responsible for deleting all of them, as well as *their* responses, and so forth. The secret to doing this is to recursively walk through the responses tree to create a list of all messages in the tree, then iterate through the list to delete those items from the main message board. This actually requires a subordinate template, called get_message_list:

```
<xsl:template name="get_message_list">
    <xsl:param name="msg"/>
    <msg id="{$msg//@id}" is_external="{$msg/is_external}"
        href="$msg/content/@href"/>
    <xsl:for-each select="//message[@parent=$msg//@id]">
        <xsl:call-template name="get_message_list">
            <xsl:with-param name="msg" select="."/>
        <xsl:call-template>
    </xsl:for-each>
</xsl:template>
```

Then we have the template to take care of the deletion:

```
<xsl:template name="delete_message">
    <xsl:param name="id"/>
    <xsl:variable name="msg" select="//message[@id=$id]"/>

    <!-- Generate list of messages to delete -->
    <xsl:variable name="messages_to_delete">
        <xsl:call-template name="get_message_list">
            <xsl:with-param name="$msg"/>
        </xsl:call-template>
    </xsl:variable>
    <!-- Delete internal linked resources -->
    <xsl:for-each select="$messages_to_delete/msg[@is_external='no']">
        <xsl:variable name="deleted_resource"
        select="state:deleteFile(string(@href))"/>
    </xsl:for-each>

    <!-- Create new message board with only those items
        not in the deleted item list. -->
    <xsl:variable name="new_message_board">
        <messages board="//messages/@board" idcounter="//message/@idcounter">
            <xsl:for-each select="//message">
                <xsl:variable name="$message_id" select="@id"/>
                <xsl:if test="not($new_message_list/msg[@id=$message_id])">
                    <xsl:copy-of select="."/>
```

```
            </xsl:if>
          </xsl:for-each>
      </messages>
  </xsl:variable>
  <!-- Save the new board -->
  <xsl:variable name="board_href"
      select="concat('msgboards/',$board,'.xml')"/>
  <xsl:variable name="persist_board"
  select="state:persistState($board_href,$new_message_board/messages)"/>
</xsl:template>
```

Thus, a list is made of those messages that need to be deleted (walking down the tree from the initial deleted node), and the internal contents of the nodes are deleted (the routine won't delete external contents, only files on the current server). Then the original list of messages is iterated, and only those messages which aren't on the deleted list are added back into the new message list.

Deletion is thus a matter of *exclusion* – you iterate through a list and only add those messages you don't want to delete. Deleting messages is one of the few places where a hierarchical arrangement may have been advantageous, but it would have still required two templates to work properly, and given that deletions are a relatively rare operation, the benefits of being able to simply terminate a node and all of its children doesn't compare to the advantages of using a linear structure here.

Viewing Lists of Messages

Of course, the ability to add or delete messages is largely irrelevant if you can't see what messages are on the boards, the contents of those messages, or if you can't write new messages to the server in the first place. Viewing messages actually constitutes three different, though related, actions:

❑ Being able see a list of messages (either all or, more likely, a limited selection)

❑ Being able to see an individual message, with the appropriate navigation to the messages "around" it

❑ Being able to edit the messages themselves

Additionally, these should tie neatly into the framework so that the code can be re-used in a reasonable fashion.

There are a number of different possible views that you can place on a message board, for example:

❑ Showing all of the messages

❑ Showing messages staggered by original post and responses

❑ Viewing only twenty messages at a time

❑ Showing messages sorted by date or user or alphabetical order

❑ Viewing messages filtered by a particular key

Using Filters

Each of these views can be represented as separate XSL filters, such as the `show_sort_table` filter below, which creates a table of pages of links, twenty at a time, showing items sorted by date, user, or alphabetical order. It has options that will let you limit content only to original posts (not responses), and can be configured to change the headers being displayed – you could, for example, incorporate abstracts in the view:

```
<!-- show_sort_table.xsl -->
<xsl:stylesheet
    xmlns:xsl="http://www.w3.org/1999/XSL/Transform"
    version="1.0">

<xsl:param name="root" select="//messages"/>
<xsl:param name="sort_field" select="'date'"/>
<xsl:param name="direction" select="'descending'"/>
<xsl:param name="include_replies" select="'yes'"/>
<xsl:param name="page" select="1"/>
<xsl:param name="messages_shown" select="20"/>
<xsl:param name="list_page" select="'show_msg_list'"/>
<xsl:param name="message_page" select="'show_msg_list'"/>

<xsl:param name="header_data">
    <field name="title" caption="Message Title"/>
    <field name="user" caption="User Name"/>
    <field name="date" caption="Date Added"/>
</xsl:param>
```

The `header_data` parameter provides a way for web designers to specify which columns they want at the top of the table, as well as providing a more legible label for that column (you could conceivably expand this to indicate whether a given field can be sorted, for example).

Sorting the Message List

The `get_processed_list` template handles the initial sorting of the messages:

```
<xsl:template name="get_processed_list">
    <!-- sort the messages by the requisite key -->
    <xsl:variable name="sorted_messages">
        <xsl:for-each select="$root/message">
            <xsl:sort select="*[name(.)=$sort_field]" direction="$direction"/>
            <xsl:choose>
                <xsl:when test="($include_replies='no')">
                    <xsl:if test="not(/@parent)">
                        <xsl:copy-of select="."/>
                    </xsl:if>
                </xsl:when>
                <xsl:otherwise>
                    <xsl:copy-of select="."/>
                </xsl:otherwise>
            </xsl:choose>
        </xsl:for-each>
    </xsl:variable>
```

```
<!-- retrieve the messages in the range from the first message on a given page
to one less than the number of messages per page added to the first message-->
  <xsl:variable name="start_msg"
    select="(number($page)-1)*number(messages_shown)+1"/>
  <xsl:variable name="filtered_messages">
      <xsl:for-each
      select="$sorted_messages//message[position() &gt;=$start_msg]
      [position() &lt; number($start_msg)+number($messages_shown)]">
          <xsl:copy-of select="."/>
      </xsl:for-each>
  </xsl:variable>
</xsl:template>
```

The XPath expression `*[name(.)=$sort_field]` iterates through the children of each `message` object until it matches the name of the sort field, then orders it relative to the pre-existing objects. This is a considerably slower process than being able to specify the field directly, so if you always know you'll be sorting by reverse date it may be easier to use this:

```
<xsl:sort select="date" direction="descending" />
```

However, the method chosen works well when you have multiple possible search values.

Let's take a look at a view of the message list. The messages are displayed in reverse chronological order, although you can choose to select a different sorting mechanism to change the ordering:

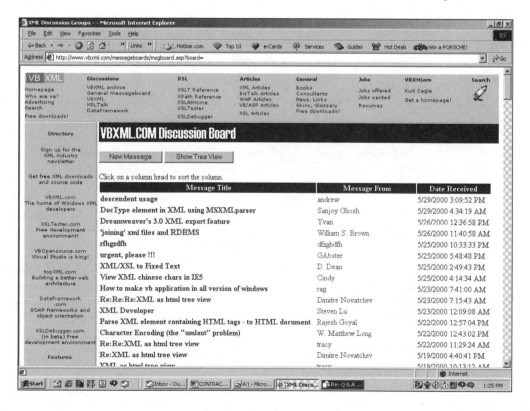

Viewing Replies

The `get_processed_list` template also includes a test to see whether replies should be incorporated into the list. It may be preferable to turn reply display off, since you can still see them in the individual message views. This is especially useful when the primary pages consist of articles and the responses make up user feedback.

Paging the Messages

The final part of the `get_processed_list` template iterates through the remaining messages and retrieves only those messages that fall within a given page (where a page typically contains 20 messages, but this can be adjusted via the `messages_shown` parameter).

Retrieving the Messages

The `get_header_link` and `get_body_link` templates move the hypertext links to retrieve the appropriate pages out of the primary HTML display:

```
<xsl:template name="get_header_link">
    <xsl:param name="field"/>
    <xsl:param name="content"/>
    <a><xsl:attribute name="href">xmlserver.asp?list_page=<xsl:value-of
    select="$list_page"/>&amp;message_page=<xsl:value-of
    select="$message_page"/>&amp;sort_field=<xsl:value-of
    select="$field/@name"/>&amp;direction=<xsl:choose><xsl:when
    test="$direction='ascending'">descending</xsl:when>
    <xsl:otherwise>ascending</xsl:otherwise></xsl:choose>&amp;page
    =<xsl:value-of select="$page"/>&amp;messages_shown=<xsl:value-of
    select="$messages_shown"/></xsl:atttribute><xsl:value-of
    select="$content"/></a>
</xsl:template>

<xsl:template name="get_body_link">
    <xsl:param name="msg_id"/>
    <xsl:param name="content"/>
    <a><xsl:attribute name="href">xmlserver.asp?filter=<xsl:value-of
    select="$message_page"/>&amp;msg_id=<xsl:value-of
    select="$msg_id"/></xsl:atttribute><xsl:value-of select="$content"/></a>
</xsl:template>
```

The sample shown here uses anchors and links to handle the routines that will do such things as change the sort column (or invert the current column) or jump to the appropriate page display for a given link. This section could have just as readily been re-written using a combination of JavaScript and the POST method on the client, (which I leave as an exercise to the reader).

The only disadvantage with the framework approach is that the XSLT filter that displays the table is not the same one that displays the page the table is in. Thus, you do need to set the `list_page` and `message_page` parameters to the name of the page which contains the list (the current XHTML page) and the page that displays the entire message (see the `xp:apply` sample below for an example).

Navigating Between Messages

The navigational controls move you back or forth in the message space a page at a time:

```
<xsl:template name="nav_controls">
    <xsl:variable name="msg_count" select="count(//message)"/>
    <xsl:variable name="page_count" select="(((number($msg_count-1)) -
    ((number($msg_count)-1) mod number($messages_shown)) div
    number($messages_shown))+1"/>
    <xsl:if test="$page &gt; 1">
    <input type="button" value="Previous"><xsl:attribute
    name="onclick">location='xmlserver.asp?list_page=<xsl:value-of
    select=" $list_page"/>&amp;message_page=<xsl:value-of
    select="$message_page"/>&amp;sort_field=<xsl:value-of
    select="$sort_field"/>&amp;direction=<xsl:value-of
    select="$direction"/>&amp;page=<xsl:value-of
    select="number($page)-1"/>&amp;messages_shown=<xsl:value-of
    select="$messages_shown"/>'</xsl:attribute></input>
    </xsl:if>
    <xsl:if test="number($page)&lt; $page_count">
    <input type="button" value="Next"><xsl:attribute
     name="onclick">location='xmlserver.asp?list_page=<xsl:value-of
     select=" $list_page"/>&amp;message_page=<xsl:value-of
     select="$message_page"/>&amp;sort_field=<xsl:value-of
     select="$sort_field"/>&amp;direction=<xsl:value-of
     select="$direction"/>&amp;page=<xsl:value-of
     select="number($page)+1"/>&amp;messages_shown=<xsl:value-of
     select="$messages_shown"/>'</xsl:attribute></input>
    </xsl:if>
    <span>Page <input type="text" name="new_page" id="new_page"
    value="{$page}"/> of <xsl:value-pof select="$page_count"/></span>
    <input type="button" value="Go"><xsl:attribute
    name="onclick">location='xmlserver.asp?list_page=<xsl:value-of
    select="$list_page"/>&amp;message_page=<xsl:value-of
    select="$message_page"/>&amp;sort_field=<xsl:value-of
    select="$sort_field"/>&amp;direction=<xsl:value-of
    select="$direction"/>&amp;page='+new_page.value+'&amp;messages_shown=
    <xsl:value-of select="$messages_shown"/>'</xsl:attribute></input>
    <input type="button" value="New"><xsl:attribute
    name="onclick">location='xmlserver.asp?filter=<xsl:value-of
    select="$message_page"/>&amp;is_new=yes</xsl:atttribute><xsl:value-of
    select="$content" </input>
</xsl:template>
```

The sample shown here is fairly simple, consisting of a "Previous" button, a "Next" button, a legend "Page X of Y" where the first number is contained in a text box, and a "Go" button that will let you jump to a given page by typing its number in the text box. Note that if the page number exceeds the number of pages (or is less than zero) then no messages will be displayed, but nor will an error code.

The final button, the New button, jumps to the message page with the is_new parameter set to "yes". This tells the XML server to create a new message as a root level object and display it in edit mode. Any user can choose to edit or delete her own messages, so if a user is unsatisfied with a page they created, they can purge it from the system.

The List View

The term "list-view" is actually a little deceptive – this is essentially a table view, with each message constituting one row of the table:

```
        <!-- Display as a table. -->
    <xsl:template match="draw_table">
        <table class="xp_dynamic_table">
            <tr class="xp_header_row">
                <xsl:for-each select="$header_data/field">
                <th class="xp_header_cell">
                    <xsl:call-template name="get_header_link">
                        <xsl:with-param name="field"
                                select="."/>
                        <xsl:with-param name="content"
                                select="@caption"/>
                    </xsl:call-template>
                </th>
                </xsl:for-each>
            </tr>
            <xsl:for-each select="$filtered_messages">
                <tr class="xp_body_row">
                <xsl:variable name="msg" select="."/>
                <xsl:for-each select="$header_data/field">
                    <xsl:variable name="field" select="."/>
                    <td class="xp_body_cell">
                        <xsl:call-template
                            name="get_body_link">
                        <xsl:with-param name="msg_id"
                            select="$msg/@id"/>
                        <xsl:with-param name="content"
                            select="$msg/*[name()=
                            $field/@name]"/>
                        </xsl:call-template>
                    </td>
                </xsl:for-each>
            </xsl:for-each>
            <tr><td colspan="{count($header_data/field)}">
                <xsl:call-template name="nav_controls"/>
                </td>
            </tr>
        </table>
    </xsl:template>
</xsl:template>
</xsl:stylesheet>
```

The goal that I had in writing this style sheet was to make it as generic as possible, so that it could be used to generate any number of tables that followed this same basic structure (which includes the user list and one view of the message boards list). One advantage of this approach is that it makes it easier to incorporate this into a framework setting. For example, it might be possible to make this an xp:apply element in the framework:

```
<xp:apply sort_field="title" direction="ascending" include_replies="no" page="4"
messages_shown="30" list_page="showMessagePages" message_page="showMessage">
<xp:param name="header_data">
   <field name="title" caption="Message Title"/>
   <field name="abstract" caption="Abstract"/>
</xp:param>
</xp:apply>
```

This would show the fourth page (records 91 to 120) of primary messages (no replies) sorted alphabetically in ascending order. It will display only two columns, however – the `title` column and the `abstract` column, which gives a summary of the message.

A Few Thoughts on Online Editors

One of the more intriguing aspects about HTML is the fact that it is possible to create it with a text editor, even if that "editor" is simply a `TEXTAREA` box on a page, and the amount of information that can be captured in this manner can produce a staggeringly complex set of possibilities. Additionally, you can use the built-in editing capabilities of some of the more recent web browsers (such as Microsoft's Internet Explorer 5.5, which allows you to edit text in any container, not just a `TEXTAREA` box) to generate HTML code in a WYSIWYG environment.

One benefit of using an XML-based framework is that you can in fact design interface components targeted to specific browsers without sacrificing the "down-stream" market of older browsers, Personal Digital Assistants (better known as PDAs) running WAP, or even voice-based "browsers" running over your telephone.

Most HTML WYSIWYG editors, however, build really horrendous code, at least as far as XML is concerned. Opening tags (especially such tags as the `<P>` paragraph tag) frequently do not have equivalent closing tags. Tag overlap is possible:

```
<B>This <I>is a </B>Test</I>
```

and can easily be generated, for example, while it is far more rare to the see the XML compliant:

```
<B>This <I>is a </I></B><I> Test</I>
```

created by an editor such as Front Page (in fairness, Microsoft Front Page 2000 is considerably better about even HTML compliance than previous versions, but it still tends to do awkward things to HTML code).

Perhaps one of the more pervasive and troubling problems in generated HTML code is the fact that id attributes, so important in both HTML and XML, seem universally to lack any quotation marks – this one improvement in current editors would radically simplify the conversion of HTML to XML.

In other words, regardless of whether the text is entered by hand or generated by an inline HTML editor, the chances are that anything that your users type will not be XML compliant. How do you get around this when writing your editors? One way is to assume that any text that is entered in an online editor should be treated as simple text with all tags stripped off. You can then use tags such as the `<PRE>` tag to retain formatting information, keeping everything a uniform font style.

However, this solution tends to create very flat-looking text and also suffers from having paragraphs of text display as single long lines that exceed the display width of the screen several times over. A second solution is to parse the incoming text, replacing carriage returns with break (`<BR/>`) elements. The output can then be displayed in a `DIV` or similar block element. This is one of the solutions that the discussion group framework offers. This information can then be kept within an enclosed CDATA section in the page's XML document, perhaps as part of a generic `DIV` element.

A third solution is to use a WYSIWYG type editor and JavaScript to create the contents of a message, then wrap the resulting HTML in a CDATA section as with the second solution. This solution is of course dependent upon having a browser sufficiently advanced to allow for such an editor (or the use of a Java applet or ActiveX component) to provide this level of functionality.

Another approach is to let your users type HTML code directly into the editor, which will then be output by the browser when it's displayed in view mode. Unfortunately, the danger with this is that it allows users to write potentially dangerous script code directly into the site.

Finally, there are two *external* solutions that you can apply. The first is to upload one or more local files to the site and then create a reference to them from within the page. While simple in theory, the exact methods for handling file upload vary dramatically from system to system, and administering these resources can be complicated. The second remote alternative is to create a link to an existing web site or online resource when the page is created, either to upload the resources into a local cache or to just be kept as a remote link.

One of the advantages of maintaining resources as remote links is that they can similarly be produced by XML-based servers. Since such servers are typically parametric in scope (they work by taking commands from query string or form parameters), this means the XML thus created is likely to be dynamic – with the framework architecture given here, this means that parameters can conceivably be passed through the framework to the target resource URL.

Editing and Viewing Individual Messages

The creation and processing of forms makes up a significant amount of the total HTML web pages out there. From the standpoint of the XMLServer architecture, a form is simply a mechanism for populating a form `Request` object, and the server makes little distinction between parameters passed as part of a form and parameters passed as part of a query string – both pass parametric information back to the XMLServer to process as necessary.

One of the problems I've always found with forms, however, is that the visual presentation of the form can often obscure the underlying code for it, especially when, for aesthetic purposes, a form is embedded in a table. The `tabular_form.xsl` filter was intended to address that issue. It converts an XML structure (contained in the `<items>` element as a parameter) that holds the various form types, labels, and content information and then converts it into a table with the labels positioned correctly relative to the form controls (text boxes, combo boxes, etc.).

The editing frame is actually an instance of the `tabular_form.xsl`, which associates specific form field names and ids with their corresponding parameter names in the target modules:

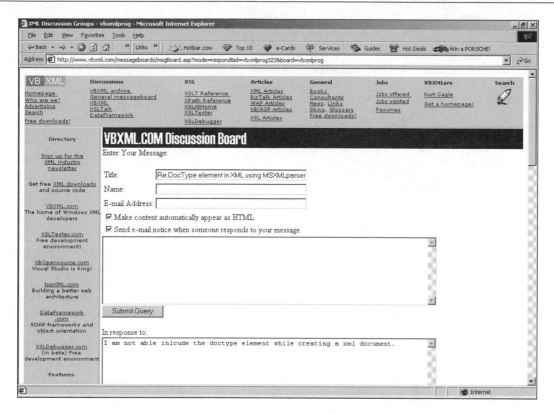

The `tabular_form.xsl` is easily one of the most complicated samples in this case study. The primary reason for this is that each form control requires its own template since both the requirements and the capabilities of each control are so different from one another. Note, when looking at this section, the use of the `mode` XSLT element. The `tabular_form` template may (and almost always will, come to that) be called up as a named template in some other XSLT filter. Rather than making each of the items in the form themselves named templates (which increases the risk of namespace confusion) the templates that find a given element are matching templates, but the `mode` identifies them as belonging to `tabular_form.xsl`, so that the chance for namespace collision drops dramatically.

The `xsl:param` element named `"items"` contains the actual items that make up the form, with the name of each element corresponding with the type of the form element (i.e., `<text …>` replaces `<input type="text"/>`, `<hidden …>` replaces `<input type="hidden"/>`. Additionally, the `textarea` object is treated like any other element.

The first part of the style sheet exposes the parameters, providing substitute values when no value is explicitly stated in the called document. The default method for sending the information through the `tabular_form` object is (not surprisingly) POST, which is the way that forms routinely send information. However, you can also send this via a GET mechanism if you need to pass a URL:

```
<?xml-stylesheet type="text/xsl" href="tabular_form.xsl" ?>
<xsl:stylesheet xmlns:xsl="http://www.w3.org/1999/XSL/Transform" version="1.0">
  <xsl:output method="xml" omit-xml-declaration="yes"/>
```

601

```
<xsl:param name="form_id" select="'form1'"/>
<xsl:param name="action" select="'xmlserver.asp'"/>
<xsl:param name="method" select="'post'"/>
<xsl:param name="filter" select="'show_message_page'"/>
<xsl:param name="items">
  <text id="title" caption="Title" value="Title"/>
  <textarea id="body" caption="Message" value=" "/>
  <checkbox id="cbox" caption="Selection" value="yes"/>
  <hidden id="hidden" value="HiddenValue"/>
  <reset id="reset" caption="Reset"/>
  <button id="button" caption="Button"
            onclick="window.status='You have just pressed a button.'"/>
  <file id="file" caption="File"/>
  <image id="image" caption="Image" src="d:\bin\images.jpg"/>
  <password id="password" caption="Password"/>
  <submit/>
</xsl:param>
```

The CSS style sheet is also included as a parameter here, providing a sufficient amount of information to ensure that elements appear more or less properly styled. You could replace this with a style sheet of your own (note the `.tabular_form` prefixes, which identify appropriate classes specifically for this kind of an object), or use the `@style` directive to import a style sheet from an external file (refer back to Chapter 3 for more details on this).

```
<xsl:param name="tabular_form_css">
  <style>
  .tabular_form_table {width:70%;}
  .tabular_form_row {}
  .tabular_form_cell_label {width:20%;}
  .tabular_form_cell_content {width:80%}
  .tabular_form_textarea {width:100%;}
  .tabular_form_submit {width:100%;}
  .tabular_form_reset {width:100%;}
  .tabular_form_button {width:100%;}
  .tabular_form_file {width:100%;}
  .tabular_form_image {width:100%;}
  .tabular_form_password {width:100%;}
  </style>
</xsl:param>
```

The `tabular_form` named template illustrates a common trend in working with imported style sheets – call the name of the style sheet the same as the name of the primary interface (think of it as being analogous to a class) in the style sheet. This template echoes the parameters of the document itself, a process which ensures that parameters can be passed into the named template with the `<xsl:with-param>` element, but that they also have consistent default values.

Note that the `tabular_form` template is actually quite small, and serves to generate a form (after inserting the CSS for the form) with methods and actions corresponding to the requested parameters. It then iterates over each child item from `<xsl:param name="items"/>` element.

```
<xsl:template name="tabular_form">
  <xsl:param name="form_id" select="$form_id"/>
  <xsl:param name="action" select="$action"/>
```

```
        <xsl:param name="method" select="$method"/>
        <xsl:param name="filter" select="$filter"/>
        <xsl:param name="items" select="$items"/>
        <xsl:copy-of select="$tabular_form_css"/>
        <form action="{$action}" method="{$method}" id="{$id}" name="{$id}">
          <input id="filter" name="filter" type="hidden" value="{$filter}"/>
          <table class="tabular_form_table">
          <xsl:for-each select="$items/*">
            <xsl:apply-templates select="." mode="tabular_form"/>
          </xsl:for-each>
          </table>
        </form>
      </xsl:template>
```

Each of the subsequent match templates attempts to match the name of the item nodes with a given template, working within the `tabular_form` modality. Because these items are being output to an HTML table to better position the elements, most of the actual code involves creating HTML-like DHTML code. First there is the template for a hidden type of input:

```
    <xsl:template match="hidden" mode="tabular_form">
      <input type="hidden" id="{@id}" name="{@id}" value="{@value}"/>
    </xsl:template>

    <xsl:template match="text" mode="tabular_form">
      <tr class="tabular_form_row">
      <td class="tabular_form_cell_label"><xsl:value-of select="@caption"/></td>
      <td class="tabular_form_cell_content">
        <input id="{@id}" name="{@id}" type="text" class="tabular_form_text">
        <xsl:if test="@value">
          <xsl:attribute name="value">
            <xsl:value-of select="@value"/>
          </xsl:attribute>
        </xsl:if>
        <xsl:for-each select="@*[starts-with(name(.),'on')]">
          <xsl:attribute name="{name(.)}"><xsl:value-of select="."/></xsl:attribute>
        </xsl:for-each>
        </input>
      </td>
      </tr>
    </xsl:template>
```

Next there is a file template:

```
    <xsl:template match="file" mode="tabular_form">
      <tr class="tabular_form_row">
      <td class="tabular_form_cell_label"><xsl:value-of select="@caption"/></td>
      <td class="tabular_form_cell_content">
        <input id="{@id}" name="{@id}" type="file" class="tabular_form_file">
        <xsl:if test="@value">
          <xsl:attribute name="value">
            <xsl:value-of select="@value"/>
          </xsl:attribute>
        </xsl:if>
        <xsl:for-each select="@*[starts-with(name(.),'on')]">
```

```
      <xsl:attribute name="{name(.)}"><xsl:value-of select="."/></xsl:attribute>
    </xsl:for-each>
    </input>
  </td>
  </tr>
</xsl:template>
```

Following this is the password template:

```
<xsl:template match="password" mode="tabular_form">
  <tr class="tabular_form_row">
  <td class="tabular_form_cell_label"><xsl:value-of select="@caption"/></td>
  <td class="tabular_form_cell_content">
    <input id="{@id}" name="{@id}" type="password"
         class="tabular_form_password">
    <xsl:if test="@value">
      <xsl:attribute name="value">
        <xsl:value-of select="@value"/>
      </xsl:attribute>
    </xsl:if>
    <xsl:for-each select="@*[starts-with(name(.),'on')]">
      <xsl:attribute name="{name(.)}"><xsl:value-of select="."/></xsl:attribute>
    </xsl:for-each>
    </input>
  </td>
  </tr>
</xsl:template>
```

Then a submit button template:

```
<xsl:template match="submit" mode="tabular_form">
  <tr class="tabular_form_row">
  <td class="tabular_form_cell_label">
    <input>
      <xsl:attribute name="class">tabular_form_submit</xsl:attribute>
      <xsl:attribute name="type">submit</xsl:attribute>
      <xsl:if test="@id">
      <xsl:attribute name="id"><xsl:value-of select="@id"/></xsl:attribute>
      <xsl:attribute name="name"><xsl:value-of select="@name"/></xsl:attribute>
      </xsl:if>
      <xsl:if test="@caption">
      <xsl:attribute name="value">
        <xsl:value-of select="@caption"/>
      </xsl:attribute>
      </xsl:if>
      <xsl:for-each select="@*[starts-with(name(.),'on')]">
        <xsl:attribute name="{name(.)}">
          <xsl:value-of select="."/>
        </xsl:attribute>
      </xsl:for-each>
    </input>
  </td>
  </tr>
</xsl:template>
```

604

A reset button template:

```xsl
<xsl:template match="reset" mode="tabular_form">
  <tr class="tabular_form_row">
  <td class="tabular_form_cell_label">
    <input>
      <xsl:attribute name="class">tabular_form_reset</xsl:attribute>
      <xsl:attribute name="type">reset</xsl:attribute>
      <xsl:if test="@id">
      <xsl:attribute name="id"><xsl:value-of select="@id"/></xsl:attribute>
      <xsl:attribute name="name"><xsl:value-of select="@name"/></xsl:attribute>
      </xsl:if>
      <xsl:if test="@caption">
      <xsl:attribute name="value">
        <xsl:value-of select="@caption"/>
      </xsl:attribute>
      </xsl:if>
      <xsl:for-each select="@*[starts-with(name(.),'on')]">
        <xsl:attribute name="{name(.)}">
          <xsl:value-of select="."/>
        </xsl:attribute>
      </xsl:for-each>
    </input>
  </td>
  </tr>
</xsl:template>
```

The button template:

```xsl
<xsl:template match="button" mode="tabular_form">
  <tr class="tabular_form_row">
  <td class="tabular_form_cell_label">
    <input>
      <xsl:attribute name="class">tabular_form_button</xsl:attribute>
      <xsl:attribute name="type">button</xsl:attribute>
      <xsl:if test="@id">
      <xsl:attribute name="id"><xsl:value-of select="@id"/></xsl:attribute>
      <xsl:attribute name="name"><xsl:value-of select="@name"/></xsl:attribute>
      </xsl:if>
      <xsl:if test="@caption">
      <xsl:attribute name="value">
        <xsl:value-of select="@caption"/></xsl:attribute>
      </xsl:if>
      <xsl:for-each select="@*[starts-with(name(.),'on')]">
        <xsl:attribute name="{name(.)}">
          <xsl:value-of select="."/></xsl:attribute>
      </xsl:for-each>
    </input>
  </td>
  </tr>
</xsl:template>
```

The checkbox template:

```
<xsl:template match="checkbox" mode="tabular_form">
  <tr class="tabular_form_row">
    <td class="tabular_form_cell_label" colspan="2">
      <input class="tabular_form_checkbox" type="checkbox" id="{@id}"
             name="{@id}"><xsl:if test="@value='yes' or @value='true'">
             <xsl:attribute name="checked">yes</xsl:attribute></xsl:if>
             <xsl:for-each select="@*[starts-with(name(.),'on')]">
             <xsl:attribute name="{name(.)}"><xsl:value-of select="."/>
             </xsl:attribute></xsl:for-each><xsl:value-of select="@caption"/>
      </input>
    </td>
  </tr>
</xsl:template>
```

The textarea template:

```
<xsl:template match="textarea" mode="tabular_form">
  <tr class="tabular_form_row">
  <td class="tabular_form_cell_label" colspan="2">
    <xsl:value-of select="@caption"/></td>
  </tr>
  <tr>
  <td class="tabular_form_cell_content" colspan="2">
    <div>
    <textarea id="{@id}" name="{@id}" style="width:100%;height:200;">
    <xsl:for-each select="@*[starts-with(name(.),'on')]">
      <xsl:attribute name="{name(.)}">
        <xsl:value-of select="."/>
      </xsl:attribute>
    </xsl:for-each>
    <xsl:choose>
      <xsl:when test="@value">
        <xsl:value-of select="@value"/>
      </xsl:when>
      <xsl:otherwise>
        <xsl:text> </xsl:text>
      </xsl:otherwise>
    </xsl:choose>
    </textarea>
    </div>
  </td>
  </tr>
</xsl:template>
```

There is a template for form image maps:

```
<xsl:template match="image" mode="tabular_form">
  <tr class="tabular_form_row">
  <td class="tabular_form_cell_label" colspan="2">
  <input type="image" id="{@id}" name="{@id}" src="{@src}"/>
  <xsl:if test="@caption">
  <xsl:attribute name="alt"><xsl:value-of select="@caption"/></xsl:attribute>
```

```
      </xsl:if>
      </td>
      </tr>
   </xsl:template>
```

Finally the very last template is the root node match template, which matches the start of any document. By including such a match, you can use the same script as part of the framework and as an independent transformation:

```
   <xsl:template match="/">
     <xsl:call-template name="tabular_form"/>
     </xsl:call-template>
   </xsl:template>
  </xsl:stylesheet>
```

In addition to setting some parameter information, the `tabular_form` template also allows you to define the output in its own little mini-xsl. For example, when run as its own default filter, the template specifically uses the expressions:

```
   <xsl:param name="items">
     <text id="title" caption="Title" value="Title"/>
     <textarea id="body" caption="Message" value=" "/>
     <checkbox id="cbox" caption="Selection" value="yes"/>
     <hidden id="hidden" value="HiddenValue"/>
     <reset id="reset" caption="Reset"/>
     <button id="button" caption="Button"
        onclick="window.status='You have just pressed a button.'"/>
     <file id="file" caption="File"/>
     <image id="image" caption="Image" src="d:\bin\images.jpg"/>
     <password id="password" caption="Password"/>
     <submit/>
   </xsl:param>
```

The framework contains complete documentation for these pseudo-XSL elements. Once the elements are in place, by the way, this template can be used via parameter calls. Thus, for instance, the file `edit_message_page.xsl`, shown below, actually serves up the results from `tabular_form` and places the results into the output stream of `edit_message_pearl`:

```
  <xsl:stylesheet xmlns:xsl="http://www.w3.org/1999/XSL/Transform"
      xmlns:msxsl="urn:schemas-microsoft-com:xslt"
   xmlns:xp="http://www.vbxml.com/utilities"
   version="1.0">
   <xsl:import href="property_table.xsl"/>
   <xsl:import href="dates.xsl"/>
   <xsl:import href="state.xsl"/>
   <xsl:import href="tabular_form.xsl"/>

   <xsl:param name="board_name" select="'development'"/>
   <xsl:param name="id" select="1"/>
   <xsl:param name="message_board">
     <xsl:copy-of select="xp:document(concat($board_name,'.xml'))"/>
   </xsl:param>
   <xsl:param name="msg" select="$message_board//message[@id=$id]"/>
```

```
    <xsl:template name="body">
      <xsl:copy-of select="xp:document(string($msg//link/@href))"/>
    </xsl:template>

<xsl:template match="/">
<html>
<head>
  <title>Message - <xsl:value-of select="$msg/title"/></title>
</head>

<body>
<h1>Editor</h1>
<xsl:variable name="content"><xsl:call-template name="body"/></xsl:variable>
<xsl:call-template name="tabular_form">
  <xsl:with-param name="id" select="'form1'"/>
  <xsl:with-param name="action" select="'xmlserver.asp'"/>
  <xsl:with-param name="method" select="'post'"/>
  <xsl:with-param name="filter" select="'update_message_page'"/>
  <xsl:with-param name="items">
    <hidden id="id" caption="Title" value="{$id}"/>
    <text id="title" caption="Title" value="{$msg/title}"/>
    <xsl:if test="$content">
    <textarea id="body" caption="Body" value="{$content}"/>
    </xsl:if>
    <submit/>
  </xsl:with-param>
</xsl:call-template>
</body>
</html>
</xsl:template>
</xsl:stylesheet>
```

While this document bears a faint resemblance to HTML, the use of the call-template lets you create very robust applications without needing to write as much code.

Summary

The full framework being developed here comprises several dozen objects with more being added over time, so what is shown makes up only a very small portion of the whole project. However, in most cases, the technique is the same – build XSLT classes that can either stand alone as filters or be invoked by name. These classes in turn are used to build more advanced classes, until ultimately you reach the class that performs the actual generation of HTML. This approach bears a number of similarities to the ways that Java programs are laid out, with the name of the class being the name of the first "public" method.

The XMLPipes framework can be seen in action at the VBXML website (http://www.vbxml.com), along with a host of new templates for generating a wide range of results, from hierarchical treeview controls to specialized tables. The XMLServer.asp approach described here can be fairly readily mimicked in a Java environment as well as the Internet Explorer/IIS environment mentioned previously. While the back-end code can occasionally look a little forbidding, once these back-end pieces *are* implemented then incorporating them into your XSL becomes much easier.

Case Study 3: XML for a Business-to-Business Application

George Santayana once said *"those who fail to learn from history are doomed to repeat it"*. The aim of this case study is to give you enough history to help you learn from our experiences on a real-world XML Business-to-Business project – to pick up the good points and learn from the mistakes.

I'll take you through a solution developed by members of **BASDA**, the **Business and Accounting Software Developers Association**. Under the **eBIS-XML** banner, BASDA has produced XML schemas for e-commerce. So far, there are schemas for purchase orders and invoices, with others, such as delivery advice, planned.

So how does this help, when **Electronic Data Interchange** (**EDI**) already has mechanisms for doing the same thing? Perhaps surprisingly, much of the secret lies with XSL. We'll see why the EDI approach is not necessarily the best.

So in this case study, I'll take you through the development of a real-life complex schema and describe the associated style sheet. Although I will use a fictional character to illustrate the issues that led to this work, the schemas are in live use, with (in May 2000) five systems already carrying the eBIS-XML logo and over a hundred more working towards it.

At the time of writing (and at the time these schemas were developed), there were several options for the schema syntax to use. For reasons explained later, the current eBIS-XML schemas are coded using Microsoft's XML Data Reduced (XDR) syntax, but I'll translate this to the latest draft from the W3C for the purpose of this exercise, since that is what is covered in this book, and is less dependent on one software vendor. Similarly, the style sheets use the version of XSL in Microsoft's original IE5 release, but I've redeveloped them in XSLT, as this is what we'll want for the future.

You will therefore learn:

❑   More about e-business

❑   About the principles behind the BASDA work

❑   About the schema itself, including why certain decisions were made

❑   About the style sheets, from which I hope you'll pick up some useful tips and tricks

❑   About a couple of useful XML tools

This case study should help to reinforce the knowledge you've acquired throughout the book, in particular Chapters 4, 5, 9, 10 and 11 where we first discussed XSLT and validation methods.

Because of the huge scale of the project, it would be very difficult to implement on a development machine. So for this case study you can leave your PC switched off. It's the principles behind the project, the decision processes we went through, and the overview of how XML technologies can be put into practice that you'll learn about here. And don't worry if you don't understand it all straight away. This is a description of a major real-world project more complex than anyone could reasonably expect from a beginner. Learn what you can from it, then come back and read it again once you have gained more experience. That way, you will double the value you get from it.

> *And my involvement? As a freelance XML consultant, I was commissioned by Microsoft in September 1999 to develop the XSL style sheets for the project, and later by BASDA to move the schema from version 2.4 to version 3.*

Let's start by taking a look at the kind of e-business problem we're trying to solve.

An E-Commerce Problem and Our Solution

Arthur Discspinner was sitting in his office towards the end of the last century, thinking about how he runs his music wholesaling business. Arthur buys CDs from the publishers using Electronic Data Interchange or by faxing orders, then sells to shops, taking his orders by mail, phone or fax. He also sells directly to DJs, who generally order over the Web or by e-mail. Sometimes they just turn up on his doorstep, expecting him to give them what they want straight away. He considered each of these in turn:

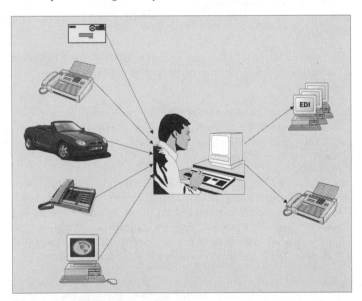

Being a sophisticated type of guy, Albert can produce orders by fax directly from his accounting system. This is at least an improvement on printing out and posting his orders, and they arrive a day earlier. These are automatically sent to his supplier, who then fulfils the order and invoices by fax. Albert types the invoice information from the fax into his accounting system. This manual process continues when he hand-writes a check, prints off a remittance advice and posts them to the record company.

Unfortunately, his ordering using EDI is actually worse rather than better than fax. Although EDI held the promise of linking supply chains electronically, the reality is that the big business (the record company) benefits, while the small guy (Arthur) suffers. Arthur uses EDI for four of his suppliers because otherwise they won't do business with him. Unfortunately, the nature of the EDI world is such that they use different EDI standards, and he needs to support them all. He therefore has four PCs, one for each supplier, and some expensive software to produce EDI Orders and accept EDI Invoices. And still he has to copy the information into his accounting system since none of the systems links to this (at least, not without replacing his accounting system with one fifty times the price).

What about supplying his customers? When the information comes in by fax, e-mail, letter, phone or hand carried, he manually enters it into his accounting system, fulfils the order, prints out an invoice and sends it off. Is it any better when he deals over the Web? Being a small company, his web site is hosted by an Internet Service Provider. The ISP provides credit card clearing facilities, but the order itself is still sent as an e-mail to Albert, who prints it out and enters it into his system.

Clearly, although Arthur's initials are AD, his systems are positively BC (or should that be BeC – Before e-Commerce?). Arthur may be fictitious, but he's not stupid, and his problems are real enough. He doesn't see why, when documents are being produced electronically, he should have to take a paper copy and re-enter the information into his computer. A little research (such as reading BASDA's "A Practical View of eCommerce", October 1999) tells him that 95% of documents manually entered into computer systems were produced by other computing systems. And 95% of web-based e-commerce systems are not connected to the accounting systems of the supplier. Computer systems and networks have been around for years, so what went wrong?

Now that we're all XML experts, we want to know how XML can help.

E-Commerce Requirements

So what are Arthur's requirements? First and foremost, he wants to eliminate duplicate data entry. If someone somewhere has entered information into a computer system, he doesn't want to have to do it again. Taking a less selfish view, if he has entered information into his systems, his suppliers and customers shouldn't have to do it again either. After all, if he can improve the buying experience, he'll get more business, and if he can reduce his suppliers' costs, he'll have, at minimum, better supplier relationships. He might even be able to negotiate better prices.

What else would Arthur like? How about eliminating specialist stationery? Here in the UK, for reasons that the cynical might put down to lack of planning by the relevant authorities, our telephone numbers change every few years. (Having seen the latest change, I suspect that this is not about to end.) So eliminating the cost, not only of the stationery, but of throwing it away and replacing it every time there's a change, is a great benefit. Not to mention the storage space freed up, from what could be regarded as overhead material. Arthur can now use this for stocks of his products, thus keeping his customers happier.

Of course, Arthur wants to get rid of the cost of the four PCs and system he uses for EDI. He wouldn't mind reducing his postage, phone and fax costs as well. And while he's about it, reducing the time between a customer sending an order and Arthur fulfilling it would be handy too.

And Arthur doesn't want to learn a new accounting system, pay for an upgrade or pay for a consultant to configure everything for him. What's more, he wants to use the same system with *all* his suppliers.

In short – Arthur is a typical customer for a software solution. He wants everything, he wants it for nothing and he wants it now. In fact, I remember Queen writing a song about him.

Luckily, with the help of XML and the co-operation of a large number of software vendors, he can have all of this (and potentially more).

Why Doesn't EDI Achieve This?

EDI has been with us for many years, but it has not reached its full potential, with very little support outside the major supply-chain driven industries such as automobile manufacture. Let's just look briefly at a few reasons why EDI has not reached the mass market.

In concept, EDI is a way of delivering business documents electronically. It does this by providing coding and transport mechanisms. The coding uses **delimited** formats, with each field being separated by a reserved character. There are two basic standards for EDI – ANSI X.12 used in North America, and EDIFACT used throughout most of the rest of the world.

These messages are carried over **Value Added Networks** (VANs) between the trading parties. These are managed networks, providing a secure and robust service at a high cost. Compare this to the Internet, which currently provides a less secure, less robust service at a low cost. Of course, much work is being done to increase the security and robustness of the Internet, but it does not yet compare to a VAN.

Ignoring the headers that are part of the EDI standards, some information coded in EDI might look like this:

```
"Arthur Discspinner Music","Music distributor","Arthur
Discspinner","arthur@discspinner.co.uk"
```

So what is the problem? One problem stems from the delimited nature of the coding. You can tell (because, as a human being, you can place the words in a context) that Arthur Discspinner Music is the name of a business, and that it is probably a music distributor. Arthur Discspinner is probably the person to contact, as it is clearly his e-mail address that follows.

Alternatively, this message might be a query, and Arthur Discspinner Music might be looking to find a music distributor with which to work. And Arthur remains the person to contact. The point is that EDI is not **self describing**, so you cannot be sure. In XML, we might describe the same information as:

```
<Company>Arthur Discspinner Music</Company>
<MarketSector>Music distributor</MarketSector>
<Contact>
  <Name>Arthur Discspinner</Name>
  <Email>arthur@discspinner.co.uk</Email>
</Contact>
```

Now we know what the data is about. More importantly, if we add a new field, our programs can still interpret the data, even if they cannot handle the additional information. In EDI, we could try:

```
"Arthur Discspinner Music","Music distributor","Arthur Discspinner","0118 912
3456","arthur@discspinner.co.uk"
```

614

In general, an EDI system will report an error, since it is finding a phone number when it expects an e-mail address. An XML system, by contrast, will still find the e-mail address because it will be looking for it by element name:

```
<Company>Arthur Discspinner Music</Company>
<MarketSector>Music distributor</MarketSector>
<Contact>
   <Name>Arthur Discspinner</Name>
   <Phone>0118 912 3456</Phone>
   <Email>arthur@discspinner.co.uk</Email>
</Contact>
```

Of course, the EDI format is much more concise, reflecting the fact that it was developed at a time of high communications costs. However, it has lost all flexibility. The XML format, on the other hand, gains flexibility at the expense of verboseness.

The result of this is that EDI systems must be 100% compatible in the message structures they understand. And if we want to use EDI across industries, the EDI message must be a superset of all the possible requirements. Of course, however hard you try to do this, you will miss something, or a new requirement will come along (who would have included a web address ten years ago?). So companies get together to define standards for use in their industry and companies wanting to trade together start to use proprietary extensions to meet more specific needs. And that is why Arthur needs separate systems to talk to each of his EDI-equipped suppliers.

When you add to this the costs of the value added networks, you can see why EDI has not made the mass market. That is not to say it doesn't have its place. If you are an auto manufacturer using just-in-time systems, you need the reliability and service level agreements inherent in the EDI infrastructure. You have a specific set of suppliers who can program your part numbers into their systems. And, although these suppliers might not like having to implement specific systems just to deal with you, that is the price they pay to do business in a market where the customer is dominant.

The eBIS-XML Concept

Before we start on how eBIS-XML is going to help, let's just review the current situation. PCs are thousands of times faster than they were when EDI was first developed. (The fuel injection system on the typical automobile has more processing power than was used to put Neil Armstrong on the Moon.) We have a global network capable of linking businesses instantly, but still Arthur is retyping orders and invoices and, even more unbelievably, taking checks to his bank and queuing to pay them into his account. No surprise that he wants to know what went wrong. So let's look at the solution.

For the mass market – for people like Arthur – what we're looking for is a system that can link accounting systems over the Web or by e-mail, since these are cheap and ubiquitous mechanisms for transferring information. That's virtually what EDI does. However, we want a "many-to-many" solution, whereby Arthur, with his low-end accounting system, can link not only to his music publishers with their Enterprise Resource Planning (ERP) systems, but also to his stationery supplier, his local taxi company, his web site and his customers.

We have seen how EDI provides a "one-to-many" solution that requires 100% compatibility between end systems. One effect of this requirement is that we can be sure that the data we receive contains exactly the information we need, so we can read it straight into our computer systems. Another effect is that we do not get the ability to handle messages with missing data or to easily extend the information we are sending. Because he is linking to so many disparate systems, Arthur needs to be able to handle messages that are lacking important (to him) information, like part numbers.

At BASDA, we use the term **flexible interoperability** to describe the fact that systems can work together without being 100% compatible.

And finally, for those who don't have compatible systems, he should also be able to send a document exactly as he would to a compatible system, but the receiver should be able to view it in a browser and print it out. And this is the eBIS-XML concept.

Receiving an Order

Let's look at what happens when Arthur receives an eBIS-XML purchase order. When the order arrives, rather than the information being posted directly by his system, the system will effectively pre-populate the order entry screen. So the information that has been entered by someone else is not lost, but if, for example, his customer has ordered records by name and not included the bar code information that Arthur uses internally, he can add that information. If his customer does not know the customer reference that Arthur uses for him, Arthur can add that too. So we are not *competing* with the 100% compatibility and automatic posting of EDI, we are *complementing* it by developing a system for the mass market.

Sending an Invoice

At some point, Arthur will send an invoice to his customer. Suppose his customer does not have an eBIS-XML enabled system. No problem! Using an XSL style sheet, the customer can view the document in his browser and print it out. Of course, not everyone currently has an XML-enabled browser and, because the standards are new, support might be different across browsers. So we will see shortly that, as an interim measure, Arthur's system might process the XML through the style sheet itself and send both XML and HTML versions of the invoice.

Communicating via the Web Site

And what about his web site? This can generate the order itself and send it directly into Arthur's system. Of course, here he has more control over the information provided, so this might be posted directly by his system, rather than being opened for editing first.

The diagram below shows the concept. The fully integrated system can communicate with another fully integrated system, but it can also send information directly to a browser. Within the web marketplace, a web site can send an order to Arthur in much the same way as a customer can from an eBIS-XML enabled system:

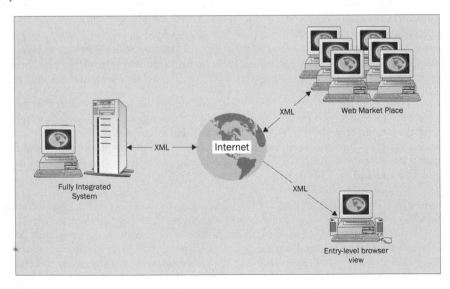

So now we have several differences from EDI: while EDI is intended purely for system-to-system use, we are now able to get a friendly display. And while EDI requires 100% compatibility, we can now link systems that are not 100% compatible.

Placing an Order

When Arthur places an order with one of his suppliers, everything works in the same way. Arthur has his low-end accounting system. This system generates an order that is going to contain all the essential information, such as:

❑   What he wants

❑   Where he wants it delivered

❑   Whom to invoice

At least, that's the information that *Arthur* deems essential. As before, the *supplier*'s ERP system might also need to know stock numbers and other information. But we now have a mechanism where the order can be imported into the ERP system, then edited before posting. In fact, that's just what would happen with a manual data entry, except that the information supplied by Arthur doesn't have to be re-entered. So we have the ability to *add* data at the receiving end.

Receiving an Invoice

Now let's look in more detail at the invoice Arthur receives. This includes prices, discounts, tax and payment terms. This information is essential to Arthur's accounts, and so needs to be imported into his accounting system. The invoice might also add other information such as special offers. Arthur might want to know about these, but his accounting system does not. This is another benefit of the style sheet. Although Arthur has an eBIS-XML enabled system, this will just post the *accounting* information. Arthur can then use the style sheet to see and print the complete document with all its additional information. In other words, his accounting system can *subtract* information without Arthur losing it.

So What (exactly) is eBIS-XML?

After many years when there was no mechanism for exchanging business documents on a many-to-many basis, once XML and XSL came along, the solution quickly became obvious. We have just seen that we can send our documents as XML, allow editing before posting, and use XSL style sheets to add a display capability. This is inexpensive, as the tools are cheap and the messages can be sent over the Internet.

Of course, if we are to use XML to exchange data, we need some mechanism for describing the details of the message structure. Two mechanisms are available for this – DTDs and XML Schemas, which were explained in Chapter 9 and 10 respectively. We will see shortly why schemas were chosen.

Rather than insist on 100% compatibility between end systems, we insist that they allow missing information to be added. In other words, instead of posting the information as it arrives, we hold it in its original form, then when someone comes to process it, we pre-populate the data entry screen. So we're not replacing the fully automated systems in sophisticated supply chains like those in the automobile industry – we're producing systems for the other 95% of the world.

As well as pre-populating the screens, we supply an XSL style sheet so the full document can be viewed and printed. We then have everything we need in our accounting or ERP system, whether or not it was in the original document, and we have the full information from the document, whether or not our accounting system requires it. And who should supply the style sheet? Clearly, the supplier of the system sending the message, as only it knows which parts of the standard it is using.

So we have a mechanism that uses:

- ❑ XML as its **data coding** mechanism

- ❑ XML schemas as its **language definition** mechanism

- ❑ The Internet as its **data transport** mechanism

- ❑ XSL as its **display** mechanism

Although many people think of standards like eBIS-XML in terms of an XML schema, we have seen that this is more than just a schema. That is why the last section was called "The eBIS-XML Concept". We have already seen that this concept includes not only the data formats described in the schemas we will be seeing shortly, but also the requirement to allow data to be edited before posting, and a way in which XSL style sheets are applied to the data to provide a viewable and printable document.

Security Issues

That is the current status of the standard. However, I mentioned earlier that a benefit of EDI is its use of robust and secure networks. In eBIS-XML at the moment, we are using e-mail, which is intrinsically neither robust nor secure. In doing this, we are no worse off than putting a printed document in an envelope and sending it through the post, but we could do better. BASDA decided not to define standards in this area itself, but instead to work with other standards bodies that are working on the types of systems needed. So the eBIS-XML standard is evolving. The basic concepts of flexible interoperability using style sheets and editing messages before posting are there. The data encoding is there. And there is a mechanism (e-mail) for delivering documents. Better delivery mechanisms will follow.

An Existing eBIS-XML Application

We'll look in detail at how we can use XML and style sheets to produce our business-to-business (B2B) documents shortly. But first, just to prove that this is really happening out there, here is a screen shot from Exchequer Enterprise (http://www.exchequer.com) – one of the first accounting systems to support the eBIS-XML standard:

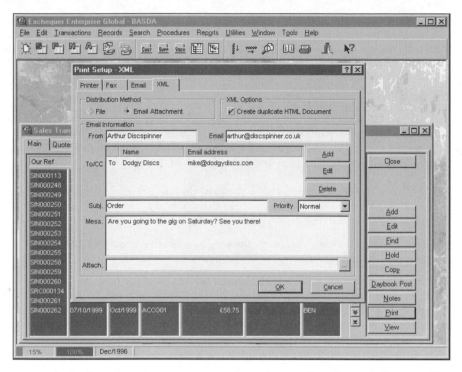

As you can see, the order is being sent as an e-mail attachment that allows Arthur to add a message. At the receiving end, a compliant system will poll the mailbox for eBIS-XML messages and list them in the system ready for processing. The e-mail address of Dodgy Discs has been configured into the system, so that has been added automatically, as has Arthur's own e-mail address. There is also the option to add a text message and copy the e-mail to others, just like a normal e-mail system.

As I mentioned earlier, there's also a facility to add a duplicate HTML attachment. This will use Exchequer's style sheet to produce an HTML image of the XML document. Doesn't this defeat the object of sending the message as XML? Well, only partly, and it provides a work-around until everyone has an XML-aware browser to view the document.

Decisions, Decisions

Like all good technical books, this one has been about the latest standards and how to use them. Unfortunately, in the real world, we cannot always use the latest technology. And with a case study based on a real project, we will inevitably fall even further behind.

The eBIS-XML schemas I will describe in detail later were started as a result of an e-mail from Microsoft to BASDA in May 1999, so that is the start point of the story. At the time of writing (a week after the anniversary of that initial e-mail), version 3 of the schemas has just been released.

> I appreciate that there are different views on Microsoft's strategy of developing systems based on draft versions of XML standards. Personally, I'm glad that it put software out as part of IE5 so that a large audience could get used to working with the tools. Others think it should have waited for the standards to be finalized. Microsoft is as committed to the standards as other suppliers, and upgrades its software as the standards are released. Similarly, eBIS-XML will update the standards it uses as the tools to use them become available.

619

The good news is that, as this case study illustrates, it's possible to *redevelop* a style sheet in XSLT and the exact syntax used by the schema is no more important than the native file format used by your word processor. As with the word processor, what counts is that the schema syntax supports all the facilities we need.

DTD versus Schema

In the middle of 1999, the choice for defining the eBIS-XML language was between DTDs, a draft version of the W3C Schema Definition Language (XSDL) that contained the warning "*the Working Group anticipates substantial changes*" and Microsoft's XML Data Reduced (XDR) schema language. Let's take ourselves back in time to look at the pros and cons of each of these:

- ❑ The DTD has the advantage that it's a standard (in fact, remembering that we have traveled back to 1999, it is the only one of the three that is). It also has good tool support. Against it, it's not strong on specifying data types, and we know that W3C's XSDL will replace it.

- ❑ The W3C schema language is clearly the way to go in the long term, but we know it will change and it has (at this time) poor tool support.

- ❑ XDR has the advantage that it meets most of the needs of the project (including having a data typing mechanism) and it has a validating parser (Microsoft's MSXML). Against this, it was a *proposal* to the W3C, rather than an output of the W3C. So, while it has many similarities to the current W3C working draft, it is only supported by Microsoft tools. We also know that it will be superseded by the W3C standard when it's released.

Within the XML community, many people have religious arguments about DTDs and schemas. Some will also hate the idea of using a Microsoft proprietary technology. But, as I'll show later, it really makes very little difference which you choose, as long as it does the job. In this case, BASDA went with XDR as tools were readily available to work with it, and it is used by BizTalk, which, as we will see later, is an important part of eBIS-XML.

> For now think of BizTalk as a library of business schemas – by using a suitable schema from this library, businesses can save the effort of developing their own and can be sure they are using the same schema as their customers and suppliers.

Style Sheets and XSL

Here we're back to making choices. Should we use CSS or XSL? If we use XSL, which version (since XSLT was not a full recommendation at the time)?

In Chapter 3, we saw some good examples of how CSS can be used to render XML for display in a browser (or to other media such as print). We also saw the disadvantages. Principally, CSS uses a "push" model – the layout of the rendered page is driven by the order of elements in the XML source document. This is great for a mainly textual document such as a book or company report.

By contrast, XSLT can use either a "push" or a "pull" model, where the layout of the rendered page is driven by the style sheet itself. When dealing with the type of data present in a business document such as a purchase order or invoice, the structure of the document will not generally be driven by display requirements – and in fact different companies might want to display the content in very different formats. In these circumstances, the "pull" model is the one we need.

You might, as an exercise, try to render an eBIS-XML document using CSS (you can download one from http://www.biztalk.org/BizTalk/default.asp). If you do, don't forget that it must display at different screen resolutions, so go easy with your use of absolute positioning!

A second problem with CSS is that it's a client-side technology, and the latest features incorporated in CSS2 are not well supported in current browsers. While Netscape 6 is looking good, IE5, for example, doesn't support creating tables using CSS – something that is very useful when creating the columnar format typical of a purchase order or invoice. And of course, version 4 browsers don't support processing XML on the client at all.

OK, so we need XSL for this. Again, at the time, there was a W3C draft and a Microsoft implementation based on an earlier draft. One key requirement during development was that it should be easy for people to render the documents for display. We weren't concerned if people all had to use a specific browser while developing the systems – the point was that it had to be easy. This mandated the use of the Microsoft version used in IE5. As you saw in the screen shot earlier, Exchequer Enterprise can also create an HTML document to send with the XML document, so we can maintain compatibility with multiple browsers.

Style Sheet Tools

The tools available for style sheet development were not strong in 1999, but have come a long way since. I guess I'm like those developers who still write their C++ code in a text editor rather than an integrated development environment – I started writing XSL before there were tools available, and still find it quicker to use a good text editor. However, recently I have started to try Excelon's **XML Stylus** (http://www.excelon.com), and have found features such as previewing the display as it would appear in IE5, color coding of syntax, auto-completion of element names, and the ability to set breakpoints very useful. Perhaps I will switch soon.

Tools for Developing Schemas

Here again, in May 1999, the tools available for developing schemas were not well developed. BASDA therefore commissioned DecisionSoft (http://www.decisionsoft.com) to produce scripts for their **X-Tract** tool, to create XDR schemas from comma-separated files. BASDA could then use a spreadsheet to define the schemas, and process them to XDR.

Here's an extract from a spreadsheet that was created at the time. It describes the INVOICELINE element of our schema:

Type	Name	Description	Required	Occurs	Type
ELEMENT	INVOICELINE	Invoice line			
ATTRIBUTE	LINETYPE	Invoice line type			string
ATTRIBUTE	LINEACTION	Invoice line action code			string
DATA	LINETYPEDESC	Invoice line type description		ONE	string
DATA	LINEACTIONDESC	Invoice line action description		ONE	string
DATA	LINENO	Invoice line number	M	ONE	int
DATA	LINETOTAL	Extended line value		ONE	float
CHILD	PRODUCT	Product Identification	D	MANY	
CHILD	QUANTITY	Order quantity	D	MANY	
CHILD	PRICE	Product price(s)		MANY	
CHILD	DISCOUNT	Discounts		MANY	
CHILD	LINETAX	Tax details	R	ONE	
CHILD	DATEINFO	Date information		MANY	
CHILD	DIMENSION	Dimensions		MANY	
CHILD	REFERENCE	Line References	D	MANY	
CHILD	DELIVSCHED	Line Delivery Schedule		MANY	
CHILD	NARRATIVE	Line narrative	D	MANY	
CHILD	LOTSERIAL	Lot / Serial number information		MANY	

Here we can see that an INVOICELINE element has two attributes (LINETYPE and LINEACTION). The first defines the type of line (for example, does the line refer to goods and services or freight charges). The second describes an action. This will normally be to add a line, but if the invoice is a modification to a previous invoice, it could be to change or delete a line. The empty cells in the Required column indicate that these are not mandatory, and the Type column shows that they are both text data.

The next four rows indicate a group of child elements that contain only text nodes (this is indicated by the DATA in the first column). These can all occur a maximum of once each, but only the LINENO is mandatory, as indicated by an M in the Required column.

The remaining rows refer to child elements that have child elements of their own. From the chapter on schemas (Chapter 10), you will remember that these have an eltOnly content model. This shows that, for example, the PRICE element contains not just a number, but further structure. This covers areas such as tax details and delivery dates. Note that the Required column contains the characters R and D as well the M for mandatory. These indicate that an element is recommended or that there is a dependency. These can't be coded into a schema, so the information must be treated as a business rule for the human reader.

Earlier, I mentioned that the choice of schema type was not so important – what is the schema in this case? Is it the spreadsheet, which people used to develop their systems, and which contains additional information such as information about dependencies? Or is it the XDR document, which is only used by the system test suite? Of course, systems could use this XDR schema to validate input documents, but this is a big processing overhead. In practice, they rely on a certification program, and assume that certified products are producing valid documents.

> **Basically, schemas need to be understood by systems, and by you and me as developers – and our needs are very different from those of the systems.**

Using the spreadsheet to produce the XDR schema is one solution. Later we'll see the inverse – using a tool to generate the schema, then using a style sheet to display the schema in a human-friendly form.

Version 3

So that was the position in 1999. Towards the end of the year, the schema was released as version 2.4 and lodged with BizTalk. Early in 2000, the BASDA members, that is, the developers of accounting systems such as Exchequer, Scala and TAS that would have to use the schemas, decided to redevelop the schemas in the light of the knowledge they had gained.

On that basis, the BASDA members took the brave decision to go ahead with a new version of the schema. Why brave? Because several of them were close to releasing eBIS-XML compliant upgrades to their systems and so could lose their advantage. On the other hand, these were the most enthusiastic about the change.

While the spreadsheet approach had been a great way to start, its limitations were beginning to show. It was easy to use, and the spreadsheets were very easy to understand, but it had not been designed to implement every feature of the schema language. For example, it was not possible to create elements that contained both attributes and text nodes. Also, while it was possible to create attributes, there was no facility for providing enumerated attribute values or defaults. During discussions with DecisionSoft about adding additional features, it became clear that we really needed the full power of XDR and that there were now standard products that could do the job without custom scripts. On the basis of recommendations such as the review of the product at ASP Today (http://www.asptoday.com/articles/20000301.htm), we evaluated and selected **XML Authority** (http://www.extensibility.com) and have been developing the eBIS-XML schemas with this ever since.

The disadvantage of this approach was that users of the schemas liked their spreadsheet view – it might not have all the power of the underlying schema language, but it was easy to read. So rather than develop a spreadsheet and create a schema, we created a schema and generated a spreadsheet.

> **I believe that, for any XML schema development, the needs of the validating parsers and the needs of the people have to be treated separately. If you develop schemas, you need a good way of documenting them.**

So for a schema of any significant size, tools for developing and viewing schemas are essential. At BASDA, I developed XSL style sheets to show three views of the schemas in a browser, one of which looked rather like the spreadsheet.

The three schema views developed for this project were designed for printed documentation. Since then, I've developed more browser-oriented views, which I'll using here. In fact, by the time this book is published, I hope to have made these available on the Web, so if you want to see different views of your own schemas, have a look at http://www.boynings.co.uk.

623

eBIS-XML Schemas

So now that we've had an overview of what eBIS-XML is all about, it's time to take a closer look at how BASDA went about developing the eBIS-XML schemas.

The first complete version was released in late 1999, and was referred to as version 2.4. In January 2000, we started to design version 3. I will be referring to both here – it is obvious which is which, as version 2.4 used all uppercase characters for both element and attribute names, while version 3 uses what is known as upper camel case, where each word, including the first, starts with an upper case letter. So, for example, the version 2.4 INVOICELINE element became the version 3 InvoiceLine element.

Developing the v2.4 eBIS-XML Schemas

Before describing the detail of the schema, let's look at the general structure. The diagram here displays the basic structure of the Invoice schema using another of the views I generated, this one displaying the structure as a map:

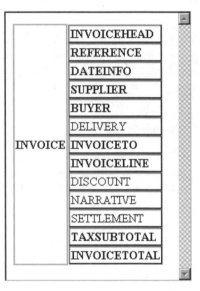

I am showing just the document element and its immediate children. The dark elements are required, the pale ones optional. In later diagrams, we will see that the same is true for attributes, which are prefixed by an @ sign. I can select the element from which to start the display (in this case, the document element INVOICE) and see a map of its children. Clicking on an element will collapse or expand it (using CSS to change the border style to outset when it's collapsed, much as we saw in Chapter 3). Double clicking on an element will open a new window showing more detail:

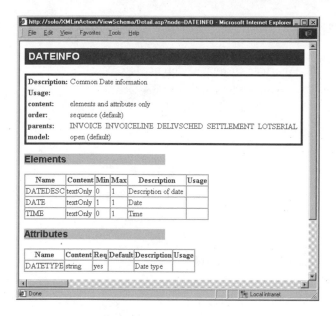

We can see here the basic structure of an invoice. The Order schema is very similar, omitting elements that will not appear in an order, such as those relating to tax, and making optional elements such as PRICE that will always be required in an invoice but can be left out of an order. (After all, when I send you an invoice, the aim is to tell you how much to pay me.)

Most of the elements are self-explanatory. The INVOICEHEAD contains information about the invoice document itself – what we now refer to as *metadata*. For example, this is where we specify the currency in which we are invoicing. The next element, REFERENCE, is our placeholder for any references we need to include. For example, we will put the customer's original order number here, along with any project number that we have been given. The DATEINFO element tells us the date of the invoice, while the SUPPLIER and BUYER elements tell us the major parties involved. Optionally, we might include delivery information, such as a delivery address and the name of the carrier we are using. We then include an invoice address (which, in a large company, might well be different from the buyer's address), before we get to the meat of the document – the INVOICELINE elements that tell us the products and prices. Following this, we have discount information, followed by one or more free text NARRATIVE elements. These can be used, for example, to indicate special offers in which the customer might be interested. Following the SETTLEMENT element, which indicates the terms under which we expect to be paid (and any discounts for early settlement), we include tax information and the total value of the invoice.

We saw earlier that INVOICELINE has a REFERENCE child, and now we see that INVOICE does as well. The REFERENCE element looks like this:

Type	Name	Description	Required	Occurs	Type
ELEMENT	REFERENCE	Common Reference format			
ATTRIBUTE	REFTYPE	Reference type	M		string
DATA	REFDESC	Description of reference	R	ONE	string
DATA	REFCODE	Reference Code	D	ONE	string
DATA	REFCODESC	Reference Code Description		ONE	string
DATA	REFVALUE	Reference Value	D	ONE	string

The type of reference we have is indicated by a code in the REFTYPE attribute, with a textual description in the REFDESC element. The codes are taken from a code list:

ACR	Alternate customer reference
ASR	Alternate supplier's reference
BLO	Associated Blanket Order
COC	Cost Centre
COM	Company
CON	Consignment note / manifest No
CUR	Customer's reference (PO – OurRef : INVOICE – YourRef)
CUT	Customers VAT / TAX Number
DEP	Department
GLR	General Ledger reference
INV	Invoice reference number
OAN	Order amendment number - not supported in this version
ORD	Order reference number
OLN	Order line number
PRR	Project reference
PRA	Project Analysis / Action Code
SUR	Supplier's reference (PO – YourRef : INVOICE – OurRef)
SUT	Supplier's VAT / TAX Number
TRR	Transmission reference number
USR	User definable description

So the INVOICE element might have a reference to an order number, while the INVOICELINE has a reference to an order line number. This keeps the schema small by only including a single REFERENCE element definition, while the code list is used to define the exact meaning of the element.

Since different reference types might be allowed in different contexts, this is a clear indication that a schema might not tell the whole story – in most practical uses of XML schemas, there will be business rules of some kind that cannot be coded into the schema. In this case, we will see soon how we changed things in version 3 to avoid the problem, and the trade-off we had to make. However, I have yet to see a significant XML language (and what we are describing here *is* a significant XML language) that does not require some document other than the schema to describe rules that cannot be coded into the schema. In many cases, the description element of the schema can be used to document these for the human reader, but sometimes a separate document is required.

You can minimize these circumstances by trying to eliminate dependencies between elements and other elements and between elements and attributes, but you might not always be able to do so. Just think of the forms you have completed in the past. How often have you seen a statement such as "if your answer is 'yes' go to question 6, otherwise go to question 7"? In schema terms, whether question 6 is mandatory depends on a previous answer and so cannot be coded into the schema.

626

So checking that an XML document is correct for a specific use involves three levels of checking:

- ❑ Is the document well-formed XML?
- ❑ Does the document match the schema (is it valid)?
- ❑ Does the document meet the business rules?

The XML parser will do the first two for us. So the more business rules we can put in the schema, the less error checking code we have to write ourselves.

Moving On Up – Version 3

Let's look at one or two of the changes in version 3. Being a browser screen shot, rather than a spreadsheet, I couldn't show the column headings. The first two are the same as before, while the others are, in order, Content, Req, Max and Default.

Here's the same element that we saw above, using the version 3 invoice schema:

ELEMENT	InvoiceLine	eltOnly		
ATTRIBUTE	Action	Add | Delete | Change	no	Add
ATTRIBUTE	TypeCode	string	no	
ATTRIBUTE	TypeDescription	string	no	
ATTRIBUTE	TypeCodelist	string	no	
DATA + ATT	LineNumber	int	yes	1
DATA	SuppliersProductCode	string	no	1
DATA	BuyersProductCode	string	no	1
CHILD	InvoiceLineReferences		no	1
CHILD	Product		no	MANY
CHILD	Quantity		no	1
CHILD	Price		yes	MANY
CHILD	PercentDiscount		no	MANY
CHILD	AmountDiscount		no	MANY
CHILD	LineTax		no	1
DATA	LineTotal	float	yes	1
CHILD	Delivery		no	MANY
DATA	InvoiceLineInformation	string	no	MANY
DATA	ExtendedDescription	string	no	MANY
DATA	Narrative	string	no	MANY
CHILD	LotSerial		no	MANY

Again, I've left out comment columns for clarity. The columns are slightly different because of the different structure of the schema. We'll look more at this in a moment.

I mentioned that the original script implemented a subset of XDR. Since the design of the v2.4 schemas didn't allow elements to have both text and attributes, this was not implemented in the script. In v3 we use this ability, so the first column has a new DATA+ATT element type. We've also changed the Type column to Content. As well as describing the data type of textOnly elements, this shows the possible values of enumerated attributes (and the new Default column shows default values where they are defined). The Req column now only shows a yes or no – gone are the concepts of "recommended" and "dependency", which can be put in the description fields as business rules.

At the time version 2.4 was released, the schemas that we have seen were thought to include all the information we needed. However, people were becoming uncomfortable with the coding of the data, partly for reasons such as the inability to specify what references were allowed in what context, but also for other reasons. These are the main weaknesses we saw:

- Interdependencies make validation hard

- Having both codes and descriptions makes documents long

- Similar elements had different definitions

- No use was made of enumerations and default attribute values

- There was no indication of which Order elements to use as references in the Invoice

- We used a proprietary extensibility mechanism (for example the USR code in the code list we saw earlier)

But above all, it was just too hard to understand and use, which was discouraging some major vendors of accounting systems from adopting it.

Then there were some points that seem less important. For example, the upper case element names were not really typical of XML documents. This might not seem important, but when we want eBIS-XML to gain acceptance as a worldwide standard, it is important that our documents should look like other XML documents. The change we made to upper camel case (and avoiding abbreviations in names) had a side benefit I had not foreseen – it is much easier for programmers whose first language is not English to understand names when they can see where the word boundaries are.

Here is a comparison of the top-level structure of the v2.4 (left) and v3 (right) schemas. As you can see, they are very similar, reflecting the fact that we did not want to change the *data*, only the way it is *encoded*:

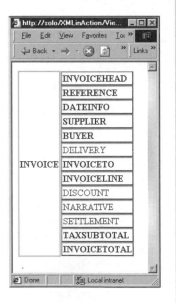
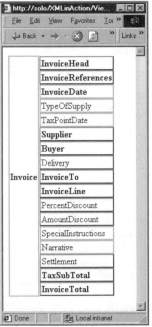

However, if we expand to see the invoice references, we can see the change we have made to improve the ability of the XML parser's validation to check that the correct references are included:

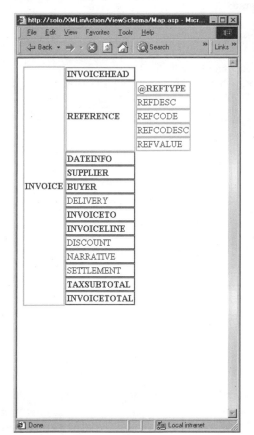

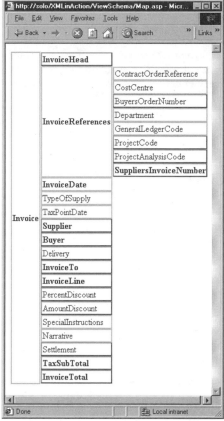

The result of changes like this was that, when I completed the first draft of version 3, we found that documents were just over half as long for the same information, that the schema provided better validation and that it was easier to understand. Look at an example of a purchase order number in version 2.4:

```
<REFERENCE REFTYPE="CUR">
  <REFDESC>Customer's reference</REFDESC>
  <REFCODE>BAS10325</REFCODE>
</REFERENCE>
```

This uses a generic REFERENCE element, with an attribute to describe its meaning. It then has a description of the attribute value (so it's human readable and can be displayed by a style sheet without lookup tables) and the actual purchase order number. So what is wrong with this?

This schema was accompanied by the code list we saw earlier showing the allowed REFTYPE codes. So we had a customer's reference, in this case as a child of the INVOICE element. Clearly, since we must include the customer's original order number in the invoice, the REFERENCE element must be mandatory here. And it must have maxOccurs=* to allow other references such as a project reference. But a reference of type, say, OLN (Order Line Number) would be meaningless here.

629

The use of an attribute to further describe the element type has prevented the parser from checking that the specific reference type is allowed, or even that mandatory types are present. Here's an equivalent extract from a document using the version 3 schema:

```
<BuyersOrderNumber>BAS10325</BuyersOrderNumber>
```

This is clearly a lot simpler, but there is a trade-off. I can now insist that there is a BuyersOrderNumber as a child of Invoice, but I have to list every one of the allowed reference types everywhere they can occur in my schema. The result looks like this:

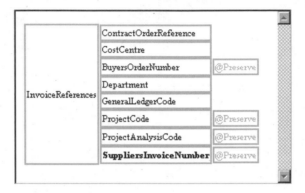

So now we have specific reference types in their correct place, allowing the schema itself to define the correct usage. This change was probably the most fundamental of all those we made in the move from v2.4 to v3.

Using Attributes

However, there are still times when it is appropriate to use an attribute to further define an element. When might this be? Well consider discounts. This is the definition in v2.4:

And here is the code list giving the possible values of the DISCTYPE attribute:

SPD	Special Discount
LID	Line Discount
VOD	Volume Discount
ESD	Early Settlement Discount

LPI	Late payment interest charge
RED	Recipe Discount – dependent on other items
TRD	Trade Discount

These codes don't affect the processing of the discount in the same way that references with different REFTYPES will be treated in different ways. They are just there to add a bit of further explanation. In this case, the code list is retained in version 3. There is one change – the Early Settlement Discount only appears in one place in the invoice, where it is the only discount type allowed. So this is pulled out as a separate element within the Settlement element:

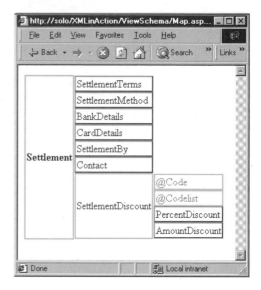

Working with References

At the beginning of our discussion of the v3 schemas, I mentioned the inability of the older schema to indicate which information in an order should be included as a reference in the invoice. We changed this by adding a Preserve attribute in v3. You might have been wondering what the purpose of the FIXED keyword in a DTD was – I certainly used to. Here's an example. We've already seen the example of the customer's order number from the order becoming a reference in the invoice. The Preserve attribute indicates that we have a value that must be carried forward in this way. It's therefore an indication to the systems developer, and will always have the value true. Further information is provided in the description element within the schema. In my web view of the schema outline, I can double click on any element to get detailed information about the element and its attributes and child elements. This includes any information included in description elements.

You will also see a Usage description here. XML Authority 1.2 allows notes of different types and indicates their type with an attribute. I used this attribute in my XSL style sheet to pull out usage notes. However, because the attribute is used without defining its own namespace, the XDR schema produced by XML Authority is, if you use this feature, technically invalid. If you try to open the schema in a validating XML editor, it will report an error. I didn't know of this error when first generating the schemas, and it is not a problem as we strip the comments out of the schemas before using them (they are only there so we can automatically create the documentation). However, I would not recommend the use of the Usage feature of XML Authority until this error is fixed.

The Final Schema

So where are we with the schema? Here is a map of the mandatory elements of an invoice:

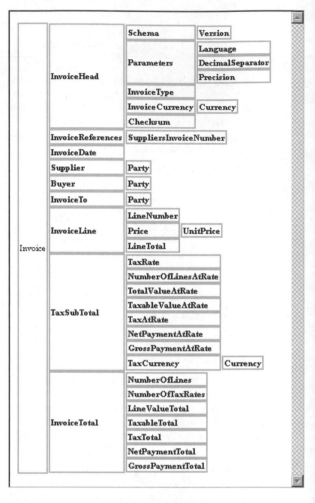

This clearly shows the minimum requirements of an eBIS-XML invoice. By contrast, if I were to print the full schema, including attributes and all optional elements, it would take seven pages. This is the strength of the eBIS-XML concept – the complete schema is a *superset* of requirements, but a systems developer need only include the elements he or she requires.

Furthermore, if any developer finds they need an element that is not included (and the specific requirements of turkey farmers only just made it into this release, so there will be industries and systems that require more), they can use the extensibility mechanism of XML to add further elements for display with their style sheet.

Earlier, I mentioned that dependencies between elements and between elements and attributes handicapped us when defining which elements were mandatory. While the map above looks like the outline of an invoice, the equivalent for v2.4 does not:

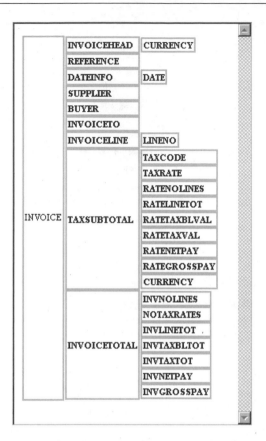

While the SUPPLIER, BUYER and INVOICETO elements are mandatory, they contain no mandatory sub-elements, so we don't even know who we're invoicing, and worse, they won't know who to pay! And look at the INVOICELINE element. All that's mandatory is the LINENO. Everything else has dependencies that stop us making any other elements mandatory. However, if you look back at the InvoiceLine of the v3 schema, even this is not perfect from this point of view. Because we can describe a product either by one of several part numbers or using a text description, we can't make any mandatory. It's back to the business rules to define what's required.

I won't go through the complete schema element by element, but just pick out a few points.

InvoiceHead

The first of these are some elements of InvoiceHead. The complete map of this element (although I've collapsed the tax-related Intrastat element to reduce the size) is:

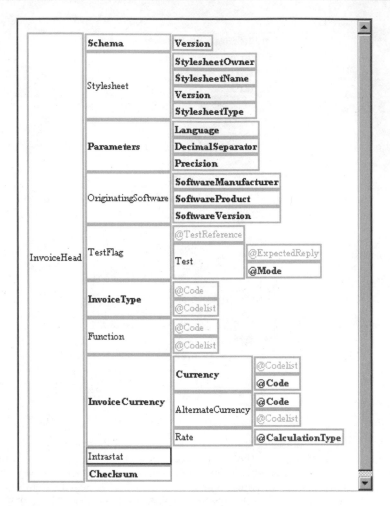

This element gives some basic information about the document, such as the language and decimal separator used. The elements I want to mention here are `OriginatingSoftware` and `TestFlag`. I now include elements like these on all e-commerce related schemas.

The first is useful if the receiving software detects errors in the specific messages or the flow of messages it receives. The information provided allows someone to identify the system sending the message and report the fault. This is especially useful in circumstances where a single entity is receiving messages from multiple sources. For example, in the UK, we can submit our tax information over the Internet using an XML schema. Several suppliers of tax calculation software support this process. If one is consistently giving errors, it is much better for the Inland Revenue (the UK equivalent of the IRS) to contact the supplier directly with suitable information, rather than to contact each citizen individually and expect them to report the fault.

The `TestFlag` element does exactly what it says, plus a bit more. In normal use, the element will either be absent or contain the value 0. If it is present with a non-zero value, this is an instruction to the receiving system that this is a test message. The certification system for eBIS-XML compliant systems will use this so that they can receive messages and know what to do with them.

They will also be told what tests to perform and which of several possible replies to send. The flag also allows bilateral testing between eBIS-compliant systems, something that is used heavily during the development stage.

Address

One element that's always controversial is the `Address`. Some accounting systems break down address information into individual fields such as "Street" and "Zip Code". Others just store each line without assigning any meaning. We decided to support both using the following representation, where the `AddressLine` element supports the free format style:

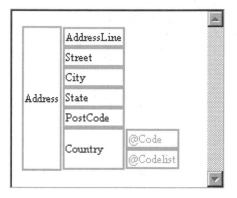

Because we're supporting both styles, we had to make all elements optional. Again, this is a weakness of current schema mechanisms that don't allow inter-element dependencies, such as you must have *either* this element *or* that element.

Summary of Schema Development Tips

So what have we learnt about schemas through this example?

❑   Firstly, you never really saw any schema code except in screen shots. This reflects the fact that, if you use a schema development tool, you will avoid the need to work with the detail of the schema language syntax.

❑   Then next we saw the benefit of avoiding dependencies between elements and between elements and attributes. We saw how steps were taken when developing v3 to reduce these interdependencies within the schema, and so increase the value of the schema.

❑   And finally, we saw that, however hard we try, the schema is unlikely to be a full description of an XML language. We used the case of a simple questionnaire to illustrate how there might even be dependencies between the data entered and the validity constraints in the XML.

A Reprise on the Tools Used

You never really saw any schema code except in screen shots exactly because of the point I made that schemas have two audiences – human and machine. Assuming you're all human, I've therefore used human-friendly forms of describing the eBIS-XML language – tables, maps and textual descriptions.

And this brings me back to my point that the exact syntax is not so important. We have used a combination of tools to produce and view the schemas – XML Authority for production and style sheets for viewing.

Let's look at a small sample from the invoice schema shown in different ways:

- ❑ A map
- ❑ A detailed description
- ❑ A DTD
- ❑ An XDR schema
- ❑ A schema meeting the W3C April 2000 schema draft

As a Map

We'll look at the `Quantity` element, which is a child of the `InvoiceLine`. Firstly, the map shows the general structure very succinctly:

We can see here that the element has three attributes. We can see their names (`UOMCode`, `UOMDescription` and `UOMCodelist`) and that they are optional (they are in faint text), but that is all.

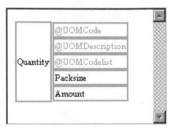

We can also see two optional elements (`PackSize` and `Amount`) and that (since the border is faint gray, rather than "Outset" style you can see in earlier screenshots, which darkens the right and bottom edges), they do not have any attributes or child elements.

A Detailed View

If we double click on the `Quantity` element, we can see all the information in the schema for the `Quantity` element and some information about its children:

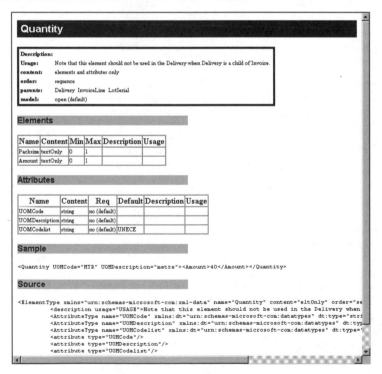

In this case, there is no description (which would be contained in a `description` element with no `usage` attribute in the schema), but there is a usage description. Remember the warning I gave earlier about the use of this feature of XML Authority – the `usage` attribute technically makes the schema itself invalid since it is not declared in the DTD that describes the XDR language.

Below this, we show the type of content allowed within this element, and the order constraints for the children. These reflect the `content` and `order` attributes of the `ElementType` element of the schema, as we will see in a moment.

Finally, we show whether the element uses an open or closed model. Here, the text **open (default)** indicates that the model is open because the attribute was not included and so the default value has been used.

After this, we see the child elements using the spreadsheet-like view we saw earlier. This now gives us more detail than we had in the map view, for example, indicating that, not only are the elements optional, but there can be a maximum of one instance of each.

We show similar information for the attributes, including that the code list used is a United Nations one unless a different one is specified.

Then we show two pieces of XML. The first is taken from a sample document that uses the schema. The style sheet simply extracts the first instance of the element type from the document. Using XSLT, this could be using the `xsl:document` element, but since I did not have full XSLT support available (this style sheet has to run the release version of IE5), I use a little piece of JavaScript to "glue" the sample document to the end of the schema. Of course, I need a single document element in the resulting XML, so I put the resulting XML within a new element.

The final piece of XML shows the actual schema source. In this case, it is in XDR, and so is slightly different from the syntax you have been learning. In a moment, I will show both versions so you can easily see the differences.

As a DTD

This is the same information expressed as a DTD, which describes the element in a traditional way:

```
<!ELEMENT Quantity  (Packsize? , Amount? )>
<!ATTLIST Quantity  UOMCode        CDATA  #IMPLIED
                    UOMDescription CDATA  #IMPLIED
                    UOMCodelist    CDATA  'UNECE' >

<!ELEMENT Packsize  (#PCDATA )>

<!ELEMENT Amount    (#PCDATA )>
<!ATTLIST Amount    e-dtype NMTOKEN  #FIXED 'float' >
```

As XDR and XSD Schemas

The XDR schema is what we actually used on the project:

```
<?xml version ="1.0"?>
<!--Generated by XML Authority. Conforms to XML Data subset for IE 5-->
<Schema name="quantity.xdr"
    xmlns="urn:schemas-microsoft-com:xml-data"
```

```
    xmlns:dt="urn:schemas-microsoft-com:datatypes">
  <ElementType name="Quantity" content="eltOnly" order="seq">
   <AttributeType name="UOMCode" dt:type="string"/>
   <AttributeType name="UOMDescription" dt:type="string"/>
   <AttributeType name="UOMCodelist" dt:type="string" default="UNECE"/>
   <attribute type="UOMCode"/>
   <attribute type="UOMDescription"/>
   <attribute type="UOMCodelist"/>
   <element type="Packsize" minOccurs="0" maxOccurs="1"/>
   <element type="Amount" minOccurs="0" maxOccurs="1"/>
  </ElementType>

  <ElementType name="Packsize" content="textOnly"/>
  <ElementType name="Amount" content="textOnly" dt:type="float"/>
</Schema>
```

and the XSD schema is what you have been learning in this book:

```
<?xml version ="1.0"?>
<!--Generated by XMLAuthority. Conforms to w3c http://www.w3.org/1999/XMLSchema-->
<schema xmlns="http://www.w3.org/1999/XMLSchema">
  <element name="Quantity">
    <complexType content="elementOnly">
      <sequence>
        <element ref="Packsize" minOccurs="0" maxOccurs="1"/>
        <element ref="Amount" minOccurs="0" maxOccurs="1"/>
      </sequence>
      <attribute name="UOMCode" type="string"/>
      <attribute name="UOMDescription" type="string"/>
      <attribute name="UOMCodelist" use="default" value="UNECE"
      type="string"/>
    </complexType>
  </element>

  <element name="Packsize" type="string"/>
  <element name="Amount" type="float"/>
</schema>
```

XML Authority

And how did I create all these so easily (believe me, it was easy)? The answer is in lines like:

```
<!--Generated by XML Authority. Conforms to XML Data subset for IE 5-->
```

Tools like XML Authority allow you to create a schema easily, and export it to different formats:

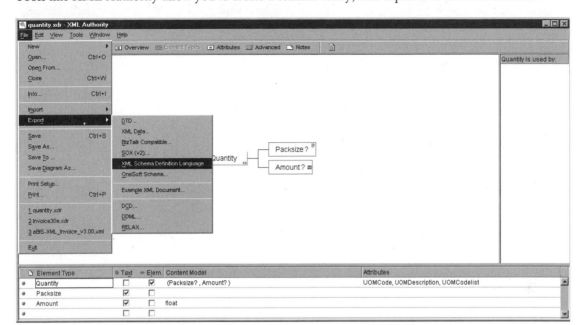

The diagram shows the file being saved as a W3C XSD schema, as well as the other options available. It also shows the main schema design screen, with a simple map of the elements and descriptions underneath. It is these descriptions that we edit to produce the schemas. A different screen allows us to set the parameters for attributes, such as their data types, whether they are required, and enumerated values.

That's all I have to say about the eBIS-XML schemas. Let's have a look at how style sheets allow us to exchange documents when the communicating systems implement different subsets of the standard.

eBIS-XML Style Sheets

We saw earlier that one way eBIS-XML copes with multiple diverse systems that are not 100% compatible with each other is through XSLT style sheets. It is the combination of flexible interoperability and style sheets that is central to the eBIS-XML concept. To understand how these style sheets work, let's examine the way eBIS-XML deals with invoices.

A Simple Invoice

Here's a simple invoice containing pretty much the minimum information required for a commercial transaction. I have provided some notes as we go through the document. The first line after the XML declaration is the document element `Invoice`. This sets a default namespace for the complete document.

```
<?xml version="1.0"?>
<Invoice xmlns="urn:www.basda.org/schema/eBIS-XML_invoice_v3.00.xml">
```

We then have the `InvoiceHead` element, which, as we saw earlier, contains data about the invoice such as the associated style sheet and the decimal separator (dot or comma) used within the document body. This is the *metadata* for the document – it does not tell us about the transaction being invoiced, but about the structure and coding of the document.

```
<InvoiceHead>
  <Schema>
    <Version>3.00</Version>
  </Schema>
  <Stylesheet>
    <StylesheetOwner>BASDA</StylesheetOwner>
    <StylesheetName>eBIS-XML3_simple.xsl</StylesheetName>
    <Version>3.00</Version>
    <StylesheetType>xsl</StylesheetType>
  </Stylesheet>
  <Parameters>
    <Language>en_GB</Language>
    <DecimalSeparator>.</DecimalSeparator>
    <Precision>20.3</Precision>
  </Parameters>
  <InvoiceType>Commercial Invoice</InvoiceType>
  <InvoiceCurrency>
    <Currency Code="GBP">Pounds Sterling</Currency>
  </InvoiceCurrency>
  <Checksum>61491</Checksum>
</InvoiceHead>
```

Following this, we have two references. The first is the order number to which the invoice refers, and the second is the invoice number itself. This is followed by the invoice date:

```
<InvoiceReferences>
  <BuyersOrderNumber>PO1001</BuyersOrderNumber>
  <SuppliersInvoiceNumber>INV3625</SuppliersInvoiceNumber>
</InvoiceReferences>
<InvoiceDate>2000-04-18</InvoiceDate>
```

We follow this with the `Supplier` details, in this case, just a name and address. We have seen that we could also include references here, but this is a simple invoice, so does not include such information.

```
<Supplier>
  <Party>A Supplier Ltd</Party>
  <Address>
    <Street>1 Some Street</Street>
    <City>Anytown</City>
    <State>Berks</State>
    <PostCode>RG1 1XX</PostCode>
  </Address>
</Supplier>
```

The structure of the `Buyer` information and the description of where to send the invoice are similar in structure:

```
<Buyer>
   <Party>BASDA Ltd</Party>
   <Address>
      <Street>530 The Linen Hall</Street>
      <Street>162-168 Regent Street</Street>
      <City>London</City>
      <PostCode>W1R 5TB</PostCode>
   </Address>
</Buyer>
<InvoiceTo>
   <Party>BASDA Ltd</Party>
   <Address>
      <Street>530 The Linen Hall</Street>
      <Street>162-168 Regent Street</Street>
      <City>London</City>
      <PostCode>W1R 5TB</PostCode>
   </Address>
</InvoiceTo>
```

We then have the `InvoiceLine` itself:

```
<InvoiceLine>
   <LineNumber>1</LineNumber>
   <InvoiceLineReferences>
      <OrderLineNumber>1</OrderLineNumber>
   </InvoiceLineReferences>
   <Product>
      <Description>Bicycles</Description>
   </Product>
   <Quantity>
      <Amount>3</Amount>
   </Quantity>
   <Price>
      <UnitPrice>129.99</UnitPrice>
   </Price>
   <LineTax>
      <TaxRate Code="S">17.5</TaxRate>
      <TaxValue>68.24</TaxValue>
   </LineTax>
   <LineTotal>389.97</LineTotal>
</InvoiceLine>
```

This starts with a line number and refers to the line number of the original order to which it refers. Some accounting systems use this information to reconcile invoices against orders, and so this line number is a required element. For the product, we are just providing a description, which we follow with a quantity and a unit price. These both have more structure than might seem necessary, but that is because quantity and price information might be more complex. For example, as a supermarket, I might order 1000 chickens, but my supplier might invoice me by total weight. This additional structure allows for such scenarios. I then have the tax charged for this line and the total pre-tax value of the goods.

No, the `TaxRate` value is not a typo – we really do charge that rate in the UK (and other parts of Europe charge even more)!

```
<TaxSubTotal>
  <TaxRate Code="S">17.5</TaxRate>
  <NumberOfLinesAtRate>1</NumberOfLinesAtRate>
  <TotalValueAtRate>389.97</TotalValueAtRate>
  <TaxableValueAtRate>389.97</TaxableValueAtRate>
  <TaxAtRate>68.24</TaxAtRate>
  <NetPaymentAtRate>458.21</NetPaymentAtRate>
  <GrossPaymentAtRate>458.21</GrossPaymentAtRate>
  <TaxCurrency>
    <Currency Code="GBP">Pounds Sterling</Currency>
  </TaxCurrency>
</TaxSubTotal>
```

The `TaxSubTotal` element provides a summary of the tax for the complete invoice. This element is repeated for each tax rate used within the invoice. This is followed by the `InvoiceTotal`, which provides a summary of the complete document:

```
<InvoiceTotal>
  <NumberOfLines>1</NumberOfLines>
  <NumberOfTaxRates>1</NumberOfTaxRates>
  <LineValueTotal>389.97</LineValueTotal>
  <TaxTotal>68.24</TaxTotal>
  <NetPaymentTotal>458.21</NetPaymentTotal>
  <GrossPaymentTotal>458.21</GrossPaymentTotal>
</InvoiceTotal>
</Invoice>
```

Shown in another tool from Extensibility, this time a preview copy of their **XML Instance Editor** (http://www.extensibility.com), we can see the top level elements used in the message:

Comparing this to the schema map we saw earlier, we can see that this contains only the mandatory elements. This follows right through the document, which contains hardly more than the minimum information to buy three bicycles. (Although it is the norm in the UK for companies to provide senior staff with cars, these are pretty well useless in London where, as long as you don't get killed by a delivery driver on the way, a bicycle is a much faster way to travel.)

When we look at this in IE5 (using the XSLT-compliant March 2000 developer preview of MSXML), we see it as a paper document. I have marked up the screen shot to indicate which elements of the message generate which parts of the image:

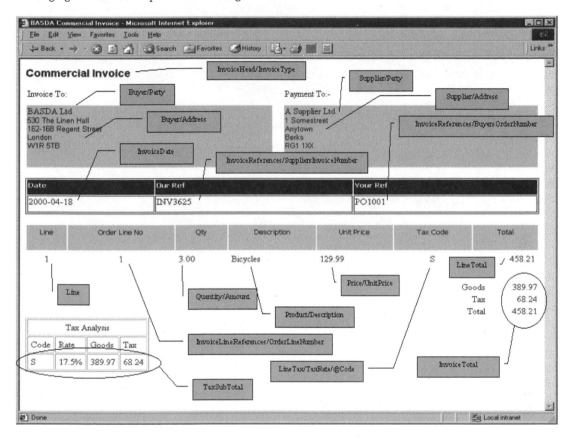

Push and Pull Models

Earlier, I introduced the idea of "push" and "pull" models for rendering documents. In the "push" model, as used by CSS, the structure of the output is controlled by the structure of the document. This is great for intrinsically linear documents, such as a company annual report (or even a book about XML) but, as we saw, is less than suitable for documents such as our invoice. Here, we want the style sheet to control the layout of the resulting image, which is why we'll use a "pull" model.

In practice, though, we actually use a bit of a hybrid. Although the basic layout is controlled by the style sheet, the lines of the address, for example, are displayed in the order they appear in the document – i.e. using a "push" model.

So how does the structure of the style sheet determine the model we're using? Typically, for a "push" model, we'll have lots of small templates, each indicating how to display that particular element. The template for the document root might just perform an `xsl:apply-templates` on all its children, and so the document will be rendered in the order of the elements in the source XML.

643

With a "pull" model, there'll usually be one large template creating the HTML framework, and pulling in data from the XML source as and when it is required. In our style sheet, this is a very large template, but the structure of it is simple:

```
<xsl:template match="Invoice">

<!-- process the heading -->
<!-- create a table for the invoice addresses and process them -->
<!-- create a table for the invoice dates, references etc and process them -->
<!-- create a table for the invoice lines and process them -->
<!-- create a table for the invoice totals and process them -->
<!-- create a table for the tax table and add the tax information -->
<!-- add any narrative text -->

</xsl:template><!-- "Invoice" -->
```

We'll look at some of these areas in more detail later.

More About the Invoice Style Sheet

When we look at the displayed invoice, there's no space for the optional delivery address. And the individual invoice lines only show a small amount of information – the line number, quantity, description, unit price, tax code and total.

This is a summary of the `InvoiceLine` element and the full description of the product:

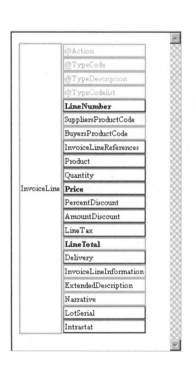
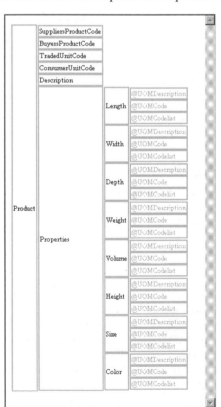

Allowing space for all that information would mean the document would never fit on either a screen or a printed page (although this could be a good opportunity to buy stock in the manufacturers of large-format printers).

So does each document need a different style sheet? That would never work. The answer is to make the style sheet **dynamic**.

The XML for our Invoice Data

Since this is a case study about Arthur Discspinner, what would an invoice to him look like? Here is an invoice for five copies of each of three CDs. Where the structure is much as the bicycle invoice, I will not comment on it – just use it to refer back to see the code that has generated parts of the browser display that follows:

```
<?xml version ="1.0"?>
<Invoice>
  <InvoiceHead>
    <Schema>
      <Version>3.00</Version>
    </Schema>
    <Stylesheet>
      <StylesheetOwner>BASDA</StylesheetOwner>
      <StylesheetName>eBIS-XML3_simple.xsl</StylesheetName>
      <Version>3.00</Version>
      <StylesheetType>xsl</StylesheetType>
    </Stylesheet>
    <Parameters>
      <Language>en_GB</Language>
      <DecimalSeparator>.</DecimalSeparator>
      <Precision>20.3</Precision>
    </Parameters>
    <InvoiceType>Commercial Invoice</InvoiceType>
    <InvoiceCurrency>
      <Currency Code = "GBP">Pounds Sterling</Currency>
    </InvoiceCurrency>
    <Checksum>85237</Checksum>
  </InvoiceHead>
```

Note that we now have far more references. For example, the original order contained a general ledger code, so this has been included in the invoice.

```
  <InvoiceReferences>
    <CostCentre>364</CostCentre>
    <BuyersOrderNumber>ADPO1254</BuyersOrderNumber>
    <Department>CEO</Department>
    <GeneralLedgerCode>123-456</GeneralLedgerCode>
    <SuppliersInvoiceNumber>DDINV1341</SuppliersInvoiceNumber>
  </InvoiceReferences>
  <InvoiceDate>2000-05-11</InvoiceDate>
  <Supplier>
    <SupplierReferences>
      <BuyersCodeForSupplier>DODGYDI</BuyersCodeForSupplier>
      <TaxNumber>123 4567 89</TaxNumber>
    </SupplierReferences>
```

```
      <Party>Dodgy Discs</Party>
      <Address>
        <Street>1 The Cut</Street>
        <City>Reading</City>
        <State>Berks</State>
        <PostCode>RG1 IXX</PostCode>
        <Country Code = "GBR">Great Britain</Country>
      </Address>
```

As well as the address, Dodgy Discs has included contact information:

```
      <Contact>
        <Department>Sales</Department>
        <DDI>0118 912 3456</DDI>
        <Email>dick@dodgydiscs.com</Email>
        <Mobile>07957 123456</Mobile>
      </Contact>
    </Supplier>
    <Buyer>
      <BuyerReferences>
        <SuppliersCodeForBuyer>DISCSPIN</SuppliersCodeForBuyer>
      </BuyerReferences>
      <Party>Arthur Discspinner</Party>
      <Address>
        <Street>12 Altwood Avenue</Street>
        <City>Maidenhead</City>
        <State>Berks</State>
        <PostCode>SL6 4ZZ</PostCode>
      </Address>
      <Contact>
        <DDI>01628 654321</DDI>
        <Name>Arthur Discspinner</Name>
        <Fax>01628 654322</Fax>
        <Email>arthur@discspinner.co.uk</Email>
      </Contact>
    </Buyer>
```

Dodgy Disks has also included delivery information, which it will have taken from the original order. In many cases, this will be different from the `Buyer` address as a purchasing department might be on a different site from the department that will actually use the goods.

```
      <Delivery>
        <DeliverTo>
          <Party>Arthur Discspinner</Party>
          <Address>
            <Street>12 Altwood Avenue</Street>
            <City>Maidenhead</City>
            <State>Berks</State>
            <PostCode>SL6 4ZZ</PostCode>
          </Address>
          <Contact>
            <Name>Arthur Discspinner</Name>
            <DDI>01628 654321</DDI>
          </Contact>
```

```
      </DeliverTo>
    </Delivery>
    <InvoiceTo>
      <Party>Arthur Discspinner</Party>
      <Address>
        <Street>12 Altwood Avenue</Street>
        <City>Maidenhead</City>
        <State>Berks</State>
        <PostCode>SL6 4ZZ</PostCode>
      </Address>
    </InvoiceTo>
```

Now we start on the `InvoiceLine` elements. In this case, we have three. These lines refer to a `ConsumerUnitCode` element. In effect, this is the bar code on the CD case. In many cases, companies will order using a `TradedUnitCode`. While the `ConsumerUnitCode` refers to the items you and I might buy in the shop (in this case, a single CD), the `TradedUnitCode` refers to a commercial purchase, which might be for a box of 100 CDs, or a pallet of boxes of breakfast cereal.

```
    <InvoiceLine Action = "Add" TypeCode = "GDS" TypeDescription =
    "Goods and Services">
      <LineNumber>1</LineNumber>
      <InvoiceLineReferences>
        <OrderLineNumber>1</OrderLineNumber>
      </InvoiceLineReferences>
      <Product>
        <ConsumerUnitCode>9362-45024-2</ConsumerUnitCode>
        <Description>Eric Clapton Unplugged (Eric Clapton)</Description>
      </Product>
      <Quantity>
        <Amount>5</Amount>
      </Quantity>
      <Price>
        <UnitPrice>7.99</UnitPrice>
      </Price>
      <LineTax>
        <TaxRate Code = "S">17.5</TaxRate>
        <TaxValue>6.99</TaxValue>
      </LineTax>
      <LineTotal>39.95</LineTotal>
    </InvoiceLine>
    <InvoiceLine Action = "Add" TypeCode = "GDS" TypeDescription =
    "Goods and Services">
      <LineNumber>1</LineNumber>
      <InvoiceLineReferences>
        <OrderLineNumber>1</OrderLineNumber>
      </InvoiceLineReferences>
      <Product>
        <ConsumerUnitCode>7777-91843-23</ConsumerUnitCode>
        <Description>Hunky Dory (David Bowie)</Description>
      </Product>
      <Quantity>
        <Amount>5</Amount>
      </Quantity>
```

```
    <Price>
      <UnitPrice>7.99</UnitPrice>
    </Price>
    <LineTax>
      <TaxRate Code = "S">17.5</TaxRate>
      <TaxValue>6.99</TaxValue>
    </LineTax>
    <LineTotal>39.95</LineTotal>
</InvoiceLine>
<InvoiceLine Action = "Add" TypeCode = "GDS" TypeDescription =
"Goods and Services">
    <LineNumber>1</LineNumber>
    <InvoiceLineReferences>
      <OrderLineNumber>1</OrderLineNumber>
    </InvoiceLineReferences>
    <Product>
      <ConsumerUnitCode>7599-27439-2</ConsumerUnitCode>
      <Description>Alice's Restaurant (Arlo Guthrie)</Description>
    </Product>
    <Quantity>
      <Amount>5</Amount>
    </Quantity>
    <Price>
      <UnitPrice>7.99</UnitPrice>
    </Price>
    <LineTax>
      <TaxRate Code = "S">17.5</TaxRate>
      <TaxValue>6.99</TaxValue>
    </LineTax>
    <LineTotal>39.95</LineTotal>
</InvoiceLine>
<Narrative>If you spend over £1000 with us this month, we will give
you a free weekend at Disneyland Paris</Narrative>
<Settlement>
    <SettlementTerms Code = "30I">30 days from invoice</SettlementTerms>
</Settlement>
<TaxSubTotal>
    <TaxRate Code = "S">17.5</TaxRate>
    <NumberOfLinesAtRate>3</NumberOfLinesAtRate>
    <TotalValueAtRate>119.85</TotalValueAtRate>
    <TaxableValueAtRate>119.85</TaxableValueAtRate>
    <TaxAtRate>20.97</TaxAtRate>
    <NetPaymentAtRate>140.82</NetPaymentAtRate>
    <GrossPaymentAtRate>140.82</GrossPaymentAtRate>
    <TaxCurrency>
      <Currency Code = "GBP">Pounds Sterling</Currency>
    </TaxCurrency>
</TaxSubTotal>
<InvoiceTotal>
    <NumberOfLines>3</NumberOfLines>
    <NumberOfTaxRates>1</NumberOfTaxRates>
    <LineValueTotal>119.85</LineValueTotal>
    <TaxableTotal>119.85</TaxableTotal>
    <TaxTotal>20.97</TaxTotal>
```

```
      <NetPaymentTotal>140.82</NetPaymentTotal>
      <GrossPaymentTotal>140.82</GrossPaymentTotal>
    </InvoiceTotal>
  </Invoice>
```

This is rather longer than before, not only because it contains three `InvoiceLine` elements, but because it contains additional information such as a delivery address. Here it is displayed in a browser:

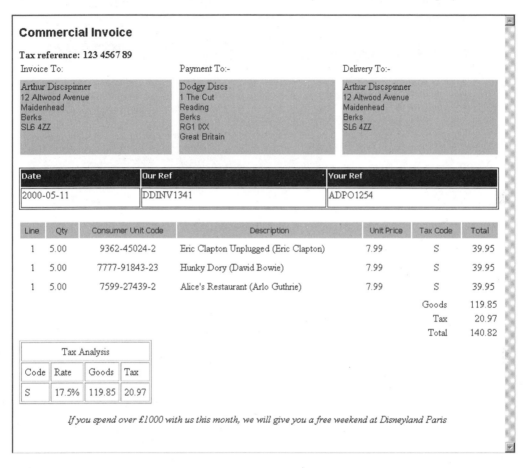

Not only has the data changed, but also the layout of the invoice: we've added the "Delivery To" address and a Consumer Unit Code field to the invoice lines themselves.

We can take this further with another example:

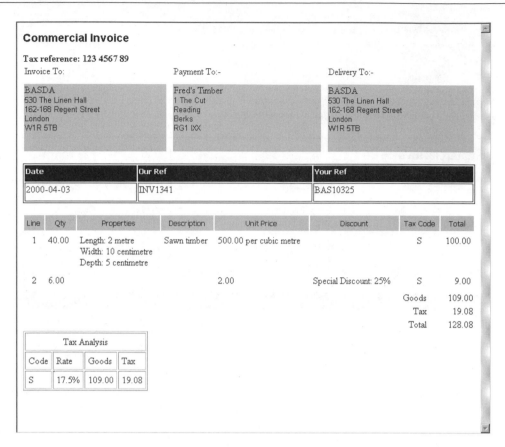

Commercial Invoice

Tax reference: 123 4567 89

Invoice To:	Payment To:-	Delivery To:-
BASDA 530 The Linen Hall 162-168 Regent Street London W1R 5TB	Fred's Timber 1 The Cut Reading Berks RG1 IXX	BASDA 530 The Linen Hall 162-168 Regent Street London W1R 5TB

Date	Our Ref	Your Ref
2000-04-03	INV1341	BAS10325

Line	Qty	Properties	Description	Unit Price	Discount	Tax Code	Total
1	40.00	Length: 2 metre Width: 10 centimetre Depth: 5 centimetre	Sawn timber	500.00 per cubic metre		S	100.00
2	6.00			2.00	Special Discount: 25%	S	9.00
						Goods	109.00
						Tax	19.08
						Total	128.08

Tax Analysis			
Code	Rate	Goods	Tax
S	17.5%	109.00	19.08

We now have a **Properties** field showing the size of the timber, the **Unit Price** is indicating the quantity in which it's measured and the second item has had a **Discount** applied. This illustrates the point I made earlier about needing structure in the `Quantity` and `Price` elements. Here they are for this example:

```
<Quantity UOMCode="MTR" UOMDescription="metre">
  <Packsize>10</Packsize>
  <Amount>40</Amount>
</Quantity>
<Price UOMCode="MTQ" UOMDescription="cubic metre">
  <Units>0.4</Units>
  <UnitPrice>500.00</UnitPrice>
</Price>
```

We can see that we now have information in the `Quantity` such as the size of the pack and the units in which we are measuring the wood. The `Price` then shows that we are charging for 0.4 cubic metres of timber.

So, the final document that we display in our browser is different depending on what data is present in our XML documents.

The Dynamic Style Sheet

All we have to do to achieve this flexibility is test whether *any* of the InvoiceLine elements has a specific descendant. If it has, we can then include a column in the invoice lines area of the document for the field. Since the invoice lines are in a table, this is easy to do, although the test needs to be done twice – once for the heading and once for each row of the table body. With so many elements, it gets a little messy, but at least it can be done. So perhaps it's time to sell that stock in the printer manufacturer that you bought a few pages back.

We can use a similar logic to decide whether we need to display a **Delivery To**: address. We check if the Delivery element has a child named DeliverTo, and if it does, we create a new column in the table that contains the addresses and output the data it contains. Since this is a simpler example than the InvoiceLine, I will describe it first. This is the complete code:

```
<table border="0" width="100%">
  <tr>
    <td width="32%" height="23" valign="top">Invoice To:</td>
    <td width="1%" height="150" valign="top" rowspan="2"></td>
    <td width="33%" height="23" valign="top">Payment To:-</td>
    <xsl:if test="Delivery/DeliverTo">
      <td width="1%" height="150" valign="top" rowspan="2"></td>
      <td width="33%" height="23" valign="top">Delivery To:-</td>
    </xsl:if>
  </tr>
  <tr>
    <td valign="top" bgcolor="#C0C0C0">
      <xsl:value-of select="Buyer/Party"/>
      <xsl:apply-templates select="Buyer/Address"/>
    </td>
    <td valign="top" bgcolor="#C0C0C0">
      <xsl:value-of select="Supplier/Party"/>
      <xsl:apply-templates select="Supplier/Address"/>
    </td>
    <xsl:if test="Delivery/DeliverTo">
      <td valign="top" bgcolor="#C0C0C0">
        <xsl:value-of select="Delivery/DeliverTo/Party"/>
        <xsl:apply-templates select="Delivery/DeliverTo/Address"/>
      </td>
    </xsl:if>
  </tr>
</table>
```

Here we use two xsl:if statements: one to create the table column and put in the heading, and the other to call a template to put in the address. These lines create the table column:

```
<xsl:if test="Delivery/DeliverTo">
  <td width="1%" height="150" valign="top" rowspan="2"></td>
  <td width="33%" height="23" valign="top">Delivery To:-</td>
</xsl:if>
```

The first of the td elements just provides some separation between this and the previous address information. The second creates a cell with the text **Delivery To:-**. Both are created only if there is a Delivery/DeliverTo element in the document.

651

We can then populate the address information, using the same test to create the table cell only if required:

```
<xsl:if test="Delivery/DeliverTo">
  <td valign="top" bgcolor="#C0C0C0">
    <xsl:value-of select="Delivery/DeliverTo/Party"/>
    <xsl:apply-templates select="Delivery/DeliverTo/Address"/>
  </td>
</xsl:if>
```

My simple style sheet was designed only to handle the examples here, so it doesn't contain every element of the InvoiceLine. However, this is the code that creates the table:

```
<table border="0" width="100%" height="108" cellpadding="5">
  <tr bgcolor="#C0C0C0" style="font-size:10pt;font-family:Tahoma">
    <td align="center">Line</td>
    <xsl:if test="//InvoiceLine/InvoiceLineReferences/ProjectCode">
      <td align="center">Project Code</td>
    </xsl:if>
    <xsl:if test="//InvoiceLine/InvoiceLineReferences/ProjectAnalysisCode">
      <td align="center">Project Analysis Code</td>
    </xsl:if>
    <xsl:if test="//InvoiceLine/InvoiceLineReferences/BuyersOrderNumber">
      <td align="center">Order No</td>
    </xsl:if>
    <xsl:if test="//InvoiceLine/InvoiceLineReferences/OrderLineNumber">
      <td align="center">Order Line No</td>
    </xsl:if>
    <xsl:if
    test="//InvoiceLine/InvoiceLineReferences/BuyersOrderLineReference">
      <td align="center">Order Line Ref</td>
    </xsl:if>
    <td align="center">Qty</td>
    <xsl:if test="//InvoiceLine/Product/Properties">
      <td align="center">Properties</td>
    </xsl:if>
    <xsl:if test="//InvoiceLine/Product/SuppliersProductCode">
      <td align="center">Our Product Ref</td>
    </xsl:if>
    <xsl:if test="//InvoiceLine/Product/BuyersProductCode">
      <td align="center">Your Product Ref</td>
    </xsl:if>
    <xsl:if test="//InvoiceLine/Product/TradedUnitCode">
      <td align="center">Traded Unit Code</td>
    </xsl:if>
    <xsl:if test="//InvoiceLine/Product/ConsumerUnitCode">
      <td align="center">Consumer Unit Code</td>
    </xsl:if>
    <td align="center">Description</td>
    <td align="center">Unit Price</td>
    <xsl:if test="//InvoiceLine[PercentDiscount | AmountDiscount]">
      <td align="center">Discount</td>
    </xsl:if>
```

```
      <xsl:if test="//InvoiceLine/LineTax">
        <td align="center">Tax Code</td>
      </xsl:if>
      <td align="center">Total</td>
    </tr>

    <xsl:apply-templates select="InvoiceLine"/>

  </table>
```

Table columns that will always be needed, such as `Qty`, are included every time. Others use an `xsl:if` to create them. For example, in the line:

```
      <xsl:if test="//InvoiceLine/Product/BuyersProductCode">
```

the test will return `true` if there is any occurrence in the document of a `BuyersProductCode` element in the correct context. The following line:

```
      <td align="center">Your Product Ref</td>
```

then creates and populates the table cell.

The template for `InvoiceLine`, called at the end of this section of code, does much the same for the body of the table, so we'll only look at one of the more complex parts – the one that showed the dimensions of the wood in the previous invoice:

```
      <xsl:if test="//InvoiceLine/Product/Properties">
        <td align="left">
          <xsl:for-each select="Product/Properties/*">
            <div>
              <xsl:value-of select="name(.)"/>: <xsl:value-of select="."/>
               <xsl:value-of select="@UOMDescription"/>
            </div>
          </xsl:for-each>
        </td>
      </xsl:if>
```

Here, we use an `xsl:for-each` element to process each property, whatever its name. We then create an HTML `div` (which as you will remember from Chapter 3 contains an intrinsic `display:block` style) to ensure that each appears on a separate line. Inside this, we put the name of the property followed by a colon, a space, the value of the text node, another space, and the description of the units of measure. I have two comments to make on this.

Firstly, I'm normally opposed to displaying the name of an element using a style sheet. For one thing, it's an unnecessary restriction on the element name. It can also cause problems once you try to make a style sheet multi-lingual. Although the element name stays the same, the display has to change. The alternatives are to code the display text into the element (using the `xml:lang` attribute to allow multiple languages in one document), or to create a lookup table in the style sheet using an `xsl:choose` element. However, in this case, I was just developing a basic style sheet from which BASDA members could develop more sophisticated solutions, so the simple solution was adequate.

Secondly, we have two different ways of displaying a space – the first time I've just used a space character, the second time I've used the   character reference, which is equivalent to an HTML . Why is this?

Think back to the discussion of white space in Chapter 5. In the first instance, the XSL processor knows that there is a text node because of the colon. It will therefore preserve white space. In the second case, there is no text between the end-tag of one xsl:value-of and the start-tag of the next. Any white space is therefore ignored. The character reference is one way of enforcing a space. Using xsl:text would be another:

```
<xsl:text> </xsl:text>
```

There is a third: we could put a small DTD at the start of our XSL file to define our own nbsp character entity:

```
<!DOCTYPE xsl:stylesheet [
        <!ENTITY nbsp " ">
]>
```

This would make our style sheet more familiar to HTML programmers. "You pays your money and you takes your choice." It's entirely up to you which you use in *your* applications.

Doing it the Easy Way?

I mentioned earlier that I didn't use an XSL development tool, but I would show one later. Here's a screenshot from Excelon Stylus:

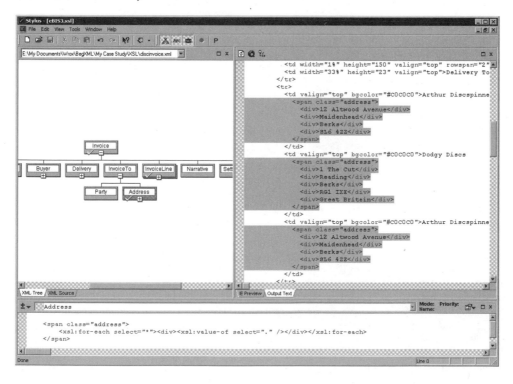

On the left, we can see the structure of the document. Elements with a tick against them have templates in the style sheet.

On the right, we can see the generated HTML. Alternatively, we could look at the result as it would appear in IE5, using the IE Preview tab.

And down at the bottom, we can see (and edit) the template itself. In this case, I have clicked on the Address element in the upper-left pane. This displays the template in the lower pane, and highlights those parts of the generated HTML that result from executing this template.

There's a lot more to the tool than this, so try downloading the evaluation version from http://www.excelon.com and test it for yourself. In fact I would say the same about any of these tools. I can't always give recommendations as I do not have time to try all the tools available – I just tell you what *I* use, and you can try the tools for yourself.

Summary of the Style Sheet

So there we have it. We've seen:

- ❏ How each manufacturer of an eBIS-XML compliant system must produce style sheets for their documents
- ❏ How to make these style sheets dynamic so that they only create elements on the generated document where there is data in the XML document
- ❏ The difference between "push" and "pull" models
  - ❏ When each is suitable
  - ❏ How style sheets can be structured to use one or the other (or a hybrid)
- ❏ (Briefly), one of the tools used for XSL development

Next, we'll look at some other aspects of e-commerce, and how eBIS-XML needs to develop in the future.

Have We Met Arthur's Requirements?

These are the requirements I described earlier:

- ❏ Eliminate duplicate data entry
- ❏ Eliminate specialist stationery
- ❏ Get rid of the cost of value added networks
- ❏ Reduce postage, phone, and fax costs
- ❏ Reduce time from customer order to fulfillment
- ❏ Keep the same accounting system
- ❏ Keep any upgrade simple to configure

Let's look at them one at a time.

Eliminate Duplicate Data Entry

Well clearly, we have done that. If Arthur's customers have eBIS-XML enabled accounting systems, they can place an order which will be sent via e-mail as an XML message to Arthur. The order entry module of Arthur's accounting system can then poll his mail server to see if there are any eBIS-XML messages, pull these out and list them. Arthur can work through this list, adding any additional information required, then post the orders into his system. When he comes to place an order with his supplier, he uses a similar process – enter the data once, and send it off. And when the invoice comes back, this can be automatically reconciled against the order.

What about those who use his web site? We have not covered this so far in the case study, but the method is very similar. Arthur's customers can fill in a web form with all the required information. The web server can then take this information and, using the Document Object Model, create an eBIS-XML Order message. A simple component can then be used on the web server to add this as an attachment to an e-mail and send it to Arthur. When his system generates an invoice, this can be mailed as an XML document. As we saw with Exchequer Enterprise earlier, the translation to HTML could also be done within Arthur's accounting system and an HTML message sent as well.

Eliminate Specialist Stationery

Again, this was easily done. Remember that eBIS-XML documents have two audiences – human and machine. The machine doesn't care about headed paper, and the style sheet can have suitable information and logos built in for the human.

Get Rid of the Cost of VANs

Earlier, we mentioned the high cost of Value Added Networks. Removing the requirement for these comes as part of the system. We are now using the Internet and, as we all know, the Internet is free.

Reduce Postage, Phone, and Fax Costs

Arthur is now placing all his orders by e-mail. Since he pays next to nothing for this, he is immediately cutting overhead costs.

Reduce Time from Customer Order to Fulfillment

Not only is the Internet free, it's also instant (OK, so e-mail uses a store and forward mechanism, but we're talking minutes rather than days). Typically, a customer might print out an order on Monday, miss the last post of the day, so the order reaches Arthur on Wednesday. He is out of stock, so he places an order with his suppliers, again by post. A whole week has gone by in passing messages that could be done instantly. By that time, the record is probably out of the charts and everyone has forgotten the name of the performer.

Keep the Same Accounting System

We've seen how eBIS-XML is being built into Exchequer Enterprise. BASDA claims to represent the manufacturers of 80% of the world's accounting systems, and have over a hundred currently working with eBIS-XML. So there is a good chance that an upgrade will be available for Arthur's system before long.

Keep any Upgrade Simple to Configure

Again, we saw in Exchequer Enterprise that no configuration was required. Sending using XML is just an option when a message is being sent. Compare this to EDI systems that require 100% compatibility between the systems in the supply chain.

Next Steps

We've now seen the eBIS-XML concept, the structure of the Invoice schema (the Order schema is very similar) and the way style sheets are used to allow co-working between disparate systems.

So far, we have a document that we can send using e-mail between systems in much the same way that we would send a paper document by post. This already achieves our aim of eliminating duplicate data entry, and also eliminates postal delays. In fact, it's probably just what Arthur needs.

But what happens when Arthur has a particularly important order and sends it by recorded delivery mail? Is there an Internet equivalent for that? This is just one of several improvements that can (and will) be made. Here are a few possibilities:

- ❑ Encrypt the message to keep it away from prying eyes

- ❑ Provide stronger protection against tampering than the fairly simple calculation currently used to create the checksum

- ❑ Provide a mechanism to confirm delivery

- ❑ Allow both SMTP (e-mail) and HTTP (web) delivery, and allow each party to the transaction to use different mechanisms

If we get these in place, we have a mechanism whereby:

- ❑ Nobody can claim that they didn't receive a document

- ❑ Nobody can claim that the document they received was different from the one sent

- ❑ Everyone is safe from industrial espionage

- ❑ Larger companies with permanent e-mail connections can use instant HTTP delivery, while smaller companies with dial-up connections can use slower e-mail delivery – but they can still talk to each other

The encryption and protection against tampering can use standard mechanisms, such as the secure sockets layer (SSL) for web transactions, but the other areas need some thought. Let's start with mixing HTTP and SMTP.

Simple Routing

To provide this interchange between systems using different transport mechanisms, we clearly need some kind of gateway. Luckily, there are plenty around (not all of them released at the time of writing). Four of the higher profile products are:

- ❑ Microsoft's BizTalk server (http://www.microsoft.com/biztalk)

- ❑ IBM's B2B server (http://www.ibm.com)

- ❑ Netfish's XDI eProcess platform (http://www.netfish.com)

- ❑ Excelon's B2B Integration Server (http://www.excelon.com)

These will all provide the translations required, and do a lot more besides.

Clearly, if we're going to address our messages to such a server rather than the end recipient, we need to add some additional information. This is, again, just like the postal service. We could take our documents straight to the recipient without any additional information, but if we use a third party (the Post Office) we place the document in an envelope containing the recipient and sender's addresses. There are several competing standards for such envelopes (the United Nations Economic Commission for Europe – UNECE – is currently working on a standard). Remembering that the original suggestion for eBIS-XML came from Microsoft, it is not surprising that BASDA chose to use Microsoft's BizTalk envelope. As well as being supported by BizTalk server, this is also supported by other systems and is an important input to the UNECE effort. As in other areas where the standards are not yet in place, I am sure BASDA will support any international standard once it is ratified and supported by standard products.

The BizTalk Header

When we have one document (the invoice) embedded in another (the BizTalk envelope) we need to identify the appropriate language for each element. Of course, you'll immediately realize by this stage in the book that we do that using XML namespaces, which were explained in Chapter 8.

Here's an invoice in its envelope:

```xml
<?xml version="1.0"?>
<?xml-stylesheet type="text/xsl" href="eBIS3.xsl"?>
<biztalk_1 xmlns="urn:schemas-biztalk-org:biztalk/biztalk_1.xml">
  <header>
    <delivery>
      <message>
        <messageID>163845</messageID>
        <sent>2000-05-015T19:00:01+01:00</sent>
        <subject>Invoice</subject>
        <basda:SENDER xmlns:basda="urn:basda.org:header">
          Arthur Discspinner
        </basda:SENDER>
        <basda:RECIPIENT xmlns:basda="urn:basda.org:header">
          Dodgy Discs Ltd
        </basda:RECIPIENT>
      </message>
      <to>
        <address>http://www.dodgydiscs.com/recv.asp</address>
        <state>
          <referenceID/>
          <handle/>
          <process/>
        </state>
      </to>
      <from>
        <address>mailto:orders@discspinner.co.uk</address>
        <state>
          <referenceID>123</referenceID>
          <handle>7</handle>
          <process>myprocess</process>
        </state>
      </from>
```

```
      </delivery>
      <manifest>
      </manifest>
    </header>
    <body>
      <Invoice xmlns="urn:www.basda.org/schema/eBIS-XML_invoice_v3.00.xml">
        <!-- Invoice content goes here -->
      </Invoice>
    </body>
  </biztalk_1>
```

This clearly shows the namespaces used and the information provided. We can also see two extension elements in the BizTalk header:

```
<basda:SENDER xmlns:basda="urn:basda.org:header">
  Arthur Discspinner
</basda:SENDER>
<basda:RECIPIENT xmlns:basda="urn:basda.org:header">
  Dodgy Discs Ltd
</basda:RECIPIENT>
```

These extend the BizTalk language using a BASDA namespace. By doing this, the message will still pass any BizTalk validation.

The key elements in the envelope are the to and from elements. These identify the sender and recipient of the message, and so ensure delivery. There is also additional information provided, which is well described in the BizTalk documentation.

So the last thing we need to do is provide a mechanism for knowing that documents arrive and can be processed. Such mechanisms are generally described as **choreography**.

Choreography

Currently, the choreography that Arthur uses is very simple, and, using a military analogy, is known as "fire and forget". The "forget" part is not, contrary to the opinion of his friends, an inheritance of his lifestyle during the '60s, but is due to his being at the bleeding edge of XML-based e-commerce.

When Arthur is placing an order, he presses the button on his accounting system, and the message is sent as an e-mail attachment to his supplier. How does he know it arrived? Because the discs arrive a couple of days later. This is fine for him, and probably for 90% of the world's transactions, but we can do better.

This is another area that the UNECE is working on, with a plan to introduce a multi-stage process. This will provide confirmation to Arthur, firstly that his message has arrived, secondly that it is an eBIS-XML Order message passing the validation rules, and thirdly that the order meets Dodgy Disc's own business rules. (For example, that the goods are in stock and that the purchase does not take Arthur over his credit limit.) Once he has received these three messages (which will be handled automatically by his accounting system) he will know that the order has been accepted.

More Futures

Although the routing mechanisms are not yet in place, they are planned and will happen. When we move on from there, we enter the realms of speculation.

Once gateways are in place, what else can we do? And what opportunities are there for the suppliers of accounting systems to contribute to the future? If you thought accounting systems were boring, you're rather behind the times!

The first facility to be provided by the gateways will be **schema translation**. While eBIS-XML is currently the only many-to-many schema deployed, there are plenty of industry-specific schemas. The gateways promise to translate between these. After working with e-commerce schemas for a while now, I suspect that this is not as easy as the gateway vendors think – but we shall see.

Other areas promised are product catalogues and B2B auctions. And it's here that accounting systems can really start to bring some benefit to their users. If there are gateways on the Internet supplying multi-vendor catalogues, Arthur need no longer decide to place his order with Dodgy Discs. Instead, he can say what products he wants and when he needs them, and his accounting system can go out to the Internet and identify possible vendors. It can then list these in order of price, highlighting those who are already Arthur's approved suppliers. One click and the order goes.

Or if he's placing a big order, his accounting system could automatically place an invitation to bid on a gateway. Supplier ERP systems will be automatically tracking activity on the gateway, so they'll see Arthur's invitation to bid, check their stocks and prices, and place a bid. At midday the next day Arthur can just take the best offer. Even better for Arthur, this could be run as a supplier's auction. Each bid is visible, and Arthur just decides when to stop and take the latest (and lowest) one.

And If We Were to Start Now?

I have been asked what, with hindsight, I think is good about the approach we used and what we would do differently if we were to start this project again now. The nature of a case study is that material will be out of date by the time it is published, since it relates to past work. When we are all working in Internet time, and especially XML time, which seems to move even faster, this can make material irrelevant by the time it is published.

That is not quite the case here, since I am writing in May 2000, and, although the project started in July 1999, we had a major re-think in January and used the opportunity to change not only the schemas, but also the way in which they were generated. So to some extent, the answer to what we would do differently is "very little".

One thing we clearly did right was to get the project moving and make sure we had a delivery in the shortest possible timescale. Others are also working on B2B schemas, but they tend to be going for the "100% interoperability" EDI approach, and are spending much longer ensuring that they have a complete superset of the possible requirements. I firmly believe that BASDA's "flexible interoperability" approach is the main reason it will be successful. This approach not only means that users of eBIS-XML enabled systems can communicate with non-enabled systems, but it allows easy extensibility for specific requirements and when requirements change. Even better, the way in which we use style sheets ensures that using this extensibility will not prevent systems from inter-working.

The major change I would make to the approach we used is the way in which we modeled data. We started with the spreadsheets that not only modeled the data, but also the way in which it would be encoded in XML. This means that, when the most important thing was to get the data model right, in order to document it we also had to decide where we would use elements and where we would use attributes. Starting again, I would separate these two stages – first model the data we wanted to encode, then decide on the exact encoding. That way, we are always concentrating on the most important aspect of the development at any time.

Other changes are more obvious, and reflect the advance of standards while we were developing. XSLT is now a full W3C Recommendation, and XML Schema Definition Language is close to ratification. Starting now, I would therefore be using these. However, we had the foresight to ensure the flexibility to change to the latest standards, and this will happen soon. For the schemas, this is just a case of asking XML Authority to save in a different format, and perhaps later manually optimizing to use features of XSDL, such as inheritance, that are not included in XDR. For XSL, Microsoft has developed a style sheet that makes a fair attempt to translate the original IE5 style sheets to XSLT. This is available from http://msdn.microsoft.com/xml. So again, the change is easy – process with the style sheet, then manually optimize.

Summary

In this case study, we've seen how eBIS-XML is enabling e-commerce for the small and medium enterprise. It's not competing with the big supply-chain ERP systems, but will interact with them to make life easier for the huge number of smaller companies out there.

We couldn't discuss every aspect of eBIS-XML in detail, but we have looked at the schema, and I hope picked up a few tips from real experience to supplement the knowledge of the schema syntax that you gained earlier. We've also seen some tools that make the specific schema syntax rather unimportant to most of us.

Then we saw how eBIS-XML uses XSL style sheets to allow the systems to take only what they need from the message, but allow the human reader to see it all. This ensures the "flexible interoperability" that is a key feature of the standard. We saw the importance of making style sheets for such a task as flexible as possible – there is potentially a lot of data in the message, but each message will only contain a subset, so we want our style sheet to only provide space for what's there.

Finally we saw how the e-commerce world is moving, with B2B gateways providing translations at both transport and message structure levels, and some speculation on how automatic tendering and auctions could revolutionize the whole purchasing process.

A single chapter of a book does not normally have an "acknowedgements" section, but I would like to thank Dennis Keeling, CEO of BASDA, not only for the huge amount of skill and effort he put into making this project a success, but also for permission to publish information that is not in the public domain. Also to BASDA members for the work they put into the schema, and Exchequer Software Ltd for helping me set up a copy of Enterprise for the screen shot that proves that this is a real-world case study with products already deployed.

Let me leave you with a quotation from an article in the March/April 2000 edition of Application Development Advisor: "... *in the e-commerce arena, XML only stands a chance of success if there is as little complication and confusion as possible, and that will only come about if there is strong adherence to initiatives such as BASDA's eBIS-XML*".

The XML Document Object Model

This appendix lists all of the interfaces in the DOM Level 2 Core, both the **Fundamental Interfaces** and the **Extended Interfaces**, including all of their properties and methods. Examples of how to use these interfaces were given in Chapter 6.

Further information on these interfaces can be found at http://www.w3.org/TR/1999/CR-DOM-Level-2-19991210/core.html.

Fundamental Interfaces

The DOM Fundamental Interfaces are interfaces that *all* DOM implementations must provide, even if they aren't designed to work with XML documents.

DOMException

An object implementing the DOMException interface is raised whenever an error occurs in the DOM.

Property	Description
code	An integer, representing which **Exception Code** this DOMException is reporting.

The code property can take the following values:

Exception Code	Integer Value	Description
INDEX_SIZE_ERR	1	The index or size is negative, or greater than the allowed value.
DOMSTRING_SIZE_ERR	2	The specified range of text does not fit into a DOMString.

Table continued on following page

Exception Code	Integer Value	Description
HIERARCHY_REQUEST_ERR	3	The node is inserted somewhere it doesn't belong.
WRONG_DOCUMENT_ERR	4	The node is used in a different document than the one that created it, and that document doesn't support it.
INVALID_CHARACTER_ERR	5	A character has been passed which is not valid in XML.
NO_DATA_ALLOWED_ERR	6	Data has been specified for a node which does not support data.
NO_MODIFICATION_ ALLOWED_ERR	7	An attempt has been made to modify an object which doesn't allow modifications.
NOT_FOUND_ERR	8	An attempt was made to reference a node which does not exist.
NOT_SUPPORTED_ERR	9	The implementation does not support the type of object requested.
INUSE_ATTRIBUTE_ERR	10	An attempt was made to add a duplicate attribute.
INVALID_STATE_ERR	11	An attempt was made to use an object which is not, or is no longer, useable.
SYNTAX_ERR	12	An invalid or illegal string was passed.
INVALID_MODIFICATION_ERR	13	An attempt was made to modify the type of the underlying object.
NAMESPACE_ERR	14	An attempt was made to create or change an object, in a way which is incompatible with namespaces.
INVALID_ACCESS_ERR	15	A parameter was passed or an operation attempted which is not supported by the underlying object.

Node

The Node interface is the base interface upon which most of the DOM objects are built, and contains methods and attributes which can be used for all types of nodes. The interface also includes some helper methods and attributes which only apply to particular types of nodes.

Property	Description
nodeName	The name of the node. (Will return different values, depending on the nodeType, as listed in the next table.)

Property	Description
nodeValue	The value of the node. (Will return different values, depending on the nodeType, as listed in the next table.)
nodeType	The type of node. Will be one of the values from the next table.
parentNode	The node that is this node's parent.
childNodes	A NodeList containing all of this node's children. If there are no children, an empty NodeList will be returned, not NULL.
firstChild	The first child of this node. If there are no children, this returns NULL.
lastChild	The last child of this node. If there are no children, this returns NULL.
previousSibling	The node immediately preceding this node. If there is no preceding node, this returns NULL.
nextSibling	The node immediately following this node. If there is no following node, this returns NULL.
attributes	A NamedNodeMap containing the attributes of this node. If the node is not an element, this returns NULL.
ownerDocument	The document to which this node belongs.
namespaceURI	The namespace URI of this node. Returns NULL if a namespace is not specified.
prefix	The namespace prefix of this node. Returns NULL if a namespace is not specified.
localName	Returns the local part of this node's QName.

The value of the nodeName and nodeValue properties depend on the value of the nodeType property, which can return one of the following constants:

nodeType property constant	nodeName	nodeValue
ELEMENT_NODE	Tag name	NULL
ATTRIBUTE_NODE	Name of attribute	Value of attribute
TEXT_NODE	#text	Content of the text node
CDATA_SECTION_NODE	#cdata-section	Content of the CDATA section
ENTITY_REFERENCE_NODE	Name of entity referenced	NULL
ENTITY_NODE	Entity name	NULL
PROCESSING_INSTRUCTION_NODE	Target	Entire content excluding the target

Table continued on following page

nodeType property constant	nodeName	nodeValue
COMMENT_NODE	#comment	Content of the comment
DOCUMENT_NODE	#document	NULL
DOCUMENT_TYPE_NODE	Document type name	NULL
DOCUMENT_FRAGMENT_NODE	#document-fragment	NULL
NOTATION_NODE	Notation name	NULL

Method	Description
insertBefore(newChild, refChild)	Inserts the newChild node before the existing refChild. If refChild is NULL, inserts the node at the end of the list. Returns the inserted node.
replaceChild(newChild, oldChild)	Replaces oldChild with newChild. Returns oldChild.
removeChild(oldChild)	Removes oldChild from the list, and returns it.
appendChild(newChild)	Adds newChild to the end of the list, and returns it.
hasChildNodes()	Returns a Boolean; true if the node has any children, false otherwise.
cloneNode(deep)	Returns a duplicate of this node. If the Boolean deep parameter is true, this will recursively clone the sub-tree under the node, otherwise it will only clone the node itself.
normalize()	If there are multiple adjacent Text child nodes (from a previous call to Text.splitText()) this method will combine them again. It doesn't return a value.
supports(feature, version)	Indicates whether this implementation of the DOM supports the feature passed. Returns a Boolean, true if it supports the feature, false otherwise.

Document

An object implementing the Document interface represents the entire XML document. This object is also used to create other nodes at run time.

The Document interface extends the Node interface.

Property	Description
`doctype`	Returns a `DocumentType` object, indicating the document type associated with this document. If the document has no document type specified, returns `NULL`.
`implementation`	The `DOMImplementation` object used for this document.
`documentElement`	The root element for this document.

Method	Description
`createElement(tagName)`	Creates an element, with the name specified.
`createDocumentFragment()`	Creates an empty `DocumentFragment` object.
`createTextNode(data)`	Creates a `Text` node, containing the text in `data`.
`createComment(data)`	Creates a `Comment` node, containing the text in `data`.
`createCDATASection(data)`	Creates a `CDATASection` node, containing the text in `data`.
`createProcessingInstruction(target, data)`	Creates a `ProcessingInstruction` node, with the specified `target` and `data`.
`createAttribute(name)`	Creates an attribute, with the specified `name`.
`createEntityReference(name)`	Creates an entity reference, with the specified `name`.
`getElementsByTagName(tagname)`	Returns a `NodeList` of all elements in the document with this `tagname`. The elements are returned in document order.
`importNode(importedNode, deep)`	Imports a node `importedNode` from another document into this one. The original node is not removed from the old document, it is just cloned. (The Boolean `deep` parameter specifies if it is a deep or shallow clone: deep – sub-tree under node is also cloned, shallow – only node itself is cloned.) Returns the new node.
`createElementNS(namespaceURI, qualifiedName)`	Creates an element, with the specified namespace and QName.
`createAttributeNS(namespaceURI, qualifiedName)`	Creates an attribute, with the specified namespace and QName.

Table continued on following page

667

Method	Description
`getElementsByTagNameNS` (*namespaceURI*, *localName*)	Returns a `NodeList` of all the elements in the document which have the specified local name, and are in the namespace specified by *namespaceURI*.
`getElementByID`(*elementID*)	Returns the element with the ID specified in *elementID*. If there is no such element, returns `NULL`.

Note: all of the `createXXX()` *methods return the node created.*

DOMImplementation

The `DOMImplementation` interface provides methods which are not specific to any particular document, but to any document from this DOM implementation. You can get a `DOMImplementation` object from the `implementation` property of the `Document` interface.

Method	Description
`hasFeature`(*feature*, *version*)	Returns a Boolean, indicating whether this DOM implementation supports the *feature* requested. *version* is the version number of the feature to test.
`createDocumentType`(*qualifiedName*, *publicID*, *systemID*, *internalSubset*)	Creates a `DocumentType` object, with the specified attributes.
`createDocument`(*namespaceURI*, *qualifiedName*, *doctype*)	Creates a `Document` object, with the document element specified by *qualifiedName*. The *doctype* property must refer to an object of type `DocumentType`.

DocumentFragment

A document fragment is a temporary holding place for a group of nodes, usually with the intent of inserting them back into the document at a later point.

The `DocumentFragment` interface extends the `Node` interface, without adding any additional properties or methods.

NodeList

A `NodeList` contains an ordered group of nodes, accessed via an integral index.

Property	Description
length	The number of nodes contained in this list. The range of valid child node indices is 0 to length-1 inclusive.
item(*index*)	Returns the Node in the list at the indicated *index*. If *index* is the same as or greater than length, returns NULL.

Element

Provides properties and methods for working with an element.

The Element interface extends the Node interface.

Property	Description
tagName	The name of the element.

Method	Description
getAttribute(*name*)	Returns the value of the attribute with the specified *name*, or an empty string if that attribute does not have a specified or default value.
setAttribute(*name*, *value*)	Sets the value of the specified attribute to this new *value*. If no such attribute exists, a new one with this *name* is created.
removeAttribute (*name*)	Removes the specified attribute. If the attribute has a default value, it is immediately replaced with an identical attribute, containing this default value.
getAttributeNode (*name*)	Returns an Attr node, containing the named attribute. Returns NULL if there is no such attribute.
setAttributeNode (*newAttr*)	Adds a new attribute node. If an attribute with the same name already exists, it is replaced. If an Attr has been replaced, it is returned, otherwise NULL is returned.
removeAttributeNode (*oldAttr*)	Removes the specified Attr node, and returns it. If the attribute has a default value, it is immediately replaced with an identical attribute, containing this default value.
getElementsByTagName (*name*)	Returns a NodeList of all descendents with the given node *name*.

Table continued on following page

Method	Description
getAttributeNS(*namespaceURI*, *localName*)	Returns the value of the specified attribute, or an empty string if that attribute does not have a specified or default value.
setAttributeNS(*namespaceURI*, *qualifiedName*, *value*)	Sets the value of the specified attribute to this new *value*. If no such attribute exists, a new one with this namespace URI and QName is created.
removeAttributeNS(*namespaceURI*, *localName*)	Removes the specified attribute. If the attribute has a default value, it is immediately replaced with an identical attribute, containing this default value.
getAttributeNodeNS(*namespaceURI*, *localName*)	Returns an Attr node, containing the specified attribute. Returns NULL if there is no such attribute.
setAttributeNodeNS(*newAttr*)	Adds a new Attr node to the list. If an attribute with the same namespace URI and local name exists, it is replaced. If an Attr object is replaced, it is returned, otherwise NULL is returned.
getElementsByTagNameNS *namespaceURI*, *localName*)	Returns a NodeList of all of the elements matching these criteria.

NamedNodeMap

A named node map represents an unordered collection of nodes, retrieved by name.

Property	Description
length	The number of nodes in the map.

Method	Description
getNamedItem(*name*)	Returns a Node, where the nodeName is the same as the *name* specified, or NULL if no such node exists.
setNamedItem(*arg*)	The *arg* parameter is a Node object, which is added to the list. The nodeName property is used for the name of the node in this map. If a node with the same name already exists, it is replaced. If a Node is replaced it is returned, otherwise NULL is returned.
removeNamedItem(*name*)	Removes the Node specified by *name*, and returns it.

Method	Description
item(*index*)	Returns the Node at the specified *index*. If *index* is the same as or greater than length, returns NULL.
getNamedItemNS (*namespaceURI, localName*)	Returns a Node, matching the namespace URI and local name, or NULL if no such node exists.
setNamedItemNS(*arg*)	The *arg* parameter is a Node object, which is added to the list. If a node with the same namespace URI and local name already exists, it is replaced. If a Node is replaced it is returned, otherwise, NULL is returned.
removeNamedItemNS (*namespaceURI, localName*)	Removes the specified node, and returns it.

Attr

Provides properties for dealing with an attribute.

The Attr interface extends the Node interface.

Property	Description
name	The name of the attribute.
specified	A Boolean, indicating whether this attribute was specified (true), or just defaulted (false).
value	The value of the attribute.
ownerElement	An Element object, representing the element to which this attribute belongs.

CharacterData

Provides properties and methods for working with character data.

The CharacterData interface extends the Node interface.

Property	Description
data	The text in this CharacterData node.
length	The number of characters in the node.

Table continued on following page

Method	Description
substringData(*offset*, *count*)	Returns a portion of the string, starting at the *offset*. Will return the number of characters specified in *count*, or until the end of the string, whichever is less.
appendData(*arg*)	Appends the string in *arg* to the end of the string.
insertData(*offset*, *arg*)	Inserts the string in *arg* into the middle of the string, starting at the position indicated by *offset*.
deleteData(*offset*, *count*)	Deletes a portion of the string, starting at the *offset*. Will delete the number of characters specified in *count*, or until the end of the string, whichever is less.
replaceData(*offset*, *count*, *arg*)	Replaces a portion of the string, starting at the *offset*. Will replace the number of characters specified in *count*, or until the end of the string, whichever is less. The *arg* parameter is the new string to be inserted.

Text

Provides an additional method for working with text nodes.

The Text interface extends the CharacterData interface.

Method	Description
splitText(*offset*)	Separates this single Text node into two adjacent Text nodes. All of the text up to the *offset* point goes into the first Text node, and all of the text starting at the *offset* point to the end goes into the second Text node.

Comment

Encapsulates an XML comment.

The Comment interface extends the CharacterData interface, without adding any additional properties or methods.

Extended Interfaces

The DOM Extended Interfaces need only be provided by DOM implementations that will be working with XML documents.

CDATASection

Encapsulates an XML CDATA section.

The CDATASection interface extends the Text interface, without adding any additional properties or methods.

ProcessingInstruction

Provides properties for working with an XML processing instruction (PI).

The `ProcessingInstruction` interface extends the `Node` interface.

Property	Description
target	The PI target, in other words the name of the application to which the PI should be passed.
data	The content of the PI.

DocumentType

Provides properties for working with an XML document type. Can be retrieved from the `doctype` property of the `Document` interface. (If a document doesn't have a document type, `doctype` will return `NULL`.)

`DocumentType` extends the `Node` interface.

Property	Description
name	The name of the DTD.
entities	A `NamedNodeMap` containing all entities declared in the DTD (both internal and external). Parameter entities are not contained, and duplicates are discarded, according to the rules followed by validating XML parsers.
notations	A `NamedNodeMap` containing the notations contained in the DTD. Duplicates are discarded.
publicID	The public identifier of the external subset.
systemID	The system identifier of the external subset.
internalSubset	The internal subset, as a string.

Notation

Provides properties for working with an XML notation. Notations are read-only in the DOM.

The `Notation` interface extends the `Node` interface.

Property	Description
publicID	The public identifier of this notation. If the public identifier was not specified, returns `NULL`.
systemID	The system identifier of this notation. If the system identifier was not specified, returns `NULL`.

Entity

Provides properties for working with parsed and unparsed entities. `Entity` nodes are read-only.

The `Entity` interface extends the `Node` interface.

Property	Description
`publicID`	The public identifier associated with the entity, or `NULL` if none is specified.
`systemID`	The system identifier associated with the entity, or `NULL` if none is specified.
`notationName`	For unparsed entities, the name of the notation for the entity. `NULL` for parsed entities.

EntityReference

Encapsulates an XML entity reference.

The `EntityReference` extends the `Node` interface, without adding any properties or methods.

SAX 1.0: The Simple API for XML

This appendix contains the specification of the SAX interface, version 1.0, much of which is explained in Chapter 7. It is taken largely verbatim from the definitive specification to be found on http://www.megginson.com/sax/, with editorial comments added in italics.

The classes and interfaces are described in alphabetical order. Within each class, the methods are also listed alphabetically.

The SAX specification is in the public domain: see the web site quoted above for a statement of policy on copyright. Essentially the policy is: do what you like with it, copy it as you wish, but no-one accepts any liability for errors or omissions.

The SAX distribution also includes three "helper classes":

- ❑   AttributeListImpl is an implementation of the AttributeList interface
- ❑   LocatorImpl is an implementation of the Locator interface
- ❑   ParserFactory is a class that enables you to load a parser identified by a parameter at run-time

The documentation of these helper classes is not included here. For this, and for SAX sample applications, see the SAX distribution available from http://www.megginson.com.

Class Hierarchy

```
class java.lang.Object
        interface org.xml.sax.AttributeList
        class org.xml.sax.helpers.AttributeListImpl
                (implements org.xml.sax.AttributeList)
        interface org.xml.sax.DTDHandler
        interface org.xml.sax.DocumentHandler
        interface org.xml.sax.EntityResolver
        interface org.xml.sax.ErrorHandler
        class org.xml.sax.HandlerBase
                (implements org.xml.EntityResolver,
                            org.xml.sax.DTDHandler,
                            org.xml.sax.DocumentHandler,
                            org.xml.sax.ErrorHandler)
        class org.xml.sax.InputSource
        interface org.xml.sax.Locator
        class org.xml.sax.helpers.LocatorsImp
                (implements org.xml.sax.Locator)
        interface org.xml.sax.Parser
        class org.xml.sax.helpers.ParserFactory
        class java.lang.Throwable
                (implements java.io.Serializable)
        class java.lang.Exception
                class org.xml.sax.SAXExeception
                        class org.xml.sax.SAXParseException
```

The diagram above shows the class hierarchy of SAX 1.0. We covered many of these classes in Chapter 7, although some were left out as they are outside of the scope of what you will most likely need to know. However, this appendix covers them all, and further details can be found at the SAX web site.

Interface org.xml.sax.AttributeList

An AttributeList is a collection of attributes appearing on a particular start tag. The Parser supplies the DocumentHandler with an AttributeList as part of the information available on the startElement event. The AttributeList is essentially a set of name-value pairs for the supplied attributes; if the parser has analyzed the DTD it may also provide information about the type of each attribute.

Interface for an element's attribute specifications

The SAX parser implements this interface and passes an instance to the SAX application as the second argument of each startElement event.

The instance provided will return valid results only during the scope of the startElement invocation (to save it for future use, the application must make a copy: the AttributeListImpl helper class provides a convenient constructor for doing so).

An AttributeList includes only attributes that have been specified or defaulted: #IMPLIED attributes will not be included.

There are two ways for the SAX application to obtain information from the AttributeList. First, it can iterate through the entire list:

```
public void startElement (String name, AttributeList atts) {
  for (int i = 0; i < atts.getLength(); i++) {
    String name = atts.getName(i);
    String type = atts.getType(i);
    String value = atts.getValue(i);
    [...]
  }
}
```

(Note that the result of `getLength()` will be zero if there are no attributes.)

As an alternative, the application can request the value or type of specific attributes:

```
public void startElement (String name, AttributeList atts) {
  String identifier = atts.getValue("id");
  String label = atts.getValue("label");
  [...]
}
```

The `AttributeListImpl` helper class provides a convenience implementation for use by parser or application writers.

getLength	Return the number of attributes in this list.
public int getLength()	The SAX parser may provide attributes in any arbitrary order, regardless of the order in which they were declared or specified. The number of attributes may be zero.
	Returns:
	The number of attributes in the list.
getName	Return the name of an attribute in this list (by position).
public String getName (int index)	The names must be unique: the SAX parser shall not include the same attribute twice. Attributes without values (those declared #IMPLIED without a value specified in the start tag) will be omitted from the list.
	If the attribute name has a namespace prefix, the prefix will still be attached.
	Parameters:
	index – The index of the attribute in the list (starting at 0).
	Returns:
	The name of the indexed attribute, or null if the index is out of range.

Table continued on following page

679

getType	Return the type of an attribute in the list (by position).
public String getType (int index)	The attribute type is one of the strings "CDATA", "ID", "IDREF", "IDREFS", "NMTOKEN", "NMTOKENS", "ENTITY", "ENTITIES", or "NOTATION" (always in upper case).
	If the parser has not read a declaration for the attribute, or if the parser does not report attribute types, then it must return the value "CDATA" as stated in the XML 1.0 Recommendation (clause 3.3.3, "Attribute-Value Normalization").
	For an enumerated attribute that is not a notation, the parser will report the type as "NMTOKEN".
	Parameters:
	index – The index of the attribute in the list (starting at 0).
	Returns:
	The attribute type as a string, or null if the index is out of range.
getType	Return the type of an attribute in the list (by name).
public String getType (String name)	The return value is the same as the return value for getType(int).
	If the attribute name has a namespace prefix in the document, the application must include the prefix here.
	Parameters:
	name – The name of the attribute.
	Returns:
	The attribute type as a string, or null if no such attribute exists.

getValue	Return the value of an attribute in the list (by position).
public String getValue (int index)	If the attribute value is a list of tokens (IDREFS, ENTITIES, or NMTOKENS), the tokens will be concatenated into a single string separated by whitespace.
	Parameters:
	index – The index of the attribute in the list (starting at 0).
	Returns:
	The attribute value as a string, or `null` if the index is out of range.
getValue	Return the value of an attribute in the list (by name).
public String getValue (String name)	The return value is the same as the return value for `getValue(int)`.
	If the attribute name has a namespace prefix in the document, the application must include the prefix here.
	Parameters:
	name – The name of the attribute.
	Returns:
	The attribute value as a string, or `null` if no such attribute exists.

Interface org.xml.sax.DocumentHandler

Every SAX application is likely to include a class that implements this interface, either directly or by subclassing the supplied class `HandlerBase`. See Chapter 6 for a full discussion of the various methods.

Receive notification of general document events

This is the main interface that most SAX applications implement: if the application needs to be informed of basic parsing events, it implements this interface and registers an instance with the SAX parser using the setDocumentHandler method. The parser uses the instance to report basic document-related events like the start and end of elements and character data.

The order of events in this interface is very important, and mirrors the order of information in the document itself. For example, all of an element's content (character data, processing instructions, and/or subelements) will appear, in order, between the startElement event and the corresponding endElement event.

Application writers who do not want to implement the entire interface can derive a class from `HandlerBase`, which implements the default functionality; parser writers can instantiate `HandlerBase` to obtain a default handler. The application can find the location of any document event using the Locator interface supplied by the Parser through the `setDocumentLocator` method.

---

characters
 	
public void characters(
 	
      char ch[],
      int start,
      int length)
 	
throws SAXException
	Receive notification of character data.
	
	The Parser will call this method to report each chunk of character data. SAX parsers may return all contiguous character data in a single chunk, or they may split it into several chunks; however, all of the characters in any single event must come from the same external entity, so that the Locator provides useful information.
	
	The application must not attempt to read from the array outside of the specified range *and must not attempt to write to the array*.
	
	Note that some parsers will report whitespace using the `ignorableWhitespace()` method rather than this one (validating parsers must do so).
	
	Parameters:
	
	ch - The characters from the XML document.
	
	start - The start position in the array.
	
	length - The number of characters to read from the array.
	
	Throws: SAXException
	
	Any SAX exception, possibly wrapping another exception.

endDocument public void endDocument() throws SAXException	Receive notification of the end of a document. The SAX parser will invoke this method only once *for each document*, and it will be the last method invoked during the parse. The parser shall not invoke this method until it has either abandoned parsing (because of an unrecoverable error) or reached the end of input. **Throws**: SAXException Any SAX exception, possibly wrapping another exception.

endElement

public void endElement(

    String name)

throws SAXException

Receive notification of the end of an element.

The SAX parser will invoke this method at the end of every element in the XML document; there will be a corresponding `startElement()` event for every `endElement()` event (even when the element is empty).

If the element name has a namespace prefix, the prefix will still be attached to the name.

Parameters:

name – The element type name.

Throws: SAXException.

Any SAX exception, possibly wrapping another exception.

ignorableWhitespace

public void
ignorableWhitespace
    (char ch[],
    int start,
    int length)

throws SAXException

Receive notification of ignorable whitespace in element content.

Validating parsers must use this method to report each chunk of ignorable whitespace (see the W3C XML 1.0 recommendation, section 2.10): non-validating parsers may also use this method if they are capable of parsing and using content models.

SAX parsers may return all contiguous whitespace in a single chunk, or they may split it into several chunks; however, all of the characters in any single event must come from the same external entity, so that the Locator provides useful information.

The application must not attempt to read from the array outside of the specified range.

Parameters:

ch – The characters from the XML document.

start – The start position in the array.

length – The number of characters to read from the array.

Throws: SAXException.

Any SAX exception, possibly wrapping another exception.

Table Continued on Following Page

processingInstruction
 	
public void
processingInstruction(
      String target,
 	
      String data)
 	
throws SAXException
	Receive notification of a processing instruction.
	
	The parser will invoke this method once for each processing instruction found: note that processing instructions may occur before or after the main document element.
	
	A SAX parser should never report an XML declaration (XML 1.0, section 2.8) or a text declaration (XML 1.0, section 4.3.1) using this method.
	
	Parameters:
	
	target - The processing instruction target.
	
	data - The processing instruction data, or null if none was supplied.
	
	Throws: SAXException
	
	Any SAX exception, possibly wrapping another exception.

setDocumentLocator public void setDocumentLocator (Locator locator)	Receive an object for locating the origin of SAX document events. A SAX parser is strongly encouraged (though not absolutely required) to supply a Locator: if it does so, it must supply the Locator to the application by invoking this method before invoking any of the other methods in the `DocumentHandler` interface. The Locator allows the application to determine the end position of any document-related event, even if the parser is not reporting an error. Typically, the application will use this information for reporting its own errors (such as character content that does not match an application's business rules). The information returned by the locator is probably not sufficient for use with a search engine. Note that the locator will return correct information only during the invocation of the events in this interface. The application should not attempt to use it at any other time. **Parameters:** locator – An object that can return the location of any SAX document event.

startDocument	Receive notification of the beginning of a document.
public void startDocument()	The SAX parser will invoke this method only once *for each document*, before any other methods in this interface or in `DTDHandler` (except for `setDocumentLocator`).
throws SAXException	
	Throws: SAXException
	Any SAX exception, possibly wrapping another exception.
startElement	Receive notification of the beginning of an element.
public void startElement (	The parser will invoke this method at the beginning of every element in the XML document; there will be a corresponding `endElement()` event for every `startElement()` event (even when the element is empty). All of the element's content will be reported, in order, before the corresponding `endElement()` event.
String name, AttributeList atts)	
throws SAXException	If the element name has a namespace prefix, the prefix will still be attached. Note that the attribute list provided will contain only attributes with explicit values (specified or defaulted): #IMPLIED attributes will be omitted.
	Parameters:
	name - The element type name.
	atts - The attributes attached to the element, if any.
	Throws: SAXException
	Any SAX exception, possibly wrapping another exception.

Interface org.xml.sax.DTDHandler

This interface should be implemented by the application, if it wants to receive notification of events related to the DTD. SAX does not provide full details of the DTD, but this interface is available because without it, it would be impossible to access notations and unparsed entities referenced in the body of the document.

Notations and unparsed entities are rather specialized facilities in XML, so most SAX applications will not need to use this interface.

Receive notification of basic DTD-related events

If a SAX application needs information about notations and unparsed entities, then the application implements this interface and registers an instance with the SAX parser using the parser's setDTDHandler method. The parser uses the instance to report notation and unparsed entity declarations to the application.

The SAX parser may report these events in any order, regardless of the order in which the notations and unparsed entities were declared; however, all DTD events must be reported after the document handler's startDocument event, and before the first startElement event.

It is up to the application to store the information for future use (perhaps in a hash table or object tree). If the application encounters attributes of type "NOTATION", "ENTITY", or "ENTITIES", it can use the information that it obtained through this interface to find the entity and/or notation corresponding with the attribute value.

The HandlerBase class provides a default implementation of this interface, which simply ignores the events.

notationDecl	Receive notification of a notation declaration event.
public void notationDecl (String name, String publicId, String systemId)	It is up to the application to record the notation for later reference, if necessary.
throws SAXException	If a system identifier is present, and it is a URL, the SAX parser must resolve it fully before passing it to the application.
	Parameters:
	name – The notation name.
	publicId – The notation's public identifier, or null if none was given.
	systemId – The notation's system identifier, or null if none was given.
	Throws: SAXException.
	Any SAX exception, possibly wrapping another exception.

unparsedEntityDecl

public void unparsedEntityDecl
       (String name,
        String publicId,
        String systemId,
        String notationName)

throws SAXException

Receive notification of an unparsed entity declaration event.

Note that the notation name corresponds to a notation reported by the `notationDecl()` event. It is up to the application to record the entity for later reference, if necessary.

If the system identifier is a URL, the parser must resolve it fully before passing it to the application.

Parameters:

name - The unparsed entity's name.

publicId - The entity's public identifier, or `null` if none was given.

systemId - The entity's system identifier (it must always have one).

notationName - The name of the associated notation.

Throws: SAXException.

Any SAX exception, possibly wrapping another exception.

Interface org.xml.sax.EntityResolver

When the XML document contains references to external entities, the URL will normally be analyzed automatically by the parser: the relevant file will be located and parsed where appropriate. This interface allows an application to override this behavior. This might be needed, for example, if you want to retrieve a different version of the entity from a local server, or if the entities are cached in memory or stored in a database, or if the entity is really a reference to variable information such as the current date.

When the parser needs to obtain an entity, it calls this interface, which can respond by supplying any `InputSource` *object.*

Basic interface for resolving entities

If a SAX application needs to implement customized handling for external entities, it must implement this interface and register an instance with the SAX parser using the parser's `setEntityResolver` method.

The parser will then allow the application to intercept any external entities (including the external DTD subset and external parameter entities, if any) before including them.

687

Many SAX applications will not need to implement this interface, but it will be especially useful for applications that build XML documents from databases or other specialized input sources, or for applications that use URI types other than URLs.

The following resolver would provide the application with a special character stream for the entity with the system identifier "http://www.myhost.com/today":

```
import org.xml.sax.EntityResolver;
import org.xml.sax.InputSource;

public class MyResolver implements EntityResolver {
  public InputSource resolveEntity (String publicId, String systemId)
  {
    if (systemId.equals("http://www.myhost.com/today")) {
                            // return a special input source
      MyReader reader = new MyReader();
      return new InputSource(reader);
    } else {
                            // use the default behavior
      return null;
    }
  }
}
```

The application can also use this interface to redirect system identifiers to local URIs or to look up replacements in a catalog (possibly by using the public identifier).

The HandlerBase class implements the default behavior for this interface, which is simply always to return null (to request that the parser use the default system identifier).

resolveEntity	Allow the application to resolve external entities.
public InputSource resolveEntity (String publicId, String systemId) throws SAXException, IOException	The parser will call this method before opening any external entity except the top-level document entity (including the external DTD subset, external entities referenced within the DTD, and external entities referenced within the document element): the application may request that the parser resolve the entity itself, that it use an alternative URI, or that it use an entirely different input source.
	Application writers can use this method to redirect external system identifiers to secure and/or local URIs, to look up public identifiers in a catalogue, or to read an entity from a database or other input source (including, for example, a dialog box).
	If the system identifier is a URL, the SAX parser must resolve it fully before reporting it to the application.

resolveEntity (cont.)	**Parameters:**
	publicId – The public identifier of the external entity being referenced, or `null` if none was supplied.
	systemId – The system identifier of the external entity being referenced.
	Returns:
	An `InputSource` object describing the new input source, or `null` to request that the parser open a regular URI connection to the system identifier.
	Throws: SAXException.
	Any SAX exception, possibly wrapping another exception.
	Throws: IOException.
	A Java-specific IO exception, possibly the result of creating a new `InputStream` or `Reader` for the `InputSource`.

Interface org.xml.sax.ErrorHandler

You may implement this interface in your application if you want to take special action to handle errors. There is a default implementation provided within the `HandlerBase` *class.*

Basic interface for SAX error handlers

If a SAX application needs to implement customized error handling, it must implement this interface and then register an instance with the SAX parser using the parser's `setErrorHandler` method. The parser will then report all errors and warnings through this interface.

The parser shall use this interface instead of throwing an exception: it is up to the application whether to throw an exception for different types of errors and warnings. Note, however, that there is no requirement that the parser continue to provide useful information after a call to `fatalError` (in other words, a SAX driver class could catch an exception and report a `fatalError`).

The `HandlerBase` class provides a default implementation of this interface, ignoring warnings and recoverable errors and throwing a `SAXParseException` for fatal errors. An application may extend that class rather than implementing the complete interface itself.

error	Receive notification of a recoverable error.
public void error (SAXParseException exception) throws SAXException	This corresponds to the definition of "error" in section 1.2 of the W3C XML 1.0 Recommendation. For example, a validating parser would use this callback to report the violation of a validity constraint. The default behavior is to take no action.

Table continued on following page

error (cont.)	The SAX parser must continue to provide normal parsing events after invoking this method: it should still be possible for the application to process the document through to the end. If the application cannot do so, then the parser should report a fatal error even if the XML 1.0 recommendation does not require it to do so.
	Parameters:
	exception – The error information encapsulated in a SAX parse exception.
	Throws: SAXException.
	Any SAX exception, possibly wrapping another exception.
fatalError	Receive notification of a non-recoverable error.
public void fatalError (SAXParseException exception)	This corresponds to the definition of "fatal error" in section 1.2 of the W3C XML 1.0 Recommendation. For example, a parser would use this callback to report the violation of a well-formedness constraint.
throws SAXException	The application must assume that the document is unusable after the parser has invoked this method, and should continue (if at all) only for the sake of collecting additional error messages: in fact, SAX parsers are free to stop reporting any other events once this method has been invoked.
	Parameters:
	exception – The error information encapsulated in a SAX parse exception.
	Throws: SAXException.
	Any SAX exception, possibly wrapping another exception.

warning	Receive notification of a warning.
public void warning (SAXParseException exception)	SAX parsers will use this method to report conditions that are not errors or fatal errors as defined by the XML 1.0 recommendation. The default behavior is to take no action.
throws SAXException	The SAX parser must continue to provide normal parsing events after invoking this method: it should still be possible for the application to process the document through to the end.
	Parameters:
	exception – The warning information encapsulated in a SAX parse exception.
	Throws: SAXException.
	Any SAX exception, possibly wrapping another exception.

Class org.xml.sax.HandlerBase

This class is supplied with SAX itself: it provides default implementations of most of the methods that would otherwise need to be implemented by the application. If you write classes in your application as subclasses of HandlerBase, you need only code those methods where you want something other than the default behavior.

Default base class for handlers

This class implements the default behavior for four SAX interfaces: EntityResolver, DTDHandler, DocumentHandler, and ErrorHandler.

Application writers can extend this class when they need to implement only part of an interface; parser writers can instantiate this class to provide default handlers when the application has not supplied its own.

Note that the use of this class is optional.

In the description below, only the behavior of each method is described. For the parameters and return values, see the corresponding interface definition.

characters	By default, do nothing. Application writers may override this method to take specific actions for each chunk of character data (such as adding the data to a node or buffer, or printing it to a file).
public void characters (char ch[], int start, int length)	
throws SAXException	

Table continued on following page

endDocument

public void endDocument()

throws SAXException

Receive notification of the end of the document.

By default, do nothing. Application writers may override this method in a subclass to take specific actions at the beginning of a document (such as finalizing a tree or closing an output file).

endElement

public void endElement
      (String name)

throws SAXException

By default, do nothing. Application writers may override this method in a subclass to take specific actions at the end of each element (such as finalizing a tree node or writing output to a file).

error

public void error
      (SAXParseException e)

throws SAXException

The default implementation does nothing. Application writers may override this method in a subclass to take specific actions for each error, such as inserting the message in a log file or printing it to the console.

fatalError

public void fatalError
      (SAXParseException e)

throws SAXException

The default implementation throws a SAXParseException. Application writers may override this method in a subclass if they need to take specific actions for each fatal error (such as collecting all of the errors into a single report): in any case, the application must stop all regular processing when this method is invoked, since the document is no longer reliable, and the parser may no longer report parsing events.

ignorableWhitespace

public void ignorableWhitespace
      (char ch[],
      int start,
      int length)

throws SAXException

By default, do nothing. Application writers may override this method to take specific actions for each chunk of ignorable whitespace (such as adding data to a node or buffer, or printing it to a file).

notationDecl

public void notationDecl
      (String name,
      String publicId,
      String systemId)

By default, do nothing. Application writers may override this method in a subclass if they wish to keep track of the notations declared in a document.

processingInstruction
 	
public void processingInstruction
        (String target,
        String data)
 	
throws SAXException
	By default, do nothing. Application writers may override this method in a subclass to take specific actions for each processing instruction, such as setting status variables or invoking other methods.

resolveEntity
 	
public InputSource resolveEntity
        (String publicId,
        String systemId)
 	
throws SAXException
	Always return null, so that the parser will use the system identifier provided in the XML document.
	
	This method implements the SAX default behavior: application writers can override it in a subclass to do special translations such as catalog lookups or URI redirection.

setDocumentLocator public void setDocumentLocator (Locator locator)	By default, do nothing. Application writers may override this method in a subclass if they wish to store the locator for use with other document events.
startDocument public void startDocument() throws SAXException	By default, do nothing. Application writers may override this method in a subclass to take specific actions at the beginning of a document (such as allocating the root node of a tree or creating an output file).

startElement
 	
public void startElement
        (String name,
        AttributeList attributes)
 	
throws SAXException
	By default, do nothing. Application writers may override this method in a subclass to take specific actions at the start of each element (such as allocating a new tree node or writing output to a file).

unparsedEntityDecl
 	
public void unparsedEntityDecl
        (String name,
        String publicId,
        String systemId,
        String notationName)
	By default, do nothing. Application writers may override this method in a subclass to keep track of the unparsed entities declared in a document.

Table continued on following page

693

warning public void warning (SAXParseException e) throws SAXException	The default implementation does nothing. Application writers may override this method in a subclass to take specific actions for each warning, such as inserting the message in a log file or printing it to the console.

Class org.xml.sax.InputSource

An InputSource object represents a container for the XML document or any of the external entities it references (technically, the main document is itself an entity). The InputSource class is supplied with SAX: generally the application instantiates an InputSource and updates it to say where the input is coming from, and the parser interrogates it to find out where to read the input from.

The InputSource object provides three ways of supplying input to the parser: a System Identifier (or URL), a Reader (which delivers a stream of Unicode characters), or an InputStream (which delivers a stream of uninterpreted bytes).

A single input source for an XML entity

This class allows a SAX application to encapsulate information about an input source in a single object, which may include a public identifier, a system identifier, a byte stream (possibly with a specified encoding), and/or a character stream.

There are two places that the application will deliver this input source to the parser: as the argument to the Parser.parse method, or as the return value of the EntityResolver.resolveEntity method.

The SAX parser will use the InputSource object to determine how to read XML input. If there is a character stream available, the parser will read that stream directly; if not, the parser will use a byte stream, if available; if neither a character stream nor a byte stream is available, the parser will attempt to open a URI connection to the resource identified by the system identifier.

An InputSource object belongs to the application: the SAX parser shall never modify it in any way (it may modify a copy if necessary).

If you supply input in the form of a Reader or InputStream, it may be useful to supply a system identifier as well. If you do this, the URI will not be used to obtain the actual XML input, but it will be used in diagnostics, and more importantly to resolve any relative URIs within the document, for example entity references.

InputSource public InputSource()	Zero-argument default constructor.
InputSource public InputSource (String systemId)	Create a new input source with a system identifier. Applications may use setPublicId to include a public identifier as well, or setEncoding to specify the character encoding, if known.

InputSource (cont.)	If the system identifier is a URL, it must be fully resolved.
	Parameters:
	systemId – The system identifier (URI).
InputSource public InputSource (InputStream byteStream)	Create a new input source with a byte stream. Application writers may use `setSystemId` to provide a base for resolving relative URIs, `setPublicId` to include a public identifier, and/or `setEncoding` to specify the object's character encoding.
	Parameters:
	byteStream – The raw byte stream containing the document.
InputSource public InputSource (Reader characterStream)	Create a new input source with a character stream. Application writers may use `setSystemId()` to provide a base for resolving relative URIs, and `setPublicId` to include a public identifier.
	The character stream shall not include a byte order mark.
setPublicId public void setPublicId (String publicId)	Set the public identifier for this input source. The public identifier is always optional: if the application writer includes one, it will be provided as part of the location information.
	Parameters:
	publicId – The public identifier as a string.
getPublicId public String getPublicId ()	Get the public identifier for this input source.
	Returns:
	The public identifier, or `null` if none was supplied.

Table continued on following page

setSystemId public void setSystemId (String systemId)	Set the system identifier for this input source. The system identifier is optional if there is a byte stream or a character stream, but it is still useful to provide one, since the application can use it to resolve relative URIs and can include it in error messages and warnings (the parser will attempt to open a connection to the URI only if there is no byte stream or character stream specified). If the application knows the character encoding of the object pointed to by the system identifier, it can register the encoding using the `setEncoding` method. If the system ID is a URL, it must be fully resolved. **Parameters:** systemId – The system identifier as a string.
getSystemId public String getSystemId ()	Get the system identifier for this input source. The `getEncoding` method will return the character encoding of the object pointed to, or `null` if unknown. If the system ID is a URL, it will be fully resolved. **Returns:** The system identifier.
setByteStream public void setByteStream (InputStream byteStream)	Set the byte stream for this input source. The SAX parser will ignore this if there is also a character stream specified, but it will use a byte stream in preference to opening a URI connection itself. If the application knows the character encoding of the byte stream, it should set it with the `setEncoding` method. **Parameters:** byteStream – A byte stream containing an XML document or other entity.

getByteStream public InputStream getByteStream()	Get the byte stream for this input source. The getEncoding method will return the character encoding for this byte stream, or null if unknown. **Returns:** The byte stream, or null if none was supplied.
setEncoding public void setEncoding (String encoding)	Set the character encoding, if known. The encoding must be a string acceptable for an XML encoding declaration (see section 4.3.3 of the XML 1.0 recommendation). This method has no effect when the application provides a character stream. **Parameters:** encoding – A string describing the character encoding.
getEncoding public String getEncoding()	Get the character encoding for a byte stream or URI. **Returns:** The encoding, or null if none was supplied.
setCharacterStream public void setCharacterStream (Reader characterStream)	Set the character stream for this input source. If there is a character stream specified, the SAX parser will ignore any byte stream and will not attempt to open a URI connection to the system identifier. **Parameters:** characterStream – The character stream containing the XML document or other entity.
getCharacterStream public Reader getCharacterStream()	Get the character stream for this input source. **Returns:** The character stream, or null if none was supplied.

Table continued on following page

Interface org.xml.sax.Locator

This interface provides methods that the application can use to determine the current position in the source XML document.

Interface for associating a SAX event with a document location

If a SAX parser provides location information to the SAX application, it does so by implementing this interface and then passing an instance to the application using the document handler's `setDocumentLocator` method. The application can use the object to obtain the location of any other document handler event in the XML source document.

Note that the results returned by the object will be valid only during the scope of each document handler method: the application will receive unpredictable results if it attempts to use the locator at any other time.

SAX parsers are not required to supply a locator, but they are very strongly encouraged to do so. If the parser supplies a locator, it must do so before reporting any other document events. If no locator has been set by the time the application receives the `startDocument` event, the application should assume that a locator is not available.

getPublicId public String getPublicId()	Return the public identifier for the current document event. **Returns:** A string containing the public identifier, or `null` if none is available.
getSystemId public String getSystemId()	Return the system identifier for the current document event. If the system identifier is a URL, the parser must resolve it fully before passing it to the application. **Returns:** A string containing the system identifier, or `null` if none is available.
getLineNumber public int getLineNumber()	Return the line number where the current document event ends. Note that this is the line position of the first character after the text associated with the document event. In practice some parsers report the line number and column number where the event starts. **Returns:** The line number, or -1 if none is available.
getColumnNumber public int getColumnNumber()	Return the column number where the current document event ends. Note that this is the column number of the first character after the text associated with the document event. The first column in a line is position 1. **Returns:** The column number, or -1 if none is available.

Interface org.xml.sax.Parser

Every SAX parser must implement this interface. An application parses an XML document by creating an instance of a parser (that is, a class that implements this interface) and calling one of its `parse()` *methods.*

Basic interface for SAX (Simple API for XML) parsers

All SAX parsers must implement this basic interface: it allows applications to register handlers for different types of events and to initiate a parse from a URI, or a character stream.

All SAX parsers must also implement a zero-argument constructor (though other constructors are also allowed).

SAX parsers are reusable but not re-entrant: the application may reuse a parser object (possibly with a different input source) once the first parse has completed successfully, but it may not invoke the `parse()` methods recursively within a parse.

parse	Parse an XML document.
public void parse (InputSource source)	The application can use this method to instruct the SAX parser to begin parsing an XML document from any valid input source (a character stream, a byte stream, or a URI).
throws SAXException, IOException	Applications may not invoke this method while a parse is in progress (they should create a new Parser instead for each additional XML document). Once a parse is complete, an application may reuse the same Parser object, possibly with a different input source.
	Parameters:
	source – The input source for the top-level of the XML document.
	Throws: SAXException.
	Any SAX exception, possibly wrapping another exception.
	Throws: IOException.
	An IO exception from the parser, possibly from a byte stream or character stream supplied by the application.
parse	Parse an XML document from a system identifier (URI).
public void parse (String systemId)	This method is a shortcut for the common case of reading a document from a system identifier. It is the exact equivalent of the following:
throws SAXException, IOException	`parse(new InputSource(systemId));`
	If the system identifier is a URL, it must be fully resolved by the application before it is passed to the parser.

Table continued on following page

parse (cont.)	**Parameters:** systemId – The system identifier (URI). **Throws:** SAXException. Any SAX exception, possibly wrapping another exception. **Throws:** IOException. An IO exception from the parser, possibly from a byte stream or character stream supplied by the application.
setDocumentHandler public void setDocumentHandler (DocumentHandler handler)	Allow an application to register a document event handler. If the application does not register a document handler, all document events reported by the SAX parser will be silently ignored (this is the default behavior implemented by HandlerBase). Applications may register a new or different handler in the middle of a parse, and the SAX parser must begin using the new handler immediately. **Parameters:** handler – The document handler.
setDTDHandler public void setDTDHandler (DTDHandler handler)	Allow an application to register a DTD event handler. If the application does not register a DTD handler, all DTD events reported by the SAX parser will be silently ignored (this is the default behavior implemented by HandlerBase). Applications may register a new or different handler in the middle of a parse, and the SAX parser must begin using the new handler immediately. **Parameters:** handler – The DTD handler.

setEntityResolver

public void setEntityResolver
        (EntityResolver resolver)

Allow an application to register a custom entity resolver.

If the application does not register an entity resolver, the SAX parser will resolve system identifiers and open connections to entities itself (this is the default behavior implemented in `HandlerBase`).

Applications may register a new or different entity resolver in the middle of a parse, and the SAX parser must begin using the new resolver immediately.

Parameters:

resolver – The object for resolving entities.

setErrorHandler

public void setErrorHandler
        (ErrorHandler handler)

Allow an application to register an error event handler.

If the application does not register an error event handler, all error events reported by the SAX parser will be silently ignored, except for `fatalError`, which will throw a `SAXException` (this is the default behavior implemented by `HandlerBase`).

Applications may register a new or different handler in the middle of a parse, and the SAX parser must begin using the new handler immediately.

Parameters:

handler - The error handler.

setLocale

public void setLocale
        (Locale locale)

throws SAXException

Allow an application to request a locale for errors and warnings.

SAX parsers are not required to provide localization for errors and warnings; if they cannot support the requested locale, however, they must throw a SAX exception. Applications may not request a locale change in the middle of a parse.

Table continued on following page

701

setLocale (cont.)	**Parameters:**
	locale – A Java Locale object.
	Throws: SAXException.
	Throws an exception (using the previous or default locale) if the requested locale is not supported.

Class org.xml.sax.SAXException

This class is used to represent an error detected during processing either by the parser or by the application.

Encapsulate a general SAX error or warning

This class can contain basic error or warning information from either the XML parser or the application: a parser writer or application writer can subclass it to provide additional functionality. SAX handlers may throw this exception or any exception subclassed from it.

If the application needs to pass through other types of exceptions, it must wrap those exceptions in a SAXException or an exception derived from a SAXException.

If the parser or application needs to include information about a specific location in an XML document, it should use the SAXParseException subclass.

getMessage	Return a detail message for this exception.
public String getMessage()	If there is a embedded exception, and if the SAXException has no detail message of its own, this method will return the detail message from the embedded exception.
	Returns:
	The error or warning message.
getException	Return the embedded exception, if any.
public Exception getException()	**Returns:**
	The embedded exception, or null if there is none.
toString	Convert this exception to a string.
public String toString()	
	Returns:
	A string version of this exception.

Class org.xml.sax.SAXParseException

Extends `SAXException`.

This exception class represents an error or warning condition detected by the parser or by the application. In addition to the basic capability of `SAXException`, a `SAXParseException` allows information to be retained about the location in the source document where the error occurred. For an application-detected error, this information might be obtained from the `Locator` object.

Encapsulate an XML parse error or warning

This exception will include information for locating the error in the original XML document. Note that although the application will receive a `SAXParseException` as the argument to the handlers in the `ErrorHandler` interface, the application is not actually required to throw the exception; instead, it can simply read the information in it and take a different action.

Since this exception is a subclass of `SAXException`, it inherits the ability to wrap another exception.

SAXParseException
 	
public SAXParseException
      (String message,
      Locator locator)
	Create a new `SAXParseException` from a message and a Locator.
	
	This constructor is especially useful when an application is creating its own exception from within a `DocumentHandler` callback.
	
	Parameters:
	
	message – The error or warning message.
	
	locator – The locator object for the error or warning.

SAXParseException
 	
public SAXParseException
      (String message,
      Locator locator,
      Exception e)
	Wrap an existing exception in a `SAXParseException`.
	
	This constructor is especially useful when an application is creating its own exception from within a `DocumentHandler` callback, and needs to wrap an existing exception that is not a subclass of `SAXException`.
	
	Parameters:
	
	message – The error or warning message, or `null` to use the message from the embedded exception.
	
	locator – The locator object for the error or warning.
	
	e – Any exception.

Table continued on following page

SAXParseException	Create a new `SAXParseException`.
public SAXParseException (String message, String publicId, String systemId, int lineNumber, int columnNumber)	This constructor is most useful for parser writers. If the system identifier is a URL, the parser must resolve it fully before creating the exception. **Parameters:** message – The error or warning message. publicId – The public identifier of the entity that generated the error or warning. systemId – The system identifier of the entity that generated the error or warning. lineNumber – The line number of the end of the text that caused the error or warning. columnNumber – The column number of the end of the text that caused the error or warning.
SAXParseException public SAXParseException (String message, String publicId, String systemId, int lineNumber, int columnNumber, Exception e)	Create a new `SAXParseException` with an embedded exception. This constructor is most useful for parser writers who need to wrap an exception that is not a subclass of `SAXException`. If the system identifier is a URL, the parser must resolve it fully before creating the exception. **Parameters:** message – The error or warning message, or `null` to use the message from the embedded exception. publicId – The public identifier of the entity that generated the error or warning. systemId – The system identifier of the entity that generated the error or warning. lineNumber – The line number of the end of the text that caused the error or warning. columnNumber – The column number of the end of the text that caused the error or warning. e – Another exception to embed in this one.

getPublicId

public String getPublicId()

Get the public identifier of the entity where the exception occurred.

Returns:

A string containing the public identifier, or `null` if none is available.

getSystemId

public String getSystemId()

Get the system identifier of the entity where the exception occurred. *Note that the term "entity" includes the top-level XML document.*

If the system identifier is a URL, it will be resolved fully.

Returns:

A string containing the system identifier, or `null` if none is available.

getLineNumber

public int getLineNumber()

The line number of the end of the text where the exception occurred.

Returns:

An integer representing the line number, or -1 if none is available.

getColumnNumber

public int getColumnNumber()

The column number of the end of the text where the exception occurred. The first column in a line is position 1.

Returns:

An integer representing the column number, or -1 if none is available.

ASP Quick Start Tutorial

One of the many exciting uses for XML is for transmitting data via the Web. Throughout the book, as we learn about the various XML technologies, we cover numerous examples of this, but occasionally assume some knowledge of web programming in general and **Active Server Pages** (**ASP**) in particular. This appendix is intended to help if you have *limited* previous ASP experience, or simply need a refresher. It is not intended to teach you everything there is to know about ASP – this is the subject of many other books, such as *Beginning ASP 3.0* (ISBN 1-861003-38-2) from Wrox Press. But it should give you enough of an understanding to be able to follow along with our examples of using XML and ASP together, such as in Case Study 2.

ASP is a great tool for creating dynamic web pages. It is a Microsoft technology, which works by allowing us the functionality of a programming language, using the programming code to dynamically generate HTML for our web pages. Using ASP you can do many things. You are able to draw upon the wealth of data available to you on the server and across the enterprise in various databases, including XML-based data stores. You are able to customize pages to the needs of each different user that comes to your web site. In addition, by keeping your code on the server-side you can build a library of functionality. This library can be drawn upon again and again to further enhance other web sites. Best of all, using server-side script libraries will allow your web sites to scale to multi-tier, or distributed, web applications.

To be able to do these things, you need a good understanding of the HTTP protocol, and how an HTTP server interacts with a browser. This model is important to understand when developing web applications that exist on the client and server side. We'll go through HTTP and give a simplified overview of how the protocol works. Then we'll give you a quick run through of Active Server Pages, or ASP.

ASP can be used to create everything from simple, static web pages, to database-aware dynamic sites, using HTML and scripting. Its other important use is as programming *glue*. Through the use of ASP, you can create and manipulate server-side components. These components can perhaps provide data to your application such as graphic image generation, or maybe link to a mainframe database, or an XML application. ASP does nothing but facilitate the use of these components on the web. ASP comes with some built-in objects that are important to understand before their full potential can be unleashed. We will cover each of these objects in depth. Finally, we'll look at some real-world examples of using ASP on a web site.

The Anatomy of the HTTP Protocol

As you know, surfing the Web is as simple as clicking a link on your browser. But do you know what really goes on beneath the hood of your web browser? It can be quite complex, but isn't too difficult to understand. More importantly, it will help you to understand the intricacies of client and server-side scripting.

Overview

The **Hypertext Transfer Protocol**, or **HTTP**, is an *application level* TCP/IP protocol. An application level protocol is one that travels on top of another protocol. In this instance, HTTP travels on top of TCP, which is also a protocol. When two computers communicate over a TCP/IP connection, the data is formatted and processed in such a manner that it is guaranteed to arrive at its destination. This elaborate mechanism is the TCP/IP protocol.

HTTP takes for granted, and largely ignores, the entire TCP/IP protocol. It relies instead on text commands like GET and PUT. Application level protocols are implemented, usually, within an application (as opposed to at the driver level), hence the name. Some other examples of application level protocols are the **File Transfer Protocol** (FTP) and the mail protocols, **Standard Mail Transfer Protocol** (SMTP) and the **Post Office Protocol** (POP3). Pure binary data is rarely sent via these protocols, but when it is, it is encoded into an ASCII format. This is inefficient at best, and future versions of the HTTP protocol will rectify this problem. The most up-to-date version of HTTP is version 1.1, and almost all web servers available today support this version.

There is also a new HTTP protocol in development called HTTP-NG, or HTTP-Next Generation. This newer, robust protocol will utilize bandwidth more efficiently and improve on many of the original HTTP's shortcomings. The biggest improvement in the new protocol is that data will be transferred in binary format as opposed to text, thus making transactions quicker. More technical information about HTTP-NG is available from the W3C at http://www.w3.org/Protocols/HTTP-NG/Activity.html.

The HTTP Server

To carry out an HTTP request, there must be an HTTP or web server running on the target machine. This server is an application that listens for and responds to HTTP requests on a certain TCP port (by default, port 80). An HTTP request is for a single item from the web server. The item may be anything from a web page to a sound file. The server, upon receipt of the request, attempts to retrieve the data asked for. If the server finds the correct information, it formats and returns the data to the client. If the requested information could not be found, the server will return an error message.

Pulling up a single web page in your browser may cause dozens of HTTP transactions to occur. Each element on a web page that is not text needs to be requested from the HTTP server individually. The main point of all this is that each HTTP transaction consists of a request and a response:

And it is in this transaction model that you must place yourself when you are programming web applications.

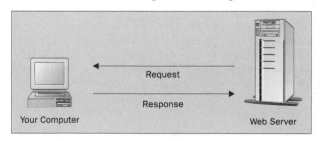

Protocol Basics

There are four basic states that make up a single HTTP transaction. They are:

- ❑ The Connection
- ❑ The Request
- ❑ The Response
- ❑ The Disconnection

A client connects to a server and issues the request. It waits for a response, then disconnects. A connection typically lasts only for a few seconds. On web sites like Yahoo where the data is not laden with graphics, and the information is fairly static, requests last less than one second.

The Connection

The client software, a web browser in this case, creates a TCP/IP connection to an HTTP server on a specific TCP/IP port. Port 80 is used if one is not specified; this is considered the default port for an HTTP server. A web server may, however, reside on any port allowed. It is completely up to the operator of the web server, and port numbers are often deliberately changed as a first line of defense against unauthorized users.

The Request

Once connected, the client sends a request to the server. This request is in ASCII, and must be terminated by a carriage-return/line-feed pair. Every request must specify a method, which tells the server what the client wants. In HTTP 1.1, there are eight methods: OPTIONS, GET, HEAD, POST, PUT, DELETE, TRACE, and CONNECT. For more information about the different methods and their use, check out the HTTP specification on the W3C web site. For the purpose of this quick start tutorial, we are going to focus on the GET method.

The GET method asks the web server to return the specified page. The format of this request is as follows:

```
GET <URL> <HTTP Version>
```

You can make HTTP requests yourself with the **telnet** program. Telnet is a program that is available on most computer systems and it was originally designed for use on UNIX systems. Since basic UNIX is character-based, one could log in from a remote site and work with the operating system. Telnet is the program that allows you to connect to a remote machine and all versions of Windows come with a telnet program. The screenshot overleaf shows what it looks like.

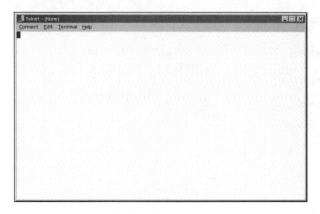

*Microsoft's telnet leaves much to be desired. Thankfully, a company called Van Dyke Technologies
(www.vandyke.com) created an excellent telnet program called CRT.*

Telnet defaults to TCP/IP port 23. On UNIX systems, in order to telnet into a machine, that machine
must be running a telnet server. This server listens for incoming telnet connections on port 23.
However, almost all telnet programs allow you to specify the port on which to connect. It is this feature
that we can utilize to examine HTTP running under the hood.

If you choose not to download the Van Dyke telnet client, you can test this by running Window's own
telnet. Windows has no predefined menu item for this program, but it can usually be found at
C:\WINDOWS\TELNET.EXE. To run it, press the Start button and select Run. Type in telnet and press
Enter. You should see a telnet window similar to the one above.

Select Remote System from the Connect menu and you'll be presented with the following dialog:

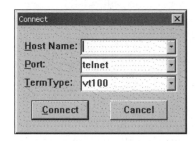

Type in the name of any web server; we chose http://www.mindbuilder.com. Then enter the web
server's port. This is almost always 80.

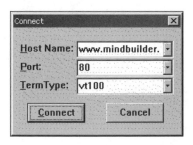

Once you are connected, the title bar will change to contain the name of the server to which you are connected. There is no other indication of connection. It is at this point that you need to type in your HTTP command. Type in the following, all in upper case:

```
GET / HTTP/1.0
```

Note that unless you have turned on Local Echo in the Preferences, you will not see what you type. After you've entered the command you must send a carriage return (*Ctrl-M*) followed by a line feed (*Ctrl-J*). The following screenshot shows what is returned – this is the response to your HTTP request:

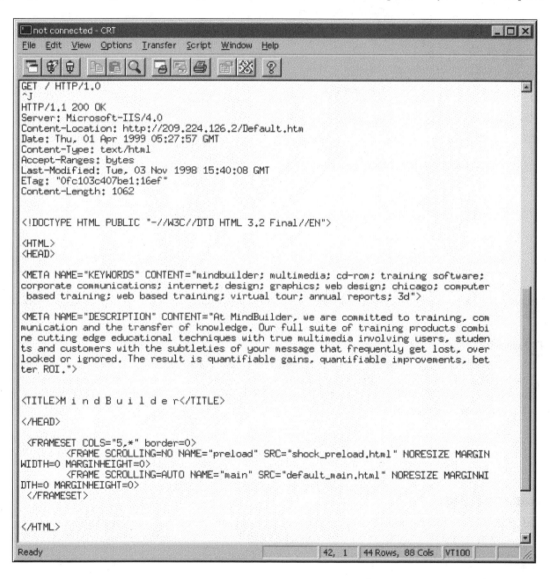

The Response

Upon receipt of the request, the web server will answer. This will most likely result in some sort of HTML data as we just saw. However, you may get an error as in the following example:

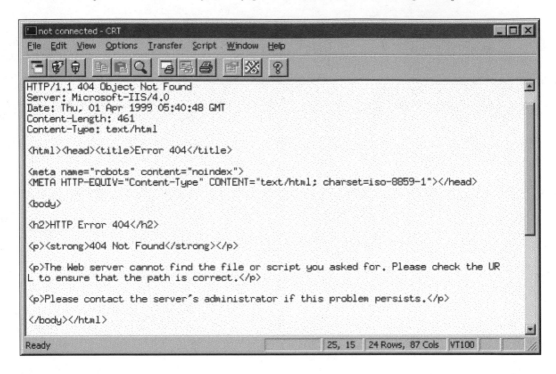

Again, the response is in HTML, but the code returned is an error code (404) instead of an OK (200). In this case the wrong URL was entered and the file could not be found.

HTTP Headers

What was actually returned is a two-part response. The first part consists of HTTP headers. These headers provide information about the actual response to the request, the most important header being the status header. In the listing above, it reads **HTTP/1.1 404 Object Not Found**. This indicates the actual status of the request.

The other headers that were returned with this request are Server, Date, Content-Length, and Content-Type. There are many different types of headers, and they are all designed to aid the browser in easily identifying the type of information that is being returned.

Disconnecting

After the server has responded to your request, it closes the connection thus disconnecting you. Subsequent requests require you to re-establish your connection with the server.

Introducing Active Server Pages

With the HTTP architecture laid out in the last section, you can clearly see that the real heart of the HTTP protocol lies in the request and the response. The client makes a request to the server, and the server provides the response to the client. What we're looking at here is really the foundation of client/server computing. A client makes a request from a server and the server fulfills that request. We see this pattern of behavior throughout the programming world today, not only in web programming.

Microsoft recognized this pattern and developed a new technology that rendered web programming a much more accessible technique. This technology is Active Server Pages or ASP for short. ASP is a server-side scripting environment that comes with Microsoft's Internet Information Services. ASP allows you to embed scripting commands inside your HTML documents. The scripting commands are interpreted by the server and translated into the corresponding HTML and sent back to the server. This enables the web developer to create content that is dynamic and fresh. The beauty of this is that it does not matter which browser your web visitor is using, because the server returns only pure HTML. Sure you can extend your returned HTML with browser specific programming, but that is your choice. By no means is this all that ASP can do, but we'll cover more of its capabilities, such as form validation and data manipulation, later in this chapter.

Although you can use languages such as JavaScript or even Perl, by default the ASP scripting language is VBScript.

How the Server Recognizes ASPs

ASP pages do not have an `html` or `htm` extension; they have an `.asp` extension instead. The reason for this is twofold. First, in order for the web server to know to process the scripting in your web page, it needs to know that there is some in there. Well, by setting the extension of your web page to `.asp`, the server can assume that there are scripts in your page.

A nice side effect of naming your ASP pages with the `.asp` extension is that the ASP processor knows that it does not need to process your HTML files. It used to be the case, as in ASP 2.0, that any page with the `.asp` extension, no matter whether it contained any server side scripting code or not, was automatically sent to the server, and would thereby take longer to process. With the introduction of ASP 3.0 in Windows 2000, the server is able to determine the presence of any server side code and process or not process the page accordingly. This increases the speed of your HTML file retrieval and makes your web server run more efficiently.

Secondly, using an `asp` extension (forcing interpretation by the ASP processor every time your page is requested) hides your ASP scripts. If someone requests your `.asp` file from the web server, all they are going to get back is the resultant processed HTML. If you put your ASP code in a file called `mycode.scr` and request it from the web server, you'll see all of the code inside.

ASP Basics

ASP files are really just HTML files with scripting embedded within them. When a browser requests an ASP file from the server, it is passed on to the ASP-processing DLL for execution. After processing, the resulting file is then sent on to the requesting browser. Any scripting commands embedded from the original HTML file are executed and then removed from the results. This is excellent, in that all of your scripting code is hidden from the person viewing your web pages. That is why it is so important that files containing ASP scripts have an `.asp` extension.

The Tags of ASP

To distinguish the ASP code from the HTML inside your files, ASP code is placed between <% and %> tags. This convention should be familiar to you if you have ever worked with any kind of server-side commands before in HTML. The tag combination implies to the ASP processor that the code within should be executed by the server and removed from the results. Depending on the default scripting language of your web site, this code may be VBScript, JScript, or any other language you've installed.

All of our ASP scripts in this appendix will be in VBScript, since that is the default.

In the following snippet of HTML, you'll see an example of some ASP code between the <% and %> tags:

```
<TABLE>
<TR>
<TD>
<%
    x = x + 1
    y = y - 1
%>
</TD>
</TR>
</TABLE>
```

<SCRIPT> Blocks

You may also place your ASP code in <SCRIPT></SCRIPT> blocks. However, unless you direct the script to run at the server level, code placed between these tags will be executed at the client as normal client-side scripts. To direct your script block to execute on the server, use the RUNAT="Server" command within your <SCRIPT> block as follows:

```
<SCRIPT Language="VBScript" RUNAT="Server">
... Your Script ...
</SCRIPT>
```

The Default Scripting Language

As stated previously, the default scripting language used by ASP is VBScript. However, you may change it for your entire site, or just a single web page. Placing a special scripting tag at the beginning of your web page does this. This tag specifies the scripting language to use for this page only:

```
<%@ LANGUAGE=ScriptingLanguage%>
```

ScriptingLanguage can be any language for which you have the scripting engine installed. ASP comes with JScript, as well as VBScript.

If you are using the <SCRIPT> tags, you can specify which language to use by adding the Language attribute as shown:

```
<SCRIPT Language="VBScript" RUNAT="Server">
```

You can set the default scripting language for the entire application by changing the Default ASP language field in the Internet Service Manager on the App Options tab.

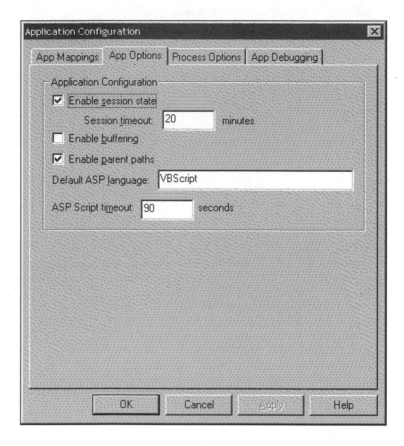

Mixing HTML and ASP

You've probably guessed by now that one can easily mix HTML code with ASP scripts. VBScript has all of the flow control mechanisms like If Then, For Next, and Do While loops. But with ASP you can selectively include HTML code based on the results of these operators. Let's look at an example.

Suppose you are creating a web page that greets the viewer with a "Good Morning", "Good Afternoon", or "Good Evening" depending on the time of day. This can be done as follows:

```
<HTML>
<BODY>
<P>The time is now <%=Time()%></P>
<%
  Dim iHour

  iHour = Hour(Time())

  If (iHour >= 0 And iHour < 12 ) Then
%>
Good Morning!
<%
```

```
    ElseIf (iHour > 11 And iHour < 5 ) Then
%>
Good Afternoon!
<%
   Else
%>
Good Evening!
<%
End If
%>
</BODY>
</HTML>
```

First we print out the current time. The `<%=` notation is shorthand to print out the value of an ASP variable or the result of a function call. We then move the hour of the current time into a variable called `iHour`. Based on the value of this variable we write our normal HTML text.

Notice how the HTML code is outside of the ASP script tags. When the ASP processor executes this page, the HTML that lies between control flow blocks that aren't executed is discarded, leaving you with only the correct code. Here is the source of what is returned from our web server after processing this page (at 19:48:37):

```
<HTML>
<BODY>
<P>The time is now 7:48:37 PM</P>

Good Evening!

</BODY>
</HTML>
```

As you can see, the scripting is completely removed leaving only the HTML tags and text.

The other way to output data to your web page viewer is using one of ASP's built-in objects called `Response`. We'll cover this approach in the next section as you learn about the ASP object model.

Commenting Your ASP Code

As with any programming language, it is of the utmost importance to comment your ASP code as much as possible. However, unclear comments are not worth putting in your code.

Comments in ASP are identical to comments in VBScript. When ASP comes across the single quote character it will graciously ignore the rest of the line:

```
<%
Dim iLumberJack

'I'm a comment and I'm O.K.
iLumberJack = iLumberJack + 1
%>
```

The Active Server Pages Object Model

ASP, like most Microsoft technologies, utilizes a Component Object Model, or COM, to expose functionality to consumer applications. ASP is actually an extension to your web server that allows server-side scripting. At the same time it also provides a compendium of objects and components, which manage interaction between the web server and the browser. These objects form the **Active Server Pages Object Model**. These objects can be manipulated by scripting languages. Take a look at the following diagram:

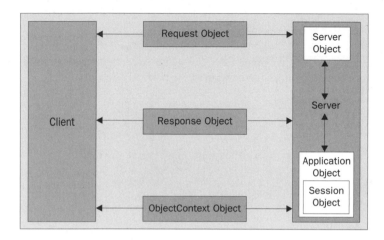

ASP 2.0 neatly divides up into six objects, which manage their own part of the interaction between client and server. As you can see in the diagram, at the heart of the interaction between client and server are the Request and Response objects, which deal with the HTTP request and response; but we will be taking a quick tour through all of the different objects and components that are part of ASP.

The object model consists of six core objects, each one with distinct properties and methods. The objects are:

- ❑   Request
- ❑   Response
- ❑   Application
- ❑   Session
- ❑   Server
- ❑   ObjectContext

Each of the objects, barring the Server and ObjectContext object, can use collections to store data. Before we look at each object in turn we need to take a quick overview of collections.

Collections

Collections in ASP are very similar to their VBScript namesakes. They act as data containers that store their data in a manner close to that of an array. The information is stored in the form of name/value pairs.

The `Application` and the `Session` object have a collection property called `Contents`. This collection of variants can hold any information you wish to place in it. Using these collections allows you to share information between web pages.

To place a value into the collection, simply assign it a key and then assign the value, such as:

```
Application.Contents("Name") = "Evil Knievel"
```

Or:

```
Session.Contents("Age") = 25
```

Fortunately for us, Microsoft has made the `Contents` collections the default property for these two objects. Therefore the following shorthand usage is perfectly acceptable:

```
Application("Name") = "Evil Knievel"
Session("Age") = 25
```

To read values from the `Contents` collections, just reverse the call:

```
sName = Application("Name")
sAge = Session("Age")
```

Iterating the Contents Collection

Because the `Contents` collections work like regular VBScript collections, they are easily iterated. You can use the collections' `Count` property, or use the `For Each` iteration method:

```
For x = 1 to Application.Contents.Count
  ...
Next

For each item in Application.Contents
  ...
Next
```

> Note that the `Contents` collections are 1 based. That is to say that the first element in the collection is at position 1, not 0.

To illustrate this, the following ASP script will dump the current contents of the `Application` and `Session` objects' `Contents` collections:

```
<HTML>
<BODY>
<P>The Application.Contents</P>
```

```
<%
    Dim Item

    For Each Item In Application.Contents
     Response.Write Item & " = [" & Application(Item) & "]<BR>"
    Next
%>
<P>The Session.Contents</P>
<%
    For Each Item In Session.Contents
     Response.Write Item & " = [" & Session(Item) & "]<BR>"
    Next
%>
</BODY>
</HTML>
```

Removing an Item from the Contents Collection

The `Application` object's `Contents` collection contains two methods, and these are `Remove` and `RemoveAll`. These allow you to remove one or all of the items stored in the `Application.Contents` collection. At the time of writing, there is no method to remove an item from the `Session.Contents` collection.

This is how we'd add an item to the `Application.Contents` collection, and then remove it:

```
<%
    Application("MySign") = "Pisces"
    Application.Contents.Remove("MySign")
%>
```

Or we could just get rid of everything:

```
<%
    Application.Contents.RemoveAll
%>
```

Not all of the collections of each object work in this way, but the principles remain the same and we will explain how each differs when we discuss each object.

The Request Object

When your web page is requested, much information is passed along with the HTTP request, such as the URL of the web page requested and format of the data being passed. It can also contain feedback from the user such as the input from a text box or drop down list box. The `Request` object allows you to get at information passed along as part of the HTTP request. The corresponding output from the server is returned as part of the `Response`. The `Request` object has several collections to store information that warrant discussion.

The Request Object's Collections

The Request object has five collections. Interestingly, they all act as the default property for the object. That is to say, you may retrieve information from any of the five collections by using the abbreviated syntax, for example:

```
ClientIPAddress = Request("REMOTE_ADDR")
```

The REMOTE_ADDR value lies in the ServerVariables collection. However, through the use of the collection cascade, it can be retrieved with the above notation. Note that for ASP to dig through each collection, especially if they have many values, to retrieve a value from the last collection is inefficient. It is always recommended to use the fully qualified collection name in your code. Not only is this faster, but it improves your code in that it is more specific, and less cryptic.

ASP searches through the collections in the following order:

- ❑ QueryString
- ❑ Form
- ❑ Cookies
- ❑ ClientCertificate
- ❑ ServerVariables

If there are variables with the same name, only the first is returned when you allow ASP to search. This is another good reason for you to fully qualify your collection.

QueryString

Contains a collection of all the information attached to the end of a URL. When you make a URL request, the additional information is passed along with the URL to the web page, appended with a question mark. This information takes the following form:

```
URL?item=data[&item=data][…]
```

The clue to the server is the question mark. When the server sees this, it knows that the URL has ended, and variables are starting. So an example of a URL with a query string might look like this:

```
http://www.buythisbook.com/book.asp?bookname=BeginningXML
```

We stated earlier that the collections store information in name/value pairs. Despite this slightly unusual method of creating the name/value pair, the principle remains the same. bookname is the name and BeginningXML is the value. When ASP gets hold of this URL request, it breaks apart all of the name/value pairs and places them into this collection for easy access. This is another excellent feature of ASP. Query strings are built up using ampersands to delimit each name/value pair so if you wished to pass the user information along with the book information, you could pass the following:

```
http://www.buythisbook.com/book.asp?bookname=BeginningXML&buyer=ChrisUllman
```

Query strings can be generated in one of three ways. The first is, as discussed, by a user-typed URL. The second is as part of a URL specified in an anchor tag:

```
<A HREF="book.asp?bookname=BeginningXML">Go to book buying page</A>
```

So when you click on the link, the name/value pair is passed along with the URL. The third and final method is via a form sent to the server with the GET method:

```
<FORM ACTION="book.asp" METHOD="GET">
Type your name: <INPUT TYPE="TEXT" NAME="buyer"><BR>
Type your requested book:  <INPUT TYPE="TEXT" NAME="bookname" SIZE=40><BR>
<INPUT TYPE=SUBMIT VALUE=Submit>
</FORM>
```

You input the information into the text boxes on the form. The text is submitted when you click on Submit and two query strings are generated.

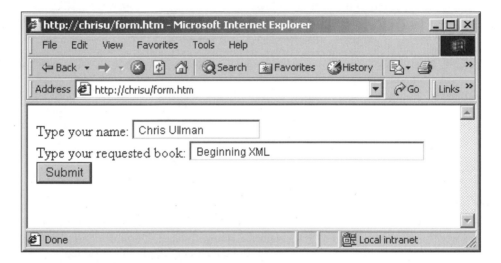

Next you need to be able to retrieve information, and you use this technique regardless of which of the three methods were used to generate the query string:

```
Request.QueryString("buyer")
Request.QueryString("bookname")
```

Note that these lines won't display anything by themselves, you need to add either the shorthand notation (equality operator) to display functions in front of a single statement, or when a number of values need displaying then use Response.Write to separately display each value in the collection.

E.g. <%=Request.QueryString("buyer")%> or Response.Write(Request.QueryString("bookname"))

The first of the two `Request` object calls should return the name of `Chris Ullman` on the page and the second of the two should return `Beginning XML`. Of course you could always store this information in a variable for later access:

```
sBookName = Request.QueryString("bookname")
```

Form

Contains a collection of all the form variables posted to the HTTP request by an HTML form. Query strings aren't very private as they transmit information via a very visible method, the URL. If you want to transmit information from the form more privately then you can use the `Form` collection to do so – it sends its information as part of the HTTP `Request` body. This easy access to form variables is one of ASP's best features.

If we go back to our previous example, the only alteration we need to make to our HTML form code is to change the `METHOD` attribute. Forms using this collection must be sent with the `POST` method and not the `GET` method. It is actually this attribute that determines how the information is sent by the form. So if we change the method of the form as follows:

```
<FORM ACTION="book.asp" METHOD="POST">
Type your name: <INPUT TYPE="TEXT" NAME="buyer"><BR>
Type your requested book:  <INPUT TYPE="TEXT" NAME="bookname" SIZE=40><BR>
<INPUT TYPE=SUBMIT VALUE=Submit>
</FORM>
```

Once the form has been submitted in this style, then we can retrieve and display the information using the following:

```
<%=Request.Form("buyer")%>
```

Cookies

Contains a read-only collection of cookies sent by the client browser along with the request. Because the cookies were sent from the client, they cannot be changed here. You must change them using the `Response.Cookies` collection. A discussion of cookies can be found a little later on when we look at the `Response` object.

ClientCertificate

When a client makes a connection with a server requiring a high degree of security, either party can confirm who the sender/receiver is by inspecting their digital certificate. A digital certificate contains a number of items of information about the sender, such as the holder's name, address and length of time the certificate is valid for. A third party, known as the Certificate Authority or CA, will have previously verified these details.

The `ClientCertificate` collection is used to access details held in a client side digital certificate sent by the browser. This collection is only populated if you are running a secure server, and the request was via an https:// call instead of an http:// call. This is the preferred method to invoke a secure connection.

ServerVariables

When the client sends a request and information is passed across to the server, it's not just the page that is passed across, but information such as who created the page, the server name, and the port that the request was sent to. The HTTP header that is sent across together with the HTTP request also contains information of this nature, such as the type of browser, and type of connection. This information is combined into a list of variables that are predefined by the server as environment variables. Most of them are static and never really change unless you change the configuration of your web server. The rest are based on the client browser.

These server variables can be accessed in the normal way. For instance, the server variable `HTTP_USER_AGENT`, which returns information about the type of browser being used to view the page, can be displayed as follows:

```
<%=Request.ServerVariables("HTTP_USER_AGENT")%>
```

Alternatively you can print out the whole list of server variables and their values with the following code:

```
For Each key in Request.ServerVariables
    Response.Write "<B>" & (key) & "</B> "
    Response.Write (Request.ServerVariables(key)) & "<BR>"
Next
```

This displays each key of the `ServerVariables` collection in bold, and the contents of the key (if any) after it. The final product looks like this:

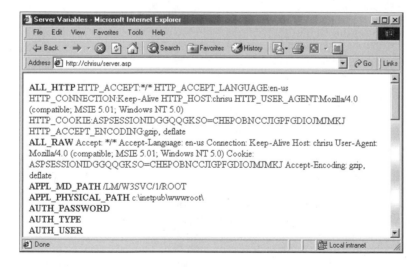

Server variables are merely informative, but they do give you the ability to customize page content for specific browsers, or to avoid script errors that might be generated.

Request Object Property and Method

The `Request` object contains a single property and a single method. They are used together to transfer files from the client to the server. Uploading is accomplished using HTML forms.

TotalBytes Property

When the request is processed, this property will hold the total number of bytes in the client browser request. Most likely you'd use it to return the number of bytes in the file you wish to transfer. This information is important to the `BinaryRead` method.

BinaryRead Method

This method retrieves the information sent to the web server by the client browser in a `POST` operation. When the browser issues a `POST`, the data is encoded and sent to the server. When the browser issues a `GET`, there is no data other than the URL. The `BinaryRead` method takes one parameter, the number of bytes to read. So if you want it to read a whole file, you pass it the total number of bytes in the file, generated by the `TotalBytes` property.

This method is very rarely applied because `Request.QueryString` and `Request.Form` are much easier to use. That's because `BinaryRead` wraps its answer in a safe array of bytes. For a scripting language that essentially only handles variants, that makes life a little complicated. However this format is essential for file uploading when the file contains something other than pure text. You can find full details on how to upload files and then decode a safe array of bytes in an excellent article at: http://www.15seconds.com/Issue/981121.htm.

The Response Object

After you've processed the request information from the client browser, you'll need to be able to send information back. The `Response` object is just the ticket. It provides you with the tools necessary to send anything you need back to the client.

The Response Object's Collection

The `Response` object contains only one collection: `Cookies`. This is the version of the `Request` object's `Cookies` collection that can be written to.

If you've not come across them before, cookies are small (limited to 4kb of data) text files stored on the hard drive of the client that contain information about the user, such as whether they have visited the site before and what date they last visited the site. There are lots of misapprehensions about cookies being intrusive as they allow servers to store information on the user's drive. However you need to remember that firstly the user has to voluntarily accept cookies or activate an Accept Cookies mechanism on the browser for them to work, secondly this information is completely benign and cannot be used to determine the user's e-mail address or such like. They are used to personalize pages that the user might have visited before. Examples of things to store in cookies are unique user IDs, or user names; then, when the user returns to your web site, a quick check of cookies will let you know if this is a return visitor or not.

You can create a cookie on the user's machine as follows:

```
Response.Cookies("BookBought") = "Beginning XML"
```

You can also store multiple values in one cookie using an index value key. The cookie effectively contains a VBScript `Dictionary` object and using the key can retrieve individual items. The way it functions is very similar to an array.

```
Response.Cookies("BookBought")("1") = "Beginning XML"
Response.Cookies("BookBought")("2") = "Professional XML"
```

A cookie will automatically expire – disappear from the user's machine – the moment a user ends their session. To extend the cookie beyond this natural lifetime, you can specify a date with the `Expires` property. The date takes the following format: *WEEKDAY DD-MON-YY HH:MM:SS*, for example:

```
Response.Cookies("BookBought").Expires = #31-Dec-99#
```

The # sign can be used to delimit dates in ASP (as in VBScript).

Other properties that can be used in conjunction with this collection are:

❑ `Domain`: a cookie is only sent to pages requested within the domain from which it was created

❑ `Path`: a cookie is only sent to pages requested within this path

❑ `HasKeys`: specifies whether the cookie uses an index/`Dictionary` object or not

❑ `Secure`: specifies whether the cookie is secure – a cookie is only deemed secure if sent via the HTTPS protocol

You can retrieve the cookie's information using the `Request` object's `Cookies` collection, mentioned earlier. To do this you could do the following:

```
You purchased <%=Request.Cookies("BookBought")%> last time you visited the site.
```

If there were several cookies in the collection you could iterate through each cookie and display the contents as follows:

```
For Each cookie in Request.Cookies
    Response.Write (Request.Cookies(cookie))
Next
```

The Response Object's Methods

To understand what the `Response` object's methods and properties do, we need to examine in more detail the workings of how ASP sends a response. When an ASP script is run, an **HTML output stream** is created. This stream is a receptacle in which the web server can store details and create the dynamic/interactive web page. As mentioned before, the page has to be created entirely in HTML for the browser to understand it (excluding client-side scripting, which is ignored by the server).

The stream is initially empty when created. New information is added to the end. If any custom HTML headers are required then they have to be added at the beginning. Then the HTML contained in the ASP page is added to the script, so anything not encompassed by <% %> tags is added. The `Response` object provides two ways of writing directly to the output stream, either using the `Write` method or its shorthand technique. We've already seen examples of both of these – let's look at them in more detail.

Write

Probably the most frequently used method of all the built-in objects, `Write` allows you to send information back to the client browser. You can write text directly to a web page by encasing the text in quotation marks:

```
Response.Write "Hello World!"
```

Or to display the contents of a variant you just drop the quotation marks:

```
sText = "Hello World!"
Response.Write sText
```

For single portions of dynamic information that only require adding into large portions of HTML, you can use the equality sign as shorthand for this method, as specified earlier, for example:

```
My message is <% =sText %>
```

This technique reduces the amount of code needed, but at the expense of readability. There is nothing to choose between these techniques in terms of performance.

AddHeader

This method allows you to add custom headers to the HTTP response. For example, if you were to write a custom browser application that examined the headers of your HTTP requests for a certain value, you'd use this method to set that value. Usage is as follows:

```
Response.AddHeader "CustomServerApp", "BogiePicker/1.0"
```

This would add the header `CustomServerApp` to the response with the value of `BogiePicker/1.0`. There are no restrictions regarding headers and header value.

AppendToLog

Calling this method allows you to append a string to the web server log file entry for this particular request. This allows you to add custom log messages to the log file.

BinaryWrite

This method allows you to bypass the normal character conversion that takes place when data is sent back to the client. Usually, only text is returned, so the web server cleans it up. By calling `BinaryWrite` to send your data, the actual binary data is sent back, bypassing that cleaning process.

Clear

This method allows you to delete any data that has been buffered for this page so far. See the discussion of the `Buffer` property for more details.

End

This method stops processing the ASP file and returns any currently buffered data to the client browser.

Flush

This method returns any currently buffered data to the client browser and then clears the buffer. See the discussion of the `Buffer` property for more details.

Redirect

This method allows you to relinquish control of the current page to another web page entirely. For example, you can use this method to redirect users to a login page if they have not yet logged on to your web site:

```
<%
If (Not Session("LoggedOn") ) Then
    Response.Redirect "login.asp"
End If
%>
```

The Response Object's Properties

Buffer

You may optionally have ASP buffer your output for you. The `Buffer` property tells ASP whether or not to buffer output. Usually, output is sent to the client as it is generated. If you turn buffering on (by setting this property to `True`), output will not be sent until all scripts have been executed for the current page, or the `Flush` or `End` methods are called.

`Response.Buffer` has to be inserted after the language declaration, but before any HTML is used. If you insert it outside this scope you will most likely generate an error. A correct use of this method would look like:

```
<@ LANGUAGE = "VBSCRIPT">
<% Response.Buffer = True %>
<HTML>
. . .
```

The `Flush` method is used in conjunction with the `Buffer` property. To use it correctly you must set the `Buffer` property first and then at places within the script you can flush the buffer to the output stream, while continuing processing. This is useful for long queries, which might otherwise worry the user that nothing was being returned.

The `Clear` method erases everything in the buffer that has been added since the last `Response.Flush` call. It erases only the response body, however, and leaves the response header intact.

CacheControl

Generally when a proxy server retrieves an ASP web page, it does not place a copy of it into its cache. That is because by their very nature ASP pages are dynamic and, most likely, a page will be stale by the next time it is requested. You may override this feature by changing the value of this property to `Public`.

Charset

This property will append its contents to the HTTP content-type header that is sent back to the browser. Every HTTP response has a content-type header that defines the content of the response. Usually the content-type is "text/html". Setting this property will modify the type sent back to the browser.

ContentType

This property allows you to set the value of the content-type that is sent back to the client browser.

Expires

Most web browsers keep web pages in a local cache. The cache is usually kept as long as you keep your browser running. Setting the Expires property allows you to limit the time the page stays in the local cache. The value of the Expires property specifies the length of time in minutes before the page will expire from the local cache. If you set this to zero, the page will not be cached at all.

ExpiresAbsolute

Just like the Expires property, this property allows you to specify the exact time and date on which the page will expire.

IsClientConnected

This read-only property indicates whether or not the client is still connected to the server. Remember that the client browser makes a request then waits for a response? Well, imagine you're running a lengthy script and during the middle of processing, the client disconnects because he was waiting too long. Reading this property will tell you if the client is still connected or not. Unfortunately in ASP 2.0, this property doesn't seem to function correctly, and has only been repaired within ASP 3.0 in Windows 2000.

Status

This property allows you to set the value returned on the status header with the HTTP response.

The Application and Session Objects

The Application and Session objects, like Request and Response, work very closely together. Application is used to tie all of the pages together into one consistent application, while the Session object is used to track and present a user's series of requests to the web site as a continuous action, rather than as an arbitrary set of requests.

Scope Springs Eternal

Normally, you will declare a variable for use within your web page. You'll use it, manipulate it, then perhaps print out its value, or whatever. But when your page is reloaded, or the viewer moves to another page, the variable, with its value, is gone forever. By placing your variable within the Contents collection of the Application or Session objects, you can extend the life span of your variable!

Any variable or object that you declare has two potential scopes: procedure and page. When you declare a variable within a procedure, its life span is limited to that procedure. Once the procedure has executed, your variable is gone. You may also declare a variable at the web page level but like the procedure-defined variable, once the page is reloaded, the value is reset.

Enter the `Application` and `Session` objects. The `Contents` collections of these two objects allow you to extend the scope of your variables to session-wide, and application-wide. If you place a value in the `Session` object, it will be available to all web pages in your site for the life span of the current session (more on sessions later). Good session scope variables are user IDs, user names, login time, etc.; things that pertain only to the session. Likewise, if you place your value into the `Application` object, it will exist until the web site is restarted. This allows you to place application-wide settings into a conveniently accessible place. Good application scope variables are font names and sizes, table colors, system constants, etc.; things that pertain to the application as a whole.

The global.asa File

Every ASP application may utilize a special script file. This file is named `global.asa` and it must reside in the root directory of your web application. It can contain script code that pertains to the application as a whole, or each session. You may also create ActiveX objects for later use in this scripting file.

The Application Object

ASP works on the concept that an entire web site is a single web application. Therefore, there is only one instance of the `Application` object available for use in your scripting at all times. Note that it is possible to divide up your web site into separate applications, but for the purposes of this discussion we'll assume there is only one application per web site.

Collections

The `Application` object contains two collections: `Contents` and `StaticObjects`. The `Contents` collection was discussed earlier. The `StaticObjects` collection is similar to `Contents`, but only contains the objects that were created with the `<OBJECT>` tag in the scope of your application. This collection can be iterated just like the `Contents` collection.

> *You cannot store references to ASP's built-in objects in* `Application`'s *collections.*

Methods

The `Application` object contains two methods:

❑ The `Lock` method is used to "lock-down" the `Contents` collection so that it cannot be modified by other clients. This is useful if you are updating a counter, or perhaps grabbing a transaction number stored in the `Application`'s `Contents` collection.

❑ The `Unlock` method "unlocks" the `Application` object thus allowing others to modify the `Contents` collection.

Events

The `Application` object generates two events: `Application_OnStart` and `Application_OnEnd`. The `Application_OnStart` event is fired when the first view of your web page occurs. The `Application_OnEnd` event is fired when the web server is shut down. If you choose to write scripts for these events they must be placed in your `global.asa` file.

The most common use of these events is to initialize application-wide variables; with items such as font names, table colors, database connection strings or perhaps to write information to a system log file. The following is an example `global.asa` file with script for these events:

```
<SCRIPT LANGUAGE=VBScript RUNAT=Server>
Sub Application_OnStart
    'Globals…
    Application("ErrorPage") = "handleError.asp"
    Application("SiteBanAttemptLimit") = 10
    Application("AccessErrorPage") = "handleError.asp"
    Application("RestrictAccess") = False

    'Keep track of visitors…
    Application("NumVisits") = Application("NumVisits") + 1
End Sub
</SCRIPT>
```

The Session Object

Each time a visitor comes to your web site, a `Session` object is created for the visitor if the visitor does not already have one. Therefore, there is an instance of the `Session` object available to you in your scripting as well. The `Session` object is similar to the `Application` object in that it can contain values. However, the `Session` object's values are lost when your visitor leaves the site. The `Session` object is most useful for transferring information from web page to web page. Using the `Session` object, there is no need to pass information in the URL.

The most common use of the `Session` object is to store information in its `Contents` collection. This information would be session-specific in that it would pertain only to the current user.

Many web sites today offer a "user personalization" service, that is, to customize a web page to their preference. This is easily done with ASP and the `Session` object. The user variables are stored in the client browser for retrieval by the server later. Simply load the user's preferences at the start of the session and then, as the user browses your site, utilize the information regarding the user's preferences to display information.

For example, suppose your web site displays stock quotes for users. You could allow users to customize the start page to display their favorite stock quotes when they visit the site. By storing the stock symbols in your `Session` object, you can easily display the correct quotes when you render your web page.

This session management system relies on the use of browser cookies. The cookies allow the user information to be persisted even after a client leaves the site. Unfortunately, if a visitor to your web site does not allow cookies to be stored, you will be unable to pass information between web pages within the `Session` object.

Collections

The `Session` object contains two collections: `Contents` and `StaticObjects`. The `Contents` collection we discussed earlier. The `StaticObjects` collection is similar to `Contents`, but only contains the objects that were created with the `<OBJECT>` tag in your HTML page. This collection can be iterated just like the `Contents` collection.

Properties

The following table contains the properties that the `Session` object exposes for your use:

Property	Description
CodePage	Setting this property will allow you to change the character set used by ASP when it is creating output. This property could be used if you were creating a multi-national web site.
LCID	This property sets the internal locale value for the entire web application. By default, your application's locale is your server's locale. If your server is in the US, then your application will default to the US. Much of the formatting functionality of ASP utilizes this locale setting to display information correctly for the country in question. For example, the date is displayed differently in Europe versus the US. So based on the locale setting, the date formatting functions will output the date in the correct format.
	You can also change this property temporarily to output data in a different format. A good example is currency. Let's say your web site had a shopping cart and you wanted to display totals in US dollars for US customers, and Pounds Sterling for UK customers. To do this you'd change the LCID property to the British locale setting, and then call the currency formatting routine.
SessionID	Every session created by ASP has a unique identifier. This identifier is called the SessionID and is accessible through this property. It can be used for debugging ASP scripts.
Timeout	By default, ASP sessions will timeout after 20 minutes of inactivity. Every time a web page is requested or refreshed by a user, the internal ASP time clock starts ticking. When the time clock reaches the value set in this property, the session is automatically destroyed. You can set this property to change the timeout period if you wish.

Methods

The Session object contains a single method, Abandon. This instructs ASP to destroy the current Session object for this user. This method is what you would call when a user logs off your web site.

Events

The Session object generates two events: Session_OnStart and Session_OnEnd. The Session_OnStart event is fired when the first view of your web page occurs. The Session_OnEnd event is fired when the web server is shut down. If you choose to write scripts for these events they must be placed in your global.asa file.

The most common use of these events is to initialize session-wide variables – items like usage counts, login names, real names, user preferences, etc. The following is an example global.asa file with script for these events:

```
<SCRIPT LANGUAGE=VBScript RUNAT=Server>
Sub Session_OnStart
    Session("LoginAttempts") = 0
    Session("LoggedOn") = False
End Sub
```

731

```
Sub Session_OnEnd
    Session("LoggedOn") = False
End Sub
</SCRIPT>
```

The Server Object

The next object in the ASP object model is the Server object. The Server object enables you to create and work with ActiveX controls in your web pages. In addition, the Server object exposes methods that help in the encoding of URLs and HTML text.

Properties

ScriptTimeout

This property sets the time in seconds that a script will be allowed to run. The default value for all scripts on the system is 90 seconds; if a script has run for longer than 90 seconds, the web server will intervene and let the client browser know something is wrong. If you expect your scripts to run for a long time, you will want to use this property.

Methods

CreateObject

This method is the equivalent to VBScript's CreateObject, or using the New keyword – it instantiates a new instance of an object. The result can be placed into the Application or Session Contents collection to lengthen its life span.

Generally you'll create an object at the time the session is created and place it into the Session.Contents collection. For example, let's say you've created a killer ActiveX DLL with a really cool class that converts Fahrenheit to Celsius and vice versa. You could create an instance of this class with the CreateObject method and store it in the Session.Contents collection like this:

```
Set Session("MyConverter") = Server.CreateObject("KillerDLL.CDegreeConverter")
```

This object would be around as long as the session is and will be available for you to call. This method is invaluable when working with database connections.

ASP comes with its own built in set of components that you can create instances of using the CreateObject method. These are:

❑ **AdRotator** – used to display a random graphic and link every time a user connects to the page

❑ **Browser Capabilities** – manipulates a file called browscap.ini contained on the server computer to determine the capabilities of a particular client's browser

❑ **Content Linker** – provides a central repository file from where you manage a series of links and their URLs, and provides appropriate descriptions about them

❑ **ContentRotator** – a cut down version of the Ad Rotator that provides the same function but without optional redirection

❑ **PageCounter** – counts the number of times a page has been hit

❑ **PermissionChecker** – checks to see if a user has permissions before allowing them to access a given page

❑ **Counters** – counts any value on an ASP page from anywhere within an ASP application

❑ **MyInfo** – can be used to store personal information about a user within an XML file

❑ **Status** – used to collect server profile information

❑ **Tools** – a set of miscellaneous methods that are grouped under the generic heading of Tools

❑ **IISLog** – allows you to create an object that allows your applications to write to and otherwise access the IIS log

Execute

This method executes an ASP file and inserts the results into the response. You can use this call to include snippets of ASP code, like subroutines.

GetLastError

This method returns an `ASPError` object that contains all of the information about the last error that has occurred.

HTMLEncode

This method encodes a string for proper HTML usage. This is useful if you want to actually display HTML code on your web pages.

MapPath

This method returns a string that contains the actual physical path to the file in question. Subdirectories of your web site can be virtual. That is to say that they don't physically exist in the hierarchy of your web site. To find out the true whereabouts of a file, you can call this method.

Transfer

The `Transfer` method allows you to immediately transfer control of the executing page to another page. This is similar to the `Response.Redirect` method except for the fact that the `Transfer` method makes all variables and the `Request` collections available to the called page.

URLEncode

This method, as the title suggests, encodes a URL for transmission. This encoding includes replacing spaces with a plus sign (+) and replacing unprintable characters with hexadecimal values. You should always run your URLs through this method when redirecting.

The ObjectContext Object

The final object we shall consider is the `ObjectContext` object, which comes into play when you use transactions in your web page. When an ASP script has initiated a transaction, it can either be committed or aborted by this object. It has two methods to do this.

SetAbort

`SetAbort` is called when the transaction has not been completed and you don't want resources updated.

SetComplete

`SetComplete` is called when there is no reason for the transaction to fail. If all of the components that form part of the transaction call `SetComplete`, then the transaction will complete.

Using Active Server Pages Effectively

Is it true that a little bit of knowledge is a bad thing? In the realm of ASP, I think not. A little bit of knowledge is probably just piquing your interest. For the final part of this appendix we're going to build a web site to demonstrate some of the features of ASP. This sample site will demonstrate many of the ASP features and principles described earlier.

Designing the Site

Before we start creating our new web site, we should discuss the design. For your first ASP application, we'll keep it quite simple. What we want to create is an HTML form that accepts for input the following information: first name, last name, and e-mail address. After the user submits the form, our ASP page will reformat the first and last name, and check the e-mail address for proper syntax.

The user will be given three attempts to enter the information correctly or else a warning message will display at the bottom of the screen. The input page will look like this:

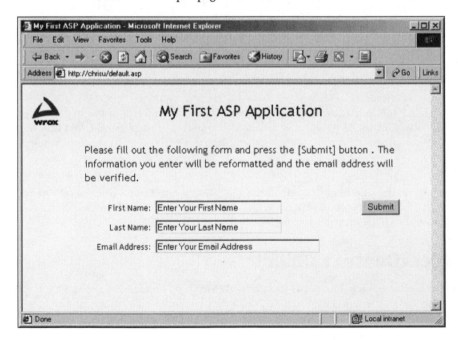

Creating the global.asa File

The first step in creating a new ASP application is to create your `global.asa` file. This is the file that houses your event handlers for the `Application` and `Session` objects. In addition, in this file you may set application-wide and session-wide variables to their default values. To create this file, in the root of your web server directory create a file called `global.asa`. Here is the content of our sample `global.asa`:

```
<SCRIPT LANGUAGE=VBScript RUNAT=Server>
Sub Application_OnStart
    Application("AllowedErrorsBeforeWarning") = 3
End Sub

Sub Session_OnStart
    Session("ErrorCount") = 0
End Sub

Sub Session_OnEnd
    'Nothing to do here...
End Sub

Sub Application_OnEnd
    'Nothing to do here...
End Sub
</SCRIPT>
```

Our file has handlers defined for `Application_OnStart`, `Application_OnEnd`, `Session_OnStart`, and `Session_OnEnd`. The `Application_OnEnd` and `Session_OnEnd` events are not used in this example, but are shown above for completeness.

We want to set a limit on the number of submissions the user can make before a warning message is shown. Since this is a feature of the application and affects all users, we will store this constant in the `Application.Contents` collection. This is done in the `Application_OnStart` event. We add to the collection an item named `AllowedErrorsBeforeWarning` and set its value to 3.

Now that we know how many times a user *can try* to get it right, we need a place to store the number of times the user *has tried* to get it right. Since this counter is different for each user, we'll place this into the `Session.Contents` collection. We initialize our variable to 0. This is done in the `Session_OnStart` event. We add to the collection an item named, appropriately, `ErrorCount`, with a value of 0.

Creating our Main Page

Now that we've laid the groundwork for our ASP application, it's time to build the main page. Since this is a simple example, we will only utilize a single web page. Let's begin by creating this single page.

Create a new web page on your site and name it `default.asp`. This is the file name used by IIS as the default web page. The default web page is the page that is returned by a web server when no web page is specified. For example, when you call up http://www.wrox.com/, you aren't specifying a web page. The server looks through its list of default file names and finds the first match in the web site's root directory.

The page is quite long. But it breaks logically into two distinct sections: the ASP/VBScript portion, and the HTML portion. Let's examine each section individually.

The ASP/VBScript Section

The top half of our file is where the ASP code lives. This is the code that is executed by the server before the page is returned to the browser that requested it. As you've seen, any code that is to be executed on the server before returning is enclosed in the special <% and %> tags.

For clarity (and sanity!), the ASP code has been divided into subroutines. This not only makes the code more readable, but also will aid in its reuse. Our code has two routines: Main, and InitCap.

Before we do anything else however, we declare some variables:

```
<%@ Language=VBScript %>
<%
Dim txtFirstName, txtLastName, txtEmailAddr
Dim sMessage
```

When variables are declared outside of a subroutine in an ASP page, the variables retain their data until the page is completely processed. This allows you to pass information from your ASP code to your HTML code, as you'll see.

After our variables have been declared, we have our Main routine. This is what is called by our ASP code every time a browser retrieves the page. The Main subroutine is not called automatically: we must explicitly call it ourselves.

```
'*********************************************************************
'* Main
'*
'* The main subroutine for this page...
'*********************************************************************

Sub Main()
  '  Was this page submitted?
  if ( Request("cmdSubmit") = "Submit" ) Then
  ' Reformat the data into a more readable format...
    txtFirstName = InitCap(Request("txtFirstName"))
    txtLastName = InitCap(Request("txtLastName"))
    txtEmailAddr = LCase(Request("txtEmailAddr"))
    ' Check the email address for the correct components...
    if ( Instr(1, txtEmailAddr, "@") = 0 or Instr(1, txtEmailAddr, ".") = 0 ) Then
      sMessage = "The email address you entered does not appear to be valid."
    Else
      '  Make sure there is something after the period..
      if ( Instr(1, txtEmailAddr, ".") = Len(txtEmailAddr) & _
         or Instr(1, txtEmailAddr, "@") = 1 or & _
         (Instr(1, txtEmailAddr, ".") = Instr(1, txtEmailAddr, "@") + 1) ) Then
        sMessage = "You must enter a complete email address."
      end if
    End If
```

```
        'We passed our validation, show that all is good...
        if ( sMessage = "" ) Then
          sMessage = "Thank you for your input. All data has passed verification."
        else
          Session("ErrorCount") = Session("ErrorCount") + 1

        if ( Session("ErrorCount") > Application("AllowedErrorsBeforeWarning") ) then
            sMessage = sMessage & "<P><Font Size=1>You have exceeded the" & _
                    " normal number of times it takes to get this right!</Font>"
        end if
      End If
    Else
      ' First time in here? Set some default values...
      txtFirstName = "Enter Your First Name"
      txtLastName = "Enter Your Last Name"
      txtEmailAddr = "Enter Your Email Address"
    End If
End Sub
```

First we see if the form was actually submitted by the user, otherwise we initialize our variables. To determine if the page has been submitted, we check the value of the cmdSubmit Request variable. This is the button on our form. When pressed, the form calls this page and sets the value of the cmdSubmit button to Submit. If a user just loads the page without pressing the button, the value of cmdSubmit is blank (" "). There are other ways to determine if a web page was submitted, but this method is the simplest.

After we have determined that the page was in fact submitted, we run the names through the second function on this page: InitCap. InitCap is a quick little function that will format a word to proper case. That is to say that the first letter will be capitalized, and the rest of the word will be lower cased. Here is the function:

```
'*********************************************************************
'* InitCap
'*
'* Capitalizes the first letter of the string
'*********************************************************************

Function InitCap(sStr)
    InitCap = UCase(Left(sStr, 1)) & LCase(Right(sStr, Len(sStr) - 1))
End Function
```

Now that we've cleaned up the names, we need to check the e-mail address for validity. To do this we ensure that it contains an "@" sign and a period (.). Once past this check, we make sure that there is data after the period and that there is data before the "@" sign. This is 'quick and dirty' e-mail validity checking.

If either of these checks fail, we place a failure message into the string sMessage. This will be displayed in our HTML section after the page processing is complete.

Now, if our e-mail address has passed the test, we set the message (sMessage) to display a thank you note. If we failed our test, we increment our error counter that we set up in the global.asa file. Here we also check to see if we have exceeded our limit on errors. If we have, a sterner message is set for display.

737

Finally, the last thing in our ASP section is our call to `Main`. This is what is called when the page is loaded:

```
'****************************************************************
'* Call our main subroutine
'****************************************************************


Call Main()
```

The HTML Section

This section is a regular HTML form with a smattering of ASP thrown in for good measure. The ASP that we've embedded in the HTML sets default values for the input fields, and displays any messages that our server side code has generated:

```
<HTML>
<HEAD>
   <META NAME="GENERATOR" Content="Microsoft FrontPage 3.0">
   <TITLE>My First ASP Application</TITLE>
</HEAD>

<BODY>
<TABLE border="0" cellPadding="0" cellSpacing="0" width="600">
<TBODY>
  <TR>
     <TD width="100"><A href="http://www.wrox.com" target="_blank"
     border=0 alt><IMG border=0 title="Check out the Wrox Press Web Site!"
     src="images/wroxlogo.gif" WIDTH="56" HEIGHT="56"></A></TD>
     <TD width="500"><CENTER><FONT size="5" face="Trebuchet MS">My First
     ASP Application</FONT></CENTER></TD>
  </TR>

  <TR>
     <TD width="100"> </TD>
     <TD width="500" align="left"><FONT face="Trebuchet MS"><BR>
     Please fill out the following form and press the [Submit] button. The
     information you enter will be reformatted and the email address will
     be verified.</FONT>
     <FORM action="default.asp" id="FORM1" method="post" name="frmMain">
      <TABLE border="0" cellPadding="1" cellSpacing="5" width="100%">
       <TR>
         <TD width="100" nowrap align="right">
           <FONT size="2" face="Trebuchet MS">First Name:</FONT>
         </TD>
         <TD width="350"><FONT size="2" face="Trebuchet MS">
           <INPUT title="Enter your first name here" name="txtFirstName"
           size="30" value="<%=txtFirstName%>" tabindex="1"></FONT></TD>
         <TD width="50"><DIV align="right"><FONT size="2" face="Trebuchet MS">
           <INPUT type="submit" title="Submit this data for processing..."
           value="Submit" name="cmdSubmit" tabindex="4"></FONT></TD>
       </TR>

       <TR>
         <TD width="100" nowrap align="right">
```

```
                <FONT size="2" face="Trebuchet MS">Last Name:</FONT></TD>
             <TD width="400" colspan="2">
                <FONT size="2" face="Trebuchet MS">
                <INPUT title="Enter your last name here" name="txtLastName"
                size="30" value="<%=txtLastName%>" tabindex="2"></FONT></TD>
          </TR>

          <TR>
             <TD width="100" nowrap align="right">
                <FONT size="2" face="Trebuchet MS">Email Address:</FONT>
             </TD>
             <TD width="400" colspan="2"><FONT size="2" face="Trebuchet MS">
             <INPUT title="Enter your valid email address here"
             name="txtEmailAddr" size="40" value="<%=txtEmailAddr%>"
             tabindex="3"></FONT></TD>
          </TR>
          <TR>
             <TD nowrap width=500 colspan="3" align="center">
             <FONT face="Trebuchet MS"><BR>
             <STRONG><%=sMessage%></STRONG> </FONT></TD>
          </TR>
        </TABLE>
      </FORM>
      <P> </TD>
    </TR>
</TBODY>
</TABLE>
</BODY>
</HTML>
```

The most important part of the HTML is where the ASP code is embedded. The following snippet illustrates this:

```
<INPUT title="Enter your first name here" name="txtFirstName" size="30"
 value="<%=txtFirstName%>" tabindex="1">
```

Here we see a normal text input box. However, to set the value of the text box we use the Response.Write shortcut (<%=) to insert the value of the variable txtFirstName. Remember that we dimensioned this outside of our ASP functions so that it would have page scope. Now we utilize its value by inserting it into our HTML. We do exactly the same thing with the Last Name and Email Address text boxes.

The last trick in the HTML section is the display of our failure or success message. This message is stored in the variable called sMessage. At the bottom of the form, we display the contents of this variable like so:

```
<TD nowrap width=500 colspan="3" align="center">
   <FONT face="Trebuchet MS">
   <BR>
   <STRONG>
   <%=sMessage%>
   </STRONG>
   </FONT>
</TD>
```

The beauty of this code is that if sMessage is blank then nothing is shown, otherwise the message is displayed.

Summary

In this ASP Quick Start tutorial we first looked at how HTTP is the transaction system that sends web pages to requesting clients. It is a very important piece of the puzzle. We then discussed Active Server Pages, or ASP. You learned how ASP pages are created, and what special HTML tags you need to include in your files to use ASP. We looked through the ASP object model and saw that the Request and Response objects are used to manage details of the HTTP request and responses. We saw that the Application object is used to group pages together into one application and we saw that the Session object is used to create the illusion that the interaction between user and site is one continuous action. Finally, we created a small application that demonstrates two uses for ASP: form validation and data manipulation.

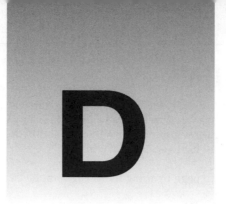

JavaScript Quick Start Tutorial

JavaScript is one of the main languages used for programming web pages. It is well suited to Internet development, because it's a **scripting language** (which is interpreted at the moment it is run), rather than a **compiled language**.

For a compiled language, the programmer writes some **source code**, which is text in an English-like language, and then puts the code through a compiler, which translates the programmer's instructions into machine language. The compiled code is then run. This makes the code very fast, but also ties the program to a particular type of operating system. For example, code compiled for a computer running Windows NT will not run on a computer running UNIX.

For a scripting language, however, there is no compiler, so the code always stays in source code form. When it is time to run the code, a **scripting engine** must interpret the code while it's running it, which makes the code run slower. The computer translates a line of source code into machine language and runs it, then translates another line, etc. Most scripting engines are probably smarter than that, but this is the basic idea. Scripting code is more portable, however, because it can run on *any* computer that has an appropriate scripting engine. That is, if I write some JavaScript, that code can run on a Windows NT machine, a UNIX machine, or a Macintosh machine. As long as the machine has a JavaScript scripting engine installed, the code will run.

> *JavaScript was first created by Netscape to provide a scripting language for web browsers. Microsoft developed a similar language, also based on the syntax of Java, called **JScript**. A variant of JavaScript was released under the name of **ECMAScript**, to provide a standardized language for web browsers to use. Both Microsoft and Netscape are working to make their individual scripting languages compliant with ECMAScript. For the most part, JavaScript, JScript, and ECMAScript are almost identical.*

This appendix does not aim to teach you everything there is to know about JavaScript, but is intended to give you enough knowledge to help you follow along with the code examples in the rest of the book.

JavaScript and HTML

Since HTML documents are text-only documents, and since they're intended to be viewable on any machine running any operating system, scripting languages like JavaScript go very well with HTML. There are other scripting languages around, like **VBScript** and **Python**, but the only language that's really well supported in *multiple* browsers is JavaScript.

You can insert script into a web page by using the HTML <SCRIPT> element, like this:

```
<SCRIPT language="JavaScript">
<!--
  alert("Hello World!");
//-->
</SCRIPT>
```

The language attribute specifies the scripting language we're using. Since some older browsers don't understand the <SCRIPT> element, many DHTML (Dynamic HTML) developers hide scripting code inside HTML comments, as shown above. This will prevent the script from being shown in the text of an HTML document.

There's also a <NOSCRIPT> element; browsers that understand the <SCRIPT> element will ignore the contents of a <NOSCRIPT> element:

```
<NOSCRIPT>
  <P>
    This page requires JavaScript, which your browser doesn't understand.
  </P>
</NOSCRIPT>
```

Browsers will try to display any text within an element they don't understand. A non scripting-aware browser would first try to display the text inside the <SCRIPT> element; however, since all of the text is inside an HTML comment, the browser thinks that there's nothing to display. Then it gets to the <NOSCRIPT> element, and there is text to display, so users with non scripting-aware browsers will get this message.

JavaScript and Java

JavaScript doesn't really have any relation to the Java programming language, except that the syntax of the language looks very similar to that of Java. This is different from a language like VBScript, which is *subset* of the Visual Basic programming language. However, if you are a Java programmer, JavaScript will seem very familiar to you, and learning JavaScript will be very much like learning a subset of Java.

Running the Examples in this Appendix

All of the examples in this appendix were tested on both Internet Explorer and Netscape Navigator. To facilitate this testing, I threw together a very simple HTML page (`JavaScriptTester.htm`) like this:

```
<HTML>
<HEAD><TITLE>JavaScript tester</TITLE>

<SCRIPT language="JavaScript"><!--
   //JavaScript code goes here!
//--></SCRIPT>
<NOSCRIPT>
  <P>This page requires JavaScript, and you don't have it.</P>
</NOSCRIPT>

</HEAD><BODY>
  <P>This is my JavaScript tester page.</P>
</BODY>
</HTML>
```

We can then insert any JavaScript code to be tested at that highlighted line, between the `<SCRIPT>` start and end-tags. As the browser is loading this page, it will execute the JavaScript it finds there. This makes it possible to debug the JavaScript in exactly the same way that many HTML authors debug their web pages, like this:

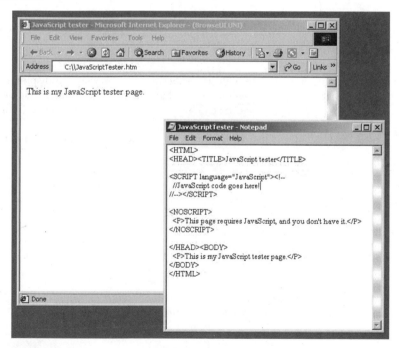

As you make the changes in Notepad, you simply go to **File/Save** and save the document. Then go to IE or Netscape and hit refresh/reload, and see the changes in the browser.

Note that JavaScript is case sensitive, so be careful when typing in code.

745

Statements

Any programming language is really just a number of instructions for a computer to perform. These instructions are broken up into **statements**, where each statement is usually one instruction to the computer.

You might not initially understand some of the statements in this section, but all will become clear as we study more JavaScript concepts in upcoming sections.

A JavaScript statement looks like this:

```
strFirstName = "John";
```

Each statement is ended with a semicolon. We could, if we wanted, put more than one statement on a line, separated by semicolons. However, you'll find it makes your code much more readable to put each statement on a separate line, wherever possible.

In JavaScript, as in most programming languages, the "=" character is used to **assign** a value to a variable; in this case, we are assigning the string "John" to the variable strFirstName. The value on the right hand side of the "=" character is always assigned to the variable on the left hand side. (More on variables in the next section.)

We can also call **functions** (chunks of code which are given unique names), using a syntax like this:

```
alert("Hello world!");
```

This will call a function called alert(), a built-in JavaScript function that will display a message box. The text "Hello world!" which is between the "( )" characters is a **parameter** that we're passing to the function. In this case, the value we pass to alert() will be the text that's displayed in the message box.

A statement can have more than one instruction in it; for example, consider the following:

```
strFirstName = getFirstName();
```

This actually tells the computer to do two things:

❑   First, call the getFirstName() function

❑   Next, take the return value from that function, and assign it to the strFirstName variable

*A number of statements can also be grouped together in a **block**, which is delimited by { } characters, but we'll study blocks when we look at functions in more detail.*

Comments

Along with the instructions for the computer, we also have the ability to annotate our code with **comments**. Comments are ignored by the scripting engine, and only serve to help humans understand what your code means. This could be other developers, who are looking at code you have written, or it could be yourself. Remember: code you wrote six months ago may look as foreign to you as code someone else wrote, so including comments in your code to explain why you did what you did may save you some frustration later on.

There are two kinds of comments we can include in JavaScript: **single line comments** and **multi-line comments**.

Single Line Comments

Single line comments begin with two forward slashes (//). Everything after these two slashes, to the end of the line, is ignored by the scripting engine. For example:

```
strFirstName = "John";   //assign a value to strFirstName
alert("Hello world!");
```

The first line begins with a statement, but then includes a comment. The text "assign a value to strFirstName" will be ignored by the scripting engine, as if it wasn't there at all. The comment ends at the end of the line, so the call to the alert() function will still be executed by the scripting engine.

Multi-line Comments

Multi-line comments begin with /*, and end with */. Scripting engines ignore all of the text within those two delimiters, even if there are newlines or JavaScript code included. For example:

```
/*
   This is an example of a large comment.

   alert("Hello world!");

   It is ignored by the scripting engine.
*/
```

All of this text will be ignored by the scripting engine, including the line that looks like a function call. As far as JavaScript is concerned, this is all just a comment, and it's therefore ignored. Be careful how you use multi-line comments, though, because you might run into problems like this:

```
strFirstName = "John";   /*assign a value to strFirstName
alert("Hello world!");    which will be used later*/
```

In this code snippet, the call to alert() is inside the comment, and therefore won't be executed by the scripting engine! To make this work properly, we have to either do this:

```
strFirstName = "John";   /*assign a value to strFirstName*/
alert("Hello world!");   /*which will be used later*/
```

or this:

```
strFirstName = "John";   //assign a value to strFirstName
alert("Hello world!");   //which will be used later
```

Better yet, we would probably want to do one of these:

```
strFirstName = "John";   //assign a value to strFirstName
                         //which will be used later
alert("Hello world!");
```

or:

```
strFirstName = "John";   /*assign a value to strFirstName
                         which will be used later*/
alert("Hello world!");
```

This makes things much clearer, since future developers will be able to see at a glance that the comment only applies to the first JavaScript statement.

Variables

In order to get our JavaScript to do useful things, we're going to need to keep track of some information. We can do this using **variables**.

> **A variable is just a way of pointing to a section of the computer's memory, which holds a particular value that you want to remember and make use of.**

A variable is declared using the `var` keyword, like this:

```
var strFirstName;
```

This declares to the scripting engine that we're creating a variable called `strFirstName`. There isn't any value in that variable yet, but we could put one there if we wanted, using our earlier statement:

```
strFirstName = "John";
```

We can also assign a variable its value at the same time we create it, like so:

```
var strFirstName = "John";
```

This creates the variable, *and* gives it an initial value.

A variable's value can be changed at any time – that's why they call it a *variable*:

```
var strFirstName = "John";      //the value is John
strFirstName = "Andrea";        //the value is now Andrea
strFirstName = 1;               //now it is 1
```

In some cases, the `var` keyword is not necessary to declare our variables; we can start using a new variable right away, and JavaScript will automatically create it for us. For example:

```
var strFirstName = "John";
strLastName = strFirstName;
```

Even though we didn't actually declare our `strLastName` variable, JavaScript creates it for us, and we can use it in our code. Regardless of this automatic behavior, it's considered good practice to declare all of your variables explicitly with the `var` keyword, and not rely on JavaScript to create them for you.

Unfortunately, there is no way to *enforce* this best practice in JavaScript, as there is in other programming languages. When writing JavaScript, it's up to you the programmer to make sure your variables are properly defined before using them.

Data Types

There are different types of data that we can work with in our JavaScript code. These are:

❑ numbers

❑ strings

❑ Booleans

❑ objects

There are also three special values:

❑ `null` – used to indicate that the variable is deliberately empty

❑ `undefined` – the value a variable has when it is first created, before it is assigned a value

❑ `NaN` – a special value indicating that the variable is "Not A Number"

As opposed to most programming languages, JavaScript variables don't have any particular type, but just assume the type of whatever information is given to them. For example, take a look at the following code, written in Java:

```
int iAge;
iAge = 10;          //this is okay
iAge = "a string";  //this will raise an error in Java
```

In Java, since we declare variables to have a certain type, they can only ever store values of that type. So we have declared a variable called `iAge`, which can store integer values. That means that if we try to assign the variable a string, as we do in the second assignment, we will get an error. On the other hand, take a look at this JavaScript code:

```
var iAge;
iAge = 10;              //this is okay
iAge = "a string";  //this is also okay in JavaScript
```

In JavaScript, since the type of a variable changes with its data, we can assign any kind of data to our variables. For the first assignment, `iAge` becomes a numeric variable, since it's storing a number; in the second example it changes to become a string variable, because that's what it's storing.

Boolean variables can be assigned the values `true` and `false`. These are JavaScript reserved words, so if we do this:

```
iAge = true;
```

`iAge` is now a Boolean.

We'll study the last type of variable, an object variable, in a later section.

Variable Names

There are a few rules on what kinds of names you can give your variables, so that scripting engines will be able to tell your variables apart from other things in your code. They are as follows:

❑   The first character must be a letter, an underscore, or a dollar sign.

❑   The variable name can't be a word that is already a part of the JavaScript language. (So you couldn't name a variable `var`, or `true`, for example.)

❑   After the first character, numbers are also allowed in the name.

> **You should also note that variable names are case-sensitive.**

This means that a variable named `strFirstName` is different from a variable named `strfirstname`. However, it would usually be a very bad idea to create two variables names that are exactly the same except for case! Unfortunately, this can sometimes cause accidental confusion, and difficult-to-solve bugs in your code. For example, consider the following:

```
var strFirstName;
strFirstname = "John";
alert(strFirstName);
```

This will pop up a message box with the text **undefined**. What? Wait a second, why does it say undefined? Well, if you look very closely, you'll notice that when we assigned the value `John` to our variable in the second statement, we spelled it wrong (with a small n for name); in this case, JavaScript thinks we're declaring a *new* variable, named `strFirstname`, and helpfully goes ahead and creates it for us. So when we try to access the `strFirstName` variable, it still hasn't been assigned a value, which means it's `undefined`.

Under normal circumstances, you will know what kind of information will be stored in your variables. For example, I know that the `strFirstName` variable will always hold a string, and that the `iAge` variable will always hold a number.

For this reason, it's usually a good idea to add a **prefix** to your name, with a short lower case string that declares what type of variable it is. This is commonly called **Hungarian Notation** (the practice was started at Microsoft, by Dr. Charles Simonyi). There are different variations of Hungarian Notation around, so you should pick a notation that's easily recognizable and consistent for you. In my case, I'm using the prefix `str` to indicate that the variable will hold a string, and the prefix `i` to indicate that the variable will hold an integer, but you might choose different prefixes in your code.

Operators

JavaScript provides many **operators**, which can be used in mathematical expressions, Boolean conditions, etc. This section won't cover all of them, just the most common ones.

Mathematical

The most obvious operators needed in a programming language are mathematical operators. Most of these operators are pretty obvious:

- ❑ Addition is done using a +
- ❑ Subtraction is done using a –
- ❑ Division is done using a /
- ❑ Multiplication is done using a *
- ❑ Comparisons are made using the equality operator ==

For example:

```
varA = 1 + 1; //addition
varA = 2 - 1; //subtraction
varA = 4 / 2; //division
varA = 2 * 2; //multiplication
```

There is also a **modulus** operator, %, which divides two numbers and returns the remainder. For example, to test whether a number is even, you would divide by 2 and see if the remainder is 0, like this:

```
if(varA % 2 == 0)
  alert("It's even.");
```

Finally, there are two very handy operators: the increment (++) and decrement (--) operators. In programming, one of the most common actions you'll perform is to add 1 to a variable's value, something like this:

```
varA = varA + 1;
```

This is a bit simpler with the increment operator, which is ++. It works like this:

```
varA++;          //equivalent to varA = varA + 1
```

The decrement operator works the same way, and subtracts 1 from a number:

```
varA--;          //equivalent to varA = varA - 1
```

Assignment

We have already seen the most basic assignment operator, =, which assigns the value on the right to the variable on the left:

```
varA = 2;
```

Along with the normal assignment operator, however, there are also **compound assignment operators**, which work along with the earlier mathematical operators. They work something like this:

```
varA += 2;        //equivalent to varA = varA + 2
```

This means "take the value that is in varA, add 2 to it, and then assign that back to varA", in effect, adding 2 to varA. Compound operators include:

❑   addition (+=)

❑   subtraction (-=)

❑   multiplication (*=)

❑   division (/=)

❑   modulus (%=)

Logical (Boolean)

There are a number of operators provided that can be used to make decisions. The easiest is used to test if two values are the same, using the equality operator, like this:

```
varA == varB
```

JavaScript will evaluate this expression as a Boolean; it will be true if varA is the same as varB, or false otherwise. (Note: be careful to use the equality operator == and not the assignment operator =.)

We can also do the opposite:

```
varA != varB
```

which will evaluate to true if varA is *not* the same as varB.

We can take the opposite of any statement, by using the ! (NOT) operator. For example, we could also have written the above like this:

```
!(varA == varB)
```

Similarly, we can test if the values are less than or greater than other values:

```
varA <  varB  //true if varA is less than varB
varA >  varB  //true if varA is greater than varB
varA <= varB  //true if varA is less than, or equal to, varB
varA >= varB  //true if varA is greater than, or equal to, varB
```

These separate expressions can also be combined together, in powerful AND and OR statements. For example, consider the following:

```
(varA > varB) && (varA < 1000)
```

That && is the logical AND operator. This will evaluate to `true` if varA is greater than varB, *and* varA is less than 1,000. (Notice that I have included parentheses, to make things more explicit.) That is, if either of these conditions is `false`, the whole expression will evaluate to `false`. On the other hand, consider this:

```
(varA > varB) || (varA < 1000)
```

The `||` is the logical OR operator. This will evaluate to `true` if varA is greater than varB, *or* if varA is less than 1,000. That is, if either of these expressions is `true`, the whole expression is `true`.

We'll see some places where logical operators are used a little later on, when we get to the section on "Conditional Code".

Precedence of Operators

In some cases, you might have a number of operators all strung together in one statement, and JavaScript will have to figure out which operators to execute first. For example, consider the following:

```
varA = 25 + 10 * 12;
```

If JavaScript were to execute this line from left to right, then we would get 25 + 10, which is 35, times 12, which is 420. However, in mathematics, multiplication has a higher precedence than addition, which means that really we're supposed to multiply the 10 by 12 first, giving us 120, and then add the 25, which is 145. So which is it?

JavaScript does things in proper mathematical order, so the answer to the above would indeed be 145. In fact, there are a lot of rules in JavaScript concerning which order things get done. However, you can always override JavaScript's rules by using parentheses. So we could have achieved each of the above results, by doing this:

```
varA = (25 + 10) * 12;   //420
```

or:

```
varA = 25 + (10 * 12);   //145
```

Whenever there is even the slightest confusion as to which order things might get processed, you should use parentheses. Even if you'll be specifying the same order that JavaScript would have done it anyway, it's better to be safe than sorry, and it helps to make things clear for other programmers.

Functions

From time to time you're going to come across a section of code that you will be calling multiple times, from multiple places in your code. Or maybe you have code that you just want to group together, to separate it from the rest of your code, and make things more readable and easier to understand. In either of these cases, what you're looking for is a **function**.

Creating Functions

We can create a function like this:

```
function getFirstName()
{
  return "John";
}
```

First comes the keyword `function`, followed by the name we're giving this function, and parentheses "( )". Functions must be named using the same naming conventions as JavaScript variables.

After this comes a block of code, delimited by the "{ }" characters, and inside this block is the code for the function. Note that the "{ }" characters don't have to go on separate lines as we've shown them here; many developers prefer to write their JavaScript functions like this:

```
function getFirstName() {
  return "John";
}
```

This example is very simple and most JavaScript functions in real life would be much longer or more complicated.

Returning Information from a Function

In many cases, we'll want to be able to return information from our functions. This is done via the `return` keyword. Anything after the `return` keyword, and before the semicolon, is returned from the function. So in the following code, the value of `strFirstName` will end up being "John":

```
strFirstName = getFirstName();

function getFirstName()
{
  return "John";
}
```

The first statement calls the function, and the rest of the code snippet defines the function. Notice that in JavaScript we don't have to define our functions before we use them.

Passing Information to a Function

So far so good, but what if our function needs some information in order to do its work? We can pass this information to the function via **parameters**. These are declared when we create the function, by putting them inside the parentheses, like this:

```
function getGreater(first, second)
{
  if(first > second)
    return first;
  else
    return second;
}
```

We would then call the function like so:

```
var blah1, blah2, iGreater;
blah1 = 10;
blah2 = 20;

iGreater = getGreater(blah1, blah2);
```

Notice that we don't need to use the same names as we declared for our parameters in the function; we can pass in variables with any names we desire. The variables we pass are assigned to the parameters in the order specified, so here `first` will be assigned the value of 10 and `second` will be given 20.

Built-in Functions

In addition to the functions you create yourself, there are a number of built-in functions provided by JavaScript. For example, we've been using the `alert()` function, which pops up a message box containing the text you pass to it.

There's also an `eval()` function, which will take a string representing a mathematical expression, and perform that expression:

```
var blah1, blah2;

blah1 = "2 + 2";
blah2 = blah1;

alert(blah2);
```

This will pop up a message box with the text 2 + 2. However, if we change the previous code to this:

```
var blah1, blah2;

blah1 = "2 + 2";
blah2 = eval(blah1);

alert(blah2);
```

The new message box will have the text 4. This is because the eval() function takes the passed string, translates it to a mathematical expression, evaluates it, and returns the results from that.

Be careful that the string you pass to eval() really is a mathematical expression, though, or you might get into trouble. For example, consider the following:

```
alert(eval("hello world"));
```

In this case, eval() can't change "hello world" to a proper expression. Both IE and Netscape Navigator return an error that the statement is missing a ";". (This also illustrates that JavaScript error messages, like many other programming languages, can provide misleading information.)

This example also shows how the return value of one function can be directly passed as the parameter of another function. In this case, JavaScript executes the functions from inside to out; in other words, the eval() function will be executed, and the return value of eval() will be passed as the parameter to alert(), which will then be executed. JavaScript programmers do this a lot, so you should get used to seeing it, even if you don't do it yourself.

Program Flow

So far all of our JavaScript examples have been pretty simple: do this, then do this, and then you're done. Unfortunately, in the real world programs are rarely that simple. In many cases we're going to need to make decisions (for example if this is true, then do this, otherwise, do this). We're also going to have to repeat sections of code multiple times.

Conditional Code

JavaScript provides several statements that let us make decisions:

- ❑ if
- ❑ if … else
- ❑ switch

The if Statement

You can make decisions in your JavaScript code using the if statement. It looks something like this:

```
var blah = 10;

if(blah > 5)
{
  strMessage = "Blah is greater than 5.";
  alert(strMessage);
}
```

JavaScript translates whatever is inside the parentheses to a Boolean, which is called the **condition**. If that condition is `true`, the contents of the `if` statement's code block are executed. If the condition is not `true`, the contents of this code block are ignored.

If there is only one statement to be executed, the code block becomes optional, in which case the `if` statement can be written one of two ways:

```
if(blah > 5)
  alert("Blah is greater than 5.");
```

or:

```
if(blah > 5) alert("Blah is greater than 5.");
```

Basically, anything up to the end of the next semicolon is part of the `if` statement, regardless of what white space exists in between.

When leaving out the block characters, `{ }`, it's always a good idea to indent the statement that will be executed when the `if` condition is `true`, to keep it visually separate from the rest of your code. For example, we could write:

```
if(blah > 5)
strMessage = "Blah is greater than 5.";
alert(strMessage);
```

In this case, if the `blah` variable is greater than 5, `strMessage` will be assigned the text `Blah is greater than 5`. However, regardless of the outcome of our `if` condition, the `alert()` function will still be called! To make it easier to recognize the conditional code, we would have been better off indenting the second line, like this:

```
if(blah > 5)
  strMessage = "Blah is greater than 5.";
alert(strMessage);
```

Now it's more clear what will be happening, and under what conditions. (Personally, I usually prefer to include the `{ }` characters, even when there is only one statement being executed.)

if ... else

Now suppose we wanted to output one of two messages: one if `blah` is greater than 5, or a different one if it is less than or equal to 5. We could do this:

```
if(blah > 5)
  alert("Blah is greater than 5.");
if(blah <= 5)
  alert("Blah is not greater than 5.");
```

But there must be an easier way. And, in fact, there is, using the `else` keyword, like so:

```
if(blah > 5)
    alert("Blah is greater than 5.");
else
    alert("Blah is not greater than 5.");
```

The `else` is now part of the overall `if` statement. If our condition is `true`, the first block will be executed, otherwise, the second block will be executed. And, most importantly, only one of the two statements will ever be executed; they're mutually exclusive.

You can also chain `if` statements together, something like this:

```
if(blah == 1)
    alert("1");
else if(blah == 2)
    alert("2");
else
    alert("not 1 or 2");
```

The switch Statement

In addition to chaining `if` statements together, JavaScript also provides the `switch` statement. This can execute any number of statements, based on your condition, and can be more readable than chaining together `if`s.

We could have written the above like this:

```
switch(blah)
{
    case 1:
        alert("1");
        break;
    case 2:
        alert("2");
        break;
    default:
        alert("not 1 or 2");
        break;
}
```

JavaScript will execute whichever `case` statement matches the `switch` statement's condition. If no `case` statement matches the condition, the `default` statement will be run. (If no `case` statement matches, and there is no `default` statement, nothing will happen.)

Notice also those `break` statements in there; once JavaScript starts executing any of the `case` or `default` statements, it keeps on going until it comes across a `break` statement, or the end of the `switch` statement. So, say we rewrote the above like this:

```
switch(blah)
{
  case 1:
    alert("1");
  case 2:
    alert("2");
    break;
  default:
    alert("not 1 or 2");
    break;
}
```

Since there's no break statement for the first case, we'll get two message boxes if blah is 1: one saying 1, and one saying 2. Sometimes this is the desired behavior, and sometimes not. When you do leave out the break statement, it's called a **fall through**, and it's always a good idea to comment your code, so that people know you're falling through on purpose, like this:

```
switch(blah)
{
  case 1:
    alert(1);
    //fall through
  case 2:
    alert(2);
    break;
  default:
    alert("not 1 or 2");
    break;
}
```

Now there won't be any confusion as to whether this fall through is on purpose or is simply a typographical error.

Loops

A **loop** is a construct whereby you tell the computer to repeat the same section of code over and over, usually for a specified number of iterations. There are a number of ways to create loops in JavaScript, but we'll just study the most common ones:

- ❑ The for loop
- ❑ The while loop
- ❑ The do ... while loop
- ❑ The break and continue statements

The for Loop

First of all, we have the `for` loop. This is a simple loop where you tell JavaScript exactly how many times you want the code executed. For example:

```
for(var i = 0; i < 10; i++)
{
  alert(i);
}
```

Just like `if` statements, the block characters are optional if the loop will only be executing one statement, but I usually include them anyway. Notice there are three pieces of information we specify to the `for` loop, separated by semicolons:

❑ First, we initialize a **counter** for the loop. This is a variable that will keep track of where we are in the loop; if we don't have one, we can create one right in the `for` loop (as we've done here) so long as we initialize it.

❑ The second piece of information is the **test condition**. As long as this test evaluates to `true`, the loop will continue, but when the test evaluates to `false`, the loop will stop. In this case, our loop will keep running as long as our counter is less than 10.

❑ Finally, we have an **action**, which updates the counter or affects the test condition. In this case, we increment our counter by 1 after every iteration. We have initially set our counter to 0, will update it by 1 every time, and will finish when the counter is equal to or greater than 10. That means this loop will run exactly 10 times.

If we were to run this code we would get message boxes saying 0, 1, 2 ... up until 9, and then the loop would stop.

> Notice that I've named my counter **i**, which isn't exactly a descriptive name for a variable. However, since loop counters are so common, and aren't usually used for anything else, it has become conventional to use **i** for loop counters. In cases where loops are nested, and therefore can't all use **i**, programmers often use **i**, then **j**, then **k**, etc.

Because we can do whatever we want in our action, we have great control over our loop. For example, this loop will only pop up message boxes for even numbers:

```
for(var i = 0; i < 10; i += 2)
{
  alert(i);
}
```

while and do ... while Loops

Sometimes we won't know in advance exactly how many times we want to execute the loop. In that case, we have two other choices:

❑ A `while` loop

❑ A `do ... while` loop

For example, suppose we want to pop up a message box over and over and over again saying It's morning!. And, of course, we only want that message box in the morning hours, not in the afternoon. Terribly annoying, but it will demonstrate the concepts well enough. We have two choices for constructing this loop. (Warning! If you're typing in these examples, you might not want to try this one, because you'll have trouble making it stop – especially if it's morning!)

First, the `while` loop:

```
var dtTheDate = new Date();

while(dtTheDate.getHours() < 12)
{
  alert("It's morning!");
}
```

Or, we could use the `do ... while` loop:

```
var dtTheDate = new Date();

do
{
  alert("It's morning!");
} while(dtTheDate.getHours() < 12)
```

The only difference between these two types of loops is the number of times the loop executes. In the `while` loop, the condition will be tested *before* the loop is executed even once, meaning that if it fails, the loop will never execute. On the other hand, for the `do ... while` loop, the condition is tested *after* the loop runs, meaning that the loop will be executed at least once, even if the condition is `false`. Which is preferable depends on your situation; in our case, the `while` loop is more appropriate. (If we used the `do ... while` loop, we would get a message box saying It's morning! even if it's afternoon.)

The break and continue Statements

Sometimes there will be special conditions under which we have to stop running the loop prematurely. Or, alternatively, we might want to just stop this iteration, and move on to the next iteration. JavaScript provides the means to do this, using the `break` and `continue` statements.

The `break` statement, which we saw before in our discussion of the `switch` statement, can also be used to break out of a loop. For example, an alternative way to write the previous loops might have been to do it like this:

```
while(true)
{
  if(dtTheDate.getHours() >= 12)
    break;

  alert("It's morning!");
}
```

The condition for our while statement is now true, which will always be true, meaning that this loop will run forever unless we specifically break out of it! (An improperly written loop, which will continue forever, is called an **infinite loop**.) However, inside the loop we then check the time, and if it's afternoon, we call break to exit the loop.

We could also rewrite our earlier example, which showed message boxes for all even numbers between 0 and 10, using the continue statement, as follows:

```
for(var i = 0; i < 10; i++)
{
  if(i % 2 != 0)
    continue;

  alert(i);
}
```

We iterate through all of the numbers. However, if the number isn't exactly divisible by 2 (that is, it is not an even number), we just move on to the next one, without processing it, by calling continue. Notice that when we use the continue statement the counter is automatically updated.

Objects

Since **Object Oriented Programming** is one of the more powerful concepts to come out of the software engineering world, it's no surprise that JavaScript provides functionality for working with objects. There are some built-in object types in the language, as well as limited functionality for creating your own objects, in recent versions of the ECMAScript specification.

An object is a special kind of variable, because it contains not only data, but functions for working with that data. A function built into an object is called a **method**. Objects also provide **properties**, which allow you to set and retrieve information in the object.

Every object contains a very special method, called a **constructor**, which is used when the object is instantiated (in other words first created, to initialize it). The constructor always has the same name as the object itself, and is called in JavaScript using the new keyword. For example, JavaScript provides a built-in String object, which you would instantiate like this:

```
var strMyString = new String();
```

The variable strMyString now contains a String object, which at this point is empty, and the String object's constructor has initialized the object. If there are parameters to the constructor, they can be passed just as with any function. For example, the String constructor allows you to pass in the string you want to create, like this:

```
var strMyString = new String("Hi");
```

strMyString now contains a String object, and that object contains the string Hi.

The rest of this section will cover some of the more common built-in JavaScript objects. (Building your own objects is outside the scope of this introduction to JavaScript.)

String

Probably the most common object that exists in JavaScript is the `String` object, which provides many useful properties and methods for dealing with strings. Any work done with strings in JavaScript is done via the `String` object, even if it isn't explicitly used.

For example, consider the following:

```
var varA = "Hello";
```

In this case, although we didn't explicitly create a `String` object, JavaScript will create one for us, and `varA` will hold that object, just as though we had called the `String` constructor.

The toLowerCase and toUpperCase Methods

Two very simple, and handy, methods are `toLowerCase()` and `toUpperCase()`. These are pretty self-explanatory, but we'll demonstrate them anyway:

```
var strMyString = new String("This is my 2nd string!");

alert(strMyString.toUpperCase());   //returns "THIS IS MY 2ND STRING!"
alert(strMyString.toLowerCase());   //returns "this is my 2nd string!"
alert(strMyString);                 //returns "This is my 2nd string!"
```

As you can see, only characters are affected by these methods; numbers and punctuation are not changed. But wait, when we called `alert()` that last time, it turns out the string didn't change!

Okay, so the methods weren't so self-explanatory. It turns out that many of the methods on the `String` object won't actually *modify* the string itself; they'll return a new `String` object, containing the results. In order to make the changes to the object itself, we'd have to do something like this:

```
strMyString = strMyString.toUpperCase();
```

Methods to Return Strings and Characters

Specific characters can be retrieved from a string using the `charAt()` and `charCodeAt()` methods, which return the character or its Unicode code respectively. Sub-strings can be returned from the `substr()` and `substring()` methods, which return a sub-string based on its length or its position in the string, respectively. All of these work on the string based on its index (which is zero based, in other words the first item is index 0, the second item is index 1, etc.).

Consider the following examples:

```
var strMyString = new String("Hello World!");

//returns the character at position 4, or "o"
alert(strMyString.charAt(4));

//returns the character code of the character at position 4, or 111
alert(strMyString.charCodeAt(4));
```

```
//returns 2 characters starting at the 3rd, or "lo"
alert(strMyString.substr(3, 2));

//returns the characters starting at the 3rd, up to the 5th, or "lo"
alert(strMyString.substring(3, 5));
```

Methods to Search Strings

You can also search the contents of a string. For example, the `indexOf()` and `lastIndexOf()` methods will return the character position where the first or last occurrence of a character occurs, respectively.

The `search()` method is similar, except that it searches for more than one character and returns the index of the first character in the string being searched for:

```
var strMyString = new String("This is my 2nd string!");

alert(strMyString.search("2nd"));   //returns 11
```

Joining Strings

And finally, we can also join strings together, using the `concat()` method. Like the `toUpperCase()` and `toLowerCase()` methods, `concat()` doesn't alter the strings: it returns a new one. Consider the following examples:

```
var strBlah1 = new String("string1");
var strBlah2 = new String("string2");

alert(strBlah1.concat(strBlah2));   //returns "string1string2"
alert(strBlah2.concat(strBlah1));   //returns "string2string1"
```

But there's an easier way to concatenate strings – using the + operator:

```
var strBlah1 = new String("string1");
var strBlah2 = new String("string2");

alert(strBlah1 + strBlah2);   //returns "string1string2"
alert(strBlah2 + strBlah1);   //returns "string2string1"
```

There are other methods available from the `String` object, but we won't cover them all here.

Number

JavaScript automatically creates and uses a `Number` object for every number it uses. However, there is only really one method you would use for `Number`, which is `toString()`. And even the `toString()` method doesn't need to be called explicitly that often, because JavaScript will automatically convert numbers to strings when needed.

For example, consider the following code:

```
var Blah1 = new String("1"); //string object
var Blah2 = 5;               //number

alert(Blah1 + Blah2);
```

This will produce a message box with the message 15. You see, whenever JavaScript comes across the + operator, if any of the values involved are strings, JavaScript converts *all* of the values to strings. So, since Blah1 is a String object, JavaScript converts Blah2 to a String, then uses the + operator to concatenate them together. The last statement is equivalent to doing this:

```
alert(Blah1.concat(Blah2.toString ()));
```

This can be useful when formatting numbers for output, or writing numbers in XML.

Math

The JavaScript Math object is an interesting one; you never need to create a Math object of your own using the new keyword. In fact, you *can't* create a Math object. So, you need to use the properties and methods of Math directly, without an object.

You would use it like this:

```
varA = Math.PI;
```

The PI property returns the value of pi (3.141592...).

As you've probably guessed, Math provides a number of mathematical methods. We won't cover them here, but they're the usual ones you'd expect: things like sin(), tan(), atan(), etc. But we'll study a couple of the more fun ones: max(), min(), and random().

The max() and min() methods are pretty easy. Simply pass in two numbers, and they will send back to you the one which is bigger, or the one which is smaller, respectively:

```
varA = 1;
varB = 2;

alert(Math.max(varA, varB));   //returns 2
alert(Math.min(varA, varB));   //returns 1
```

Be careful that the variables you pass to these methods are actually numbers, though:

```
varA = "!";
varB = "a";

alert(Math.max(varA, varB));   //returns NaN
alert(Math.min(varA, varB));   //returns NaN
```

In JavaScript, NaN stands for Not a Number.

The random() method is used to create a random number, between 0 and 1. (For example, .6654666833980297.) As in all programming languages that provide random numbers, the number isn't *completely* random; it's based on some mathematical expression, probably including the time of day, date, etc. But for almost all applications, it's as close to randomness as you'll ever need.

Date

Another common activity programmers need to perform is working with dates and times. JavaScript provides the Date object for this, which provides many, *many* methods for getting the date and time from the computer on which it is running, and working with dates and times in general. Examples include:

- ❑ getDate – returns the day of the month (1 to 31)

- ❑ getDay – returns the day of the week (0 to 6, where 0 is Sunday)

- ❑ setMonth(*monthvalue*) – sets the month to the *monthvalue* given (0 to 11 where 0 represents January)

There are just way too many methods to go into here, so you'll just have to take my word for it that Date is a useful object. If you need to work with dates and times in your code, any good JavaScript reference should list all of Date's methods for you.

Arrays

There are times when a simple variable won't do, and you need a number of pieces of information, grouped together in a list. JavaScript provides **arrays** to do this. Arrays are created like this:

```
var arArray = new Array("Mon", "Tues", "Wed", "Thurs", "Fri");
var i;

for(i in arArray)
  alert(arArray[i]);
```

There's a whole bunch of new stuff in here, so we'll take it piece by piece.

First of all, there is the first line, which creates our array. This looks just like creating an object, and that's exactly what it is: an array is just a special object, which contains a list of other objects. There is even a length property, which returns the number of items in the array.

Next, we have a for ... in loop. This is a special JavaScript loop, which can be used to iterate through the items in an array. We used i as a counter variable, just like a regular for loop. The difference is that instead of providing a condition for exiting the loop, this loop will automatically run for every item in the array, incrementing the counter each time, and when it runs out of items, the loop will stop. We could also have written this as follows:

```
for(i = 0; i < arArray.length; i++)
{
alert(arArray[i]);
}
```

And finally, we access the individual members of the array by using the square brackets "[]", and inserting the index of the item we want to retrieve. So arArray[0] would retrieve the first item in the array, and arArray[4] would retrieve the fifth item.

Summary

This appendix has covered enough JavaScript to get you started, and to enable you to understand the code used in some of the chapters in this book. If you want to learn more about JavaScript, there are many useful publications, including Instant JavaScript (ISBN 1-861001-27-4) and, for a more advanced coverage, Professional JavaScript (ISBN 1-861002-70-X) both from Wrox Press.

Support, Errata, and P2P.Wrox.Com

One of the most irritating things about any programming book is when you find that bit of code you've just spent an hour typing simply doesn't work. You check it a hundred times to see if you've set it up correctly and then you notice the spelling mistake in the variable name on the book page. Of course, you can blame the authors for not taking enough care and testing the code, the editors for not doing their job properly, or the proofreaders for not being eagle-eyed enough, but this doesn't get around the fact that mistakes do happen.

We try hard to ensure no mistakes sneak out into the real world, but we can't promise that this book is 100% error free. What we can do is offer the next best thing by providing you with immediate support and feedback from experts who have worked on the book, and try to ensure that future editions eliminate these gremlins.

We also now commit to supporting you not just while you read the book, but once you start developing applications as well, through our online forums, where you can put your questions to the authors, reviewers, and fellow industry professionals.

In this appendix we'll look at how to:

❑ Enroll in the peer to peer forums at http://p2p.wrox.com

❑ Post and check for errata on our main site, http://www.wrox.com

❑ E-mail technical support with a query or feedback on our books in general

Between all three support procedures, you should get an answer to your problem very quickly.

The Online Forums at P2P.Wrox.Com

You can join the XML mailing list (or any others which are of interest to you) for author and peer support. Our system provides **programmer to programmer™ support** on mailing lists, forums and newsgroups, all in addition to our one-to-one e-mail system, which we'll look at in just a while. Be confident that your query is not just being examined by a support professional, but by the many Wrox authors and other industry experts present on our mailing lists.

How to Enroll for Online Support

Just follow this four-step system:

1. Go to p2p.wrox.com in your favorite browser. Here you'll find any current announcements concerning P2P – new lists created, any removed and so on:

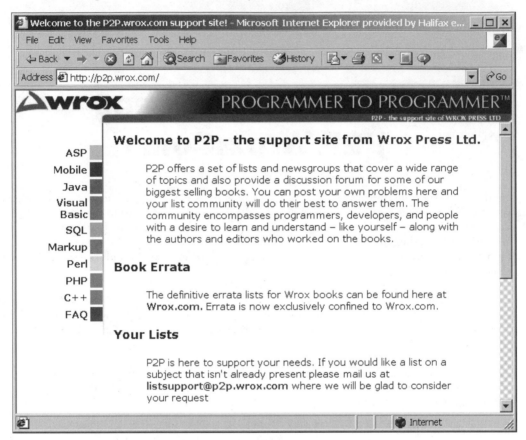

2. Click on the Markup button in the left hand column.

3. Choose to access the xml list.

4. If you are not a member of the list, you can choose to either view the list without joining it or create an account in the list, by hitting the respective buttons.

5. If you wish to join, you'll be presented with a form in which you'll need to fill in your e-mail address, name and a password (of at least 4 characters). Choose how you would like to receive the messages from the list and then hit Save.

6. Congratulations. You're now a member of the xml mailing list.

Why this System Offers the Best Support

You can choose to join the mailing lists and you can receive a weekly digest of the list. If you don't have the time or facility to receive the mailing list, then you can search our online archives. You'll find the ability to search on specific subject areas or keywords. As these lists are moderated, you can be confident of finding good, accurate information quickly. Mails can be edited or moved by the moderator into the correct place, making this a most efficient resource. Junk and spam mail are deleted, and your own e-mail address is protected by the unique Lyris system from web-bots that can automatically hoover up newsgroup mailing list addresses. Any queries about joining, leaving the lists or any query about the list should be sent to: listsupport@p2p.wrox.com.

Support and Errata

The following section will take you step by step through the process of posting errata to our web site to get book-specific help. The sections that follow, therefore, are:

❑ Wrox Developer's Membership

❑ Finding a list of existing errata on the web site

❑ Adding your own errata to the existing list

There is also a section covering how to e-mail a question for technical support. This comprises:

❑ What your e-mail should include

❑ What happens to your e-mail once it has been received by us

So that you only need view information relevant to yourself, we ask that you register (for FREE) as a Wrox Developer Member. This is a quick and easy process, that will save you time in the long-run. If you are already a member, just update your membership to include this book.

Wrox Developer's Membership

To get your FREE Wrox Developer's Membership click on Membership in the top navigation bar of our home site – http://www.wrox.com. This is shown in the screenshot opposite:

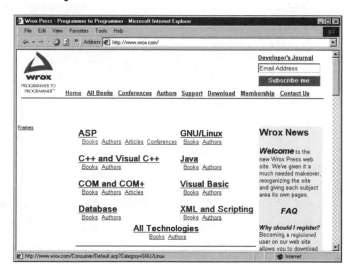

Then, on the next screen, click on **New User**. This will display a form (not shown). Fill in the details on the form and submit the details using the **Register** button at the bottom. Before you can say 'The best read books come in Wrox Red' you will get this screen (but with your own user name shown):

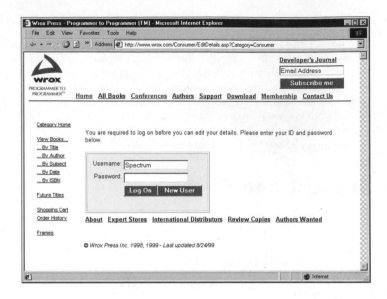

Type in your password once again and click **Log On**. The following page (also not shown) allows you to change your details if you need to, but now you're logged on, you have access to all the source code downloads and errata for the entire Wrox range of books.

Finding an Erratum on the Web Site

Before you send in a query, you might be able to save time by finding the answer to your problem on our web site – http:\\www.wrox.com.

Each book we publish has its own page and its own errata sheet. You can get to any book's page by clicking on **Support** from the top navigation bar.

Halfway down the main support page is a section called **Book Errata** which has a drop-down list of titles. Simply scroll down the list until you see **Beginning XML**, select it and then hit **Errata**.

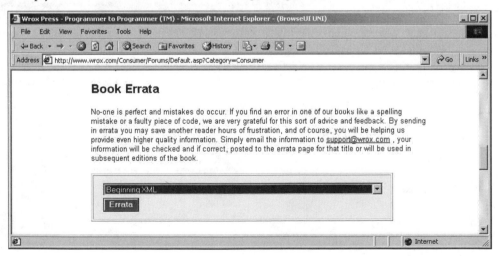

This will take you to the errata page for the book. Select the criteria by which you want to view the errata, and click the Apply criteria button. This will provide you with links to specific errata. For an initial search, you are advised to view the errata by page numbers. If you have looked for an error previously, then you may wish to limit your search using dates. We update these pages frequently to ensure that you have the latest information on bugs and errors. An example of an errata page is shown:

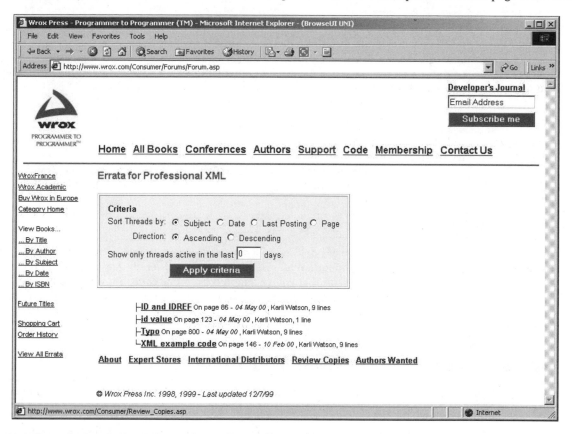

Add an Erratum: E-mail Support

If you wish to point out an erratum to put up on the web site, or directly query a problem in the book with an expert who knows the book in detail, then e-mail support@wrox.com. A typical e-mail should include the following things:

❑ The **book name**, **last four digits of the ISBN** and **page number** of the problem in the Subject field

❑ Your **name**, **contact info** and details of the **problem** in the body of the message

We won't send you junk mail. We need the details to save your time and ours. When you send an e-mail it will go through the following chain of support.

Customer Support

Your message is delivered to one of our customer support staff who are the first people to read it. They have files on most frequently asked questions and will answer anything general immediately. They answer general questions about the book and the web site.

Editorial

Deeper queries are forwarded to the technical editor responsible for that book. They have experience with the programming language or particular product and are able to answer detailed technical questions on the subject, directly related to the book's contents. Once an issue has been resolved, the editor can post errata to the web site or reply directly to your e-mail as appropriate.

The Authors

Finally, in the unlikely event that the editor can't answer your problem, they will forward the request to the author. We try to protect the author from any distractions from writing. However, we are quite happy to forward specific requests to them. All Wrox authors help with the support on their books. They'll mail the customer and the editor with their response, and again all readers should benefit.

What We Can't Answer

Obviously with an ever-growing range of books and an ever-changing technology base, there is an increasing volume of data requiring support. While we endeavor to answer all questions about the book, we can't solve bugs in your own programs that you've adapted from our code. So, while you might have loved the online "Lydia's Lugnuts" store in Case Study 1, don't expect too much sympathy if you cripple your company with a live adaptation you customized from the case study code. But do tell us if you're especially pleased with the routine you developed with our help.

How to Tell Us Exactly What You Think

We understand that errors can destroy the enjoyment of a book and can cause many wasted and frustrated hours, so we seek to minimize the distress that they can cause.

You might just wish to tell us how much you liked or loathed the book in question. Or you might have ideas about how this whole process could be improved. In which case you should e-mail feedback@wrox.com. You'll always find a sympathetic ear, no matter what the problem is. Above all you should remember that we do care about what you have to say and we will do our utmost to act upon it.

Useful Web Resources

This appendix is a compilation of some of the most useful web bases resources relating to XML and the surrounding technologies.

W3C web site

http://www.w3.org

XML specification

http://www.w3.org/TR/1998/REC-xml-19980210#sec-intro

Microsoft MSXML parser

http://msdn.microsoft.com/downloads/webtechnology/xml/msxml.asp

James Clark's xp parser

http://www.jclark.com/xml/xp/

Expat parser (information)

http://www.jclark.com/xml/expat.html

Expat parser (download)

ftp://ftp.jclark.com/pub/xml/expat.zip

Vivid Creations XML tools, including ActiveDOM

http://www.vivid-creations.com

DataChannel parser

http://xdev.datachannel.com/directory/xml_parser.html

Apache Software Foundation's Xerces parser

http://xml.apache.org/

IBM xml4j parser

http://alphaworks.ibm.com/tech/xml4j

XML tools

http://www.xmlsoftware.com/parsers/

CSS2 specification

http://www.w3.org/TR/1998/REC-CSS2

VOXML browser

http://www.voxml.com

XSL

http://www.w3.org/Style/XSL

XSLT specification

http://www.w3.org/TR/xslt

XSL Formatting Objects specification

http://www.w3.org/TR/xsl/

XSL tutorials

http://www.xslinfo.com/tutorials/
http://www.xslt.com

James Clark's XT

http://www.jclark.com/xml/xt.html

Teun Duynstee's XSLT reference

http://www.vbxml.com

DOM

http://www.w3.org/TR/DOM-Level-2/
http://www.w3.org/TR/1999/CR-DOM-Level-2-19991210/core.html

CueXML

http://www.cuesoft.com

SAX

http://www.megginson.com/SAX/

SAX 2.0

http://www.megginson.com/SAX/Java/index.html

History of SAX

http://www.megginson.com/SAX/history.html

SAX-aware parsers

http://www.megginson.com/SAX/

Sun Project X

http://java.sun.com/products/xml/

Java Development Kit

http://java.sun.com/products/jdk/1.1/download-jdk-windows.html

XML Namespaces specification

http://www.w3.org/TR/1999/REC-xml-names

URI syntax

http://www.ietf.org/rfc/rfc2396.txt

URN syntax

http://www.ietf.org/rfc/rfc2141.txt

URL syntax

http://www.ietf.org/rfc/rfc1738.txt

XML 1.0 DTD syntax

http://www.w3.org/TR/1998/REC-xml

Document Content Description (DCD)

http://www.w3.org/TR/1998/NOTE-dcd

XML Schema Part 0: Primer

http://www.w3.org/TR/xmlschema-0

XML Schema Part 1: Structures

http://www.w3.org/TR/xmlschema-1

XML Schema Part 2: Datatypes

http://www.w3.org/TR/xmlschema-2

XML-Data

http://www.w3.org/TR/1998/NOTE-XML-data

XML-Data-Reduced

http://msdn.Microsoft.com/xml/reference/schema/start.asp

XPath specification

http://www.w3.org/TR/xpath

XPointer specification

http://www.w3.org/TR/xptr

XLink specification

http://www.w3.org/TR/xlink/

XML Query Working Group

http://www.w3.org/TR/xmlquery-req

XML databases – eXcelon

http://www.exceloncorp.com/

Oracle's Technology Network and XML Developer's Kit

http://technet.oracle.com/tech/xml/

XML-RPC protocol

http://www.xmlrpc.com/

SOAP

http://msdn.microsoft.com/xml/general/soapspec-v1.asp

DevelopMentor

http://www.develop.com/soap/issues.htm

RDF and Dublin Core standard specifications

http://www.w3.org/RDF/

Tim Bray's "RDF and Metadata"

http://www.xml.com/pub/98/06/rdf.html

John Cowan's "RDF Made Easy"

http://www.ccil.org/~cowan/XML/rdf-made-easy.ppt

Schematron web site

http://www.ascc.net/xml/resource/schematron/schematron.html

Schematron XSLT style sheet

http://www.ascc.net/xml/resource/schematron/schematron.xsl

Miloslav Nic's Schematron tutorials

http://zvon.vscht.cz/HTMLonly/SchematronTutorial/General/contents.html

Visual Basic code generator for XML Schema documents

http://msdn.microsoft.com/xml/articles/generat.asp

XML-DEV mailing list (now hosted by OASIS)

http://www.oasis-open.org/

XML Schema Datatypes

In this appendix, we'll fill in some of the details about XML Schema datatypes that we introduced in Chapter 10. As we saw in that chapter, XML Schema provides two basic kinds of datatypes:

- **primitive datatypes** – those that are not defined in terms of other types
- **derived datatypes** – types that are defined in terms of existing types

There are three W3C documents of interest: XML Schema Part 0: Primer, XML Schema Part 1: Structures, and XML Schema Part 2: Datatypes [all 7 April 2000], at http://www.w3.org/TR/xmlschema-0, http://www.w3.org/TR/xmlschema-1, and http://www.w3.org/TR/xmlschema-2, respectively. Together, these comprise the Last Call Working Draft of XML Schema, for which the comment period ended on 12 May 2000.

XML Schema is based on XML 1.0, but also requires the use of Namespaces in XML [14 January 1999], available at http://www.w3.org/TR/REC-xml-names.html.

Primitive Types

The following are the primitive datatypes that are built-in to XML Schema:

- `string` – a finite-length sequence of UCS characters
- `boolean` – a two-state "`true`" or "`false`" flag
- `float` – a 32-bit single-precision floating-point number
- `double` – a 64-bit double-precision floating-point number
- `decimal` – a decimal number of arbitrary precision
- `timeDuration` – a duration of time
- `recurringDuration` – a recurring duration of time
- `binary` – text-encoded binary data

- ❑ uriReference – a standard Internet URI
- ❑ ID – equivalent to the XML 1.0 ID attribute type
- ❑ IDREF – equivalent to the XML 1.0 IDREF attribute type
- ❑ ENTITY – equivalent to the XML 1.0 ENTITY attribute type
- ❑ NOTATION – equivalent to the XML 1.0 NOTATION attribute type
- ❑ QName – a legal QName string (name with qualifier), as defined in *Namespaces in XML*

Let's take a closer look at these.

string

A finite-length sequence of UCS characters, as defined in ISO 10646 and Unicode. Value and lexical spaces are identical. This datatype is ordered by UCS code points (integer character values).
For example:

```
<an_element>This sentence is a legal string literal with élan.</an_element>
```

Built-in derived types: language, NMTOKEN, and Name.

boolean

A binary value. True may be represented as "true" or "1" (one), and false may be either "false" or "0" (zero).

```
<an_element flag1="true" flag2="1" />    <!-- two flags, equivalent values -->
<an_element flag3="false" flag4="0" />   <!-- ditto -->
```

This datatype is not ordered, and there are no built-in derived types.

decimal

An arbitrary precision decimal number, with values in the range $i \times 10^n$, where i and n are integers (with n being the scale of the value space). This datatype is ordered by numeric value.

The lexical representation is represented by a finite-length sequence of decimal digits separated by a period (.) as a decimal indicator, and an optional leading sign (+ or –). If the sign is omitted, it's assumed to be a plus. The representation is further constrained by the scale and precision facets. Leading and/or trailing zeroes are optional. For example, each of the following is a valid decimal:

```
<an_element num1="-1.23" num2="3.1416" num3="+042" num4="100.00" />
```

Built-in derived type: integer.

float

An IEEE single-precision 32-bit floating-point number as specified in IEEE 754-1985.

> *The IEEE Standard for Binary Floating-Point Arithmetic (IEEE 754-1985) is available at http://standards.ieee.org/reading/ieee/std_public/description/busarch/754-1985_desc.html. (Someone needs to talk to these people about using simpler and more reasonable URLs!)*

The value space includes all values $m \times 2^e$, where m is an integer whose absolute value is less than 2^{24}, and e is an integer between **-149** and **104**, inclusive. There are also five special values in a float's value space: positive and negative zero (represented as "**0**" and "**-0**"), positive and negative infinity ("**INF**" and "**-INF**"), and not-a-number ("**NAN**"). This datatype is ordered by numeric value.

The lexical representation is a mantissa (which must be a decimal number) optionally followed by the character **E** or **e**, followed by an exponent (which must be an integer). If the **E**/**e** and exponent are omitted, an exponent value of 0 (zero) is assumed. For example:

```
<an_element num1="-1E4" num2="3.1416" num3="12.78e-1" num4="NAN" />
```

There are no built-in derived types.

double

An IEEE double-precision 64-bit floating-point number as specified in IEEE 754-1985.

The value space includes all values $m \times 2^e$, where m is an integer whose absolute value is less than 2^{53}, and e is an integer between **-1075** and **970**, inclusive. There are also the same five special values as defined for the `float` type. This datatype is ordered by numeric value.

The lexical representation is the same as the `float` type. For example:

```
<an_element num1="-1E666" num2="3.1416" num3="12.78e-1040" num4="INF" />
```

There are no built-in derived types.

timeDuration

A duration of time, with a countably infinite value space, as specified in ISO 8601.

> **ISO 8601:Representations of dates and times,** 1988-06-15 *is one of the few ISO standards that is available on the WWW (at http://www.iso.ch/markete/8601.pdf). Ordering information for the new draft and its corrections are at http://www.iso.ch/cate/d15903.html and http://www.iso.ch/cate/d15905.html.*

The lexical representation is the ISO 8601 extended format: P*n*Y*n*M*n*DT*n*H*n*M*n*S. The upper-case letters P, Y, M, D, T, H, M, and S in this format are called designators. The "P" stands for "period" (as in a duration of time) and is required to be the first character of any timeDuration string. The recurring "*n*" represents number, so *n*Y is the number of years, *n*M the number of months, *n*D of days, T is the date/time separator, *n*H is hours, the second *n*M is minutes, and *n*S is seconds. Seconds may be any decimal number of arbitrary precision.

For example:

```
<an_element duration="P12Y10M2DT0H40M27.87S" />
```

This represents a timeDuration of 12 years, 10 months, 2 days, 0 hours, 40 minutes, and 27.875 seconds.

Truncated lexical representations of this format are allowed provided they conform to the following:

❑   Lowest order items may be omitted. If so, their value is assumed to be zero.

❑   The lowest order item may have a decimal fraction of arbitrary precision.

❑   If any of the number values equals zero, the number and its corresponding designator may be omitted. However, at least one number and its designator must always be present.

❑   The designator **T** must be absent if all time items are omitted.

❑   The leading designator **P** must always be present.

For example:

```
<an_element duration="P12Y10M2DT40M27.87S" />
```

represents the same timeDuration as the previous example – except here we're using one of the truncated forms (hours have been omitted).

An optional preceding minus sign (–) is also allowed, to indicate a negative duration; if the sign is omitted, a positive duration is assumed

One more example: the durations in the first line below are all legal (meaning 500 years, 42 months, 1 year + 6 months + 2 hours, and 42 days + 1 hour + 57 minutes, respectively), whilst the subsequent two lines are both *illegal*:

```
<an_element d1="P500Y" d2="P42M" d3="P1Y6MT2H" d4="P42DT1H57M" />
<an_element d="P-1347M" />      <!-- minus sign must precede the P -->
<an_element d="P1Y2MT" />       <!-- T must be omitted in this case -->
```

There are no built-in types derived from timeDuration.

recurringDuration

A `timeDuration` that recurs with a specific `timeDuration` starting from a specific origin. The value space is countably infinite. (See also §5.5.3.2 of ISO 8601.)

The lexical representation is the ISO 8601 extended format `CCYY-MM-DDThh:mm:ss.sss`. The `CC` represents the century, `YY` the year, `MM` the month and `DD` the day. The `T` is the date/time separator. The `hh`, `mm`, and `ss.sss` represent hours, minutes and seconds respectively. Additional digits may be used to increase the precision of the fractional seconds, and additional digits can be added to `CC` to accommodate year values greater than 9999. An optional preceding minus sign (-) is allowed to indicate a negative duration; if the sign is omitted, a positive duration is assumed.

The basic string may be immediately followed by a `Z` to indicate Coordinated Universal Time (UTZ).

> *UTZ is the internationally-accepted apolitical term for the world's base time zone on the Zero Meridian, commonly-known in Anglo-countries as Greenwich Mean Time.*

A local time zone offset (the difference between the local time zone and UTZ) may also be indicated by adding another string with the format: `±hh.mm`, where `hh` and `mm` are defined as above, and the sign may be either plus or minus. The two time zone options (UTZ and local) are mutually exclusive

The primary purpose, and only legal use, of `recurringDuration` is as a base type for some derived date/time type. This derived type must specify both the duration and period constraining facets. This primitive datatype *may not be used directly in a schema* – though it may be used indirectly via a derived type.

Built-in derived types: `recurringDate`, `recurringDay`, `time`, `timeInstant`, and `timePeriod` (all of these, except the first, use truncated versions of the above lexical representation).

The two required facets are specified using the same lexical format as `timeDuration`. These facets specify the length of the duration (`duration`) and after what duration it recurs (`period`). If `duration`'s value is zero, it means that the duration is a single instant of time. If the `period` is zero, the duration doesn't recur, in other words there's only a single occurrence.

binary

Some arbitrary binary data, which is any finite-length sequence of binary octets (8-bit bytes). This datatype is not ordered.

The lexical representation of this datatype depends upon the choice of encoding facet (see its description in the previous section). For example:

```
<an_element encoding="hex">312D322D33</an_element>
```

This example shows the hex encoding of the ASCII string `"1-2-3"`.

There are no built-in derived types.

This type *may not be used directly in a schema* – it may only be used indirectly via a derived type.

uriReference

An absolute or relative Uniform Resource Identifier (URI) Reference that may have an optional fragment identifier. This datatype is not ordered.

The lexical representation of this datatype is any string that matches the URI-reference production in Section 4 of RFC 2396. For example:

```
<an_element link="http://www.w3.org" />              <!-- HTTP -->
<an_element link="ftp://ftp.is.co.za/rfc/rfc2396.txt" /> <!-- FTP -->
<an_element link="mailto://sales@wrox.com" />        <!-- email -->
<an_element link="telnet://melvyl.ucop.edu" />       <!-- Telnet -->
```

ID

A datatype that is equivalent to the ID attribute type as defined in the XML 1.0 recommendation (see also Chapter 11). This datatype is not ordered, and the following validity constraints apply:

❑　The value of the ID string must uniquely identify its associated element

❑　It must be used once, and only once, in a document instance

The lexical representation of this datatype is any NCName string (name without colon), as defined in *Namespaces in XML*. For example:

```
<an_element its_id="AGENT_ID_007" />
```

There are no built-in derived types.

IDREF

A datatype that is equivalent to the IDREF attribute type as defined in the XML 1.0 recommendation (see also Chapter 9). The value of the IDREF string must match the value of an element or attribute of type ID, somewhere within the same document instance. This datatype is not ordered.

The lexical representation of this datatype is any NCName string (name without colon), as defined in *Namespaces in XML*. For example:

```
<an_element codename="AGENT_ID_007" />
```

Built-in derived type is: IDREFS.

For compatibility with XML 1.0 DTDs, this datatype should only be used for attributes.

ENTITY

A datatype that's equivalent to the ENTITY attribute type as defined in the XML 1.0 recommendation (see also Chapter 11), with a value space that's scoped to a specific document instance. The ENTITY value must match an unparsed entity name that's declared in the schema. This datatype is not ordered.

The lexical representation of this datatype is any NCName string (name without colon), as defined in *Namespaces in XML*.

Built-in derived type: ENTITIES.

For compatibility with XML 1.0 DTDs, this datatype should only be used for attributes.

NOTATION

A datatype that's equivalent to the NOTATION attribute type as defined in the XML 1.0 recommendation (see also Chapter 11), with a value space that is scoped to a specific document instance. The NOTATION value must match a notation name that is declared in the schema. This datatype is not ordered.

The lexical representation of this datatype is any NCName string (name without colon), as defined in *Namespaces in XML*.

There are no built-in derived types.

For compatibility with XML 1.0 DTDs, this datatype should only be used for attributes.

QName

A qualified name, as defined in *Namespaces in XML*. Each qualified name is comprised of a pair of names, separated by the namespace delimiter (:) character, the namespace name (which is a uriReference), and the local name (which is an NCName). This datatype is not ordered.

The lexical representation of this datatype is any legal QName string (name with qualifier). For example:

```
<a_ns_name:an_element_name> .. </a_ns_name:an_element_name>
```

There are no built-in derived types.

Constraining Facets for Primitive Types

The usable constraining facets for each of the 14 primitive datatypes are:

	length	min Length	pattern	enumeration	min/max Exclusive/ Inclusive	scale, precision	encoding	duration, period
string	X	X	X	X	X			
boolean			X					
float			X	X	X			
double			X	X	X			

Table continued on following page

	length	min Length	pattern	enumeration	min/max Exclusive/ Inclusive	scale, precision	encoding	duration, period
decimal			X	X	X	X		
timeDuration			X	X	X			
recurring Duration			X	X	X			**X** (*req*)
binary	X	X	X	X			**X** (*req*)	
uriReference	X	X	X	X				
ID	X	X	X	X	X			
IDREF	X	X	X	X	X			
ENTITY	X	X	X	X	X			
NOTATION	X	X	X	X	X			
QName	X	X	X	X	X			

Those facets labeled "(req)" are always required for any derived types based on this base datatype.

Built-in Derived Types

The following are the derived datatypes that are built-in to XML Schema:

- ❑ language – a natural language identifier, as defined by RFC.1766
- ❑ Name – a legal XML 1.0 name
- ❑ NCName – a legal XML 1.0 "non-colonized" name, as defined in *Namespaces in XML*
- ❑ integer – an integer number
- ❑ negativeInteger – an integer number with a value < 0
- ❑ positiveInteger – an integer number with a value > 0
- ❑ nonNegativeInteger – an integer number with a value ≥ 0
- ❑ nonPositiveInteger – an integer number with a value ≤ 0
- ❑ byte – an integer number with a value in the range -128 to +127 (inclusive)
- ❑ short – an integer number with a value in the range -32,768 to +32,767 (inclusive)

- `int` – an integer number with a value in the range -2,147,483,648 to +2,147,483,647 (inclusive)

- `long` – an integer number with a value in the range -9,223,372,036,854,775,808 to +9,223,372,036,854,775,807 (inclusive)

- `unsignedByte` – a non-negative integer number with a value in the range 0 to +255 (inclusive)

- `unsignedShort` – a non-negative integer number with a value in the range 0 to +65,535 (inclusive)

- `unsignedInt` – a non-negative integer number with a value in the range: 0 to +4,294,967,295 (inclusive)

- `unsignedLong` – a non-negative integer number with a value in the range 0 to +18,446,744,073,709,551,615 (inclusive)

- `year` – a Gregorian calendar year

- `month` – a Gregorian calendar month

- `century` – a Gregorian calendar century (a year without the two rightmost digits)

- `date` – a Gregorian calendar date (a single day)

- `recurringDate` – a Gregorian calendar date that recurs once every year

- `recurringDay` – a Gregorian calendar date that recurs once every month

- `time` – an instant of time that recurs every day

- `timeInstant` – a specific instant in time

- `timePeriod` – a specific period of time with a given start and end

- `IDREFS` – equivalent to the XML 1.0 `IDREFS` attribute type

- `NMTOKEN` – equivalent to the XML 1.0 `NMTOKEN` attribute type

- `NMTOKENS` – equivalent to the XML 1.0 `NMTOKENS` attribute type

- `ENTITIES` – equivalent to the XML 1.0 `ENTITIES` attribute type

Let's look at examples of some of these datatypes:

language

A natural language identifier, as defined by RFC 1766.

```
<LanguageOfOrigin>en-GB</LanguageOfOrigin>
<an_element xml:lang="en-US" > ... </an_element>
```

The first of these two examples shows an element that has its content constrained to be the `language` datatype. The second exploits a little-known attribute defined in the XML 1.0 REC, which uses the same type of values.

name, NCName

Respectively a legal XML 1.0 name and a legal XML 1.0 "non-colonized" name, as defined in *Namespaces in XML*.

```
<somens:an_element_name> ... </somens:an_element_name>
<an_element_name> ... </an_element_name>
```

Both of the above examples are legal XML names that conform to the name datatype. The first is also a QName, i.e. a namespace-qualified name. The latter is a non-qualified ("non-colonized") name that conforms to the NCName datatype, a more restrictive version of name.

integer, negativeInteger, positiveInteger, nonNegativeInteger, nonPositiveInteger

These five datatypes are all integers, but negativeInteger, positiveInteger, nonNegativeInteger, and nonPositiveInteger are constrained to specific ranges of values. For example, a negativeInteger is any integer value less than zero. The difference between a negativeInteger and a nonPositiveInteger (or positiveInteger and nonNegativeInteger) is that the latter also includes zero in its value space.

byte, short, int, long

These four datatypes are all integer types, and are all constrained to finite ranges of values.

unsignedByte, unsignedShort, unsignedInt, unsignedLong

These four datatypes are all nonNegativeInteger types, and are also constrained to finite ranges of values (as shown in the table below).

century, year, month, date

These four datatypes are all derived from another derived datatype, the timePeriod type. They represent Gregorian calendar dates based upon the formats defined in §5.2.1 of ISO 8601, as shown in the following examples:

```
<Century>19</Century>
<Year>2525</Year>
<Month>08</Month>
<Date>31</Date>
```

Note that the names of the elements are also just examples – the correlation between these names and the datatype names is strictly illustrative. Dates in XML are always represented using numbers, in the form "YYYY-MM-DD", where "YYYY" is the year, "MM" is the month, and "DD" is the day of the month. This minimizes any confusion based upon language or cultural differences.

The century datatype is used to represent the leftmost digits of the year (<u>underlined</u> in the preceding format example). It is important to note that this is not the commonly used ordinal century (e.g. the 1900s were known as the "20th century" – strictly speaking this century was the years 1901-2000, since there is no year 0 in the Gregorian calendar). Rather, a century is the two (or more) leftmost digits of a year, up to and including the hundreds digits ("19" is the century of the year "1999").

A year or century may be preceded by a minus sign (–) to indicate years BCE (Before Common Era). Additional digits may be added to the left of these to represent years before -9999 BCE and after 9999 CE.

recurringDate, recurringDay

These two datatypes are derived from the recurringDuration primitive type. The former must always be represented in the truncated date form of "--MM-DD", the latter as "---DD".

```
<AnnualAppointment>--04-15</AnnualAppointment>
<MonthlyAppointment>---10</MonthlyAppointment>
```

The above examples show the date/day of two different appointments: the first on the 15th of April, the second on the 10th of every month.

time, timeInstant, timePeriod

These three datatypes are derived from the recurringDuration primitive type. The first two use similar formats. A time always uses the 24-hour clock in the form "HH:MM:SS.SSS HH:MM", where "HH" is hours (0-24), "MM" is minutes, "SS.SSS" is seconds. The fractional seconds and the decimal point are optional, as is the " HH:MM", which is used to show the difference between local time zone and UTZ (also known as GMT). Data of the timeInstant type must always include the full date, as well as the time-of-day.

```
<TheTimeNowIs>20:14:57+07:00</TheTimeNowIs>
<ThisInstantIs>2000-05-28T20:14:57+07:00</ThisInstantIs>
<Duration>P12Y10M2DT0H40M27.87S</Duration>
```

The timePeriod type uses same representation as its base type, recurringDuration. See its definition in the **Primitive Types** section above (the above example uses the same value as the examples in that section, only this time it's shown as the content of an element rather than the value of an attribute).

Constraining Facets for Derived Types

The usable constraining facets for each of the built-in derived datatypes are:

	length	min Length /max Length	pattern	enumeration	min/max Exclusive/ Inclusive	scale, precision	duration, period
language	X	X	X	X	X		
Name	X	X	X	X	X		
NCName	X	X	X	X	X		
integer			X	X	X	X	
negativeInteger			X	X	X	X	
positiveInteger			X	X	X	X	
nonNegativeInteger			X	X	X	X	
nonPositiveInteger			X	X	X	X	
byte			X	X	X	X	
short			X	X	X	X	
long			X	X	X	X	
int			X	X	X	X	
unsignedByte			X	X	X	X	
unsignedShort			X	X	X	X	
unsignedLong			X	X	X	X	
unsignedInt			X	X	X	X	
year			X	X	X		X
month			X	X	X		X
century			X	X	X		X
date			X	X	X		X
recurringDate			X	X	X		X
recurringDay			X	X	X		X
time			X	X	X		X
timeInstant			X	X	X		X

	length	min Length /max Length	pattern	enumeration	min/max Exclusive/ Inclusive	scale, precision	duration, period
timePeriod			X	X	X		X
IDREFS	X	X		X			
NMTOKEN	X	X	X	X	X		
NMTOKENS	X	X		X			
ENTITIES	X	X		X			

Index

A Guide to the Index

The index is arranged hierarchically, in alphabetical order, with symbols preceding the letter A. Most second-level entries and many third-level entries also occur as first-level entries. This is to ensure that users will find the information they require however they choose to search for it.

Symbols

' (apostrophe), entity references, 426
! (exclamation mark), DTDs, 337
(hash mark), character references, 424
#, URL fragment identifier, 334
% (percent sign), parameter entities, 423
& (ampersand), parsed entities, 423
 , space character, 654
&amp, & character, 53
&apos, ' character, 54
&gt, > character, 54
&lt, < character, 53
 , white space, 36
&quot, 54
( ), functions in XPath, 146
*, cardinality operator, 345
, (comma), list operator character, 343
/*...*/, comments in stylesheets, 71
/, document root in XPath, 143
//, recursive descent operator, XPath, 143
: (colon)
  pseudo-classes, 78
  namespaces, 298
; (semi-colon), parsed entities, 423
? (question mark), cardinality operator, 345
@ symbol in XPath, 143
[ ], location paths, XPath, 144
| (vertical bar), list operator character, 343
+, cardinality operator, 345
<!--...-->, comments, 43
  adding automatically, 254
  in stylesheets, 71
<?...?> tags, processing instructions, 51
==, comparisons in Java,, 283

A

about attribute
  <rdf:description> element, 530
absolute position, CSS, 104
abstract attribute
  <complexType> element, 401
  <simpleType> element, 398
:active pseudo-class, 79
ActiveDOM, 57, 219
ActiveX Data Objects. See ADO
actuate attribute, XLink, 450, 452
  arc-type elements, 459
add_message template
  bulletin board system, 588
Addresses in schemas, 635
ADO
  Connection object, 486
  databases, connecting to, 486
  Recordset object, 484
  SQL queries, capturing results of, 480
advertising on bulletin boards, 573
:after pseudo-class, 81
alert() function, Document object, 19
alignment, 122
all media group, 89
<all>, XML schema, 409
American Standard Code for Information
    Interchange (ASCII), 48
&amp, & character, 53
ampersand (&), parsed entities, 423
ancestors, 20
anchors, 465
<annotation> element, 412, 418
annotations in XML Schema, 418–19
anonymous type, 405
ANSI X1.2, EDI standard, 614

ANY category
ELEMENT declarations, 339
<any> element, XML schema, 410
&apos, ' character, 54
apostrophe ('), entity references, 426
appendChild method
Node interface, 232
appendData() method
CharacterData interface, 250
<appInfo> element, 418
applications
communication between using XML, 485
requirements for XML, 320
scalability, 526
arc-type elements, XLink, 450
extended links, 459
Arthur Discspinner. See music wholesaling case study
ASCII, 48
ASP, 707-40
instantiator page, 525
sending data to, 504
<assert> element
Schematron, 532
async property
MSXML, 230
asynchronous file loading, 230
atomic datatypes, 388
list datatypes derived from, 400
ATTLIST declarations, 337, 349-58
attribute default parameter, 356
attribute types, 351
BookCatalog example, 360-73
CDATA attribute type, 351
enumerated values attribute type, 352
ID attribute type, 353
IDREF attribute type, 353
IDREFS attribute type, 353
NMTOKEN attribute type, 355
NMTOKENS attribute type, 355
shortcut using parameter entity references, 430, 431
Attr interface, DOM, 242, 247, 671
name property, 248
ownerElement property, 247
specified property, 248
using, 248
value property, 248
attrDefault parameter
ATTLIST declarations, 350
attribute default parameter, 356
default values, 358
#FIXED, 357
#IMPLIED, 357
#REQUIRED, 357

<attribute> element
constraints, 414-16
form attribute, 414
id attribute, 414
name attribute, 414
ref attribute, 414
type attribute, 414
use attribute, 414
value attribute, 414
XML Schema, 414-17
attribute groups, 416-17
attribute-list declaration. See ATTLIST declarations
<attributeGroup> element, 416-17
AttributeList object, 276
getLength method, 277
getName method, 277
getType method, 277
getValue method, 277, 278
attributes, 38-42, 349
adding, 39
dynamically, 178-81
case-sensitivity, 353
dependencies between elements and, 632
dynamically adding with XSLT, 178-81
vs. elements, 41-42
extracting with SAX, 276-81
global attributes, 306
namespaces, 305-7
plain text, 351
reasons for using, 41
related groups of, 179
sets, 179
types, 351
using, 365-73
without values, 493
attributes axis, XPath, 158
attributes property
Node interface, 228, 245
attrName parameter
ATTLIST declarations, 350
aural media, 89
stylesheets for, 125-27
Author element
BookCatalog example, 325
auto property, positioning schemes, 106
axis names, XPath, 156-60
attributes, 158
child, 157
descendant, 158
following-sibling, 158
namespace, 158
parent, 158
preceding-sibling, 158
self, 157
azimuth property, 126

B

B2B auctions, 660

B2B e-commerce. *See* **business to business e-commerce**

B2B Integration Server (Excelon), 657

B2B server (IBM), 657

B2C transactions, 24

background
color, 95
creating, 102
images, 99–104
positioning and repeating images, 101
properties, combining, 102

bare names syntax, XPointer, 468, 469

BASDA, 611

base attribute
<complexType> element, 401
<simpleType> element, 398

base datatypes, 386

BBS. *See* **bulletin board system**

:before pseudo-class, 81

behavior attributes, XLink, 452

binary files, 10

binary primitive datatype, XML schema, 386
encoding constraining facet, 394

binding, constants, 203

bitmap media group, 89

bits, 10

BizTalk, 620
header, 658
framework, 485
server, 657

block attribute
<complexType> element, 402

block elements
box model, 90

bold fonts, 117

Book element
BookCatalog example, 325, 328

BookCatalog example
ATTLIST declarations, 360–65
shortcut using parameter entities, 431
attributes, using, 365–73
Author element, 325
basic data model, 325–29
Book element, 325, 328
Catalog element, 325, 328
conditional sections, 440
data model, 326–29
extending, 358–59
Document Type Declaration, 333

DTD, 324
expanded, 363
internal and external subsets, 439
linking to document, 335–36
ELEMENT declarations, 347
external unparsed entities, using, 436
notation, 436
parameter entities, 431
parent-child relationships, 325
Publisher element, 325, 328
ID attribute, 370
vocabulary, 324
XML, reason for using, 324

boolean functions in XPath, 150–52

boolean primitive datatype, XML schema, 386

boolean() function, XPath, 151

borders, 96–99

bounds fundamental facet, 392
value spaces, 390

box model, 90–94
block elements, 90
display properties, 91
inline elements, 90

**
 tag in XML, 550**

branches, 20

browsers. *See also individual browsers*
colors, 95
CSS, 61, 208
ISO character entities, supporting, 434

built-in datatypes, 387
XML schema, 385, 790–93

bullet characters, 113
fancy, 75
graphical, 114
positioning, 114

bulletin board system, 567
access, 575
add_message template, 588
advertising, 573
architecture, 567
button template, 605
CDATA sections, 589
checkbox template, 606
deiete_message template, 592
designing, 576
file template, 603
form image maps template, 606
get_body_link template, 596
get_header_link template, 596
get_message_list template, 592
get_processed_list template, 594
heirarchical structure, 576
problems with, 578
linear structure, 578
advantages of, 582

bulletin board system (continued)
list view, 597
membership directories, 573
message ancestor tree, 580
message child tree, 580
message sibling tree
next, 581
previous, 582
messages
creating, 583
dating, 589
deleting, 592
editing, 590
linking to, 589
lists of, viewing, 593
navigating between, 596
paging, 596
retrieving, 596
sorting, 594
uniquely identifying, 588
viewing, 600
namespaces, 583
next response, 581
password template, 604
personalization, 573
private content, 573
Re: characters, 588
recursive templates, 580
replies, viewing, 596
reset button template, 605
root node match template, 607
security access, 573
submit button template, 604
tabular_form.xsl, 600
output defining, 607
textarea template, 606
threading, 568
user IDs, 576
Business and Accounting Software Developers Association, 611
business cards example, 209
Business Objects layer, 482
business to business e-commerce, 24, 324, 611
See also music wholesaling case study
XSLT, 135
business to customer transactions, 24
button template
bulletin board system, 605

C

Cagle, Kurt, 567
Candidate Recommendation, W3C nomenclature, 379
cardinality fundamental facet, 392
value spaces, 390
cardinality operators, 340, 341, 345

carriage return character, 37
cascading class selectors, 75
Cascading Stylesheets. *See* **CSS**
case conversion, 155
case-order attribute
<xsl:sort> element, 195
case-sensitivity
of attributes, 353
of tags, 34
casting, 223
Catalog element
BookCatalog example, 325, 328
catch blocks
exception handling, 226
CDATA attribute type, 351
cdata-section-elements attribute
<xsl:output> element, 175
CDATA sections, 54–57
adding automatically, 254
bulletin board system, 589
extracting with SAX, 273–76
CDATASection interface, DOM, 254, 672
centimeters, font sizes in, 116
CGI
XML-RPC cheat, 521
character code, 47
Character Data. *See* **CDATA**
character encoding, 47
character-points, XPointer, 471
character references, 54, 424
CharacterData interface, DOM, 249, 671-72
appendData() method, 250
data property, 249
deleteData() method, 250
insertData() method, 250
length property, 249
replaceData() method, 251
substringData() method, 250
characters() method
DocumentHandler interface, 273
checkbox template
bulletin board system, 606
Chemical Markup Language. *See* **CML**
child axis, XPath, 157
child elements
content models, 340
default namespaces for, 302
child sequence syntax, XPointer, 468, 469
childNodes property
Node interface, 230
children of objects
serialization of, 510–11

<choice> element, 405
choice groups
  XML schema, 408
choice lists, 341
  using, 343
choreography, 659
citizens, 573
Clark, James, 132
class attribute, CSS, 71–78
class selectors, 73
  cascading, 75
  inheriting, 75
classes, 221
  in HTML, 71–78
  pseudo-classes, 78–81
  in XML, 84
CLASSPATH environment variable, 266
clip property
  positioning schemes, 108
cloneNode method
  Node interface, 233
CML, 17
COBRA, 485, 519
code generator from Oracle, 494
collapsed ranges, XPointer, 471
colon (:)
  pseudo-classes, 78
  namespaces, 298
color property, borders, 96
colors, 94–96
  hexadecimal codes, 95
columns, databases, 478
COM, 485
  associating COM objects with namespaces, 583
comma (,), list operator character, 343
Comment interface, DOM, 254, 672
comment() function, XPath, 147
comments, 42–45
  displaying, 44
  in stylesheets, 71
commit/rollback functionality, serialization, 517
Common Object Request Broker Architecture, 485,
    519
compact display property, 91
comparisons in Java, (==), 283
Complex Type Definition, 397, 400–406
<complexType> element, 401
  block attribute, 402
  content attribute, 401, 405
  converting to from DTDs, 402–6
  final attribute, 402

Component Object Model. See COM
compression, 14, 42
concat() function, XPath, 153
concatenation of strings, 153, 155
conditional sections, 439–43
  dynamic stylesheets, 651
  in XSLT, 182–87
  nesting, 443
Connection object, 486
  Execute() method, 486
constants in XSLT, 201–4
  binding, 203
constraining facets, datatypes, 390, 392–95,
    789-90
  duration, 395
  encoding, 394
  enumeration, 394
  length, 393
  maxExclusive, 394
  maxInclusive, 394
  maxlength, 393
  minExclusive, 394
  minInclusive, 394
  minlength, 393
  pattern, 393
  period, 395
  precision, 394
  scale, 394
container node, XPointer, 470
contains() function, XPath, 153
content attribute
  <complexType> element, 405
  <simpleType> element, 401
content
  blindness of CSS to, 208
  in elements, categories of, 338–40
  flow of in box model, 90
  from multiple sources, incorporating, 557–63
content models, 340–47
  cardinality, 345
  choice lists, 343
  element content, 341
  mixed content, 342
  PCDATA content, 340
  sequence lists, 343
  XML schema, 382, 397, 406–11
    cardinality, 407
    choice groups, 408
    content from another schema, 410
    element content categories, 407
    mixed content, 409
    model groups, 411
    sequence groups, 408
Content/Presentation paradigm, 65
contentHandler interface, SAX 2.0, 291

context node, XPath, 141
  attributes of, 158
  copying, 192
  templates, effect of, 165
contextual information, loss of through proliferation of tags, 64
continuous media group, 89
copying source tree, 190–92
count() function, XPath, 149
createAttribute() method
  Document interface, 236
createDocument() method
  DOMImplementation interface, 238
createElement() method
  Document interface, 236
createNodeType() method
  Document interface, 236
cryptography, 657
CSS, 61
  absolute position, 104
  :active, 79
  :after, 81
  alignment, 122
  background
    combining properties, 102
    creating, 102
    images, 99–104
    positioning images, 101
    repeating images, 101
  :before, 81
  borders, 96–99
  box model, 90–94
  browser support, indifference to, 208
  bullet characters, 113
  cascading, 68–71
  cascading class selectors, 75
  class attribute, 71–78
  clip property, 108
  colors, 94–96
  content blindness of, 208
  external stylesheets, 81–82
    in XML, 83–86
  :first-child, 78
  :first-letter, 80
  :first-line, 80
  fixed position, 105
  float property, 109
  :focus, 79
  font-family property, 118
  font manipulation, 116–19
  height property, 107
  :hover, 79
  images, 100
  @import directive, 82
  indenting text, 120
  inherited position, 105
  interactivity limitations, 208

  internal stylesheets, 87
  kerning, 121–22
  :lang, 80
  letter spacing, 121
  line height, 121
  :link, 79
  <LINK> element, 81
  lists, 111–15
  margins, 120
  @media directive, 88
  media types, 87–89
  order, sensitivity to, 208
  origins of, 66
  overflow property, 108
  padding, 120
  page breaks, 124
  @page directive, 124
  positioning schemes, 104–11
  printing, 122–25
  push model, 620, 643
  reasons for using, 62–63
  relative position, 104
  Ruby characters, 122
  setting positions, 105
  static position, 104
  tables, 111–15
  text manipulation, 116–19
  url() function, 99
  :visited, 79
  width property, 107
  XML, 83
    displaying, 23
  <?xml-stylesheet?> processing instruction, 83
  XSL Formatting Objects, 213
  XSLT, 208–13
cue property, 127
CueXML, 219

D

data
  binary, 10
  describing, 15
  retrieving from multiple tables, 480
  structured, 21
data coding mechanism, XML as, 618
data model
  BookCatalog example, 326–29
    basic, 326–29
    extending, 358–59
Data Objects layer, 482
  simplifying, 489
  XML, returning from, 486
data property
  CharacterData interface, 249
  ProcessingInstruction interface, 256

Data service layer, 482
data-type attribute
   <xsl:sort> element, 195
data types. *See datatypes*
databases
   connecting to, 486
   data retrieval, 480
   integrity, 479
   joins, 480
   n-tier architecture, 482–87
   normalization, 481
   primary keys, 480
   relational, 478
   situations when not needed, 496–97
   SQL, 479–80
   staging, 488
   types of, 478
   uniqueness, 479
   vendors and XML, 490–96
   XML, 487–89
    storing, 487
DataChannel, 57
datatype extension, 385, 397
datatype restriction, 385, 397
datatypes
   atomic, 388
   bounds, 392
   cardinality, 392
   definitions, 397
    complex, 397, 400–406
    simple, 397, 398–400
   derived, 385, 387
    by list, 400
    by restriction, 399
   DOMString, 219
   DTDs, weakness of, 374
   equality, 391
   facets, 389, 390
    constraining, 392-95, 789-95
    fundamental, 390–92
   lexical space, 389, 390
   list, 388
   order, 391
   primitive, 385, 386
   value spaces, 389, 390
   XML schema, 382-83, 385, 783-95
date datatype, XML Schema, 387
date format, ISO standard, 328
DB2 parser
   XML schema support, 384
DCOM, 485, 519
   firewalls prevent use of, 520
debugging
   newline and tabs, 509
   Schematron, 531
   serialization, 503
    historical information, 518

decimal numbers in character references, 424
decimal primitive datatype, XML schema, 386
   precision constraining facet, 394
   scale constraining facet, 394
declarations. *See also* XML declaration
   XML schema, 384
declarative programming, 138–40
   vs. imperative, 137–40
deep clones
   cloneNode method, 233
default attribute
   <element> element, 412
default namespaces, 300–303
   canceling, 303
   on specific elements, 302
   using, 301
default templates, XSLT, 165
default XLink attributes, 463
definitions
   XML schema, 384
deleteData() method
   CharacterData interface, 250
delimited formats, EDI, 614
denormalization in databases, 481
dependency in elements, 622, 628
   and attributes, 632
   eliminating, 626
derived datatypes, 385, 387
   built-in, 387
   contraining facets for, 794-95
   by list, 400
   by restriction, 399
derivedBy attribute
   <complexType> element, 401
   <simpleType> element, 398
descendant axis, XPath, 158
descendants, 20
deserialization, 503
DHTML, 19, 223
disable-output-escaping atttribute
   <xsl:value-of> element, 171
Discspinner, Arthur. *See music wholesaling case study*
discussion groups. *See bulletin board system*
display attributes in XML, 86, 91
   block, 90
   inline, 90
   other values, 91
   tables, 114
   visibility property, compared, 92
display mechanism, XSL as, 618
distributed objects, 485
Distributed COM. *See DCOM*

distributed computing, 519–26
firewalls, 520

\<DIV\> element, 69, 653

DOCTYPE declaration. *See Document Type Declaration*

document element name
Document Type Declaration, 333

document entity, 422

document instances, 321

Document interface, DOM, 235, 666-68
createAttribute() method, 236
createElement() method, 236
createNodeType() method, 236
documentElement property, 235
factory methods, 236
getElementsByTagName() method, 236
importNode() method, 234

document object (DOM), 19

Document object (ADO)
xml property, 487

Document Object Model. *See DOM*

document root in XPath, 142
matching template against, 198

Document Type Declaration, 331–36
document element name, 333
DTD source, 333
example, 335–36
PUBLIC locations, 334
structure and syntax, 332–35
SYSTEM locations, 333

Document Type Definitions. *See DTDs*

document types, 21–22
namespaces, 293–97
XML vocabulary, 321

\<documentation\> element, 418

documentElement property
Document interface, 235

DocumentFragment interface, DOM, 239, 668

DocumentHandler interface, SAX, 268
characters() method, 273
endDocument() method, 268, 270
endElement() method, 274
HandlerBase implementation, 268
ignorableWhitespace() method, 288
processingInstruction() method, 289
SAXException object, 281
setDocumentLocator() method, 284
startDocument() method, 268, 270
startElement() method, 271

documents
attributes, using to describe metadata, 349
DTDs, associating, 331–36
example, 335–36
elements, retrieving from, 468

entities, 422
events
end of document, 270
start of document, 270
linking to specific parts of, 464–74
loading from servers, 523
namespaces, adding, 298–99
nodes, 142
adding, 236
schemas, including from various sources, 404
tree, traversing, 230
validating with Schematron, 530–33
Web page, transforming to, 198
XML schema, associating, 395

DocumentType interface, 673

DOM, 19, 23, 217, 663-74
Attr interface, 242, 671
CDATASection interface, 254, 672
CharacterData interface, 249, 671-72
Comment interface, 254, 672
Document interface, 235, 666-68
DocumentFragment interface, 239, 668
DocumentType interface, 673
DOMImplementation interface, 238, 668
DTDs, not supported by, 375
Element interface, 242
Entity interface, 674
EntityReference interface, 674
exceptions, 226
implementations, 223
features, finding which supported, 238
interfaces, 220 (*See also individual interfaces*)
MSXML extensions to, 490
NamedNodeMap interface, 245, 670-71
NodeList interface, 240
Notation interface, 673
Oracle XML parsers' extensions to, 494
owner documents, 232
ProcessingInstruction interface, 256
Text interface, 249, 672
tree, traversing, 230
XML, 219

DOM Core, 224
interfaces, 224
Extended, 224
Fundamental, 224
namespace-aware functions, 226

DOM CSS, 224

DOM HTML, 224

DOMException interface, 227, 663-64

DOMImplementation interface, DOM, 238, 668
createDocument() method, 238
hasFeature() method, 238

DOMString data type, 219

double primitive datatype, XML schema, 386

double quotation marks, attributes, 38

downloading fonts, 119
Driver, SAX Parser class (xp), 270
drop-caps, 78, 109
.dtd files, 330
DTD source
Document Type Declaration, 333
DTDs, 23, 289, 319
alternatives to, 329
ATTLIST declaration, 337, 349–58
<complexType> element, converting to, 402-6
conditional sections, 439–43
content models (See content models)
data types, weakness, 374
default XLink attributes, 463
DOM not supported, 375
EBNF, 375
ELEMENT declaration, 337, 338–49
content categories, 338–40
content models, 340–47
example, 347
entities (See entities)
ENTITY declaration, 337
external subset, 330–31, 438–39
hierarchies, describing in, 329
inheritance, lack of, 375
internal subset, 330–31, 438–39
limitations of, 373–75, 530
markup, 337
namespaces, limited support of, 374
non-extensibile, 374
NOTATION declaration, 337
one per document, 374
optional elements, 345
overriding, 375
reasons for using, 320
repetitive declarations, shortcut for, 430
sharing, 322, 324
tools, limited, 375
validating parsers, 322–23
XML 1.0, 321
XML declaration, 332
XML documents, associating with, 331–36
example, 335–36
vs. XML schema, 380, 620
XML vocabulary, 321
Dublin Core vocabulary, 324, 438, 529
duplicate attribute error, 38
duration constraining facet, 395
Dynamic HTML. See DHTML
dynamic schemas, 383
dynamic stylesheets, 651
dynamically adding attributes with XSLT, 178–81
dynamically creating elements with XSLT, 175-78

E

e-commerce. See also eBIS-XML
B2B auctions, 660
choreography, 659
EDI, failings of, 614
product catalogues, 660
requirements, 613
met by eBIS-XML, 655
schema translation, 660
XML, using in, 24
XSLT, importance of, 134–37
EBCDIC, 48
eBIS-XML, 611, 615, 617
e-commerce requirements met by, 655
Exchequer Enterprise, 618
invoices
receiving, 617
sending, 616
map, viewing schema as, 636
orders
placing, 617
receiving, 616
schema vs. DTD, 620
schemas, 624
Address, 635
attributes, using, 630
detailed view of, 636
developing, 624
as DTD, 637
final version, 632
InvoiceHead, 633
REFERENCE element, 629
references, working with, 631
REFTYPE attribute, 626
showing in different ways, 636
version 2.4 weaknesses, 628
as XDR schema, 637
XML Authority, 638
as XSD schema, 637
security issues, 618
stylesheets, 620, 639
dynamic, 645
invoice, 639, 644
version 3, 623
schema, 627
XML-Data Reduced, 620
XSL, 620
EBNF
DTDs, 375
ebXML schema, 383
EDI, 324, 611
disadvantages of, 613
failings of, 614
XML compared, 614
EDIFACT, EDI standard, 614

editors, 599

eight-bit ASCII encoding, 48

Electronic Data Interchange. *See EDI*

element content, 20
XML schema, 407

ELEMENT declarations, 337, 338–49
content categories, 338–40
content models, 340–47
  cardinality operators, 345
example, 347
XML schema, 411–13

<element> element, 405, 412–13
default attribute, 412
fixed attribute, 412
id attribute, 412
maxOccurs attribute, 412
minOccurs attribute, 412
name attribute, 412
ref attribute, 412
type attribute, 412

element equivalent classes, XML schema, 412

Element interface, DOM, 242, 669-70
getAttribute() method, 242
getAttributeNode() method, 242
getElementsByTagName() method, 242
removeAttribute() method, 242
removeAttributeNode() method, 242
setAttribute() method, 242
setAttributeNode() method, 242
tagName property, 242
using, 243

elementName parameter
ATTLIST declarations, 350

elements, 28
vs. attributes, 41–42 (*See also* attributes)
CDATA, extracting, 273–76
content, 20, 28
  categories of, 338–40
content models, 341
dependencies, 622, 628
in different namespaces, outputting, 311-12
dynamically creating in XSLT, 175–78
empty, 46
end of element event, 274
ID attributes, 353
illegal PCDATA characters, 53–57
information, accessing with Node interface, 229
names, 33
namespaces, 293–97
  default, 300–303
  prefixes, 294–96
  qualified names, 297
  on specific elements, 301
relationships between, 353
retrieving from documents, 468
root, 33

rules for, 31–37
start and end tags, 31
start of element event, 271
  namespaces, 305–7
wrappers, 362, 543
XSLT, containing as variables, 202

<em> tags, 117

EMPTY category
ELEMENT declarations, 339

empty elements, 46, 339

encoding, 47–49
Unicode, 48

encoding attribute
<xsl:output> element, 173

encoding constraining facet, 394

encryption, 657

endDocument() method, 268, 270

endElement() method
DocumentHandler interface, 274

end-point() function, XPointer, 474

end-tags, 28, 31

entities, 422
conditional sections, 439–43
general, 422, 424–29
ISO entity set, 432–34
limitations, 426
<!NOTATION> declaration, 435
parameter, 422, 430–32
parsed, 422, 425–29
  external, 427
  internal, 425
references (See entity references)
unparsed, 429

ENTITIES attribute type, 351, 435–38

ENTITY attribute type, 351, 435–38

<!ENTITY> declaration, 422

ENTITY declarations (DTDs), 337

Entity interface, DOM, 674

ENTITY primitive datatype, XML schema, 386

entity references, 53, 423–24
character references, 424
delimiters, 426
parsed entities, 422
recursive, 426

EntityReference interface, DOM, 674

enumerated values attribute type, 351, 352

enumeration constraining facet, 394, 404

equality fundamental facet, 391
value spaces, 390

Err object, 227

error handling. *See also* exceptions; errors
SAXException, 281–88

error() method
ErrorHandler interface, 286
errorCode property
parseError object, 524
ErrorHandler interface, 286–88
error() method, 286
fatal() method, 286
warning() method, 286
errors, 58. *See also* **exceptions; error handling**
Locator object, 284–86
parser, 286–88
reporting with Schematron, 530–33
escaping characters, 53
Event object, 518
events
end of document, 270
end of element, 274
from parsers, catching, 270
SAX, 262
DocumentHandler interface, 268
receiving, 268–73
serialized object models, capturing in, 518
start of document, 270
start of element, 271
Excelon, 490
B2B Integration Server, 657
XML Stylus, 621, 654
exception handlers, 226
exceptions, 226. *See also* **errors.**
Locator object, 284–86
SAXException object, 281
throws exception, 270
Exchequer Enterprise, 618
exclamation mark (!), DTDs, 337
Execute() method
Connection object, 486
Expat, 57
expressions, XPath, 141
Extended Backus Naur Form. *See* **EBNF**
Extended interfaces, DOM Core, 224
extended links, 454, 456–63
arc-type elements, 459
creating, 457
remote resources, adding, 458
resource-type elements, 461
title-type elements, 463
extended-type elements, XLink, 450, 457
extending interfaces, 225
Extensible Markup Language. *See* **XML**
Extensible Stylesheet Language. *See* **XSL**
Extensible Stylesheet Language for Transformations. *See* **XSLT**
external entity references, 352

external parsed entities, 425, 427
advantages and disadvantages of, 427
text declarations, 428
external stylesheets, 81–82
in XML, 83–86
external subset, DTDs, 330–31
vs. internal subsets, 438–39
PUBLIC locations, 334
SYSTEM locations, 333
when to use, 330
external unparsed entities, 429
notation, 436
extraneous white space, 37

F

facets, datatypes, 389, 390
constraining, 392–95, 789-90
fundamental, 390–92
factory methods
Document interface, 236
false() function, XPath, 151
fatal errors, 58
fatal() method
ErrorHandler interface, 286
fields, databases, 479
file template
bulletin board system, 603
files
binary, 10
text, 11
filters, using in XPath location paths, 145
final attribute
<complexType> element, 402
firewalls and distributed computing, 520
:first-child pseudo-class, 78
:first-letter pseudo-class, 80
:first-line pseudo-class, 80
firstChild property
Node interface, 230
#FIXED, 357
fixed attribute, <element> element, 412
fixed position, CSS, 105
flexible interoperability, 616
float primitive datatype, XML schema, 386
float property
positioning schemes, 109
sidebars, 110
:focus pseudo-class, 79
following-sibling axis, XPath, 158
@font-face, 117

<FONT> tag
colors, 95
deprecated, 116
fonts
downloading, 119
@font-face, 117
font family, 117
kerning, 121–22
manipulation of, 116–19
sizes, 116
small caps, 119
styles, 117
underlining, 119
weight, 117
FOR XML EXPLICIT clause, 492
FOR XML RAW clause, 491
form attribute
<attribute> element, 414
<form> element
id and name attributes, 504
form image maps template
bulletin board system, 606
formatting XSLT ouput, 174
framework system in XHTML, 568
function of, 570
rq namespace, 571
server, defining, 572
XMLPipes, 569
xmlserver.asp file, 572
xp namespace, 571
xpo:page object, 571
from attribute, XLink, 450, 453
arc-type elements, 459
Front Page, 599
fully qualified names, namespaces, 298
functions in XPath, 146
boolean, 150–52
node, 146–48
numeric, 149–50
positional, 148–49
recursion, 193
string, 152–56
fundamental facets, datatypes, 390
bounds, 392
cardinality, 392
equality, 391
numeric/non-numeric, 392
order, 391
Fundamental interfaces, DOM Core, 224
fxp parser, 322

G

general entities, 422, 424–29
entity references, 423
parsed, 425–29
parsed entities, 422
unparsed, 429
getAttribute() method
Element interface, 242
getAttributeNode() method
Element interface, 242
getColumnNumber() method
Locator object, 285
getElementsByTagName() method, 490
Document interface, 236
Element interface, 242
getLength method
AttributeList object, 277
getLineNumber() method
Locator object, 285
getName method
AttributeList object, 277
getNamedItem() method
NamedNodeMap interface, 245
getPublicId() method
Locator object, 285
getSystemId() method
Locator object, 285
getType method
AttributeList object, 277
getValue method
AttributeList object, 277, 278
global attributes, 306
XLink, 448
global constants, 203
grid media group, 89
<group> element, XML schema, 411
&gt, > (greater than) character, 54

H

HandlerBase class
DocumentHandler interface, 268
ErrorHandler interface, 286–88
hasChildNodes method
Node interface, 231
hasFeature() method
DOMImplementation interface, 238

hash mark (#), character references, 424
height property
    positioning, 107
helper applications
    associating using <!NOTATION> declaration, 436
here() function, XPointer, 474
hexadecimal color codes, 95
hexadecimal numbers in character references, 424
hierarchical databases, 478
hierarchies of information, 18–20
    in HTML, 19
    in XML, 19
historical information, serialization, 518–19
:hover pseudo-class, 79
href attribute, XLink, 449, 451
HTML
    anchors, 465
    and ASP, 715-16
    colors, 94–96
    from XML, 497
    hierarchies in, 19
    history, 12, 63–65
    hyperlinks, 446–47
    integrating XML data into, 545
    and JavaScript, 744
    maintenance, 540
    markup, origins of, 63
    object model, 223
    style attribute, 67
    <style> element, 67
    style sheets, 65
    styling, 63–65, 66–68
    white space, 35
    XML, difference from, 18, 62
HTTP, 708-12
    SQL queries through, 491, 495
hyperlinks, 12, 446–47
Hypertext Markup Language. *See* HTML

I

id attribute
    <attribute> element, 414
    <attributeGroup> element, 417
    BookCatalog example, 370
    <element> element, 412
    <form> element, 504
ID attribute type, 351, 353
ID primitive datatype, XML schema, 386
IDREF attribute type, 351, 353
    one-to-one links, establishing, 354
IDREF primitive datatype, XML schema, 386

IDREFS attribute type, 351, 353
    limitation of, 372
    one-to-many links, establishing, 355
ignorableWhitespace() method
    DocumentHandler interface, 288
IGNORE keyword, conditional sections, 440
IIOP, 519
    firewalls prevent use of, 520
IIS Request parameters, 571
illegal PCDATA characters, 53–57
    CDATA sections, 54–57
    escaping characters, 53
<IMG/> tag in XML, 550
images
    background, 99–104
    CSS, 100
    unparsed entities, using to refer to, 429
imperative programming, 137
    vs. declarative, 137–40
implementing interfaces, 221
#IMPLIED, 350, 357
    shortcut, 430
@import directive, 82
importNode() method
    Document interface, 234
inches, font sizes in, 116
INCLUDE keyword, conditional sections, 440
indent attribute
    <xsl:output> element, 174
indentation, 119–20
indexes, XPointer, 470
infinite loops, 202
information, hierarchies of, 18–20
inherit display property, 91
inheritance
    lack of in DTDs, 375
    in XML schema, 382
inherited position, CSS, 105
inline elements
    box model, 90
inline links, 454–56
inline-table display property, 91, 115
insertBefore method
    Node interface, 233
insertData() method
    CharacterData interface, 250
instantiator pages, 521–26, 525
    benefits of, 526
integer datatype, XML Schema, 387
integrity in databases, 479

inter-enterprise communications with XML, 485
inter-object communications with XML, 484
interactive media, 89
  limitations of CSS in, 208
interfaces, 221
  DOM, 220
  DOM Core, 224
  extending, 225
  implementing, 221
  multiple, 222
  SAX, implementing, 268
internal parsed entities, 425
  format, 425
internal stylesheets, 87
internal subset, DTDs, 330–31
  vs. external subsets, 438–39
  when to use, 330
internally-defined entity references, 352
internationalization, 346
  Unicode, 48
Internet
  encryption, 657
  instant nature of, 656
  resources, 312
Internet Explorer, 57
  default XSL stylesheet, 213
  DOM, 219
  ISO character entities, 434
  MSXML, 219
  XML-Data Reduced, 329
  XML files, opening in, 14
Internet Inter-ORB Protocol. *See* IIOP
ISAPI filters, 491
ISO entity set, 432–34
ISO Latin1 entity set, 432
ISO standard date format, 328
ISO-8859-1, 48
italics, 117
item() method
  NamedNodeMap interface, 245
  NodeList interface, 240

J

Java
  class paths, modifying, 266
  class that implements SAX interface, 268
  comparisons, (==), 283
  exception handling, 226
  interfaces, implementing, 222
  and JavaScript, 744
  main() method, 270
  namespaces, 296

  read() method, 270
  SAX, 261
  throws exception, 270
  void, meaning of, 270
  XSLT, calling routines from, 583
Java DataBase Connectivity, 485
Java Project X TR2 parser, 322
JavaScript, 743-67
  imperative programming, 137
  object model simulation, 503–8
  try and catch exception handling supported, 227
  XML parsers, preventing from being parsed by, 55
JavaSoft
  free JDK, 261
JDBC, 485
JDK
  installing, 264
  tools, executing, 267
Jelliffe, Rick, 530
joins, 480

K

kerning, 121–22

L

labels for resources, 451
:lang pseudo-class, 80
language datatype, XML Schema, 387
**language definition mechanism, XML schema as,
  618**
Last Call Working Draft, W3C nomenclature, 379
last() function, XPath, 149
lastChild property
  Node interface, 230
layers, logical, n-tier architecture, 482
leaves, 20
length constraining facet, 393
length property
  CharacterData interface, 249
  NamedNodeMap interface, 245
  NodeList interface, 240
letter spacing, 121
lexical space, datatypes, 389, 390
  encoding constraining facet, 394
line feed character, 37
line height, 121
<LINK> element, 81
:link pseudo-class, 79
link source, 354

link target, 354
linking
 arcs, 459
 defining functionality of, 452
 directionality, 453
 extended links, 454, 456–63
  creating, 457
 hyperlinks, 446–47
 inline links, 454–56
 labeling resources, 451
 out of line links, 456–63
 simple links, 454–56
 to specific parts of documents, 464–74
 XLink, 447, 448–64
  attributes, 449–53
 XML, 447–48
 XPointer, 447, 464–74
  locations, 470
  points, 470
  ranges, 471–74
  schemes, 467
  shorthand syntaxes, 468–70
  URIs, appending to, 465
  XPath, extensions to, 474
list datatypes, 388
 derived from atomic datatypes, 400
list operator characters, 343
list, derivation of datatypes by, 400
list-item display property, 91
lists, 111–15
 bullet characters, 113
 in HTML, 75
 in XML, 113
load() method, 225, 523
loadXML() method, 225
local constants, 203
local resources
 extended links, adding to, 461
location paths, XPath, 141, 142–46
 building, 143
 specific, 144–46
location sets, XPointer, 464, 470
locations, XPointer, 464, 470
locator attribute, XLink, 451
Locator object, 284–86
 getColumnNumber() method, 285
 getLineNumber() method, 285
 getPublicId() method, 285
 getSystemId() method, 285
 setDocumentLocator() method, 284
 using, 285
locator-type elements, XLink, 450, 458
logical layers, n-tier architecture, 482
< < (less than) character, 53

lugnuts Web store case study, 537
 complexity, 538
 conditional processing, 556
 content from multiple sources, incorporating, 557–63
 future of, 565
 HTML code, 539
 maintenance, 540
 metadata, 556
 namespaces, 560
 Nut Haus
  templates, 562
  XML product listing, 559
 Nuts. Nuts? Nuts!
  templates, 561
  XML product listing, 558
 products, grouping together, 544
 suppliers, incorporating information from, 557–63
 templates, 549, 552
  currency, 555
 XML, 540–45
  displaying, 545–57
  elements, wrapping, 543
  files, creating, 542
  structure, designing, 540
 XSLT stylesheet, 549
  output, formatting, 555
Lyndia. See lugnuts Web store case study

M

Macintosh computers, newline characters on, 37
main() method, Java, 270
margins, 119–20
marker display property, 91
markup
 contextual information, loss of, 64
 history, 12–13
 origins of, 63
 for Web, 64
 white space, 37
 XML, containing as a variable, 202
match attribute
 <xsl:template> element, 133, 167, 194
MathML, 17
maxExclusive constraining facet, 394
maxInclusive constraining facet, 394
maxlength constraining facet, 393
maxOccurs attribute
 <element> element, 412
 XML schema, 407
@media directive, 88
media groups, 89
media types, CSS, 87–89

Megginson, David, 264

membership directories, 573
  access, 575
  member records, 575

message boards. See bulletin board system

metadata
  attributes, 41, 349
  binary files, 10
  lugnuts Web store case study, 556
  RDF, 528–30
  in text files, 12

method attribute
  <xsl:output> element, 173

methods, 19
  overriding, 268

Microsoft, XML technologies of, 490–93

Miloslav, Nic, 533

minExclusive constraining facet, 394

minInclusive constraining facet, 394

minlength constraining facet, 393

minOccurs attribute
  <element> element, 412
  XML schema, 407

mixed content, 20
  content models, 342

mode attribute
  <xsl:apply-templates> element, 168, 197–201
  <xsl:template> element, 168, 197–201

modes, 197–201
  transforming XML documents to Web pages, 198
  using, 198

MSXML parser, 322, 490
  async property, 230
  COM objects, associating with namespaces, 583
  DOM implementation, 219
    load() method, 225, 523
    loadXML() method, 225
    save() method, 225
  parseError object, 524
  selectSingleNode() method, 524
  XML-Data Reduced, 329
  XML documents, creating, 486
  XSLT, 132

msxsl namespace, 583

msxsl:script element, 584

multi-tier architecture. See n-tier architecture

multiple classes in XML, 84

multiple interfaces, implementing, 222

music wholesaling case study, 612
  choreography, 659
  dynamic stylesheets, 645
  e-commerce requirements, 613
  e-mail, 656
  eBIS-XML, 615, 617
    schemas, 624
  EDI, failings of, 614
  entry duplication, elimination of, 656
  internet, instant nature of, 656
  invoices
    receiving, 617
    sending, 616
  orders
    placing, 617
    receiving, 616
  specialist stationery, elimination of, 656
  upgrading, 656
  VANs, elimination of, 656
  Web site, 616

N

\n character, newlines, 505, 509

n-tier architecture, 482–87
  advantages of, 483
  Data Objects, returning XML from, 486
  XML, using in, 484–87

name attribute
  <attribute> element, 414
  <attributeGroup> element, 417
  <complexType> element, 401
  <element> element, 412
  <form> element, 504
  <simpleType> element, 398
  <xsl:element> element, 175
  <xsl:template> element, 168

Name datatype, XML Schema, 387

name property
  Attr interface, 248

name tokens, 351
  enumerated values attribute type, 352

name() function, XPath, 147

NameChar characters, 338
  NMTOKEN / NMTOKENS attribute types, 355

named templates, 168, 201–4

NamedNodeMap interface, DOM, 245, 670-71
  getNamedItem() method, 245
  item() method, 245
  length property, 245
  removeNamedItem() method, 245
  setNamedItem() method, 238, 245

namespace-aware functions, DOM Core, 226

namespace axis, XPath, 158

Namespace Identifier, URNs, 313

Namespace Specific String, URNs, 313

namespace-uri() function, 310

namespaces, 23
  attributes, 305–7
  BizTalk header, 658
  default, 300–303
    canceling, 303

namespaces (*continued***)**
  of descendants, 301
  DTDs' limited support of, 374
  fully qualified names, 298
  lugnuts Web store case study, 558, 560
  namespace URIs, meaning of, 315
  notations, 303–5
  objects, associating with, 583
  ouputting, 311–12
  prefix approach, 294–96
  qualified names, 297
  reasons for using, 293–97, 316–17
  on specific elements, 301
  URLs, 314–15
  XHTML, 316
  in XML, 297–307
  XML schema, specifying for, 396
  xmlns attribute, 297
  XSLT, 308–12
    outputting namespaces, 311–12
    using in, 309–10
naming elements, 33
  case-sensitivity, 34
** nbsp, white space, 36**
NCName datatype, XML Schema, 387
NDATA keyword, unparsed entities, 429
negativeInteger datatype
  derived by restriction, 399
nesting conditional sections, 443
nesting tags, 32
Netscape Navigator
  ISO character entities, 434
newline characters, 37, 505, 509
NextSibling property
  Node interface, 230
NIDs, URNs, 313
NMTOKEN attribute type, 351, 355
NMTOKENS attribute type, 351, 355
node functions in XPath, 146–48
Node interface, DOM, 227, 664-66
  appendChild method, 232
  attributes property, 228, 245
  childNodes property, 230
  cloneNode method, 233
  element information, accessing, 229
  firstChild property, 230
  hasChildNodes method, 231
  insertBefore method, 233
  lastChild property, 230
  nextSibling property, 230
  nodeName property, 228
  nodeType property, 227
  nodeValue property, 228
  ownerDocument property, 232
  parentNode property, 230

  previousSibling property, 230
  removeChild method, 233
  replaceChild method, 233
  tree
    modifying, 234
    navigating, 232
node-points, XPointer, 470
node-sets, 142
node() function, XPath, 147
NodeList interface, DOM, 240, 668-69
  accessing items in, 241
  item() method, 240
  length property, 240
  returning, 230
nodeName property
  Node interface, DOM, 228
nodes, 142
  adding and removing, 232
  children of, 231
    checking existence of, 231
  copying, 233
  documents, 235
    adding to, 236
  information, retrieving, 227
  NamedNodeMaps, accessing in, 245
  ordered collections of, 240
  processing on several, 187–90
  retrieving parts of, 470
  unordered collections of, 245
nodeType property, 227
nodeValue property
  Node interface, DOM, 228
non-XML data, 434–38
  ENTITIES attribute type, 435–38
  ENTITY attribute type, 435–38
  NOTATION attribute type, 435
  <!NOTATION> declaration, 435
none display property, 91
normalization in databases, 481
  staging database, 488
not() function, XPath, 151
NOTATION attribute type, 351, 435
<!NOTATION> declaration, 337, 422, 429, 435
  helper applications, associating, 436
Notation interface, DOM, 673
NOTATION primitive datatype, XML schema, 386
notations
  non-XML data, 434–38
NOTE, W3C nomenclature, 379
NSS, URNs, 313
number() function, XPath, 150
numeric functions in XPath, 149–50
numeric/non-numeric datatypes
  fundamental facet, 392
  value spaces, 390

Nut Haus, lugnuts case study
templates, 562
XML product listing, 559
Nuts. Nuts? Nuts!, lugnuts case study
templates, 561
XML product listing, 558

O

object models, 19
DOM (*See* DOM)
JavaScript simulation, 503–8
serializing, 502–19
children of objects, 510–11
commit/rollback functionality, 517
empty objects, 517
Event object, 518
events, capturing, 518
historical information, keeping track of, 518–19
serialize() method, 511–16
to XML, 503
text nodes, 509
XML as, 218
object oriented databases, 478
Object, RDF, 528
objects
associating with namespaces, 583
communication with XML, 484
deserialization, 503
distributed, 485
script blocks, loading into, 586
serialization, 502–19
children of objects, 510–11
stateless, 526–28
string functions, handling with, 586
omit-xml-declaration attribute
<xsl:output> element, 173
On Error Resume Next, 227
online editors, 599
optional elements, 345
Oracle
vs. SQL Server, 496
XML parsers, 494
XML technologies, 494–96
order attribute
<xsl:sort> element, 195
order fundamental facet, 391
value spaces, 390
order sensitivity of CSS, 208
ordered lists, tags for, 75
ordinal references, XPointer, 468
org.sax.xml.Parser. *See under* **SAX, interfaces**
origin() function, XPointer, 474
out of line links, 456–63

output, XSLT, 173–75
lugnuts Web store case study, 555
overflow property
positioning schemes, 108
overlap of tags, 32
overriding methods, 268
ownerDocument property
Node interface, 232
ownerElement property
Attr interface, 247

P

padding, 119–20
page breaks, 124
@page directive, 124
paged media, 89
parameter entities, 422, 430–32
conditional sections, 439–43
declaration format, 430
entity references, 423
limitations, 431
uses, 430
parameters, 205–8
parent axis, XPath, 158
parent/child relationships, XML, 19
parentNode property
Node interface, 230
parse() method, 270
Parsed Character DATA, 28
parsed entities, 422, 425–29
entity references, 423–24
external, 425, 427
internal, 425
parseError object
MSXML, 524
parsers, 16
asynchronous file loading, 230
comments, displaying, 44
endDocument() method, 270
endElement() method, 274
errors, 286–88
events from, catching, 270
exceptions, 281–88
extraneous white space, 37
Locator object, 284–86
MSXML, 486
namespaces, 298
associating objects with, 583
Parser object, 270
SAX-aware, 263
setDocumentHandler() method, 270
startDocument() method, 270

parsers (*continued*)
   startElement() method, 271
   synchronous file loading, 230
   validating, 321
   XML schema, support for, 384
   xp, installing, 265
parsing XML, 57–58
password template
   bulletin board system, 604
pattern constraining facet, 393
pause property, 127
PCDATA, 28
   content models, 340
   illegal characters, 53–57
percent sign (%), parameter entities, 423
percentages, using in positioning schemes, 106
period constraining facet, 395
personalization, 573
PIs. See processing instructions
pitch property, 126
pitch-range property, 126
pixels, font sizes in, 116
   vs. points, 123
play-during property, 127
points, sizing fonts with, 123
points, XPointer, 464, 470
   character-points, 471
   defining, 470
   node-points, 470
position() function, XPath, 149
positional functions in XPath, 148–49
positioning background images, 101
positioning schemes, 104–11
   absolute position, 104
   auto, 106
   clip property, 108
   fixed position, 105
   float property, 109
   height property, 107
   inherited position, 105
   overflow property, 108
   percentages, 106
   relative position, 104
   setting positions, 105
   static position, 104
   width property, 107
<PRE> tag, 36
preceding-sibling axis, XPath, 158
precision constraining facet, 394
Predicate, RDF, 528
prefixes to define namespaces, 294–96
   URIs, use of to eliminate ambiguity, 296–97

Presentation layer, 482
PreviousSibling property
   Node interface, 230
primary keys, databases, 480
primitive datatypes, 385, 386, 783-90
printing, 122–25
   using scripting, 125
priority attribute
   <xsl:template> element, 168
private content on bulletin boards, 573
processContents attribute
   <any> element, 410
processing-instruction() function, XPath, 147
processing instructions, 51–53
   stylesheets, associating with documents using, 134
ProcessingInstruction interface, DOM, 256, 673
   data property, 256
   target property, 256
processingInstruction() method
   DocumentHandler interface, 289
product catalogues, 660
programming
   imperative vs. declarative, 137–40
   side effects in, 140–41
properly nesting tags, 32
properties, 19
   setting on stateless objects, problems of, 527
Proposed Recommendations, W3C nomenclature, 379
pseudo-classes, 78–81
   :active, 79
   :after, 81
   :before, 81
   :first-child, 78
   :first-letter, 80
   :first-line, 80
   :focus, 79
   :hover, 79
   :lang, 80
   :links, 79
   :rect, 108
   :visited, 79
PUBLIC locations, external DTDs, 334
Publisher element
   BookCatalog example, 325, 328
pull model, 643
   XSLT, 620
push model, 643
   CSS, 620
   XSLT, 620

Q

QName. *See qualified names*
QName primitive datatype, XML schema, **386**
qualified names, **297**
   to define behaviors of actuate attribute, XLink,
     452
&quot, **54**
quotation marks
   attributes in XML, 38
   XPath, 145

R

range() function, XPointer, **474**
range-inside() function, XPointer, **474**
ranges, XPointer, **464, 470, 471–74**
   collapsed, 471
   with multiple locations, 472
   selecting, 472
RDF, **528–30**
   how it works, 529
   search engines, 529
<rdf:description> element, **530**
Re: characters on bulletin boards, **588**
read() method, Java, **270**
reason property
   parseError object, 524
REC, W3C nomenclature, **379**
records, databases, **479**
Recordset object
   returning, 486
   in SQL queries, 484
:rect pseudo function, **108**
recurringDuration primitive datatype, XML schema,
     386
   duration constraining facet, 395
   period constraining facet, 395
recursion, **193**
   bulletin board system case study, 580
recursive descent operator (//), XPath, **143**
ref attribute
   <attribute> element, 414
   <attributeGroup> element, 417
   <element> element, 412
regex, **393**
regular expressions, **393**
related groups of attributes, **179**
relational databases, **478**
relative position, CSS, **104**
Remote Procedure Calls, **24, 519-26**

remote resources, **458**
removeAttribute() method
   Element interface, 242
removeAttributeNode() method
   Element interface, 242
removeChild method
   Node interface, 233
removeNamedItem() method
   NamedNodeMap interface, 245
repeating background images, **101**
replaceable content, entities, **422**
replaceChild method
   Node interface, 233
replaceData() method
   CharacterData interface, 251
replacement text, **422**
<report> element
   Schematron, 533
#REQUIRED, **350, 357**
   shortcut, 430
reset button template
   bulletin board system, 605
Resource Description Framework. *See RDF*
resource-type elements, XLink, **450**
   extended links, 461
resources, **312**
   displaying, 453
   extended links, adding to, 461
   labels for, 451
   multiple, 453
   remote, adding to extended link, 458
   specifying when retrieved, 452
responses on message boards, **581**
restriction, datatypes derived by, **399**
result tree, **133**
   elements in different namespaces, outputting to,
     311–12
   namespaces, outputting to, 309–10
   sections of, copying from source tree, 190–92
reusability in n-tier architecture, **484**
role attribute, XLink, **449, 451**
   arc-type elements, 459
rollback/commit functionality, serialization, **517**
root element, **33**
   Document Type Declaration, 333
   namespaces, 301
root node match template
   bulletin board system, 607
routing, **657**
rows, databases, **478**
RPC, **24, 519–26**
rq namespace, **571**

Ruby characters, 122
rules, style sheets, 67
run-in display property, 91
RXP parser, 322

S

Santayana, George, 611
save() method, 225
SAX, 23, 677-705
  advantages of, 290
  attributes, extracting, 276–81
  CDATA, extracting, 273–76
  class paths, modifying, 266
  DocumentHandler interface, 268
    HandlerBase implementation, 268
  drawbacks of, 290
  event-driven, 262
  events
    receiving, 268–73
  installing, 264
  interfaces
    Parser, 270
    using, 264–89
  Locator object, 284–86
  Megginson, David, 264
  obtaining, 263–64
  parsing, 269
  reason for development of, 261
SAX 2.0, 291
  contentHandler interface, 291
  XMLReader interface, 291
SAXException object, 281
  startElement() method, 276
scalability
  of n-tier architecture, 484
  stateless objects, 526–28
Scalable Vector Graphics. See SVG
scale constraining facet, 394
<schema> element, 395, 406
  XML-Data Reduced, 396
schemas, 23, 379
  associating with documents, 395
  dependency in elements, 622
  documenting, 623
  Schematron (See Schematron)
  tools for developing, 621
  translation of, 660
  X-Tract tool, 621
  XML Authority, 638
  XML Schema (See XML Schema)
Schematron, 530–33
  <assert> element, 532
  <report> element, 533
  using, 531

schemes, XPointer, 467
scope, constants, 203
scripting
  loading objects into script blocks, 586
  printing using, 125
SDD. See Standalone Document Declaration
search engines, 529
  Web spiders and data types, 382
security access on bulletin boards, 573
security in n-tier architecture, 484
select attribute
  <xsl:apply-templates> element, 168
  <xsl:copy> element, 190
  <xsl:sort> element, 195
  <xsl:variable> element, 203
SELECT statement, 479
selectNodes() method, 490, 494
selectors, style sheets, 68
selectSingleNode() method, 490, 494, 524
self axis, XPath, 157
semantic attributes, XLink, 451
  extended links, 457
semi-colon (;), parsed entities, 423
sequence groups
  XML schema, 408
sequence lists, 341
  using, 343
serialize() method
  creating, 511–16
serializing object models, 502–19
  children of objects, serialization of, 510–11
  commit/rollback functionality, 517
  deserialization, 503
  empty objects, 517
  events, capturing, 518
  historical information, keeping track of, 518–19
  newlines, 505, 509
  tabs, 505, 509
  to XML, 503
servers. See Web servers
setAttribute() method
  Element interface, 242
setAttributeNode() method
  Element interface, 242
setDocumentHandler() method, 270
setDocumentLocator() method, 284
setFeature() method
  XMLReader interface, 291
setNamedItem() method
  NamedNodeMap interface, 238, 245
setting positions, 105
seven-bit ASCII encoding, 48

SGML, 12
   complexity of, 42
shallow clones
   cloneNode method, 233
sharing DTDs, 324
shorthand syntaxes of XPointer, 468–70
show attribute, XLink, 449, 453
   arc-type elements, 459
sibling/sibling relationships, XML, 19
side effects in programming, 140–41
sidebars, 110
Simple API for XML. *See* SAX
simple content, 20
simple links, 454–56
Simple Object Access Protocol. *See* SOAP
Simple Type Definition, 387, 397, 398–400
   derivation by list, 400
   derivation by restriction, 399
simple-type elements, XLink, 450
<simpleType> element, 387, 398
single quotation marks, attributes, 38
small caps, 119
SOAP, 485, 521
   XMLPipes framework, 572
sorting in XSLT, 195–97
sound, 125–27
source tree, 133
   copying to result tree, 190–92
   namespaces, using, 309–10
<span> elements
   drop-caps, 78
speak property, 127
specified property
   Attr interface, 248
speech-rate property, 126
splitText() method
   Text interface, 251
splitting text, 251
SQL, 479–80
   HTTP, making queries available over, 491, 495
   joins, 480
   queries, capturing results of, 480
   stored procedures, 483
   XML documents, tool for generating from queries, 494
SQL Server
   FOR XML EXPLICIT clause, 492
   FOR XML RAW clause, 491
   vs. Oracle, 496
   using, 492
   XML support, 491–93

SQL Update Grams, 492
<sql:query> element, 491
   attributes without values, 493
SQLXML ISAPI, 497
staging databases, 488
   historical information, 518
standalone attribute
   DTDs, 332
   external resources, setting for, 439
   XML declaration, 328
   <xsl:output> element, 173
Standalone Document Declaration, 49
standards, 619
start-point() function, XPointer, 474
start-tags, 28, 31
startDocument() method, 268, 270
startElement() method, 271
   AttributeList parameter, 276
   SAXException parameter, 276
starts-with() function, XPath, 153
state:document() function, 584
state:encapsulateXML() function, 584
state:getCurrentDate() function, 584
state:persistDocument() function, 584
state:transformDocument() function, 584
stateless objects, 526–28
   example, 528
static media group, 89
static position, CSS, 104
STG Validator parser, 322
stored procedures, 483
strikethrough, 119
string functions
   objects for handling, 586
   in XPath, 152–56
string primitive datatype, XML schema, 386
string() function, XPath, 152
string-length() function, XPath, 146, 153
strings
   concatenating, 153, 155
      in serialization of object model, 504
   handling, 249
   modifying, 250
   translating, 155
<strong> tags, 117
structured data, 21
Structured Query Language. *See* SQL
structures, 397
   XML schema, 383
style attribute, HTML, 67

<style> element, 67
class attribute, 72
overriding styles, 70
style property, borders, 96
stylesheets, 67
associating with documents using processing
instructions, 134
aural, 125–27
cascading, 68–71
classes, 71–78
comments in, 71
default in Internet Explorer, 15
dynamic, 645, 651
eBIS-XML, 620, 639
external, 81–82, 83–86
HTML, 65
integrating XML data into, 545
@import directive, 82
internal, 87
<LINK> element, 81
namespaces, 308–12
reason for using, 62–63
tools, 621
sub-strings, handling, 250
Subject, RDF, 528
submit button template
bulletin board system, 604
substring-after() function, XPath, 154
substring-before() function, XPath, 154
substring() function, XPath, 154
substringData() method
CharacterData interface, 250
sum() function, XPath, 150
Sun Project X, 263
SVG, 17
synchronous file loading, 230
SYSTEM locations
external DTDs, 333

T

\t character, tabs, 505, 509
table-caption display property, 92, 115
table-cell display property, 92, 115
table-column-group display property, 92, 115
table display property, 91, 115
table-footer-group display property, 92, 115
table-header-group display property, 92, 115
table of contents, generating, 570
table-row display property, 92, 115
table-row-group display property, 91, 115
tables (CSS), 111–15

tables (databases), 478
data, retrieving from, 480
denormalization, 481
joins, 480
normalization, 481
tabs, 505, 509
helper function for generating, 512
tabular_form.xsl
bulletin board system, 600
tactile media group, CSS, 89
tagName property
Element interface, 242
tags, 28
case-sensitivity, 34
colors, 95
contextual information, loss of through misuse of,
64
end, 28, 31
in HTML vs. XML, 62, 550
properly nesting, 32
start, 28, 31
target property
ProcessingInstruction interface, 256
templates, 163–65
calling other templates, 168–71
context node, effect on, 165
declarative programming, 138–40
default, 165
defining, 167–68
lugnuts case study, 549, 552
matching against document root, 198
modes, 197–201
named, 168, 204
order of operations, 164
parameters, 205–8
priority, 167
recursion, 193
bulletin board system case study, 580
transforming XML documents to Web pages, 198
<xsl:for-each> element, 187–90
XSLT stylesheets, 133–34
text
alignment, 122
colors, 95
flowing around blocks, 109
indenting, 119
kerning, 121–22
line height, 121
manipulation of, 116–19
positioning schemes, 104–11
replacement, 422
result tree, inserting into, 181–82
sidebars, 110
splitting, 251
text declarations
external parsed entities, 428

text editors, 599
text files, 11
Text interface, DOM, 249, 672
    splitText() method, 251
text nodes
    adding to object model, 509
text() function, XPath, 148
textarea template
    bulletin board system, 606
third normal form, 481
this object, 270
threading on bulletin boards, 568
throws exception, 270
time datatype, XML Schema, 387
timeDuration primitive datatype, XML schema, 386
title attribute, XLink, 449, 451
    arc-type elements, 459
title property
    document object, 19
title-type elements, XLink, 450
    extended links, 463
to attribute, XLink, 450, 453
    arc-type elements, 459
tool tips, 452
top-level elements, 173
translate() function, XPath, 154
trees, 20
    modifying, 234
    traversing with DOM, 230
    XPath, 158
true() function, XPath, 151
try blocks
    exception handling, 226
type attribute
    <attribute> element, 414
    <element> element, 412
    XLink, 449, 450
Type Definition Hierarchy, 397
type-specific searching, 382

U

underlining text, 119
UNECE
    choreography, 659
Unicode, 48, 352
    character references, 424
uniqueness in databases, 479
Unix, newline characters in, 37
unordered lists, tags for, 75

unparsed entities, 422, 429
    notation, 422, 434, 436
unsequenced group, XML schema, 409
ur-type definition, 397
UriReference primitive datatype, XML schema, 386
URIs, 312–15
    namespace URIs, meaning of, 315
    using to define namespaces, 296-97
    XPointer expressions, appending to, 465
URL fragment identifier (#), 334
url() function, CSS, 99
URLs, 312
    namespaces, 314–15
URNs, 313
use attribute
    <attribute> element, 414
user agents and media groups, 89
user-derived datatypes
    XML schema, 385
user IDs on bulletin boards, 576
UTF-16, 48
    DOMString, 220
    external parsed entities, 429
UTF-8, 48
    external parsed entities, 429

V

valid element names, 33
valid XML, 321–24
    advanced, 421
    schemas, 379
validating parsers, 321, 322–23
Value Added Networks, EDI, 614
value attribute
    <attribute> element, 414
value property
    Attr interface, 248
value spaces, datatypes, 389, 390
values of attributes, 38
variables in XSLT, 201–4
    binding, 203
version attribute
    <xsl:output> element, 173
    <xsl:stylesheet> element, 308
vertical bar (|), list operator character, 343
visibility property
    display property compared, 92
:visited pseudo-class, 79
Visual Basic
    code generator, 491
    exception handling, 226

visual media group, 89
vocabularies
RDF, 529
XML, 17, 21, 321, 438
voice-family property, 126
void, meaning of in declarations, 270
volume property, 126

W

W3C. *See* **World Wide Web Consortium**
warning() method
ErrorHandler interface, 286
Web, markup for, 64
Web pages
custom fonts, 119
indentation, 119–20
margins, 119–20
padding, 119–20
positioning schemes, 104–11
printing, 122–25
transforming XML documents to, 198
Web servers
reducing load on with XML, 24
XML documents, loading from, 523
XML, using to post information to, 503–8
Web site
Web sites
communicating via, 616
content with XML, 24
Web spiders
and XML schema data types, 382
well-formed XML, 27, 321
white space, 35–37
end-of-line, 37
ignorableWhitespace() method, 289
in markup, 37
preserving by using <xsl:text>, 182
width property
borders, 96
positioning, 107
Windows
newline characters, 37
windows-1252, 48
Working Draft(s), W3C nomenclature, 379
World Wide Web Consortium, 22
CSS, 66
nomenclature, 379
wrapper elements, 362
WYSIWYG editors, 599

X

X-Tract tool, 621
XDI eProcess platform, 657
XDK, 494
XML SQL Utility for Java, 494
XDR. *See* **XML-Data Reduced**
Xerces, 58, 263
Xerxes-C++, 322
Xerxes-J, 322
XHTML
framework system, 568
function of, 570
namespace, 298, 316
XHTML server, 569
XInclude
XML schema, can use with, 381
XJParser, 322
XLink, 447, 448–64
actuate attribute, 452
default attributes, 463
extended links, 454, 456–63
creating, 457
from attribute, 453
global attributes, 448, 449–53
href attribute, 451
role attribute, 451
show attribute, 453
simple links, 454–56
title attribute, 451
to attribute, 453
type attribute, 450
XML schema, can use with, 381
XML, 13–15
attributes, 38–42
comments, 42–45
CSS (*See* CSS)
Data Objects, returning from, 486
databases, 487–89
storing in, 487
vendors, 490–96
displaying, 23, 545–57
DOM, 219
DTDs, 319
EDI compared, 614
errors, 58
extensibility of, 17
hierarchies in, 19
HTML
difference from, 18, 62
transforming to, 497
internationalization, 346
linking, 447–48
Microsoft technologies, 490–93

XML (*continued*)
n-tier architecture, using in, 484–87
namespaces, 297–307
object model, 218
Oracle technologies, 494–96
parsers (*See* parsers)
parsing, 57–58
potential uses for, 501
reasons for using, 15–17
SAX (*See* SAX)
serializing objects to, 503
SQL Server, 491–93
SQL Update Grams, 492
stateless objects, 527
valid (*See* valid XML)
well-formed, 27, 321
where used, 23–24
white space, 36

<?xml...?> tags, XML declarations, 47

XML 1.0 specification, 23
DTDs, 321

XML Authority, 623, 638
XML schema support, 384

XML-Data
as alternative to DTDs, 329

XML-Data Reduced, 380
as alternative to DTDs, 329
eBIS-XML, 620
proprietary schema language, 384
<Schema> element, 396

XML declaration, 47, 328
character encoding, specifying, 48
DTDs, 332
not a processing instruction, 51
standalone attribute (*See* standalone attribute)

XML Developers Kit. *See* XDK

XML document types. *See* document types

XML documents. *See* documents

XML-DR. *See* XML-Data Reduced

XML Instance Editor, 642

XML Linking Working Group, 447–48

XML NameChar characters, 338
NMTOKEN / NMTOKENS attribute types, 355

XML Parser for Java v2, 322
XML schema support, 384

XML Processors. *See* parsers

xml property
Document object, 487

XML-RPC, 519–26
cheat, 521–26
instantiator pages, 521–26
benefits of, 526
XML, communication using, 485

XML schema, 379
<all>, 409
as alternative to DTDs, 329
<annotation> element, 418
annotations, 418–19
<any>, 410
<appInfo> element, 418
associating with documents, 395
atomic datatypes, 388
<attribute> element, 414–17
constraints, 414–16
<attributeGroup> element, 416–17
basic principles, 383
built-in datatypes, 385
Complex Type Definition, 397, 400–406
content models, 382, 397, 406–11
cardinality, 407
choice and sequence groups, 408
content from another schema, 410
element content categories, 407
mixed content, 409
model groups, 411
data typing, 382
datatypes, 383, 385, 783-95
facets, 390
lexical space, 390
value spaces, 390
declarations, 384
definitions, 384
derived datatypes, 385, 387
built-in, 387
<documentation> element, 418
vs. DTDs, 380, 620
dynamic, 383
element declarations, 411–13
<element> element, 412–13
element equivalent classes, 412
extensibility of, 382
<group>, 411
including schemas from various sources, 404
limitations of, 530
list datatypes, 388
maxOccurs, 407
minOccurs, 407
multiple, 383
namespaces, specifying, 396
parser support, 384
preamble, 395
primitive datatypes, 385, 386
requirements of, 380
Simple Type Definition, 387, 397
structures, 383, 397
syntax, 381
version, specifying, 396

XML Spy 3.0
XML schema support, 384

XML SQL Utility for Java, 494

<?xml-stylesheet?> processing instruction, 83

XML Stylus, 621, 654

XML template files, 491

XML vocabulary, 321

XML4c 3.1.0 parser, 322
  XML schema support, 384

XML4J parser, 58, 263, 322
  XML schema support, 384

xmlns attribute, namespaces, 297
  default namespaces, canceling, 303

xmlns:xsl attribute
  <xsl:stylesheet> element, 166

XMLPipes, 567
  framework, 569

XMLReader interface, SAX 2.0
  setFeature() method, 291

xp namespace, 571

xp parser
  Driver, 270
  installing, 265
  SAX, 263–64
  SAX Parser interface, 270

xp.jar file, 265

XPath, 23, 131, 141
  @ symbol, 143
  attributes axis, 158
  axis names, 156–60
  boolean() function, 151
  child axis, 157
  comment() function, 147
  complex expressions, 145
  concat() function, 153
  contains() function, 153
  context node, 141
  count() function, 149
  descendant axis, 158
  document root, 142
  expressions, 141
   using axes, 159
  false() function, 151
  following-sibling axis, 158
  functions, 146
   boolean, 150–52
   node, 146–48
   numeric, 149–50
   positional, 148–49
   string, 152–56
  last() function, 149
  location paths, 141, 142–46
   more specific, 144–46
  MSXML, expressions used by, 490
  name() function, 147
  namespace axis, 158
  namespaces, 310
  node() function, 147
  nodes, 142

not() function, 151
number() function, 150
parent axis, 158
pattern, 167
position() function, 149
preceding-sibling axis, 158
processing-instruction() function, 147
quotation marks, 145
recursive descent operator (//), 143
Schematron, 530–33
self axis, 157
starts-with() function, 153
string() function, 152
string-length() function, 146, 153
substring() function, 154
sum() function, 150
text() function, 148
translate() function, 154
true() function, 151
XML schema, can use with, 381
XML syntax, reason for not using, 144
XPointer extensions to, 474

xpo:page object
  framework system in XHTML, 571

XPointer, 447, 464–74
  bare name syntax, 468, 469
  child sequence syntax, 468, 469
  elements, retrieving from documents, 468
  location sets, 464, 470
  locations, 464, 470
  multiple expressions, 465
  points, 464, 470
  ranges, 464, 470, 471–74
   with multiple locations, 472
   selecting, 472
  schemes, 467
  shorthand syntaxes, 468–70
  URIs, appending expressions to, 465
  XPath, extensions to, 474

xsd namespace identifier, 396

xsi namespace identifier, 396

XSL, 133. See also XSLT
  CSS, distinction between, 208
  as display mechanism, 618
  eBIS-XML, 620
  in real world, 213
  result tree, 133
  source tree, 133
  XML, displaying, 23, 545–57

XSL elements
  separating from other elements, 308

XSL Formatting Objects, 133, 209
  CSS, 213

XSL processors
  XML namespaces, 308

XSL transformations
MSXML support, 490
Oracle, 496
<xsl:apply-templates> element, 165, 168–71
mode attribute, 197–201
<xsl:attribute> element, 178–81
<xsl:attribute-set> element, 178–81
<xsl:call-template> element, 204
<xsl:choose> element, 182–87
<xsl:copy> element, 192–94
<xsl:copy-of> element, 190–92
<xsl:element> element, 175–78
<xsl:for-each> element, 139, 164, 187–90
using, 188
<xsl:if> element, 182–87
dynamic stylesheets, 651
lugnuts Web store case study, 556
<xsl:otherwise> element, 183
<xsl:output> element, 173–75
<xsl:param> element, 205
bulletin board system, 601
<xsl:sort> element, 195–97
<xsl:stylesheet> element, 166–67
version attribute, 308
<xsl:template> element, 133, 167–68
mode attribute, 197–201
named templates, 204
using, 168
<xsl:text> element, 181–82
<xsl:transform> element, 166
<xsl:value-of> element, 134, 139, 164, 171–72
using, 172
<xsl:variable> element, 202
<xsl:when> element, 183
<xsl:with-param> element, 205
XSLISAPI, 497
XSLT, 131, 497. *See also* XSL
attribute namespaces, 306
attributes, dynamically adding, 178–81
business to business example, 135
conditional processing, 182–87, 556
constants, 201–4
CSS, 208–13
default template, 165
e-commerce, Importance In, 134–37
elements
containing as variables, 202
in different namespaces, outputting, 311-12
dynamically adding, 175–78

embedding HTML documents in, problems with, 568
modes, 197–201
named templates, 201–4
namespaces, 308–12
outputting, 311–12
using, 309–10
order of operations, 164
ouput, specifying, 173–75
parameters, 205–8
push and pull models, 620
in real world, 213
recursive templates, 193
bulletin board system case study, 580
Schematron, 530–33
side effects, lack of, 140–41
sorting, 195–97
templates, 163–65
context node, effect on, 165
text, inserting into result tree, 181–82
variables, 201–4
XML, displaying, 23, 535-57
<xsl:apply-templates> element, 168–71
<xsl:attribute> element, 178–81
<xsl:attribute-set> element, 178–81
<xsl:choose> element, 182–87
<xsl:copy> element, 192–94
<xsl:copy-of> element, 190–92
<xsl:element> element, 175–78
<xsl:for-each> element, 187–90
<xsl:if> element, 182–87
<xsl:output> element, 173–75
<xsl:param> element, 205
<xsl:sort> element, 195–97
<xsl:stylesheet> element, 166–67
<xsl:template> element, 167–68
<xsl:text> element, 181–82
<xsl:value-of> element, 171
<xsl:variable> element, 202
XSLT engines, 132
declarative programming, 139
XSLT stylesheets, 132
associating using processing instructions, 134
how they work, 133–34
templates, 163–65
XSQL Servlet, 495
XT, 132
Java routines from XSLT, 583

Y

Yahoo!, 529
Yankovic, Wierd Al, 29

wrox
PROGRAMMER TO PROGRAMMER™

Wrox writes books for you. Any suggestions, or ideas about how you want information given in your ideal book will be studied by our team.
Your comments are always valued at Wrox.

Free phone in USA 800-USE-WROX
Fax (312) 893 8001

UK Tel. (0121) 687 4100   Fax (0121) 687 4101

Beginning XML - Registration Card

Name _____

Address _____

_____

_____

_____

City_____ State/Region _____

Country_____ Postcode/Zip _____

E-mail _____

Occupation _____

How did you hear about this book? _____

☐ Book review (name) _____

☐ Advertisement (name) _____

☐ Recommendation _____

☐ Catalog _____

☐ Other _____

Where did you buy this book? _____

☐ Bookstore (name)_____ City _____

☐ Computer Store (name)_____

☐ Mail Order _____

☐ Other _____

What influenced you in the purchase of this book?

☐ Cover Design
☐ Contents
☐ Other (please specify) _____

How did you rate the overall contents of this book?

☐ Excellent   ☐ Good
☐ Average   ☐ Poor

What did you find most useful about this book? _____

What did you find least useful about this book? _____

Please add any additional comments. _____

What other subjects will you buy a computer book on soon? _____

What is the best computer book you have used this year? _____

Note: This information will only be used to keep you updated about new Wrox Press titles and will not be used for any other purpose or passed to any other third party.

Check here if you DO NOT want to receive support for this book ☐

wrox
PROGRAMMER TO PROGRAMMER™

NB. If you post the bounce back card below in the UK, please send it to:

Wrox Press Ltd., Arden House, 1102 Warwick Road,
Acocks Green, Birmingham B27 6BH. UK.

Computer Book Publishers